ADVANCES IN PARTICLE PHYSICS
Volume 2

An Interscience Series

# Advances in
# PARTICLE PHYSICS

Edited by

**R. L. COOL**
*Department of Physics*
*Brookhaven National Laboratories*
*Upton, Long Island, New York*

**R. E. MARSHAK**
*Department of Physics*
*University of Rochester*
*Rochester, New York*

Volume 2

INTERSCIENCE PUBLISHERS
a division of John Wiley & Sons, New York · London · Sydney · Toronto

Library of Congress Catalog Card Number 67-13955
SBN 470 170573
Printed in the United States of America.

# Foreword

The late Sulamith Goldhaber intended to co-author an article on "Meson Resonances" with Gerson Goldhaber for this volume of *Advances in Particle Physics*. She was enthusiastic about the idea of writing a comprehensive review article with her husband on a subject to which they had been giving special attention in recent years. The present volume, which contains "their" article as well as several others by friends and colleagues, is dedicated to her memory.

R. L. Cool
R. E. Marshak

# Sulamith Goldhaber (1923–1965)

Sulamith Low was born in Vienna, Austria, on November 4, 1923. Her family emigrated from Austria and she grew up in Palestine, where she met Gerson Goldhaber when they were both students at the Hebrew University. They received their masters degrees in 1947, the year they were married. They then came to the United States, where they attended the University of Wisconsin and earned their doctorates. From 1951 to 1953 Gerson had a junior faculty appointment at Columbia, working with the cyclotron, and Sula was a research associate in radiochemistry. Radiochemistry was an "intermediate state" that permitted her to learn and apply the techniques of nuclear physics and thereby make the otherwise "forbidden transition" from her original field of physical chemistry to high energy physics.

By the time Gerson came to Berkeley as an assistant professor in 1953, he and Sula had become one of the most competent American teams in the art and science of nuclear emulsion technology. They worked long hours together, setting up developing facilities for their emulsions and training a team of scanners and measurers. They had their eyes firmly on the Bevatron, which was about to become the world's most powerful accelerator. From its earliest operating days, one or both of them seemed always to be waiting in a corner of the control room, in the hope that the busy crew would grant them a quick exposure of some kind. Because of their perseverence, they were rewarded with some of the earliest and most interesting observations of the interactions of negative $K$ mesons with protons.

Sula gave a memorable introductory talk on heavy mesons and hyperons at the 1956 Rochester Conference; much of what she reported was her own work. More than any other event in the history of the Rochester Conferences, her talk marked the turning point in the study of strange particles. Before then, cosmic ray physicists had reported almost all the experimental data; from then on, the field belonged almost exclusively to accelerator users.

Sula's bibliography shows many important papers among the 25 publications that resulted from her concentrated attack on Bevatron problems using the nuclear emulsion techniques. As examples, she and Gerson were the first to observe the mass splitting of the charged $\Sigma$ hyperons, and she, working with most of the Berkeley exponents of the nuclear emulsion technique, observed the first nuclear interactions of the newly discovered antiprotons.

In the early 1960's, it became apparent that Sula Goldhaber should switch her attention from nuclear emulsions to bubble chambers. So she and Gerson teamed with George Trilling in the formation of what is frequently called the Goldhaber-Trilling Group. After a transition period in which she published simultaneously on nuclear events in emulsion, propane, and hydrogen, she concentrated her scientific attention on liquid hydrogen bubble chambers for the rest of her life.

Sula attacked the problems of hydrogen bubble chamber physics with the enthusiasm and vigor that had characterized all her earlier work. She was soon an acknowledged expert in the field, as her list of invited papers amply demonstrates. She was in great demand as a speaker at international conferences; she always had important things to say, and she expressed herself beautifully. Her contributions in this last period of her life are so well known that they hardly need to be recalled. She and her associates were long the world's experts on the interactions of $K^+$ mesons with nucleons, and she played important roles in the discoveries of several "resonant states," most notably the $A$ mesons. She and Gerson first measured the spin of the $K^*$ meson; they are credited with the first study of the simultaneous production of pairs of resonant states, and they devised the "triangle diagram" to aid in such studies.

In the fall of 1965, Sula and Gerson started around the world on a sabbatical tour, visiting high energy physics laboratories, attending conferences, and giving lectures. Their first stop was at Oxford, to attend the biennial European conference on high energy physics. Sula had invested much of her last year in turning the Berkeley Hough-Powell device into a productive system, so she visited CERN to exchange ideas on automatic film measurement. She then lectured at Ankara, and spent the month of November at the Weizmann Institute, preparing the series of lectures she was to give in Madras.

But in Madras, she was suddenly stricken with a brain hemorrhage. Exploratory surgery revealed a brain tumor, and she died without recovering consciousness. To her countless friends all over the world, it was an unbelievable shock. It did not seem possible that someone who personified so much that was youthful and vivacious could suddenly be removed from our midst.

Sula had a fierce loyalty to all the things she loved, and they were many: her family, her religion, her two adopted countries, her science, her laboratory, and her friends. She managed concurrently to be several quite different, always attractive and effective persons: a distinguished scientist, a remarkable homemaker and hostess, and a devoted wife and mother. She will be missed for her important contributions to the many fields in which she labored, but most of all she will be missed for the personal warmth she always radiated. She was a fine scientist and a real woman.

September 1968

Dr. Luis Alvarez
*Lawrence Radiation Laboratory*
*University of California*
*Berkeley, California*

# Contents

# Recent Developments in Boson Resonances *

GERSON GOLDHABER AND SULAMITH GOLDHABER†

*Department of Physics and Lawrence Radiation Laboratory,*
*University of California, Berkeley, California*

## Contents

* The framework of this article is based on a talk by one of us (G.G.) at the 2nd Coral Gables Conference on Symmetry Principles at High Energy, Coral Gables, Florida, January 20–22, 1965, and a series of lectures by the other (S.G.) presented at the 5th Session of the Spring School of Experimental and Theoretical Physics, Nor-Hambert Erevan, Armenia, May 18–27, 1965. The experimental data presented is in part from the 13th International Conference on High-Energy Physics held in Berkeley, August 1966, and is augmented by data presented up to and including the 1967 Heidelberg Conference on elementary particles.

† Deceased. Sulamith Goldhaber ל″ז died suddenly on December 11, 1965. At the time she held a Guggenheim fellowship and the appointment of Visiting Professor at the Institute of Mathematical Sciences in Madras, India.

# I. Prologue

The advances in the study of strongly interacting particles and resonances have been a continuous race between theorists and experimentalists. Once experimentalists established the existence of the proton and neutron as the building blocks of the nucleus, Yukawa predicted the need for a meson in 1935. The theorists were then ahead by a definite prediction. By 1947 the experimentalists had finally discovered the right kind of meson, the pion. In doing this they tapped such a bountiful source, cosmic rays, that they were able to throw in four more particles, the $K$, $\Sigma$, $\Lambda$, and soon thereafter the $\Xi$. With this step, the experimentalists regained the lead. No one had predicted such particles, nor did there appear to be any particular need for them in contemporary theories.

The advent of high-energy accelerators was followed by a period of rapid experimental progress: the discovery of the $\pi^0$ in 1949, the discovery of the first resonance $N^*(1238)$ in 1953, the discovery of associated production in 1954, and the discovery of the antiproton (confirming Dirac's theory) in 1955. The proposals by Pais on associated production and of Gell-Mann and Nishijima on strangeness gave a framework to the experimental discoveries; the theorists drew abreast. These ideas were soon confirmed from the study of the nature of the interactions of $K^+$ and $K^-$ mesons in emulsions and later in hydrogen bubble chambers. The complete picture was confirmed with the discovery of the $\Xi^0$. Meanwhile, from a different and unexpected source, the experiments on electron–proton scattering, data on the proton and neutron form factors began to accumulate. From these data a number of theorists predicted the existence of vector mesons. While the search for these particles was in progress, the first "modern" resonance, the $Y^*(1385)$, was discovered (1960). This was followed in rapid succession by the discovery of the $K^*(890)$, the $\rho$, the $\omega$, and many others. With the $\rho$ and $\omega$ the need for vector mesons appeared satisfied; with all the additional resonances observed there again was a surplus. However, as soon as a definite pattern began to emerge from the data, Gell-Mann and Ne'eman introduced $SU_3$, and Gell-Mann and Okubo introduced the mass splitting formula. They were able to predict the presence of new resonances as well as all their quantum numbers. The discovery of the $\eta$ and the measurements of the spin and parity of the $\eta$ and $K^*$ were the first confirmations, establishing the pseudoscalar and vector meson octets experimentally.

The discovery of the $\Xi^*(1530)$ coupled with the apparent absence of any positive strangeness hyperons led to the most striking prediction of $SU_3$—the $\Omega^-$. The gargantuan effort which led to the discovery of the $\Omega^-$ is well known. The physics community is now the proud possessor of some 12 recorded examples of this particle. At this point one can say that the experimentalists were on a par with the theorists. But now there is radical change: the theorists no longer talk of groups of 8, or 10, or possibly 27 particles; with the introduction of $SU_6$ (and up) they are talking of groups with 405 and more states. In spite of the fact that they are counting spin projections as distinct states as well, with such numbers of particles the experimentalists must clearly concede that the theorists are way ahead at present.

This brings us to the subject of this article. The phenomenal progress of the last few years has yielded a pseudoscalar octet and singlet or "nonet," a vector nonet, and, more recently, a tensor nonet of bosons. Aside from these well established and classified particles and resonances, there exist a number of other resonances, peaks and "bumps." Some of them are definite resonances but are not yet classified in a specific group; some may not be resonances at all, but rather another type of phenomenon. These too we will describe in this article.

In the case of the first few resonances observed, the experimentalists worked very hard to convince themselves, and others, that this was indeed the correct interpretation for the phenomenon under study. The shoe is now on the other foot. In view of the large number of resonances already established, and the enormous numbers still envisaged by our theoretical friends, a resonance would appear to be the simplest explanation for any statistically significant "bump." It is thus up to us experimentalists to exercise self-restraint, and to explore every individual "bump" carefully in order to ascertain whether the simplest explanation is indeed the correct one.

## II. Quantum Number Determination

### 1. Definitions

To qualify as a particle or a resonance, a "bump" must have a well-defined set of quantum numbers associated with it. These correspond to the conservation laws which hold for strong interactions.

$B$     Baryon number, $B = N - \bar{N}$, where $N$ and $\bar{N}$ are the number of nucleons and antinucleons in the system, $B = 0$ for bosons.

$Y$     Hypercharge, $Y = B + S$, where $S$ is the strangeness.

$I$     Isotopic spin. The multiplicity of charge states is given by $2I + 1$.

$J$     Total angular momentum or spin.

$P$     Intrinsic parity, defined relative to the proton for non-strange bosons, relative to the $\Lambda$ for $S = Y = 1$ bosons.

$C$     Charge conjugation. Only the neutral member of the $2I + 1$ states of an isotopic spin multiplet can be eigenstate of $C$. For strange mesons certain linear superpositions of $K^0$ and $\bar{K}^0$ states are eigenstates of $CP$.

$G$     $G$ conjugation or $G$ parity. Applicable for nonstrange ($Y = S = 0$) bosons only.

Finally, for a definite charge state one can further specify:

$I_z$     The particular $z$ component of isotopic spin.

$Q$     The charge, related to $I_z$ and $Y$ by the Gell-Mann–Nishijima relation $Q = I_z + Y/2$.

All these quantum numbers—and perhaps others we are not aware of as yet—are conserved in particle or resonance *production*. However, this is not necessarily so in the decay. In fact, it is here that the distinction arises between "particles" and "resonances." A state is referred to as a "particle" when no channel is available for decay via strong interactions. The decay of a particle thus proceeds via electromagnetic interaction (e.g., $\eta \rightarrow \pi^+\pi^-\pi^0$, or $\pi^0 \rightarrow \gamma + \gamma$) with the violation of $G$ or, if that process is forbidden as well, via weak interactions (e.g.,

$\pi^+ \to \mu^+ + \nu_\mu$, $K^+ \to \pi^+\pi^-\pi^0$, etc.) violating $Y$, $I$, $P$, $C$, and $G$. In the latter case the decay rate is sufficiently low that the "particle" can travel a measurable distance before decay, thus leaving a track in a bubble chamber, for example. The mean distance traversed is given by $L = \beta\gamma c\tau$, where $\tau$ is the mean life of the particle [e.g., $\tau(\pi^+) = 2.61 \times 10^{-8}$ sec, $\tau(K^+) = 1.23 \times 10^{-8}$ sec] and $\beta\gamma = P/mc$.

We refer to a state as a "resonance" when an open channel for decay via strong interactions *is* available (e.g., $K^{*+} \to K^+ + \pi^0$, $\omega \to \pi^+\pi^-\pi^0$, etc.), in this case all the above-mentioned quantum numbers are conserved. Here $\tau$ is related to the resonance width $\Gamma$ by the Heisenberg uncertainty relation $\tau\Gamma \approx \hbar$. Here we can express $\hbar c$ as $\hbar c = 197$ MeV $-$ fermis. Thus for $\Gamma = 100$ MeV, for example, $\tau \approx 6 \times 10^{-24}$ sec, giving a distance traversed of $L \approx 2 \times 10^{-13}$ cm or 2 fermis, which is of course much too small to observe directly. The presence of a resonance and its quantum numbers can thus only be determined from a study of the decay products or the recoiling reaction products.

The complete equivalence between particles and resonances is demonstrated particularly clearly in the case of the $J^P = \frac{3}{2}^+$ baryon decouplet (see Fig. 1). Here we have a number of states belonging to the

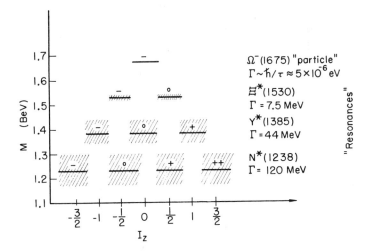

FIG. 1. The baryon decouplet illustrating "resonances" and "particles" in a single multiplet. $J^P = \frac{3}{2}^+$.

same $SU(3)$ representation. Of these the isotopic spin quartet [the four $N^*(1238)$ or $\Delta(1238)$ charge states], the isotopic spin triplet [the three $Y^*(1385)$ charge states], and the isotopic spin doublet [the two $\Xi^*(1530)$ charge states] are all resonances; the tenth member, the isotopic spin singlet, the $\Omega^-(1675)$, is a particle.

## 2. The Internal Quantum Numbers B, Y, and I

The determination of $B$ is trivial. For bosons no (single) baryon can occur among the decay products, although baryon–antibaryon pairs can of course occur if the mass is high enough, $M > 2M_p$.

The determination of $Y$ is similarly straightforward. For all bosons we can appeal to strangeness conservation in the production process to determine $Y$. For resonances the same is also true for the decay process. For particle decay we can use the $\Delta S = \pm 1$ rule in the weak decay processes.

The determination of $I$ is carried out by a search for the maximum value of $I_z$ which shows the resonance. Then $I_z$ obeys the relation $|I_z| \leq I$. As an example, let us consider $K^*(890)$ production in the reaction $K^+ + p \rightarrow K^+\pi^-\pi^+p$. This reaction in a pure isotopic spin state ($I = 1$) proceeds to a considerable extent via $K^{*0} + N^{*++}$ double resonance formation with $I_z(K^+\pi^-) = -\frac{1}{2}$ and $I_z(p\pi^+) = \frac{3}{2}$. Figure 2a shows the phase space triangle plot where $M(K^+\pi^-)$ is plotted versus $M(p\pi^+)$. The two resonances show up very clearly. Figure 2b shows the same data plotted as $M(K^+\pi^+)$ vs. $M(p\pi^-)$. Here we note that while some $N^{*0}$ formation is evident, no enhancement occurs in the $I_z = \frac{3}{2}$, $K^+\pi^+$ channel.

From isotopic spin conservation we can, however, deduce the expected amount of $K^+\pi^+$ resonance production if the $K^*(890)$ were an $I = \frac{3}{2}$ resonance. We must thus compare the two channels

$$K^+ + p \rightarrow (K^+\pi^-) + (p\pi^+) \tag{1}$$

$$K^+ + p \rightarrow (K^+\pi^+) + (p\pi^-) \tag{2}$$

where each parenthesis is considered to be an isotopic spin $\frac{3}{2}$ state for the moment.

Thus we must compare the Clebsch-Gordan coefficients ($I_1$, $I_2$, $I_{z1}$, $I_{z2}/I$, $I_z$) which become ($\frac{3}{2}$, $\frac{3}{2}$, $-\frac{1}{2}$, $\frac{3}{2}/1$, 1) for Eq. (1) and ($\frac{3}{2}$, $\frac{3}{2}$, $\frac{3}{2}$, $-\frac{1}{2}/1$, 1) for Eq. (2). In this case these are equal to one another. The experimental data can clearly rule out equal $K^*$ enhancements in the case of Eqs. (1) and (2), showing that $I < \frac{3}{2}$, leaving $I = \frac{1}{2}$

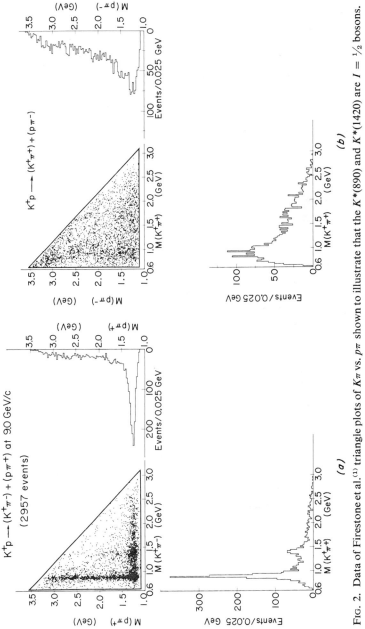

Fig. 2. Data of Firestone et al.[1] triangle plots of $K\pi$ vs. $p\pi$ shown to illustrate that the $K^*(890)$ and $K^*(1420)$ are $I = \frac{1}{2}$ bosons.

for the $K^*(890)$. Thus the correct assignment for the $K^*$ state is $|K^+\pi^-\rangle = |\frac{1}{2}, -\frac{1}{2}\rangle$. This was already noted in the experiment of Alston et al.[2] in the reaction $K^-p \rightarrow K^{*0} + \Lambda$, the experiment in which the $K^*(890)$, the first boson resonance, was discovered.

A particularly simple situation arises if one of two decay products is an $I = 0$ state—the $\omega$ in the decay $B \rightarrow \pi\omega$, for example. Then the $I$ spin is the same as that of the other decay product, i.e., $I(B) = I(\pi) = 1$.

## 3. The Spin and Parity $J^P$

The spin $J$ of a resonance is usually the quantum number which is hardest to determine. The procedures differ, depending on the number of decay particles and on whether more than one decay mode is observed. We will discuss these in turn.

### A. Two-Particle Decay

In most instances ($\bar{p}p$ annihilation at rest is a notable exception) resonance production proceeds through peripheral reactions. Furthermore, these frequently behave as if they proceed primarily via the exchange of a particular virtual particle, e.g., $\pi$, which is isovector-pseudoscalar, i.e., $I^G J^P = 1^- 0^-$ exchange, or $\rho$, which is isovector-vector, i.e., $I^G J^P = 1^+ 1^-$ exchange, or $\omega$, which is isoscalar–vector, i.e., $I^G J^P = 0^- 1^-$ exchange.

We will now consider two limiting cases: pseudoscalar (e.g., $\pi$) exchange and vector (e.g., $\rho$ or $\omega$) exchange. For these the method of alignment of the resulting resonance is readily described in simple terms.

*a. Boson Resonance Production by Pseudoscalar Exchange.* The basic principle is to study the boson resonance production vertex in the resonance center of mass with the incident particle direction as the axis of quantization. Classically we know that angular momentum is given by $\mathbf{l} = \mathbf{r} \times \mathbf{p}$; hence $\mathbf{l}$ is perpendicular to $\mathbf{p}$. Quantum mechanically this translates into the fact that the amplitudes corresponding to $m_l \neq 0$ vanish for the above axis of quantization, and only the amplitude corresponding to the projection $m_l = 0$ is present. Since the incident and exchange particles in the case of interest here are both pseudoscalar, the spin (and parity) of the resulting boson resonance are determined by $l$. In fact $J^P$ are given by $J = l$ and $P = (-1)^l$. Furthermore $m_J = m_l$, so the absence of $m_l \neq 0$ amplitudes implies that the boson resonance is aligned with $m_J = 0$ (see Fig. 3). If $J = 1$ this gives a

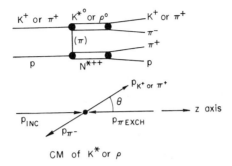

Fig. 3. (*Top*) Feynman diagram for vector meson production by virtual pion exchange. (*Bottom*) Description of the decay angle in the vector meson center of mass.

decay angular distribution of $|Y_1^0 (\cos \theta)|^2 \propto \cos^2 \theta$, and for $J = 2$ we get $|Y_2^0 (\cos \theta)|^2 \propto (9 \cos^4 \theta - 6 \cos^2 \theta + 1)$. These features are well approximated in the examples of $K^*(890)$ production, $J^P = 1^-$, and $K^*(1420)$ production, both in reaction (1) at 4.6 and 9 GeV/c (see Fig. 4). For the $K^*(1420)$ the distribution is consistent with $J^P = 2^+$.

*b. Spin 1 Boson Resonance Production by Vector Exchange.* Here again alignment of the boson resonance is expected. To form a $1^-$ resonance we must add angular momentum $l^P = 1^-$ to the incident particle $J^P = 0^-$ and the exchange particle $J^P = 1^-$. The addition of the two magnetic substates $m_l$ and $m_{(\text{vector})}$ to give $M_J$ are shown in Table I. As may be noted, only the states $m_J = \pm 1$ are allowed on this

TABLE I

Composition of Magnetic Substates for the Production of a Spin $J^P = 1^-$ Particle by a Pseudoscalar Meson with Vector Meson Exchange. The Axis of Quantization $z$ is Taken Along the Incident Direction

| $M_J$ | $m_l$ | $m_{(\text{vector})}$ | Comment |
|:---:|:---:|:---:|:---|
| 1 | 0 | 1 | Allowed |
| | 1 | 0 | $m_l \neq 0$ amplitudes vanish |
| 0 | 1 | −1 | $m_l \neq 0$ amplitudes vanish |
| | 0 | 0 | Clebsch-Gordan coefficient $(1,1,0,0/1,0) = 0$ |
| | −1 | 1 | $m_l \neq 0$ amplitudes vanish |
| −1 | 0 | 1 | Allowed |
| | 1 | 0 | $m_l \neq 0$ amplitudes vanish |

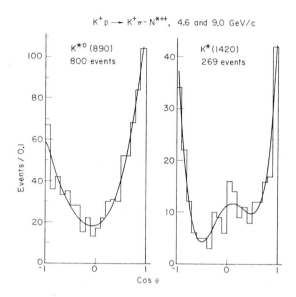

FIG. 4. Data of Fu et al.[3] decay angular distribution for the $K*(890)$ and $K*(1420)$ for the reaction shown. The curves are expansions in Legendre polynomials: $\Sigma_l a_l P_l(\cos\theta)$ with $a_1 = 0.46 \pm 0.07$, $a_2 = 1.12 \pm 0.08$, $a_3 = 0.18 \pm 0.10$, $a_4 = 0.04 \pm 0.11$ for the $K*(890)$ and $a_1 = 0.19 \pm 0.12$, $a_2 = 1.20 \pm 0.15$, $a_3 = -0.25 \pm 0.17$, $a_4 = 1.16 \pm 0.18$ for the $K*(1420)$ with $a_0$ normalized to 1.0.

model. Thus the angular distribution corresponds to $|Y_1^{\pm 1}(\cos\theta)|^2 \propto \sin^2\theta$. In practice this limiting case is never quite achieved. Thus there are angular distributions which have considerable $\sin^2\theta$ components such as the reaction $K^+p \to K^{*+}p$, but for boson resonances no pure case of complete alignment with $M_J = \pm 1$ has yet been found.†

    *c. The Spin Density Matrix Approach.* A more general approach in studying a boson resonance produced in a mixed state is to evaluate the spin density matrix $\rho_{mm'}$. Here $m$ and $m'$ are magnetic quantum numbers relative to the $z$ axis.

    This method, which is well known from atomic and nuclear physics, was applied to particle physics primarily by Jackson and co-workers.[4]

---

† A very clear-cut case of alignment due to vector exchange ($\rho$) occurs in the production of the baryon resonance $N*(1238)$ in the reactions $K^+p \to K^0\pi^+p$ and $\pi^+p \to \pi^0\pi^+p$. Here the meson vertex cannot emit a virtual $\pi$ due to spin parity conservation $0^- + 0^- \not\to 0^-$.

The matrix $\rho_{mm'}$ can be written as:

$$\rho_{mm'} = \begin{bmatrix} \rho_{11} & \rho_{10} & \rho_{1-1} \\ \rho_{01} & \rho_{00} & \rho_{0-1} \\ \rho_{-11} & \rho_{-10} & \rho_{-1-1} \end{bmatrix}$$

for the $J = 1$ case.

The spin density matrix has the following properties which will be stated here without proof:

1. The matrix is hermitian: $\rho_{mm'} = \rho^*_{m'm}$. Consequently, the diagonal elements are real.

2. The sum of the diagonal elements is unity.

$$Tr(\rho) = \Sigma \rho_{mm} = 1$$

3. All diagonal elements are positive.

$$\rho_{mm} \geqq 0$$

4. Parity conservation in the production process gives the following relation between the elements:

$$\rho_{-m,-m'} = (-1)^{m-m'} \rho_{m,m'}$$

Applying these properties to the above example gives:

$$\rho_{mm'} = \begin{bmatrix} \rho_{11} & \rho_{10} & \rho_{1,-1} \\ \rho^*_{10} & 1 - 2\rho_{11} & -\rho^*_{10} \\ \rho_{1,-1} & -\rho_{10} & \rho_{11} \end{bmatrix}$$

Here $\rho_{11}$ and $\rho_{1,-1}$ are real and $\rho_{10}$ is complex. We are thus left with four numbers which completely describe the spin density matrix. Three of these numbers, $\rho_{11}$, $\rho_{1,-1}$, and Re $\rho_{10}$, can be obtained directly from the experimental measurements through the relation:

$$W(\theta, \phi) = C\{\rho_{11} \sin^2 \theta + (1 - 2\rho_{11}) \cos^2 \theta - \rho_{1,-1} \sin^2 \theta \cos 2\phi$$
$$- \sqrt{2} \text{ Re } \rho_{10} \sin^2 \theta \cos \phi\}$$

where $W(\theta, \phi)$ is the experimental angular distribution in terms of the resonance decay angles $\theta$ and $\phi$, as defined in Figure 5. The azimuthal angle $\phi$ is usually called the Treiman-Yang angle. Here $\rho_{00}$, which is sometimes quoted, is given by $\rho_{00} = 1 - 2\rho_{11}$.

The limiting case of pure pseudoscalar exchange corresponds to $\rho_{11} = 0$ or $\rho_{00} = 1$ giving the $\cos^2 \theta$ distribution, $\rho_{1,-1} = 0$ giving the isotropic Treiman-Yang angular distribution, and Re $\rho_{1,0} = 0$ giving no

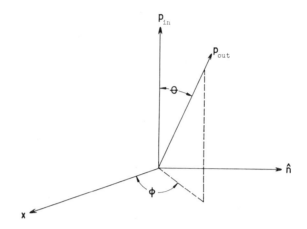

FIG. 5. Definition of the decay angle $\theta$ and Treiman-Yang angle $\phi$ in the resonance center of mass. $\mathbf{p}_{\text{in}}$ is the direction of the incident particle, $\hat{n}$ is the normal to the production plane, and $\hat{x} = \hat{n} \times \hat{p}_{\text{in}}$.

$\theta\phi$ correlation. In reality, absorption effects in the initial and final states cause sizeable changes from the simple model. This subject has been treated in great detail in the literature, particularly by Jackson.[4]

A number of special methods have recently been developed for spin analysis; for details we refer the reader to some of the original papers.[5]

### B. Three-Particle Decay

In the case of three-particle decay we have two ways to handle the problem of the spin determination.

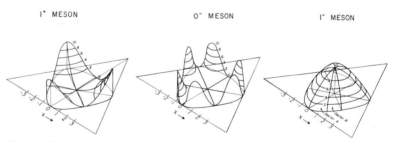

FIG. 6. Three-dimensional graphs of the square of the matrix elements for $1^+$, $0^-$, and $1^-$ decay into three pions. From Stevenson et al.

*1.* We can again evaluate the direction of the polarization vector. In this case this is the normal to the decay plane in the center of mass of the boson resonance. The polar coordinates $\theta$ and $\phi$ of the normal relative to the incident direction thus play the same role here as discussed in the previous section.

*2.* A study of the density distribution in a Dalitz plot may reveal the characteristic symmetry pattern of the decay matrix. The classic examples are the $\tau$, for which the method was introduced, as well as more recently the $\omega$ and $\eta$ decays. Figure 6 shows a density distribution of the Dalitz plot (in three dimensions) for the matrix elements corresponding to $J^P = 1^+$, $0^-$, and $1^-$ mesons from Stevenson et al.[6] Figure 7 shows the pattern of the Dalitz plot of a three-pion system for matrix elements corresponding to various $I$, $J^P$ values according to

| Spin | $I = 0$ | $I = 1$ (except $3\pi_0$) | $I = 2$ $\pi_+ \pi_- \pi_0$ | $I = 2$ other modes | $I = 1$ ($3\pi_0$ only) and $I = 3$ |
|------|---------|---------------------------|-----------------------------|---------------------|--------------------------------------|
| $0^-$ | | | | | |
| $1^+$ | | | | | |
| $2^-$ | | | | | |
| $3^+$ | | | | | |
| $1^-$ | | | | | |
| $2^+$ | | | | | |
| $3^-$ | | | | | |

FIG. 7. Location of the zeros in the matrix elements for three-pion decay according to Zemach. The vanishing of the matrix element is indicated by a heavy black dot or heavy black curve. If both coincide it indicates a vanishing to higher order.

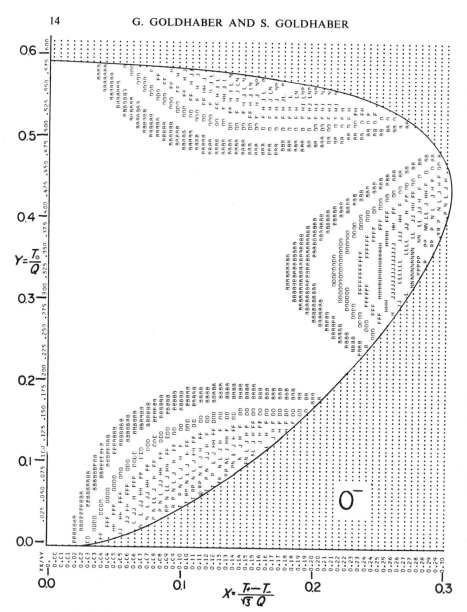

FIG. 8. (a)–(e) Contour maps for the square of the matrix elements of $I = 0$ $\pi^+\pi^-\pi^0$ decay. The contours are given in 5% steps by the letters A—T with every other letter omitted for clarity. The figures give the right-hand half of the Dalitz plot.

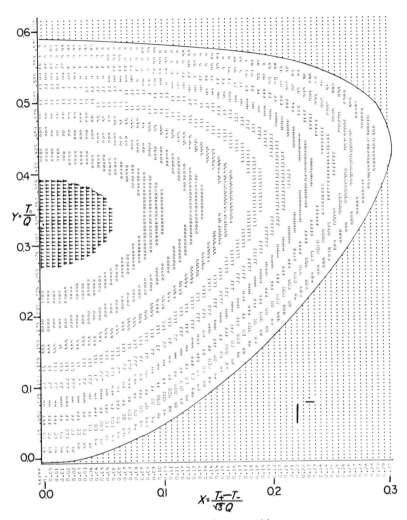

FIG. 8*b*. See caption on p. 14.

Zemach.[7] The regions of the Dalitz plot where the density must vanish because of symmetry requirements are shown in the figure as heavy black dots or heavy black curves.

Further details on the simplest matrix elements for the $I = 0$ states are given in Table II and Figure 8. The distributions in Figure 8

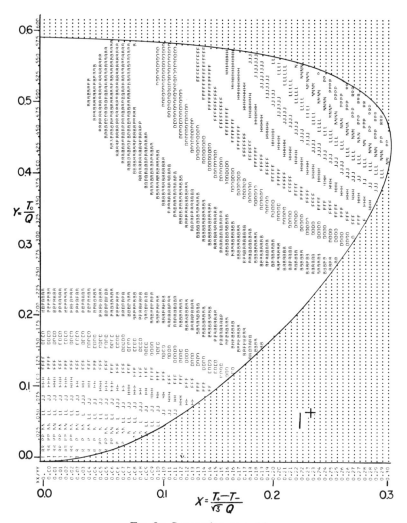

FIG. 8c. See caption on p. 14.

correspond to contour maps of the various matrix elements squared in 5% steps. The letters *A–T* designate the 20 levels, where every other letter has been left blank for clarity.

Figure 9 shows the location of the peaks in the density distributions which correspond to the areas encompassing roughly 50% of the

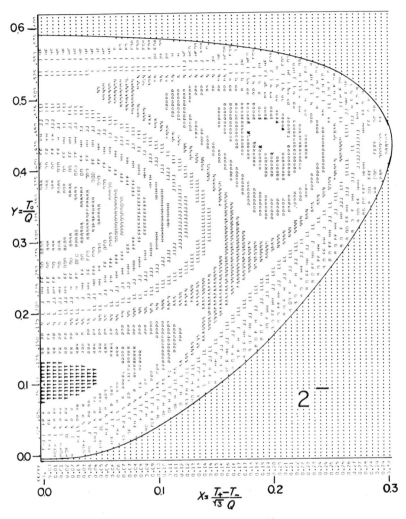

FIG. 8d. See caption on p. 14.

population for each of the matrix elements (i.e., 50% of the number of events corresponding to the spin state $J^P$ should occur inside these areas). The fact that these areas are largely mutually exclusive raises the possibility that, once sufficient data is available, one may be able to perform a systematic "mass sweep" in search of new resonances, even if

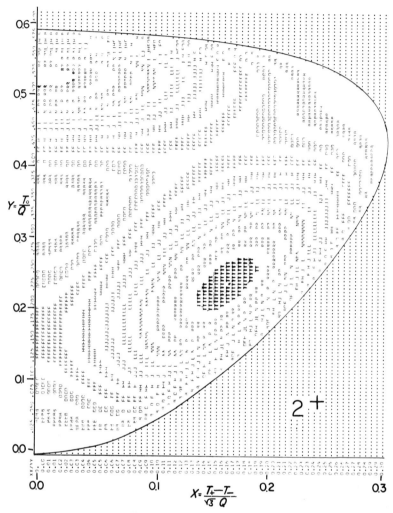

FIG. 8e. See caption on p. 14.

these resonances do not show up as distinct bumps.[8] This is equivalent to finding the distribution in energy of the various coefficients in an expansion of the differential cross section in Legendre polynomials. Some of the higher $N^*$ resonances, for example, show up as only very

to $G = (-1)^{l+I}$ where $l$ is the angular momentum between them. Thus $G(K\bar{K}) = (-1)^{l+I}$; also $C(K\bar{K}) = (-1)^l$. For decay into $K^0\bar{K}^0$ there is the additional restriction that $K_1^0 K_1^0$ or $K_2^0 K_2^0$ are $C = +1$ states and hence will only occur for even $l$, and $K_1^0 K_2^0$ is a $C = -1$ state and will thus occur for odd $l$ only.[14]

c. *Decay into* $K\bar{K}\pi$, $I = 0$. To make use of our knowledge of $G(\pi)$ and $G(K\bar{K})$ it is expedient to carry out the decomposition of the $K\bar{K}\pi$ system in the $K\bar{K}$ center of mass with angular momentum $l$ between $K\bar{K}$ and $l_\pi$ between $\pi$ and the $K\bar{K}$ system. Here now $G(K\bar{K}\pi) = G(K\bar{K})G(\pi)$; also as $I(\pi) = 1$ to get $I(K\bar{K}\pi) = 0$ we need $I(K\bar{K}) = 1$. Thus $G(K\bar{K}\pi) = (-1)^l$. Also $P(K\bar{K}\pi) = (-1)^l(-1)^{l_\pi}P(K)P(\bar{K})P(\pi) = (-1)^{l+l_\pi+1}$.

### C. Production from the $\bar{p}p$ State at Rest

An ingenious method for the spin-parity determination of the $K^*(890)$ was proposed by Schwartz[15] and carried out by Armenteros et al.[16] This utilizes the phenomenon predicted by Day, Sucher, and Snow[17] that $\bar{p}p$ annihilations at rest occur overwhelmingly from $S$ states. The proof that $\bar{p}p$ annihilations at rest occur from the $S$ state was carried out by Armenteros et al. by studying the reaction $\bar{p}p \to K^0\bar{K}^0$ for a sample of stopped antiprotons. Since for two pseudo-scalar mesons $P = (-1)^l$ the final state can only be $J^P = 0^+$, $1^-$, etc. Thus of the two $\bar{p}p$ initial $S$ states $^1S_0(J^{PC} = 0^{-+})$ and $^3S_1(J^{PC} = 1^{--})$ only $^3S_1$ can contribute. Hence for $S$-wave capture $C = -1$. Thus of the $K^0\bar{K}^0$ states only $K_1K_2$ and not $K_1K_1$ or $K_2K_2$ can contribute. The observed interaction was $\bar{p}p \to K_1^0K_2^0$, i.e., single $V$-events only, which allowed them to set a low limit on non $S$-wave capture. Schwartz suggested that the reaction

$$\left.\begin{array}{c}\bar{p}p \to K^{*0}\bar{K}^0 \\ \to \bar{K}^*K^0\end{array}\right\} \to K^0\bar{K}^0\pi^0$$

could test whether the spin of the $K^*$ is $0^+$ or not. If $J^P = 0^+$ for the $K^*$, then only the $^1S_0$ state can contribute to the above reaction. Thus as $C(\pi^0) = +1$ we must have $C(K\bar{K}) = +1$ and hence the $K_1^0K_1^0\pi^0$ final state. The experiment gave events with the $K_1K_2\pi^0$ final state as well and hence suggested that $J(K^*) \geqq 1$.

### III. An Experimental Survey of the Boson Resonances

In this section we will review some of the recent experimental data on the boson resonances. In each case we will emphasize those features which are currently being investigated. In any such survey one is faced with the question of how to group the bosons. This was no problem as long as there was a handful of known particles, but now, as the number of known particles becomes comparable to the number of chemical elements, this problem is becoming serious. Rather than choose an ordering by mass, or an alphabetic list, we will group the bosons according to $SU(3)$ assignments and furthermore according to the quark model of Gell-Mann and Zweig. In view of the tentative nature of some of the data and of the model as well, there will undoubtedly be some wrong assignments. The spirit of this discussion will thus be in terms of the following question.

*1. Do the Known Bosons Fit the Quark Model?*

From the presently known experimental evidence it is clear that there are three well-established octets and singlets, the $J^{PC} = 0^{-+}$, $1^{--}$, and $2^{++}$ multiplets.† Furthermore, at least within the $1^{--}$ and $2^{++}$ multiplets, there is extensive mixing between the $I = 0$ member of the octet and the $SU(3)$ singlet, so that we are effectively dealing with nonets. New data on these multiplets, as well as some of the remaining questions concerning them, will be discussed below. Aside from the established multiplets there is a considerable amount of fragmentary information on other bosons. We will examine the evidence for these states from the point of view of whether they fit the quark model, or more precisely, the $q\bar{q}$ model for bosons.

Here it must be stressed that the $q\bar{q}$ model, in particular as developed by Dalitz,[20] is the simplest model that is compatible with most of the experimental data. We will thus pursue some detailed comparisons between the data and this model. However, the reader should be careful to note that the model is not definitely established at present. Thus the detailed comparisons are aimed at finding either agreement with or deviations from the model.

Aside from the question whether or not the $q\bar{q}$ model represents the "ultimate" physical truth, it certainly has a tremendous mnemonic

† In this section the emphasis will be on recent data rather than on the "historical" development. We apologize to our colleagues whose very important original discoveries may not be mentioned. Many of these references can be found in the excellent review by Miller.[18] A complete set of references is available in the data collection of Rosenfeld et al.[19]

value, in that it allows us to keep some order in what would otherwise be a jumble of unrelated facts and numbers.

Finally, if it should turn out that the $q\bar{q}$ model is in good agreement with the data, it is still not clear whether this would imply that quarks actually exist, perhaps to be found one day at 200–300 BeV accelerators, or whether the quark concept is just the simplest way of expressing a more complicated physical system.

### A. Some Features of the $q\bar{q}$ Model

The $q\bar{q}$ model assumes that the octet plus singlet structure of the pseudoscalar and vector mesons, each in good agreement with $SU(3)$, are not isolated occurrences but rather are members of a higher symmetry. In this instance they are considered to be the two possible $L = 0$ states of the $q\bar{q}$ system. When we come to the $J^{PC} = 2^{++}$ mesons, then even within the framework of the quark model we can take one of two directions. Either they correspond to the $q\bar{q}$ states with $L = 1$ or they are more complex quark systems, in this case $qq\bar{q}\bar{q}$. In the former case all mesons will correspond to octets and singlets, which can yield nonets through mixing. In the latter case we should get additional multiplets belonging to the groups **10**, $\overline{\textbf{10}}$, **27**, and even higher.

As mentioned above, for bosons the simplest possible hypothesis is the $q\bar{q}$ model. Thus we will only consider multiplets of higher dimension if and when compelling experimental evidence requires. Clear-cut evidence would be the presence of "exotic" particles, particles which *cannot* be fitted into singlets, octets, and, in the case of baryons, decuplets as well.[21] For bosons these could be $S = 2$ states such as $K^+K^+$, $I = {}^3\!/_2$ states such as $K^+\pi^+\pi^0$, or $I = 2$ states such as $\pi^+\pi^+$. The evidence for exotic bosons has been discussed elsewhere.[21,22]

In the $q\bar{q}$ model, the $J^{PC} = 2^{++}$ mesons are ${}^3P_2$ states. We thus expect to find the other three $L = 1$ states ${}^1P_1$, ${}^3P_1$, and ${}^3P_0$ as well, nonets with $J^{PC} = 1^{+-}, 1^{++}$, and $0^{++}$. Similarly there can be states with $L = 2$ and higher. The qualitative spectrum of nonets, with spin–spin splitting between the two $S$ state nonets and spin-orbit splitting between the four $L = 1$ and four $L = 2$ state nonets, is illustrated in Figure 12. Furthermore, if it should turn out that the spin-orbit splitting (which splits nonets of a given $L$) is substantially smaller than the splitting due to orbital angular momentum (which splits nonets having different $L$),

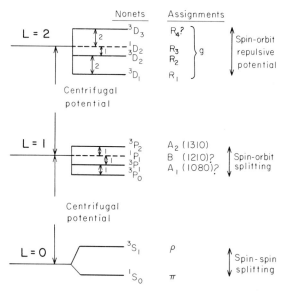

FIG. 12. Qualitative sketch of the distribution of nonets on the $q\bar{q}$ model. (Not to scale.) $SU_3$ splitting not shown.

we would expect to observe "boson $L$ clusters" consisting of the four nonets of a given $L$ value. It might then be difficult to resolve the clusters into nonets, unless high resolution methods become available. This question will be discussed in Section III-4 below.

## 2. The Pseudoscalar and Vector Mesons or the $L = 0$ $q\bar{q}$ States

### A. The Pseudoscalar Mesons or the $^1S_0$ States ($J^{PC} = 0^{-+}$)

The pseudoscalar and vector mesons are illustrated in Figure 13. The $\pi$ and $K$ have been known for a long time and we will say no more about them. The reason we will not discuss the $K$ is not that there is no new information, but rather that starting with the discovery of $CP$ violation in $K_2^0$ decay[12] there is *so much* new and exciting information that any discussion of the $K$ would run way beyond the scope of this article. The $\eta$, because of its unique properties—a decay presumably via the electromagnetic interaction which violates $G$ parity—is currently

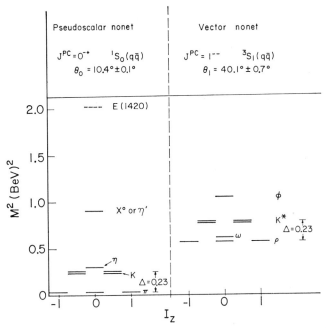

FIG. 13. The two $L = 0$ nonets. Note that there is a tenth candidate for the pseudoscalar mesons, the $E(1420)$. Should this be the $\eta'$, the mixing angle $\theta_0$ is reduced to $\sim 6°$. $\Delta$ is the separation between the isovector and isodoublet in (BeV)$^2$. Data as of October 1967.

the subject of very intensive study and considerable controversy. Some aspects of the $\eta$ meson will be discussed below.

The pseudoscalar singlet associated with the pseudoscalar octet to form a nonet has been called $\eta'$. There are several problems which have come up recently with regard to it. In the past[137] the $X^0(960)$ was considered to be the $\eta'$. This assignment was questioned by the reported discovery of the $\delta^-(963)$, an $I \geqq 1$ meson, by the CERN missing-mass experiment. Confirmatory evidence for the $\delta$ was presented at the 1966 Berkeley Conference from a measurement of the recoil deuteron momentum distribution in the reaction $pp \rightarrow d + \delta^+(966)$ carried out at Saclay. This reaction implied $I(\delta) = 1$. While neither of those experiments looked completely convincing, the combined evidence was hard to dispute. In view of the apparent mass degeneracy between $X^0(960)$ and $\delta$, considerable effort at the 1966 Berkeley conference[23] and the 1967 Heidelberg conference[24] went into successfully proving that the $X^0(960)$ is indeed an $I = 0$ meson and is thus distinct from the neutral member of the $\delta$ isotopic triplet. The latest development on this subject is that at the 1967 Heidelberg conference the supporting evidence for the $\delta$ vanished as the result of an improved version of the $d$-recoil experiment at Saclay.[25] Thus we will not consider the $\delta$ until additional evidence becomes available. However, there is a further difficulty: the CERN-Paris groups conclude that the $E(1420)$ meson is very likely to have $I^G J^P = 0^+ 0^-$. Thus there are, to the best of our present knowledge, two candidates for the "$\eta'$ slot." In principle, the $q\bar{q}$ model can accommodate more than one multiplet with the same $J^{PC}$ values by considering them, for example, as having different radial excitations. However, if this is indeed the case it is puzzling that only one member of such a nonet has been observed so far. We will discuss the $X^0(960)$ and the $E(1420)$ below.

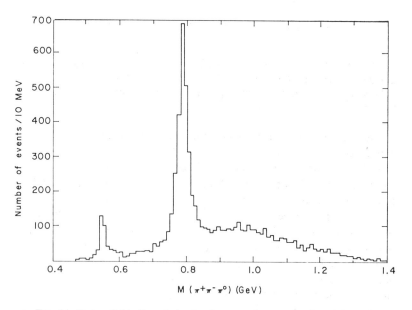

FIG. 14. Data of Abolins et al. showing $\eta$ and $\omega$ production. Histogram of $M(\pi^+ \pi^- \pi^0)$ for 6804 events from the reaction $\pi^+ d \rightarrow p_{sp} p \pi^+ \pi^- \pi^0$ with $p_{sp} < 300$ MeV/c.

*a. Some Recent Experimental Results on the $\eta$ Meson.* A recent mass distribution for neutral mesons decaying into $\pi^+\pi^-\pi^0$ obtained in the reaction $\pi^+ + d \rightarrow pp\pi^+\pi^-\pi^0$ is shown in Figure 14 from the data of Abolins et al.[26] This is the same reaction in which the $\eta$ was first observed by Pevsner et al.[27] at a $\pi^+$ momentum of 1.23 BeV/c. The quantum numbers of the $\eta$ were deduced by Bastien et al.[28] and confirmed by Alff et al.[29] by observing that the $\eta$ decay distribution in a Dalitz plot did not fit into any of the $I = 0$ patterns shown in Section II-3-B above: there appeared to be no vanishing of the $\eta$ decay matrix element on any point on the periphery or on the symmetry axes. In addition, the $\eta$ Dalitz plot did not exhibit sextant symmetry, but rather indicated a decrease of the matrix element with increasing $T_{\pi^0}$. The conclusion was that the $\eta$ is an $I^G J^P = 0^+ 0^-$ particle which decays electromagnetically into an $I^G J^P = 1^- 0^-$ state, thus violating (at least) $I$ and $G$ conservation.

## 1. The $\eta$ Lifetime or Decay Width

A method suggested by Primakoff[30] based on the principle of detailed balance has been used to measure the decay width of the $\eta$ meson. This method makes use of the fact that mesons which decay into the $\gamma\gamma$ mode can be produced by the inverse reaction, namely by the interaction of a photon with a virtual photon from the Coulomb field of a heavy nucleus. This method was successfully employed earlier[31] for an independent determination of the $\pi^0$ lifetime.

The differential cross section for the Primakof effect $d\sigma_P/d\Omega$ is related to the partial decay width $\Gamma_{\gamma\gamma}$ by

$$\frac{d\sigma_P}{d\Omega} = 8\alpha\Gamma_{\gamma\gamma}Z^2 \frac{\beta^3 E^4}{\mu^3} \frac{|F_{em}(Q)|^2}{Q^4} \sin^2\theta$$

where $\alpha$ is the fine structure constant, $Z$ is the nuclear charge number, $\beta$, $\mu$, and $\theta$ are the meson velocity, mass, and production angle, respectively, $E$ is the incident photon energy, which to a good approximation is equal to the total energy of the resulting $\eta$, $Q$ is the momentum transfer, and $F_{em}(Q)$ is the electromagnetic form factor of the nucleus with corrections for $\eta$ reabsorption included.

The experiment by Bemporad et al.[32] consisted in measuring both the angles and energies of $\gamma$-$\gamma$ coincidence events in lead glass Čerenkov counters. The measurements detect the decay mode $\eta \rightarrow \gamma\gamma$. Figure 15 shows a log-log scatter plot of the two $\gamma$-ray energies measured as well

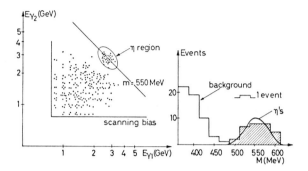

Fig. 15. Typical plot from the data of Bemporad et al. of the pulse height correlation for good $\gamma\gamma$ events. The $m = 550$ MeV line is the predicted locus of the $\eta$ events in the hypothesis of point counters; the elliptic locus is that predicted by the Monte Carlo calculation taking into account the finite dimensions of the Čerenkov apertures. The mass histogram on the right is derived from the $E_{\gamma_1}$ vs. $E_{\gamma_2}$ plot. The solid line represents the mass distribution as calculated by the Monte Carlo program.

as a mass histogram. It shows that the $\eta$ events were clearly resolved from background.

Figure 16 gives the observed counting rate which shows the characteristic peak ascribed to the Primakoff effect at angles $<1°$. According to the above equation, the Primakoff effect should actually vanish at $\theta = 0°$ but rises very rapidly to a maximum at $\theta \simeq 0.3°$. This rise is not resolved in the experimental data. Bemporad et al. conclude from the analysis of their experiment that the partial decay width $\Gamma_{\gamma\gamma}$ for $\eta \to \gamma\gamma$ is $\Gamma_{\gamma\gamma} = (1.21 \pm 0.26)$ keV. With the latest branching ratio for $\gamma\gamma$ decay quoted at Heidelberg[24] this becomes $\Gamma_{\gamma\gamma} = 0.88 \pm 0.19$ keV. Note that actually $\Gamma_{\gamma\gamma}$ comes into the equation twice, as the $\gamma\gamma$ decay mode is used for $\eta$ detection.

## 2. The Main $\eta$ Decay Branching Ratios

There has recently been considerable controversy on the $\eta$ decay branching ratios. The reason for this is that nearly $\frac{3}{4}$ of the total $\eta$ decay rate goes into all neutral particles, $\gamma\gamma$, $\pi^0\pi^0\pi^0$, and possibly $\pi^0\gamma\gamma$. The problem has been that it is no easy task to disentangle these decay modes experimentally. The ratio between all neutral decays and decays into charged particles, primarily $\pi^+\pi^-\pi^0$ and $\pi^+\pi^-\gamma$, is fairly well known and generally agreed upon. The disagreement has occurred on

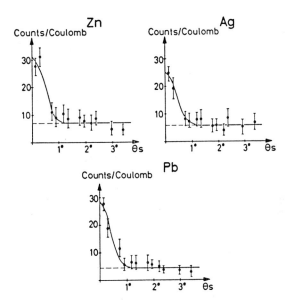

FIG. 16. Data of Bemporad et al. on the Primakoff effect. Experimental yields in the 5.5 GeV measurements on zinc, silver, and lead (bremsstrahlung end point energy 6.0 GeV). The errors are mainly statistical, but also include the uncertainties in the separation of the $\eta$ events from the background in plots like the one shown in the previous figure. The solid lines represent fits to the data which give values for $\Gamma_{\gamma\gamma}$.

the rate into the $\pi^0\gamma\gamma$ mode. If this rate is found to be large, then the $\eta \to 3\pi^0$ rate is assessed as small, which leads to difficulties with the ratio $R = \Gamma(\eta \to 3\pi^0)/\Gamma(\eta\to\pi^+\pi^-\pi^0)$. This ratio should be $R \approx 1.5$ (except for small phase space corrections) if $\Delta I = 1$ in $\eta$ decay. Considerably smaller values for $R$ could mean the presence of $\Delta I = 3$ components. We will mention five recent experiments.

(i) Feldman et al.[33] observed the $\eta$ decay into neutral particles with a series of anticoincidence counters and lead-plate spark chambers surrounding a hydrogen target. $\eta$'s were produced by 0.7-BeV/c $\pi$'s in the reaction $\pi^-p \to n + \eta$. Identification was by neutron time-of-flight counters. The numbers of events with 1–6 $\gamma$-rays converted in their system were counted. They then evaluated the rates into the various neutral decay modes by using a Monte Carlo program to determine the number of converted $\gamma$-rays expected from each mode. The

TABLE IV

Data of Feldman et al.[33] Experimental and Best Fit 1–6 $\gamma$ Distributions. The Experimental Distribution is Prior to Corrections for Premature Conversion in the Hydrogen Target and Dalitz Pairs. The Last Three Columns Give the Probability for $n\gamma$'s Converting in the Spark Chamber for Various $\eta$ Decay Modes

| Number $n$ of gammas | Exptl. | Best fit | $\gamma$ Conversion probability for | | |
|---|---|---|---|---|---|
| | | | $2\gamma$ | $\pi^0\gamma\gamma$ | $3\pi^0$ |
| 0 | — | — | 0.189 | 0.028 | 0.005 |
| 1 | $1087 \pm 137$ | 1162 | 0.384 | 0.177 | 0.048 |
| 2 | $1656 \pm 193$ | 1520 | 0.427 | 0.375 | 0.171 |
| 3 | $471 \pm 65$ | 470 | | 0.325 | 0.310 |
| 4 | $245 \pm 31$ | 253 | | 0.095 | 0.297 |
| 5 | $86 \pm 13$ | 80 | | | 0.142 |
| 6 | $13 \pm 4$ | 15 | | | 0.027 |

experimental results and the best fit to the data are shown in Table IV with the Monte Carlo calculations of the conversion probabilities for each decay mode. They concluded that:

$$R_1 = 2\gamma/\text{all neutrals} \quad = 57.9 \pm 5.2\%$$
$$R_2 = \pi^0\gamma\gamma/\text{all neutrals} = 24.4 \pm 5.0\%$$
$$R_3 = 3\pi^0/\text{all neutrals} \quad = 17.7 \pm 3.5\%$$

where the errors are statistical and include a $\pm 5\%$ uncertainty in the $\gamma$ conversion efficiency and scanning efficiency.

These results give a rather small value of $0.57 \pm 0.13$ for $R$. One possible difficulty with this method is that any uncertainty in conversion efficiency of the spark chambers comes in as a high power, that of the number of converted $\gamma$-rays.

The four other experiments we will describe represent the most recent results. They are consistent with each other, but disagree with the above in that they find $R \sim 1.5$.

(ii) Baltay et al.[34] studied the neutral decay modes of the $\eta$ using a bubble chamber filled with deuterium. They looked for the reaction $\pi^+ d \to pp + \text{neutral(s)}$ at 820 MeV/c with one external $\gamma$-ray conversion in the chamber.

After suitable fiducial-volume cuts they observed 2014 such events. Figure 17 shows the missing-mass squared distribution $M_x{}^2$ based

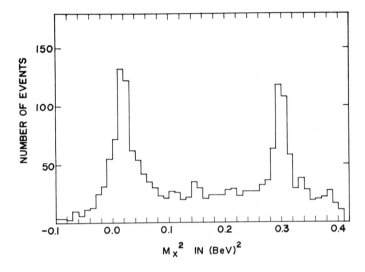

FIG. 17. Data of Baltay et al. Distribution in the mass squared $(m_x{}^2)$ for the reaction $\pi^+ + d \rightarrow p + p + x^0$ with one associated, converted $\gamma$-ray observed.

purely on the measurements of the incoming $\pi^+$ and the two outgoing protons. The $\pi^0$ as well as the $\eta^0$ peaks are clearly visible together with background from $2\pi^0$ and $3\pi^0$ production. Figure 18a shows the computed $\gamma$-ray spectrum for the three reactions considered $\eta \rightarrow 3\pi^0$, $\eta \rightarrow \pi^0\gamma\gamma$, and $\eta \rightarrow \gamma\gamma$ for equal branching ratios. The dashed curves are the theoretical spectra, and the solid curve is the expected result with detection efficiencies and experimental resolution folded in. The experimental $\gamma$-ray spectrum as obtained from the measurement on each $e^+e^-$ pair, transformed into the $x^0$ center of mass, is shown in Figures 18b, c, and d: part (c) corresponds to the $\eta$ mass band and (b) and (d) to background control regions. The only significant contributions to the region $E_\gamma{}^* = 210 \pm 30$ MeV come from the conjectured $\pi^0\gamma\gamma$ decay mode. The data is consistent with no contribution from such a decay mode. This conclusion is strengthened by the results shown in Figure 19 which gives the $M_x{}^2$ distribution for various bands in $E_\gamma{}^*$. Here the 180–240 MeV band shows no appreciable $\eta^0$ signal, as would be expected if the band is primarily populated with background, non $\eta$ events, while an actual fit gives no $\pi^0\gamma\gamma$ events. Baltay et al. state their result as an upper limit $\Gamma(\eta^0 \rightarrow \pi^0\gamma\gamma)/\Gamma(\eta^0 \rightarrow \gamma\gamma) \leqq 0.28$ with 95%

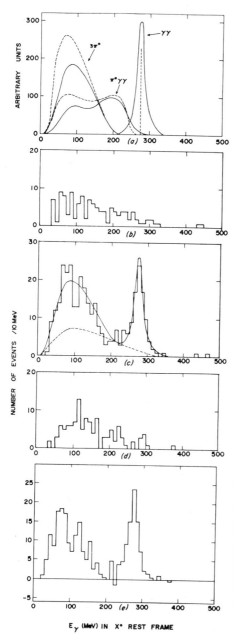

$E_\gamma$ (MeV) IN X° REST FRAME

FIG. 18. Data of Baltay et al. Distributions of the $\gamma$-energy in the missing mass rest frame. The dashed curves in (a) show the theoretical distributions for three decay modes of the $\eta^0$, and the solid curves represent the expected distributions modified by the experimental resolution and $\gamma$-detection efficiencies; (b)–(d) show the experimental distributions for the $\eta^0$ and two control regions; (e) shows the data after a bin-by-bin subtraction of the background. (b) $0.24 \leqq m_x^2 \leqq 0.28$. (c) $0.28 \leqq m_x^2 \leqq 0.32$. (d) $0.32 \leqq m_x^2 \leqq 0.36$. (e) $0.28 \leqq m_x^2 \leqq 0.32$.

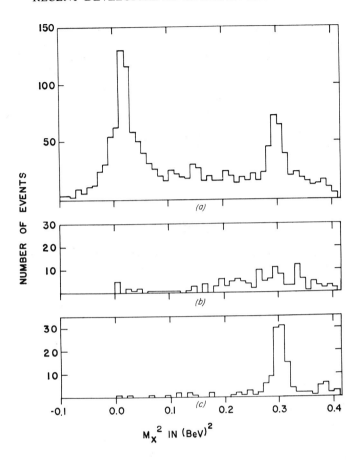

FIG. 19. Data of Baltay et al. Distribution in $m_x{}^2$ for events with $E_\gamma{}^*$ (a) below 180, (b) 180–240, and (c) 240–300 MeV.

confidence level. Their conclusions in terms of the ratio to all neutral decays are:

$$R_1 = 2\gamma/\text{all neutrals} \quad = 53.3 \pm 4.6\%$$
$$R_2 = \pi^0\gamma\gamma/\text{all neutrals} \leq 15\%$$
$$R_3 = 3\pi^0/\text{all neutrals} \quad = 46.7 \pm 6.7\%$$

Furthermore, they have also carried out a direct measurement of the charged decay modes in their data. After various corrections this gives

$\Gamma(\eta^0 \to \pi^+\pi^-\gamma)/\Gamma(\eta^0 \to \pi^+\pi^-\pi^0) = 0.24 \pm 0.04$ where the experimental separation between the $\gamma$ and the $\pi^0$ is shown in Figure 20. And finally, from their measurement of $(\eta^0 \to \text{neutrals})/(\eta^0 \to \text{charged modes}) = 2.64 \pm 0.23$, they obtain $R = 1.58 \pm 0.25$. This experiment looks very convincing, in that it allows one to see the detailed internal checks as shown above.

(*iii*) Baglin et al.[35] studied $\eta$ production by $\pi^-$ mesons in a heavy liquid bubble chamber. This enabled them to measure the ratio $R$ directly by observing

and

$$\eta \to \pi^+\pi^-\pi^0$$
$$\quad \hookrightarrow 2 \text{ converted } \gamma\text{-rays}$$

They obtain the conversion probability $p_6$ for 6 $\gamma$-rays from a Monte Carlo program to be $p_6 = 0.025$ for a 50% Freon–propane mixture and $p_6 = 0.126$ for pure Freon. Pictures with both these liquids were used in this study. They conclude from their data on the basis of 55 6$\gamma$-ray events that

$$R = 1.3 \pm 0.4$$

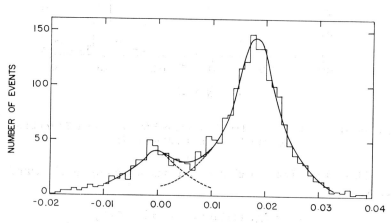

Fig. 20. Data of Baltay et al. Missing mass spectrum ($m_y{}^2$) for four-prong events $\pi^+ d \to p p \pi^+\pi^- + y^0$ in the $\eta$ region. The curve represents the resolution function. $0.27 \leqq m_x{}^2 \leqq 0.33$ (BeV)$^2$.

(*iv*) Bonamy and Sonderegger[36] have performed a measurement of the branching ratio $\eta \to \pi^0\gamma\gamma$ to $\eta \to \gamma\gamma$. This was done with a $\pi^-$ beam on a liquid hydrogen target and energy-sensitive spark chambers. The experiment consisted of the observation (with high efficiency) of the $\pi^- p \to 4\gamma + n$ reaction. They found 754 such events and from kinematic fitting procedures assigned them to the reactions

$$\begin{aligned}\pi^- p &\to \pi^0\gamma\gamma n \\ &\to \pi^0\pi^0 n \\ &\to \pi^0\eta^0 n \\ &\to \eta^0\eta^0 n\end{aligned}\Big\}\eta^0 \to 2\gamma$$

Events with more than 4$\gamma$'s, with additional $\gamma$'s falling outside their 0.45 sterad spark chamber assembly, were eliminated by (high efficiency) lead scintillation anticoincidence screens. The majority of the 4$\gamma$ events were $\pi^0\pi^0 n$ events. The $\pi^0\gamma\gamma n$ candidates were separated by demanding that $M(\gamma\gamma)$ lie outside the experimental $\pi^0$ mass band, a requirement which for reasonable $\eta \to \pi^0\gamma\gamma$ matrix elements should hold for a large fraction of these events. Of the remaining candidates, only $13 \pm 6$ events were consistent with the $\eta$ mass region. From these results, and an earlier determination of the $\eta \to \gamma\gamma$ rate they conclude

$$[\Gamma(\eta \to \pi^0\gamma\gamma)]/[\Gamma(\eta \to \gamma\gamma)] = 0.05 \pm 0.04$$

or, if expressed as an upper limit, less than 0.13 with 95% confidence level. Thus this experiment yields $R$ consistent with 1.5.

(*v*) Buniatov et al.[37] carried out a thick-plate spark chamber-scintillation counter experiment at CERN. Here again the $\eta$ mass was determined from the neutron time of flight, and this experiment, although different in detail, is based on the same principles described above in the experiment of Feldman et al. The CERN-Karlsruhe experiment had somewhat higher conversion efficiency and thus a greater yield of 3, 4, 5, and 6 $\gamma$-events. This may be noted in Table V when compared with Table IV. Figure 21 shows the missing mass distribution for the 0–6 $\gamma$-events (after subtraction of accidentals). This experiment again concludes that the rate $R_2$ for $\pi^0\gamma\gamma$ decay is very low. In fact their data is consistent with zero contribution from this decay mode. They quote $R_1 = 59.0 \pm 33\%$ and $R_3 = 41.0 \pm 3.3\%$ for a fit including only the 2$\gamma$ and 3$\pi^0$ decay modes.

If the $\pi^0\gamma\gamma$ mode is included they found $R_2 = 2.8 \pm 4.4\%$. This corresponds to $R_2 < 12\%$ with 95% confidence level. This experiment gives $R = 1.38 \pm 0.15$.

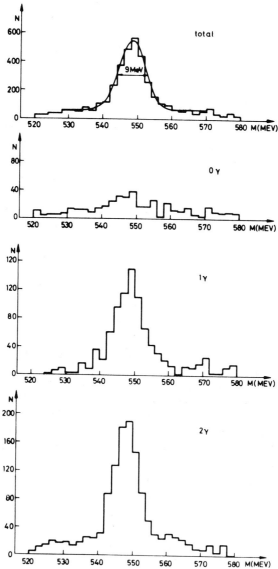

FIG. 21. Data of Buniatov et al. Missing-mass distribution for different

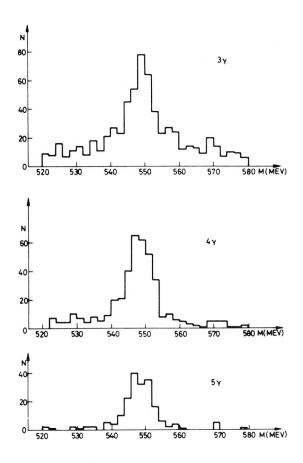

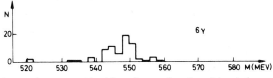

number of observed gammas. Accidentals are already subtracted.

TABLE V

Data of Buniatov et al.[37] Experimental and Best Fit Results of 0–6 $\gamma$ Events and Probabilities (for $E_c = 20$ MeV)[a] to See a 0–6 $\gamma$ Event from the Different Decay Modes. The Experimental Numbers Are Prior to Corrections for Losses Due to Dalitz Pairs and $\gamma$ Conversion in Target and Anticounters. The Number $N_0$ Was Not Used in the Fitting Procedure

| Number $n$ of gammas | Experimental $N_i$ | Best fit contribution from | | Probability to see $n\gamma$ from | | |
|---|---|---|---|---|---|---|
| | | $2\gamma$ | $3\pi^0$ | $2\gamma$ | $\pi^0\gamma\gamma$ | $3\pi^0$ |
| 0 | 122 ± 35 | 90 | 2 | 0.063 | 0.009 | 0.002 |
| 1 | 646 ± 47 | 594 | 17 | 0.418 | 0.090 | 0.019 |
| 2 | 799 ± 55 | 737 | 101 | 0.519 | 0.315 | 0.114 |
| 3 | 270 ± 36 | — | 244 | — | 0.405 | 0.273 |
| 4 | 285 ± 28 | — | 305 | — | 0.181 | 0.342 |
| 5 | 180 ± 20 | — | 178 | — | — | 0.199 |
| 6 | 57 ± 13 | — | 46 | — | — | 0 051 |

[a] Here $E_c$ is the slope of the exponential used in the shower detection efficiency curve.

Butterworth[24] quotes the latest world compilation on $\eta$ decay rates as: $\Gamma(\pi^+\pi^-\pi^0) = 22 \pm 1\%$, $\Gamma(\pi^+\pi^-\gamma) = 5 \pm 1\%$, $\Gamma(\gamma\gamma) = 41 \pm 2\%$, $\Gamma(\pi^0\gamma\gamma) = 2 \pm 2\%$, and $\Gamma(3\pi^0) = 30 \pm 2\%$, which gives $R = 1.4 \pm 0.2$.

## 3. The Search for Rare $\eta$ Decay Modes

There are several rare $\eta$ decay modes which have been investigated and for which upper limits are available. Flatté[38] has searched for the decay mode $\eta \to \pi^+\pi^-\pi^0\gamma$ in the reaction $K^-p \to \Lambda + \eta$ from 1.2–1.7 BeV/c. A sample of 31,000 events with two prongs and a visible $\Lambda$ decay were studied. Of these 14,000 events of the type $K^-p \to \Lambda\pi^+\pi^-$ + neutral(s) were singled out in the search for the above decay mode. He found 17 events which could be consistent with this decay mode but could also have arisen from the reaction $K^-p \to \Sigma^0\pi^+\pi^-\pi^0$. He quotes $\Gamma(\eta \to \pi^+\pi^-\pi^0\gamma)/\Gamma(\eta \to \pi^+\pi^-\pi^0) < 7\%$. Price and Crawford[39] have studied a sample of 219 $\eta$ decays into $\pi^+\pi^-\pi^0$ and compare this to zero observed candidates for $\eta \to \pi^+\pi^-\pi^0\gamma$ or $\eta \to \pi^+\pi^-\gamma\gamma$. The sample comes from 11,000 $\pi^+$ and $\pi^-p$ interactions giving 4 prongs in the 72-in. LRL hydrogen bubble chamber for incident momenta 1050–1170

MeV/c. Their observed missing-mass-square spectrum for the events $\eta \to \pi^+\pi^- + (x^0)$ is shown in Figure 22. They quote upper limits of $\Gamma(\pi^+\pi^-\pi^0\gamma)/\Gamma(\pi^+\pi^-\pi^0) < 0.9\%$ and $\Gamma(\pi^+\pi^-\gamma\gamma)/\Gamma(\pi^+\pi^-\pi^0) < 0.9\%$. Baltay et al.[34] in the work quoted in Section III-2-A above also find upper limits for these decay modes. They quote the 95% confidence level upper limit $(\eta^0 \to \pi^+\pi^-\pi^0\gamma + \eta \to \pi^+\pi^-\gamma\gamma)/(\eta^0 \to \pi^+\pi^-\pi^0) \leqq 1.6\%$.

Baglin et al.[40] have looked for the $C$ violating decay mode $\eta \to \pi^0 e^+ e^-$ in the Ecole Polytechnique heavy-liquid bubble chamber exposed to a 950-MeV/c $\pi^-$ beam. The film examined contained a sample of 752 $\eta \to \pi^0\pi^+\pi^-$ decays with direct $\pi^0$ detection by conversion $\gamma$-rays. They quote $\Gamma(\eta^0 \to \pi^0 e^+ e^-)/\Gamma(\eta \to$ all modes) $< 0.9 \times 10^{-3}$ with 90% confidence level.

More recently Billing et al.[41] have carried out a similar experiment in the University College London–Rutherford Laboratory heavy-liquid bubble chamber. This was done with a 830-MeV/c $\pi^+$ beam. The sample they studied corresponds to an effective number of $\eta$ decays, by all decay modes, of 600. They found no case corresponding to the

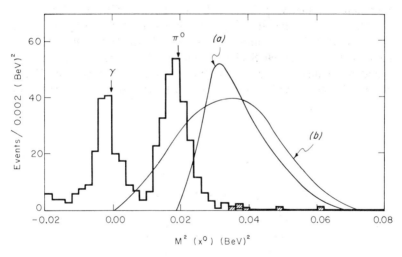

FIG. 22. Spectrum of (mass)$^2$ of missing neutral for $\eta \to \pi^+\pi^- + (x^0)$ in the data of Price and Crawford. At this stage the $4C$ events have been removed, but the remaining events have not been examined on the scanning table. The shaded events were found upon examination at the scanning table to be spurious and were removed. Curves (a) and (b) correspond to the expected spectra for $\eta$ decay into $\pi^+\pi^-\pi^0\gamma$ and $\pi^+\pi^-\gamma\gamma$, respectively.

$\eta \to \pi^0 e^+ e^-$ decay mode and thus conclude $\Gamma(\eta^0 \to \pi^0 e^+ e^-)/\Gamma(\eta \to$ all modes) $< 3.7 \times 10^{-4}$ with 90% confidence level.

## 4. The Search for Asymmetries in the Average $\pi^+$ and $\pi^-$ Energies in $\eta$ Decay

Ever since the discovery of $CP$ violation in $K_2^0$ decay,[12] there has been an intensive search for other interactions which might reveal the nature of this violation. In particular, because it is an example of a $G = +1$ particle decaying into 3 pions ($G = -1$), Friedberg, Lee, and Schwartz[42] singled out the $\eta$ as a promising candidate for detailed studies of decay asymmetries which would indicate violation of $C$. In his rapporteur talk at the 1966 Berkeley meeting, Fitch quoted five experiments which looked for an asymmetry in the average $\pi^+$ and $\pi^-$ energy distribution from $\eta$ decay.[42] In practice this amounts to looking for a right–left asymmetry in a Dalitz plot distribution. Of these five experiments we will discuss the two which have the highest statistics. On the basis of 1351 $\eta$ decay events observed in the reaction $\pi^+ d \to \eta p p$ in a deuterium bubble chamber, a Columbia-Stony Brook group[43] noted an asymmetry of 7.8 $\pm$ 2.8% which is an effect of 2.5 standard deviations. This is the same exposure from which the $\eta$ decay branching ratio (Section III-2-A above) was carried out later. On the other hand, a CERN–Zurich–Saclay[44] spark chamber-counter experiment found no significant asymmetry (0.3 $\pm$ 1.0%) on the basis of 10,665 events. Figures 23 and 24 show the distributions of events over the six

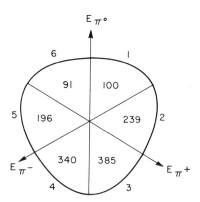

FIG. 23. Dalitz plot for $\eta \to \pi^+ \pi^- \pi^0$ from the Columbia-Stony Brook bubble chamber experiment.

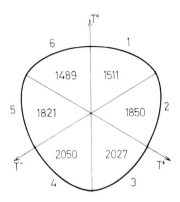

FIG. 24. Dalitz plot for $\eta \to \pi^+\pi^-\pi^0$ from the CERN-Zurich-Saclay spark chamber-counter experiment.

sextants of the $\eta$ decay Dalitz plot for the two experiments. Aside from the left–right asymmetry effects looked for in these experiments one may note the well-known variation of density along the $T_{\pi^0}$ axis mentioned above. The fact that this variation is considerably smaller in the spark chamber experiment is related to detection efficiency which should, however, not affect the left–right asymmetry effects. The conclusion from the presently available experiments is that so far no significant asymmetry has been observed. Considerably higher statistics experiments are currently in progress.[45]

b. *The Quantum Numbers and Decay Modes of the* $X^0(960)$ *or* $\eta'$. We will review the current status of the $I^G$, $J^P$ assignment for the $X^0$. These are based on the following experimental observations:

(a)
$$X^0 \to \pi\pi\eta$$
$$X^0 \not\to \pi\pi\pi$$

Hence, $G = +1$, assuming strong decay.

(b)
$$X^0 \to \pi^+\pi^-\gamma$$

with strong indication for $\rho$ formation. Hence, for

$$X^0 \to \rho^0\gamma$$

we obtain $C = +1$. This then implies that $I = 0$.

(c) The $J^P = 0^-$ assignment comes primarily from the decay angular distribution of the $\pi\pi\gamma$ mode. The $\pi^+\gamma$ angle in the $\rho^0$ center of mass is consistent with a $\sin^2 \theta$ distribution. From this it follows that $J^P = 0^-$ or $0^+$. The odd parity assignment is arrived at on the assumption that $\pi\pi\eta$ and $\pi\pi\gamma$ are decay modes of the same particle. While the mass coincidence looks very good, this can only be established by observing $X^0$ branching ratios for radically different production processes. The following series of figures [from the data of Rittenberg[46]] illustrate the above assertions.

To answer the question of how well the $\pi\pi\gamma$ mode is established—a somewhat tricky measuring and fitting problem—we show Figure 25, which is a correlation between two missing mass squared values: for the reaction,

$$K^-p \rightarrow \Lambda + (\pi^+ + \pi^- + MM)$$

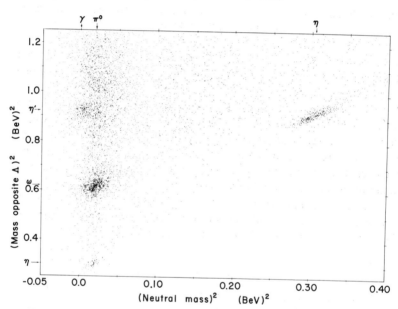

FIG. 25. The data of Rittenberg presented at the 1966 Berkeley Conference on the $K^-p$ interaction from 2.1–2.7 BeV/c. The data shown is a missing mass scatter plot from the reaction $K^-p \rightarrow \Lambda\pi^+\pi^- +$ neutrals. The plot shows clearly that in the region of the $X^0$ (or $\eta'$) the missing mass is in the region of $(MM)^2 = 0$. The points plotted represent unfitted data. The region corresponding to the decay of the $X^0$ into $\pi\pi\eta$, with $\eta$ decay into neutral modes, is seen as the accumulation of points on the right-hand side of the figure. The peculiar shape of this accumulation is due to correlation between the errors contributing to the two missing masses that are plotted.

the plot corresponds to the mass squared of the quantity in the bracket (mass opposite $\Lambda$) versus the neutral mass squared $(MM)^2$. Here we note various clusters of events. At the $X^0$ (or $\eta'$) mass value we see the $\eta$ (proceeding via its neutral decay modes) on the right, as well as an accumulation near the $\pi^0$ mass value but definitely extending to the

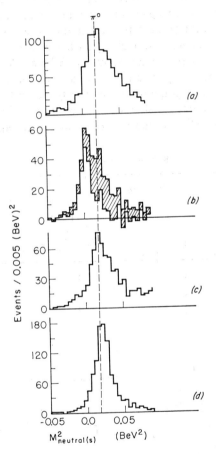

FIG. 26. Data of Rittenberg. Projection of the scatter plot in the previous figure for various slices of the $(\pi^+\pi^- + MM)^2$. The region of the $X^0$ (or $\eta'$) again clearly shows the decay $\pi\pi\gamma$. (a) $0.95 \le M^2_{vs.\Lambda} \le 1.15$ (BeV)$^2$, control region (b) $0.89 \le M^2_{vs.\Lambda} \le 0.95$ (BeV)$^2$ ($\eta'$ region). Cross-hatched area indicates subtraction based on regions below and above $\eta'$ region. (c) Control region $0.70 \le M^2_{vs.\Lambda} \le 0.89$ (BeV)$^2$. (d) $0.50 \le M^2_{vs.\Lambda} \le 0.70$ (BeV)$^2$ ($\omega$ region.)

$(MM)^2 = 0$ region (i.e., $\gamma$ production). Thus the $\pi^0$ peak (vertical band) which goes with $\eta \to \pi^+\pi^-\pi^0$ and $\omega \to \pi^+\pi^-\pi^0$ events is noticeably to the right of the $\gamma$ peak, as is the general continuous $\pi^0$ production background (vertical band). In this plot $\Lambda^0\pi^+\pi^-$ events (4 constraint fits) and $\Sigma^0\pi^+\pi^-$ events (2 constraint fits) have been eliminated. Also a $\Delta^2 < 0.5$ (BeV/c)$^2$ cutoff has been applied. The mass squared projections corresponding to this plot are shown in Figures 26 and 27. Figure 26 shows the neutral $(MM)^2$ projection for $(\pi^+\pi^- + MM)^2$ bands corresponding to the $\omega$, a control region below the $X^0$ mass, the $X^0$ mass band, and a control region above the $X^0$ mass. For the $X^0$ mass band the background expected from the neighboring control bands is shown as shaded. This graph illustrates clearly the shift to $(MM)^2 = 0$, i.e., $\gamma$ production. Figure 27 shows the $(\pi^+\pi^- + MM)^2$ distribution for bands around $(MM)^2 = 0$ and $(MM)^2 = m_\pi{}^2$. Here again one notes

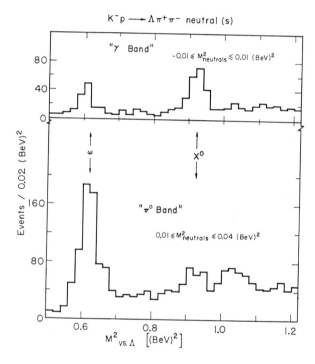

FIG. 27. Data of Rittenberg. The other projection of the scatter plot in Fig. 25 for bands around the $\gamma$ and $\pi^0$ masses, respectively.

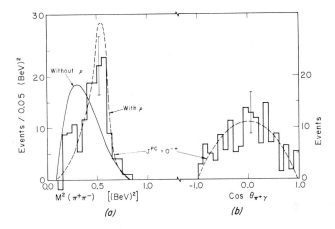

FIG. 28. Data of Rittenberg. (a) Evidence for the decay $X^0 \to \rho^0\gamma$. (b) The distribution of the $\pi^+\gamma$ angle. $K^-p \to \Lambda\eta'$, $\eta' \to \pi^+\pi^-\gamma$. 146 events.

that the $X^0$ lies primarily in the former band while the $\omega$ lies primarily in the latter band. We stress that the observation of the $\omega$ in the $(MM)^2 = 0$ band should not be interpreted as evidence for a $\pi^+\pi^-\gamma$ decay mode of the $\omega$ but rather is an indication of the mass resolution of the experiment. Figure 28 shows the $\pi^+\pi^-$ mass distribution for the $X^0 \to \pi\pi\gamma$ events, indicating the evidence for $\rho$ formation, as well as the $\pi^+\gamma$ angular distribution indicating the $\sin^2\theta$ character.

c. *New Data on the E(1420) Meson.* Baillon et al.[47] have published a considerably more detailed study of the $E$ meson in the reaction

$$\bar{p}p \to K\bar{K}\pi\pi\pi$$

The sample studied represented $1.4 \times 10^6$ annihilations at rest. The particular reactions are:

$$\bar{p}p \to K_1^0 K^\pm \pi^\mp \pi^+ \pi^- \qquad \text{600 events} \qquad (3)$$
$$\to K_1^0 K^\pm \pi^\mp (\pi^0\pi^0) \qquad \text{273 events} \qquad (4)$$
$$\to K_1^0 K_1^0 \pi^0 \pi^+ \pi^- \qquad \text{657 events} \qquad (5)$$
$$\to K_1^0 (K^0\pi^0) \pi^+ \pi^- \qquad \text{757 events} \qquad (6)$$
$$\to K^+ K^- \pi^0 \pi^+ \pi^- \qquad \text{760 events} \qquad (7)$$

Of these reactions (4) and (6) cannot be fitted but are inferred from the $MM$ fit for the particles in brackets, and reaction (7) was obtained for about $\frac{1}{4}$ the total sample.

Figure 29 shows the five $(K\bar{K}\pi)$ mass squared distributions for reactions (3)–(7). We note that:

*1.* $I(E) = 0$ because $(K\bar{K}\pi)^{\pm}$ and $(K\bar{K}\pi)^{\pm\pm}$ do not show the $E$.

*2.* $C(E) = +1$ (most likely) because $E \to K_1{}^0 K_1{}^0 \pi^0$ (83 $\pm$ 21 events in Fig. 29) and not $C = -1$ because $E \nrightarrow K_1 K_2 \pi^0$ (20 $\pm$ 25 events in Fig. 29).

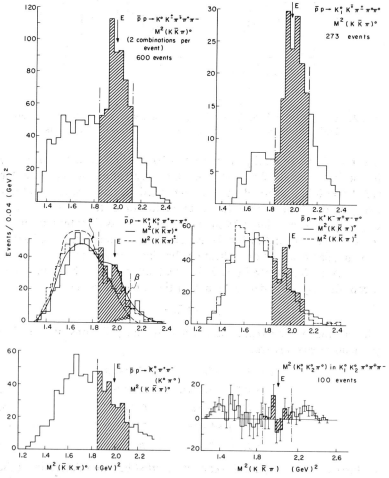

FIG. 29. Data of Baillon et al. Evidence for the $E$ meson from various reactions with antiproton annihilations at rest.

3. From the above two results it follows that $G(E) = +1$. Baillon et al. further conclude that

4. $M(E) = 1425 \pm 7$ MeV, $\Gamma(E) = 80 \pm 10$ MeV.

5. $\Gamma(E \rightarrow K^*\overline{K}$ or $\overline{K}^*K)/\Gamma(E \rightarrow K\overline{K}\pi) \approx 0.5$. Finally they discuss the $J^P$ value of the $E$. They have performed a very elaborate analysis involving the decay $K\pi$ and $K\overline{K}$ mass distributions, Figure 30, as well as decay and production angular distributions shown in Figure 31.

6. From the $(K\overline{K})$ enhancement (Fig. 30) as $E \rightarrow (K\overline{K})\pi$ and as $G(\pi) = -1$ and $I(\pi) = 1$ it follows that $G(K\overline{K}) = -1$ and that $I(K\overline{K}) = 1$. It further follows that $l(K\overline{K})$ is even giving $J^P(K\overline{K}) = 0^+$, $2^+$, if we accept $J^P(K\overline{K}) = 0^+$ then $J^P(E) = 0^-, 1^+, 2^-, \ldots$. However, to have $J^P(K\overline{K}) = 0^+$ compatible with the distribution $W_1(\cos\theta)$, which is nonisotropic, we must invoke $K^*$ interference effects.

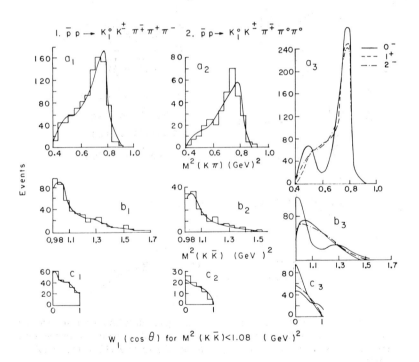

FIG. 30. Data of Baillon et al. Mass distributions and angular distributions relating to the spin determination for the $E$ meson.

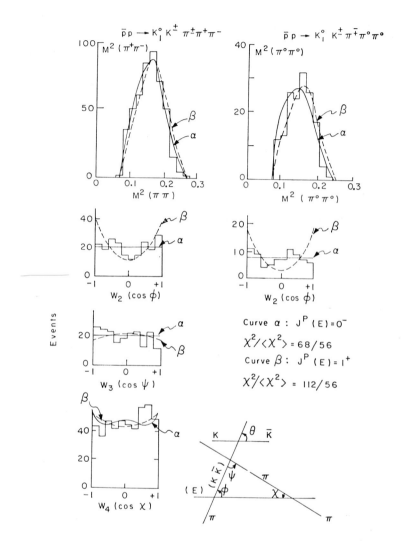

Fɪɢ. 31. Data of Baillon et al. Mass and angular distributions relating to spin determination of the $E$ meson. The angles are defined in the insert on the lower right. Curve $\alpha$: $J^P(E) = 0^-$, $\chi^2/\langle\chi^2\rangle = 68/56$. Curve $\beta$: $J^P(E) = 1^+$, $\chi^2/\langle\chi^2\rangle = 112/56$.

7. The authors express strong preference for $J^P = 0^-$ over $J^P = 1^+$ (and rule out $J^P = 2^-$ as very unlikely). This is based to a large extent on the $W_2(\cos \phi)$ distributions in Figure 31, as well as on further details given in their paper. These results were strengthened recently by a reanalysis by Montanet et al.[48] using an improved treatment of the background and no $0^+$ resonance assumption for the $K\bar{K}$ state.

## B. The Vector Mesons or the $^3S_1$ $(J^{PC} = 1^{--})$ States

Of the nine vector mesons illustrated in Figure 13, the $\rho(760)$, $\omega(783)$, $K^*(890)$, and $\phi(1019)$ are presently very well established. Current research on these particles thus concerns itself mainly with cross-section and decay-correlation measurements; interference phenomena between $\rho$ and $\omega$ (discussed below), between $\rho$ and a conjectured scalar meson (discussed in Sect. III-3-C) between $K^*$ and a possible $S$ wave $K\pi$ background (also discussed in Sect. III-3-C); the search for fine structure: and studies of the rare decay modes.

The $\rho$, $\omega$, and $K^*$ masses give a very poor fit to the Gell-Mann–Okubo octet mass (squared) formula,

$$M_{\omega_8}^2 = \tfrac{4}{3}M_{K^*}^2 - \tfrac{1}{3}M_\rho^2$$

This was rectified on the discovery of the $\phi$ and the concept of singlet mixing introduced by Sakurai. The two physical isosinglet states $\omega$ and $\phi$ are superpositions of the octet and unitary singlet states $\omega_8$ and $\omega_1$ given by:

$$\omega = \omega_1 \cos \theta_1 + \omega_8 \sin \theta_1$$
$$\phi = -\omega_1 \sin \theta_1 + \omega_8 \cos \theta_1$$

where $\theta_1$ is the $J = 1$ mixing angle. The masses are related by:

$$\tan^2 \theta_1 = (M_\phi^2 - M_{\omega_8}^2)/(M_{\omega_8}^2 - M_\omega^2)$$

The vector mesons are actually close to an "ideal nonet" in which the $\phi$ is considered to be composed of the $\bar{\lambda}\lambda$ quarks and the $\omega$ of the quark state $(\bar{p}p + \bar{n}n)\sqrt{2}$.

a. $\phi$ and $\omega$ Production Processes. Dahl et al.[10] show definite evidence for $\phi$ production in the reaction $\pi^- p \to \phi n$ where the $\phi$ decay is observed in the $K^+ K^-$ mode. The $\phi$ meson has been observed in reactions such as $K^- p \to \Lambda \phi$ involving incident strange particles and

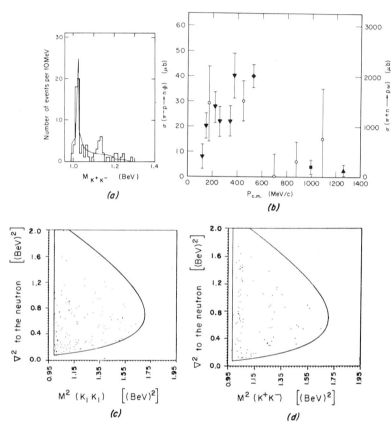

FIG. 32. Data of Dahl et al. on the $\pi^- p$ interaction at a series of momenta from 3 to 4 BeV/c. (*a*) The evidence for $\phi$ production in these reactions. 86 events. (*b*) The cross section for $\phi$ production as a function of $\phi$ momentum in the center-of-mass system. This is compared with the cross section for $\omega$ production now plotted against the $\omega$ center-of-mass momentum. Both these cross sections drop off severely for center-of-mass momenta above 800 MeV/c. The ratio between the two cross sections, left-hand scale vs. right-hand scale is $\sigma(\phi)/\sigma(\omega) \approx 1/50$. (▼) Kraemer et al. $\omega$ (◆) Bacon et al. $\omega$ (■) Cohn et al. $\omega$ (▲) Forino et al. $\omega$ (○) Dahl et al. $\phi$ (*c*) Chew-Low plots for $K_1 K_1$ production and (*d*) for $K^+ K^-$ production which indicate the nonperipheral production of $\phi$ mesons.

strange particle exchange. In the $\pi^- p$ reaction $\phi$ production is highly suppressed, which has been interpreted on the quark model as mentioned above. Similarly $\phi$ decay proceeds primarily through $K_1 K_2$ and $K^+ K^-$; however, a definite $12 \pm 4\%$ $\pi^+ \pi^- \pi^0$ component (including $\pi\rho$) has been observed.[19] This represents the admixture of nonstrange quarks in the $\phi$. Dahl et al. compare the $\phi$ production cross section with $\omega$ production in the reaction $\pi^+ n \to p + \omega$, and find the ratio of about $1:50$ in the cross sections when plotted against the center-of-mass momentum in each case (see Fig. 32). They note that both the $\phi$ production and $\omega$ production appear to go up near threshold and then drop off sharply at higher center-of-mass momenta. One other interesting feature is that $\phi$ production appears to be strongly nonperipheral. This is to be contrasted with the production of the $K_1 K_1$ enhancement of similar mass which is highly peripheral (see Figs. 32c, d).

b. $\omega$-$\rho$ Interference (?). There have been a number of theoretical papers predicting a small branching ratio for $G$ parity violating electromagnetic decay of the $\omega \to \pi^+ \pi^-$. If this occurs there could then be interference phenomena with $\rho^0 \to \pi^+ \pi^-$ decay. Flatté et al.[50] have studied the reactions $K^- p \to \Lambda \pi^+ \pi^- \pi^0$ and $K^- p \to \Lambda \pi^+ \pi^-$ at 1.42–1.7 GeV/c. These have a large cross section for $\omega$ production and not so large for $\rho$ production. In a study of 3887 events (after the competing reactions $K^- p \to Y^* + \pi$ are cut out) they had observed what they consider a statistically significant peak in the $\pi^+ \pi^-$ spectrum at the $\omega$ mass which could be interpreted as either $\omega$-$\rho$ interference or a distinct resonance (if further established) (see Fig. 33). They have published a value of $\Gamma(\omega \to \pi^+ \pi^-)/\Gamma(\omega \to \pi^+ \pi^- \pi^0) = (0.17 \pm 0.03)^2 = 2.9 \times 10^{-2}$ for "complete coherence" and $= (8.2 \pm 2) \times 10^{-2}$ with "complete incoherence." Button-Shafer[51] has reinvestigated this problem with $K^- p$ at 1.7 BeV/c. On the basis of 618 events she quotes the ratio $\Gamma(\omega \to \pi^+ \pi^-)/\Gamma(\omega \to \pi^+ \pi^- \pi^0) = (0.04 \pm 0.10)^2$ for complete coherence, i.e., consistent with the earlier value but also consistent with no effect. The ratios are quoted as the square of the amplitudes rather than the intensities because the error for complete coherence is gaussian for the amplitude.

Roos[52] has recently compiled a very large sample of events with the $\pi^+ \pi^-$ and $\pi^\pm \pi^0$ masses in the $\rho$ band. While there are some indications of anomalies in the data near the $\omega$ mass, the statistics are still not adequate for a definite conclusion. Figure 34 shows a typical sample from his compilation.

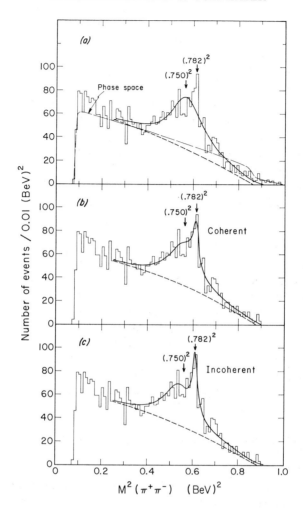

Fig. 33. Data of Flatté et al. Histogram of $M^2(\pi^+\pi^-)$ for $K^-p \rightarrow \Lambda\pi^+\pi^-$ events that are *not* $K^-p \rightarrow Y_1^*(1385) + \pi$; 1.0 to 1.8 BeV/c. (*a*) The solid curve is the fit to $\rho$ alone; the phase-space (dashed) curve is normalized to the total number of background events. The other dashed curve is the background curve (assumed to be parabolic). (*b*) The solid curve is the fit to $\rho$ and $\omega$ with completely coherent amplitudes. The dashed curve is background. (*c*) The solid curve is the fit to $\rho$ and $\omega$ with completely incoherent amplitudes. The dashed curve is background.

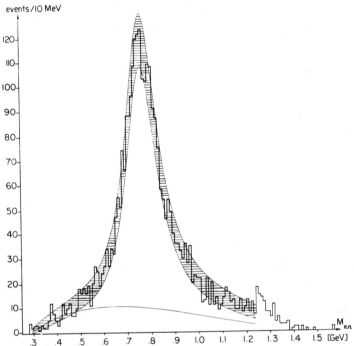

events/10 MeV

FIG. 34. Compilation by Roos to search for $\rho$–$\omega$ interference. $\pi^+ p \rightarrow \pi^+ \pi^- N_{33}^{*++}$. $t < 30$. 3236 events.

This problem is clearly not settled at present and considerably more work will be needed before it is fully understood.

    *c. Vector Meson Decay into Lepton Pairs and the Inverse Process.* There are several recent experiments which have studied the decay of the vector meson—in particular the $\rho^0$—into $\mu^+\mu^-$ as well as $e^+e^-$ pairs. Very recently the inverse process—a colliding $e^-e^+$ beam experiment yielding $\rho^0$ mesons—has also been reported. These experiments, which measure the branching ratio for the decay into lepton pairs, give the coupling constant $\gamma_v$ between the vector mesons and the photon.

### 1. $\rho^0$ Decay into $\mu^+\mu^-$ Pairs

    We will discuss two recent experiments here. Wehmann et al.[53] have studied $\mu$ pair production with 12 GeV/c incident $\pi^-$ meson on iron and carbon targets at the AGS in Brookhaven. These targets were in the form of plates in a spark chamber. The experimental layout is shown in Figure 35. The technique consisted of detecting $\mu$ pairs in a series of range spark chambers. The $\mu$ mesons were separated from $\pi$ mesons by use of a 6.5-ft iron "filter." $\rho^0$ mesons are produced on the complex nuclei by pion exchange. Those decaying into $\mu$ pairs can then be detected in the apparatus. The reaction can be considered as:

$$\pi^- + \pi^+ \text{ (virtual)} \rightarrow \rho^0 \rightarrow \gamma \rightarrow \mu^- + \mu^+$$

For one pion exchange the $\rho^0$ mesons are produced aligned with $m_J = 0$ along the incident direction (see Sect. II-1). If the $\rho^0$ then decays into $\pi^+\pi^-$ pairs these have a $\cos^2 \theta$ angular distribution. However a photon with the corresponding polarization gives rise to a lepton pair with a $\sin^2 \theta$ distribution relative to the incident direction. The alignment of the $\rho^0$ as measured through either of these two angular distributions corresponds to the density matrix element $\rho_{00} \approx 1$. Figure 36 shows the $\mu^+\mu^-$ pair mass distribution and Figure 37 the decay angular distributions and momentum transfer distribution. As may be noted a clear $\rho^0$ signal is observed and the angular distributions of the $\mu$ pairs are indeed consistent with one pion exchange. By comparing their data on carbon and iron with $\rho^0$ production by 16-GeV/c $\pi^-$ mesons in the

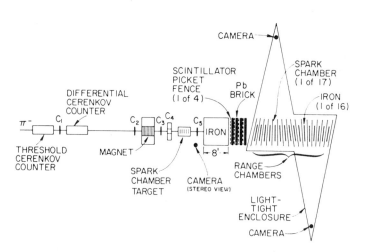

Fig. 35. Experimental layout of Wehmann et al.

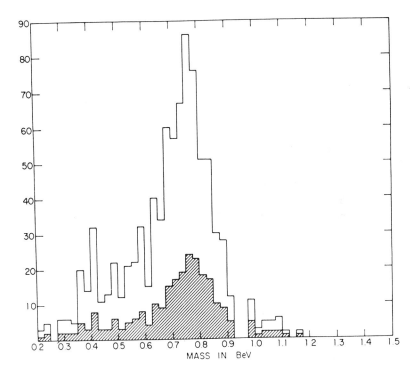

FIG. 36. Data of Wehmann et al. Invariant-mass spectrum of muon pairs. (□) Weighted event. (■) Raw events, unweighted. $|t| < 0.3$ (BeV/c)$^2$.

Ecole Polytechnique heavy-liquid bubble chamber as well as with hydrogen bubble chamber data, Wehmann et al. deduce the branching ratio:

$$(\rho^0 \to \mu^+ + \mu^-)/(\rho^0 \to \pi^+ + \pi^-) = (5.1 \pm 1.2) \times 10^{-5}$$

They also point out that for $|t| < 0.3$ (GeV/c)$^2$ the density matrix elements deduced from their data are consistent with the absorption model (see Fig. 38). For $|t| > 0.3$ the decay angular distribution changes; this may be due to the presence of the $\omega \to \mu^+\mu^-$ decay mode. The decay angular distribution is consistent with this decay mode; however, the width of the corresponding $\mu^+\mu^-$ mass distribution gives no indication of a distinct $\omega$ peak. They do, however, allow an 11% correction for this decay mode.

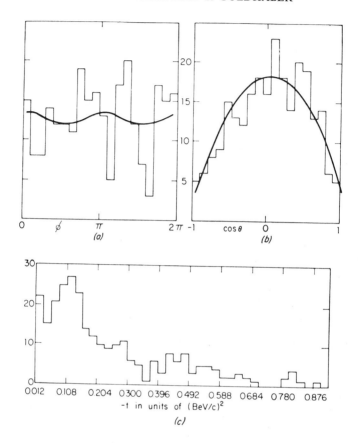

FIG. 37. Data of Wehmann et al. (*a*) Distribution of Treiman-Yang angles. (*b*) Distribution of polar angles vs. cos $\theta$. (*c*) Distribution of momentum transfer.

In a similar experiment Hyams et al.[54] used an 11.2-GeV/c $\pi^-$ beam on LiH at the CERN proton synchrotron. This experimental layout is shown in Figure 39. In this experiment they measured both the $\rho^0 \to \mu^+\mu^-$ and $\rho^0 \to \pi^+\pi^-$ decay modes directly, the latter by removing the iron and lead "filters." Figure 40 shows the resulting $\mu^+\mu^-$ and $\pi^+\pi^-$ mass spectra. From these, and by taking the different decay angular distributions into account, Hyams et al. deduce the branching ratio

$$(\rho^0 \to \mu^+ + \mu^-)/(\rho^0 \to \pi^+ + \pi^-) = (9.7^{+2}_{-2.3}) \times 10^{-5}$$

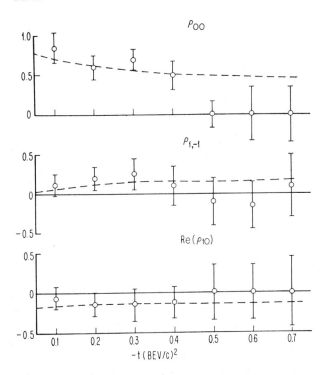

FIG. 38. Data of Wehmann et al. Decay-correlation matrix elements for combined carbon and iron events in the dimuon mass range $600 < M_{\mu\mu} < 900$ MeV plotted as a function of four-momentum transfer. These matrix elements were obtained by making maximum-likelihood fits to weighted distributions, with the weights proportional to the efficiency of the experimental detection system. The dashed line represents predictions of a one-pion exchange model including absorption.

Hyams et al. note that their angular distribution differs from that of the above experiment. They deduce $\rho_{00} = 0.07^{+0.24}_{-0.07}$ from their $\mu$ pairs and thus suggest that $\omega$ interference may not be negligible. Earlier determinations for the above branching ratio are Zdanis et al.[55] $(10^{+12}_{-8}) \times 10^{-5}$ and de Pagter et al.[56] $(4.4^{+1.6}_{-0.07}) \times 10^{-5}$.

## 2. Evidence for $\phi$ Decay into $\mu^+\mu^-$ Pairs

Wehmann et al.[53] also used the small (3%) $K^-$ component in their beam to look for $\phi$ production. As may be seen in Figure 41 they observed a definitive $\phi \rightarrow \mu^+\mu^-$ signal in this case.

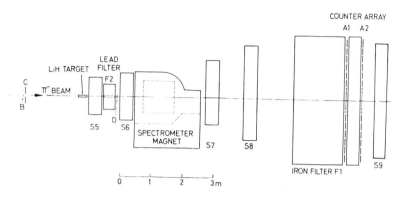

FIG. 39. Experimental arrangement of Hyams et al. $B$, $C$, $D$, $A_1$, and $A_2$ are scintillation counters. $S_5 \ldots S_8$ are thin foil, and $S_9$ are thick plate spark chambers.

### 3. $\rho^0$ Decay into $e^+e^-$ Pairs

The branching ratio $B$ of $(\rho^0 \rightarrow e^+e^-)/(\rho^0 \rightarrow \pi^+\pi^-)$ has been measured very recently by Asbury et al.[57] at DESY. The measurements were carried out with a double-arm spectrometer and threshold Čerenkov counters as well as lead-lucite shower counters to separate the electrons and pions. The experiment was done by use of a $\gamma$-beam impinging on a carbon target. Here $\rho$ production occurs via a diffraction process[58] as was demonstrated by the authors by studying various target materials from beryllium to lead.

The resulting mass distributions are shown in Figure 42. The branching ratio deduced is $B = (6.5 \pm 1.4) \times 10^{-5}$. The authors also point out that photoproduction of $\omega$ mesons—which could contribute in the same mass region—is small. Bubble chamber experiments indicate it to be $\approx 10\%$ of $\rho^0$ production.

### 4. $\rho^0$ Production in an Electron–Position Colliding Beam Experiment

Very recently Auslander et al.[59] presented preliminary results of an electron–positron colliding beam experiment. In this experiment they studied the reaction

$$e^- + e^+ \rightarrow \pi^- + \pi^+$$

in a spark chamber-counter array placed perpendicular to the VEPP-2 colliding beam storage ring at Novosibirsk. The experimental layout is

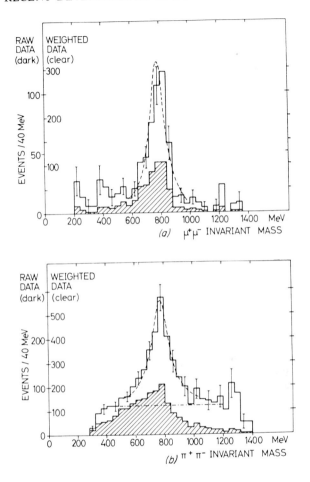

FIG. 40. Data of Hyams et al. Invariant mass of $\mu$ pairs (*a*), and $\pi$ pairs (*b*), with $E \geqq 10$ GeV. Hatched area shows raw data. Higher histograms show weighted data on arbitrary scale. Dashed curves show best fit Breit-Wigner resonances.

shown in Figure 43. In the experiment described they observed 303 collinear events in 742 hr of running time spread out over a period of 5 months. The events were identified as 186 $e^- e^+$ elastic scatters, 109 $\pi^- \pi^+$ production events, and 8 $\mu^- \mu^+$ pairs. The measurement consists of finding the ratio of pion pair production cross section $\sigma_\pi$ and

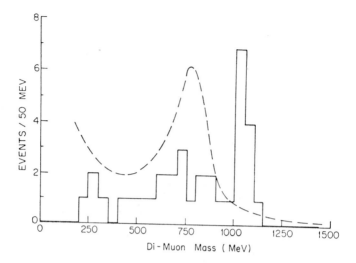

FIG. 41. Data of Wehmann et al. Evidence for $\phi \rightarrow \mu^+\mu^-$. Dimuon mass spectrum for 34 events produced with 12-BeV/c $K^-$ mesons incident on carbon and iron. For comparison the mass spectrum produced with 12-BeV/c $\pi^-$ mesons incident on carbon and iron is also shown (–––), scaled down by a factor of 50. (The incident 12-BeV/c beam contained about 3% $K^-$ meson.)

the $e^- e^+$ elastic scattering cross section $\sigma_e$. This ratio is expressed as

$$\sigma_\pi / \sigma_e = (\beta_\pi^3 / a) F^2(E)$$

where $\beta_\pi$ corresponds to the pion velocity, $a$ is a geometric constant which for 90° production is $a = 18$, and $F^2(E)$ is the pion production form factor which can be expressed by a Breit-Wigner formula:

$$F^2(E) = k m_\rho^4 / [(4E^2 - m_\rho^2)^2 + m_\rho^2 \Gamma_\rho^2]$$

Figure 44 shows a plot of $F^2$ against the total energy $2E$ of the $e^- e^+$ system. The $\rho^0$ peak shows up clearly and a fit of the Breit-Wigner formula gives $k = 0.59 \pm 0.15$, $m_\rho = 764 \pm 11$ MeV, and $\Gamma_\rho = 93 \pm 15$ MeV, where the remarkable feature is the narrow width $\Gamma_\rho$ observed for the $\rho$ meson. The entire pion pair production is consistent with $\rho^0$ production. At the peak the cross section is $\sigma_\rho = 1.2 \pm 0.2 \,\mu\text{b}$.

### 3. Mesons Which May Correspond to the $L = 1$ $q\bar{q}$ States

The phenomena which may correspond to the $L = 1$ states are sketched in Figure 45. Here only the $J^{PC} = 2^{++}$ states can be considered as established.

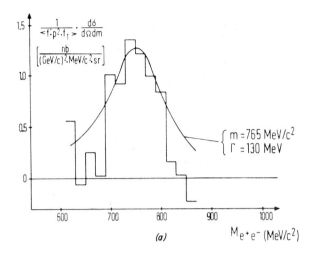

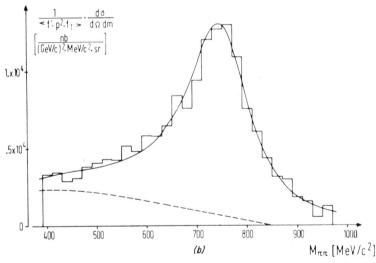

Fig. 42. Data of Asbury et al. (a) Pair yield from $\rho^0 \rightarrow e^+e^-$ as function of invariant mass. Bethe-Heitler background has been subtracted, and the magnitude of the yield includes the effect of the complete polarization of the $\rho^0$ mesons. The peak bremsstrahlung energy $k_{max} = 6.0$ GeV. 94 events. (b) Pair yield from $\rho^0 \rightarrow \pi^+\pi^-$ as function of invariant mass. Again the effect of polarization of the $\rho^0$ mesons is included in the calculation of the yield. The momentum $p$ is 2.8 GeV/c, and $k_{max} = 6.0$ GeV. 15,649 events.

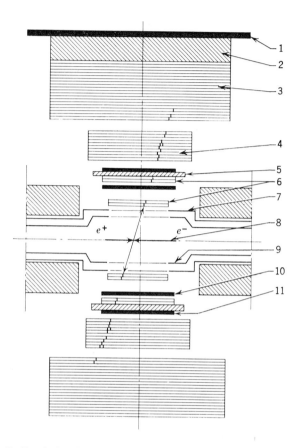

FIG. 43. Spark chamber-counter system at the VEPP-2 colliding beam storage ring at Novosibirsk. (*1*) Anticoincidence scintillation counter; (*2*) lead absorber 20 cm thick; (*3*) "range" spark chamber; (*4*) "shower" spark chamber; (*5*) Dur-aluminum absorber 2 cm thick; (*6*) thin-plate spark chambers; (*7*) window of outer vacuum chamber; (*8*) interaction region; (*9*) inner vacuum chamber; (*10*) storage ring magnet; and (*11*) scintillation counters.

## A. The Tensor Mesons or the $^3P_2$ ($J^{PC} = 2^{++}$) States

One isotopic spin singlet of the $J^P = 2^+$ nonet, the $f^0$, has been known for a comparatively long time.[60] Next came the isotopic triplet,[61] the $A_2$, followed by the two doublets, the $K^*(1420)$ and its antiparticle.[62] Initial attempts to fit these components into an octet

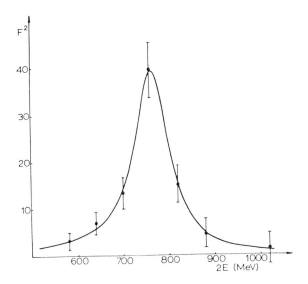

FIG. 44. $\rho^0$ production in the Novosibirsk $e^- e^+$ colliding beam experiment. The peak corresponds to a cross section $\sigma(e^- e^+ \to \pi^- \pi^+) = 1.2 \pm 0.2 \,\mu\text{b}$.

failed because they did not fulfill the Gell-Mann–Okubo mass formula. It was only with the discovery of the other singlet,[63] the $f^*(1500)$, that it was realized that here again, as in the $J^P = 1^-$ nonet, very considerable octet–singlet mixing must be occurring.[64] Thus the broad outlines concerning the nine tensor mesons $A_2(1300)$, $f^0(1250)$, $K^*(1420)$, and $f^*(1500)$ appear well established at present. There are, however, a number of finer details such as the minor decay modes which are still not settled. Furthermore, there are some new indications of additional structure in the $A_2$ which bring the simple $q\bar{q}$ model into question. These features will be discussed below.

a. *The $A_2(1300)$ Meson.* The decay modes observed for the $A_2$ meson are:

$$\begin{aligned} A_2 &\to \pi\rho \quad \text{principal decay mode} \\ &\to K\bar{K} \\ &\to \pi\eta \end{aligned} \Bigg\} \text{minor decay modes}$$

There is good evidence that $J^P = 2^+$ for the $K\bar{K}$ decay mode.[65] Considerable controversy has, however, occurred on the $J^P$ value as

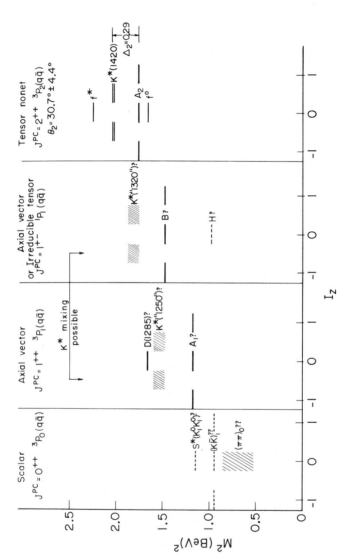

FIG. 45. A (mass)² vs. $I_z$ diagram for the $J^{PC} = 2^{++}$ tensor nonet as well as the tentative assignments for the other three $L = 1$ nonets. Where the exact mass of the proposed resonance is not known, it is indicated by a shaded region ,(———),(?), and (??) all indicate various degrees of tentative assignments.

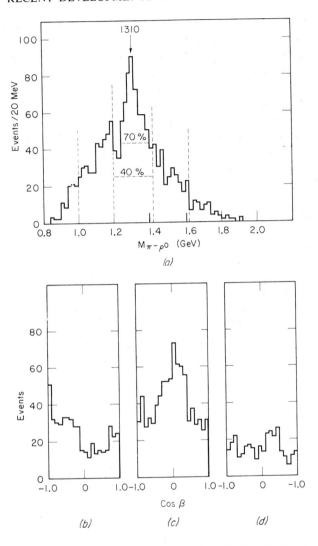

FIG. 46. Data of Chung et al. on the spin determination for the $A_2 \to \pi^- \rho^0$ decay mode. (a) The $M_{\pi^- \rho^0}$ spectrum for $\rho^0$ events [outside the diffraction region to reduce $A_1$ effects, with $\Delta_p{}^2 < 0.65$ (GeV/c)$^2$]. 1461 events. The vertical dashed lines indicate the $A_2$ region as well as the control regions, and the horizontal dashed lines indicate background levels in the $A_2$ region. (b)–(d) Distributions in cos $\beta$ for the three $M_{\pi^- \rho^0}$ intervals indicated in (a), where $\beta$ is the angle between $\pi^+$ and the "bachelor" $\pi^-$ evaluated in the $\rho^0$ rest frame. (b) 372 events, $M_{\pi^- \rho^0}(1.0 - 1.2)$. (c) 663 events, $M_{\pi^- \rho^0}(1.2 - 1.42)$. (d) 268 events, $M_{\pi^- \rho^0}(1.42 - 1.62)$.

determined from the $\pi\rho$ decay mode. It is clear that the $A_2$ meson is sitting on very substantial background. It turns out that the spin determination is strongly dependent on how one carries out the background subtraction. We show the analysis by Chung et al.[65] as an example of how the background affects the spin determination. If one uses a zero background subtraction, the solution $2^-$ is preferred. However, as the amount of background is increased, $2^+$ becomes more probable (see Figs. 46–48). This same conclusion has been arrived at in many recent experiments[66] studying the decay of the $A_2^0 \to \rho^\pm\pi^\mp$. On the other hand, the $A_2^+$ decay in the 8-GeV/c $\pi^+p$ experiment[67] appears to yield results preferring $J^P = 2^-$ or $1^+$. It must be mentioned, however, that even in the latter experiments with $\Delta^2$ cuts which suppress diffraction dissociation the $2^+$ solution occurs at about the 1% probability level.

*1. Evidence for Structure in the $A_2$ Mass Region.* A phenomenon that is at present obscure—and does not appear to fit into the $q\bar{q}$ model —is the splitting of the $A_2$ peak observed by Chikovani et al. in the CERN missing-mass-spectrometer experiment.[68]

The experimental evidence looks good; they observed a six standard deviation dip in the center of the $A_2$ peak. There is one small point one should perhaps worry about. The runs from different years give a shift

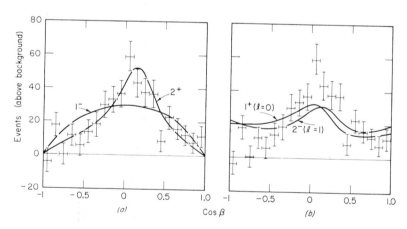

FIG. 47. Data of Chung et al. Comparison of the experimental $\cos\beta$ distributions in the $A_2$ region at the 50% background level with the theoretical curves for the $J^P = 1^-$, $2^+$, $1^+$ ($l = 0$) and $2^-$ ($l = 1$).

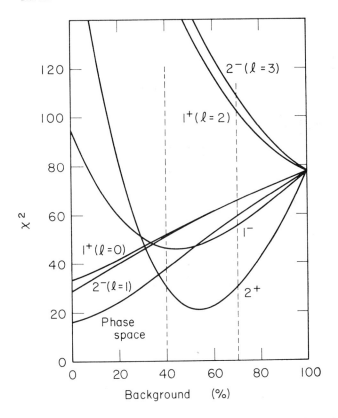

FIG. 48. Data of Chung et al. Variation of $\chi^2$ (19 degrees of freedom) for various $J_P$ assignments for the $A_2$ as a function of the background level.

in the $A_2$ central mass values; in the final distribution they were combined by superimposing these respective central mass values. However, as the authors point out, since the absolute value of the beam momentum is only known to 2%, the apparent shifts appear reasonable.

The combined data is shown in Figure 49. The authors interpret this data as:

(*a*) two incoherent resonances at

$$M_1 = 1.275(\pm 0.016) \text{ GeV} \qquad \Gamma_1 = 0.020(\pm 0.01) \text{ GeV}$$
$$M_2 = 1.318(\pm 0.016) \text{ GeV} \qquad \Gamma_2 = 0.020(\pm 0.01) \text{ GeV}$$

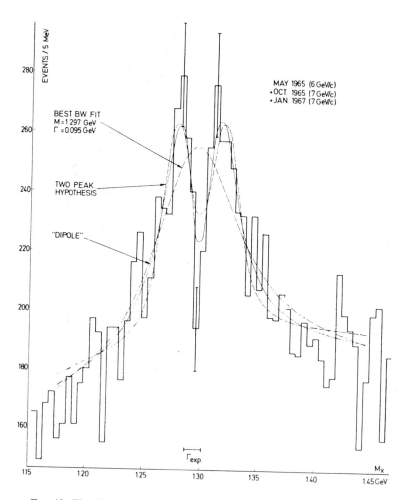

FIG. 49. The CERN missing-mass spectrometer analysis of the $A_2$ meson.

or (b) two coherent resonances, or a "dipole," i.e., two resonances with equal amplitudes and widths

$$N(M) \sim [\Gamma^2(M - M_0)^2]/\{(M - M_0)^2 + \tfrac{1}{4}\Gamma^2\}^2$$

with $M_0 = 1.296 \pm 0.016$ GeV and $\Gamma = 0.028 \pm 0.003$ GeV. The single resonance hypothesis which ignores the dip gives only a 1% $\chi^2$

probability. Here it is important to remember that this experiment represents a measurement in one small region of four-momentum transfer squared; namely the $t$ interval 0.31–0.39 $(GeV/c)^2$.

Morrison[67] has suggested from a study of the production cross section of the $A_2$, the above-mentioned different $J^P$ assignments, and discrepancies in the $A_2$ branching ratios, that there may be two distinct objects in this peak—a $2^+$ resonance as well as another one with $2^-$ or $1^+$. According to Morrison, the production cross section for boson resonances follow the empirical relation:

$$\sigma = K p_{lab}^{-n}$$

where $K$ is a constant and $p_{lab}$ the incident laboratory momentum.[107] Various exchange mechanisms can be classified according to the value of $n$. He finds that for Pomeron exchange or diffraction dissociation $n \approx 0$, for meson exchange $n \approx 2$, and for baryon exchange $n \approx 4$. For $A_2$ production he deduced the experimental value $n = 0.5 \pm 0.2$ and hence suggests that a mixture of two resonances may be involved. Further work will be needed to check the validity of this suggestion and to understand the significance of the splitting.

*b. The K\*(1420) Branching Ratio.* Bassano et al.[69] have recently reevaluated the $K\pi/(K\pi + K\pi\pi)$ branching ratio of the $K^*(1420)$. In this work based on $K^-p$ data at 4.6 and 5 BeV/c they have made judicious use of the $\Delta^2$ dependence of the $K^*(1420)$ relative to other nearby $K^*$ effects (namely, the $Q$ enhancement, see Sect. III-3-B-c). The $K^*(1420)$ $\Delta^2$ distribution is considerably wider. Thus a lower bound for $\Delta^2$ at 0.2 $(BeV/c)^2$ together with an upper bound at 2 $(BeV/c)^2$ for background elimination yields a particularly clean sample for the determination of the branching ratio (see Fig. 50). They conclude

$$K\pi/(K\pi + K\pi\pi) = 0.39 \pm 0.11$$

The same authors have also evaluated the $K\rho$ and $K^*\pi$ branching ratio based on the reaction $K^-p \rightarrow \bar{K}^0\pi^+\pi^-n$. The charge exchange reaction at the nucleon vertex has the property that the $Q$ peak does not appear to be produced, thus allowing the study of the $K^*(1420)$ effect with considerably reduced background (see Fig. 108 in Sect. III-4-B-c). The various branching ratios for the entire $2^+$ nonet are given in Section III-3-A-d below, where they are compared with a least square fit to the $SU(3)$ rates. Here we must note that the values of the above branching ratio are not yet completely settled. Thus the Argonne-Northwestern

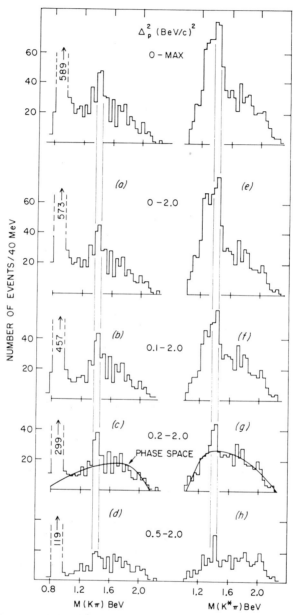

FIG. 50. Data of Bassano et al. Variation of $K\pi$ and $K^*\pi$ mass spectra (from $\bar{K}^0\pi^-p$ and $\bar{K}^0\pi^-p\pi^0$ final states, respectively), for a fixed upper cutoff and a *variable* lower cutoff in $\Delta^2(p)$.

groups ($K^-p$ at 4–5.5 GeV/c) quote[24] $K^*\pi/K\pi = 0.62 \pm 0.11$ and $K\rho/K\pi = 0.31 \pm 0.16$, which yields a $K\pi/K\pi\pi$ ratio close to unity.

c. *Further Study of the $f^*$(1520).* Barnes et al.[70] have continued their study of the $f^*$(1520) in the $K^-p \rightarrow (\Lambda^0, \Sigma^0)K\bar{K}$ reactions at 4.6 and 5 BeV/c. Figure 51 shows their data for $f^*$ decay into the $K^+K^-$, $K^0\bar{K}^0$, and $K_1^0K_1^0$ modes for peripheral production (or backward $\Lambda$ production) defined as $-1 \leqq \cos \theta_\Lambda \leqq -0.6$. By fitting a Breit-Wigner distribution to this data they find mass and width values of $M = 1513 \pm 7$ MeV and $\Gamma = 87 \pm 15$ MeV for the $f^*$. They have also carried out a search for various other decay modes of the $f^*$, namely

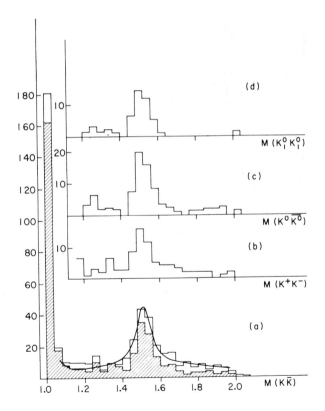

FIG. 51. The data of Barnes et al. showing $\phi$ and $f^*$ production. (a) $K\bar{K}$ mass spectrum. The shaded region corresponds to $\cos \theta_\Lambda < -0.6$. (b)–(d) Peripheral mass spectra for decay modes indicated in the figure.

$K\pi\pi$, $\pi^{+}\pi^{-}$, $\pi\pi\eta$, and $\eta\eta$ by the study of ($\Lambda^{0}$, $\Sigma^{0}$) production together with the above particle groups. They found that the $K\pi\pi$ mode is smaller than they originally estimated, upper limits for the $\pi^{+}\pi^{-}$ and $\eta\eta$ mode (as deduced from the $MM$ spectrum) and a possible small (2 standard deviation) signal for the $\pi\pi\eta$ mode. The results are illustrated in Figure 52. The quantitative data is given in Section III-3-A-d below. Finally, they also discuss the quantum numbers of the $f^{*}$. From the fact that $f^{*} \rightarrow K_{1}{}^{0}K_{1}{}^{0}$ it follows that $C = +1$.

This may be expressed quantitatively by a study of the ratio $R = (N_{2} - N_{1})/N_{2} + N_{1})$, where $N_{1}(N_{2})$ is the number of events with

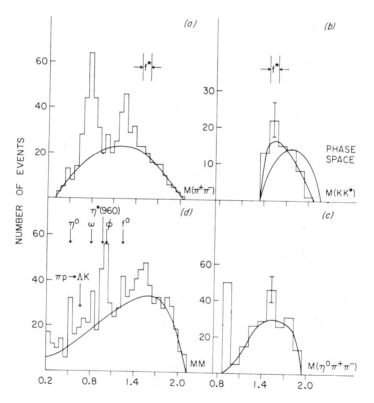

FIG. 52. Mass spectra used in search for various $f^{*}$ decay modes by Barnes et al. (a) $K^{-}p \rightarrow (\Lambda^{0},\Sigma^{0})\pi^{+}\pi^{-}$, $\cos\theta_{\Lambda} < -0.6$. (b) $K^{-}p \rightarrow (\Lambda^{0},\Sigma^{0})K\bar{K}^{*} \rightarrow (\Lambda^{0},\Sigma^{0})\bar{K}K^{*}$. $\cos\theta_{\Lambda} < -0.6$. (c) $K^{-}p \rightarrow \Lambda^{0}\eta^{0}\pi^{+}\pi^{-}$, $\Delta^{2}_{p\Lambda} < 0.9$ (BeV/c)$^{2}$. (d) $K^{-}p \rightarrow \Lambda^{0}MM$, $\cos\theta_{\Lambda} < 0.6$.

one (two) visible $K_1^0$ decays. For a $C = -1$ meson $N_2 = 0$ and thus $R = -1$, for a $C = +1$ meson one obtains from the $K_1^0 \to \pi^+\pi^-$ to $K_1^0 \to \pi^0\pi^0$ ratio that $R = +\frac{1}{5}$. Experimentally they find $R(f^*) = 0.46 \pm 0.2$. Having established $C = +1$ for the $f^*$ the allowed $J^P$ values are $0^+$, $2^+$, $4^+$, .... Figure 53 shows the $f^* \to K_1^0 K_1^0$ decay angular distribution as well as the distribution of the moments $a_l^m$ as a function of $M(K\bar{K})$ for all $K\bar{K}$ decay modes. Here the decay angular distribution $f(\theta, \varphi)$ is expressed as $f(\theta, \varphi) = \sum_{l=0}^{2J} \frac{1}{2} a_l^m [Y_l^m(\theta, \varphi) + Y_l^{-m}(\theta, \varphi)]$. Both methods indicate $J^P > 0^+$ and probably $2^+$ although $4^+$ cannot be ruled out.

Ammar et al.[71] have studied the $f^*$ in the $K^-p$ interaction at 5.5 GeV/c. Their data differs from the above primarily in that they observe a considerably narrower decay width (see Fig. 54). They find

$$M(f^*) = 1515 \pm 7 \text{ MeV}$$

and

$$\Gamma(f^*) = 35 \pm 25 \text{ MeV}$$

Furthermore, they see no evidence for the $\pi\pi\eta$, $\pi\pi$, and $(K^*\bar{K} + \bar{K}^*K + K\bar{K}\pi)$ decay modes and quote $0 \pm 0.3$, $0 \pm 0.2$, and $0 \pm 0.4$ of the $K\bar{K}$ mode as limits on these. From angular distribution studies they concur with $J^P = 2^+$ or $4^+$. As far as the comparison with $SU(3)$ is concerned (see Table VI) the lower value for $\Gamma(f^*)$ suggested here actually appears to give a better agreement.

It is interesting to note here that the $\pi^+\pi^-$ branching ratio of the $f^*$ is very low. This would thus imply that, just as in the case of the $\varphi$ (for which the $\pi\rho$ branching ratio is very low), the $f^*$ may also be primarily composed of the $\lambda\bar{\lambda}$ quarks. As a consequence of this, one would expect $f^*$ production in $\pi^-p$ reactions, in which the $f^0$ shows up very strongly, to be suppressed.

*d. Comparison with SU(3).* Bassano et al.[69] have also reexamined the fit of the decay rates of the $2^+$ nonet with the predictions of $SU(3)$. The two-body decay rate $\Gamma$ for a member of an $SU(3)$ multiplet can be expressed in terms of

$$\Gamma = |M|^2 C^2 (p/m^2)[p^2 X^2/(p^2 + X^2)]^2$$

where $M$ is the decay matrix element which in unbroken $SU(3)$ should be a constant for all the members of a multiplet, $C$ is an $SU(3)$ Clebsch-

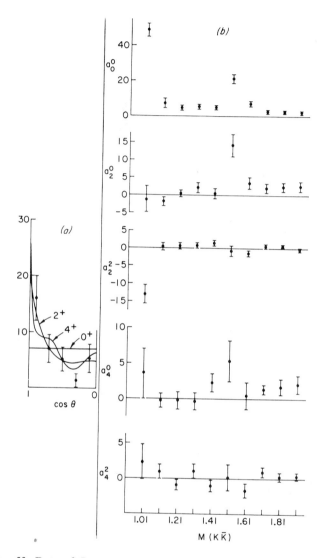

FIG. 53. Data of Barnes et al. (a) Polar angle distribution of decay kaon from $f^* \to K_1^0 + K_1^0$ in $f^*$ rest frame. (b) Moments $(a_l^m)$ distribution of $K\bar{K}$ events plotted against $K\bar{K}$ effective mass.

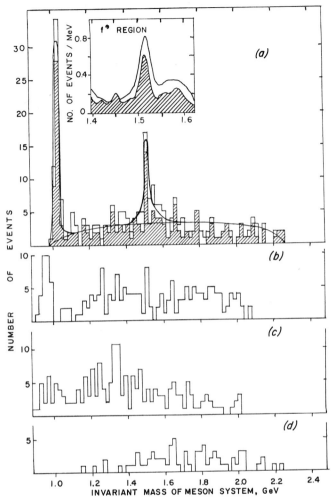

FIG. 54. Data of Ammar et al. for $K^- p$ at 5.5 GeV/c. (a) The invariant mass distribution for a total of 246 events fitting the hypothesis $K^- p \to \Lambda K \bar{K}$. The $\Lambda K^+ K^-$ events are differentiated from the $\Lambda K^0 \bar{K}^0$ events by cross-hatching. The curve consists of two Breit-Wigner functions plus phase space, fitted to the entire sample of both types of events. The insert shows a more detailed mass ideogram in the region of the $f^*$. (b) Missing mass (MM) distribution in the reaction $K^- p \to \Lambda + MM$ for those events that fit the hypothesis $K^- p \to \Lambda \pi^+ \pi^- \eta$. Only those events with $\Delta^2(MM) \leqq 0.7$ (GeV/c)$^2$, and having a mass for the missing $\eta$ within $\pm 50$ MeV of the known $\eta$ mass, have been plotted. (c) Invariant mass distribution of the $\pi^+ \pi^-$ system for events fitting the hypothesis $K^- p \to \Lambda \pi^+ \pi^-$ and having $\Delta^2(\pi^+ \pi^-) \leqq 0.7$ (GeV/c)$^2$. (d) Invariant mass distribution of the $K \bar{K} \pi$ system for events fitting $\Lambda K^0 \bar{K}^0 (\pi^0)$ or $\Lambda K^+ \pi^- \bar{K}^0$ or $\Lambda K^- \pi^+ K^0$, for which at least two neutral decays were detected.

TABLE VI

Comparison of the Decay Rates of the Tensor Nonet with $SU(3)$ According to Bassano et al.[69]

| Decay mode | $\Gamma_{\text{expt}}$, MeV | $SU(3)$ coefficients | $SU(3)$ rates $\Gamma$, MeV |
|---|---|---|---|
| | Type $A$ decays $2^+ \rightarrow 1^- + 0$ | | |
| $A_2(1320) \rightarrow \rho\pi$ | $56 \pm 19$ | $4$ | $67$ |
| $K^*(1420) \rightarrow K^*\pi$ | $34 \pm 12$ | $3/2$ | $22$ |
| $K^*(1420) \rightarrow \rho K$ | $10 \pm 9$ | $3/2$ | $6$ |
| $K^*(1420) \rightarrow \omega^0 K$ | $4 \pm 3$ [a] | $\frac{3}{2} \sin^2 \theta_1$ | $2$ |
| $f^*(1500) \rightarrow K^*K$ | $9 \pm 9$ [a] | $6 \cos^2 \theta_2$ | $10$ |
| | Type $B$ decays $2^+ \rightarrow 0^- + 0^-$ | | |
| $A_2 \rightarrow K\bar{K}$ | $2.5 \pm 2$ | $12$ | $4$ |
| $A_2 \rightarrow \eta^0\pi$ | $6.5 \pm 6$ | $8$ | $7$ |
| $K^*(1420) \rightarrow K\pi$ | $29 \pm 13$ | $18$ | $29$ |
| $K^*(1420) \rightarrow K\eta^0$ | $3 \pm 3$ [a] | $2$ | $1$ |
| $f^0 \rightarrow \pi\pi$ | $117 \pm 21$ | $3(2 \sin \theta_2 + \alpha \cos \theta_2)^2$ | $121$ |
| $f^0 \rightarrow K\bar{K}$ | $0 \pm 12$ | $4(\sin \theta_2 - \alpha \cos \theta_2)^2$ | $7$ |
| $f^0 \rightarrow \eta^0\eta^0$ | $0 \pm 12$ [a] | $(2 \sin \theta_2 - \alpha \cos \theta_2)^2$ | $1$ |
| $f^* \rightarrow \pi\pi$ | $0 \pm 6$ [a] | $3(2 \cos \theta_2 - \alpha \sin \theta_2)^2$ | $1$ |
| $f^* \rightarrow K\bar{K}$ | $62 \pm 15$ | $4(\cos \theta_2 + \alpha \sin \theta_2)^2$ | $33$ |
| $f^* \rightarrow \eta^0\eta^0$ | $0 \pm 16$ [a] | $(2 \cos \theta_2 + \alpha \sin \theta_2)^2$ | $8$ |

[a] Only two standard deviation *upper limits* appear to be significant for these rates. For the purpose of fitting, such upper limits are recorded as zero $\pm$ one standard deviation.

Gordan coefficient which also includes the octet–singlet mixing effects, $p$ is the decay momentum in the center of mass, $p/m^2$ is a phase space factor, and $X$ is an inverse interaction radius. It was shown earlier by Goldberg et al.[132] that the results are very insensitive to $X$ for values $> 200$ MeV.

One must distinguish between two types of decay: $2^+ \rightarrow 1^- + 0^-$ (type $A$) and $2^+ \rightarrow 0^- + 0^-$ (type $B$). For the former there are only two parameters to fit $|M_A|^2$ and $X_A$. In the latter case there are three parameters $|M_B|^2$, $X_B$, and $\alpha$, where $\alpha$ is proportional to the ratio of singlet to octet decay amplitudes. The experimental decay rates and the fitted rates are given in Table VI. A reasonable fit can be obtained, but as the authors point out, one will need considerably greater accuracy in the decay rates before a sensitive test of agreement with $SU(3)$ can be made.

Here it should also be noted that substantially higher values for the ratio $A_2 \rightarrow \eta\pi/\pi\rho$ have been quoted at the Heidelberg Conference.[24] These are:

| | | |
|---|---|---|
| Genova–Hamburg–Milano–Scalay | 11 GeV/c $\pi^-$ | 26 ± 9% |
| Bonn–Durham–Nijmegen–Paris–Torino | 5 GeV/c $\pi^+$ | 24 ± 8% |
| Urbana | 5 GeV/c $\pi^-$ | 23 ± 8% |

Higher values for $A_2 \rightarrow K\bar{K}/\pi\rho$ are also discussed in Section III-3-C-b below.

### B. Evidence for Some $^3P_1$ and $^1P_1$ ($J^{PC} = 1^{++}$ and $1^{+-}$) States

None of the candidates for the two $1^+$ nonets $^3P_1$ and $^1P_1$ expected on the $q\bar{q}$ model can be considered as fully established at present. We will discuss a number of phenomena which are candidates for these nonets. Should it turn out that none of these assignments is correct, it would throw serious doubts on the validity of the $q\bar{q}$ model. We will thus proceed with our discussion as if the $q\bar{q}$ model holds, keeping in mind that the validity of the assignments represent a test of the model.

*a. The $A_1$, the Candidate for $I^GJ^P = 1^-1^+$.* The $A_1$ effect is beset by a number of difficulties:

#### 1. Kinematic Effects

It is possible to reproduce a peak at low $M(\pi\rho)$ values through $\pi$ exchange and scatter at the nucleon vertex [known as the Deck effect[72]], $\rho$ exchange and scatter at the nucleon vertex, and diffraction dissociation.[133] Recently Ross and Yam[73] have suggested that these three effects may be comparable and that one needs to take a coherent superposition of all three effects (see Fig. 55). More recently, Berger[74] has suggested Regge pole exchange which gives rise to narrower peaks. There is no doubt that the kinematic effects are really present as was shown by Shen et al.,[75] for example. However, so far no such model has reproduced all the experimental data on the $A_1$ in a quantitative fashion.

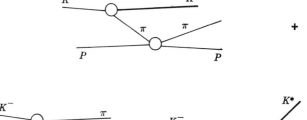

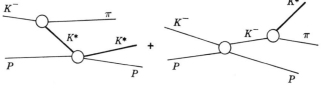

Fig. 55. The Feynman diagrams for the three amplitudes of Ross and Yam illustrated here for the reaction $K^- p \to K^* \pi p$.

## 2. Experimental Observation

There are a number of good experiments in which a definite, sharp $A_1$ peak is observed, but there are also some other equally good experiments at different momenta where no such peak is visible and at best a shoulder is observed (see Figs. 56–59). Finally, some experiments have observed an apparent clear signal at the $A_1$ peak in their initial observation of the effect, but the signal has considerably decreased with improved statistics (see Figs. 60 and 61).

## 3. Indications of More Structure

In some of the higher momentum experiments some evidence for additional structure, the $A_{1.5}$ has been observed. Figure 57 is a compilation by Butterworth from his rapporteur talk at the 1967 Heidelberg Conference which illustrates this effect. The perturbing feature is that the $A_{1.5}$ is narrow but does not occur at the same mass in all instances!

A possible resolution of this dilemma is that if the $A_1$ is a $J^P = 1^+$ resonance which is produced by Pomeranchuk exchange, as all angular distribution data appear to indicate, then there will be interference between it and the amplitudes due to the kinematical effects (which, furthermore, interfere among themselves).

Such interference effects can in principle[21,73] give rise to the vanishing of the $A_1$ peak for some incident momenta as well as possibly

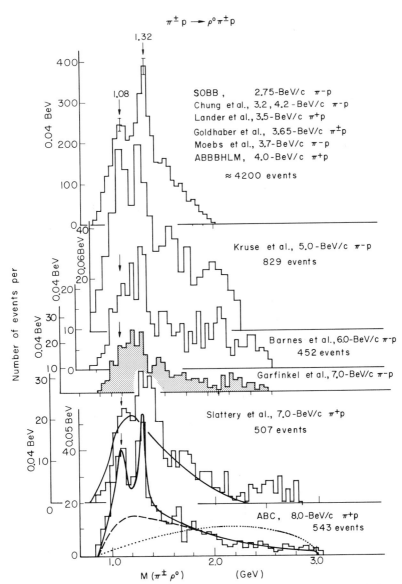

FIG. 56. Compilation by Goldhaber and Shen of the $\pi^\pm \rho^0$ mass distribution before the 1966 Berkeley Conference.

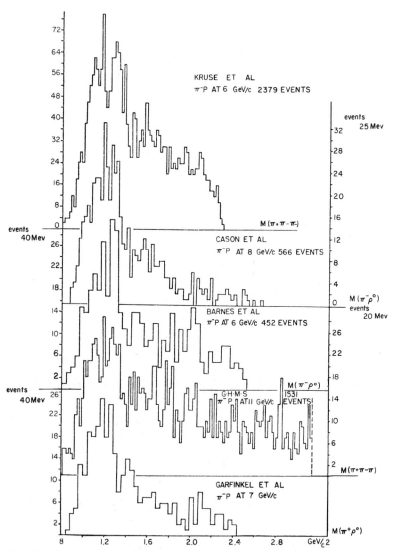

FIG. 57. Compilation by Butterworth of the $3\pi$ or $\pi\rho$ mass distributions showing the evidence for the $A_{1.5}$.

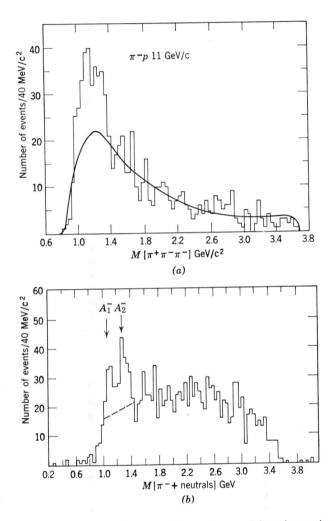

FIG. 58. Data of Genova-Hamburg-Milano-Saclay collaboration on the $A_1$ and $A_2$ production. (a) $\pi^- p \rightarrow \pi^- p \pi^+ \pi^-$, 758 events, $\rho_{in}^o$. (b) $\pi^- p \rightarrow \pi^- p$ + neutrals, 1491 events.

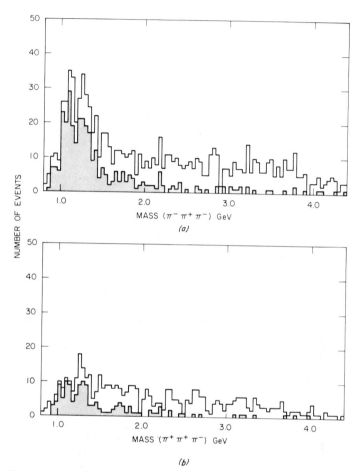

FIG. 59. Data of Ballam et al. on $A_1$ and $A_2$ production in $\pi^- p$ and $\pi^+ p$ reactions at 16 GeV/c. (a) $\pi^- p \rightarrow p\pi^- \pi^+ \pi^-$, 911 events, shaded curve shows $\rho^0 \pi^-$ events with $N^*$ excluded. (b) $\pi^+ p \rightarrow p\pi^+ \pi^+ \pi^-$, 454 events, shaded curve shows $\rho^0 \pi^+$ events with $N^*$ excluded.

shifts of the mass value. Here again no detailed quantitative calculations are available as yet. Whether such an interpretation can account for a narrow, wandering $A_{1.5}$ as well is not clear at present.

There is a new result by Bellini et al.[76] on the alternate decay mode of what may be the $A_1^-$. In the work on 16-GeV/c $\pi^-$ mesons on heavy

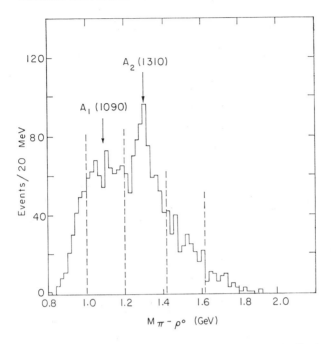

FIG. 60. Latest results from Chung et al. on the $\pi^- \rho^0$ mass distribution, 1917 events.

nuclei they had previously demonstrated the coherent production of $\pi^- \rho^0$, giving a general peak in the region of the $A_1$, although wider than just the $A_1$ effect (see Fig. 62). They have now also studied the events with $\pi^- \pi^0 \pi^0$ production by observing the $\gamma$ rays converted to electron pairs in the chamber. They find essentially the same coherent production phenomenon for $\pi^0 \rho^-$ in this case. Figure 63 shows the mass peak which looks essentially like the one in the previous figure.

Ideally, one would like to observe the $A_1$ meson in a reaction which is "immune" to kinematical effects. Recently some indication of the peaks in the $A_1$ and $A_2$ mass region have been observed in $\bar{p}p$ annihilation experiments into 7 pions.[77,134] In view of the complexity of these reactions the interpretation and statistical significance of these peaks is not clear at present (see Sect. III-4-B).

Taking all these points into consideration we are at present not in a position to consider the $A_1$ as an *established* resonance, but one cannot help but share Butterworth's opinion[24] that it must exist.

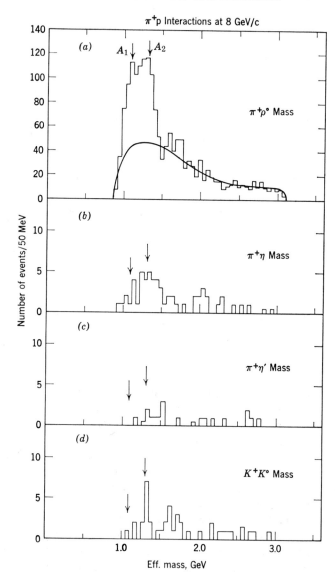

FIG. 61. Data of the ABC collaboration showing a study of the decay modes indicated for the $A_1$ and $A_2$ mesons. $\pi^+ p$ interactions at 8 GeV/c. (a) $\pi^+ p \rightarrow p\pi^+ \rho^0 \rightarrow p\pi^+ \pi^+ \pi^-$, $N^{*++}$ excluded, 1685 events, (———) O.P.E. calculation. (b) $\pi^+ p \rightarrow p\pi^+ \eta \rightarrow p\pi^+ \pi^+ \pi^- \pi^0$, $N^{*++}$ excluded. (c) $\pi^+ p \rightarrow p\pi^+ \eta' \rightarrow p\pi^+ \pi^+ \pi^- Z^0$ $N^{*++}$ excluded, $Z^0$ in $\eta$. (d) $\pi^+ p \rightarrow pK^+ K^0$.

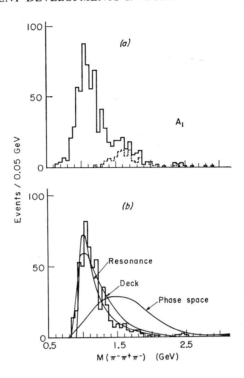

FIG. 62. Data from the heavy liquid bubble chamber of experiment 16-GeV/c $\pi^-$ in $C_2F_5Cl$ (Orsay-Saclay-Milan-Berkeley). Note the dashed histogram in part (a) corresponding to $\pi f^0$ formation. (——) 744 $\pi^-\pi^+\pi^-$. (---) 129 $\pi^-f^0$. (b) 563 $\pi^-\rho^0$.

b. *The B(1220), the Candidate for* $I^G J^P = 1^+ 1^+$. The $B$ phenomenon has been observed in the decay mode[78-80]

$$B^{\pm}(1220) \to \pi^{\pm}\omega$$

This implies directly that $G = +1$ (4$\pi$'s in final state) and $I = 1$ [since $I(\omega) = 0$], and hence $C = -1$.

In an experiment on $\bar{p}p$ annihilation at rest going to 5 pions, Baltay et al.[81] have observed confirmatory evidence for the $B$ meson:

$$\bar{p}p \to B^{\pm}\pi^{\mp}$$
$$\phantom{\bar{p}p \to B^{\pm}} \hookrightarrow \omega^0\pi^{\pm}$$
$$\phantom{\bar{p}p \to B^{\pm}\omega^0} \hookrightarrow \pi^+\pi^-\pi^0$$

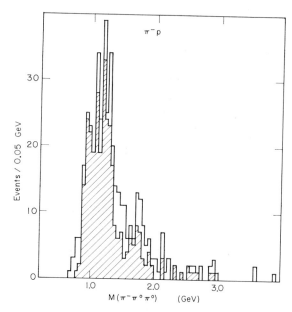

Fig. 63. Data of Bellini et al. at 16 GeV/c $\pi^-$ in a heavy liquid bubble chamber. 431 events. Shaded area with at least $1\rho^-$, $0.6 \leqq M_\rho \leqq 0.85$ GeV, 304 events.

Previous to this, the identification of the $B$ as a meson has been brought into question by two experiments.

*1.* In our own work[80] we observed that the $B$ enhancement appeared to be associated primarily with the periphery of the $\omega$ decay Dalitz plot, a region in which the background to "true $\omega$" ratio is maximal. This effect, if not an enormous statistical fluctuation (which can occur, as we all know only too well), could be due to some peculiar interference with the background. While confirmed in some experiments[82] it was not observed by Chung et al.[79] nor in the $\bar{p}p$ experiments.

*2.* Chung et al. suggested on the basis of their $\pi^-p$ data that the $B$ could be due to a kinematical effect involving virtual $\rho p \rightarrow \pi p$ scattering at the nucleon vertex.

The results of Baltay et al. (see Figs. 64 and 65) and the similar data of a CERN-College de France experiment[24] (see Fig. 66) tend to overrule both of these objections to the identification of the $B$ as a meson. As for the $J^P$ value for the $B$, we can rule out $1^-$, $2^+$ because

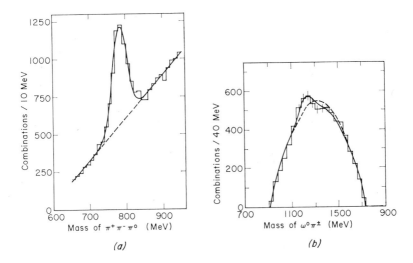

FIG. 64. Data of Baltay et al. ($a$) The $\pi^+\pi^-\pi^0$ mass distribution showing the $\omega$ meson production, $\bar{p} + p \rightarrow \pi^+ + \pi^+ + \pi^- + \pi^- + \pi^0$, at rest. ($b$) The $\omega\pi^\pm$ mass distribution showing the $B$ production, $\bar{p} + p \rightarrow \omega^0 + \pi^+ + \pi^-$, at rest, 7524 combinations.

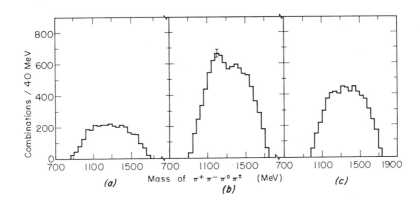

FIG. 65. Data of Baltay et al. showing $B$ production as well as the absence of the $B$ when control regions below and above the $\omega$ are taken. ($a$) Lower control region, $705 \leqq m(\pi^+\pi^-\pi^0) \leqq 745$. ($b$) $\omega^0$ region, $765 \leqq m(\pi^+\pi^-\pi^0) \leqq 805$. ($c$) Upper control region, $825 \leqq m(\pi^+\pi^-\pi^0) \leqq 865$.

the $\pi\pi$ decay mode is absent. Furthermore, the CERN-College de France experiment[24] does not favor $0^-$ or $2^-$. This leaves $1^+$ as a possibility, but this is, however, certainly not established as yet.

    *c. Evidence for Two Axial Vector $K^*$'s.* A very large enhancement in the $K\pi\pi$ mass system has been observed in a series of experiments both in $K^+p$ and $K^-p$ reactions for incident momenta from 2.6 to 13 BeV/c.[83] This enhancement lies roughly in the mass region 1.1–1.5 BeV. Most experiments agree that the enhancement consists of *at least* two phenomena:

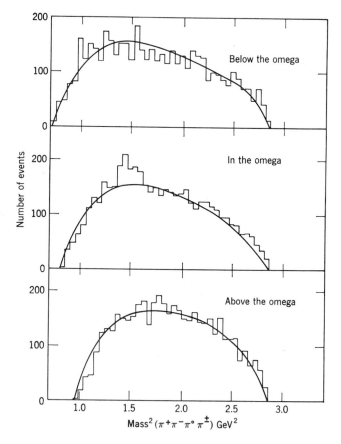

FIG. 66. Similar results to those in Fig. 65 from the CERN-College de France experiment.

*1.* The $K^*(1420)$ in the $K\pi\pi$ decay mode. This has been clearly resolved from the main enhancement in a number of experiments.[84,85]

*2.* A large enhancement, roughly in the mass region 1.1–1.4 BeV, recently called the "$Q$ enhancement" by Berlinghieri et al.[86] The cross section for the $Q$ enhancement does not vary much with incident momentum. The structure of the $Q$ enhancement, however, has shown distinct, statistically significant differences for various incident momenta. This is illustrated for four $K^+p$ experiments in Figure 67.[84,85,87,88] It is the latter feature we wish to discuss here.

### 1. The Observation of Two Peaks in the $Q$ Enhancement

The recent data[88] at 9-GeV/c $K^+p$ is shown in more detail in Figure 68. Two mass peaks centered at 1250 and 1400 MeV above a broad background can be clearly distinguished. These two peaks are well resolved by a 60-MeV wide dip of about 3.2 standard deviations, and are respectively 7 and 6 standard deviation effects above background.

Figure 68*b–d* show various regions of four-momentum transfer to the proton, $\Delta_p{}^2$. As may be noted the $K^*(1420)$ has a $\Delta_p{}^2$ distribution somewhat wider than those of the $K^*(1250)$ and $K^*(1320)$, and appears clearly for $\Delta_p{}^2 \geq 0.3$ (BeV/c)$^2$ in the shaded histogram in Figure 68*d*. The unresolved peak at 1400 MeV in Figure 68*a* is interpreted to consist of two parts: the $K^*(1420)$ and a peak at 1360 MeV, which is conjectured to be the same as the $K^*(1320)$. The 1360 MeV peak appears most clearly in the $0.1 \leq \Delta_p{}^2 < 0.3$ region. The apparent resonance parameters observed in the experiment are thus:

$$M = 1250 \pm 10 \text{ MeV} \qquad \Gamma = 50 \pm 20 \text{ MeV}$$
$$M = 1360 \pm 10 \text{ MeV} \qquad \Gamma = 80 \pm 20 \text{ MeV}$$
$$M = 1420 \pm 10 \text{ MeV} \qquad \Gamma = 80 \pm 20 \text{ MeV}$$

On the basis of the angular distribution for $K^*(890)$ decay (which is of the form $\cos^2 \theta$ for both peaks in the $Q$ enhancement), it is further argued that the data is consistent with the interpretation that the $K^*(1250)$ and $K^*(1320)$ resonances are of $J^P = 1^+$, are produced by Pomeranchuk exchange, and decay mainly by $S$ wave into $K^*(890) + \pi$.

### 2. The Possibility of $K^*$ Mixing

If we consider the $K^*$'s belonging to the four $L = 1$ nonets we find the following simplest allowed decay modes:

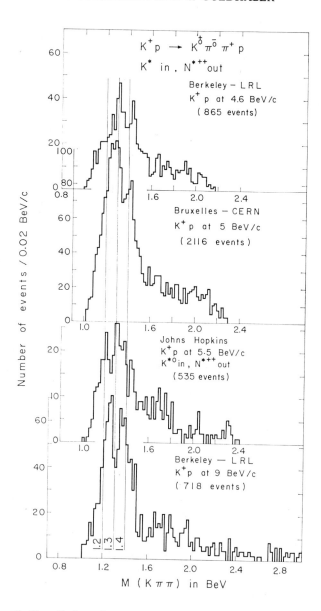

FIG. 67. Compilation of the $K\pi\pi$ mass distribution for various incident momenta as shown. As may be noted from the location of the three vertical lines at 1.2, 1.3, and 1.4 BeV there are statistically significant differences between the various mass distributions.

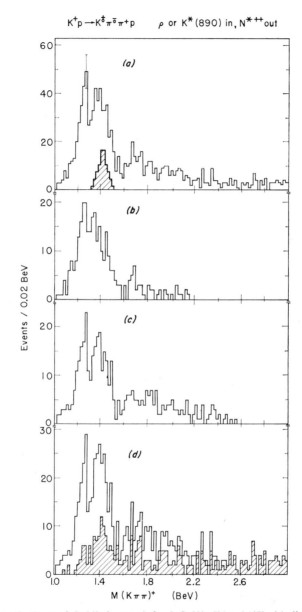

FIG. 68. Data of Goldhaber et al. for 9-GeV/c $K^+ p$. $M(K\pi\pi)^+$ distributions for events in the $\rho$ meson or $K^*(890)$ bands with $N^{*++}$ band removed for (a) all $\Delta_p{}^2$, 1058 events. The shaded area in (d) represents an estimate of the $K^*\pi$ and $K\rho$ decay modes of the $K^*(1420)$. (b) $\Delta_p{}^2 < 0.1$ (BeV/c)$^2$, 308 events. (c) $0.1 \leqq \Delta_p{}^2 < 0.3$ (BeV/c)$^2$, 423 events. (d) $\Delta_p{}^2 \geqq 0.1$ (BeV/c)$^2$, 750 events; shaded area $\Delta_p{}^2 \geqq 0.3$ (BeV/c)$^2$, 327 events.

$$K^*(^3P_0) \to K\pi$$
$$K^*(^3P_1) \to K^*(890)\pi \quad \text{or} \quad K\rho \to K\pi\pi$$
$$K^*(^1P_1) \to K^*(890)\pi \quad \text{or} \quad K\rho \to K\pi\pi$$
$$K^*(^3P_2) \to K\pi \quad \text{and} \quad K^*(890)\pi \quad \text{or} \quad K\rho \to K\pi\pi$$

where the last one is already identified as $K^*(^3P_2) \equiv K^*(1420)$.

Aside from $K^*(1420)$ we thus expect two more distinct $K^*$'s in the $K\pi\pi$ mass spectrum, both with $J^P = 1^+$. In connection with these a new and so far unique situation can arise. The two isovector mesons corresponding to the $^3P_1$ and $^1P_1$ states, presumably the $A_1(1080)$ and $B(1220)$, are eigenstates of $G$ (and their neutral components are eigenstates of $C$), and thus form distinct entities with $I^G J^P = 1^- 1^+$ and $1^+ 1^+$, respectively. The same also holds for the four possible isoscalars belonging to these two nonets. On the other hand, the $K^*$'s are not eigenstates of $C$, in fact the values of $C$ here can be considered[89] to refer to the two different $q\bar{q}$ structures $^3P_1$ and $^1P_1$. The possibility thus exists that the two $K^*$'s will mix so that the two physical particles, say $K_\text{I}$ and $K_\text{II}$, may each be a mixture of the $^3P_1$ and $^1P_1$ states.[90,91] Thus in this particular instance the two $1^+$ nonets may be tied together. Gatto et al.[90] have called the resulting structure of 18 particles an "octodecimet."

## 3. Interference in the Mass Distributions

In addition to, and aside from, the possibility of particle mixing, if we are dealing with two adjacent states with the same $J^P$ values, we may expect interference effects in the $K\pi\pi$ mass distributions.[92] In general a mass distribution corresponds to an average over all decay angular distributions. Thus $K^*$'s with different $J^P$ values, such as a $1^+ K^*$ and the $2^+ K^*(1420)$, will not give any interference effect in the $K\pi\pi$ mass distributions and the amplitudes will add incoherently. However, two $K^*$'s each with $J^P = 1^+$ will add coherently.

A very simple model corresponding to the coherent addition of two resonances together with a third added incoherently has been suggested.[92] Here we express each resonance by a Breit-Wigner amplitude and allow an arbitrary phase between two of them.

Let $B_k = \frac{1}{2}\Gamma_k/(E_k - E - i\frac{1}{2}\Gamma_k)$, with $k = 1, 2,$ and $3$, correspond to the Breit-Wigner amplitude for each of these resonances; then the resulting mass distribution can be expressed as

$$\frac{d\sigma}{dM} \propto (|a_1 B_1 + B_2 e^{i\phi}|^2 + |a_3 B_3|^2)P$$

where $E_k$ and $\Gamma_k$ are the resonant masses and widths respectively, $\phi$ is a relative phase angle, and $a_1$ and $a_3$ relative amplitudes, all of which must be determined from experiment, and $P$ is a phase-space factor. As an illustration, this expression was evaluated for $E_1 = 1250$ MeV, $\Gamma_1 = 50$ MeV, $E_2 = 1320$ MeV, $\Gamma_2 = 80$ MeV, $E_3 = 1420$ MeV, $\Gamma_3 = 90$ MeV, $a_1 = 1$, $a_3 = 1/\sqrt{2}$, and values of $\phi$ from 0 to $9\pi/5$ in ten equal steps. Figure 69 shows the resulting mass distribution. As may be noted, aside from the $K^*(1420)$ peak, the shape of the mass distribution in the $Q$ enhancement can appear as a single peak at $E_2$ for $\phi \approx 6\pi/5$, a broad, flat-topped peak centered at $\approx (E_1 + E_2)/2$ for $\phi \approx \pi$, indications of a single peak at $E_1$ for $\phi \approx 3\pi/5$, and two separate peaks at $\approx E_1$ and $\approx E_2$ for $\phi \approx \pi/5$ or lower, as well as for $\phi \approx 8\pi/5$. Thus in a variation of $\phi$ the mass distribution can go through an entire

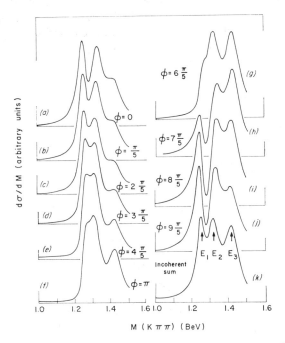

FIG. 69. Computation of the interference patterns in the $K\pi\pi$ mass distribution for two $K^*$ resonances at 1250 and 1320 MeV added coherently and a third at 1420 MeV added incoherently. The computation was done for a series of values of the phase angle $\phi$ between the two coherent amplitudes as described in the text, and is shown in (a)–(j). (k) is the incoherent sum of the three resonances.

gamut of shapes, some of which are very similar to the experimental $K^+p$ data in the 4.6–9 BeV/c region.

There is little doubt that a considerable amount of background amplitude must be present in addition to the resonances discussed above. Just as in the case of the $A_1$ meson discussed above the three contributing amplitudes[73] will also lead primarily to $J^P = 1^+$. A more realistic model must therefore include both a coherent and an incoherent background term, where the phase of the former can also vary relative to the two Breit-Wigner amplitudes.

### 4. The $C(1230)$ and $C'(1320)$ Mesons from $\bar{p}p$ Annihilation at Rest

Montanet et al. [as quoted by Butterworth[24]] have reached very similar conclusions from their data on the $C^0(1230) \rightarrow K\pi\pi$ effect.[93] It has been a mystery for a long time why the $C$ occurred only in the neutral form. At the same time they had observed a small enhancement, $C'$ at 1320 MeV which occurred only in the charged mode (see Fig. 70 from the CERN-College de France groups as well as Fig. 71 showing

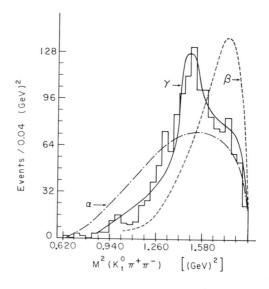

FIG. 70. Data on the $C$ meson from $\bar{p}p$ annihilations at rest by the CERN-Paris groups. $\bar{p} + p \rightarrow K_1^0 K_1^0 \pi^+ \pi^-$, $M^2(K_1^0 \pi^+ \pi^-)$. The curves shown are: $\alpha$, phase space; $\beta$, $(K\rho)$ phase space in $\bar{p}p \rightarrow K_1^0 K_1^0 \rho$; $\gamma$, 40% phase space + 60% $\bar{p}p \rightarrow K^0 C^0$ with $C^0 \rightarrow K^0 \rho^0$.

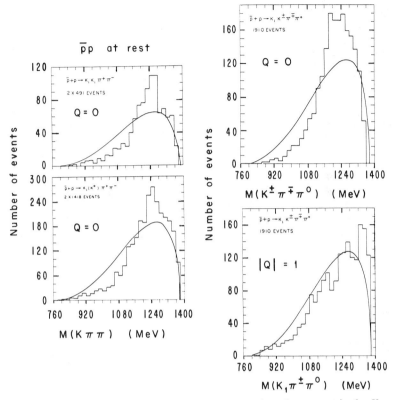

FIG. 71. Data of Barash et al. at Columbia on the enhancement in the $K\pi\pi$ mass distribution at 1250 MeV for the neutral system and 1320 MeV for the charged system.

similar data from the Columbia group).[94] It was emphasized by Lipkin[90] that as the initial state in $\bar{p}p$ annihilation is a mixed $I = 1$ and 0 state, interference effects between two $K^*$'s can take such a form.

## 5. Kinematic Effects

Just as in the case of the $A_1$ the $Q$ enhancement could also be due to kinematic effects. In fact Dornan et al.[95] feel that their data for $K^-p$ at 4.6 and 5 GeV/c can be interpreted in this fashion. Our feeling is that while kinematic effects are certainly present,[136] the sharp peaks discussed above must be of resonant origin. In this connection it is relevant to consider the data of Crennell et al.,[96] who observe a peak at 1300 MeV in the reaction

$$\pi^- p \to \Lambda(K\pi\pi)^0$$

This cannot be due to a kinematic origin of the types discussed here (see Fig. 72).

## 6. Another Interpretation of the $Q$ Enhancement

Bassompierre et al.[85] have analyzed their data from 5-GeV/c $K^+p$ (shown in Fig. 67 above) by a number of different cuts. (*a*) They first eliminate very low $\Delta_p{}^2$ values and choose $\Delta_p{}^2 > 0.1$ to avoid kinematic effects. (*b*) They then choose equatorial and polar regions in $\cos\theta_{KK}$, the $K^*(890)$ decay angle. This has the effect of enhancing the $|1, \pm 1\rangle$ and $|1,0\rangle$ states, respectively, with the incident $K$ as the axis of quantization. With these selections they claim three resonances in the $Q$ peak; that is four in all, including the $K^*(1420)$ (see Fig. 73). Namely, 1230 and 1320 MeV for polar and 1280 MeV for equatorial alignment. They furthermore indicate these have different $\Delta_p{}^2$ distributions.

In view of the complication of possible interference effects between two resonances and coherent background, this interpretation does not seem compelling on the basis of the presently available data.

*e. The $D(1285)$, a Candidate for $I^G J^P = 0^+1^+$.* The $D$ meson with the decay mode $D \to K\bar{K}\pi$ has been observed in a study of the reactions

$$\pi^- p \to K_1{}^0 K_1{}^0 \pi^- p \tag{8}$$
$$K_1 K^- \pi^0 p \tag{9}$$
$$K^+ K^- \pi^- p \tag{10}$$
$$K^- K_1{}^0 \pi^+ n \tag{11}$$
$$K^+ K_1{}^0 \pi^- n \tag{12}$$

by Miller et al.[97] at 3.2–4 GeV/c and in a study of the reactions

$$\bar{p}p \to K_1 K^\pm + n\pi \tag{13}$$
$$\to K_1 K_1 + n\pi \tag{14}$$

by d'Andlau et al. at 1.2 GeV/c.[98] Dahl et al.[10] have recently performed a careful attempt to arrive at the quantum numbers of the $D$ meson in a further study of reactions (8)–(12). In this analysis both $D(1285)$ and $E(1420)$ which are produced in reactions (11) and (12) have been studied.

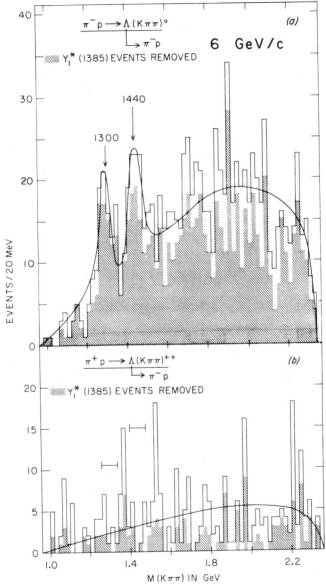

FIG. 72. Evidence for a $K^*(1300)$ from a reaction which is "immune" from the usual kinematic effects. (a) 1048 events, (b) 290 events. From Crennell et al. at Brookhaven.

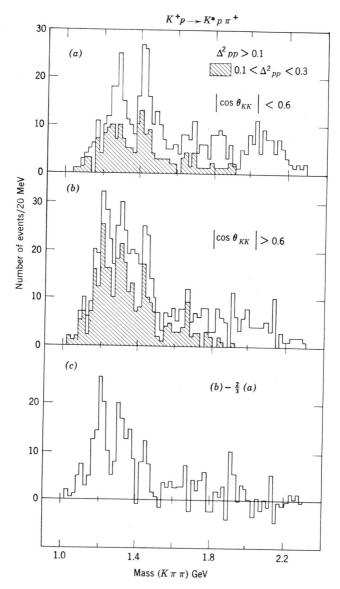

FIG. 73. Data of Bassompierre et al. on the $K^*\pi$ mass distribution for $K^+p$ at 5 GeV/c. These authors suggest that with the cuts shown on the figure they observe three distinct peaks in the $Q$ enhancement.

They find from the reaction $\pi^- p \to n D(1285)$

*1.* $M_D = 1283 \pm 5$ MeV, $\Gamma_D = 35 \pm 10$ MeV.

*2.* $I$ for $D$ and $E$ is most likely 0, as may be noted from the comparison of $(K\bar{K}\pi)^0$ and $(K\bar{K}\pi)^-$ in Figure 74.

*3.* An attempt to measure $G$ directly by observing $K_1 K_1 \pi^0 (G = +1)$ or $K_1 K_2 \pi^0 (G = -1)$ did not yield enough events for a conclusive test.

*4.* A $K\bar{K}$ enhancement at low masses is observed in the $D$ (and $E$) decay. However, they could not determine whether the cause for this is the $I = 1$ $K\bar{K}$ state or constructive interference between $K^*(890)$ and $\bar{K}^*(890)$.

*5.* By comparing the $\bar{K}K$ mass distribution and the internal decay angle $\theta_{K\bar{K}}$ distribution with the matrix element calculation shown in Section II-3, Figure 11, they favor $J^{PG} = 1^{++}$ with $2^{-+}, 0^{-+}$, and $1^{+-}$ as "next most likely" (see Fig. 75).

The curves for the $E$ favor $J^{PG} = 1^{++}$ with $2^{-+}$ and $0^{-+}$ as "next most likely." Their result on the $E$ thus arrives at the opposite conclusion of the CERN-College de France group; in view of the limited statistics in the present experiment this disagreement cannot be taken as completely compelling (see Sect. III-2-A). It is clear however that further study of this question is indicated.

*e. The H(990) (?), a Candidate for $I^G J^P = 0^- 1^+$.* Evidence for the $H$ meson ($M = 975$ MeV) with the decay mode $H^0 \to \rho\pi$ was first observed by the ABBBHLM[82] collaboration in the reaction:

$$\pi^+ p \to (\pi\rho)^0 + N^{*++} \quad \text{at} \quad 4 \text{ BeV/c}$$

In our own work[82] studying the same reaction at 3.65 BeV/c we observed a similar phenomenon but of considerably lower intensity so that we could not consider this as a confirmation of the effect. Benson et al.[99] reported data on the reaction:

$$\pi^+ d \to pp(\pi\rho) \quad \text{at} \quad 3.65 \text{ BeV/c}$$

in which they observed a statistically significant signal for the $H$ meson. They observe the mass at $\sim 1000$ MeV (see Fig. 76). The effect is, however, not observed by the BBFO collaboration[100] who studied the same reaction at 5.1 GeV/c (see Fig. 77).

There is one other subtle point to consider about the $H$. Experimentally it is very difficult to distinguish between the decay modes:

$$H^0 \to \rho^0 \pi^0 \tag{15}$$

and

$$X^0 \to \rho^0 \gamma \tag{16}$$

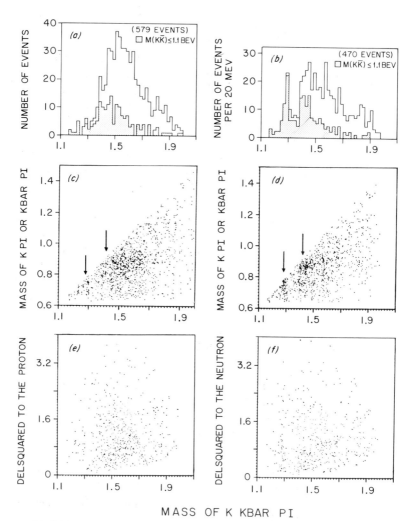

MASS OF K KBAR PI

FIG. 74. Data of Dahl et al. on the $pK\bar{K}\pi$ final states $(a)$, $(c)$, and $(e)$, and $nK\bar{K}\pi$ final states $(b)$, $(d)$, and $(f)$, for beam momenta of 2–4 BeV/c. $(a)$ and $(b)$ Effective mass histograms of $K\bar{K}\pi$. $(c)$ and $(d)$ Scatter plots of the $K\pi$ and $\bar{K}\pi$ effective masses vs. the $K\bar{K}\pi$ effective mass. Two points plotted per event. $(e)$ and $(f)$ Scatter plots of $\Delta^2$ to the nucleon vs. the $K\bar{K}\pi$ effective mass. The effective masses are in units of BeV, $\Delta^2$ is in units of $(BeV/c)^2$.

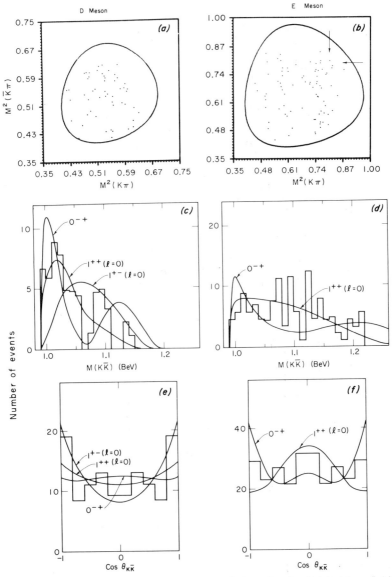

FIG. 75. Data of Dahl et al. Decay correlations for the $D$ ($a$), ($c$), and ($e$) (1.245 BeV $\leqq M_{K\bar{K}\pi} \leqq$ 1.325 BeV) and the $E$ ($b$), ($d$), and ($f$) (1.360 BeV $\leqq M_{K\bar{K}\pi} \leqq$ 1.480 BeV) mesons. ($a$) and ($b$) Decay Dalitz plots. Arrows indicate the $K^*(891)$ and $\bar{K}^*(891)$ bands. The envelopes are for ($a$) 1.325 BeV and ($b$) 1.480 BeV. ($c$) and ($d$) $K\bar{K}$ effective-mass distributions. ($e$) and ($f$) Distribution in cos $\theta_{K\bar{K}}$; each event plotted twice. Curves represent predictions of the more likely $J^P$ assignments. Coordinates of the Dalitz plots are in BeV². Each event has been weighted to correct for detection efficiency. ($c$) 60.77 events. ($d$) 132.38 events.

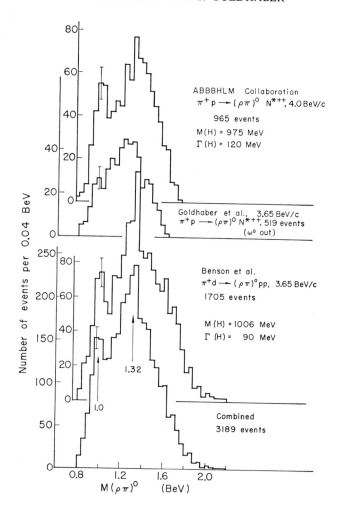

FIG. 76. A compilation of data relating to the $H$ meson.

However the two experiments which have observed the clear signal for the $H$ meson assert that the $\rho^0\pi^0$, $\rho^+\pi^-$, and $\rho^-\pi^+$ decay modes of the $H$ are roughly equal. This would indicate that the $H$ phenomenon appears distinctly different from the erroneous fits obtained from $X^0$ decay, as the latter will not give apparent $\rho^\pm\pi^\mp$ decay modes.

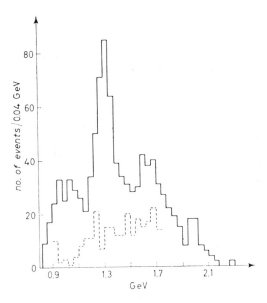

Fig. 77. Data of Armenise et al. for $\pi^+ d \to pp\pi^+\pi^-\pi^0$ at 5.1 GeV/c. $M(\pi^+\pi^-\pi^0)$ spectrum of 938 events having at least one of the three possible $M(\pi\pi)$ combinations in the $\rho$ region (0.66–0.86 GeV). (---) $M(\pi^+\pi^-\pi^0)$ for the events with no $\rho$ associated. This data shows a clear $A_2$ peak but no evidence for $H$ production.

Barbaro-Galtieri et al.[101] have reported possible evidence for the $H$ from the reaction:

$$K^- n \to \sum{}^- \pi^+\pi^-\pi^0$$

A peak is observed at 2.1 GeV/c but no significant peak for 2.6 GeV/c (see Fig. 78). The small signal at 2.6 GeV/c is consistent with $X^0$ production. At 2.1 GeV/c one-third of the signal can be ascribed to $X^0$ and $\phi$ contamination, leaving a signal of 2.5 standard deviation.

If the $H$ exists, and this is still in question according to Butterworth,[24] $G = -1$ from the decay mode. The mass of the $H$ is such that the location of the $\rho$ bands dictate the population of the corners of the Dalitz plot (see illustration in Fig. 79). Thus $J^P = 1^+$ is slightly preferred but could be influenced by $\pi\rho$ nonresonant background. Evidence for $I = 0$ is shown in Figure 80 which compares charged and neutral $\pi\rho$ combinations. The suggestion has actually been made[19] that the $H$

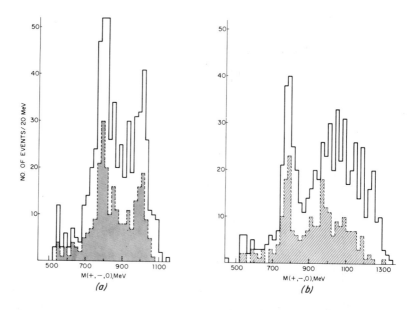

FIG. 78. Data presented at Heidelberg by Barbaro-Galtieri on possible confirmatory evidence for the $H$ meson from the reaction $K^- n \to \Sigma^- \pi^+ \pi^- \pi^0$. Shaded events correspond to $\Delta^2 < 0.6$ (GeV/c)². (a) 2.1 GeV/c; (b) 2.6 GeV/c.

enhancement may be the neutral $A_1$ peak displaced (presumably by some interference phenomenon). This suggestion then hinges on the question whether or not the $H^0 \to \rho^0 \pi^0$ mode can be reliably substantiated. More work on this phenomenon is clearly needed.

    *f. The Need for More Isoscalars.* To round out the picture of the two $^3P_1$ and $^1P_1$ nonets we are still short by two isoscalars. So far, if we accept the transfer of the $E(1420)$ to $J^P = 0^-$ as final, there are no obvious candidates.

### C. The Search for Scalar Mesons or $^3P_0$ ($J^{PC} = 0^{++}$) States

    Of all the bosons described so far the scalar mesons (assuming they exist) are perhaps the most difficult to come to grips with. The quantum numbers $J^{PC} = 0^{++}$ are such that the allowed decay modes are quite restricted. Some of these are shown in Figure 119 in Section III-4-E-d. Thus for $I^G = 0^+$ we can have the decay modes $\pi^+ \pi^-$ and $\pi^0 \pi^0$. where

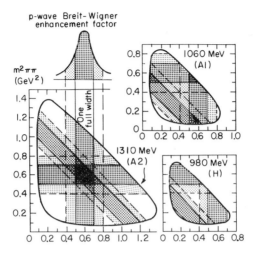

FIG. 79. Sketch from Rosenfeld et al. illustrating the location of the $\rho$ bands for $I = 0$ mesons located in the $A_2$, $A_1$, and $H$ mass region. All three bands appear for $I = 0$ resonances. For the $A_1$ and $A_2$ only two bands $\rho^{\pm}\pi^{\mp}$, but not $\rho^0\pi^0$, will occur.

the latter is not allowed for the $\rho$ meson, as well as $K_1{}^0K_1{}^0$, $K\bar{K}$, and $4\pi$. For $I^G = 1^-$ we can have $\pi\eta$, $K_1{}^0K_1{}^0$, and $K\bar{K}$ and for the $K^*$ we can have the $K\pi$ decay mode.

At the moment none of these states are firmly established, although there are indications for a number of them.

   *a. The Evidence for an $I = 1$ $K\bar{K}$ State Near Threshold.* Conforto et al.[102] have recently completed a very detailed study of the $\bar{p}p$ annihilation process at rest based on $1.35 \times 10^6$ events and in particular on the reactions:

$$\bar{p}p \rightarrow K_1{}^0K^{\pm}\pi^{\mp} \qquad \text{2000 events} \qquad (17)$$

$$\bar{p}p \rightarrow K_1{}^0K_1{}^0\pi^0 \qquad \text{364 events} \qquad (18)$$

The main features of reaction (17) can be seen from the Dalitz plot in Figure 81. As may be noted there are five distinct effects: *(1)* the horizontal $K^{*0}$ band, *(2)* the vertical $K^{*\pm}$ band, *(3)* the $A_2(1280)$ band, *(4)* the $K\bar{K}(990)$ band, and *(5)* $K\pi$ threshold enhancement bands. Here we are primarily concerned with *(4)*, the $I = 1$ $K\bar{K}$ band. Figure 82 shows the $K_1{}^0K^{\pm}$ mass squared distribution and Figure 83 the same distribution after the $K^*$ bands have been removed.

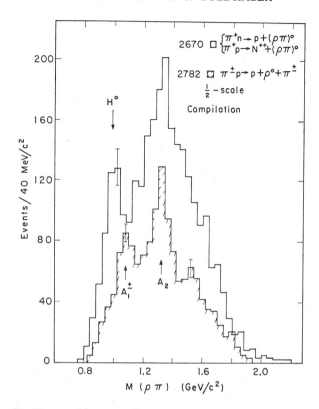

FIG. 80. The outer histogram gives the neutral $\pi\rho$ mass distribution, from the data of Benson et al. and the ABBBHLM collaboration, which are the two experiments which show the most pronounced evidence for the $H^0$ meson. The shaded histogram shows for comparison the charged $\pi\rho$ mass distribution to indicate that the $A_1$ is considerably displaced from the $H^0$ meson. The $A_2$ is observed in both cases.

Conforto et al. find that this effect can be fitted about equally well by three different models:

(a) The $K\bar{K}$ amplitude can be described by an $S$-wave scattering length $A_0$; the expression for the amplitude is thus

$$1/(1 - iA_0 p_{K\bar{K}})$$

Here $A_0$ is real and is given by $A_0 = 2.0^{+1.0}_{-0.5}F$.

(b) They obtain an equally good fit for a negative $A_0$ and in fact a complex value $A_0 = a_0 + ib_0$ with $a_0 = -2.3^{+0.3}_{-4.0}$ and $b_0 = 0^{+0.5}_{-0.0}F$.

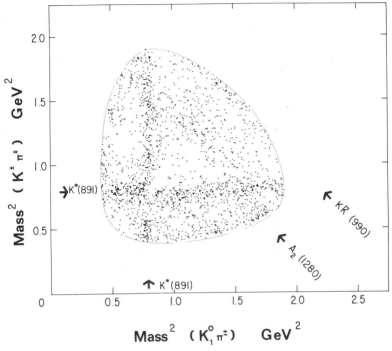

FIG. 81. Data of Conforto et al. Effective mass squared Dalitz plot for $\bar{p}p \rightarrow$ $K_1^0 K^{\pm} \pi^{\mp}$ (2000 events). Four accumulations of events are visible: the $K^{*0}(891)$, $K^{*\pm}(891)$, $K\bar{K}(1280)$, and $K\bar{K}(990)$. They are indicated by the arrows.

This would thus correspond to a rather narrow virtual bound state at $M = 972$ MeV. Dalitz had in fact suggested such a complex scattering length by starting out with the $\delta(963)$, although the latter effect is presently uncertain.

(c) They can also interpret their result in terms of a resonance just above threshold. By evaluating the Breit-Wigner amplitude they obtain

$$M_0 = 1016 \pm 6 \text{ MeV}$$
$$\Gamma \sim 25 \text{ MeV}$$

Thus, if either of the last two interpretations is correct we have a resonance, either at 972 or 1016 MeV, whose $S$-wave character is inferred from an isotropic decay angular distribution. In either case the $\pi\eta$ decay mode should show up, but has not been seen as yet.

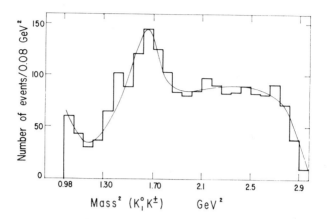

FIG. 82. Data of Conforto et al. $(K_1^0K^\pm)$ effective mass squared distribution for $\bar{p}p \to K_1^0K^\pm\pi^\mp$. The curve corresponds to the theoretical distribution as given by the best fit taking effects (1)–(5) into account. The accumulations of events at 990 MeV and at 1280 MeV (effective mass squared of 0.98 and 1.64 GeV²) are clearly visible.

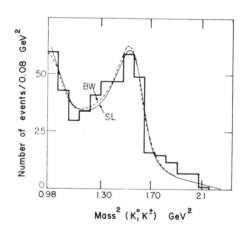

FIG. 83. Same distribution as in Fig. 82 for $M^2(K\pi) > 0.9$ GeV². Curve $SL$ represents the theoretical distribution as given by the fit when an $S$-wave scattering length of $2F$ is introduced for the $K\bar{K}$ threshold effect. Curve $BW$ represents the theoretical distribution as given by the fit when a Breit-Wigner form factor is introduced for the $K\bar{K}$ threshold effect.

Conforto et al. have also accounted for the other items in the Dalitz plot by one overall fit. The structure of the $K^*$ bands and the displacement of the $A_2$ band to the lower mass value of 1280 MeV can be understood by interference effects. The $K\pi$ enhancement near threshold can be accounted for by an $S$-wave scattering length of either $a_{1/2} \simeq a_{3/2} = -0.4F$ or $a_{1/2} = 0.3F$ and $a_{3/2} = -0.3F$. In connection with the latter effect the question has also been raised whether the two $K\pi$ and the $K\bar{K}$ threshold enhancement along with the empty region at the center of the Dalitz plot, which suggests annihilation from the $^1S_0$ state, are the result of a particular matrix element for the interaction rather than distinct threshold effects.

The $K\bar{K}$ enhancement is also observed in the decay of the $E(1420)$ and $D(1285)$ mesons, although in these cases the origin for the enhancement could be inherent in the form of the decay matrix element.

Finally, the $K\bar{K}$ enhancement has been seen in $\pi^\pm p$ interactions, where it was originally observed.[103]

b. *The Evidence for an $I = 0$ $K_1{}^0K_1{}^0$ State Near Threshold.* There are four recent experiments which have studied the $K_1{}^0K_1{}^0$ mass spectrum, three of them in the reaction

$$\pi^- p \rightarrow K_1{}^0 K_1{}^0 n$$

at various momenta and one in $\bar{p}p$ annihilation experiments.[104]

The experiments disagree on the location of the $K_1{}^0K_1{}^0$ threshold enhancement. We will discuss the three experiments on the $\pi^- p$ interaction here.

The experiment of Dahl et al.[10] has observed the $K_1{}^0K_1{}^0$ enhancement for incident $\pi^-$ momenta from 2 to 4.2 BeV/c. In this momentum interval the enhancement occurs right at threshold and can be fitted by a scattering length, but not a Breit-Wigner form as indicated in Figure 84. In the experiment by Crennell et al.[105] with 6-GeV/c $\pi^-$ mesons, a small peak in the $K_1K_1$ mass distribution is observed; however, now the location of this peak appears to be above threshold at 1068 MeV. This they have called the $S^*$. Figure 85 shows the mass distribution together with curves which indicate that a Breit-Wigner shape gives a better fit than the scattering length. Figure 86 shows their $K\bar{K}$ mass distribution both for the charged and neutral combinations. This is the evidence that their effect is an $I = 0$ enhancement. For the $K\bar{K}$ system $G = (-1)^{l+I}$. Thus for $I = 0$, $l$ must be even, giving the possible spin parity series $J^P = 0^+, 2^+, 4^+, \ldots$. The angular distributions shown in Figure 85 indicate $S$-wave decay.

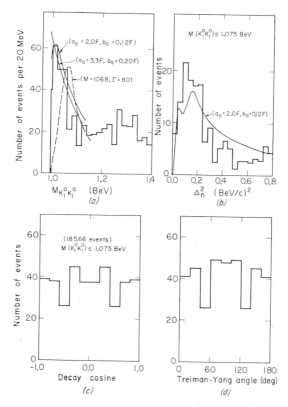

Fig. 84. Data of Dahl et al. from $nK_1^0K_1^0$ final states at all momenta. (a) $K_1^0K_1^0$ effective mass distribution. Curves compare the zero-effective-range approximation with a resonance shape at 1068 MeV. (b) Distribution of $\Delta^2$ to the neutron for events with $M_{K\bar{K}} \leqq 1075$ MeV. The curve is the prediction for one-pion exchange. (c) and (d) Histograms of cos $\theta$ and $\phi$ for events with $M_{K\bar{K}} \leqq 1075$ MeV. Two points have been plotted for each event. Each event has been weighted to correct for detection efficiency.

Beusch et al.[106] have studied the same reaction in a spark chamber experiment at CERN. The momenta studied were 5, 7, and 12 GeV/c. In this experiment they again find an $S^*$ resonance type enhancement located at 1079 MeV. Figure 87 shows their $K_1K_1$ mass distribution. Figure 88 shows an enlargement of the low mass region with background and higher resonances subtracted out. As mentioned, they suggest that the resonance interpretation can fit their data, while

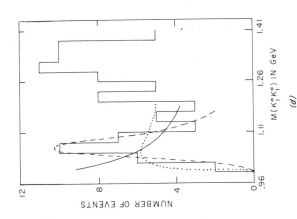

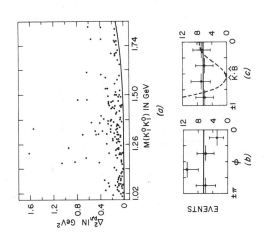

FIG. 85. Data of Crenell et al. (*a*) A section of the Chew-Low plot of $\Delta_2^{p,n}$ vs. $M(K_1^0 K_1^0)$ for the reaction $\pi^- + p \to K_1^0 + K_1^0 + n$. All of the 26 events in the $S^*$ region (below 1.12 GeV) have $\Delta^2 \leqq 0.34$ GeV$^2$; most of the $S^*$ events have $\Delta^2 \leqq 0.1$ GeV$^2$. (*b*) The Treiman-Yang angular distributions $\phi$ (folded about zero) of the 26 $S^*$ events is consistent with the flat curve shown. (*c*) The scattering angle $\cos \theta = \hat{K} \cdot \hat{B}$ (folded about zero) of one $K_1^0$ relative to the incident pion in the $S^*$ rest frame. The distribution is consistent with isotropy (solid curve), as expected for $J^P = 0^+$. The dashed curve shown is the $(3 \cos^2 \theta - 1)^2$ distribution expected for a $J^P = 2^+$ meson produced by a one-pion exchange mechanism. (*d*) A section of the $M(K_1^0 K_1^0)$ spectrum from the reaction $\pi^- + p \to K_1^0 + K_1^0 + n$ is shown. An $S$-wave resonance curve (dashed) and constant $S$-wave scattering length fits [dotted ($\pm 1.4 + 0.2iF$) and solid ($\pm 4 + 0.2iF$)] are also shown.

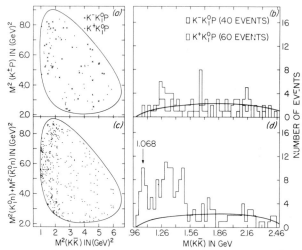

FIG. 86. Data of Crennell et al. (*a*) The $M^2(K^{\pm}p)$ vs. $M^2(K^{\pm}K_1^0)$ Dalitz plot of 100 $K^{\pm}K_1^0p$ events and (*b*) the mass projection $M(K^{\pm}K_1^0)$, with a phase-space curve (solid) normalized to the events above 1.56 GeV. (*c*) The $M^2(K_1^0n)$ vs. $M^2(K_1^0K_1^0)$ Dalitz plot of 178 $K_1^0K_1^0n$ events plotted twice (two $K_1^0n$ masses per event) and (*d*) the mass projection $M(K_1^0K_1^0)$, with a phase-space curve (solid) normalized to the events above 1.56 GeV. The $S^*$ enhancement at 1.068 GeV is indicated.

TABLE VII

Data of Beusch et al.[106] for All Momenta Combined: Percent of Events and Resonance Properties. Numbers without Errors have been Fixed in the Fitting Procedure

| Reson-ance | Per cent of events | Mass | Width |
|---|---|---|---|
| $S^*$ | $14.7 \pm 1.3$ | $1079 \pm 6$ | $168 \pm 21$ |
| $f$ | $17.4 \begin{smallmatrix} +2.6 \\ -3.4 \end{smallmatrix}$ | $1254$ | $80$ |
| $A_2$ | $18.6 \begin{smallmatrix} +4.8 \\ -3.6 \end{smallmatrix}$ | $1344 \pm 7$ | $88 \pm 23$ |
| $G$ | $6.5 \begin{smallmatrix} +2.3 \\ -2.0 \end{smallmatrix}$ | $1439 \pm 6$ | $43 \pm 18$ |

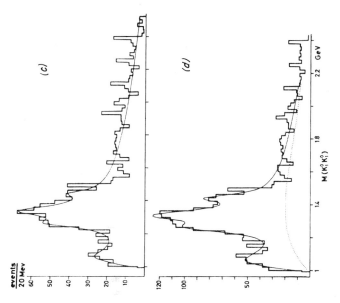

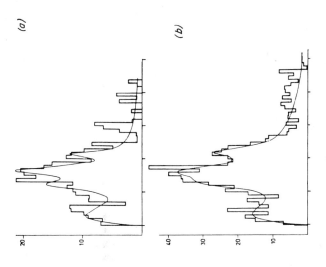

Fig. 87. Data of Beusch et al. of the spark-chamber experiment at CERN. Weighted $K_1K_1$ mass spectra. The solid line is the best fit of four resonances plus background; the broken line is the fitted background. Due to weighting, the scale does not correspond exactly to the number of observed events per histogram bin. One event represents 0.0545, 0.0143, and 0.0039 $\mu$b at 5, 7, and 12 GeV/c. (a) 5 GeV/c. 310 events. (b) 7 GeV/c, 721 events. (c) 12 GeV/c, 1529 events. (d) 5, 7, and 12 GeV/c, 2559 events.

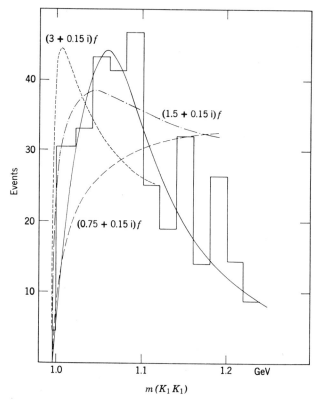

Fig. 88. Data of Beusch et al. Low mass end of the weighted $K_1K_1$ mass spectrum, all beam momenta combined. Background and higher resonances are subtracted. Comparison of various curves with the $S^*$ resonance data. (——) Breit-Wigner $S$-wave resonance. $M = 1079$ MeV. $\Gamma = 168$ MeV. (- - -) scattering length.

scattering lengths do not give a good fit. Beusch et al. furthermore suggest that the peak around the $A_2$ region consists of three distinct effects: the $f^0 \to K_1K_1$ decay, the $A_2 \to K_1K_1$ decay, and what they called the $G \to K_1K_1$ at 1439 MeV. Table VII gives their estimate of the per cent distribution of events from these four effects, as well as the central mass values and widths. Beusch et al. also noticed that the cross section for the production of the various resonance effects they have observed in the $K_1K_1$ mode follow the power law[107] $\sigma = Kp_{\text{lab}}^{-n}$. By plotting the $f^0 \to \pi\pi$ and $A_2 \to \pi\rho$ decays on the respective curves, they can deduce the branching ratios as both sets of data agree with the same power law (see Fig. 89).

The exponents $n$ in the expression for the cross section and the branching ratios are:

$$n(f^0) = 2.15 \pm 0.4$$
$$R(f^0) = \Gamma(f^0 \to K\bar{K})/\Gamma(f^0 \to \pi\pi) = 4.7 \pm 1.2\%$$
$$n(A_2) = 1.65 \pm 0.35$$
$$R(A_2) = \Gamma(A_2 \to K\bar{K})/\Gamma(A_2 \to \pi\rho) = 13 \pm 3\%$$

These branching ratios are higher than the average values currently quoted by Rosenfeld et al.[19] One interesting new phenomenon can occur here. Even though $f^0$ and $A_2$ have different $G$ values, as they both decay into the $K_1^0 K_1^0$ mode in the $J^P = 2^+$ states the overlapping resonances can interfere *in the mass distribution*. Thus one will have to be careful in interpreting these branching ratios. In this connection a comparison between the $K^+ K^-$ and $K_1^0 K_1^0$ decay modes, which should have the opposite signs in the interference effect[91] ought to prove fruitful.

*c. The Search for $I = 0$ $\pi\pi$ States.* The search for $I = 0$ $\pi\pi$ states has taken two distinct directions. The first consists of attempts to observe the $\pi^0\pi^0$ decay mode, which is forbidden by $I$ spin conservation for the $I = 1$ $\rho^0$ state. The second approach consists of attempts to deduce the presence of an $I = 0$ $\pi^+\pi^-$ state from a phase shift analysis of the $\pi^+\pi^-$ spectrum.

### 1. Measurements on the $\pi^0\pi^0$ System

So far no conclusive evidence has been obtained for a mass peak that would correspond to the $\pi^0\pi^0$ decay of an $I^G J^P = 0^+ 0^+$ meson. Some evidence reported earlier by Feldman et al.[108] at a mass of 730 MeV is not observed in more recent experiments by Buhler-Broglin et al.[109] and by Buniatov et al.[110] Figure 90 shows the result of a search in the mass region 600–900 MeV by the latter authors. While the neutral decay of the $\omega$ shows up clearly in this work, there is no evidence for a narrow peak. Aside from a relatively narrow peak searched for in the above experiments there is some evidence for a possible wider enhancement by Corbett et al.[111] and Wahlig et al.[112] On the other hand, in the $\pi^+ d \to pp$ + neutrals reaction at 5.1 GeV/c Armenise et

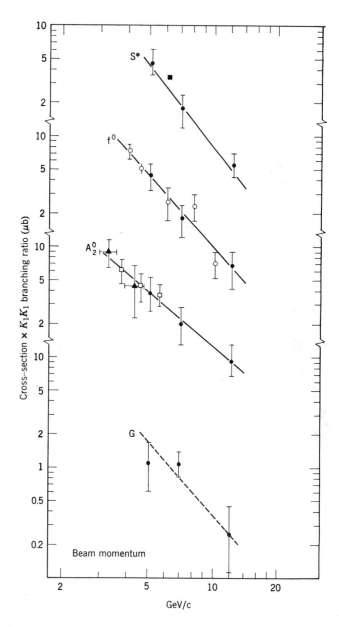

FIG. 89. Production cross sections $\sigma(\pi^- p \to B^0 n)$ and $\sigma(\pi^+ n \to B^0 p)$ of neutral resonances $B^0$, multiplied by the $K_1^0 K_1^0$ branching ratios. ($\bullet$) Data of Beusch et al. The other data points refer to bubble chamber measurements at lower energies quoted in this work. ($\bigcirc$) $\pi\pi$ ($\square$) $\pi\rho$.

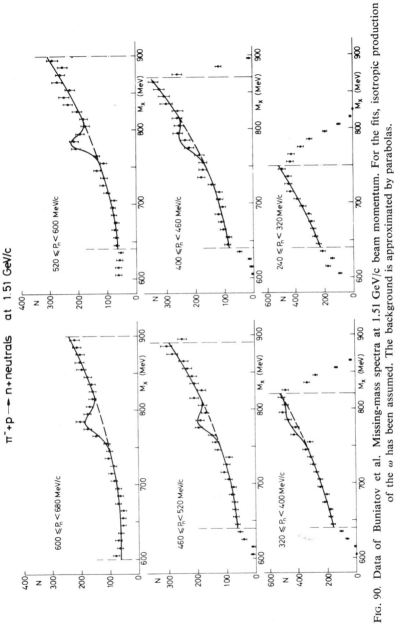

Fig. 90. Data of Buniatov et al. Missing-mass spectra at 1.51 GeV/c beam momentum. For the fits, isotropic production of the $\omega$ has been assumed. The background is approximated by parabolas.

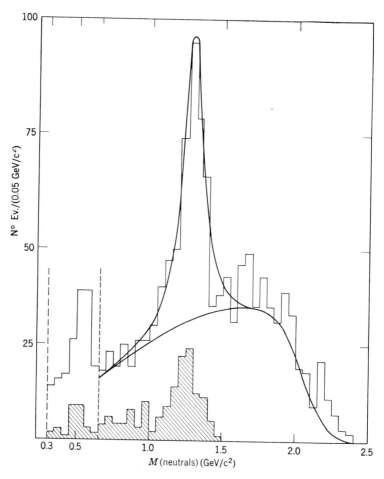

FIG. 91. Data of Armenise et al. on $\pi^+ d \to p_s p$ + (neutrals) at 5.1 GeV/c. The mass distribution of the neutral system for the conditions: $0.080 < p_{(p_s)} < 0.280$ GeV/c. All $\Delta^2$ 1570 events. Shaded $\Delta^2 < 0.08$ GeV$^2$ 174 events. The $\eta$ and $f^0$ peaks decaying into all neutrals are clearly present. No evidence for any other enhancement in the $\rho$ region is observed.

al.[113] observe a clear signal for $\eta^0$ and $f^0$ decay into neutrals, but no noticeable peak is observed between the two (see Fig. 91). A number of other indications were discussed by Butterworth[24] and we refer the reader to his talk for details.

## 2. Analysis of the $\pi^+\pi^-$ System

The suggestion that the asymmetry observed in the decay angular distribution of the $\pi^+\pi^-$ system and in particular the difference between the behavior of this system and the $\pi^\pm\pi^0$ system is due to the interference of an $S$-wave resonance with the $\rho^0$ is an old one.[135] We will discuss three analyses designed to obtain the $S$-wave phase shifts here. Recently Walker et al.[114] have compiled much of the available experimental data from the reactions

$$\pi^- p \rightarrow \pi^- \pi^+ n \tag{19}$$

and

$$\pi^- p \rightarrow \pi^- \pi^0 p \tag{20}$$

in the momentum interval 2–7 GeV/c. Here we note that the $\pi^+\pi^-$ system can be in the $I = 0, 1,$ or 2 states while the $\pi^-\pi^0$ system can only be in the $I = 1$ or 2 states as $I_z(\pi^-\pi^0) = -1$. From this data they deduce a value for the (virtual) $\pi\pi$ scattering cross section $\sigma(\pi\pi)$ from the expression:

$$\frac{d^2\sigma}{d\Delta dm^*} = Km^{*2}\sigma_{\pi\pi}f(\Delta)$$

where $f(\Delta)$ is an empirical function of $\Delta$ (the momentum transfer to the nucleon), $K$ is the pion momentum in the dipion c.m., and $m^*$ is the dipion invariant mass. (See Figs. 92 and 93.) They then perform a phase shift analysis on this data with the resulting $I = 0$ and $I = 2$ $S$-wave phase shifts shown in Figure 94, where the $I = 2$ phase shifts are first deduced from reaction (20). They get one set of phase shifts which passes through $90°$ at around 750 MeV. They consider this set to be unlikely. Another set which they favor approaches $90°$ at 850–950 MeV.

Malamud and Schlein[115] have carried an analysis on a compilation of data for reactions (19) and (20) above at momenta 2.1–3.2 GeV/c. They have attempted to make this analysis as model independent as possible. They suggest a method, based on obtaining the average values or moments of the spherical harmonics $\langle Y_l^m(\theta,\phi)\rangle$ as a function of the effective dipion mass $m_{\pi\pi}$. The method assumes that the $\pi\pi$ scattering amplitudes, considered as $S$ and $P$ wave, can be factored from the helicity amplitudes at the nucleon vertex. The latter are then obtained empirically. Figure 95 shows $\langle Y_l^0\rangle$ up to $l = 10$ averaged over large momentum intervals. This indicates that only the moments up to $l = 2$ are of importance, which corresponds to the $P$ wave (in the intensity

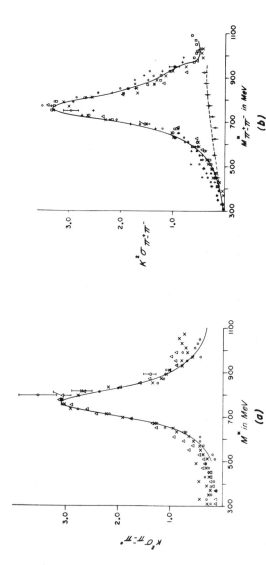

FIG. 92. Compilation and analysis by Walker et al. (a) $K^2\sigma_{\pi^- - \pi^0}$ as deduced from experiments around 2.0 and at 3.0 BeV/c. The reaction used was $\pi^- + p \rightarrow \pi^- + \pi^0 + p$. (×) 3.0 BeV, $\Delta^2 \leqq 10\mu^2$, 2511 events. (○) 3.0 BeV, $\Delta^2 \leqq 4\mu^2$, 960 events. (△) 2.0 BeV, $\Delta^2 \leqq 10\mu^2$, 3804 events. The curve is the result of fitting a $p$-wave resonance to the amplitude. $\Gamma = 160 \pm 10$ MeV, $m_R = 760$ MeV. (b) $K^2\sigma_{\pi^+ - \pi^-}$ as deduced from experiments around 2.0, 3.0, and 7 BeV/c. The reaction used was $\pi^- + p \rightarrow \pi^- + \pi^+ + n$. (△) 7–8 BeV, $\Delta^2 \leqq 8\mu^2$, 2051 events. (×) 3.0 BeV, $\Delta^2 \leqq 4\mu^2$, 2533 events. (□) 3.0 BeV, $\Delta^2 \leqq 10\mu$, 4941 events. (○) 2.0 BeV, $\Delta^2 \leqq 10\mu^2$, 5755 events. (+) 2.0 BeV, $\Delta^2 \leqq 5\mu^2$, 2043 events. (−$\phi$−−) $S$-wave amplitude. The curve is the same as fitted to the $\pi^- - \pi^0$ and added to the $S$-wave amplitude. The $\pi^+ - \pi^-$ mass spectrum seems to be shifted to higher mass values than $\pi^- - \pi^0$ by 5–10 MeV.

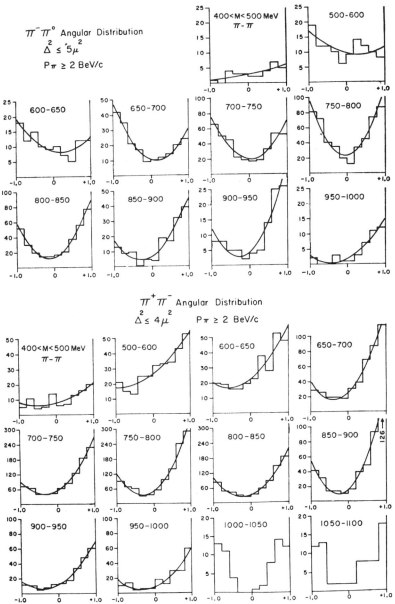

FIG. 93. The angular distributions of scattered $\pi$'s in the dipion rest frame for small momentum transfer to the nucleon. Compilation and analysis by Walker et al.

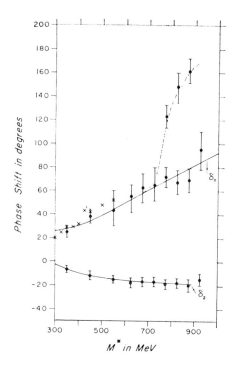

FIG. 94. The phase shift deduced by Walker et al. The branch of $\delta_0$ which passes through 90° at 750 is thought to be unlikely. That set of phase shifts would show a resonance of width about 75 MeV. ($\bar{\mathtt{I}}$) This analysis. ($\times$) Jones et al.

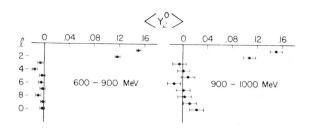

FIG. 95. Compilation and analysis by Malamud and Schlein. Moments $\langle Y_l^0 \rangle$ of the outgoing $\pi^-$ in the $\pi\pi$ rest frame of $\pi^- p \to \pi^- \pi^+ n$ with $\cos \theta_{\mathrm{c.m.}} > 0.9$. The polar axis is the helicity axis of the $\pi\pi$ system. The moments are separately given for $0.6 < m_{\pi\pi} < 0.9$ and $0.9 < m_{\pi\pi} < 1.0$ GeV.

distribution). In particular, the method gives rise to a number of internal checks, namely that the moments $N\langle Y_1^0\rangle$ and $N\langle \mathrm{Re}\ Y_1^1\rangle$ should differ only by a constant factor and similarly for $N\langle Y_2^0\rangle$, $N\langle Y_2^1\rangle$, and $N\langle Y_2^2\rangle$. These checks are well satisfied by the experimental data, as is apparent from Figure 96a, where the curves through these moments in the two instances differ by a multiplicative constant only. Three sets of resulting phase shifts are shown in Figure 97. Of these, two sets correspond to a resonance near 730 MeV. The third set

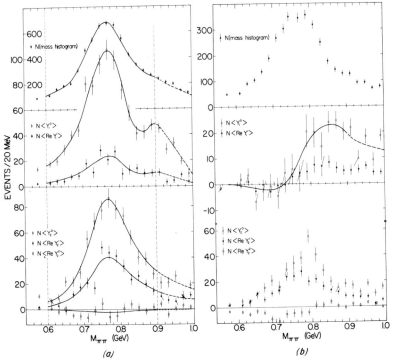

FIG. 96. Mass histograms ($N$) and moments $N\langle Y_l^m\rangle$ for (a) $\pi^-\pi^+n$ and (b) $\pi^-\pi^0p$ data with cos $\theta_{\mathrm{c.m.}} > 0.9$ from Malamud and Schlein. Only the moments $N\langle Y_1^0\rangle$ for $\pi^-\pi^0p$ were used in the fits. The curves are calculated from the "Up-Up" solution; for the three moments $N\langle Y_2^m\rangle$, curves are those of a single Breit-Wigner function and differ only by multiplicative factors. The curves on $N$ and $N\langle Y_1^m\rangle$ have been drawn smoothly to remove structure due to the fluctuations in $\delta_s$. Above 900 MeV the curves are drawn dashed to reflect the fact that the overall fit is poor in this region.

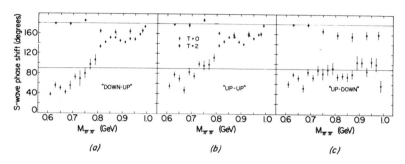

FIG. 97. Three sets of phase shifts from the analysis by Malamud and Schlein.

corresponds to a solution which hovers near 90° over the entire mass range and is thus nonresonant.

Thus in both cases there appears to be evidence for a resonance somewhere in the 730–900 MeV region, although the individual analyses differ in the exact location.

Birge et al.[116] have used the decay of $K$ mesons through the $K_{e4}$ mode:

$$K^+ \to \pi^+ \pi^- \nu e^+$$

to study the $\pi^+ \pi^-$ system. This rare decay mode ($\sim 3.6 \times 10^{-5}$) allows them to study the $\pi^+ \pi^-$ system from threshold, $2m_\pi$ to $\sim M_K$ with no other strongly interacting particles present. Their measurement gives them the difference of the $S$-wave $I = 0$ and $P$-wave $I = 1$ phase shifts: $\delta_0 - \delta_1$, averaged over the $\pi\pi$ mass region 280–400 MeV. A recent preliminary result[116] based on about 300 events gives $\delta_0 - \delta_1 = 20 \pm 12°$. As $\delta_1$ is small in this mass region this is primarily a measurement of $\delta_0$.

*d. The Search for a Scalar $K^* \to K\pi$.* We have at present no good candidate for such a state. Here again one could look for interference between an $S$-wave $K\pi$ state and the $K^*(890)$. The data of Fu et al.,[3] for example $K^+ p \to K^+ \pi^- N^{*++}$ at 4.6 and 9 GeV/c, gives the forward–backward to total ratio and shows that such interference is clearly present (see Fig. 98). Similar studies have been made by Trippe et al.[117] at 7.3 GeV/c. We are, however, far from a conclusive result as yet. There was a hint for an enhancement in the $K\pi$ system at 1080 MeV

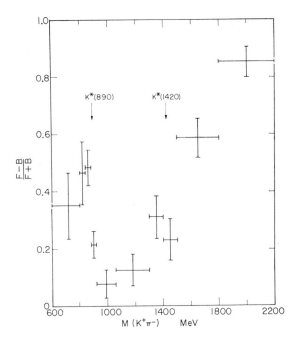

FIG. 98. Data of Fu et al. on the forward–backward asymmetry of the $K^+\pi^-$ decay angle for the reaction indicated. There is clear evidence for asymmetry and thus even-wave interference, presumably $S$-wave, in the region of the $K^*(890)$ resonance. $K^+p \to K^+\pi^-\pi^+p$ at 4.6 and 9.0 GeV/c. $N^{*++}$ in and $\Delta^2(N^{*++}) \leqq 0.6$ (GeV/c)$^2$. 2037 events.

presented by De Baere et al. at the 1966 Berkeley Conference.[82] This result again is, however, very tentative so far.

## 4. Suggestions of $L > 1$ $q\bar{q}$ States

As we go to the higher mass regions, the available experimental evidence becomes much more sparse and the interpretations become even more speculative. It is also particularly true here that different experimental techniques emphasize different aspects of the physical phenomena. We will therefore discuss individually the results from three distinct experimental investigations, namely, the CERN missing mass spectrometer work, bubble chamber work, and the Brookhaven $\bar{N}N$ total cross section work. We will then compare the various results and finally indicate what might be expected on the $q\bar{q}$ picture.

### A. The CERN Missing Mass Spectrometer Experiment and Evidence for Higher Mass Bosons

A very considerable amount of data has been reported by Maglić at the 1966 Berkeley Conference as obtained from the missing mass $(MM)$ spectrometer work at CERN. In this experiment the reaction

$$\pi^- + p \rightarrow p + (MM)^-$$

is studied by carrying out a precision angle measurement with a good momentum measurement on the recoil proton. The $\rho^-$ and $A_2^-$ show up as very prominent peaks in their work. Furthermore, they present evidence for the $\delta^-(962)$, as well as four higher mass effects, the $R^-(1691)$, $S^-(1929)$, $T^-(2195)$, and $U^-(2382)$.

*a. Some Details on the Results on the CERN Missing Mass Spectrometer Work.* Figure 99 shows a composite of all effects observed at the time of the 1966 Berkeley Conference. This graph is shown with an absolute cross section calibration, however for clarity the $\delta^-$ and $R^-$ have been multiplied by two and the $A_2$ by $\frac{1}{2}$. The figure also shows the various incident momenta at which the work was carried out and the number of events found in each peak *above* background. The dashed lines between 1 and 1.15 GeV and 1.4–1.55 GeV indicate that no high resolution mass search has yet been carried out in these regions. It is important to realize that this technique requires a considerable momentum transfer to the proton in order to work at the "Jacobian Peak" or optimum mass resolution. Thus the regions in momentum transfer explored here are in general higher than the most prominent regions observed in bubble chamber work. Furthermore $(d\sigma/dt)/\Delta M$, which is given in Figure 99, was extrapolated to a fixed value of $t$ [viz: $t = 0.2$ $(\text{GeV}/\text{c})^2$]. The extrapolation from the measured value was made according to the slope observed for diffraction scattering. This procedure need not necessarily be correct in all cases, so that the absolute values quoted should be considered with care.

Focacci et al.[118] have adopted a criterion that they will consider a peak to be physically significant when the signal exceeds the background level by more than 4.5 standard deviations.

Table VIII gives the details on all the observations. It lists: ($a$) particle name; ($b$) central mass value in MeV; ($c$) experimental resolution (which changes with mass region studied); ($d$) physical width of resonance deduced from the observations; ($e$) incident $\pi^-$ momentum

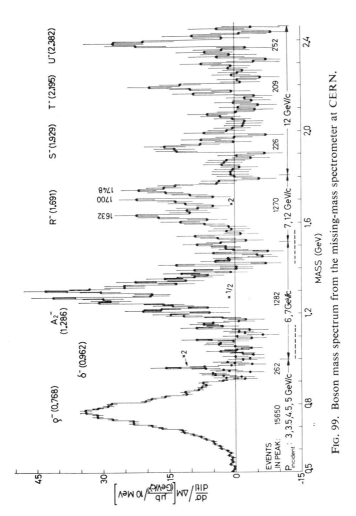

FIG. 99. Boson mass spectrum from the missing-mass spectrometer at CERN.

$p_1$; (f) statistical significance stated either as number of standard deviations or probability for the particular interpretation, such as the splitting or not splitting of the $A_2$ which is listed as equally probable; (g) number of events in peak *above* background and the statistical error on this number; (h) the signal-to-background ratio; (i) the intervals in momentum transfer squared $t$ over which the phenomenon was studied; (j) $d\sigma/dt$; and (k) the decay mode is expressed as the ratio between the different number of charged particles observed, namely $1C$ (single charged particle), $3C$ (three charged particles), and $>3C$ (more than three charged particles).

b. *General Comments.* As already mentioned, there is at present no confirmation for the $\delta^-(963)$.

A feature which is not observed in this experiment is the $A_1$. In all other work in which the $A_1$ is observed it occurs at exceptionally low $t$ values. This may explain its absence in this $MM$ spectrometer experiment.

The splitting of the $A_2$ shown here has been confirmed and amplified by the same group, as discussed in Section III-3.

c. *The Evidence for the $R^-$ Mesons.* Focacci et al. have observed a peak centered at 1691 MeV—the $R$ meson. The data consists of $973 \pm 84$ events above background. As shown in Table VIII this may actually be a boson cluster with suggested structure of $R_1(1632)$, $R_2(1700)$, and $R_3(1748)$, with $\Gamma \leqq 21$, $\leqq 30$, and $\leqq 38$ MeV, respectively. More recent data presented at Heidelberg[24] confirm these peaks and suggest a possible fourth one, $R_4$ at 1830 MeV (see Fig. 12). As will be discussed below, there is evidence from the bubble chamber data for at least two distinct objects in this mass region. Namely, both a charged and neutral $g$ meson ($g \rightarrow \pi\pi$) and thus $G = +1$, and the $A_3$ meson ($A_3^+ \rightarrow \pi^+\pi^+\pi^-$) and thus $G = -1$. The observed widths are, however, considerably greater.

d. *The Evidence for Three High Mass Bosons: $S(1929)$, $T(2195)$, and $U(2382)$.* From Table VIII we note that the peaks Focacci et al. have called $S$, $T$, and $U$ indeed fulfill their acceptance criterion. Focacci et al. have observed between 200 and 250 events above background for each of these peaks with about a 20% statistical error. These peaks were observed for a signal-to-background ratio of $\sim 1:6$. One other, and perhaps at first surprising, feature is that the peaks are all very narrow. They quote: $\Gamma(S) \leqq 35$, $\Gamma(T) \leqq 13$, and $\Gamma(U) \leqq 30$ MeV, all of which are narrower than the resolution of the instrument. Here we must note that if this same number of events, constituting a signal, had been distributed over 3 or 4 times the number of bins, such a signal would not have been detected within the statistics available so far. Thus the missing-mass measurement is most sensitive to *narrow* resonances.

### B. Evidence for Higher Mass Bosons from Bubble Chamber Work

#### a. Nonstrange Resonances in the 1650 MeV Mass Region.

1. The *g* Meson: $G = +1$, $I \geqq 0$

A compilation of the data from the reactions $\pi^- p \to \pi^- \pi^+ n$ and $\pi^+ d \to \pi^+ \pi^- pp$ prepared for the 1966 Berkeley Conference is shown in Figures 100 and 101. On all of these graphs the $\rho^0$ shows up as a very prominent structure and so does the $f^0$, which at these higher bombarding energies is nearly as prominent. The new feature first observed by Goldberg et al.[119] is a small but definite peak at 1650 MeV and $\Gamma = 150$ MeV, the *g* meson.

2. Evidence for an Enhancement with $G = +1$, $I = 1$

From a study of the reactions $\pi^\pm p \to \pi^\pm \pi^0 p$ at 6 GeV/c (for $\pi^-$) and 8 GeV/c (for $\pi^+$), there is evidence for an $\pi^\pm - \pi^0$ enhancement at 1630 MeV. With this evidence, taken in conjunction with the evidence for the $R$ from the CERN missing mass spectrometer work, we can consider the peak in this mass region with $I \geqq 1$ as established (see Figs. 102 and 103). This object presumably belongs to the same boson cluster as the *g* meson. Recently Crennell et al.[120] completed their analysis of this peak which they called the $g_1$ meson. They showed that $I = 1$ from the absence of a peak in the $\pi^+ \pi^+$ mass in the reaction $\pi^+ p \to \pi^+ \pi^+ n$. It then follows from Bose statistics that the $g_1$ meson belongs to the odd spin and parity series $J^P = 1^-, 3^-, \ldots$. From a study of the Legendre polynomial moments of the $\pi^- \pi^0$ angular distribution they suggest that $J^P = 3^-$ is preferred, although this cannot be considered as established as yet. A compilation of the available neutral ($\pi^+ \pi^-$) and charged ($\pi^\pm \pi^0$) mass distributions is shown in Figure 104. Figure 102 also shows an enhancement at 1.91 BeV observed by Deutschmann et al.[121] [According to Butterworth[24] this enhancement has decreased with improved statistics.] Here we note that both the 1.62 and 1.91-BeV peaks observed in this experiment are examples of what has been called[23] "catalytic interference" with the $N^{*++}$ band. That is, the peaks occur only in the interference region

TABLE VIII

Data on Unstable Bosons, $x^-$, Produced in Reaction $\pi^- + p \to p + x^-$, Obtained by Missing-Mass Spectrometer: $p_1 \equiv$ Lab. incident Pion Momentum; $|t| \equiv$ Square of the Momentum Transfer to Recoil Proton. [From M. N. Focacci, W. Kienzle, B. Levrat, B. C. Maglić, and M. Martin, Mass Spectrum of Bosons from 500 to 2500 MeV in the Reaction $\pi^- p \to p X^0$ Observed by a Missing-Mass Spectrometer, *Phys. Rev. Letters*, **17**, 890 (1966), with subsequent revision.]

| Particle name | Central mass value, MeV | Exptl. resolution | Physical width $\Gamma$, (deduced) | Incident $\pi^-$ momentum, $p_1$ | Statistical significance (st. dev.) | Events in peak above background and statistical error | Signal-to-background ratio | $t$ limits | $d\sigma/dt$ | Decay mode |
|---|---|---|---|---|---|---|---|---|---|---|
| $\rho^-$ | 768 ± 5 | 28 ± 5 | 127 ± 5 | 3.0<br>3.5<br>4.5<br>5.0 | | 15,600 ± 170 | 1.6:1 | 0.10 − 0.14<br>0.14 − 0.17<br>0.17 − 0.22<br>0.22 − 0.26 | 770 ± 150 [a]<br>770 ± 170<br>580 ± 100<br>370 ± 110 | $1c > 97.4\%$ |
| $\delta^-$ | 962.5 ± 5 | 24 ± 4 | ≦ 5 | 3.0<br>3.5<br>4.5<br>5.0 | 5.0 | 262 ± 52 | 1:5 | $0.11 < t < 0.21$ | 8.9 ± 3 [b] | $\geqq 1c/3c = 1.3 \begin{smallmatrix}+0.9\\-0.7\end{smallmatrix}$ |
| $A_2$ | 1,286 ± 8 | 36 ± 4 | 98 ± 5 | 6.0<br>7.0 | 17 | 1,282 ± 63 | 1:1.5 | $0.31 < t < 0.39$ | 400 ± 120 | $1c/3c = 1.05 ± 0.1$ |
| $A_2'$ | 1,260 ± 10 | | | 6.0 | 1 peak and 2 peaks equally probable: $P = 5\text{-}10\%$ | $A_2'/A_2'' \approx 1$:1 | 1:6 | | | $1c/3c \approx 1$ |
| $A_2''$ | 1,312 ± 10 | | | 7.0 | 11.6 | | | | | $1c = 0.30 ± 0.06$ [c] |

| | | | | | | | | | | |
|---|---|---|---|---|---|---|---|---|---|---|
| $R$ | $1{,}691 \pm 15$ | $31 \pm 3$ | $116 \pm 3$ | 7.0 1 peak: $P=1\%$<br>12.0 2 peaks: $P=1\%$<br>3 peaks: $P=20$<br>to 60% $(R_{1,2,3})$ | | $973 \pm 84$ | 1:6 | $0.23 < t < 0.28$ | $125 \pm 30$ | $3c = 0.67 \pm 0.10$<br>$> 3c = 0.03 \pm 0.03$ |
| $R_1$ | $1{,}632 \pm 15$ | $34 \pm 3$ | $< 21$ | | 6.7 | $360 \pm 70$ | 1:4.7 | | $35 \pm 10$ | $1c = 0.37 \pm 0.13$<br>$3c = 0.59 \pm 0.21$<br>$> 3c = 0.04 \pm 0.04$ |
| $R_2$ | $1{,}700 \pm 15$ | $30 \pm 3$ | $< 30$ | 7.0<br>12.0 | 6.1 | $485 \pm 73$ | 1:3.3 | | 43 | $1c = 0.42 \pm 0.11$<br>$3c = 0.56 \pm 0.14$<br>$> 3c = 0.01 \pm 0.01$<br>$1c = 0.14 \pm 0.08$ |
| $R_3$ | $1{,}748 \pm 15$ | $28 \pm 3$ | $< 38$ | | 7.3 | $425 \pm 74$ | 1:3.5 | | 47 | $3c = 0.80 \pm 0.18$<br>$> 3c = 0.05 \pm 0.05$<br>$1c = 0.06 \,{}^{+0.15}_{-0.06}$ |
| $S$ | $1{,}929 \pm 14$ | $22 \pm 2$ | $\leqq 35$ | 12.0 | 5.5 | $226 \pm 41$ | 1:7 | $0.22 < t < 0.36$ | $35 \pm 12$ | $3c = 0.92 \,{}^{+0.08}_{-0.20}$<br>$> 3c = 0.02 \,{}^{+0.13}_{-0.02}$ |
| $T$ | $2{,}195 \pm 15$ | $39 \pm 4$ | $\leqq 13$ | 12.0 | 5.1 | $209 \pm 41$ | 1:7 | $0.22 < t < 0.36$ | $29 \pm 10$ | $1c = 0.04 \,{}^{+0.11}_{-0.04}$<br>$3c = 0.94 \,{}^{+0.06}_{-0.19}$<br>$> 3c = 0.02 \,{}^{+0.13}_{-0.02}$ |
| $U$ | $2{,}382 \pm 24$ | $62 \pm 6$ | $\leqq 30$ | 12.0 | 5.9 | $252 \pm 43$ | 1:6 | $0.28 < t < 0.36$ | $42 \pm 14$ | $1c = 0.30 \pm 0.10$<br>$3c = 0.45 \pm 0.15$<br>$> 3c = 0.25 \pm 0.10$ |

[a] $d\sigma/dt$ normalized to 4 GeV/c (average momentum).
[b] $d\sigma/dt$ weighted between $p_1 = 3$, 3.5, and 4.5 GeV/c.
[c] Errors are one standard deviation.

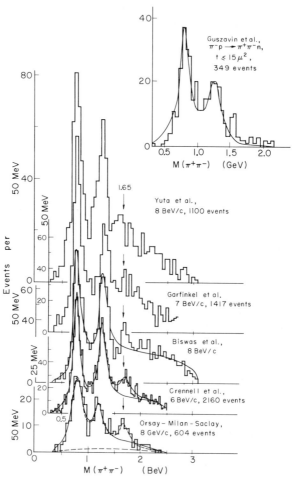

FIG. 100. A compilation prepared by Goldhaber and Shen for the 1966 Berkeley Conference of the $\pi^+\pi^-$ mass distribution for the reaction $\pi^- p \to \pi^+\pi^- n$. The evidence for the $g$ meson can be clearly noted.

with the $N^{*++}$ band. The tendency has been to cut out such interference regions but it would appear that with favorable phase relations between a new resonance and the $N^{*++}$ such resonance effects can be considerably enhanced. Thus, for example, in the reaction $K^+ p \to K^0 \pi^+ p$ there is considerable constructive interference between the $K^{*+}$ and $N^{*++}$

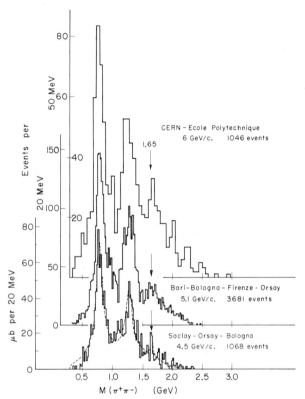

FIG. 101. A compilation prepared by Goldhaber and Shen for the 1966 Berkeley Conference of the $\pi^+\pi^-$ mass distribution for the reaction $\pi^+d \to \pi^+\pi^-pp$. The evidence for the $g$ meson can again be clearly noted.

bands both for $K^*(890)$ in experiments at 1.2 GeV/c[122] and for $K^*(1420)$ in experiments at 3.5 and 4.6 GeV/c.[3,123] Needless to say, results obtained exclusively from the catalytic interference region must be treated with care until one understands the details of the particular interference phenomenon.

## 3. The $A_3$, a $3\pi$ Enhancement of 1640 MeV with $G = -1, I \geqq 1$

A compilation by Ferbel[82] based on three sets of independent data on the $\pi^+p \to \pi^+\pi^-\pi^+p$ reaction from 7 to 8.5 GeV/c was presented at the 1966 Berkeley Conference (see Fig. 105). A very similar result was

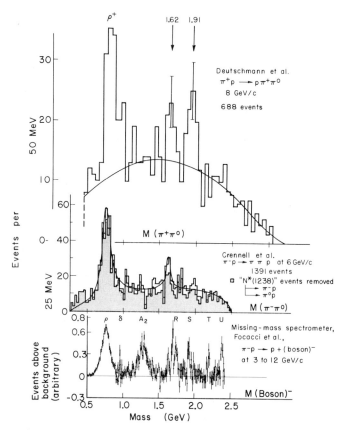

FIG. 102. A compilation of the evidence for charged $\pi\pi$ system at 1.16 and 1.91 BeV/c. The bubble chamber data in the top two figures is compared with the CERN missing-mass spectrometer work, for which the number of pions involved is not known.

also presented by Guszavin et al.[82] who studied the $\pi^-p$ reaction at 4.7 GeV/c. The statistics from the combined experiments are quite good, however the $A_3(1640)$ sits on a very large background. The signal-to-background ratio is about 1:4. The peak is primarily *not* associated with $\rho$ formation, but is observed when no cuts for the $\rho$ meson production are made. The effect could thus probably be enhanced by removing the $\rho$ band. The decay proceeds into $\pi^+\pi^-\pi^+$ as well as possibly $f^0\pi^+$. A broad enhancement in this general region in the

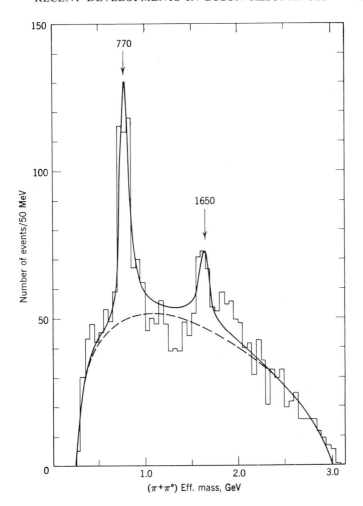

FIG. 103. New data on the $g_1$ presented at Heidelberg by the ABC collaboration. $\pi^+ p \to p\pi^+ \pi^0$ at 8 GeV/c. 2502 events. (—–) assumed background. (——) background + Breit-Wigner.

$f^0\pi^-$ mass has been noted earlier by the experiment with 16-GeV/c $\pi^-$ interactions in the Ecole Polytechnique heavy liquid chamber.[82] (See Fig. 62.) Additional confirmation for the $A_3$ was presented at Heidelberg.[24]

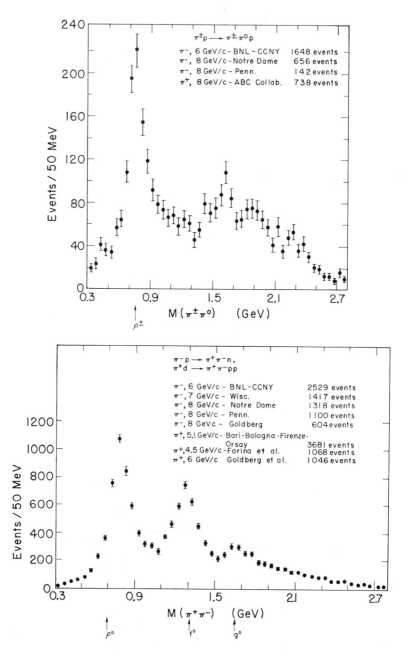

Fig. 104. A compilation prepared by Samios and Lai for the 1966 Berkeley Conference of the available data on the $\pi\pi$ mass distribution.

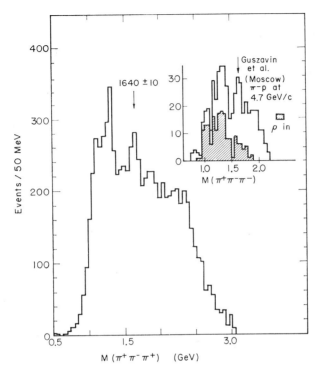

FIG. 105. The compilation by Ferbel as well as independent data by Guzavin et al. showing an enhancement at 1640 MeV which is not associated with a $\rho$ meson. This data comes from the reaction $\pi^+ p \rightarrow \pi^+ \pi^- \pi^+ p$: ($\sim$4000 events) 8.4 GeV/c (Columbia-Rutgers); ($\sim$2000 events) 7 GeV/c (Rochester-Yale); ($\sim$1700 events) 8 GeV/c (ABC collaboration).

*b. Evidence for Decay into More Complicated Systems.* If it is indeed correct that the phenomena described here represent higher angular momentum states, as has been inferred by Focacci et al. from analogy to the $\rho$ Regge trajectory and the Regge trajectories observed for baryon resonances, it is very plausible that the decay of such bosons will proceed into more complicated systems. Thus, because of centrifugal barrier factors, a decay into bosons with spin $>0$ may be more favorable than a decay into two $0^-$ mesons (when this is allowed) even though the latter decay has a higher center of mass momentum. Selection rules for decays into $J = 1$ and $J = 2$ systems ($\rho$, $\omega$, $A_2$, $f^0$, etc.) as well as for cascading to the next lower boson resonance by pion emission will be discussed in Section III-4-E below. A number of candidates for such states have been discussed by Butterworth.[24] We will give two representative examples here.

## 1. Suggestion of $\rho^0 \rho^0$ Enhancements

Danysz et al.[124] have reported data on $\bar{p}p$ annihilation to $3\pi^+ 3\pi^-$ at 2.5 and 3 GeV/c. In this data they noted two peaks in the $\pi^+ \pi^+ \pi^- \pi^-$ mass spectra.

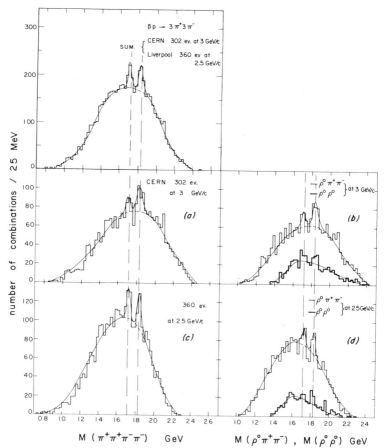

FIG. 106. Data of Danysz et al. The top figure represents the combined CERN and Liverpool $2\pi^+ 2\pi^-$ mass distributions. (a) and (b) represent the CERN data; (c) and (d) are the Liverpool data for the conditions on the figure.

$M_1(4\pi) = 1717 \pm 7$ MeV    $\Gamma_1 = 40 \pm 12$ MeV    $G = +1$
$M_2(4\pi) = 1832 \pm 6$ MeV    $\Gamma_1 = 42 \pm 11$ MeV    $G = +1$

These peaks appear to be associated (partly) with $\rho^0\pi^+\pi^-$ decay and possibly $\rho^0\rho^0$ decay (see Fig. 106). Here we must remember one problem associated with the study of large numbers of pions; each event contributes several combinations to the mass spectrum. Thus with $3\pi^+$ and $3\pi^-$ mesons one gets $(3!/2!)^2 = 9$ combinations for picking out $2\pi^+$ and $2\pi^-$ mesons. This makes the assessment of the statistical errors and reflections more difficult.

## 2. Observation of $\rho^0\omega^0$ Mass Peaks

Again in the $\bar{p}p$ annihilation at 3.0 and 3.6 GeV/c Danysz et al.[77] have observed two mass peaks in the $\bar{p}p \rightarrow 3\pi^+3\pi^-\pi^0$ reaction by studying the subsample $\bar{p}p \rightarrow \rho^0\omega^0\pi^+\pi^-$. In this case the peaks are associated with $\rho^0\omega^0$ formation.

Figure 107 shows the $M(\rho^0\omega^0)$ distribution, which indicates peaks at

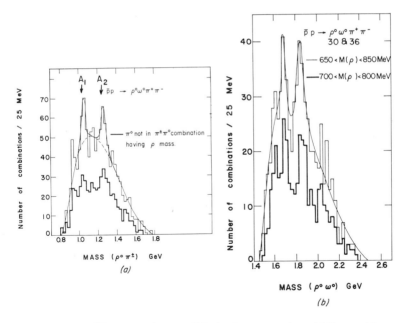

FIG. 107. Data of Danysz et al. on annihilation into seven pions. (a) Some evidence for $A_1$ and $A_2$ formation. (b) Evidence for peaks in the $\rho^0\omega^0$ mass distribution.

$M_1(\rho^0\omega^0) = 1689 \pm 10 \text{ MeV} \quad \Gamma_1 = 38 \pm 18 \text{ MeV} \quad G = -1, \; I = 1$

$M_2(\rho^0\omega^0) = 1848 \pm 11 \text{ MeV} \quad \Gamma_2 = 67 \pm 27 \text{ MeV} \quad G = -1, \; I = 1$

This same sample of events also showed what may be $A_1$ and $A_2$ formation. Figure 107 also shows the $\rho^0\pi^\pm$ mass distribution. Here

$$M(\text{``}A_1\text{''}) = 1054 \pm 7 \text{ MeV} \qquad \Gamma = 33 \pm 19 \text{ MeV}$$
$$M(\text{``}A_2\text{''}) = 1269 \pm 9 \text{ MeV} \qquad \Gamma = 45 \pm 22 \text{ MeV}$$

Indications for similar peaks in the $\rho\pi$ mass distribution in the same reaction have been quoted by Fridman et al.[134]

    *c. Evidence for Higher Mass Strange Bosons.* In a $K^-p$ experiment at 10 GeV/c the ABCLV collaboration[125] reported the observation of a $K^*$ at $1789 \pm 10$ MeV which they called the $L$ meson (see Fig. 108). Dubal et al.[82] also observed a peak at $1852 \pm 8$ MeV in the CERN missing mass spectrometer working with the small $K^-$ fraction in their negative beam. This later observation is however only a 3 standard deviation effect (see Fig. 109). On the other hand, the $K^*(1420)$ shows up in this experiment as a distinct peak. The bubble chamber work also recently gave branching ratios and further details shown in Table IX. The $L$ meson, or at any rate a somewhat broader enhancement in the same mass region, has recently been confirmed by Firestone et al.[126] In this work on $K^+p$ at 9 GeV/c in the BNL 80-in. bubble chamber,

TABLE IX

Summary of Properties for $L$-Meson According
to the ABCLV Groups[125]
Mass $= 1785 \pm 12$ MeV; Width $= 127 \pm 43$
MeV; $J^P \neq 0^-$, could be $1^+, 2^-$.

| Branching ratios | Events | % |
|---|---|---|
| $K\pi\pi$ | 194.6 | $44.5 \pm 15$ |
| $K\rho$ | 43.2 | $9.9 \pm 6$ |
| $K^*(890)\pi$ | 106.4 | $24.4 \pm 8$ |
| $K^*(1430)\pi$ | 71.9 | $16.4 \pm 8$ |
| $K\omega$ | 21.0 | $4.8 \pm 2$ |
| $K\pi$ | $< 10$ | $< 2.3$ |

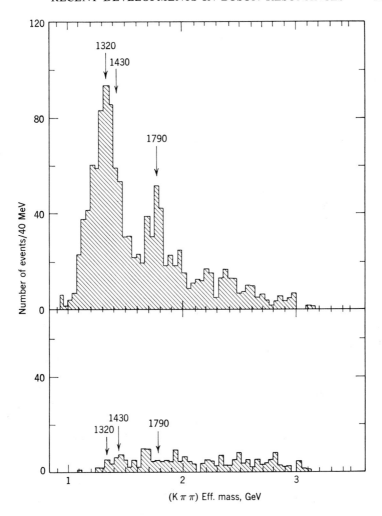

Fig. 108. New results on the $L$ meson from the ABCLV collaboration presented at Heidelberg. (Upper) $K^- p \to p K^- \pi^+ \pi^-$ at 10 GeV/c, $K^- p \to p \bar{K}^0 \pi^- \pi^0$, $N^{*++}$ excluded. $|t| < 0.6$ (GeV/c)$^2$, 1190 events. The lower part illustrates the suppression of the $Q$ enhancement as well as the $L$ meson with charge exchange at the nucleon vertex. $K^- p \to n(K\pi^+\pi^-)^0$, $|t| < 0.6$ (GeV/c)$^2$, 202 events.

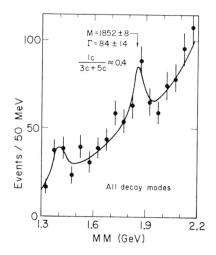

FIG. 109. Data of Dubal et al. from the CERN missing-mass spectrometer work which shows a possible peak in the general mass region of L(1790) meson.

events with a stopping proton were used and the remaining missing mass was calculated for two- and four-prong events (see Figs. 110 and 111). This thus corresponds to a use of the bubble chamber as a missing mass spectrometer with an effective momentum transfer squared cutoff at $|t| \lesssim 0.25$ $(GeV/c)^2$. A similar technique, including fitted events as well, shows a corresponding L peak from the $K^-p$ experiment[125] at 10 GeV/c (see Fig. 112). A number of other experiments quoted by Butterworth[24] with $K^+p$ and $K^-p$ interactions show evidence for the L(1790) meson. Some also indicate possible structure and a peak at 1660 MeV.

### C. The Brookhaven Precision Total $\bar{p}p$ and $\bar{p}d$ Cross Section Measurements

The $\bar{p}p$ and $\bar{p}n$ systems have baryon number zero and hence can have all the quantum numbers of the nonstrange boson states of mass $> 2M_p$. As part of a series of precision total cross section measurements, Abrams et al.[127] have measured the $\bar{p}p$ and $\bar{p}d$ cross sections for momenta from 1.0 to 3.4 GeV/c. The remarkable feature of these measurements is that despite the very large cross sections (75–120 mb for $\bar{p}p$ and 130–210 mb for $\bar{p}d$), they note distinct peaks of the order

MISSING MASS

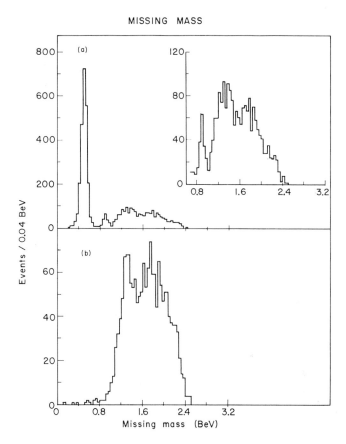

FIG. 110. Data of Firestone et al. $K^+p$ at 9 GeV/c. The missing-mass distribution for events with stopping protons. (a) Two prongs, stopping protons, 4385 events. (b) Four prongs, stopping protons, 1638 events.

of a few millibarns. (See Figs. 113–115.) The mass values and other parameters are given in Table X. One straightforward interpretation of the data is that the peaks represent higher mass bosons. In particular it is noteworthy that the peaks are consistent in mass, but not width, with the $T$ and $U$ mesons of Focacci et al.[118] One difficulty which is not yet completely resolved is that the lower peak also corresponds in mass to the threshold of the reaction,

$$\bar{p}p \to \Delta(1238)N \quad \text{or} \quad \Delta(1238)\bar{N} \qquad M = 2180 \text{ MeV}$$

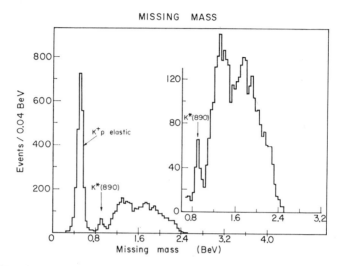

FIG. 111. The sum of the two sets of data shown in Fig. 110. In the insert the $K^*(890)$, the $Q$ peak, and a broad peak in the $L$ meson region are clearly discernible. Two and four prongs, stopping protons, 6023 events.

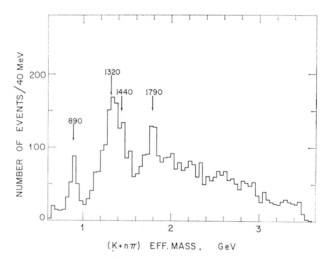

FIG. 112. Data from the ABCLV collaboration where fitted and unfitted events have been combined. Here again the effects mentioned in Fig. 111 are clearly present. $K^- p \rightarrow p(K + n\pi)^-$ at 10 GeV/c, where $n = 1, 2, 3$ and fit and no fit events taken, $N^{*++}$ excluded, 4560 events.

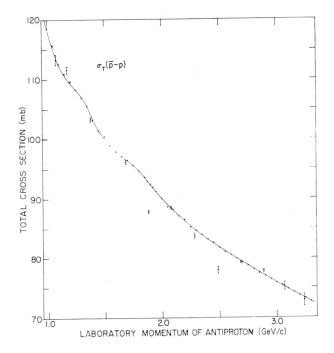

FIG. 113. The measurements of Abrams et al. on the total $\bar{p}p$ cross section ($\bigcirc$) Amaldi et al. ($\bullet$) Abrams et al.

TABLE X

Some Parameters of the Antinucleon–Nucleon Structures [a]
Data of Abrams et al.[127]

| Isotopic spin | Laboratory momentum, GeV/c | Total energy, c.m., MeV | Full width, c.m., MeV | Height, mb | $4\pi\lambda^2$, mb | $\frac{1}{2}(J + \frac{1}{2})x$ |
|---|---|---|---|---|---|---|
| 1 | 1.32 | 2190 ± 5 | 85 | 6 | 15.4 | 0.4 |
| 1 | 1.76 | 2345 ± 10 | 140 | 3 | 9.9 | 0.3 |
| 0 | 1.86 | 2380 ± 10 | 140 | 2 | 9.1 | 0.2 |

[a] These values are preliminary.

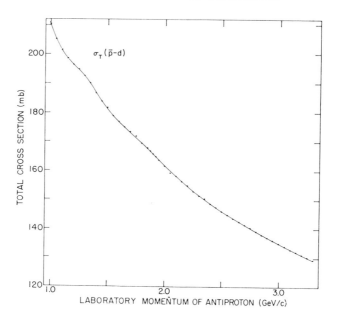

Fig. 114. The measurements of Abrams et al. on the total $\bar{p}d$ cross section.

Because of the large cross section for $\Delta$ production this reaction could in principle give rise to a peak in the total cross section which does not necessarily correspond to a boson resonance, i.e., a $t$-channel rather than an $s$-channel effect. If this is so, the situation would be analogous to the peak of Cool et al.[128] in the $K^+p$ system at 1910 MeV, which has been interpreted on the basis of nonresonant $K\Delta$ production.[129] We can compare these data with precision total cross section measurement on the $pp$ system by Bugg et al.[130] In that experiment prominent structures generally ascribed to the production of various $N^*$'s in the $t$ channel have been observed. However, the structures occur at somewhat different masses than in the $\bar{p}p$ system (see Fig. 116). A definitive interpretation of the peaks in the $\bar{p}p$ system is thus not possible without more detailed studies of the reaction products.

    *a. Preliminary Study of the Detailed Behavior of the $\bar{p}p$ Interaction at the 2200 MeV I = 1 Peak.* At the 1967 Heidelberg Conference Cooper et al.[131] have reported preliminary results on the study of the $\bar{p}p$ reaction in the 30-in. MURA hydrogen bubble chamber at Argonne. They have studied the $\bar{p}p$ reaction at several momenta between 1.24 and

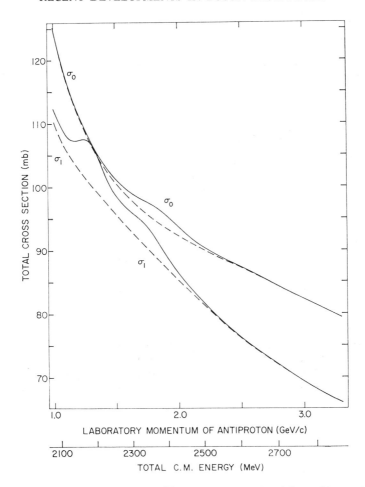

FIG. 115. The $T = 0$ and $T = 1$ $N\overline{N}$ cross sections deduced from the measurements in the previous figures of Abrams et al. at Brookhaven.

1.54 GeV/c, bracketing the 2200 MeV peak in $\sigma(\overline{p}p)$. They conclude that the $\Delta$ threshold plays only a small part in this momentum region. The $\pi N\overline{N}$ cross section amounts to only $\sim 1.5$ mb and behaves smoothly through this region. Furthermore, there is no evidence for a $\Delta$ or $\overline{\Delta}$ mass peak in the $\pi \overline{N}$ or $\pi N$ mass spectra. The large peak attributed to the $N\Delta$ production in the $pp$ experiment of Bugg et al. thus has no direct counterpart in the $\overline{p}p$ data. This may be attributable to saturation

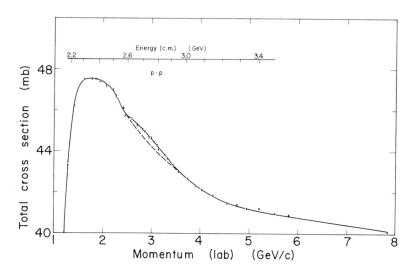

FIG. 116. The *p–p* total cross section in the same momentum region. Data from Bugg et al., Rutherford Laboratory and Cambridge.

of unitarity limits by the competing annihilation processes or perhaps to the occurrence of annihilation on rescattering subsequent to $N\overline{\Delta}$ (or $\overline{N}\Delta$) production. The preliminary results of Cooper et al. thus suggest the boson interpretation of the $\sigma(\overline{p}p)$ peak near the $T(2195)$ meson is more likely than a $t$-channel effect, although no definite conclusion is available at present.

### D. Comparison between the Various Phenomena

The phenomena described in the three previous sections clearly indicate that there is evidence for higher mass bosons. The problem is that there is no general agreement as to the relation between all the different observations. Thus there is some disagreement on the location of peaks and, in particular, severe disagreement on the widths of the peaks. Figure 117 shows a comparison compiled by Rosenfeld et al.[19] which summarizes the situation for nonstrange bosons.

Finally, in a comparison between the phenomena observed we must keep in mind some of the differences between the quantities measured as well as features which are unique to a particular approach. Two such points are discussed below.

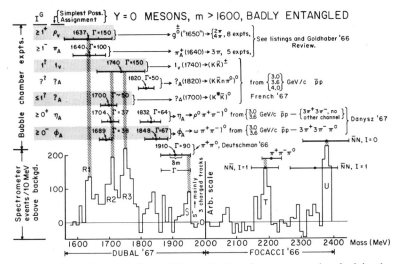

FIG. 117. Compilation by Rosenfeld et al. of various mass peaks cited in the literature in the mass region $m > 1600$ MeV.

*a. Experimental Sensitivity to Different Regions of t.* The missing-mass spectrometer work relies on precision angle measurements on a proton in the region of the "Jacobian peak." This cuts out low-momentum-transfer data. In the region of the $S(1929)$, $T(2195)$, and $U(2382)$ mesons the average momentum transfer squared value for the measurements made is $t \approx 0.3$ (GeV)$^2$. On the other hand, $\sigma(\bar{p}p)$ measurements are sensitive to all allowed values of $t$. The same is true for bubble chamber work, which in fact is most sensitive to the lowest allowed $t$ values, for which the cross sections are maximal for peripheral reactions.

*b. Partial Width for $\bar{p}p$ Decay.* The $\sigma(\bar{p}p)$ experiment will show only boson resonances for which there is a finite partial width $\Gamma(\bar{p}p)$ for $\bar{p}p$ decay in a given nonet. It is not clear at present how $\Gamma(\bar{p}p)$ depends on the quantum numbers of a particular nonet in a given $L$ cluster.

### E. Interpretation in Terms of the $q\bar{q}$ Model

In a series of lectures, Dalitz[20] has given some details on the $q\bar{q}$ model fashioned so as to fit the available data.

*a. The Bosons as "Diatomic Quark Molecules."* If the quarks are considered as very heavy objects, $M_q \gtrsim 10$ GeV, then as Dalitz points out it is possible to treat them as nonrelativistic particles in a very deep well. In analogy with a diatomic molecule, one can then think of rotational levels with different $L$ values. With a suitable choice of potential, a flat-bottom harmonic oscillator potential, one can then obtain a dependence of $E^2$ which varies linearly with $L$. The slope $\Delta(E^2)/\Delta L$ is roughly 1 (GeV)$^2$.

*b. Relation to the Regge Model, Exchange Degeneracy.* In the Regge model for baryons one finds that a Regge trajectory contains baryons having values of $J$ which differ by 2 units, so that $J_2 = J_1 + 2$. Thus baryons with opposite signature $\tau = (-1)^{J+\frac{1}{2}}$ lie on separate trajectories. The separation between two such trajectories with different signatures is ascribed to an exchange force. For bosons the $A_2$ appears to lie on the $\rho$ trajectory, and so on through $R$, $S$, $T$, and $U$, which in the spirit of the present discussion are believed to correspond to adjacent $J$ values ($J_2 = J_1 + 1$). Thus bosons with opposite signature $\tau = (-1)^J$ may lie on the same trajectory which implies that there appears to be an exchange degeneracy. Dalitz makes this plausible by pointing out that the simplest object which can be exchanged between $q$ and $\bar{q}$ must have baryon number $\frac{2}{3}$, and thus consists of two quarks $qq$ with mass $2 M_q$. The large mass of such an object would tend to suppress the exchange process.

*c. Boson-L-Clusters.* The rotational levels for the different $L$ values can thus be considered as the main splitting which occurs on this model. If this were the only mass-splitting effect, we would obtain four degenerate boson nonets for each $L$ value, namely the four states which can be formed by combining $L$ with the total quark spin $S$ for $S = 1$ or $S = 0$. These are the nonets $^3L_{L-1}$, $^3L_L$, $^1L_L$, $^3L_{L+1}$, where the symbol stands for $^{2S+1}L_J$ in the usual spectroscopic notation. An exception to this is the case for $L = 0$, where we only have two such states, the $^1S_0$ and $^3S_1$ nonets. There are, however, indications from experiment for several types of "fine structure." These suggest that the mass splittings for different $L$ values are greater than those between the four nonets corresponding to a given $L$ value. Thus we might expect to observe clusters of boson resonances which are clearly separated from each other but in which the four nonets may not always be clearly resolved. We will call these "boson $L$ clusters."

The first such boson cluster observed was the $A$ meson, which was later resolved into the $A_1$ and $A_2$ mesons. These are believed to correspond to the $P$-wave $q\bar{q}$ system. The $I = \frac{1}{2} K\pi\pi$ boson cluster centered at 1320 MeV was the next such example. Here again three objects, $K^*(1250)$, $K^*(1320)$, and $K^*(1420)$, may have been resolved as discussed in Section III-3.

Further examples of boson clusters are the $g$ or $R$ peaks, which may have their strange counterpart in the $L(1790)$ meson. These may belong to an $L = 2$ boson $L$ cluster.

## 1. Spin-Orbit Splitting

If we look at the above-mentioned $A$ and $K^*(1320)$ boson clusters, we can note the effect of spin-orbit splitting. In particular let us consider the $I = 1$ members of the four nonets $^3P_0$, $^3P_1$, $^1P_1$, and $^3P_2$. The currently popular (though yet tentative) assignment for the last three is $A_1(1080)$, $B(1220)$, and $A_2(1310)$. We note that these represent (roughly) equal (mass)$^2$ splitting. Here $\Delta(E^2) \approx 0.3$ (GeV)$^2$ for the $L = 1$ case. If we ascribe the observed splitting to a spin-orbit potential

$$\bar{V}_{so} = (\sigma + \bar{\sigma})\cdot \mathbf{L}\, V_{so}(r) = \mathbf{S}\cdot \mathbf{L}\, V_{so}(r)$$

with the mass-splitting coefficient

$$\mathbf{S}\cdot\mathbf{L} = \tfrac{1}{2}[J(J + 1) - L(L + 1) - S(S + 1)]$$

then for the four nonets this takes on the values given below:

|  | $^3L_{L-1}$ | $^3L_L$ | $^1L_L$ | $^3L_{L+1}$ |
|---|---|---|---|---|
| $\mathbf{S}\cdot\mathbf{L}$ | $-(L + 1)$ | $-1$ | $0$ | $+L$ |
| $\Delta(\mathbf{S}\cdot L)$ | | $L$ | $1$ | $L$ |

Hence on the basis of the experimental mass sequence of the $A_1$, $B$, and $A_2$, Dalitz suggests that we are dealing with a *repulsive* spin-orbit potential, that is, $V_{so}(r) > 0$. For $L = 1$ this gives *equal* (mass)$^2$ splitting in accordance with experiment. For $L = 2$ this (mass)$^2$ splitting is $2:1:2$ (see Fig. 12). The most recent data from the CERN missing-mass spectrometer[24] suggests that the $R_1(1630)$, $R_2(1700)$, $R_3(1748)$, $R_4(1830)$ (?) follow such a pattern. This would correspond to the spin parity values $J^P = 1^-$, $2^-$, $2^-$ and $3^-$, and would disagree with the $J = 3^-$ suggested[120] for the $g_1(1630)$, aside from the discrepancy in $\Gamma$. Dalitz also points out that a tensor force, which in principle could split a given $L$ cluster, is probably small, as it would give rise to unequal splitting for the $L = 1$ case.

## 2. Spin–Spin Splitting

The $L = 0$ nonets are an anomaly in that we have only spin–spin forces available for splitting the $^1S_0$ and $^3S_1$ states. These are very considerable, however, in view of the large $\pi\rho$ mass difference. The

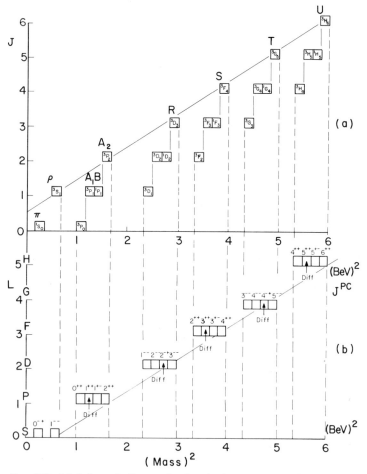

FIG. 118. (a) Schematic Regge plot for the boson nonets. (b) Plot of $L$ vs. (mass)$^2$ which shows up the suggested boson cluster effect more clearly. Note that the spin-orbit splitting is shown schematically only. (Not to scale.) The symbol Diff marks the nonets whose members can be formed by diffraction dissociation for incident $\pi$ or $K$ beams. $SU_3$ splitting not shown.

surprising feature is that this force appears to have died out for $L = 1$. This behavior can be explained by making the spin–spin force of sufficiently short range.

  *d. Some Possible Consequences of the $q\bar{q}$ Model.* To explore the model we have outlined above in further detail, we can consider the schematic Regge plot shown in Figure 118$a$, which indicates schematically what the boson clusters may look like, although, of course, the spin-orbit splitting of the higher $L$ boson clusters is not known at present. The indicated mass splitting is symbolic only and should not be taken seriously. Each square in Figure 118$a$ represents a nonet of mesons. The $SU(3)$ splitting is not shown. Presumably there can be four distinct Regge trajectories; only the $\rho$ trajectory is indicated. Figure 118$b$ shows the same plot, where now, however, $L$ is plotted against mass squared. Here the clustering is more apparent. The distributions indicated in Figure 118 represent the simplest possible situation. Should the spin-orbit splitting increase rapidly as $L$ increases, for example, we could get bosons of different $L$ superimposed on each other, and thus lose the cluster effect.

  Other causes which can complicate or even obscure the cluster effect would be:

  (*a*) The presence of bosons belonging to higher-symmetry groups such as the 27 configuration, which requires the existence of states like $K^+K^+$, $K\pi\pi$, $I = \frac{3}{2}$, $\pi^+\pi^+$, etc., or what have been called exotic particles. In our estimation, there is not yet sufficient evidence to require us to invoke such configurations. This has been discussed in detail elsewhere.[21,22]

  (*b*) Boson clusters corresponding to higher radial quantum numbers $n$. Here we must note that, until we get a clear understanding of the $q\bar{q}$ potential, it is not obvious just what $n$ represents. The $E(1420)$ meson may be an example of this for the pseudoscalar mesons.

## 1. The Allowed Decay Modes

  Continuing in the spirit of this inquiry, we can ask what are the allowed decay modes for the members of these various nonets? Some representative decay modes are illustrated in Figure 119. Here again a crude mass-squared scale is indicated. Thus, in a sense, this figure illustrates, in an approximate fashion, the mass spectrum expected for various final states. For example, the first two rows indicate the mass

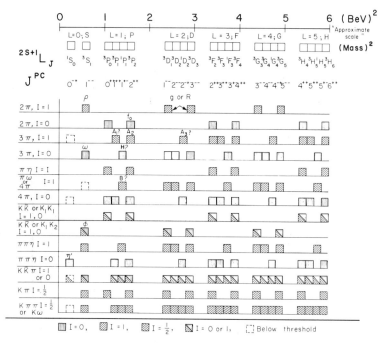

FIG. 119. Some of the allowed strong decay modes for the members of the nonets shown in Fig. 119. Again the mass scale should only be regarded as a very approximate guide. (Spin-orbit splitting not to scale, $SU_3$ splitting not shown.)

spectrum in the $I = 1$ and $I = 0$ $\pi\pi$ state, and so forth. A few of the presently known and identified states are marked with their names.

A comparison of these patterns with the experimental spectra is perhaps the most sensitive way in which to detect evidence for, or deviations from, the model described herein. Thus, for example, in the $\pi\rho$ or $\pi\pi\pi$ decay mode, in the region of the $A$ meson there is only room for two distinct mesons, corresponding to the $L = 1$ boson cluster. If the $A_1$ is established as a definite meson, and if one finds any more mesons in this region, this must indicate the presence of other effects. For example, the possible existence of the $A_{1.5}$ if it is real and distinct from the $A_1$ would be such an effect; so would the $A_2$ if it indeed has more structure, as discussed in Section III-3-A-a.

In Figure 118 is also indicated in each case which nonet would be produced by diffraction dissociation or pomeron exchange. That is, we could produce the corresponding isovector meson by pion bombardment or the $I = \frac{1}{2}$ meson by $K$ bombardment. To be produced by diffraction dissociation the boson is expected to have all the quantum numbers of the incident particle except for $J$ and $P$, which for a $0^-$ incident particle are given by adding an angular momentum $l$. This yields $J = l$ and a parity of $P = (-1)^{l+1}$ for the resulting boson state. According to a study by Morrison[107] bosons produced by this process appear to have constant cross section with increasing energy. Thus for high bombarding energies or for coherent production from heavy elements these are the ones which should dominate the cluster, while the other three nonets would presumably have cross sections that go through a maximum above threshold and then die out again with increasing energy.

For completeness we also show the corresponding decay modes for the "abnormal mode" bosons of $J^{PC} = 0^{--}, 0^{+-}, 1^{-+}$, and $2^{+-}$ in Figure 120.

Some Allowed Strong Decay Modes for "Abnormal Mode" Bosons which need $qq\bar{q}\bar{q}$ Structure at least

| $J^{PC}$ | $0^{--}$ | $0^{+-}$ | $1^{-+}$ | $2^{+-}$ | |
|---|---|---|---|---|---|
| $2\pi$, I = 1,0 | | | | | |
| $3\pi$, I = 1 | | | I = 1 | | $\pi^+\pi^-\pi^0$, $3\pi^0$ |
| $3\pi$, I = 0 | I = 0 | | | I = 0 | $\pi^+\pi^-\pi^0$<br>$3\pi^0$ forbidden |
| $\pi\eta$, I = 1 | | | I = 1 | | |
| $\pi\omega$, I = 1 (or $4\pi$) | I = 1 | | | I = 1 | $4\pi^0$ forbidden |
| $4\pi$, I = 0 | | | I = 0 | | |
| $K\bar{K}$, $K_1K_2$<br>$K_1K_1$, $K_2K_2$ | | | | | |
| $\pi\pi\eta$, I = 1 | I = 1 | | | I = 1 | $\pi^0\pi^0\eta$ forbidden |
| $\pi\pi\eta$, I = 0 | | | I = 0 | | |
| $K\bar{K}\pi$, I = 1,0 | I = 0 or 1 | | I = 0 or 1 | I = 0 or 1 | |
| $K\pi$, I = 1/2 | | I = 1/2 | I = 1/2 | I = 1/2 | |
| $K\pi\pi$, I = 1/2 | I = 1/2 | | I = 1/2 | I = 1/2 | |

I = 0, I = 1, I = 1/2, I = 0 or 1

FIG. 120. The corresponding decay modes for abnormal mode bosons. Here additional $I$ spin states corresponding to exotic particles can also occur for the allowed decay modes shown.

*e. Selection Rules for Boson Decay.* It is of interest to look in greater detail at how these boson resonances will decay.

## 1. Nomenclature

To identify the various members of a boson $L$ cluster we will use the following nomenclature: $\pi$, $\eta$, $\eta'$, and $K$ stand for the isotopic triplet, singlets, and doublet, as in Rosenfeld et al.[19] This symbol plus the quantum numbers $^{2S+1}L_J$ identify a specific $q\bar{q}$ state. For example, the $A_2$ is given as $\pi(^3P_2)$, the $\omega$ is given as $\eta(^3S_1)$. Furthermore we occasionally use the name of the isotriplet to refer to the entire nonet; thus $A_2$ nonet refers to the $^3P_2$ nonet and $\rho$ nonet refers to the $^3S_1$ nonet.

## 2. Allowed Decays into Two-Particle States

In Tables XI through XV are listed the allowed decays of the $L = 2$ to $L = 5$ bosons into some of the better known particles. The entries in the tables are the angular momentum $l$ and corresponding $P$ when the decay mode indicated is allowed via strong interactions. The threshold mass required for each given decay mode is also indicated. One very interesting feature emerges immediately from these tables: the nonet with $J = L + 1$ decays consistently through higher angular momentum states for the common decay modes than any of the other three nonets. Thus we might expect that the widths of the bosons in the $J = L + 1$ nonets could be considerably narrower than the widths of the other bosons, for the same $L$ value.

## 3. The Cascading to Lower Boson Clusters

The allowed transitions with $l = 0$ and $l = 1$ by pion emission between the two final-state particles are illustrated in Figures 121 and 122. In Figure 123 is shown the decay from the $J = L + 1$ levels. As can be noted from these figures, the three nonets with $J = L - 1$ and $J = L$ in the two charge conjugation states can each decay via an $l = 0$ transition as well as via an $l = 1$ transition. On the other hand, the nonet with $J = L + 1$ can only cascade down to the next lower similar nonet via an $l = 2$ transition. The $l = 1$ transitions within a boson cluster of given $L$ are probably forbidden by energy conservation. Thus, here too we see that the members of the $J = L + 1$ nonets have

TABLE XI

Some Possible Decay Schemes for $L = 2$ Bosons; the Entry Refers to $l^P$ Minimum for Allowed Decays

| Decay mode $J^{PC}$ (G) | $\eta(^3D_1)$ $1^{--}$ $(-)$ | $\eta(^3D_2)$ $2^{--}$ $(-)$ | $\eta(^1D_2)$ $2^{-+}$ $(+)$ | $\eta(^3D_3)$ $3^{--}$ $(-)$ | $\pi(^3D_1)$ $1^{--}$ $(+)$ | $\pi(^3D_2)$ $2^{--}$ $(+)$ | $\pi(^1D_2)$ $2^{-+}$ $(-)$ | $\pi(^3D_3)$ $3^{--}$ $(+)$ | Threshold, MeV |
|---|---|---|---|---|---|---|---|---|---|
| $\pi\pi$ | — | — | — | — | $1^-$ | — | — | $3^-$ | 280 |
| $\pi\rho$ | $1^-$ | $1^-$ | — | $3^-$ | — | — | $1^-$ | — | 905 |
| $\pi\eta$ | — | — | — | — | — | — | — | — | 690 |
| $\pi\omega$ | — | — | — | — | $1^-$ | $1^-$ | — | $3^-$ | 925 |
| $K\bar{K}$ or $K_1K_2$ | $1^-$ | — | — | $3^-$ | $1^-$ | — | — | $3^-$ | 990 |
| $\pi f^0$ | — | — | — | — | — | — | $0^+$ | — | 1390 |
| $\pi A_2$ | — | — | $0^+$ | — | $2^+$ | $0^+$ | — | $2^+$ | 1450 |
| $\rho\rho$ | — | — | $1^-$ | — | $1^-$ | $1^-$ | — | $1^-$ | 1530 |
| $\rho\omega$ | — | — | — | — | — | — | $1^-$ | — | 1550 |
| $\rho f^0$ | — | — | — | — | $0^+$ | $0^+$ | — | $0^+$ | 2015 |

TABLE XII

Boson Nonets in $L = 2$ Cluster

| Decay mode | Mass threshold | $J_1^{P1}, J_2^{P2}$ | $K(^3D_1)$ $J^{PC} = 1^{--}$ | $K(^3D_2)$ $2^{--}$ | $K(^1D_2)$ $2^{-+}$ | $K(^3D_3)$ $3^{--}$ |
|---|---|---|---|---|---|---|
| $K\pi$ | 635 | $0^-, 0^-$ | $1^-$ | — | — | $3^-$ |
| $K^*\pi$ | 1030 | $1^-, 0^-$ | $1^-$ | $1^-$ | $1^-$ | $3^-$ |
| $K\rho$ | 1260 | $0^-, 1^-$ | $1^-$ | $1^-$ | $1^-$ | $3^-$ |
| $K^*(1400)\pi$ | 1540 | $2^+, 0^-$ | $2^+$ | $0^+$ | $0^+$ | $2^+$ |
| $KA_2$ | 1810 | $0^-, 2^+$ | $2^+$ | $0^+$ | $0^+$ | $2^+$ |
| $Kf^0$ | 1745 | $0^-, 2^+$ | $2^+$ | $0^+$ | $0^+$ | $2^+$ |
| $K^*\rho$ | 1655 | $1^-, 1^-$ | $1^-$ | $1^-$ | $1^-$ | $1^-$ |
| $K^*A_2$ | 2210 | $1^-, 2^+$ | $0^+$ | $0^+$ | $0^+$ | $0^+$ |
| $K^*f^0$ | 2140 | $1^-, 2^+$ | $0^+$ | $0^+$ | $0^+$ | $0^+$ |

TABLE XIII

Some Possible Decay Schemes for $L = 3$ Bosons; the Entry Refers to $l^P$ Minimum for Allowed Decays

| Decay mode $J^{PC}$ (G) | $\eta(^3F_2)$ $2^{++}$ (+) | $\eta(^3F_3)$ $3^{++}$ (+) | $\eta(^1F_3)$ $3^{+-}$ (−) | $\eta(^3F_4)$ $4^{++}$ (+) | $\pi(^3F_2)$ $2^{++}$ (−) | $\pi(^3F_3)$ $3^{++}$ (−) | $\pi(^1F_3)$ $3^{+-}$ (+) | $\pi(^3F_4)$ $4^{++}$ (−) | Threshold, MeV |
|---|---|---|---|---|---|---|---|---|---|
| $\pi\pi$ | $2^+$ | — | — | $4^+$ | — | — | — | — | 280 |
| $\pi\rho$ | — | — | $2^+$ | — | $2^+$ | $2^+$ | — | $4^+$ | 905 |
| $\pi\eta$ | — | — | — | — | $2^+$ | — | — | $4^+$ | 690 |
| $\pi\omega$ | — | — | — | — | — | — | $2^+$ | — | 925 |
| $K\bar{K}$, $K_1K_1$ or $K_2K_2$ | $2^+$ | — | — | $4^+$ | $2^+$ | — | — | $4^+$ | 990 |
| $\pi f^0$ | — | — | — | — | $1^-$ | $1^-$ | — | $3^-$ | 1390 |
| $\pi A_2$ | $1^-$ | $1^-$ | — | $3^-$ | — | — | $1^-$ | — | 1450 |
| $\rho\rho$ | $0^+$ | $2^+$ | — | $2^+$ | — | — | $2^+$ | — | 1530 |
| $\rho\omega$ | — | — | — | — | $0^+$ | $2^+$ | — | $2^+$ | 1550 |
| $\rho f^0$ | — | — | — | — | — | — | $1^-$ | — | 2015 |

TABLE XIV

Some Possible Decay Schemes for $L = 4$ Bosons; the Entry Refers to $l^P$ Minimum for Allowed Decays

| Decay mode $J^{PC}$ (G) | $\eta(^3G_3)$ $3^{--}$ (−) | $\eta(^3G_4)$ $4^{--}$ (−) | $\eta(^1G_4)$ $4^{-+}$ (+) | $\eta(^3G_5)$ $5^{--}$ (−) | $\pi(^3G_3)$ $3^{--}$ (+) | $\pi(^3G_4)$ $4^{--}$ (+) | $\pi(^1G_4)$ $4^{-+}$ (−) | $\pi(^3G_5)$ $5^{--}$ (+) | Threshold, MeV |
|---|---|---|---|---|---|---|---|---|---|
| $\pi\pi$ | — | — | — | — | $3^-$ | — | — | $5^-$ | 280 |
| $\pi\rho$ | $3^-$ | $3^-$ | — | $5^-$ | — | — | $3^-$ | — | 905 |
| $\pi\eta$ | — | — | — | — | — | — | — | — | 690 |
| $\pi\omega$ | — | — | — | — | $3^-$ | $3^-$ | — | $5^-$ | 925 |
| $K\bar{K}$ or $K_1K_2$ | $3^-$ | — | — | $5^-$ | $3^-$ | — | — | $5^-$ | 990 |
| $\pi f^0$ | — | — | — | — | — | — | $2^+$ | — | 1390 |
| $\pi A_2$ | — | — | $2^+$ | — | — | — | — | — | 1450 |
| $\rho\rho$ | — | — | $3^-$ | — | $1^-$ | $3^-$ | — | $3^-$ | 1530 |
| $\rho\omega$ | — | — | — | — | — | — | $3^-$ | — | 1550 |
| $\rho f^0$ | — | — | — | — | $0^+$ | $2^+$ | — | $2^+$ | 2015 |
| $\rho A_2$ | $0^+$ | $2^+$ | — | $2^+$ | — | — | — | — | 2075 |

TABLE XV

Some Possible Decay Schemes for $L = 5$ Bosons; the Entry Refers to $l^P$ Minimum for Allowed Decays

| Decay mode $J^{PC}$ (G) | $\eta(^3H_4)$ $4^{++}$ $(+)$ | $\eta(^3H_5)$ $5^{++}$ $(+)$ | $\eta(^1H_5)$ $5^{+-}$ $(-)$ | $\eta(^3H_6)$ $6^{++}$ $(+)$ | $\pi(^3H_6)$ $5^{++}$ $(-)$ | $\pi(^3H_5)$ $5^{++}$ $(-)$ | $\pi(^1H_5)$ $5^{+-}$ $(+)$ | $\pi(^3H_6)$ $6^{++}$ $(-)$ | Threshold, MeV |
|---|---|---|---|---|---|---|---|---|---|
| $\pi\pi$ | $4^+$ | — | — | $6^+$ | — | — | — | — | 280 |
| $\pi\rho$ | — | — | $4^+$ | — | $4^+$ | $4^+$ | — | $6^+$ | 905 |
| $\pi\eta$ | — | — | — | — | $4^+$ | — | — | $6^+$ | 690 |
| $\pi\omega$ | — | — | — | — | — | — | $4^+$ | — | 925 |
| $K\bar{K}, K_1K_1$ or $K_2K_2$ | $4^+$ | — | — | $6^+$ | $4^+$ | — | — | $6^+$ | 990 |
| $\pi f^0$ | — | — | — | — | $3^-$ | $3^-$ | — | $5^-$ | 1390 |
| $\pi A_2$ | — | — | — | — | — | — | $3^-$ | — | 1450 |
| $\rho\rho$ | $2^+$ | $4^+$ | — | $4^+$ | — | — | $4^+$ | — | 1530 |
| $\rho\omega$ | — | — | — | — | $2^+$ | $4^+$ | — | $4^+$ | 1550 |
| $\rho f^0$ | — | — | — | — | — | — | $3^-$ | — | 2015 |
| $\rho A_2$ | — | — | — | — | $1^-$ | $3^-$ | — | $3^-$ | 2075 |

no way of decaying with angular momentum less than $l = 2$. Thus this may again indicate particularly narrow decay widths. In Figures 121–123 let $I_1$ refer to the initial boson, and $I_2$ to the final boson, which is produced along with the $\pi$ meson. Thus $\Delta I = 1 \to 1$ indicates that the transition has to occur between an isovector initial state and an isovector final state $+\pi$. Similarly $\Delta I = \pm 1$ refers to the change of $I$ spin from the initial to the final-state bosons. The selection rules for $\pi$ transitions from an initial boson state **1** to a final **2** $[I_1(L_1)_{J_1P_1C_1G_1} \to \pi + I_2(L_2)_{J_2P_2C_2G_2}]$ with angular momentum $l$ between **2** and $\pi$ are:

$$G_2 = -G_1$$
$$P_2 = P_1(-1)^{l+1}$$

for $C_2 = C_1$,    then $\Delta I = \pm 1$
for $C_2 = -C_1$,    then $I_2 = I_1 = 1$

We can then distinguish

| $l$ = even | $l$ = odd |
|---|---|
| $P_2 = -P_1$ | $P_2 = P_1$ |
| $L_2 - L_1 =$ odd | $L_2 - L_1 =$ even |

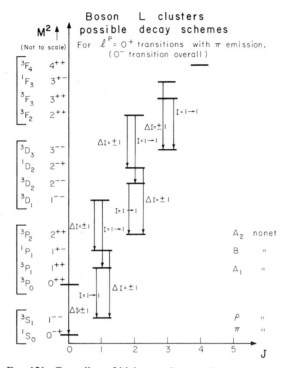

FIG. 121. Cascading of high-mass boson with $\pi$ emission.

Thus, for example,

i.e.,
$$\left.\begin{array}{l}\pi(^3P_2) \to \pi + \pi(^3S_1) \\ A_2 \to \pi + \rho\end{array}\right\}\begin{array}{l}\Delta I = 0, I_1 = I_2 = 1 \\ (l = 2)\end{array}$$

or,

i.e.,

i.e.,
$$\left.\begin{array}{l}\pi(^1P_1) \to \pi + \eta(^3S_1) \\ B \to \pi + \omega \\ \eta(^1P_1) \to \pi + \pi(^3S_1) \\ H \to \pi + \rho\end{array}\right\}\begin{array}{l}\Delta I = \pm 1 \\ (l = 0)\end{array}$$

Note that the experimental identification of the $B$ and $H$ with given quantum numbers is still tentative.

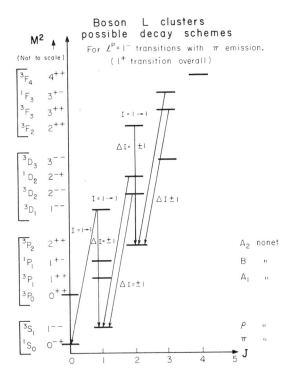

FIG. 122. Cascading of high-mass boson with $\pi$ emission.

## 4. The Width of Higher Boson Resonances

As mentioned above, the nonet with the spin $J = L + 1$, i.e., $^3L_{L+1}$, must in nearly all cases decay via higher angular momentum states than the other three nonets. The decay width $\Gamma$ for decay into two particles can be expressed as

$$\Gamma = [\gamma(k/M)][(Rk)^l/l!!]^2$$

where $k$ is the c.m. momentum, $l$ the decay angular momentum, and $M$ the mass of the boson. The coupling constant $\gamma$ and characteristic radius $R$ are, however, not known to sufficient accuracy. If we consider $\gamma$ and $R$ to be constant for a given boson $L$ cluster, it follows that members of the $J = L + 1$ nonet have a considerably narrower decay width than members of the other three nonets. Thus, for $L = 3$ and higher we might expect one narrow nonet, while it is possible that the width of the others is comparable to the spin-orbit splitting, so that they may actually not always be fully resolved from each other.

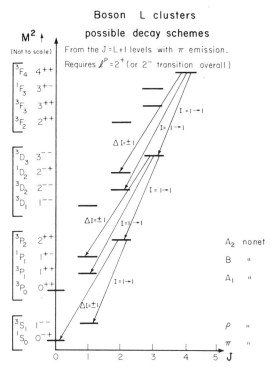

FIG. 123. Cascading of high-mass boson with $\pi$ emission.

In conclusion, it is possible that the very narrow peaks $S$, $T$, and $U$, if verified by additional experiments, may correspond to the $J = L + 1$ nonets with $L = 3$, 4, and 5. On the other hand the peaks in $\sigma(\bar{p}p)$ may correspond to either a part of, or to all of, the same boson $L$ clusters. Clearly these ideas are purely speculative at the moment and much more experimentation will be needed to test them and to establish whatever will turn out to be the correct pattern.

## Acknowledgments

We wish to thank Chumin Fu, Christina Frank, and Dr. Charles Wohl for help in various aspects of this work. This work was carried out in part while one of us (G.G.) was on sabbatical leave from the Department of Physics of the University of California and the other (S.G.) on a fellowship from the Guggenheim Memorial Foundation.

## References

1. A. Firestone, G. Goldhaber, and B. C. Shen, unpublished.
2. M. H. Alston, L. W. Alvarez, P. E. Eberhard, M. L. Good, W. Graziano, H. K. Ticho, and S. G. Wojcicki, *Phys. Rev. Letters*, **6**, 300 (1961).
3. C. Fu, I. Butterworth, A. Firestone, G. Goldhaber, S. Goldhaber, B. C. Shen, and G. H. Trilling, unpublished.
4. For example, J. D. Jackson, *Rev. Mod. Phys.*, **37**, 484 (1965), and references cited there.
5. N. Byers and S. Fenster, *Phys. Rev.*, **133**, B531 (1964); S. M. Berman and M. Jacob, *Phys. Rev.*, **139**, B1023 (1965); R. Gatto and H. P. Stapp, *Phys. Rev.*, **121**, 1553 (1961); R. H. Capps, *Phys. Rev.*, **122**, 929 (1961); M. Ademolo and R. Gatto, *Phys. Rev.*, **133**, B531 (1964).
6. L. M. Stevenson, L. W. Alvarez, B. C. Maglić, and A. H. Rosenfeld, *Phys. Rev.*, **125**, 687 (1962).
7. C. Zemach, *Phys. Rev.*, **133**, B1201 (1964).
8. G. Goldhaber, Spin Analysis for the $I = 0$ Three Pion System, UCID-2608, unpublished.
9. B. C. Shen, J. L. Brown, G. Goldhaber, S. Goldhaber, J. A. Kadyk, and G. H. Trilling, unpublished.
10. O. I. Dahl, L. M. Hardy, R. I. Hess, J. Kirz, and D. H. Miller, *Phys. Rev.*, **163**, 1377 (1967).
11. S. U. Chung, O. I. Dahl, L. M. Hardy, R. I. Hess, G. R. Kalbfleisch, J. Kirz, D. H. Miller, and G. A. Smith, *Phys. Rev. Letters*, **12**, 621 (1964).
12. J. H. Christenson, J. W. Cronin, V. L. Fitch, and R. Turlay, *Phys. Rev. Letters*, **13**, 138 (1964).
13. L. Michel, *Nuovo Cimento*, **10**, 319 (1953); T. D. Lee and C. N. Yang, *Nuovo Cimento*, **3**, 749 (1956).
14. M. Goldhaber, T. D. Lee, and C. N. Yang, *Phys. Rev.*, **112**, 1796 (1958).
15. M. Schwartz, *Phys. Rev. Letters*, **6**, 556 (1961).
16. R. Armenteros, L. Montanet, D. R. O. Morrison, S. Nilsson, A. Shapira, T. Vandermeulen, Ch. D'Andlau, A. Astier, J. Ballam, C. Ghesquière, B. P. Gregory, D. Rahm, P. Rivet, and F. Solmitz, *Proc. Intern. Conf. High-Energy Physics, CERN*, **1962**, 351.
17. T. Day, J. Sucher, and G. Snow, *Phys. Rev.*, **119**, 1100 (1960).
18. D. H. Miller, *Proc. Intern. School Phys., Enrico Fermi, Course 33*, L. W. Alvarez, Ed., Academic Press, New York, 1966, pp. 1–69.

19. A. H. Rosenfeld, A. Barbaro-Galtieri, W. J. Podolsky, L. R. Price, P. Soding, C. G. Wohl, M. Roos, and W. J. Willis, *Rev. Mod. Phys.*, **39**, 1 (1967), and more recent compilations.

20. R. H. Dalitz, rapporteur talk, *Proc. Intern. Conf. High-Energy Physics, 13th*, Berkeley, 1966, University of California Press, Berkeley, 1967, and lecture series presented at The Second Hawaii Topical Conference on Particle Physics, S. Pakvasa and S. F. Tuan, Eds., University of Hawaii Press, 1968, p. 327.

21. G. Goldhaber, lecture series presented at The Second Hawaii Topical Conference on Particle Physics, S. Pakvasa and S. F. Tuan, Eds., University of Hawaii Press, 1968, p. 165.

22. G. Goldhaber, in *Symmetry Principles at High Energy, Fourth Coral Gables Conference*, A. Perlmutter and B. Kursunoglu, Eds., W. H. Freeman and Company, San Francisco, 1967, p. 190.

23. G. Goldhaber, rapporteur talk, *Proc. Intern. Conf. High-Energy Physics, 13th*, Berkeley, 1966, University of California Press, Berkeley, 1967.

24. I. Butterworth, rapporteur talk on Mesons, *Proc. 1967 Heidelberg Intern. Conf. Elementary Particles*, H. Filthuth, Ed., North-Holland Publ. Co., Amsterdam, 1968, p. 11.

25. M. Banner, M. L. Fayoux, J. L. Hamel, J. Zsembery, J. Cheze, and J. Teiger, *Phys. Letters*, **25B**, 300 (1967); M. Banner, J. Cheze, J. L. Hamel, G. Marel, J. Teiger, J. Zsembery, P. Chavanon, M. Crozon, and L. K. Rangan, *Phys. Letters*, **25B**, 569 (1967).

26. M. A. Abolins, O. I. Dahl, J. S. Danburg, D. Davies, P. Hoch, J. Kirz, D. H. Miller, and R. Rader, contribution to the 1967 Heidelberg Intern. Conf. Elementary Particles, see ref. 24.

27. A. Pevsner, R. Kraemer, M. Nussbaum, C. Richardson, P. Schlein, R. Strand, T. Toohig, M. Block, A. Engler, R. Gessaroli, and C. Meltzer, *Phys. Rev. Letters*, **7**, 421 (1961).

28. P. L. Bastien, J. P. Berge, O. I. Dahl, M. Ferro-Luzzi, D. H. Miller, J. J. Murray, A. H. Rosenfeld, and M. B. Watson, *Phys. Rev. Letters*, **8**, 114 (1962).

29. C. Alff, D. Berley, D. Colley, N. Gelfand, U. Nauenberg, D. Miller, J. Schultz, J. Steinberger, T. H. Tan, H. Brugger, P. Kramer, and R. Plano, *Phys. Rev. Letters*, **9**, 325 (1962).

30. H. Primakoff, *Phys. Rev.*, **81**, 899 (1951).

31. G. Bellettini, C. Bemporad, P. L. Braccini, and L. Foa, *Nuovo Cimento*, **40**, 1140 (1965).

32. C. Bemporad, P. L. Braccini, L. Foa, K. Lübelsmeyer, and D. Schmitz, *Phys. Letters*, **25B**, 380 (1967).

33. M. Feldman, W. Frati, R. Gleeson, J. Halpern, M. Nussbaum, and S. Richert, *Phys. Rev. Letters*, **18**, 868 (1967). Some earlier results are as follows: G. DiGiugno, R. Querzoli, G. Troise, F. Vanoli, M. Giorgi, P. Schiavon, and V. Silvestrini, *Phys. Rev. Letters*, **16**, 767 (1966), quote for the $2\gamma$, $3\pi^0$, and $\pi^0\gamma\gamma$ branching ratios of the $\eta$ $41.6 \pm 2.2$, $20.9 \pm 2.7$, and $37.5 \pm 3.6\%$, respectively. These figures yield a $\pi^0\gamma\gamma/2\gamma$ ratio of $0.9 \pm 0.1$. M. A. Wahlig, E. Shibata, and I. Mannelli, *Phys. Rev. Letters*, **17**, 221 (1966), quote an upper limit of 0.50 (90% confidence level) for the ratio $(\eta \to \pi^0 + \gamma + \gamma)/(\eta \to 2\gamma)$. Z. S. Strugalski, I. V. Chuvilo, I. A. Ivanovska,

L. S. Okhrimenko, B. Niczyporuk, T. Kanarek, B. Stowinski, and Z. Jabłonski, quoted in ref. 23, who worked with a xenon bubble chamber, quote a $\eta \to \pi^0\gamma\gamma/\eta \to 2\gamma$ ratio of $0.84 \pm 0.4$ and $\eta \to \pi^0\pi^0\pi^0/\eta \to 2\gamma < 0.42$.

34. C. Baltay, P. Franzini, J. Kim, R. Newman, N. Yeh, and L. Kirsch, *Phys. Rev. Letters*, **19**, 1495 (1967), and C. Baltay, P. Franzini, J. Kim, L. Kirsch R. Newman, N. Yeh, J. A. Cole, J. Lee-Franzini, and H. Yarger, *Phys. Rev. Letters*, **19**, 1498 (1967).

35. C. Baglin, A. Bezaguet, B. Degrange, F. Jacquet, P. Musset, U. Nguyen-Khac, G. Nihoul-Boutang, H. H. Bingham, W. Michael, and G. Irwin, *Bull. Am. Phys. Soc.*, **12**, 567 (1967).

36. P. Bonamy and P. Sonderegger, contribution to the 1967 Heidelberg Intern. Conf. Elementary Particles, see ref. 24.

37. S. Buniatov, E. Zavattini, W. Deinet, H. Müller, D. Schmitt, and H. Staudenmaier, *Phys. Letters*, **25B**, 560 (1967).

38. S. M. Flatté, *Phys. Rev. Letters*, **18**, 976 (1967).

39. L. R. Price and F. S. Crawford, Jr., *Phys. Rev. Letters*, **18**, 1207 (1967).

40. C. Baglin, A. Bezaguet, B. Degrange, F. Jacquet, P. Musset, U. Nguyen-Khac, G. Nihoul-Boutang, H. H. Bingham, and W. Michael, *Phys. Letters*, **24B**, 637 (1967).

41. K. D. Billing, F. W. Bullock, M. J. Esten, M. Govan, C. Henderson, W. L. Knight, D. J. Miller, A. A. Owen, F. R. Stannard, E. Tompa, S. Tovey, and O. C. Waldron, *Phys. Letters*, **25B**, 435 (1967).

42. V. Fitch, rapporteur talk, *Proc. Intern. Conf. High-Energy Physics, 13th,* Berkeley, 1966, University of California Press, Berkeley, 1967, p. 63.

43. C. Baltay, P. Franzini, J. Kirsch, D. Zanello, T. Lee-Franzini, R. Loveless, J. McFadyen, and H. Yarker, *Phys. Rev. Letters*, **16**, 1224 (1966).

44. A. M. Cnops, G. Finocchiaro, J. C. Lassalle, P. Mittner, J. P. Dufey, B. Gobbi, M. A. Pouchon, and A. Muller, *Phys. Letters*, **22**, 546 (1966).

45. Wonyong Lee et al., Columbia-Brookhaven internal report, unpublished.

46. A. Rittenberg and A. Barbaro-Galtieri, presented at the International Conference on High-Energy Physics, 1966, Berkeley, California.

47. P. Baillon, D. Edwards, B. Marechal, L. Montanet, M. Tomas, C. d'Andlau, A. Astier, J. Cohen-Ganouna, M. Della-Negra, S. Wojcicki, M. Baubillier, J. Duboc, F. James, and F. R. Levy, *Nuovo Cimento*, **LA**, 393 (1967).

48. L. Montanet et al., as quoted in ref. 24.

49. The initial steps in unraveling these states were: $K^*(890)$: see ref. 2; $K^*(890)$ spin: W. Chinowsky, G. Goldhaber, S. Goldhaber, W. Lee, and T. O'Halloran, *Phys. Rev. Letters*, **9**, 330 (1962) and ref. 16; $\omega$ and its spin: B. C. Maglić, L. W. Alvarez, A. H. Rosenfeld, and M. L. Stevenson, *Phys. Rev. Letters*, **7**, 178 (1961); $\rho$: A. R. Erwin, R. March, W. D. Walker, and E. West, *Phys. Rev. Letters*, **9**, 273 (1962); $\rho$ spin: D. D. Carmony and R. T. Van de Walle, *Phys. Rev. Letters*, **8**, 73 (1962); $\phi$: L. Bertanza, V. Brisson, P. L. Connolly, E. L. Hart, I. S. Mittra, G. C. Moneti, R. R. Rau, N. P. Samios, I. O. Skillicorn, S. S. Yamamoto, M. Goldberg, L. Gray, J. Leitner, S. Lichtman, and J. Westgard, *Phys. Rev. Letters*, **9**, 180 (1962); and subsequently P. Schlein, W. E. Slater, L. T. Smith, D. H. Stork, and H. K. Ticho, *Phys. Rev. Letters*, **10**, 368 (1963).

50. S. M. Flatté, D. O. Huwe, J. J. Murray, J. Button-Shafer, F. T. Solmitz, M. L. Stevenson, and C. Wohl, *Phys. Rev. Letters*, **14**, 1095 (1965).

51. J. Button-Shafer, contribution to the International Conference on High-Energy Physics, 13th, Berkeley, 1966, unpublished.

52. M. Roos, *Nucl. Phys.*, **B2**, 615 (1967).

53. A. Wehmann, E. Engels, Jr., L. N. Hand, C. M. Hoffman, P. G. Innocenti, R. Wilson, W. A. Blanpied, D. J. Drickey, and D. G. Stairs, *Phys. Rev. Letters*, **17**, 1113 (1966); *Phys. Rev. Letters*, **18**, 929 (1967).

54. B. D. Hyams, W. Koch, D. Pellett, D. Potter, L. Von Lindern, E. Lorenz, G. Lütjens, U. Stierlin, and P. Weilhammer, *Phys. Letters*, **24B**, 634 (1967).

55. R. A. Zdanis, L. Madansky, R. W. Kraemer, S. Hertzbach, and R. Strand, *Phys. Rev. Letters*, **14**, 721 (1965).

56. J. K. dePagter, J. I. Friedman, G. Glass, R. C. Chase, M. Gettner, E. von Goeler, R. Weinstein, and A. Boyarski, *Phys. Rev. Letters*, **16**, 35 (1966).

57. J. G. Asbury, U. Becker, W. K. Bertram, P. Joos, M. Rohde, A. J. S. Smith, C. L. Jordan, and S. C. C. Ting, *Phys. Rev. Letters*, **19**, 865, 869 (1967).

58. S. M. Berman and S. D. Drell, *Phys. Rev.*, **133**, B791 (1964).

59. V. L. Auslander, G. I. Budker, Ju. N. Pestov, V. A. Sidorov, A. N. Skrinsky, and A. G. Khabakpashev, *Phys. Letters*, **25B**, 433 (1967).

60. W. Selove, V. Hagopian, H. Brody, A. Baker, and E. Leboy, *Phys. Rev. Letters*, **9**, 273 (1962).

61. G. Goldhaber, J. L. Brown, S. Goldhaber, J. A. Kadyk, B. C. Shen, and G. H. Trilling, *Phys. Rev. Letters*, **12**, 336 (1964); S. U. Chung, O. I. Dahl, L. M. Hardy, R. I. Hess, G. R. Kalbfleisch, J. Kirz, D. H. Miller, and G. A. Smith, *Phys. Rev. Letters*, **12**, 621 (1964); and Aachen-Berlin-Birmingham-Bonn-Hamburg-London(I.C.)-München Collaboration, *Phys. Letters*, **10**, 226 (1964).

62. Birmingham-Glasgow-London (I.C.)-Oxford-Rutherford Collaboration, *Phys. Letters*, **14**, 338 (1965); L. M. Hardy, S. U. Chung, O. I. Dahl, R. I. Hess, J. Kirz, and D. H. Miller, *Phys. Rev. Letters*, **14**, 401 (1965).

63. V. E. Barnes, B. B. Culwick, P. Guidoni, G. R. Kalbfleisch, G. W. London, R. B. Palmer, D. Radojicic, D. C. Rahm, R. R. Rau, C. R. Richardson, N. P. Samios, J. R. Smith, B. Goz, H. Horwitz, T. Kikuchi, J. Leitner, and R. Wolfe, *Phys. Rev. Letters*, **15**, 322 (1965).

64. S. Glashow and R. Socolow, *Phys. Rev. Letters*, **15**, 329 (1965).

65. S. U. Chung, O. I. Dahl, J. Kirz, and D. H. Miller, UCRL-16881, *Phys. Rev.*, in press.

66. G. Benson, L. Lovell, E. Marquit, B. Roe, D. Sinclair, and J. Vander Velde, *Phys. Rev. Letters*, **16**, 1177 (1966); J. Bartsch, M. Deutschmann, G. Kraus, H. Weber, P. Schmitz, C. Grote, K. Lanius, R. Leiste, S. Nowak, V. T. Cocconi, E. Flaminio, J. D. Hansen, U. Kruse, J. Loskiewicz, M. Markytan, D. R. O. Morrison, and K. Zalewski, *Phys. Letters*, **25B**, 48 (1967); N. Armenise, B. Ghidini, V. Picciarelli, A. Romano, A. Forino, R. Gessaroli, L. Lendinara, G. Quareni, A. Quareni-Vignudelli, A. Cartacci, M. G. Dagliana, G. Di Caporiacco, G. Parrini, M. Barrier, O. Goussu, J. Laberrigue-Frolow, D. Mettel, N. H. Khanh, and J. Quinquard, *Phys. Letters*, **25B**, 53 (1967); and C. Baltay, L. Kirsch, H. H. Kung, N. Yeh, and M. Rabin, *Phys. Letters*, **25B**, 160 (1967).

67. D. R. O. Morrison, *Phys. Letters*, **25B**, 238 (1967).
68. G. Chikovani, M. N. Focacci, W. Kienzle, C. Lechanoine, B. Levrat, B. Maglić, M. Martin, P. Schübelin, L. Dubal, M. Fischer, P. Grieder, H. A. Neal, and C. Nef, *Phys. Letters*, **25B**, 44 (1967).
69. D. Bassano, M. Goldberg, B. Goz, G. Pertile, V. E. Barnes, P. J. Dornan, G. R. Kalbfleisch, N. P. Samios, I. O. Skillicorn, and J. Leitner, *Phys. Rev. Letters*, **19**, 968 (1967).
70. V. E. Barnes, P. J. Dornan, G. R. Kalbfleisch, G. London, R. Palmer, R. R. Rau, N. P. Samios, I. O. Skillicorn, M. Goldberg, K. Jager, C. Y. Chang, and J. Leitner, *Phys. Rev. Letters*, **19**, 964 (1967).
71. R. Ammar, R. E. P. Davis, C. Hwang, W. Kropac, J. Mott, B. Werner, S. Dagan, M. Derrick, F. Schweingruber, and J. Simpson, *Phys. Rev. Letters*, **19**, 1071 (1967).
72. S. D. Drell and K. Hiida, *Phys. Rev. Letters*, **7**, 199 (1961); R. T. Deck, *Phys. Rev. Letters*, **13**, 169 (1964); and U. Maor and T. O'Halloran, *Phys. Letters*, **15**, 281 (1965).
73. M. Ross and Y. Y. Yam, *Phys. Rev. Letters*, **19**, 546 (1967).
74. E. L. Berger, UCRL-17825, to be published.
75. B. C. Shen, G. Goldhaber, S. Goldhaber, and J. A. Kadyk, *Phys. Rev. Letters*, **15**, 731 (1965).
76. G. Bellini, B. Daugeras, R. Huson, H. J. Lubatti, J. Six, J. J. Veillet, M. di Corato, E. Fiorini, K. Moriyasu, P. Negri, M. Rollier, H. H. Bingham, C. W. Farwell, and W. B. Fretter, contribution to the 1967 Heidelberg Intern. Conf. Elementary Particles, see ref. 24.
77. J. A. Danysz, B. R. French, and V. Simak, *Nuovo Cimento*, **LIA**, 801 (1967).
78. M. Abolins, R. L. Lander, W. A. W. Mehlhop, N. Huu Xuong, and P. M. Yager, *Phys. Rev. Letters*, **11**, 381 (1963).
79. S. U. Chung, O. I. Dahl, R. I. Hess, G. R. Kalbfleisch, J. Kirz, D. H. Miller, and G. A. Smith, *Proc. Sienna Intern. Conf. Elementary Particles*, **1**, 201 (1963); and ref. 65.
80. G. Goldhaber, S. Goldhaber, J. A. Kadyk, and B. C. Shen, *Phys. Rev. Letters*, **15**, 118 (1965).
81. C. Baltay, J. C. Severiens, N. Yeh, and D. Zanello, *Phys. Rev. Letters*, **18**, 93 (1967).
82. Quoted in ref. 23.
83. Quoted in G. Goldhaber, "Quantum Numbers of Boson Resonances," *Proc. CERN School Physics*, **3**, CERN67-24 (1967).
84. B. C. Shen, I. Butterworth, C. Fu, G. Goldhaber, S. Goldhaber, and G. H. Trilling, *Phys. Rev. Letters*, **17**, 726 (1966).
85. G. Bassompierre, Y. Goldschmidt-Clermont, A. Grant, V. P. Henri, I. Hughes, B. Jongejans, R. L. Lander, D. Linglin, F. Muller, J. M. Perreau, I. Saitov, R. Sekulin, W. de Baere, J. Debaisieux, P. Dufour, F. Grard, J. Heughebaert, L. Pape, P. Peeters, F. Vergeure, R. Windmolders, M. Jobes, and W. Matt, contribution to the 1967 Heidelberg Intern. Conf. Elementary Particles, see ref. 24.

86. J. Berlinghieri, M. S. Farber, T. Ferbel, B. Forman, A. C. Melissinos, T. Yamanouchi, and H. Yuta, *Phys. Rev. Letters*, **18**, 1087 (1967).

87. R. Zdanis, *Bull. Am. Phys. Soc.*, **12**, 567 (1967).

88. G. Goldhaber, A. Firestone, and B. C. Shen, *Phys. Rev. Letters*, **19**, 972 (1967).

89. A wider generalization of *C* referred to as "unitary-parity" has been introduced by Dothan and is called $\mathscr{C}$ in the literature. The precise definition and references are given by B. W. Lee, in "High Energy Physics and Elementary Particles," *1965 Trieste Seminars*, International Atomic Energy Agency, Vienna, 1965. See also G. L. Kane, *Phys. Rev.*, **156**, 1739 (1967).

90. R. Gatto, L. Maiani, and G. Preparata, *Nuovo Cimento*, **39**, 1192 (1965), and a recent extension by R. Gatto and L. Maiani, *The* $J^P = 1^+$ *Octodecimet of Meson Resonances*, to be published.

91. H. Lipkin, rapporteur talk, *Proc. 1967 Heidelberg Intern. Conf. Elementary Particles*, H. Filthuth, Ed., North-Holland Publ. Co., Amsterdam, 1968, p. 253.

92. G. Goldhaber, *Phys. Rev. Letters*, **19**, 976 (1967).

93. R. Armenteros, D. N. Edwards, T. Jacobsen, L. Montanet, A. Shapira, J. Vandermeulen, Ch. d'Andlau, A. Astier, P. Baillon, J. Cohen-Ganouna, D. Defoix, J. Siaud, C. Ghesquière, and P. Rivet, *Phys. Letters*, **9**, 207 (1964).

94. N. Barash, Ph.D. thesis, Columbia University, 1967.

95. P. J. Dornan, V. E. Barnes, G. R. Kalbfleisch, I. O. Skillicorn, M. Goldberg, B. Goz, R. Wolfe, and J. Leitner, *Phys. Rev. Letters*, **19**, 271 (1967).

96. D. J. Crennell, G. R. Kalbfleisch, K. W. Lai, J. M. Scarr, and T. G. Schumann, *Phys. Rev. Letters*, **19**, 44 (1967).

97. R. I. Hess, S. U. Chung, O. I. Dahl, L. M. Hardy, J. Kirz, and D. H. Miller, *Phys. Rev. Letters*, **14**, 1074 (1965).

98. C. d'Andlau, A. Astier, M. Della Negra, L. Dobrzynski, S. Wojcicki, J. Barlow, T. Jacobsen, L. Montanet, L. Tallone, M. Tomas, A.-M. Adamson, M. Baubillier, J. Duboc, M. Goldberg, E. Levy, D. N. Edwards, and J. E. A. Lys, *Phys. Letters*, **17**, 347 (1965).

99. G. Benson, E. Marquit, B. Roe, D. Sinclair, and J. Vander Velde, *Phys. Rev. Letters*, **17**, 1234 (1966).

100. CERN-Bruxelles-Birmingham Collaboration, contribution to the 1967 Heidelberg Intern. Conf. Elementary Particles, see ref. 24.

101. G. B. Chadwick, Z. G. T. Guiragossián, E. Pickup, A. Barbaro-Galtieri, M. J. Matison, and A. Rittenberg, contribution to the 1967 Heidelberg Intern. Conf. Elementary Particles, see ref. 24.

102. B. Conforto, B. Maréchal, L. Montanet, M. Tomas, C. d'Andlau, A. Astier, J. Cohen-Ganouna, M. Della Negra, M. Baubillier, J. Duboc, F. James, M. Goldberg, and D. Spencer, *Nucl. Phys.*, **B3**, 469 (1967).

103. A. R. Erwin, G. A. Hoyer, R. H. March, W. D. Walker, and T. P. Wangler, *Phys. Rev. Letters*, **9**, 34 (1962).

104. A. Astier, J. Cohen-Ganouna, M. Della Negra, B. Maréchal, L. Montanet, M. Tomas, M. Baubillier, and J. Duboc, *Phys. Letters*, **25B**, 294 (1967).

105. D. J. Crennell, G. R. Kalbfleisch, K. W. Lai, J. M. Scarr, T. G. Schumann, I. O. Skillicorn, and M. S. Webster, *Phys. Rev. Letters*, **16**, 1025 (1966).

106. W. Beusch, W. E. Fischer, B. Gobbi, M. Pepin, E. Polgar, P. Astbury, G. Brautti, G. Finocchiaro, J. C. Lassalle, A. Michelini, K. M. Terwilliger, D. Websdale, and C. H. West, *Phys. Letters*, **25B**, 357 (1967).

107. D. R. O. Morrison, 1966 Stony Brook Conference.

108. M. Feldman, W. Frati, J. Halpern, A. Kanofsky, M. Nussbaum, S. Richert, P. Yamin, A. Choudry, S. Devons, and J. Grunhaus, *Phys. Rev. Letters*, **14**, 869 (1965).

109. A. Buhler-Broglin, P. Dalpiaz, T. Massam, F. L. Navarria, M. A. Schneegans, F. Zetti, and A. Zichichi, *Nuovo Cimento*, **49**, 183 (1967).

110. S. Buniatov, E. Zavattini, W. Deinet, H. Müller, D. Schmitt, and H. Staudenmaier, contribution to the 1967 Heidelberg Intern. Conf. Elementary Particles, see ref. 24.

111. I. F. Corbett, C. J. S. Damerell, N. Middlemass, D. Newton, A. B. Clegg, W. S. C. Williams, and A. S. Carroll, *Phys. Rev.*, **156**, 1451 (1967).

112. M. Wahlig, E. Shibata, D. Gordon, D. Frisch, and J. Manelli, *Phys. Rev.*, **147**, 941 (1966).

113. N. Armenise, B. Ghidini, V. Picciarelli, A. Romano, A. Silvestri, A. Forino, R. Gessaroli, L. Lendinara, G. Quareni, A. Quareni-Vignudelli, A. Cartacci, M. G. Dagliana, G. di Caporiacco, G. Parrini, M. Barrier, J. Laberrigue-Frolow, D. Mettel, J. Quinquard, and M. Sene, contribution to the 1967 Heidelberg Intern. Conf. Elementary Particles, see ref. 24.

114. W. D. Walker, *Rev. Mod. Phys.*, **39**, 695 (1967), and W. D. Walker, J. Carroll, A. Garfinkel, and B. Y. Oh, *Phys. Rev. Letters*, **18**, 630 (1967).

115. P. E. Schlein, *Phys. Rev. Letters*, **19**, 1052 (1967); E. Malamud and P. E. Schlein, *Phys. Rev. Letters*, **19**, 1056 (1967).

116. R. W. Birge, R. P. Ely, Jr., G. Gidal, G. E. Kalmus, A. Kernan, W. M. Powell, U. Camerini, D. Cline, W. F. Fry, J. G. Gaidos, D. Murphree, and C. T. Murphy, *Phys. Rev.*, **139**, B1600 (1965). Also preliminary data presented by Singleton et al., Wisconsin-Berkeley-London (U.C.) collaboration, at the Princeton Informal Meeting on *K* Decay, October 1967.

117. T. G. Trippe, C. Y. Chien, E. Malamud, J. Mellema, P. E. Schlein, W. E. Slater, D. H. Stork, and H. K. Ticho, UCLA-1021, contribution to the 1967 Heidelberg Intern. Conf. Elementary Particles, see ref. 24.

118. M. N. Focacci, W. Kienzle, B. Levrat, B. C. Maglić, and M. Martin, *Phys. Rev. Letters*, **17**, 890 (1966).

119. M. Goldberg et al., CERN-Ecole Polytechnique-Orsay-Milan-Saclay collaboration, *Phys. Letters*, **17**, 354 (1965).

120. D. J. Crennell, P. V. C. Hough, G. R. Kalbfleisch, K. W. Lai, J. M. Scarr, T. G. Schumann, I. O. Skillicorn, R. C. Strand, M. S. Webster, P. Baumel, A. H. Bachman, and R. M. Lea, *Phys. Rev. Letters*, **18**, 323 (1967).

121. Aachen-Berlin-CERN collaboration, *Phys. Letters*, **18**, 351 (1965).

122. R. W. Bland, M. G. Bowler, J. L. Brown, G. Goldhaber, S. Goldhaber, J. A. Kadyk, and G. H. Trilling, *Phys. Rev. Letters*, **17**, 939 (1966).

123. W. De Baere et al., as quoted in ref. 23.

124. J. A. Danysz, B. R. French, J. B. Kinson, V. Simak, J. Clayton, P. Mason, H. Muirhead, and P. Renton, *Phys. Letters*, **24B**, 309 (1967).

125. J. Bartsch et al., Aachen-Berlin-CERN-London (I.C.)-Vienna collaboration, *Phys. Letters*, **22**, 357 (1966).

126. A. Firestone, G. Goldhaber, and B. C. Shen, UCRL-17833, contribution to the 1967 Heidelberg Intern. Conf. Elementary Particles, see ref. 24.

127. R. J. Abrams, R. L. Cool, G. Giacomelli, T. F. Kycia, B. A. Leontic, K. K. Li, and D. N. Michael, *Phys. Rev. Letters*, **18**, 1209 (1967).

128. R. L. Cool, G. Giacomelli, T. F. Kycia, B. A. Leontic, K. K. Li, A. Lundby, and J. Teiger, *Phys. Rev. Letters*, **17**, 102 (1966).

129. R. W. Bland, M. G. Bowler, J. L. Brown, G. Goldhaber, S. Goldhaber, V. H. Seeger, and G. H. Trilling, *Phys. Rev. Letters*, **18**, 1077 (1967).

130. D. V. Bugg, D. C. Slater, G. H. Stafford, R. F. George, K. F. Riley, and R. J. Tapper, *Phys. Rev.*, **146**, 980 (1966).

131. W. A. Cooper, L. G. Hyman, J. Loken, W. E. Manner, B. Musgrave, L. Voyvodic, contribution to the 1967 Heidelberg Intern. Conf. Elementary Particles, see ref. 24.

132. M. Goldberg, J. Leitner, R. Masto, and L. O'Raifeartaigh, *Nuovo Cimento*, **45A**, 169 (1966).

133. M. L. Good and W. D. Walker, *Phys. Rev.*, **120**, 1857 (1960); P. G. O. Freund, *Nuovo Cimento*, **44A**, 411 (1960); U. Maor and P. Yock, *Phys. Rev.*, **148**, 1542 (1966); and M. Ross and L. Stodolsky, *Phys. Rev.*, **149**, 1172 (1966).

134. A. Fridman, G. Maurer, A. Michalon, J. Oudet, B. Schiby, R. Strub, C. Voltolini, and P. Cüer, contribution to the 1967 Heidelberg Intern. Conf. Elementary Particles, see ref. 24.

135. For example, G. Puppi, *Ann. Rev. Nucl. Sci.*, **13**, 287 (1963).

136. G. Goldhaber and S. Goldhaber, "The $A_1$ and $K^{**}(1320)$ Phenomena, Kinematic Enhancement or Mesons?" in *Proceedings of the 4th Anniversary Symposium*, Institute of Mathematical Sciences, Madras, India, January 3–11, 1966, UCRL-16744, Gordon and Breach, New York, in press.

137. M. Goldberg, M. Gundzik, S. Lichtman, J. Leitner, M. Primer, P. L. Connolly, E. L. Hart, K. W. Lai, G. London, N. P. Samios, and S. S. Yamamoto, *Phys. Rev. Letters*, **12**, 546 (1964); **13**, 249 (1964); G. R. Kalbfleisch, L. W. Alvarez, A. Barbaro-Galtieri, O. I. Dahl, P. Eberhard, W. E. Humphrey, J. S. Lindsey, D. W. Merrill, J. J. Murray, A. Rittenberg. R. R. Ross, J. B. Shafer, F. T. Shively, D. M. Siegel, G. A. Smith, and R. D, Tripp, *Phys. Rev. Letters*, **12**, 527 (1964); G. R. Kalbfleisch, O. I. Dahl, and A. Rittenberg, *Phys. Rev. Letters*, **13**, 349 (1964); P. M. Dauber, W. E. Slater, L. T. Smith, D. H. Stork, and H. K. Ticho, *Phys. Rev. Letters*, **13**, 449 (1964).

# Baryon Resonances*

## ANGELA BARBARO-GALTIERI

*Lawrence Radiation Laboratory, Berkeley, California*

### Contents

* Work performed under the auspices of the U.S. Atomic Energy Commission.

175

# I. Introduction

This chapter deals with the properties of resonant states involving baryons and with the various methods used to find these properties.

A baryon is a strongly interacting particle with spin $J = \frac{1}{2} + n$, ($n$ is an integer) which decays (except for the proton) into another baryon plus one or more particles. This decay can take place through electromagnetic, weak, or strong interactions.

We will be concerned mostly with the strong interactions of baryons. These interactions take place in time of about $10^{-23}$ sec, i.e., the proton radius divided by the velocity of light, and the production cross sections are of the order of $10^{-25}$ cm$^2$ or less (i.e., $\sigma \gtrsim 100$ mb). Furthermore, we will refer to as "stable" all those particles which decay more slowly than the particles with strong interactions.

The known stable particles and the known baryons are listed in Tables I and II along with their properties.[1] For the reader's convenience we include also the table of meson states, Table III from ref. 1, since we occasionally refer to these states. Particles which decay through strong interactions are generally referred to as "resonances."

## II. General Remarks

### 1. Properties of Baryons

A strong interacting particle is characterized by a mass $M$, a lifetime $\tau$ (if stable) or a width $\Gamma$ (if subject to strong decays), and a set of quantum numbers. For baryons these are spin $J$, parity $P$, the isotopic spin $I$, the hypercharge $Y$, and, of course, the baryon number $B$.

Spin and parity of a particle are quantum numbers which have to do with its space–time properties, while isospin and hypercharge are intrinsic properties in a different space.

The intrinsic spin of particles is observed as an angular momentum. Identical particles of integral spin obey Bose statistics; i.e., wave functions describing these particles are symmetric under interchange of the coordinates of two of them (this is the case for mesons). Baryons, however, have half-odd integer spin and obey Fermi statistics; i.e., the wave function of a system of particles is antisymmetric under the interchange of the coordinates of any two.

The intrinsic parity of a particle is the parity of the wave function representing the particle at rest. It is even (odd) if the wave function does not (does) change sign under a transformation which reverses the direction of the three spatial axes. This definition holds for bosons; Table I shows the parities of $\pi$, $K$, and $\eta$ mesons to be negative. For a fermion, however, the wave function does not have a definite sign, so the absolute parity is not an observable quantity. However, since the number of fermions in any interaction is conserved, by convention the nucleon and the $\Lambda$ are assigned parity $+1$. The parities of all the baryons are measured relative to these two particles.

Particles occur in isotopic spin multiplets (for example, $\Sigma^-, \Sigma^0, \Sigma^+$) with the same mass (except for small mass differences of electromagnetic origin) and different charge, but strong interactions have proved to be charge independent, so each member of a multiplet is considered to be just a different charge state of a single particle. The charge $Q$ is related to $I$ and $Y$, by

$$Q = I_z + \tfrac{1}{2} Y$$

where $I_z$ is the $z$ component of isospin. It is often convenient to use the strangeness $S$ which is related to $Y$ and $B$ by the expression

$$Y = B + S$$

baryons which carry a strangeness are called hyperons.

The baryon number $B$ and the total angular momentum $J$ are strictly conserved in any type of interaction. Strong interactions conserve also $P, I, Y(S)$. Weak interactions do not conserve any of these, while electromagnetic interactions conserve $P$ and $Y(S)$.[2]

Our notation for the baryons is the one used in ref. 1 and it is as follows:

$$
\begin{array}{ll}
Z \text{ for } Y = 2 & I = 0,1 \\
N \text{ for } Y = 1 & I = \frac{1}{2} \\
\Delta \text{ for } Y = 1 & I = \frac{3}{2} \\
\Lambda \text{ for } Y = 0 & I = 0 \\
\Sigma \text{ for } Y = 0 & I = 1 \\
\Xi \text{ for } Y = -1 & I = \frac{1}{2} \\
\Omega \text{ for } Y = -2 & I = 0
\end{array}
$$

These symbols, without any additional notation, stand for the lower mass states, but they are also used for higher mass states; in this case the value of the mass is in parentheses following the symbol [i.e., $N(1688)$, $\Lambda(1405)$, etc.]. The more massive particles can energetically decay to a lighter particle through strong interactions; therefore, we will often refer to them as resonant states.

## 2. Methods to Detect and Study Resonant States

The properties of a resonant state are determined by studying its decay or production. There are two main types of experiments which can be performed to study a resonance: formation and production experiments. Figure 1 illustrates the two types

$$
\begin{aligned}
\text{formation:}\ & a + B \rightarrow X \rightarrow C + d \\
\text{production:}\ & a + B \rightarrow X + e \rightarrow C + d + e
\end{aligned}
$$

A resonance is made in a "formation experiment" when, bombarding a nucleon target with a meson beam ($\pi$ or $K$), the total energy in the c.m.s. corresponds to the mass of the resonance $X$. If the resonance instead is produced in association with other particles, it is made in a "production experiment"; this is always the case for $S = -2$ states, since the only targets we can build have zero strangeness, and often the case for meson resonances, since only $\bar{p} + p$ experiments have the correct quantum numbers for formation of meson states. In Sections III and IV the two types of experiments will be discussed.

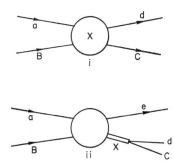

Fig. 1. Diagrams showing the two possible types of experiments to detect and study resonant states. (*i*) Formation experiments: total c.m. energy corresponds to resonance mass; (*ii*) Production experiments: the resonance is produced along with one or more other particles.

### A. Detection of Resonances

In formation experiments a resonant state normally appears as a bump in the cross section $\sigma_i$ for process $i$, when $\sigma_i$ is plotted as a function of the momentum of the bombarding particle. Figure 2 illustrates this point. All the available cross section measurements for the reaction

$$K^-p \to \bar{K}^0 n$$

have been plotted in ref. 102a as function of the $K^-$ incident momentum and clearly show the presence of resonant states. The details of this reaction will be studied in Section VI.

In production experiments the procedures to detect a resonance are different. As an example we consider the reaction

$$K^-p \to \Lambda\pi^+\pi^- \tag{2.1}$$

for only one value of the incident $K^-$ momentum. Figure 3 shows the data of Alston et al. for $P_{K^-} = 1.15$ GeV/c.[4] The elliptically shaped region represents the kinematical boundaries for the kinetic energies $T_{\pi^+}$ and $T_{\pi^-}$ of the two pions, measured in the center of mass (c.m.) frame of reaction (2.1). Each event is represented by a cross in this plot which is called a Dalitz plot (see Sect. IV-2). This plot has the property that the density of points should be uniform if the kinetic energies of the particles are statistically distributed, so that any accumulation of points reveals the energy dependence of the matrix element for that

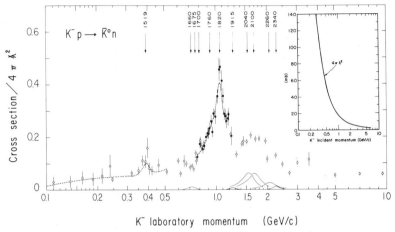

FIG. 2. Cross section (divided by $4\pi\lambda^2$) for the reaction $K^-p \to K^0n$ as a function of $K^-$ momentum.[102a] Structure is clearly shown; many of the bumps present are to be identified with resonances. The positions of the known resonances are indicated by arrows; their contributions are shown at the bottom of the graph. In the upper right corner $4\pi\lambda^2$ is shown as a function of incident momentum.

process. The projection of the points onto the two axes in Figure 3 shows a bump at a definite value of $T_{\pi^+}$ and $T_{\pi^-}$ which is evidence for the resonant state, $\Sigma(1385)$. The reaction (2.1) is, in fact, understood as a two-step process

$$K^-p \to \left\{ \begin{matrix} \Sigma(1385)^+ + \pi^- \\ \Sigma(1385)^- + \pi^+ \end{matrix} \right\} \to \Lambda\pi^+\pi^-$$

### B. Quantum Number Determination

In both types of experiments it is relatively easy to determine the hypercharge and the isospin of the resonant state $X$. Strong interactions conserve both $I$ and $Y$ and, if the decay $X \to C + d$ is a strong decay, $Y$ is derived just by adding $Y_C + Y_d$. In production experiments $X$ can be produced in various charge states, so the determination of $I$ spin is usually more direct.

The determination of $J$ and $P$ requires detailed study of the angular distribution of the decay products of $X$ and their polarization whenever possible. Usually these two quantum numbers are the last properties to be determined for a particle, because copious data and detailed analyses

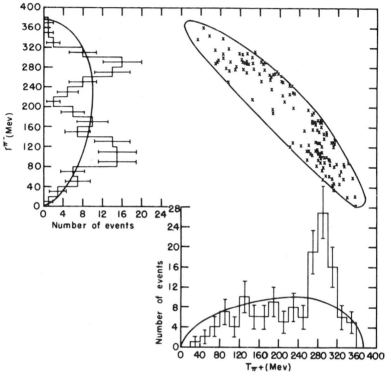

FIG. 3. Dalitz plot for the reaction $K^- p \rightarrow \Lambda \pi^+ \pi^-$ at $P_K = 1.15$ GeV/c, as obtained by Alston et al.[4] Each event is represented by a cross inside the envelope, corresponding to the kinetic energies $T_{\pi^\pm}$ of the $\pi^\pm$ in the c.m.s. of the reaction. Both the scatter plots and the projections onto the axes show evidence for the resonant state $\Sigma(1385)$.

are necessary. In Sections III and IV we will discuss some of the methods to determine $J$ and $P$.

## III. Methods of Analysis of Formation Experiments

The study of resonances in formation experiments requires the knowledge of scattering theory. The reader can find rigorous treatments of scattering theory in many textbooks.[5-7] However, it is useful to introduce the necessary formalism in a very simplified form in order to be able to proceed to the analysis of the experimental data. This section is devoted to an elementary introduction of the theoretical tools used to detect the existence of a particle in formation experiments.

## 1. Partial Wave Analysis

The scattering of a beam of particles from a target is generally described in terms of partial waves. Both initial and final state are represented by a sum of eigenfunctions of $L^2$, the square of the orbital angular momentum. Each of these eigenfunctions in the final state will have an amplitude determined by the type of interaction that produced the scattering. The differential cross section is given by the square of the magnitude of the total amplitude.

We will not give the derivation of the expression for the differential cross section, but only outline the reasoning.[5]

The scattering of a particle of mass $m$ and momentum $p$ from a potential $V(r)$ is described by the Schroedinger equation:

$$\nabla^2 \psi_f(\mathbf{r}) + [k^2 - U(\mathbf{r})]\psi_f(\mathbf{r}) = 0 \tag{3.1}$$

where $k = p/\hbar$ and $U(\mathbf{r}) = (2m/\hbar^2)V(\mathbf{r})$. (In the case of scattering of one particle from another, $p$ is the momentum in the center of mass and $m$ is the reduced mass.) If the incident particle travels along the $z$ axis the motion will be described by the plane wave:

$$\psi_i(r, \theta, \varphi) = e^{ikz} \tag{3.2}$$

which is a solution of the equation for a free particle:

$$\nabla^2 \psi_i(\mathbf{r}) + k^2 \psi_i(\mathbf{r}) = 0 \tag{3.3}$$

If spinless particles are considered, the potential $V(\mathbf{r})$ can be considered spherically symmetric. In this case the wave function will not depend on $\varphi$ and at a large distance from the scattering, i.e., for $r \to \infty$, the solution of the Schroedinger equation (3.1) will be

$$\psi_f(r, \theta) \xrightarrow[r \to \infty]{} e^{ikz} + f(\theta) e^{ikr}/r \tag{3.4}$$

where $f(\theta)$ is the scattering amplitude. Our problem now is to find an expression for $f(\theta)$.

The method of partial waves (see ref. 5, chap. 2) consists of expanding the wave functions (3.2) and (3.4) as a series of Legendre polynomials

$$\psi_i = \sum_{l=0}^{\infty} r^{-1} v_l(r) P_l(\cos \theta)$$

$$\psi_f = \sum_{l=0}^{\infty} r^{-1} u_l(r) P_l(\cos \theta)$$

(3.5)

where $v_l$ and $u_l$ are the solutions of the radial Schroedinger equations for a free particle and for scattering from a potential $U(r)$, respectively,

$$\frac{d^2 v_l(r)}{dr^2} + \left[ k^2 - \frac{l(l+1)}{r^2} \right] v_l(r) = 0$$

$$\frac{d^2 u_l(r)}{dr^2} + \left[ k^2 - U(r) - \frac{l(l+1)}{r^2} \right] u_l(r) = 0$$

(3.6)

It is possible to find asymptotic forms for $v_l(r)$ and $u_l(r)$ which satisfy Eqs. (3.6), therefore giving a solution of Eqs. (3.1) and (3.3) at large distance.

For the incident wave function the expansion (3.5) for $r \to \infty$ takes the form:

$$\psi_i = e^{ikr \cos\theta} = \frac{1}{2ikr} \sum_l (2l + 1)(e^{ikr} - e^{il\pi} - e^{-ikr}) P_l(\cos \theta) \quad (3.7)$$

where the first exponential represents an outgoing spherical wave and the second an incoming one. Each term in the expansion (3.7) is called a "partial wave," corresponding to a particular value of $l$. The scattering potential $V(r) \to 0$ for $r \to \infty$, therefore at large distance all its effect is to alter the phase of the $l$th outgoing wave by $2\delta_l$ and attenuate it by $\eta_l$ (a real number between 0 and 1). The asymptotic expansion of the final wave function is

$$\psi_f = \frac{1}{2ikr} \sum_l (2l + 1)(\eta_l e^{ikr + 2i\delta_l} - e^{il\pi} - e^{-ikr}) P_l(\cos \theta) \quad (3.8)$$

The scattered wave is the difference between Eqs. (3.7) and (3.8)

$$\psi_{\text{scat}} = \frac{1}{k} \sum_l (2l + 1) \left( \frac{\eta_l e^{2i\delta_l} - 1}{2i} \right) \frac{e^{ikr}}{r} P_l(\cos \theta) \quad (3.9)$$

From Eqs. (3.9) and (3.4) combined with Eq. (3.2) it follows:

$$f(\theta) = \frac{1}{k} \sum_l (2l + 1)\left(\frac{\eta_l\, e^{2i\delta_l} - 1}{2i}\right) P_l(\cos\theta) \qquad (3.10)$$

The differential cross section for the scattering is then

$$\frac{d\sigma_e}{d\Omega} = |f(\theta)|^2 = \lambda^2 \left|\sum_l (2l + 1)\left(\frac{\eta_l\, e^{2i\delta_l} - 1}{2i}\right) P_l\right|^2 \qquad (3.11)$$

where the wavelength $\lambda = 1/k$ has been introduced. By the orthogonality of the Legendre polynomials the total elastic cross section does not contain any products between terms with different $l$. Since

$$\int |P_l(\cos\theta)|^2\, d\cos\theta = \frac{2}{2l + 1}$$

we have

$$\sigma_e = 2\pi \int_0^\pi |f(\theta)|^2\, d\cos\theta = 4\pi\lambda^2 \sum_l (2l + 1)\left|\frac{\eta_l\, e^{2i\delta_l} - 1}{2i}\right|^2$$

$$= 4\pi\lambda^2 \sum_l (2l + 1)\,|T_l|^2 \qquad (3.12)$$

where we have introduced the scattering amplitude $T_l$ for the $l$th wave which will be discussed in Section III-4. Here the parameter $\eta_l$ is called "absorption parameter" (it should be called "transmission parameter"). For $\eta_l = 0$ there will be no outgoing wave in the final wave function because it has been completely absorbed in the scattering process; for $\eta_l = 1$ the scattered wave will contain the whole $l$th wave with a phase shift of $\delta_l$.

## 2. Cross Sections—Optical Theorem

The absorption in each wave is expressed in the reaction cross section obtained by conservation of probability by means of Eqs. (3.7) and (3.8)

$$\sigma_r = \pi\lambda^2 \sum_l (2l + 1)(1 - \eta_l^2) \qquad (3.13)$$

The total cross section is, from Eqs. (3.12) and (3.13)

$$\sigma_T = \sigma_r + \sigma_e = \pi\lambda^2 \sum_l (2l + 1)2(1 - \eta_l \cos 2\delta_l) \qquad (3.14)$$

From Eq. (3.13) it follows that the maximum value of the reaction cross section for a given $l$ is

$$(\sigma_r)_{\max} = \pi \lambda^2 (2l + 1) \quad \text{for } \eta_l = 0$$

For the elastic cross section instead, the maximum is, from Eq. (3.12)

$$(\sigma_e)_{\max} = 4\pi \lambda^2 (2l + 1) \quad \text{for } \eta_l = 1, \, \delta_l = 90°$$

The two cross sections are equal for $\eta_l = 0$, i.e., for complete absorption.

$$\sigma_e = \sigma_r = \pi \lambda^2 (2l + 1) \quad \text{for } \eta_l = 0, \text{ any } \delta_l$$

In this latter case, for $\delta_l = 0°$ the elastic scattering is called diffraction scattering.

Another important relation, which can be verified now, is the optical theorem. It relates $\sigma_T$ to the imaginary part of the forward scattering amplitude

$$\text{Im} f(0) = (1/4\pi\lambda)\sigma_T \tag{3.15}$$

In fact, from Eq. (3.10), since $P_l(1) = 1$, it follows that

$$\text{Im} f(0) = \lambda \sum_l (2l + 1) \tfrac{1}{2}(1 - \eta_l \cos 2\delta_l)$$

which is Eq. (3.14) divided by $4\pi\lambda$.

## 3. Scattering from Particles with Spin

Up to now we have ignored the fact that the target proton has spin and that energies involved might be large so that a relativistic treatment of the problem might be necessary. Again we refer the reader to a rigorous derivation of the final formulas[5,9] but repeat here the line of reasoning.

Let us call $\chi_1$ the spin state of the proton and $k$ the magnitude of the momentum in the center of mass of the proton and the incident meson. If the incident particle travels along the $z$ axis, the relative motion will be described by Eq. (3.2) modified by the presence of spin

$$\psi_{\text{inc}} = e^{ikz}\chi_1 \tag{3.16}$$

The scattered wave Eq. (3.4) will also be dependent on the spin state therefore it will be $\varphi$ dependent

$$\psi_f = e^{ikz}\chi_1 + (1/r) \, e^{ikr} \, \mathcal{M}(\theta, \varphi)\chi_1 \tag{3.17}$$

where the scattering amplitude $f(\theta)$ has been substituted by a $2 \times 2$ matrix $\mathcal{M}$ operating on two component spinors.

It turns out that $\mathcal{M}$ can be written as

$$\mathcal{M}(\theta, \varphi) = f(\theta) + g(\theta)\boldsymbol{\sigma} \cdot \mathbf{n} \tag{3.18}$$

where $\boldsymbol{\sigma}$ is the Pauli spin operator and $\mathbf{n}$ is a unit vector perpendicular to the plane of scattering. This form of $\mathcal{M}$, being a scalar, meets the requirement of conserving parity between initial and final state. If the beam direction ($z$ axis) is taken as axis of quantization $\boldsymbol{\sigma} \cdot \mathbf{n}$ involves only $\sigma_x$ and $\sigma_y$, and since they both flip the baryon spin, the amplitude $g(\theta)$ is called spin-flip amplitude. Consequently the $f(\theta)$ is called non-spin-flip amplitude.

If we call $\chi_2$ the spin state after the scattering, $\chi_2 = \mathcal{M}\chi_1$ and the differential cross section will be

$$\begin{aligned}
\frac{d\sigma}{d\Omega} = I &= \chi_2{}^{\dagger}\chi_2 = \chi_1{}^{\dagger}(f^* + g^*\boldsymbol{\sigma} \cdot \mathbf{n})(f + g\boldsymbol{\sigma} \cdot \mathbf{n})\chi_1 \\
&= |f(\theta)|^2 + |g(\theta)|^2 + (f^*(\theta)g(\theta) + f(\theta)g^*(\theta))\chi_1{}^{\dagger}\boldsymbol{\sigma} \cdot \mathbf{n}\chi_1 \quad (3.19) \\
&= |f(\theta)|^2 + |g(\theta)|^2 + 2\,\mathrm{Re}\,(f^*(\theta)g(\theta))\mathbf{P}_T \cdot \mathbf{n}
\end{aligned}$$

where $\mathbf{P}_T$ represents the polarization of the target. The polarization of the final baryon is obtained through the expression

$$I\mathbf{P}_f = \chi_2{}^{\dagger}\boldsymbol{\sigma}\chi_2 \tag{3.20}$$

In the general case $I\mathbf{P}_f$ assumes a very complicated expression. The reader can find it in ref. 9. In the case of nonpolarized target, Eqs. (3.19) and (3.20) assume the very simple forms:

$$\begin{aligned}
\left(\frac{d\sigma}{d\Omega}\right)_0 &= I_0 = |f(\theta)|^2 + |g(\theta)|^2 \\
\left(\frac{d\sigma}{d\Omega}\right)_0 \mathbf{P}_0 &= I_0\mathbf{P}_0 = 2\,\mathrm{Re}\,(f^*(\theta)g(\theta))\mathbf{n}
\end{aligned} \tag{3.21}$$

The differential cross section for polarized target is easily obtained from Eq. (3.19)

$$I_T = I_0(1 + \mathbf{P}_0 \cdot \mathbf{P}_T) \tag{3.22}$$

where $\mathbf{P}_0$ is the polarization of the final baryon for an unpolarized target.

The next problem is to find the expressions for $f(\theta)$ and $g(\theta)$. The wave functions (3.16) and (3.17) can be expanded as a sum of partial waves with the same method used to expand Eqs. (3.2) and (3.4). For each value of $l$, there will be two possible values of the total angular momentum, i.e., $J = l + \frac{1}{2}$ and $J = l - \frac{1}{2}$ and both terms will appear in the summation. The derivation is lengthy[8] and it will not be given here. The results are

$$f(\theta) = \lambda \sum_l [(l + 1)T_{l^+} + lT_{l^-}]P_l(\cos \theta) \qquad (3.23a)$$

$$g(\theta) = i\lambda \sum_l [T_{l^+} - T_{l^-}]P_l^1(\cos \theta) \qquad (3.23b)$$

where $P_l^1(\cos \theta) = \sin \theta(dP_l/d \cos \theta)$ are the first associated Legendre functions, and

$$T_{l^\pm} = \frac{1}{2i}(\eta_{l \pm \frac{1}{2}} e^{2i\delta_{l \pm \frac{1}{2}}} - 1) \qquad (3.24)$$

With this form of $T_l$ the comparison of Eq. (3.23) with Eq. (3.10) shows that the non-spin-flip amplitude $f(\theta)$ is identical to the one obtained in the spinless case, if $T_{l^+} = T_{l^-}$ which is what one would expect. Note that in this case $g(\theta)$ is zero and the differential cross section Eq. (3.21) reduces to Eq. (3.11), as expected. Furthermore, the optical theorem for the case with spin is still $\sigma_T = 4\pi\lambda \operatorname{Im} f(0)$ smce $g(0) = 0$.

Assuming only one partial wave we can find the expression for the total elastic cross section. Since

$$\int |P_l(\cos \theta)|^2 \, d \cos \theta = \frac{2}{2l + 1}$$

$$\int |P_l^1(\cos \theta)|^2 \, d \cos \theta = \frac{2(l + 1)!}{(2l + 1)(l - 1)!}$$

it is easy to show that the elastic cross section is

$$\sigma_e = 4\pi\lambda^2(J + \frac{1}{2})|T_{l\pm}|^2 \qquad (3.25)$$

where the $\pm$ sign refers to the two possible values of $J$, $J = l \pm \frac{1}{2}$.

The remaining problem is to find expressions for the amplitudes (3.23) which are valid in the relativistic case and contain the spin dependence. It turns out that if we use the Dirac equation for the proton, the formal expansion of the $f(\theta)$ and $g(\theta)$ obtained are identical to Eq. (3.23), provided that, again, the $z$ axis is taken as beam direction and quantization axis. The reader can find the derivation in Mott and Massey (ref. 5, ch. IV, p. 74).

## 4. Elastic Scattering Amplitude

From Eq. (3.24) it follows that the scattering amplitude for each value of $J$ and $l$ (or parity $P$) is:

$$T_e = (\eta \, e^{2i\delta} - 1)/2i \qquad (3.26)$$

This is the most general expression of $T$ and contains all the information on the scattering once the $\eta_{J^{\pm}}$ and $\delta_{J^{\pm}}$ are known. It is possible to calculate the form of absorption parameters and phase shifts by solving the Schroedinger equation if the potential $V(r)$ is known.[5] This has been done in cases like a square well potential [$V(r) = -D$ for $r < a$], an impenetrable sphere, a Coulomb potential and many others.

For the scattering of strongly interacting particles the exact form for the potential $V(r)$ is not known and, moreover, an exact description of the process through a differential equation does not seem to be possible. However, the Yukawa potential or a superimposition of Yukawa potentials of the form

$$V(r) = \int_{m_0}^{\infty} \rho(m) \frac{e^{-mr}}{r} \, dm$$

with $m$ the mass of the particle producing the interaction and $m_0$ the pion mass, enables one to obtain some definite predictions which have often reproduced qualitative features of strong interaction processes. The study of this problem is not the aim of this article; we will proceed, instead, to show how, from the analysis of experiments, it is possible to find $\eta_{J^{\pm}}$ and $\delta_{J^{\pm}}$, and to extract the resonant states once the scattering amplitudes are so determined. To do so, the experimental data have to be supplemented by some kind of theoretical assumption which we will specify for each case. For incident momenta lower than 300 MeV/c, the so-called "scattering length approximation" is used for the momentum dependence of $\eta$ and $\delta$. This approximate solution of the Schroedinger equations (3.6) will be discussed in Sections III-12 to III-14. For larger momenta some dispersion relation calculations have been used by some authors, as will be discussed in Section V-2.

Let us now analyze the properties of the elastic scattering amplitude [Eq. (3.26)]. The real and imaginary parts are

$$\mathrm{Re}\, T_e = (\eta/2) \sin 2\delta$$

$$\mathrm{Im}\, T_e = \tfrac{1}{2}(1 - \eta \cos 2\delta)$$

In the complex plane $T_e$ is a vector that lies on (or inside, for $\eta < 1$) a circle of radius $\frac{1}{2}$ and center on the imaginary axis at $i/2$. This circle is called the unitary circle, and the amplitude cannot be outside it because it would violate conservation of probability (the outgoing wave would be larger than the incoming wave). Figure 4 shows the graphical representation of the amplitude and the meaning of the angle $2\delta$. As the energy of the incident particle is changed, the point $T$ will move on or inside the circle (this graph is called an Argand diagram).

The fact that the circle lies on the upper part of the imaginary axis is determined by the optical theorem. In fact, if only one amplitude is present, Eqs. (3.15) and (3.23a) give

$$\sigma_T = 4\pi\lambda \, \mathrm{Im} \, f(0) = 4\pi\lambda^2(J + \tfrac{1}{2}) \, \mathrm{Im} \, T_e$$

which implies that the imaginary part of $T_e$ cannot be negative.

The elastic scattering amplitude can also be expressed in terms of a complex phase shift $\Delta = \delta + i\gamma$, where $\delta$ has the same meaning as in Eq. (3.26), and the relation between $\eta$ and $\gamma$ is $\eta = e^{-2\gamma}$. In this case we have

$$T_e = (e^{2i\Delta} - 1)/2i = e^{i\Delta} \sin \Delta = 1/(\cot \Delta - i) \qquad (3.27)$$

This form of $T_e$ is less convenient for a graphical representation, but it is often found in the literature and it will be useful later.

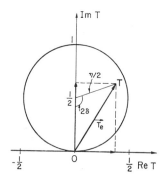

FIG. 4. The elastic scattering amplitude $T_e$ in the complex plane. For pure elastic scattering $\eta = 1$, and $T$ lies on the circle. If other channels are open, $\eta < 1$ and $T$ lies inside the circle. Each partial wave is required by unitarity to lie on or inside the unitary circle.

## 5. S, T, and K Matrices

The scattering of a particle from another particle is completely described by the elements of the scattering matrix **S**. It can be proved that the **S** matrix is unitary (conservation of probability)

$$S^\dagger S = SS^\dagger = 1$$

and symmetric (time reversal invariance) for a given $J$.

$$S_{ij} = S_{ji}$$

In the case of partial wave analysis, the **S** matrix element for elastic scattering in the partial wave $l$ (for total angular momentum $J$) is

$$S^J_{\alpha\alpha} = \eta^J_{\alpha\alpha}\, e^{2i\delta^J_{\alpha\alpha}} = e^{2i\Delta^J_{\alpha\alpha}} \tag{3.28}$$

where $\eta^J_{\alpha\alpha}$ and $\delta^J_{\alpha\alpha}$ are real and are the same of Eq. (3.26). It can be proved that, for each $J$, $S^J S^{J\dagger} = 1$ also.

The elastic scattering amplitude $T_e$ [Eq. (3.26)] is instead an element of the transition matrix **T**. The relation between the S and T matrix is the following:

$$S = 1 + 2iT \tag{3.29}$$

where **1** is the unit matrix. From Eqs. (3.28) and (3.29)

$$T^J_{\alpha\alpha} = (\eta^J_{\alpha\alpha}\, e^{2i\delta^J_{\alpha\alpha}} - 1)/2i \tag{3.30}$$

which is Eq. (3.26).

In practice it is often useful to introduce the so-called "reaction matrix" **K**, which is related to the **S** matrix and to the **T** matrix by the relations

$$S = (1 + iK)(1 - iK)^{-1} \tag{3.31}$$

$$T = K(1 - iK)^{-1}$$

or

$$T^{-1} = K^{-1} - i \tag{3.32}$$

If **S** is unitary, it follows from Eq. (3.31) that **K** is hermitian. If **S** is unitary and symmetric, it follows that **K** is a real symmetric matrix. From Eq. (3.28) we can calculate the **K** matrix element for elastic scattering for a particular $J$, in case of $\eta = 1$, to be

$$K_J = \tan \delta_J \tag{3.33}$$

which is valid only when other channels are not open.

The **K** matrix is very useful to explore energy regions close to a threshold for the opening of a new channel; in fact, the **S** matrix has a singularity at this point called the "threshold branch point." Furthermore, it follows from Eqs. (3.31) and (3.32) that the **K** matrix does not contain any of the poles of the **S** or **T** matrix. The **K** matrix will be used later in Sections III-13 to III-15 in treating the multichannel extension of the effective range theory.

### 6. Inelastic Scattering Amplitude

The matrix element which describes the scattering from channel $\alpha$ to a channel $\beta$ will be an off-diagonal element $\delta_{\alpha\beta}$. It will be

$$S_{\alpha\beta} = S_{\beta\alpha} = \eta_{\alpha\beta}\, e^{2i\delta_{\alpha\beta}} \tag{3.34}$$

Unitarity imposes some restrictions on the $\eta_{\alpha\beta}$, namely

$$0 \leq \eta_{\alpha\beta} \leq 1$$

and

$$\sum_{\beta} \eta_{\alpha\beta}^2 = 1 \tag{3.35}$$

i.e., the sum of the squares of the magnitude of the elements of a row has to be equal to unity.

Relation (3.29) implies that the off-diagonal term of the **T** matrix is

$$T_{\alpha\beta} = \eta_{\alpha\beta}\, e^{2i\delta_{\alpha\beta}}/2i \tag{3.36}$$

This expression differs from $T_{\alpha\alpha}$ [Eq. (3.30)] by the term $1/(2i)$, as expected from the partial wave expansion, since there is no inelastic channel in the incident wave. It follows that

$$\mathrm{Re}\, T_{\alpha\beta} = \tfrac{1}{2}\eta_{\alpha\beta} \sin 2\delta_{\alpha\beta}$$
$$\mathrm{Im}\, T_{\alpha\beta} = -\tfrac{1}{2}\eta_{\alpha\beta} \cos 2\delta_{\alpha\beta}$$

These represent a circle in the complex plane, as shown in Figure 5. The center is at the origin, and for $\delta = 90°$ the amplitude is pure imaginary as in the $T_{\alpha\alpha}$ case shown in Figure 4. Notice that in this case the magnitude of the amplitude is restricted to be

$$|T_{\alpha\beta}| \leq \tfrac{1}{2} \tag{3.37}$$

Furthermore, unitarity imposes another condition on the imaginary part of $T_{\alpha\beta}$. Substituting Eq. (3.29) into the unitarity condition $SS^\dagger = 1$ we get

$$\mathrm{Im}\, \mathbf{T} = \mathbf{T}^\dagger \mathbf{T}$$

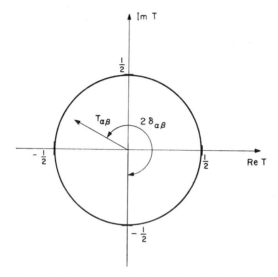

FIG. 5. The amplitude for scattering from channel $\alpha$ to an inelastic channel $\beta$. In this case the center of the circle is at the origin and the amplitude is restricted to be $|T_{\alpha\beta}| \leq \frac{1}{2}$.

or

$$\text{Im } T_{\beta\alpha} = \sum_n T_{n\beta}^* T_{n\alpha} \qquad (3.38)$$

### 7. Resonant Amplitude. Breit-Wigner Formula

The interaction between two particles is resonant when the scattering amplitude for a particular state (definite spin, parity, isotopic spin) varies rapidly, reaches a maximum and then falls again. If $T_e$ lies on the unitary circle, i.e., on the circle of Figure 4, this happens for $\delta = 90°$ (this condition, however, is, in general, neither necessary nor sufficient as we will see later). For example the $\pi N$ scattering amplitude in the $J = \frac{3}{2}^+$ state reaches $\delta = 90°$ at the total c.m. energy of 1236 MeV [$\Delta$(1236)].* For this amplitude $\eta = 1$, therefore, at $E = 1236$ MeV, $T_e = i$ [cf., Eq. (3.26)]. The contribution to the total elastic cross section due to the resonant amplitude at resonance is [from Eq. (3.25)]:

$$\sigma_e = 4\pi\lambda^2(J + \frac{1}{2})$$

* The parameters $M = 1236$ MeV and $\Gamma = 126$ MeV for this resonance have been determined using the results of phase shift analysis of Section V-2 and the resonance shape discussed in this section. These values are different from the ones quoted by other authors who did a less accurate fit to the data.

which allows us to assign the spin of the $\Delta(1236)$ as $J = \frac{3}{2}$ without further study, since $\sigma_e$ is found experimentally to be $8\pi\lambda^2$.

A resonant amplitude, in addition to being pure imaginary at the resonant energy (this is the case if no background is present as will be shown in the next section), has a particular energy dependence which is expressed by the Breit-Wigner formula (for the derivation see, for example, ref. 10):

$$T_{\alpha\alpha} = \frac{1}{2}\Gamma_{\alpha\alpha}/(E_R - E - i\Gamma/2) \qquad (3.39a)$$

where $E_R$ is the resonant energy, $\Gamma$ is the total width of the resonance, and $\Gamma_{\alpha\alpha}$ is the partial width for the channel $\alpha$. For an elastic resonance $\Gamma_{\alpha\alpha} = \Gamma$ and Eq. (3.39a) is identical to Eq. (3.27) with $\cot \delta = (E_R - E)(2/\Gamma)$. In this case it is easy to show that the amplitude $T_e$ follows the circular trajectory of Figure 4 with $\eta = 1$; for $\delta = 45°$ $E = E_R - (\Gamma/2)$, and for $\delta = 135°$, $E = E_R + (\Gamma/2)$.

The energy dependence $E_R - E$ in the denominator of Eq. (3.39a) establishes the sense of rotation in the circular trajectory as being counter clockwise. This behavior is known as the *Wigner condition*. Wigner[11] has proved that this condition follows from causality, which requires that the outgoing wave should not leave the region of interaction before the arrival of the incoming wave. This fact rules out the opposite sign $(E - E_R)$ in Eq. (3.39a). In practice it happens sometimes that the amplitude varies clockwise (see Fig. 37 in Sect. V-2), but causality is preserved because the change of phase shift is very slow, and the amplitude is not resonant. Wigner's proof applies only to elastic resonances, but Dalitz[12] has proved that it is valid in general, for inelastic resonances also.

The most general resonant amplitude is

$$T_{\alpha\beta} = \pm\frac{1}{2}\sqrt{\Gamma_\alpha\Gamma_\beta}/(E_R - E - i\Gamma/2) \qquad (3.39b)$$

where $\Gamma_\alpha$ and $\Gamma_\beta$ are the partial widths for the incident channel $\alpha$ and the outgoing channel $\beta$. The above expression is obviously equivalent to:

$$T_{\alpha\beta} = \pm\sqrt{x_\alpha x_\beta}/(\varepsilon - i) \qquad (3.40a)$$

where

$$\varepsilon = (E_R - E)/(\Gamma/2) \quad \text{and} \quad x_i = \Gamma_i/\Gamma \quad (i = \alpha, \beta) \qquad (3.40b)$$

for constant width. The $\pm$ sign in Eqs. (3.39b) and (3.40a) is related to the $SU(3)$ supermultiplet to which the resonance belongs. The points

$\varepsilon = \pm 1$ correspond to $E = E_R \mp \Gamma/2$; at these points $|\mathrm{Re}\, T_{\alpha\beta}| = |\mathrm{Im}\, T_{\alpha\beta}| = |\sqrt{x_\alpha x_\beta}|/2$. For the elastic channel it is $x_\beta = x_\alpha$ and the sign is always positive. In this case we get:

$$T_{\alpha\alpha} = x_\alpha/(\varepsilon - i) \tag{3.41}$$

which is equivalent to Eq. (3.39a). The relation between $\eta$ and $x_\alpha$ at resonance is

$$\eta = |2x_\alpha - 1|$$

The variable $x_\alpha$ is more convenient than $\eta$ when dealing with a resonance, because it represents the fraction of resonance decaying through the elastic channel; in fact it is known as the "elasticity" of the resonance. As stated before, for $\eta = 1$ ($x_\alpha = 1$) the resonant amplitude describes a circle of diameter 1, which is the unitary circle. For $x_\alpha \neq 1$ it will describe a smaller circle, inside the unitary circle, of diameter $x_\alpha$. At resonance the phase is $\delta = 90°$ for $x \geq 0.5$, $\delta = 0°$ for $x < 0.5$. Figure 6 illustrates the trajectory of $T_\alpha$ for the two cases $x = 0.75$ and $x = 0.4$. There is no qualitative difference between these two resonances, the phase of the resonant amplitude itself goes through $90°$ in both cases.

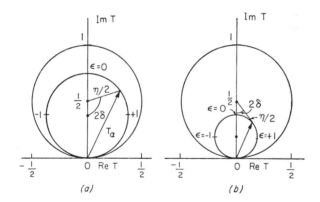

FIG. 6. The resonant amplitude for the elastic channel is shown for two different values of the elasticity $x$. (a) $x = 0.75$ and the phase shift for the amplitude goes through $90°$ at the resonant energy, (b) $x = 0.4$ and $\delta = 0°$ at the resonant energy. Notice that the phase of the resonant amplitude in the resonance circle goes through $90°$ in both cases.

Figure 7 shows the Argand diagram for $T_{\alpha\beta}$ [Eq. (3.40a)], the diameter of the circle being $|\sqrt{x_\alpha x_\beta}|$. The condition [Eq. (3.37)] on $T_{\alpha\beta}$ gives a constraint to $x_\alpha x_\beta$, in fact we have

$$|\sqrt{x_\alpha x_\beta}| \leq \tfrac{1}{2} \quad \text{or} \quad x_\alpha x_\beta < 0.25$$

*The energy dependence of* $\Gamma$ has not been introduced in Eq. (3.40b). It will modify the energy dependence of $\varepsilon$, whose expression we will find next. The energy dependence of $\Gamma$ contains a phase space factor $q$ (momentum of the outgoing particles in the center of mass) and a centrifugal barrier factor $B_l$. This factor depends on the nature of the interaction, but in first approximation we consider valid the expression of $B_l$ derived by Blatt and Weisskopf[13] for a square well potential and for nonrelativistic energies. Introducing $z = qr$, with $r$ a radius of interaction, these factors are

$$
\begin{aligned}
B_0 &= 1 & &= z^0 D_0{}^{-1} \\
B_1 &= z^2(1 + z^2)^{-1} & &= z^2 D_1{}^{-1} \\
B_2 &= z^4(9 + 3z^2 + z^4)^{-1} & &= z^4 D_2{}^{-1} \quad (3.42) \\
B_3 &= z^6(225 + 45z^2 + 6z^4 + z^6)^{-1} & &= z^6 D_3{}^{-1} \\
B_4 &= z^8(11025 + 1575z^2 + 135z^4 + 10z^6 + z^8)^{-1} &&= z^8 D_4{}^{-1}
\end{aligned}
$$

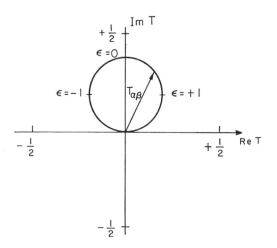

FIG. 7. The resonant amplitude for scattering into an inelastic channel. The diameter of the circle is $(x_\alpha x_\beta)^{1/2}$ and the radius of the circle has to be smaller than $\tfrac{1}{2}$. The imaginary part of the amplitude is positive or negative, depending on the $SU(3)$ supermultiplet to which the resonance belongs.

In addition to $B_l$, Layson[14] suggests a relativistic correction which amounts to $2E_R/(E_R + E)$ normalized in such a way as to be 1 at the resonant energy and smaller than 1 at higher energies. The final expression for $\Gamma$ is

$$\Gamma = \Gamma_R \frac{(qr)^{2l+1}}{D_l} \frac{2E_R}{E_R + E} \left[ \frac{D_l}{(qr)^{2l+1}} \right]_R \tag{3.43}$$

where the last factor has been introduced as a normalization factor so that $\Gamma = \Gamma_R$ for $q = q_R$. In Eq. (3.39) $\Gamma = \sum \Gamma_i$ and each $\Gamma_i$ will in general have a slightly different value of $q$. In this case $x_i = \Gamma_i/\Gamma$ will be a slowly varying function of energy. Assuming that the difference in $q$ between the various channels can be disregarded, substituting Eq. (3.43) in Eq. (3.40) we obtain:

$$T_{\alpha\beta} = \pm \sqrt{x_\alpha x_\beta}/(\varepsilon - i) \tag{3.44}$$

with

$$\varepsilon = \frac{E_R^2 - E^2}{E_R \Gamma_R} \left( \frac{q_R}{q} \right)^{2l+1} \frac{D_l(qr)}{[D_l(qr)]_R} \tag{3.45}$$

*The radius of interaction $r$* is going to affect the shape of the amplitude as function of energy. Figure 8 shows this dependence, calculated for $\Delta(1236)$, using the experimental values of the resonant mass $M = 1236$ MeV and of the total width $\Gamma_R = 126$ MeV. This resonance has an elasticity $x_\alpha = 1$ and its Argand diagram is shown in Section V-2. Figures 8a and b show Im $T$, Re $T$ for various forms of the Breit-Wigner formula: using expression (3.40b) for $\varepsilon$, with no energy dependence in $\Gamma$ (curve 1), using only the phase space factor $q/q_R$ for the energy dependence of $\Gamma$ (curve 2) and finally using the complete expression (3.45) for $\varepsilon$ with $l = 1$ (curves 3 and 4). Various values of the radius of interaction have been used in the calculation, in Figure 8 only $r = 2.0$ fermi (which corresponds to a momentum of 98.7 MeV/c) and $r = 0.7$ fermi (or 280 MeV/c momentum) are reported. The experimental points are results of phase shift analyses and are taken from McKinley[15] below $E = 1300$ MeV and from Bareyre et al.[16] above this energy.

It is easy to see that the choice of the radius of interaction is very important for energies different from $E_R$. The apparent width (width at half maximum) $\Gamma_a = E(\varepsilon = -1) - E(\varepsilon = +1)$ has a strong dependence on the radius of interaction as well as on the energy dependence of $\Gamma$, once the value of $\Gamma_R$ is fixed ($\Gamma_R = 126$ MeV for all four curves in Fig. 8). On the other hand, in the fit of experimental data the value of $\Gamma_R$ found depends on the energy dependence of $\Gamma$ and on the value of $r$ used.

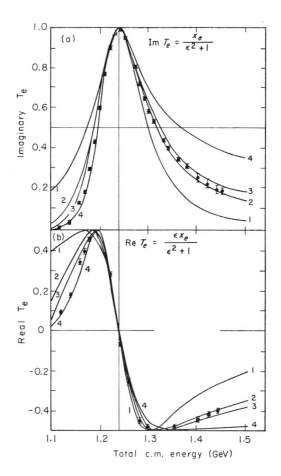

FIG. 8. Scattering amplitude for $\Delta(1236)$ with a width $\Gamma_R = 126$ MeV and elasticity equal to unity. (a) Imaginary part of $T_e$. (b) Real part of $T_e$. The experimental points are from refs. 15 and 16. The curves have been calculated as follows: 1. Breit-Wigner (BW) form with no energy dependence in $\Gamma$, 2. BW with only phase space factor for $\Gamma$, 3. BW with energy dependence in $\Gamma$ according to Eq. (3.45) and with $r = (98.7 \text{ MeV}/c)^{-1}$, 4. same as 3 with $r = (280 \text{ MeV}/c)^{-1}$. The values of the apparent widths are: $\Gamma_{a1} = 126$ MeV, $\Gamma_{a2} = 130$ MeV, $\Gamma_{a3} = 134$ MeV, and $\Gamma_{a4} = 175$ MeV.

For $\Delta(1236)$ the experimental data seem to be best in agreement with curve 3, calculated with the energy dependence [Eq. (3.45)] for $\varepsilon$ and with $r = 2$ fermi (or $q_0 = 98.7$ MeV/c). This radius is about three times larger than the value used by many authors in fitting data with a Breit-Wigner (a value of $q_0 = 300$ MeV/c has been frequently used). For resonances other than $\Delta(1236)$ the experimental data are not yet good enough to allow such determination or the behavior of the amplitude deviates from the circular path at about $\Gamma/2$ and it is not possible to determine the radius of interaction.

The conclusion we can reach looking at Figure 8 is that the form of the resonant amplitude at an energy $E \neq E_R$ depends on many factors (one being the radius of interaction) and it has to be used with caution in analyzing the experimental data.

The fractions $x_\alpha$, $x_\beta$, etc., of resonance in each channel have been assumed constant with energy. Were this not true, the resonant amplitude would deviate from a circular trajectory, since $\sqrt{x_\alpha x_\beta(E)}$ is the diameter of the circle at energy $E$. However, if a resonance decays mainly in the elastic channel $x_\alpha$ is large and the assumption of constant $x_\alpha$ is very good in the region $-1 < \varepsilon < +1$. In this case $\Gamma_\alpha$ is the major contribution to the total $\Gamma$ therefore the ratio $\Gamma_\alpha/\Gamma$ has little $q$ dependence. Below this energy region the variation of $x_\alpha$ is more affected by the large relative variation of $q$ in the various channels. Above this energy as we go further from the resonance, we might expect that other phenomena contribute to the shape of the amplitude. In addition the energy dependence of $\Gamma$ [Eq. (3.45)] might not be valid.

## 8. Effect of Background on Resonant Amplitude

The discussion of the previous section is valid if the scattering amplitude $T_{I,J,P}$ corresponding to a particular set of quantum numbers $I, J, P$, represents a pure resonant state. It is possible that when inelastic channels are open in addition to a resonance with that set of quantum numbers, there is also a slowly varying background amplitude with the same set of quantum numbers. In this case the circular path of the resonant amplitude of Figure 6 appears considerably distorted.

This problem has been treated by Dalitz[12] and more recently by Michael,[17] who has applied his formalism to the $S_{11}$ resonance in the $\pi p$ system.

Let us first consider the very simple case for which only the elastic channel is open below a threshold energy at which a two-channel resonance starts coming in. The total elastic amplitude above the threshold will be represented by a background amplitude $T_B$ and a resonant amplitude $T_R$ with elasticity $x$. The expression for $T$ is easily found using the relation (3.29) between the $S$ matrix and the $T$ matrix. If $\Delta_R$ is the phase shift produced by the resonance, the $S$ matrix element will be

$$S = e^{2i(\delta_B + \Delta_R)} = e^{2i\delta_B} e^{2i\Delta_R} = e^{2i\delta_B}(1 + 2iT_R) = 1 + 2iT$$

and through some obvious algebra we get

$$T = T_B + e^{2i\delta_B}T_R = e^{i\delta_B} \sin \delta_B + e^{2i\delta_B}T_R \qquad (3.46)$$

This expression is the same as Eq. 8 of Michael,[17] which has been derived in a more rigorous way, when the assumption of only one open channel below threshold is made. From Eq. (3.46) it is clear that the effect of the background is to rotate the resonant amplitude by the angle $2\delta_B$. If the background amplitude is constant in the energy region of the resonance, the situation is as shown in Figure 9a. The resonant circle starts at point $B$ and follows its trajectory tangent to $\overline{AB}$. The resonant energy is not at the point where the resonant amplitude is pure imaginary but it is rotated by $2\delta_B$. The diameter of the circle is the elasticity $x$. If the background amplitude changes with energy, it is obvious that the total amplitude $T$ does not follow a circular trajectory, but it is somewhat distorted; $\delta_B$ at the resonant energy will be different than that at the threshold energy and $E_R$ will not be along the line $\overline{BC}$.

A more general case is illustrated in Figure 9b. In this case more channels are open and the elastic background amplitude is not restricted to be on the unitary circle. The total elastic amplitude is now[17]

$$T_e = e^{i\Delta_0} \sin \Delta_0 + e^{2i\delta_B}T_R \qquad (3.47)$$

where $\Delta_0 = \delta_0 + i\gamma_0$ and $e^{2i\gamma_0} = \eta_0$ are the parameters for the elastic background amplitudes and $2\delta_B$ is the angle by which the resonant energy is rotated from the point of pure imaginary resonant amplitude. This phase, $\delta_B$, is different from $\delta_0$ because it contains a contribution from all the background channels including the elastic.[12,17] Note that in this case the center of the resonance circle $C'$ is no longer along the line $\overline{BC}$ because the circle is now tangent to $\overline{AB}$, which is not tangent to the unitary circle. The circular trajectory of the total amplitude $T_e$ in Figure 9b is correct only in the case of constant background throughout the resonance energy, which is very unlikely. The angle $\delta_B$ is very likely to vary with energy and the real trajectory turns out to be quite dis-

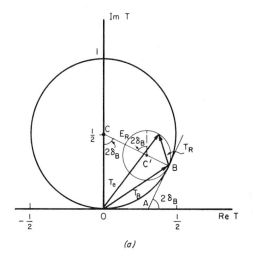

(a)

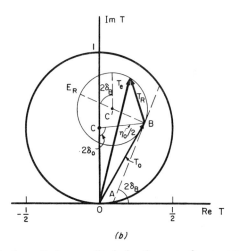

(b)

Fig. 9. Elastic scattering amplitude for the case of a resonance and a background amplitude in same $I, J, P$ state. If the background is assumed to be constant throughout the resonance region, the amplitude $\mathbf{T}$ is on the circle of center $C'$. (a) The background amplitude is pure elastic before the resonance threshold. The resonant amplitude is then rotated by $2\delta_B$, where $\delta_B$ is the phase of $\mathbf{T}_B$. (b) The background amplitude presents some absorption ($\eta < 1$). In this case the phase $2\delta_B$ by which the resonant amplitude is rotated, is not equal to the phase $2\delta_0$ of the background elastic amplitude $\mathbf{T}_0$.

torted. The reader can find two cases in which experiments have shown this particular behavior for the elastic amplitude in Section V-2. The resonances involved are the $S_{11}$ and $S_{31}$ resonance in the $\pi p$ system.

## 9. Effect of Resonances on Cross Sections

Assuming that there is no background in the same $IJP$ state as the resonance, its contribution to the total elastic cross section, from Eqs. (3.25) and (3.41), is

$$(\sigma_e)_R = 4\pi\lambda^2(J + \tfrac{1}{2})x_e^2/(\varepsilon^2 + 1) \qquad (3.48)$$

which is proportional to $x_e^2$. The factor $\lambda^2$ that appears here has the effect of displacing the position of the peak in the cross section. For example, in the case of $\Delta(1236)$, which we have taken as our model resonance, the maximum value of the scattering amplitude is at $M = 1236$ MeV as seen in Figure 8a, but the cross section has a peak at $M = 1222$ MeV as shown in Figure 10. The displacement of the peak depends on two things: the slope of the factor $4\pi\lambda^2$ and the width of the

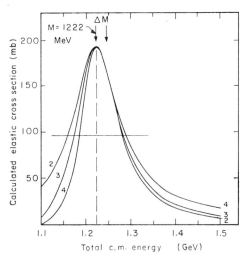

FIG. 10. Calculated elastic cross section for formation of $\Delta(1236)$, using the amplitudes of Fig. 8. Curve 1 has been omitted because its value for low masses is too large and in contradiction with experiments. The peak is displaced by $-14$ MeV with respect to the resonance mass, due to the $\lambda^2$ factor in $\sigma_e$. Comparison with Fig. 8 shows that the relative position of the curves has changed. The apparent widths are: $\Gamma_{a2} = 123$ MeV, $\Gamma_{a3} = 111$ MeV, and $\Gamma_{a4} = 100$ MeV.

resonance. The apparent width (width at a half maximum) is also affected by the factor $4\pi\lambda^2$, as can be easily seen by comparing the $\Gamma_{at}$ of Figure 10 with the $\Gamma_{ai}$ of Figure 8. For resonances with a larger $q$ and a smaller width the effect is much smaller. In any case, in studying experimental data it is more convenient to plot $\sigma/4\pi\lambda^2$ so that the behavior of the amplitude is isolated from kinematical factors. The calculated values of $\Delta M$ and of $\Gamma_a$ for some baryon resonances are reported in Table IV, where the calculations were done as for curve 3 of Figure 10.

The contribution of a resonance to the total cross section can be found using the optical theorem (3.15) and Eq. (3.23a)

$$(\sigma_T)_R = 4\pi\lambda \, \mathrm{Im}\, f(0) = 4\pi\lambda(J + \tfrac{1}{2})x_e/(\varepsilon^2 + 1) \qquad (3.49)$$

and is proportional to $x_e$. Since $x_e \leq 1$ it is easy to see that a resonance produces a larger peak in the total cross section than in the elastic cross section, if the elasticity is smaller than unity. For this reason the measurement of total cross sections is a very good way of discovering resonant states. Of course, once a bump is found in such a way, further detailed studies are necessary to ascertain the resonant behavior of the amplitude and to establish the quantum numbers of the state. The differential cross sections contain more information on the various partial waves and are the next step in understanding a bump. Figure 11 shows the

TABLE IV

Effect of Kinematical Factors on Resonance Parameters[a]

|            | $l$ | $M_R$, MeV | $\Delta M$, MeV | $\Gamma_R$, MeV | $\Gamma_{BW}$, MeV | $\Gamma_a$, MeV |
|------------|-----|------------|-----------------|-----------------|--------------------|-----------------|
| $\Delta(1236)$ | 1 | 1236 | $-14$ | 126 | 134 | 111 |
| $N(1525)$      | 2 | 1525 | $-4$  | 105 | 105 | 105 |
| $N(1688)$      | 3 | 1688 | $-3$  | 110 | 110 | 109 |
| $N(2190)$      | 4 | 2190 | $-6$  | 200 | 200 | 197 |
| $\Sigma(1660)$ | 2 | 1660 | $-1$  | 50  | 50  | 50  |
| $\Lambda(1820)$ | 3 | 1819 | $-3$ | 83  | 83  | 83  |
| $\Sigma(2035)$ | 4 | 2035 | $-7$  | 160 | 160 | 157 |

[a] The first column represents the orbital angular momentum for the elastic decay of the resonance. $M_R$ and $\Gamma_R$ are the resonance mass and width (at $M = M_R$). $\Gamma_{BW}$ is the width of the amplitude. $\Delta M$ and $\Gamma_a$ are the displacement of the resonance peak and the apparent width of the resonance as seen in total cross section.

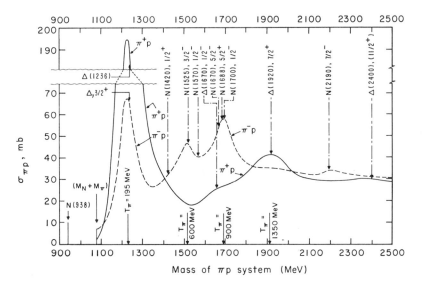

FIG. 11. The $\pi^{\pm}$ total cross sections vs. total energy in $\pi p$ c.m. system. Arrows
indicate energies where resonant states are present.

experimental data on total cross section for $\pi^{\pm}p$ interactions. The errors
are very small, so a smooth curve has been drawn through the data.[1]
All the bumps which appear in these curves turned out to contain resonances, although the situation is much more complicated than Figure 11
would indicate. The present understanding of these curves will be
discussed in Section V.

Finally the contribution to the total cross section for a particular
inelastic channel, like $Kp \rightarrow \Lambda\pi$, can be obtained from Eq. (3.44) to be

$$\sigma_{\alpha\beta} = 4\pi\lambda^2(J + \tfrac{1}{2})\,|T_{\alpha\beta}|^2 = 4\pi\lambda^2(J + \tfrac{1}{2})x_\alpha x_\beta/(\varepsilon^2 + 1) \quad (3.50)$$

Here again the factor $x_\alpha$, the elasticity of the resonance, is present. For
small $J$ and small elasticity this cross section will be small and it will be
hard to detect the resonant amplitude, unless the background is small.

### 10. Some Properties of Phase Shifts

The energy dependence and the magnitude of the phase shifts are
determined by the form of the potential; in absence of a definite form for
the potential only a few general considerations can be made. These

properties essentially derive from the sctructure of the Schroedinger equation itself. The reader can find the derivations of formulas and properties in various textbooks (see, for example, ref. 7).

The radial part of the Schroedinger equation for a particular partial wave can be written as in Eqs. (3.6), for a free particle and for a particle scattered by a potential $V(r)$ $\{U(r) = [V(r)](2m/\hbar^2)\}$:

$$v_l'' + \{k^2 - [l(l + 1)/r^2]\}v_l = 0$$
$$u_l'' + \{k^2 - [l(l + 1)/r^2] - U(r)\}u_l = 0$$

$$(3.51)$$

The asymptotic forms of $v_l$ and $u_l$ can be deduced from Section III-1. For scattering in only one channel (i.e., for $\eta_l = 1$), they are:

$$v_l(kr) \propto \sin\left(kr - l\frac{\pi}{2}\right) \qquad \text{for } r \to \infty$$
$$u_l(kr) \propto \sin\left(kr - l\frac{\pi}{2} + \delta_l\right) \quad \text{for } r \to \infty$$

$$(3.52)$$

For small $kr$, both wave functions $u_l$ and $v_l$ can be approximated with the corresponding behavior of the Bessel functions $j_l(kr)$, so

$$v_l \to u_l \to krj_l(kr) \to \frac{kr^{l+1}}{(2l + 1)!!} \quad \text{(for } kr \to 0) \qquad (3.53)$$

A useful expression for the phase shifts can be obtained by multiplying the first equation (3.51) by $u_l$, the second by $v_l$ and then subtracting and integrating over $r$ from 0 to $R$. It is easy to prove the result

$$k \sin \delta_l \propto -\int_0^\infty dr U(r)u_l(kr)v_l(kr) \qquad (3.54)$$

where the integration has been extended to $\infty$ since $u(r) = 0$ beyond $R$, the range of the interaction.

Let us now point out some properties of the phase shifts:

1. The phase shift $\delta_l$ for $l > kR$ can usually be ignored in the sum (3.11) or (3.23). In fact, the contribution of a partial wave $u_l$ is small for $l > kR$. This comes from a property of Bessel functions $j_l(kr)$. It is easily seen in the case of small $kr$ but it is a more general rule. From Eq. (3.53) we deduce that the density of partial wave is proportional to $r^2 j_l^2(kr)$ and is very low for $r < l\lambda$ ($\lambda = 1/k$ is the wavelength), reaching its

maximum for $r = l\lambda$. If the potential is zero above a range $R$ and $R < l\lambda$ the $l$th wave practically does not penetrate in the region of strong potential so it is not affected by it. Consequently $\delta_l$ is small and its contribution to the scattering is negligible.

2. From Eq. (3.54) it follows that the sign of $\delta_l$ is opposite to the sign of $U(r)$. So, an attractive potential (negative) will cause *positive* phase shifts and a repulsive potential will cause *negative* phase shifts.

3. The behavior of phase shifts for low energy can be derived from Eqs. (3.53) and (3.54).

$$\sin \delta_l \propto k^{2l+1} \quad \text{(for } k \to 0\text{)} \tag{3.55}$$

So $\delta_l \to 0$ for $k \to 0$, which implies that the scattering matrix $T \to 0$ as expected.

### 11. Effective Range Theory. Single Channel

The momentum dependence of the phase shifts $\delta$ can be obtained at low energy by solving the Schroedinger equation with some simple assumptions. This type of analysis has been introduced by Schwinger for low energy $np$ scattering and, later, by Bethe.[19] This subject is extensively treated in ref. 13, where the formulation of Bethe has been adopted. This formulation of the effective range theory has been extended to $Kp$ scattering where many channels are open at low energy and it will be treated in the next three sections.

Let us now outline the derivation of the effective range formula. For low energy ($kR < 1$) the $S$ wave is the dominant wave and its asymptotic form, from Eq. (3.52), is

$$u(r) \to \sin (kr + \delta)/\sin \delta \quad \text{(for } r \to \infty\text{)}$$

where $(\sin \delta)^{-1}$ is a normalization factor. Let us now call $w(r)$ the wave function outside the region of interaction (i.e., in the region where $V = 0$). Here this wave function will be the same as $u(r)$,

$$u(r) \xrightarrow[r \to \infty]{} w(r) \equiv \frac{\sin (kr + \delta)}{\sin \delta} \tag{3.56}$$

At the origin $u(r)$ and $w(r)$ will be different. In fact from Eq. (3.56) $w(0) = 1$, whereas $u(r)$ is affected by the potential $V(r)$ and must obey the Schroedinger equation (3.51) and Eq. (3.5); therefore $u(0) = 0$. Figure 12 shows the behavior of $u(r)$ and $w(r)$.

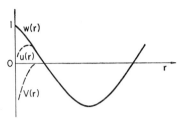

FIG. 12. The asymptotic form of the wave function $u(r) = w(r)$ is represented by the full line. The dashed line shows how $u(r)$ is modified inside the region of the interaction by the potential $V(r)$.

Let us now consider two different energies $k_1$ and $k_2$ and write Eq. (3.51) at the two energies

$$u_1'' - U(r)u_1 + k_1^2 u_1 = 0$$
$$u_2'' - U(r)u_2 + k_2^2 w_2 = 0$$

If we multiply the first equation by $u_2$ and the second by $u_1$, then subtract and integrate, we get

$$\int_0^r (u_2 u_1'' - u_2'' u_1)\, dr + (k_1^2 - k_2^2) \int_0^r u_1 u_2\, dr = 0 \qquad (3.57)$$

For $w_1$ and $w_2$ a similar expression can be written

$$\int_0^r (w_2 w_1'' - w_2'' w_1)\, d_r + (k_1^2 - k_2^2) \int_0^r w_1 w_2\, dr = 0 \qquad (3.58)$$

If we let $r \to \infty$, integrate and subtract Eqs. (3.57) and (3.58) we get [using the boundary conditions $u_1(0) = u_2(0) = 0$]:

$$w_1(0)w_2'(0) - w_2(0)w_1'(0) = (k_2^2 - k_1^2) \int_0^\infty (w_1 w_2 - u_1 u_2)\, dr \qquad (3.59)$$

Using the expression (3.56) for $w_1$ and $w_2$ and the boundary conditions $w_1(0) = w_2(0) = 1$, we have

$$-k_1 \cot \delta_1 + k_2 \cot \delta_2 = (k_2^2 - k_1^2) \int_0^\infty (w_1 w_2 - u_1 u_2)\, dr \qquad (3.60)$$

Let us now take $k_1 = 0$ and define

$$\lim_{k_1 \to 0} k_1 \cot \delta_1 = -1/a \qquad (3.61)$$

$$\rho(0, k) = 2 \int_0^\infty (w_0 w - u_0 u)\, dr \qquad (3.62)$$

Eq. (3.60) then becomes:

$$k \cot \delta = (-1/a) + \tfrac{1}{2}k^2\rho(0, k) \qquad (3.63)$$

This formula is exact. The phase shift $\delta$ is expressed as a function of $a$, the "scattering length," and a radius $\rho(0, k)$ which can be calculated, if the potential is known, after solving the Schroedinger equation for $u(kr)$.

The *scattering length a* has a geometrical meaning, shown in Figure 13 for the three cases $a < 0$, $a = \infty$, and $a > 0$, which is easy to derive using Eqs. (3.51) and (3.56). Beyond the range of the potential $V(r)$, and for $k \to 0$ the radial wave equation [Eq. (3.51)] becomes $d^2u_0/(dr^2) = 0$, which implies that $u_0$ tends to a straight line outside the range of interaction, for $k \to 0$. For the same reason $w_0$ has to be a straight line and coincide with $u_0$ outside the force range. From Eq. (3.56), $w_0(0) = 1$ and, if we call $a$ the intersection of this straight line with the $r$ axis, its equation is

$$u_0(r) = w_0(r) = 1 - r/a \quad (\text{for } k \to 0, r \to \infty)$$

From Eq. (3.56), we have that for $k \to 0$, $w_0 \to 1 + kr \cot \delta$, so, using the above expression for $w_0(r)$, we get Eq. (3.61) again.

The scattering length is also related to the total scattering cross-section at "zero energy." In fact from Eqs. (3.12) and (3.27), assuming only $S$ wave and only one channel open ($\eta = 1$), we get:

$$\sigma_0 = \lim_{k \to 0} 4\pi\lambdabar^2 |T_e|^2 = 4\pi\lambdabar^2 \lim_{k \to 0} \frac{1}{1 + \cot^2 \delta} = 4\pi a^2 \qquad (3.64)$$

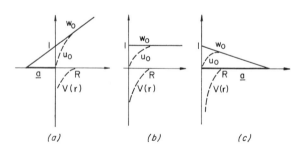

(a)              (b)              (c)

FIG. 13. It shows the three possible forms of the wave function $u(r)$ at $k = 0$. (a) The scattering length $a < 0$, no bound state is possible, (b) $a = \infty$, the potential is sufficient to produce a bound state, (c) $a > 0$, the two interacting particles form a bound state. Notice that the sign convention used here gives: $k \cot \delta = -1/a$.

However, the measurement of this cross section determines the value of $a$, but not its sign.

The sign of $a$ is related to whether or not an $S$ wave bound state is present, as can be seen from the following considerations. If we assume that $V(r)$ is a square well potential of depth $V_0$ and width $R$, it can be proved (see ref. 5, or any other quantum mechanics textbook) that a bound state occurs for $\sqrt{(U_0)}R \geq \pi/2$, i.e., for $(V_0 2\mu/\hbar^2)R^2 \geq \pi^2/4$. If $\sqrt{(U_0)}R = \pi/2$, the corresponding potential $V_b$ is sufficient to produce a bound state with zero binding energy. In this case $\delta = \pi/2$ at $k = 0$ and from Eq. (3.64) the cross section is infinite and so is $a$. This is the case in Figure 13b. For $V_0 < V_b$, $\delta \to 0$ at $k = 0$ and increases with energy, therefore $a$ is negative as in Figure 13a. For $V_0 > V_b$, the wave function tends to zero at a finite value of $r$, the two interacting particles form a bound state, $\delta = \pi$ at $k = 0$, and $a$ is positive.

In the case of $np$ scattering, it turns out that the triplet state has a large, positive scattering length, an indication of a bound state (the deuteron). The scattering length for $np$ scattering in the $I$ spin $= 0$, $J = 1$ state is in fact $a = 5.39 \pm 0.03$ fermi.[20] For the $I = 1$, $J = 0$ state $a = -23.74 \pm 0.09$ fermi[20] and no bound state is present (it is called a "virtual state" as we will see in Sect. III-16).

Turning back to Eq. (3.63), we can obtain the *effective range approximation* by substituting $\rho(0, k)$ with $\rho(0, 0)$. The integral

$$r_0 = 2 \int_0^\infty (w_0{}^2 - u_0{}^2) \, dr$$

is called the "effective range." In the case of the square well potential it is easy to prove that $r_0 = R$. This approximation is justified for low energies if the potential is larger than the energy involved, $U \gg k^2$. Now $r_0$ depends on the width and the depth of the potential and the approximation

$$k \cot \delta = -\frac{1}{a} + \tfrac{1}{2} r_0 k^2 \qquad (3.65)$$

is also called the "shape independent" approximation because $r_0$ depends only on two parameters which can be obtained with any type of potential (square well, Yukawa potential, gaussian potential, etc.)

A better approximation to Eq. (3.63) contains an extra term

$$k \cot \delta = -\frac{1}{a} + \tfrac{1}{2} r_0 k^2 - P r_0{}^2 k^4 \qquad (3.66)$$

where $P$ is called shape parameter. Of course a large amount of experimental data is needed in order to determine $P$, and in the case of $np$ scattering it turns out to be very small ($P = 0.017 \pm 0.028$ in the case of scattering in the singlet state).[20] It might be interesting to see what is the contribution from the effective range term. For triplet (spin state) $np$ scattering, $r_0 = 1.704$ fermi and at $P_n = 30$ MeV/c, it is $k \cot \delta = -0.218 + 0.020$ fermi$^{-1}$, so the contribution of the effective range is $\sim 10\%$ of the scattering length term. For singlet $np$ scattering, $r_0 = 2.67$ fermi and at $P_n = 10$ MeV/c $k \cot \delta = 0.042 + 0.003$ fermi$^{-1}$, i.e., we have to go to a lower $P_n$ to cut the contribution of the second term, since the scattering length is so large.

Equation (3.66) can also be extended to higher partial waves,

$$k^{2l+1} \cot \delta_l = -\frac{1}{a_l} + \frac{1}{2} r_l k^2 - P r_l^2 k^4 \qquad (3.67)$$

where $r_l$ does not have as simple an interpretation as $r_0$, since the centrifugal term in the Schroedinger equation alters the whole situation. For the $l$th wave Eq. (3.67) is valid only if the wave function $w_l$ does not have nodes within the range of forces, i.e., if $kR < (\pi/2)(l + 1)$.

## 12. Zero-Effective Range Approximation for Many Channels

Scattering of low energy $K^-$ ($P_K < 250$ MeV/c) has been successfully described by the effective range approximation. This description has been introduced by Jackson et al.[21] as the zero-effective range approximation. For low energy $K^-p$ interactions only the $S$ wave is present, but, unlike $np$ scattering, many channels are open, some in two possible isospin states:

$$
\begin{array}{lll}
K^-p \to K^-p & I = 0, 1 & \\
K^-p \to \bar{K}^0 n & I = 0, 1 & \\
K^-p \to \Sigma^\pm \pi^\mp & I = 0, 1 & (3.68) \\
K^-p \to \Lambda \pi^0 & I = 1 &
\end{array}
$$

The first modification of Eq. (3.65) is that $\Delta$ is now complex, since there is absorption, and therefore $a$ and $r_0$ are complex. To describe the elastic scattering there will be two complex parameters for each isotopic spin state—eight parameters in all. To reduce the number of parameters the zero-effective range has been suggested by Jackson et al.[21] The justification is that for sufficiently low momentum the range term is small compared with the scattering length term. With this approximation Eq. (3.65) becomes

$$k \cot \Delta_I = 1/A_I \qquad (3.69)$$

where the subscript $I$ refers to the isotopic spin state. (Note that the $-$ sign has been included in $A_I$, and this sign convention will be used from now on.)

Let us discuss briefly the implication of Eq. (3.69) dropping for the moment the subscript $I$. Here $\Delta = \delta + i\gamma$ and $A = a + ib$, where $a$ produces the phase shift and $b$ the absorption. For $b = 0$ we get the single channel case of Section III-11. The elastic scattering amplitude as a function of $\Delta$ can be expressed as in Eq. (3.27).

$$T = \frac{1}{\cot \Delta - i} = \frac{kA}{1 - ikA} = \frac{ka + ikb}{1 + kb - ika} \qquad (3.70)$$

From Eq. (3.12) the total elastic cross section is

$$\sigma_e = 4\pi\lambda^2 \, |T_e|^2 = 4\pi \frac{a^2 + b^2}{1 + 2kb + k^2(a^2 + b^2)} \qquad (3.71)$$

which goes to $4\pi |A|^2$ at zero energy, as expected. From Eq. (3.13) the reaction cross section is

$$\sigma_r = \pi\lambda^2(1 - \eta^2)$$

where

$$\eta = |e^{2i\Delta}| = \left| \frac{1 + i\tan\Delta}{1 - i\tan\Delta} \right| = \left| \frac{1 + ikA}{1 - ikA} \right|$$

$$\sigma_r = 4\pi\lambda \frac{b}{1 + 2kb + (a^2 + b^2)k^2} \qquad (3.72)$$

which goes like $1/k$ for $k \to 0$. For $b = 0$ the reaction cross section goes to zero, since $\eta = 1$ from the above expression for $\eta$. Therefore the parameter $b$ is directly related to the absorption in the scattering process, as it should be, since it is the imaginary part of the scattering length.

A generalization of Eqs. (3.71) and (3.72) has been made by Dalitz and Tuan[22] to take into account the $K^- - \bar{K}^0$ mass difference and Coulomb force effects. Finally, a complete new formulation of the theory through the use of the $K$ matrix has been made by Dalitz and Tuan[23,24] and by Ross and Shaw.[25,26] The latter is a very general formulation, where the use of a particular matrix ($\mathbf{M} \propto \mathbf{K}^{-1}$) allows departure from the zero-effective range approximation.

## 13. The Reaction Matrix Formalism

We will briefly recall the reaction matrix formulation of the multi-channel case; the reader can find details in refs. 23 and 24. Instead of the S matrix or **T** matrix a reaction matrix **K** is used, whose relations to **S** and **T** matrices are given in Eqs. (3.31) and (3.32).

$$\mathbf{S} = (1 + i\mathbf{K})(1 - i\mathbf{K})^{-1}$$

$$\mathbf{T}' = \mathbf{K}'(1 - ik\mathbf{K}')^{-1} \tag{3.73}$$

Notice that in Eq. (3.73) the notation is slightly different from ours. Dalitz and Tuan, in fact, define the diagonal elements of **T** as $\mathbf{T}' = e^{i\Delta} \sin \Delta/k$, which is Eq. (3.27) divided by $k$; consequently, the **K**′ matrix carries the same convention, i.e., it has the dimension of a [length]$^{-1}$ with $\hbar = c = 1$. For simplicity we follow the notation of Dalitz and Tuan in this section; the final conclusions are independent of the convention.

The method consists of writing the wave functions for all the channels in terms of a **K**′ matrix instead of a **T**′ matrix, as was done in Sections III-1 and III-2, and then using the method of *equivalent boundary conditions* for these wave functions. These particular boundary conditions turned out to be equivalent to a zero-effective range approximation. The whole treatment is done for $S$ wave only, both in the incoming channel and the outgoing ones. We will now outline the derivation of some expressions which can be used to fit the experimental data. Calling $K'_{11}$ the matrix element for the elastic scattering and $k_1$ the momentum for the same channel, for $S$ wave only, Eq. (3.8) can be written as:

$$r\psi_1{}^1 = (\sin k_1 r/k_1) - K'_{11} \cos k_1 r$$

for any inelastic channel $j$, we have

$$r\psi_j{}^1 = -K'_{j1} \cos k_j r$$

These functions satisfy the following boundary conditions at $r = 0$,

$$(r\psi_j{}^1)_0 = -K'_{j1} = -\sum_i K'_{ji}\delta_{1i} = -\sum_i K'_{ji} \left[\frac{d}{dr}(r\psi_i{}^1)\right]_0 \tag{3.74}$$

where $\delta_{1i}$ is the Kronecker symbol ($\delta_{1i} = 1$ for $i = 1$ *or* $\delta_{1i} = 0$ for $i \neq 1$). The boundary condition (3.74) is correct for any incident channel, i.e., also for any $i \neq 1$. Let us consider a two-channel case, labeled 1, 2 and with momenta $k$ and $q$. The elements of $\mathbf{K}'$ are

$$\begin{bmatrix} K'_{11} & K'_{12} \\ K_{21} & K'_{22} \end{bmatrix} = \begin{bmatrix} \alpha & \beta \\ \beta^\dagger & \gamma \end{bmatrix} \tag{3.75}$$

The $\mathbf{K}$ matrix is hermitian as seen in Section III-5, and if time reversal invariance is used, its elements are also real and $\beta^\dagger = \beta$. If we call $\chi_j$ and $\chi_j'$ the wave functions $(r\psi_j)$ and its first derivative respectively, dropping the superscript, Eq. (3.74) gives

$$(\chi_1)_0 = -\alpha(\chi_1')_0 - \beta(\chi_2')_0 \tag{3.76a}$$

$$(\chi_2)_0 = -\beta(\chi_1')_0 - \gamma(\chi_2')_0 \tag{3.76b}$$

For the incident wave in channel 1 we can also write the wave functions in terms of $\mathbf{T}'$ as

$$\chi_1 = + \sin kr/k + T'_{11} e^{ikr} \tag{3.77a}$$

$$\chi_2 = + T'_{21} e^{iqr} \tag{3.77b}$$

and from Eq. (3.77b) derive $\chi_2' = iq\chi_2$. Substituting this expression in Eq. (3.76) and eliminating $\chi_2$ we get a boundary condition for channel 1 alone

$$(\chi_1)_0 = A(\chi_1')_0 \tag{3.78}$$

where

$$A = -\alpha + i\beta q[1/(1 + i\gamma q)]\beta \tag{3.79}$$

Using Eq. (3.77a) for $\chi_1$, from Eq. (3.78) we get

$$T'_{11} = A/(1 - ikA) \tag{3.80}$$

which, with Eq. (3.27) divided by $k$ for $T'$, gives

$$k \cot \Delta = 1/A$$

This is nothing but the zero-effective range approximation Eq. (3.69); in fact $A$ is a slowly varying function of energy, if $\alpha$, $\beta$, $\gamma$ are taken to be constants. According to Eq. (3.79) $A$ can be written as

$$A = a + ib = \left( -\alpha + \frac{q^2 \beta^2 \gamma}{1 + q^2 \gamma^2} \right) + \frac{iq\beta^2}{1 + q^2 \gamma^2} \tag{3.81}$$

Notice that $b$ is always a positive quantity and for $\gamma \sim 0$, $a$ and $b$ can be taken to be constant if the energy dependence of $q$ is neglected. From Eqs. (3.76) through (3.78) we find $T'_{21}$. It is

$$T'_{21} = -[1/(1 + i\gamma q)]\beta[1/(1 - ikA)] = N/(1 - ikA) \tag{3.82}$$

For scattering in channel 2 a scattering length $B$ can be defined in the same way as $A$:

$$B = -\gamma + i\beta k[1/(1 + i\alpha k)]\beta = c + id \tag{3.83a}$$

and

$$T'_{12} = -[1/(1 + i\alpha k)]\beta[1/(1 - iq\beta)] \tag{3.83b}$$

We can now calculate the elastic cross section from Eq. (3.80) using Eq. (3.12)

$$\sigma_e = \frac{4\pi}{k^2}|T_e|^2 = 4\pi|T'_{11}|^2$$

$$= 4\pi\frac{a^2 + b^2}{1 + 2kb + k^2(a^2 + b^2)} \tag{3.84}$$

which is identical to Eq. (3.71). The reaction cross section can also be calculated. From Eq. (3.82) and the expression (3.81) for $b$, we have

$$|T'_{21}|^2 = \frac{\beta^2}{1 + \gamma^2 q^2}\frac{1}{|1 - ikA|^2} = \frac{b/q}{1 + 2kb + k^2(a^2 + b^2)} \tag{3.85}$$

From Eqs. (3.50) and (3.85) we can calculate $\sigma(1 \to 2)$; using the relation $T'_{21} = T_{21}/\sqrt{q}\sqrt{k}$ we have:

$$\sigma(1 \to 2) = \frac{4\pi}{k^2}|T_{21}|^2 = \frac{4\pi}{k}\left|\frac{T_{21}}{\sqrt{q}\sqrt{k}}\right|^2 q$$

$$= \frac{4\pi}{k}\frac{b}{1 + 2kb + k^2(a^2 + b^2)} \tag{3.86}$$

which is identical to Eq. (3.72), with $|T_{21}|^2 = (1 - \eta^2)/4$. If we express $T'_{21}$ as a function of $B = c + id$, from Eqs. (3.83) we have:

$$|T'_{21}|^2 = |T'_{12}|^2 = \frac{d/k}{1 + 2qd + q^2(c^2 + d^2)}$$

Therefore, for the cross section $\sigma(1 \to 2)$

$$\sigma(1 \to 2) = \frac{4\pi}{k^2}|T_{21}|^2 = \frac{4\pi}{k^2}\left|\frac{T_{21}}{\sqrt{q}\sqrt{k}}\right|^2 qk$$

$$= \frac{4\pi}{k^2}\frac{qd}{1 + 2qd + q^2(c^2 + d^2)} \tag{3.87}$$

This expression will be used to study the reaction $K^-p \to \Lambda\eta$ in Section VI-7.

The two-channel $\mathbf{K}'$ matrix (3.75) can be extended to many outgoing channels grouped in submatrices

$$\begin{bmatrix} K'_{11} & (K'_{12} & K'_{13} & \cdots) \\ \begin{bmatrix} K'_{21} \\ K'_{31} \\ \vdots \end{bmatrix} & \begin{bmatrix} K'_{22} & K'_{23} & \cdots \\ K'_{32} & K'_{33} \\ \vdots & \vdots \end{bmatrix} \end{bmatrix} = \begin{bmatrix} \alpha_1 & \beta_1 \\ \beta_1{}^\dagger & \gamma_1 \end{bmatrix} \tag{3.88}$$

where $\beta_1{}^\dagger$ (or in general $\beta_i{}^\dagger$) is the Hermitian conjugate of $\beta_1$ $(\beta_i)$ (equal to its transpose if time reversal holds) and includes all the elements of $\mathbf{K}'$ which describe transitions from the initial state 1 $(i)$ to all the other channels. The element $\gamma_i$ consists of all the elements of $\mathbf{K}'$ which describe transitions between the channels $f$. These matrices are related to the scattering length $A_i$ by a generalization of Eq. (3.79)

$$A_i = a_i + ib_i = -\alpha_i + i\beta_i(1 + iq_f\gamma_i)^{-1}q_f\beta_i{}^\dagger \tag{3.89}$$

and for $T'_{fi}$ we have

$$T'_{fi} = -\beta_i(1 + \gamma_i q_f)^{-1}[1/(1 - ik_iA_i)] \tag{3.90}$$

which is a generalization of Eq. (3.82). Here $q_f$ does not have the simple meaning of the two channel case. We will see an application of this more general matrix in the $I$ spin $= 1$ part of the scattering amplitude for reactions (3.68); in fact, in that case, both $\Lambda\pi$ and $\Sigma\pi$ final states contribute to the scattering amplitude.

## 14. Multichannel Effective Range Theory

In the previous section, the $\mathbf{K}'$ matrix elements $\alpha$, $\beta$, and $\gamma$ were considered energy independent in the sense that no explicit form of their energy dependence was given.

Ross and Shaw[25,26] have developed an effective range theory for systems of many coupled two-body channels, which considers an explicit energy dependence for the $\mathbf{K}$ matrix elements. This formalism can be extended to any angular momentum $l$, its range of validity in this case being smaller than in the $l = 0$ case, but for small $l$ it is still a very useful approximation. The formalism, its validity, and its applicability are extensively discussed in ref. 26; we will only report here the relevant formulas used for fitting some experimental data (Sects. V-4 and VI-4).

The scattering matrix $\mathbf{T}$ is defined in such a way that the diagonal elements are

$$T_{ii} = (e^{2i\Delta_i} - 1)/2i$$

in agreement with our convention (3.27). The relation between the **T** and **K** matrix is then

$$\mathbf{T} = \mathbf{K}(1 - i\mathbf{K})^{-1}$$

as in Eq. (3.32). The partial cross sections from channel $i$ to channel $j$ is given by

$$\sigma_{ij} = 4\pi\lambda_i^2 \frac{2J_j + 1}{2S_i + 1} |T_{ij}|^2 \tag{3.91}$$

where $J_j$ is the total spin of the final state and $S_i$ is the intrinsic spin of the initial state. All these relations apply to each single partial wave.

The authors show that by choosing a particular parameterization of the cross sections (specifically the matrix **M**) and a particular wave function ($\psi^M$), they can define in a simple manner the effective range expansion of the matrix **M**. They define

$$\mathbf{M} = \mathbf{k}^{l+\frac{1}{2}}\mathbf{K}^{-1}\mathbf{k}^{l+\frac{1}{2}} \tag{3.92}$$

where $\mathbf{k}^{l+\frac{1}{2}}$ is a diagonal matrix having elements $k_j^{l_j+\frac{1}{2}}$, the c.m. momentum of the $j$th channel to the $l_j + \frac{1}{2}$ power, $l_j$ being the orbital angular momentum of channel $j$.

The relation between **T** and **M** is:

$$\mathbf{T} = \mathbf{k}^{l+\frac{1}{2}}(\mathbf{M} - i\mathbf{k}^{2l+1})^{-1}\mathbf{k}^{l+\frac{1}{2}} \tag{3.93}$$

Below threshold we have $k \to +i|\kappa|$, so $-ik = +\kappa$. Notice that from Eq. (3.92) it follows that **M** is real and symmetric at all energies since **K** has these properties. For only one channel **M** turns out to be

$$\mathbf{M} = k^{2l+1} \cot \delta_l$$

which is Eqs. (3.92) and (3.33) combined. According to this effective range theory **M** has the following energy dependence near any energy $E_0$ (which does not have to necessarily be a threshold):

$$\mathbf{M}(E) = \mathbf{M}(E_0) + \frac{1}{2}\mathbf{R}(\mathbf{k}^2 - \mathbf{k}_0^2) \tag{3.94}$$

where $\mathbf{k}_0$ is the momentum corresponding to the energy $E_0$ and **R** is a real, energy-independent matrix. It turns out that **R** is an approximately diagonal matrix, the off-diagonal terms being the difference of two very similar integrals and therefore very close to zero. The diagonal terms $R_{ii}$ are a measure of the range of the forces in the $i$th channel. Since the $R_{ij}$ are $\sim 0$, the off-diagonal terms of **M** are constant.

Let us now write explicit expressions for a two-channel problem with $l = 0$. From Eq. (3.93), performing the inversion of the matrix $\mathbf{M} - i\mathbf{k}$, the $\mathbf{T}$ matrix will be:

$$\mathbf{T} \equiv \frac{\sqrt{k_i}\sqrt{k_j}}{D(s)} \begin{pmatrix} M_{22} - ik_2 & -M_{12} \\ -M_{12} & M_{11} - ik_1 \end{pmatrix}$$

where $D(s)$ is the determinant of the matrix $(\mathbf{M} - i\mathbf{k})$

$$D(s) = \|\mathbf{M} - i\mathbf{k}\| = (M_{11} - ik_1)(M_{22} - ik_2) - M_{12}^2$$

The scattering amplitudes can now be written as

$$\begin{aligned} T_{11} &= k_1(M_{22} - ik_2)D^{-1} \\ T_{12} &= T_{21} = -(k_1k_2)^{\frac{1}{2}}M_{12}D^{-1} \\ T_{22} &= k_2(M_{11} - ik_1)D^{-1} \end{aligned} \qquad (3.95)$$

Using Eq. (3.91), we can calculate the cross sections $\sigma_{11}$ and $\sigma_{12}$ as a function of $M_{22}$, $M_{12}$, and $M_{11}$ which are three parameters in the case of zero-effective range and five parameters if the expansion (3.94) is used.

For the reader who is more familiar with scattering length parameters, we report the relation between $\mathbf{M}_{ij}$ and $a$ and $b$. From Eq. (3.70) $T_{11}$ can be written as a function of $A_1$ (scattering length for channel 1) as

$$T_{11} = \frac{k_1}{\dfrac{1}{A_1} - ik_1} \qquad \text{with} \qquad A_1 = a_1 + ib_1$$

Dividing numerator and denominator of $T_{11}$ in Eq. (3.95) by $(M_{22} - ik_2)$ we get

$$T_{11} = \frac{k_1}{M_{11} - \dfrac{M_{12}^2}{M_{22} - ik_2} - ik_1}$$

Comparing the two expressions for $T_{11}$ we see that

$$\frac{1}{A_1} = M_{11} = \frac{M_{12}^2}{M_{22} - ik_2} \qquad \text{or} \qquad A_1 = -\frac{M_{22} - ik_2}{M_{12}^2} \qquad (3.96)$$

which implies

$$\begin{aligned} a_1 &= [M_{11}(M_{12}^2 - k_2{}^2) - M_{12}^2 M_{22}]/d \\ b_1 &= k_2 M_{12}^2/d \end{aligned}$$

where

$$d = (M_{11}M_{22} - M_{12}^2)^2 + k_2{}^2 M_{11}^2$$

In the case of $K^-p$ interactions various corrections have to be taken into account, like the electromagnetic mass splitting of $K^-$ and $\bar{K}^0$ for reactions (3.68a) and (3.68b) and coulomb scattering. These effects are included in ref. 26.

Notice that Eqs. (3.92) to (3.94) define the energy dependence of the $\mathbf{K}'$ matrix elements $\alpha$, $\beta$, and $\gamma$ of Eq. (3.75), so that Eqs. (3.80) and (3.95) are equivalent, once $A$ is expressed as a function of the $\mathbf{M}$ matrix.

## 15. Threshold Behavior and Resonances

Up to now we have not specified the energy $E_0$ about which the effective range expansion has been made. The $\mathbf{K}$ matrix formalism, as stated in Section III-5, is useful to represent the scattering in energy regions where a threshold for the opening of a new channel is present. This formalism has been used to fit the experimental data of very low energy $K^-p$ interactions. The $K^-p$ elastic scattering has its threshold at $E_0 = M_K + M_p$, but below this threshold other channels are open, i.e., $\Lambda\pi$ and $\Sigma\pi$, which cannot be directly studied below $E_0$. The formalism has also been used in a different situation, such as at threshold for $\pi p \to \eta n$ or $Kp \to \eta\Lambda$, where the elastic channel can be studied in both regions below and above threshold. The details of these reactions will be studied in Sections V-4 and VI-7.

The use of the $\mathbf{K}$ matrix formalism removes the singularity of the $\mathbf{S}$ matrix at the threshold energy $E_t$, but at the same time allows detection of the poles of the $\mathbf{S}$ matrix (or $\mathbf{T}$ matrix). From Eq. (3.80) a pole in the $K^-p$ scattering occurs at the energy where:

$$1 - ikA = 0 \tag{3.98}$$

Substituting Eq. (3.79) in Eq. (3.98) we obtain:

$$[1 + ik\alpha(E)][1 + i\gamma(E)q(E)] - q(E)k(E)\beta^2(E) = 0 \tag{3.99}$$

where $\alpha$, $\beta$, and $\gamma$ are the $\mathbf{K}$ matrix elements, functions of $E$. If only $S$ waves are considered,

$$\mathbf{K}'^{-1}(E) = \mathbf{K}'^{-1}(E_0) + \tfrac{1}{2}\mathbf{R}(\mathbf{k}^2 - \mathbf{k}_0^2) \tag{3.100}$$

which follows from Eq. (3.94). ($\mathbf{K}^{-1} \equiv \mathbf{M}$ in the notation of ref. 24).

With the assumptions of zero-effective range and $\gamma = 0$ we can find the position of the pole (therefore the resonance parameters) as a function of the constant scattering length $A = a + ib$ of Eq. (3.81). The pole is at

$$1 - ik_R(a + ib) = 1 + k_R b - ik_R a = 0 \tag{3.101}$$

If we call the complex energy at which this pole occurs $E_R$

$$E_R = M_R - i(\Gamma/2)$$

and use the relation $E_R = M_1 + M_2 + (k_R^2/2\mu)$ with $\mu$ the reduced mass of the system of particles 1 and 2, it follows from Eq. (3.101)[27] that

$$M_R = (M_1 + M_2)\left[1 - \frac{1}{2M_1M_2}\frac{a^2 - b^2}{(a^2 + b^2)^2}\right] \qquad (3.102a)$$

$$\Gamma = -\frac{M_1 + M_2}{M_1M_2}\frac{2ab}{(a^2 + b^2)^2} \qquad (3.102b)$$

This pole corresponds to a resonance if $\Gamma$ is positive, i.e., if $a$ is negative, since $b$ is always positive according to Eq. (3.81). It will be below the threshold energy $E_t = M_1 + M_2$ if $|a| > b$. This is the case for the $I$ spin $= 0$ scattering length parameters in the $K^- p$ system [corresponding to the resonance $\Lambda(1405)$ which will be discussed in Sect. VI-4]. As we will see, it is relatively easy to measure $|a|$ and $b$, but it is not possible to measure the sign of $a$, unless more than one amplitude is present so that the sign can be obtained through the study of the interference term. For $K^- p$ interactions at low energy the $I = 0$ and $I = 1$ amplitudes supply this information, since in the $\Sigma^+\pi^-$ and $\Sigma^-\pi^+$ they appear with different signs.

If Eqs. (3.102) represent a pole below threshold, it can also be found by looking for the poles of the *reduced* **K** *matrix*, which has only the terms related to the open channels below threshold. For $E < M_1 + M_2$ only one channel is open for the $K^- p$ system in the $I = 0$ state. The reduced **K** matrix, from Eq. (3.83) is $K_R = B$, i.e.,

$$K_R = -\gamma - \beta|k|\frac{1}{1 - \alpha|k|}\beta \qquad (3.103)$$

where $\gamma$ can be considered as background scattering to the resonant amplitude, represented by the second term. If we assume $\gamma \sim 0$, a pole is found at

$$1 - \alpha|k| = 0$$

From Eq. (3.81), for $\gamma \sim 0$, $\alpha = -a$ and using as before $E_R = M_1 + M_2 + (k^2/2\mu)$, we get

$$M_R = M_1 + M_2\left(1 - \frac{1}{2M_1M_2}\frac{1}{a^2}\right)$$

which is Eq. (3.102a) if $b \sim 0$ or small compared with $a$.

If we use the more general formulation of the **T** matrix in terms of the **M** matrix [Eq. (3.93)], it is clear that the poles are the zeroes of the matrix $\mathbf{M} - i\mathbf{k}^{2l+1}$, so the position of the resonances will be obtained by solving

$$\|\mathbf{M} - i\mathbf{k}^{2l+1}\| = 0 \tag{3.104}$$

For the specific case of only two channels open above a certain threshold $E_0$ and $l = 0$, it is clear from Eq. (3.95) that this condition becomes:

$$D(s) = (M_{11} - ik_1)(M_{22} - ik_2) - M_{12}{}^2 = 0 \tag{3.105}$$

This is a pole of the complete **K** matrix and will be called a pole of type (b) in the next section. In this case the pole can be below threshold or above threshold, but always in the range of validity of the effective range approximation. This pole is not different from a Breit-Wigner type of resonance, as proved by the analysis of the experimental data of the $S_{11}$ resonance of the $\pi p$ system,[28] which will be discussed in Section V-4 and of the $\Sigma(1385)$ which will be discussed in Section VI-4.

## 16. Particles as Poles of the S Matrix

From the point of view of **S** matrix theory, a stable particle (stable with respect to strong interactions) or a resonance can be identified with a pole of the **S** matrix. The position of the pole in the different sheets of the Riemann surface of the **S** or **T** matrix determines the behavior of the amplitude in the physical region, the only region accessible to experiments. Many authors have discussed this point. We refer the reader to the article by Chew.[29]

1. If the pole is on the physical sheet of the Riemann surface, it can only occur on the real axis below the lowest threshold and it represents a stable particle (like the deuteron, the $\Omega^-$, etc.).

2. The pole can also be in an unphysical sheet. If it lies at a complex point in the energy plane, very close to and just below the real axis, it will generate an amplitude in the physical region which has the familiar shape of a Breit-Wigner resonance Eq. (3.44). This kind of pole is the most familiar one and its position is sketched in Figure 14 for $\Lambda(1520)$. Fitting the data with a Breit-Wigner formula corresponds to an extrapolation from the physical region to the unphysical sheet pole. The statement that the presence of a resonance corresponds to a phase shift of 90° in the physical region is associated with the fact that the parameterization we use to extrapolate to the unphysical region, the Breit-

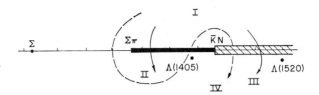

Fig. 14. Riemann surface of the $T$ matrix in the energy plane. The four possible sheets of $T(s)$ around the $KN$ threshold are shown. The arrows indicate how to reach the various sheets from the physical region. The nomenclature used for poles in the various sheets is as follows: *1.* a pole along the real axis is a "stable particle," *2.* a pole in sheet II below the $\overline{K}N$ threshold is a "virtual bound state," *3.* a pole in sheet III is a "Breit-Wigner resonance," *4.* a pole in sheet IV is a "virtual state."

Wigner amplitude, goes through 90° at the energy equal to the real part of the pole position. A pole or resonance found through $D(s) = 0$ as in Eq. (3.105) is not always associated with a phase going through 90°.

3. Special attention is required in the case in which a pole is close to a threshold for the opening of a new channel. In this case the **K** matrix formalism is used to remove the singularity of the threshold branch point, as we have seen in the previous sections. In the case of $\Lambda(1405)$ (see Sects. III-15 and VI-4), the pole lies just below threshold for $K^-N$ scattering and not far from the physical sheet and it can be found as a pole of the reduced **K** matrix which includes only the open channels. This pole has been called by Dalitz[24] a "virtual bound state." Its position is shown in Figure 14. More generally, the position of the pole may be in different sheets of the Riemann surface and it appears as a round shaped peak in the cross section for a "virtual bound state" or as a cusp for a "virtual state" depending on how far it is from the physical sheet. Fraser and Hendry,[30] among others, have studied the problem of poles close to thresholds and we refer the reader to their paper. Figure 15, reproduced from their paper, shows cusps and round-shaped peaks produced by four particular choices of the position of the pole.

A similar situation occurs when one of the two particles in the final state is an unstable particle. In this case the threshold branch point is not on the real axis, but at a complex point below it. We still have the two cases mentioned above—resonancelike peak or cusp, but the cusp in this case has been named "woolly cusp."

The point of view expressed by the authors of refs. 29 and 30 is that any effect around a threshold is always due to the presence of a pole in

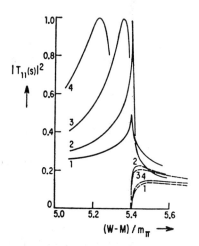

Fig. 15. Four different shapes of the elastic amplitude $|T_{11}|^2$ (solid line) near the inelastic threshold $\pi N \to N\eta$, for four different positions of the pole according to Eqs. (3.95). The parameters used are the following: $M_{11} = 10.0$, $M_{22} + \kappa_2 = 1.0$ ($k_2 = i\kappa_2$), and $\kappa_2 = -0.7$, $-0.1$, $0.5$, $1.0$ for curves $1$, $2$, $3$, and $4$, respectively. The dashed lines show the corresponding behavior of the inelastic amplitude $|T_{12}|^2$. Plot taken from Fraser and Hendry.[30]

the nearby region. Any threshold effect not produced by a pole is usually too weak to be observable.

In summary, this point of view is that any pole of the S matrix must be considered a bona fide resonance. Usually a large amount of experimental data is required in order to study the nature of a bump or anomaly in cross sections and to find the position of the pole, if a pole is at the origin of the bump or anomaly. Once the position of the pole has been identified, however, it has to be considered a particle, regardless of whether it appears on a physical sheet or off, its position being determined by the strength of the potential which produces the state.

So far, the only identified pole which lies far from the physical sheet is the pole in the singlet $np$ spin state. The triplet state, as seen in Section III-11, has a pole in the physical sheet which corresponds to the deuteron. The singlet $np$ state shows a large cusp at threshold which is produced by a pole in the unphysical sheet far from the physical sheet, called a "virtual-state pole" by Frazer and Hendry.[30] (See Sect. III-11 for the value of the scattering length corresponding to this state.) This virtual state has not been listed in Tables I and II, and the deuteron is also missing since two baryon states are not presently included in the tables. As more experimental data are collected, perhaps more of these virtual states will appear and it will be necessary to list them too.

## 17. Analysis of Experimental Data for the Scattering ($\frac{1}{2}^+0^- \to \frac{1}{2}^+0^-$)

In Section III-9 we have seen that a resonant state contributes to the total (or elastic) cross section with the product of a spin-dependent factor and the imaginary part of the amplitude at $0°$ (or the squared amplitude). This measurement alone at the resonant energy gives us the product $(J + \frac{1}{2})x_e$ [or $(J + \frac{1}{2})x_e^2$]. The study of differential cross sections is therefore necessary to find the quantum numbers of a resonance and to understand the detailed nature of a bump seen in a cross section measurement.

The scattering of a meson from a spin $\frac{1}{2}$ unpolarized target is described by Eqs. (3.21) and (3.23), which relate the measured $I_0$ and $I_0 P_0$ and the scattering amplitudes in the various partial waves. At each incident energy one can write the differential cross section and polarization in terms of the $T_{l^\pm}$ (3.24) and, if the number of data points is larger than the number of unknown quantities ($\eta_{l^\pm}$, $\delta_{l^\pm}$), one should be able to find a good fit to the data and a unique set of parameters. By performing the analysis at different energies, it should be possible to determine the energy dependence of the amplitudes $T_{l^\pm}$, and therefore isolate the ones which have a resonant behavior. In practice the situation is much more complicated.

To analyze the experimental data it is more convenient to express Eq. (3.21) as follows:

$$I_0 = \lambda^2 \sum_i A_i P_i$$

$$I_0 P_0 = \mathbf{n}\lambda^2 \sum_i B_i P_i^1$$

(3.106)

where $P_i$ are Legendre polynomials and $P_i^1$ are the first associated Legendre functions. The coefficients $A_i$ and $B_i$ now contain the scattering amplitudes squared or the products of amplitudes. Each partial wave has two possible spin states and, from now on, to identify each $J^P$ state we will use the notation $S, P, D, \ldots, H$ for $l = 0, 1, 2, \ldots, 5$ and the subscript $2J$. The expressions for $A_i$ and $B_i$ as functions of the various amplitudes through $J = \frac{9}{2}$ are given in Tables V and VI.[10] For the reader's convenience, in Table VII we list $P_i$ and $P_i^1$ up to $i = 9$. Let us now point out a few of the problems which arise in analyzing the data.

TABLE V

Coefficients of the Legendre Polynomials Expansion of the Differential Cross Section $I_0 = \lambda^2 \sum_i A_i P_i(\cos \theta)$

|  | $A_0$ | $A_1$ | $A_2$ | $A_3$ | $A_4$ | $A_5$ | $A_6$ | $A_7$ | $A_8$ | $A_9$ |
|---|---|---|---|---|---|---|---|---|---|---|
| $S_1S_1 + P_1P_1$ | 1.000 |  |  |  |  |  |  |  |  |  |
| $S_1P_1$ |  | 2.000 |  |  |  |  |  |  |  |  |
| $S_1P_3 + P_1D_3$ |  | 4.000 |  |  |  |  |  |  |  |  |
| $S_1D_3 + P_1P_3$ |  |  | 4.000 |  |  |  |  |  |  |  |
| $S_1D_5 + P_1F_5$ |  |  | 6.000 |  |  |  |  |  |  |  |
| $S_1F_5 + P_1D_5$ |  |  |  | 6.000 |  |  |  |  |  |  |
| $S_1F_7 + P_1G_7$ |  |  |  | 8.000 |  |  |  |  |  |  |
| $S_1G_7 + P_1F_7$ |  |  |  |  | 8.000 |  |  |  |  |  |
| $S_1G_9 + P_1H_9$ |  |  |  |  | 10.000 |  |  |  |  |  |
| $S_1H_9 + P_1G_9$ |  |  |  |  |  | 10.000 |  |  |  |  |
| $P_3P_3 + D_3D_3$ | 2.000 |  | 2.000 |  |  |  |  |  |  |  |
| $P_3D_3$ |  | 0.800 |  | 7.200 |  |  |  |  |  |  |
| $P_3D_5 + D_3F_5$ |  | 7.200 |  | 4.800 |  |  |  |  |  |  |
| $P_3F_5 + D_3D_5$ |  |  | 1.714 |  | 10.286 |  |  |  |  |  |
| $P_3F_7 + D_3G_7$ |  |  | 10.286 |  | 5.714 |  |  |  |  |  |
| $P_3G_7 + D_3F_7$ |  |  |  | 2.667 |  | 13.333 |  |  |  |  |
| $P_3G_9 + D_3H_9$ |  |  |  | 13.333 |  | 6.667 |  |  |  |  |
| $P_3H_9 + D_3G_9$ |  |  |  |  | 3.636 |  | 16.364 |  |  |  |
| $D_5D_5 + F_5F_5$ | 3.000 |  | 3.429 |  | 2.571 |  |  |  |  |  |
| $D_5F_5$ |  | 0.515 |  | 3.200 |  | 14.286 |  |  |  |  |
| $D_5F_7 + F_5G_7$ |  | 10.286 |  | 8.000 |  | 5.714 |  |  |  |  |
| $D_5G_7 + F_5F_7$ |  |  | 1.143 |  | 4.675 |  | 18.182 |  |  |  |
| $D_5G_9 + F_5H_9$ |  |  | 14.286 |  | 9.351 |  | 6.364 |  |  |  |
| $D_5H_9 + F_5G_9$ |  |  |  | 1.818 |  | 6.154 |  | 22.028 |  |  |
| $F_7F_7 + G_7G_7$ | 4.000 |  | 4.762 |  | 4.208 |  | 3.030 |  |  |  |
| $F_7G_7$ |  | 0.381 |  | 2.182 |  | 6.593 |  | 22.844 |  |  |
| $F_7G_9 + G_7H_9$ |  | 13.333 |  | 10.909 |  | 9.231 |  | 6.527 |  |  |
| $F_7H_9 + G_7G_9$ |  |  | 0.866 |  | 3.237 |  | 8.485 |  | 27.413 |  |
| $G_9G_9 + H_9H_9$ | 5.000 |  | 6.061 |  | 5.664 |  | 4.848 |  | 3.427 |  |
| $G_9H_9$ |  | 0.303 |  | 1.678 |  | 4.615 |  | 10.750 |  | 32.653 |

$$S_1P_3 + P_1D_3 = \mathrm{Re}(S_1{}^*P_3 + P_1{}^*D_3)$$

TABLE VI

Coefficients of the Expansion of the Polarization in First Associated Legendre Functions $I_0 P_0 = \mathbf{n}\lambda^2 \sum_i B_i P_i^1(\cos\theta)$

|  | $B_1$ | $B_2$ | $B_3$ | $B_4$ | $B_5$ | $B_6$ | $B_7$ | $B_8$ | $B_9$ |
|---|---|---|---|---|---|---|---|---|---|
| $S_1P_1$ | 2.000 | | | | | | | | |
| $S_1P_3 - P_1D_3$ | $-2.000$ | | | | | | | | |
| $S_1D_3 - P_1P_3$ | | 2.000 | | | | | | | |
| $S_1D_5 - P_1F_5$ | | $-2.000$ | | | | | | | |
| $S_1F_5 - P_1D_5$ | | | 2.000 | | | | | | |
| $S_1F_7 - P_1G_7$ | | | $-2.000$ | | | | | | |
| $S_1G_7 - P_1F_7$ | | | | 2.000 | | | | | |
| $S_1G_9 - P_1H_9$ | | | | $-2.000$ | | | | | |
| $S_1H_9 - P_1G_9$ | | | | | 2.000 | | | | |
| $P_3D_3$ | 1.600 | | 2.400 | | | | | | |
| $P_3D_5 - D_3F_5$ | $-3.600$ | | $-0.400$ | | | | | | |
| $P_3F_5 - D_3D_5$ | | 1.429 | | 2.571 | | | | | |
| $P_3F_7 - D_3G_7$ | | $-3.429$ | | $-0.571$ | | | | | |
| $P_3G_7 - D_3F_7$ | | | 1.333 | | 2.667 | | | | |
| $P_3G_9 - D_3H_9$ | | | $-3.333$ | | $-0.667$ | | | | |
| $P_3H_9 - D_3G_9$ | | | | 1.273 | | 2.727 | | | |
| $D_5F_5$ | 1.543 | | 1.600 | | 2.857 | | | | |
| $D_5F_7 - F_5G_7$ | $-5.143$ | | $-0.667$ | | $-0.190$ | | | | |
| $D_5G_7 - F_5F_7$ | | 1.333 | | 1.636 | | 3.030 | | | |
| $D_5G_9 - F_5H_9$ | | $-4.762$ | | $-0.935$ | | $-0.303$ | | | |
| $D_5H_9 - F_5G_9$ | | | 1.212 | | 1.614 | | 3.147 | | |
| $F_7G_7$ | 1.524 | | 1.455 | | 1.758 | | 3.263 | | |
| $F_7G_9 - G_7H_9$ | $-6.667$ | | $-0.909$ | | $-0.308$ | | $-0.117$ | | |
| $F_7H_9 - G_7G_9$ | | 1.299 | | 1.457 | | 1.818 | | 3.427 | |
| $G_9H_9$ | 1.515 | | 1.399 | | 1.538 | | 1.920 | | 3.628 |

$$S_1P_3 - P_1D_3 = \mathrm{Im}\,(S_1{}^*P_3 - P_1{}^*D_3)$$

TABLE VII

Legendre Polynomials and First Associated Legendre Functions

$$P_l(x) = \frac{1}{2^l l!}\frac{d^l}{dx^l}(x^2-1)^l \qquad P_l^m(x) = (1-x^2)^{|m|/2}\frac{d^{|m|}P_l}{dx^{|m|}}$$

$$\int_{-1}^{+1} P_l^2(x)dx = \frac{2}{2l+1} \qquad \int_{-1}^{+1}(P_l^m)^2dx = \frac{(l+|m|)!}{(l-|m|)!}\frac{2}{2l+1}$$

$P_0 = 1$

$P_1 = x$

$P_2 = \frac{1}{2}(3x^2 - 1)$

$P_3 = \frac{1}{2}(5x^3 - 3x)$

$P_4 = \frac{1}{8}(35x^4 - 30x^2 + 3)$

$P_5 = \frac{1}{8}(63x^5 - 70x^3 + 15x)$

$P_6 = \frac{1}{16}(231x^6 - 315x^4 + 105x^2 - 5)$

$P_7 = \frac{1}{16}(429x^7 - 693x^5 + 315x^3 - 35x)$

$P_8 = \frac{1}{128}(6435x^8 - 12012x^6 + 6930x^4 - 1260x^2 + 35)$

$P_9 = \frac{1}{128}(12155x^9 - 25740x^7 + 18018x^5 - 4620x^3 + 315x)$

$P_0^1 = 0$

$P_1^1 = \sqrt{1-x^2}$

$P_2^1 = 3\sqrt{1-x^2}\,x$

$P_3^1 = \frac{3}{2}\sqrt{1-x^2}\,(5x^2 - 1)$

$P_4^1 = \frac{5}{2}\sqrt{1-x^2}\,(7x^3 - 3x)$

$P_5^1 = \frac{15}{8}\sqrt{1-x^2}\,(21x^4 - 14x^2 + 1)$

$P_6^1 = \frac{21}{8}\sqrt{1-x^2}\,(33x^5 - 30x^3 + 5x)$

$P_7^1 = \frac{7}{16}\sqrt{1-x^2}\,(429x^6 - 495x^4 + 135x^2 - 5)$

$P_8^1 = \frac{9}{16}\sqrt{1-x^2}\,(715x^7 - 1001x^5 + 385x^3 - 35x)$

$P_9^1 = \frac{15}{128}\sqrt{1-x^2}\,(7293x^8 - 12012x^6 + 6006x^4 - 924x^2 + 21)$

*1.* First of all, we do not know at what point we have to stop the summation in Eq. (3.106). As a first approximation, angular momentum states with $l > kr$ ($r$ of the order of 1 fermi = $(197\ \text{MeV}/c)^{-1}$) can be neglected, as seen in Section III-10, but this condition is not very restrictive. Notice that from Eqs. (3.21) and (3.23) it follows that the maximum $i$ in Eq. (3.106) is $i = 2l_{max}$.

*2.* For scattering of a 0 spin particle on a spin $\frac{1}{2}$ target, the Minami ambiguity is present.[31] From the coefficients of Tables V and VI one sees that under interchange of parity for the same $J$, e.g., $S_1 \to P_1$, $I_0$ remains invariant while $I_0P_0$ changes sign. This means that measurement of angular distributions alone cannot determine the parity of the states present in the scattering.

*3.* Even if the polarization is measured the solution is still not unique, since the operation of "complex conjugation" on all amplitudes will also leave $I$ unchanged and change the sign of $IP$. Thus a further dynamical argument must be used to determine the angular momentum states. In the case of a resonance this is the Wigner condition, which requires the amplitude to move across the complex plane counter clockwise.

In practice, solving Eqs. (3.106) for phase shifts and absorption parameters requires a large amount of experimental data. Since the relations between $I$ and $IP$ and $\eta_{2J}$, $\delta_{2J}$ are so complex and the above-mentioned ambiguities are present, it is difficult to find a unique set of phase shifts and absorption parameters without the introduction of some hypotheses of another nature or some theoretical predictions. For example, at low energy it is possible to use the effective range formalism of Sections III-12 to III-14 which predicts a particular energy dependence for the amplitudes; furthermore, the $T_{l^{\pm}}$ which seem to resonate can be directly expressed as Breit-Wigner amplitudes. All these assumptions on the energy dependence of the amplitudes reduce the number of parameters and simplify the problem, although the results of the analyses are model dependent. In Sections V and VI we will see the different approaches used in the actual fitting of the experimental data.

*18. Study of Resonances Decaying into Baryons with $J > \frac{1}{2}$*

At higher energies it becomes more difficult to determine the quantum numbers of baryon resonances. The number of background amplitudes increases and the spins of the resonances tend to be large. Both facts require larger statistics in angular distributions and polarizations, since it will be necessary to determine a larger number of coefficients in the expansion (3.106) of $I$ and $IP$ in Legendre polynomials. On the other hand, a resonance with large mass has new channels open; specifically, it can decay into a lower mass resonance whose $J^P$ is known. The following processes of this type have been observed:

$$K^-p \to \Sigma(1765) \to \Lambda(1520) + \pi$$
$$K^-p \to \Lambda(1820) \to \Sigma(1385) + \pi$$

where both $\Lambda(1520)$ and $\Sigma(1385)$ have $J = \frac{3}{2}$. These decays can be used to determine the spin and parity of the higher mass resonances.

As pointed out in the previous section for decay of a state of given $J^P$ into a baryon with $J^P = \frac{1}{2}^+$ and a pseudoscaler meson, the identification of the parity state requires the measurement of the polarization because the Minami ambiguity does not permit us to determine the parity from angular distribution alone. We can easily prove this by calculating the expected angular distribution for opposite parity states using Tables V and VII, assuming that only the resonant amplitude is present. Let us calculate $I(\theta)$ for $J = \frac{3}{2}^-$

$$I(\theta) = \lambda^2 |D_3|^2 (2P_0 + 2P_2) = \lambda^2 |D_3|^2 (1 + 3 \cos^2 \theta)$$

We get the same expression for $J = \frac{3}{2}^+$ with $|P_3|^2$ instead of $|D_3|^2$. Figure 16a shows the expected angular distributions for $J = \frac{3}{2}$ and $\frac{5}{2}$. In Table VIII we report the angular dependence for various $J^P$ states.

Let us now consider the case of a resonance of a certain $J^P$ decaying into another resonance of lower $J^P$. As an example we take $\Sigma(1765) \rightarrow \Lambda(1520) + \pi$, i.e., $\frac{5}{2}^- \rightarrow \frac{3}{2}^- 0^-$. This decay can take place via $P$ or $F$ waves. If the $F$ wave is neglected, for example on the basis of its higher centrifugal barrier, the expected angular distribution for this decay can be calculated. Taking the axis of quantization along the direction of the incident $K^-$, we can write the final wave function $\mathscr{Y}_{\frac{5}{2}}^{\frac{1}{2}}$ in terms of the

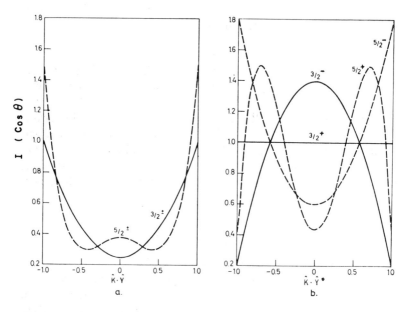

FIG. 16. (a) Angular distribution of a resonance of indicated $J^P$ decaying into spin $\frac{1}{2}$ and spin 0 particles. (b) Angular distributions for a resonance of the same $J^P$ decaying into another resonance of spin $\frac{3}{2}^-$ and a $0^-$ meson.

TABLE VIII

Meson Angular Distribution for Decay of a Resonance in a State $J^P$ into a Baryon in a State $\frac{1}{2}^+$, $\frac{3}{2}^+$, or $\frac{3}{2}^-$

| Decay | $J^P$ | $I(\theta)$ |
|---|---|---|
| $J^P \to \frac{1}{2}^+ 0^-$ | $\frac{1}{2}^\pm$ | $1$ |
| | $\frac{3}{2}^\pm$ | $1 + 3\cos^2\theta$ |
| | $\frac{5}{2}^\pm$ | $1 - 2\cos^2\theta + 5\cos^4\theta$ |
| | $\frac{7}{2}^\pm$ | $9 + 45\cos^2\theta - 165\cos^4\theta + 175\cos^6\theta$ |
| $J^P \to \frac{3}{2}^+ 0^-$ | $\frac{3}{2}^+$ | $7 - 6\cos^2\theta$ |
| | $\frac{3}{2}^-$ | $1$ |
| | $\frac{5}{2}^+$ | $1 + 2\cos^2\theta$ |
| | $\frac{5}{2}^-$ | $1 + 10\cos^2\theta - 10\cos^4\theta$ |
| | $\frac{7}{2}^+$ | $21 - 120\cos^2\theta + 465\cos^4\theta - 350\cos^6\theta$ |
| | $\frac{7}{2}^-$ | $13 - 10\cos^2\theta + 45\cos^4\theta$ |
| $J^P \to \frac{3}{2}^- 0^-$ | $\frac{3}{2}^+$ | $1$ |
| | $\frac{3}{2}^-$ | $7 - 6\cos^2\theta$ |
| | $\frac{5}{2}^+$ | $1 + 10\cos^2\theta - 10\cos^4\theta$ |
| | $\frac{5}{2}^-$ | $1 + 2\cos^2\theta$ |
| | $\frac{7}{2}^+$ | $13 - 10\cos^2\theta + 45\cos^4\theta$ |
| | $\frac{7}{2}^-$ | $21 - 120\cos^2\theta + 465\cos^4\theta - 350\cos^6\theta$ |

wave functions of all the possible angular momentum and spin states. The complete expression will be

$$\mathscr{Y}_{\frac{5}{2}}^{\frac{1}{2}} = \sqrt{\tfrac{1}{10}}\, Y_1^{-1}\chi_{\frac{3}{2}}^{\frac{3}{2}} + \sqrt{\tfrac{3}{5}}\, Y_1^0\chi_{\frac{3}{2}}^{\frac{1}{2}} + \sqrt{\tfrac{3}{10}}\, Y_1^1\chi_{\frac{3}{2}}^{-\frac{1}{2}} \qquad (3.107)$$

where $Y_1$ is the $l = 1$ angular momentum state with three possible values of the $z$ component and $\chi$ is the spin state of the decay baryon. The numerical coefficients are Clebsch-Gordan coefficients. Using the expression for the spherical harmonics $Y_l^m$ we get

$$|\mathscr{Y}_{\frac{5}{2}}^{\frac{1}{2}}|^2 \propto 1 + 2\cos^2\theta$$

Figure 16b shows this angular distribution and the ones obtained for decay of $J = \frac{3}{2}^\pm$, $\frac{5}{2}^\pm$ into a $J^P = \frac{3}{2}^-$ baryon. In Table VIII all these angular distributions are given along with the ones for decay into a $\frac{3}{2}^+$ baryon.

From Figure 16b it is possible to see that the angular distributions alone can distinguish very well between various spin-parity assignments, provided that there is little background which can alter this situation. In addition to the angular distribution, the polarization can also be studied, and it gives additional information. The effect of the background would be to introduce odd powers of cos $\theta$ in the distributions of Table VIII, coming from the inference terms. As for the $\frac{1}{2}{}^+O^-$ case of Table V, it is possible to tabulate the coefficients of the Legendre polynomial expansion of the differential cross section.

## IV. Methods of Analysis of Production Experiments

It is useful to review a few of the concepts necessary to analyze production experiments. Up to now most of the baryon resonances have been discovered and studied in formation experiments, although many resonances with $S \neq 0$ have appeared in production experiments and have subsequently been studied in formation experiments. Of course, the strangeness-2 resonances are accessible only to production experiments; therefore we outline the few methods which have been used to study resonant states in final state interactions.

### 1. Lorentz-Invariant Phase Space

A resonance can be produced in any process of the type

$$a + b \rightarrow m_1 + m_2 + m_3 + \cdots + m_n$$

where the number of particles in the final state is larger than two. Any reaction can be described in terms of a Lorentz-invariant amplitude $M$, which is related to the transition probability for unit time $w$ (with $w = \sigma v$, the cross section times the velocity in the c.m. of $a + b$) by the relation[32]

$$w = \frac{2\pi \, |M|^2 D(E)}{\prod_i 2E_i \prod_f 2E_f} = \frac{2\pi}{\prod_i 2E_i} \, |M|^2 \rho(E) \tag{4.1}$$

where $\rho(E)$ is the phase space, $\prod_{i(f)}$ is the product of twice the energies of the initial (final) particles, $E$ is the total energy in the center of mass, and $D(E)$ is the density of final states given by

$$D(E) = (2\pi)^3 \, \delta^3(\sum_i \mathbf{p}_i - \sum_f \mathbf{p}_f)\delta(\sum_i E_i - \sum_f E_f)$$
$$\times \prod_j [2\pi(2E_j)\delta(E_j^2 - p_j^2 - m_j^2) \, dE_j d^3\mathbf{p}_j(2\pi)^{-4}] \tag{4.2}$$

where $\mathbf{p}_j$ is the momentum and $E_j$ the total energy of the $j$th particle in the final state and the relativistic normalization is chosen so that there are $2E_j$ particles per unit volume.

Let us now carry out some integrations in Eq. (4.2), in order to express it in a more familiar way. Since

$$\int 2\pi(2E)\delta(E^2 - p^2 - m^2)\frac{dE}{2\pi} = 1$$

and in the c.m. of the reaction $\Sigma_i\mathbf{p}_i = 0$, Eq. (4.2) becomes

$$D(E) = (2\pi)^3\,\delta^3(\mathbf{p}_1 + \mathbf{p}_2 + \cdots\mathbf{p}_n)\delta(E - \sum_{j=1}^{n} E_j)$$

$$\times \frac{d^3\mathbf{p}_1}{(2\pi)^3}\frac{d^3\mathbf{p}_2}{(2\pi)^3}\cdots\frac{d^3\mathbf{p}_n}{(2\pi)^3} \quad (4.3)$$

where $E$ now is the total energy in the c.m.s. of the reaction. This gives, for the phase space of an $n$ body final state, the expression:

$$\rho_n(E) = (2\pi)^3 \int \frac{d^3\mathbf{p}_1\,d^3\mathbf{p}_2\ldots d^3\mathbf{p}_n}{(2\pi)^{3n}(2E_1)(2E_2)\ldots(2E_n)}$$

$$\delta^3(\mathbf{p}_1 + \mathbf{p}_2 + \cdots + \mathbf{p}_n)\delta(E - \sum_{j=1}^{n} E_j) \quad (4.4)$$

The phase space [Eq. (4.4)] contains all the dependence of $w$ on $p_j$ if the matrix element squared, $|M|^2$, is unity. Any deviation of $w$ from this form implies that $|M|^2 \neq 1$, and therefore some final state interaction is present. This is the case of interest to us, since a resonance will appear as a final-state interaction.

### 2. Three-Body Final State. Dalitz Plot

In the case of a three-body final state, it turns out that the phase space has a particular property, which can be used to investigate deviations of $|M|^2$ from unity. Let us carry out some integrations of Eq. (4.4) for this particular case. We have $\int (2\pi)^3\delta^3(\mathbf{p}_1 + \mathbf{p}_2 + \mathbf{p}_3)[d^3\mathbf{p}_3/(2\pi)^3] = 1$ for $\mathbf{p}_3 = -(\mathbf{p}_1 + \mathbf{p}_2)$; furthermore, we can put $d^3\mathbf{p}_j = p_j^2\,dp_j\,d\Omega_j$, so we get

$$D_3(E) = \frac{1}{(2\pi)^6}\,\delta(E - E_1 - E_2 - E_3)p_1^2\,dp_1\,d\Omega_1\,p_2^2\,dp_2\,d\Omega_2 \quad (4.5)$$

where

$$E_3 = \sqrt{p_1^2 + p_2^2 + 2p_1p_2\cos\theta_{12} + M_3^2} \quad (4.6)$$

We have now to integrate over the angles in Eq. (4.5). From Eq. (4.6) we have

$$\frac{d}{d\cos\theta_{12}}\,|E - E_1 - E_2 - E_3| = \frac{d}{d\cos\theta_{12}}\,\left|E - \sum_{j=1}^{3} E_j\right| = \frac{p_1 p_2}{E_3}$$

If we now take the $z$ axes along $\mathbf{p}_1$, which we can do without loss of generality, we get $\cos\theta_{12} = \cos\theta_2$ and Eq. (4.5) can be written as

$$D_3(E) = \frac{1}{(2\pi)^6}\,p_1{}^2\,dp_1\,p_2{}^2\,dp_2\,\frac{d}{d\cos\theta_2}\,\left(E - \sum_{j=1}^{3} E_j\right)$$

$$\times\;\frac{\delta(E - \sum_j E_j)}{p_1 p_2 / E_3}\;d\Omega_1\,d\Phi_2\,d\cos\theta_2$$

Here the integral of $\cos\theta_2$ has the usual form $\int dx\,\delta(x) = 1$ and the integral $\int d\Omega_1\,d\Phi_2 = 8\pi^2$, so we get

$$D_3(E) = \frac{8\pi^2}{(2\pi)^6}\,p_1{}^2\,dp_1\,p_2{}^2\,dp_2\,\frac{E_3}{p_1 p_2}$$

But $E^2 = p^2 + m^2$, so we have $p\,dp = E\,dE = E\,dT$, where $T$ is the kinetic energy; therefore, the final expression for $D_3(E)$ is now

$$D_3(E) = \frac{1}{8\pi^4}\,E_1\,dT_1 E_2\,dT_2\,E_3$$

Substituting into Eq. (4.1) gives, for the transition rate per unit energies $E_1$ and $E_2$,

$$dw_3 = \frac{1}{(4\pi)^3}\,\frac{|M|^2}{E_a E_b}\,dT_1\,dT_2 \qquad (4.7)$$

where $E_a$ and $E_b$ are the c.m. energies of the two incident particles. Equation (4.7) shows that:

$$\rho_3 \propto \int dT_1\,dT_2 \qquad (4.8)$$

This is an important result and shows the main property of the Dalitz plot[33]: if we make a scatter plot of the kinetic energies of two of the three particles in the final state, the density of points in the plot is proportional to the area $dT_1\,dT_2$. This is valid for any two particles, since the integration which led to expression (4.5) could have been done on any of the particles. Any deviation from isotropy in such a scatter plot is an indication that the matrix element $|M|^2$ of Eq. (4.7) is not a constant, but it is energy dependent.

Given a reaction like

$$K^- p \rightarrow \Lambda \pi^+ \pi^- \qquad (4.9)$$

it is more convenient to plot the square of the invariant mass of a pair of particles recoiling against the third one, because deviations from isotropy in the Dalitz plot are often indications of a resonant state decaying through a pair of particles. It is easy to prove that a scatter plot in (effective mass)$^2$ has the same properties as the one in kinetic energies. The square of the effective mass of the pair 13, for example, is

$$M_{13}^2 = (E_1 + E_3)^2 - (\mathbf{p}_1 + \mathbf{p}_3)^2 \qquad (4.10)$$

The total energy in the c.m. of the above reaction is

$$E = \sqrt{M_{13}^2 + p_2{}^2} + M_2 + T_2$$

which leads to

$$M_{13}^2 = (E - M_2)^2 - 2ET_2$$

Therefore, $dM_{13}^2 \propto dT_2$, and Eq. (4.8) becomes

$$\rho_3 \propto \int dM_{23}^2 \, dM_{13}^2 \qquad (4.11a)$$

or

$$\rho_3 \propto \int dM_{31}^2 \, dM_{21}^2 \qquad (4.11b)$$

$$\rho_3 \propto \int dM_{12}^2 \, dM_{32}^2 \qquad (4.11c)$$

The Dalitz plot for reaction (4.9) is shown in Figure 17, for an incident $K$ momentum of 1.52 GeV/c. The area inside the curve has the property of "equal number of events for equal area." The line which closes this area represents the kinematical boundaries described by energy momentum conservation in the reaction.

Let us point out a few properties of this plot.

1. A projection of this plot onto the $x$ axis is the distribution in $M_{12}^2$ so the value of $R_3(M_{12}^2)$ at a given value of $M_{12}^2 = A$ is proportional to the segment $BC$. The function $R_3(M_{12}^2)$ is the phase space distribution of $M_{12}^2$ and can be obtained through integration of Eq. (4.11c) over $dM_{23}^2$. We will see this expression later. This means that any deviation from uniformity in the Dalitz plot will show up in the projections onto the axes as a bump above the phase space curve.

2. The point $D$ represents the minimum value of $M_{12}^2$. At this point $M_{12} = M_1 + M_2$, and $p_3$ is maximum, which means that $\mathbf{p}_1$ and $\mathbf{p}_2$ have the same magnitude and the same direction.

3. The point $E$ represents the maximum value of $M_{12}^2$. At this point $M_{12} = E - M_3$, $p_3 = 0$, and $\mathbf{p}_1$ and $\mathbf{p}_2$ are equal in magnitude and opposite in direction.

4 It can be proved that the envelope of the Dalitz plot represents a situation where the 3 momentum vectors are collinear. Along $EGE'$ $p_2$ and $\mathbf{p}_3$ are parallel; along $E'FE$ they are antiparallel.

5. It can be proved that, at each point of the Dalitz plot, the following relation is valid.

$$M_{12}^2 + M_{13}^2 + M_{23}^2 = E^2 + \sum_i M_i^2$$

6. For $M_2 = M_3$, at the point $F$ (i.e., along a 45° line from the origin) $p_1 = 0$, therefore it is the point of maximum for $M_{23}^2$. Furthermore, lines perpendicular to $FG$ are lines of constant sum $M_{12}^2 + M_{23}^2$, therefore lines of constant $M_{23}^2$. This means that if we project the points of the Dalitz plot along these lines on $FG$ we obtain the $M_{23}^2$ distribution.

It is useful to find an explicit expression for the distribution of one of the variables of the three-body system, like a momentum $p_j$ or the invariant mass of two particles $M_{ij}$. In Figure 17 we have shown how to construct this distribution given the Dalitz plot envelope. This corresponds to an integral of Eq. (4.8) over one of the variables. The derivation is lengthy and we will not go through it, but the following expression in terms of $p_3$ or any other momentum can be obtained.

$$\frac{dp_3}{dp_3} \propto \frac{p_3^2\sqrt{[(E - E_3)^2 - p_3^2 - M_1^2 - M_2^2]^2 - 4M_1^2M_2^2}}{E_3[(E - E_3)^2 - p_3^2]} \quad (4.12)$$

where $E_3 = \sqrt{p_3^2 + M_3^2}$, $M_j$ ($j = 1, 2, 3$) are the masses of the three particles in the final state and $E$ is the total energy in the c.m. Given this expression we can now find $R_3(M_{12}^2)$ of Figure 17. In fact,

$$M_{12}^2 = E^2 + M_3^2 - 2EE_3$$

so

$$E_3 = \frac{-M_{12}^2 + E^2 + M_3^2}{2E} \qquad p_3 = \sqrt{E_3^2 - M_3^2} \quad (4.13)$$

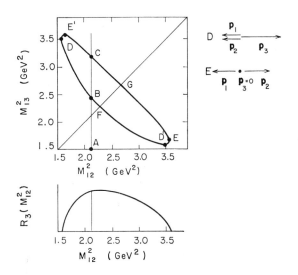

FIG. 17. The contour of the Dalitz plot for the reaction $K^- p \rightarrow \Lambda \pi^+ \pi^-$ is shown in a plot of $M_{13}^2$ vs. $M_{12}^2$. At the points $D$ and $E$ the momentum vectors for the three particles in the final state have the configuration shown at right. At point $A$ of the $M_{12}^2$ axis, the phase space available for that value of $M_{12}^2$ is represented by the segment $BC$. The curve of $R_3(M_{12}^2)$, at bottom, is obtained with this procedure. The incident $K^-$ momentum is 1.52 GeV/c.

and we can make a change of variables in Eq. (4.12). Since $R_3(M_{12}^2)\,dM_{12}^2 = (d\rho_3/dp_3)(dp_3/dM_{12}^2)\,dM_{12}^2$ and since, from Eq. (4.13), $dp_3/dM_{12}^2 = E_3/2p_3E$ we get

$$R_3(M_{12}^2) \propto \frac{p_3}{E} \cdot \frac{\sqrt{[(E - E_3)^2 - p_3{}^2 - M_1{}^2 - M_2{}^2]^2 - 4M_1{}^2 M_2{}^2}}{(E - E_3)^2 - p_3{}^2} \quad (4.14)$$

where $E_3$ and $p_3$ can now be expressed in terms of $M_{12}^2$ through expressions (4.13).

### 3. Final States with More than Three-Bodies

An $n$-body final state $(n > 3)$ does not have the property expressed in Eq. (4.8) or Eq. (4.11) for a three-body final state. The analogous expressions are more complicated and therefore, scatter plots are not as meaningful as the Dalitz plot, however, we will show that for a four-body final state it is still possible to use a scatter plot to detect final-state interactions. The phase space distributions in terms of only one variable are also more complicated than Eq. (4.14).

Srivastava and Sudarshan[34] have proved the validity of a very useful recursion relation between phase space for an $n$- and an $(n - 1)$-body final state. In terms of the momentum of the $n$th particle in the c.m. of the reaction, it is:

$$\rho_n(E) = \frac{1}{2} \int \frac{d^3 \mathbf{p}_n}{E_n} \rho_{n-1}(E') \qquad (4.15)$$

where $E' = \sqrt{(E - E_n)^2 - p_n^2}$ with $E_n$ and $p_n$ the energy and momentum of the $n$th particle. It is easy to obtain the two-body final state from expression (4.4). It is

$$\rho_2 = \pi p'/E' \qquad (4.16)$$

where $p'$ is the momentum of one of the two particles in the c.m., and $E'$ is the total energy of the two-body system. Using $\rho_2$ it is possible to deduce $\rho_3$

$$\rho_3 = \frac{1}{2} \int \frac{d^3 \mathbf{p}_3}{E_3} \rho_2(E') = \frac{4\pi}{2} \int \frac{p_3^2 \, dp_3}{E_3} \left( \frac{\pi p'}{E'} \right)$$

After evaluation of $E'$ and $p'$, $\rho_3$ assumes the form (4.12) of the previous section. If now we want to find $\rho_4$

$$\rho_4 = \frac{1}{2} \int \frac{d^3 \mathbf{p}_4}{E_4} \rho_3(E'')$$

we have to integrate $\rho_3$ over $p_3$, which is very complicated. Usually numerical integration is performed between the minimum and maximum values of $p_3$. The phase space distribution $d\rho_4/dp_4$ is therefore obtained through an integration over $p_3$ and $d\rho_n/dp_n$ requires $n - 3$ integrations.

Equation (4.15) can also be expressed in terms of the invariant mass of a pair of particles

$$\rho_n(m_1, m_2, \ldots, m_n, E)$$
$$= \int \rho_2(m_1, m_2, M_{12}) \rho_{n-1}(M_{12}, m_3, \ldots, m_n, E) \, dM_{12}^2 \quad (4.17)$$

where $\rho_2$ is the two-body Lorentz invariant phase space [Eq. (4.16)], with $E' = M_{12}$. Let us now derive the properties of a two-dimensional plot for a four-body final state

$$\rho_4(m_1, m_2, \ldots, E) = \int \rho_2(m_1, m_2, M_{12}) \rho_3(M_{12}, m_3, m_4, E) \, dM_{12}^2$$

but for $\rho_3$ we have

$$\rho_3(M_{12}, m_3, m_4, E) = \int \rho_2(m_3, m_4, M_{34})\rho_2(M_{12}, M_{34}, E) \, dM_{34}^2$$

Combining the last two expressions, we get

$$\rho_4(E) = \int \rho_2(M_{12})\rho_2(M_{34})\rho_2(M_{12}, M_{34}, E) \, dM_{12}^2 \, dM_{34}^2$$

which, using Eq. (4.16) for the two-body phase space, and leaving out the $\pi$ factors, becomes

$$\rho_4(E) \propto \int \frac{p_{12}}{M_{12}} \frac{p_{34}}{M_{34}} \frac{P}{E} \, dM_{12}^2 \, dM_{34}^2$$

In terms of $dM_{12}$, $dM_{34}$

$$\rho_4(E) = \frac{4\pi^3}{E} \int p_{12}p_{34}P \, dM_{12} \, dM_{34} \qquad (4.18)$$

where $p_{ij}$ is the absolute value of the relative momentum between particles $i$ and $j$, $\mathbf{p}_{ij} = \frac{1}{2}(\mathbf{p}_i - \mathbf{p}_j)$, $M_{ij}$ is the effective mass of the pair $ij$, and $P$ is the relative momentum between the two groups (12) and (34), i.e., $\mathbf{P} = \mathbf{p}_1 + \mathbf{p}_2 = -(\mathbf{p}_3 + \mathbf{p}_4)$, where all the $\mathbf{p}$ are in the c.m. of the reaction.

Equation (4.18) gives us the property of a scatter plot for the four-body final state: on a plot of $M_{12}$ vs. $M_{34}$, the population of events in a unit area will be proportional to $p_{12}p_{34} P$ for that unit area. This plot, however, is still useful in order to detect the presence of possible resonant states, because if the resonant cross section is not too small, it will produce a higher density along a band corresponding to a particular value of $M_{ij}$, which is easy to detect by comparison with neighboring bands. The envelope of this plot is now a triangle in which the density of points decreases to zero at the edges.

The projections of this plot on the axes will also be different from those in the case of the three-body final state. As an example, Figure 18 shows the phase space distribution for a pair of particles, for the three, four, and five-body final states in $K^- + p \rightarrow K^- + p + (n - 2)\pi^0$ at $P_K = 6.0 \text{ GeV}/c$.

## 4. Resonance Production

A multibody final state often contains pairs of particles which resonate. In this case, as we have stated before, the matrix element

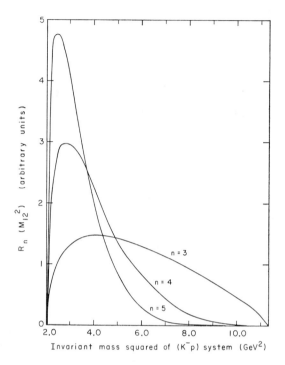

FIG. 18. Phase space distribution for the $K^- p$ system in the reaction $K^- + p \rightarrow K^- + p + (n - 2)\pi^2$ at $P_{K^-} = 6.0$ GeV/c. The three curves show the different shapes that phase space assumes for different numbers of particles in the final state.

squared, $|M|^2$ of Eq. (4.1), is not a constant. Let us consider for now the most simple case, in which only a pair of particles is in a resonant state

$$a + B \rightarrow X + m_3 + \cdots + m_n \qquad (4.19)$$
$$\phantom{a + B \rightarrow X} \quad \rightarrow m_1 + m_2$$

where $X$ is the resonance decaying into the two particles $m_1$ and $m_2$. It can be proved[35] that the presence of this resonance modifies $\sigma_X$, the cross section for production of $X + m_3 + \cdots + m_n$ in reaction (4.19), by a factor $|T_\beta|^2$. So

$$\frac{d\sigma}{dM_{12}^2} = \sigma_X(M_{12}^2) \cdot |T_\beta|^2 \qquad (4.20)$$

with

$$T_\beta = \frac{C \sqrt{\Gamma_B}}{E_R - E - i\Gamma/2} \tag{4.21}$$

where $C$ is a normalization constant, $E$ is the total energy in the c.m. of the particles $m_1$ and $m_2$, $E_R$ and $\Gamma$ are the resonance mass and width, and $\Gamma_\beta$ is the width for the particular channel $m_1 + m_2$. This form for the Breit-Wigner resonance differs from Eq. (3.39b) in the numerator, where $(\Gamma_a)^{1/2}$ is now missing, as expected, since the final state $m_1$ and $m_2$ is not coupled directly to the incoming state $a + B$, but to reaction (4.19) instead, as shown in Figure 1. The coupling to this reaction is now expressed through $\sigma_X(M_{12}^2)$ in Eq. (4.20).

The energy dependence of $\sigma_X$ depends on the particular reaction under consideration and it is often possible to construct a model for it. In Section IV-5 we will discuss the case in which the resonance $X$ is produced with small momentum transfer, i.e., the baryon $X$ carries almost all the momentum of the incoming baryon $B$. In the absence of such a model, the phase space for $(n - 1)$ bodies can be used, one of the outgoing particles being $X$, with a variable mass. However the phase space for $n$ bodies differs from the phase space for $(n - 1)$ bodies by the factor $\rho_2 = \pi p'/E' = \pi q/M_{12}$, according to Eq. (4.16), so we can replace Eq. (4.20) with

$$F(M_{12}^2) = \frac{d\sigma}{dM_{12}^2} = f(M_{12}^2)|T_\beta|^2 \tag{4.22}$$

where

$$f(M_{12}^2) = \sigma_X(M_{12}^2)$$

if production mechanism is known, and

$$f(M_{12}^2) = \frac{R_n M_{12}}{\pi q}$$

if phase space is used, $q$ being the momentum of $m_1$ and $m_2$ in their rest frame.

### A. Position of the Peak in Production Experiments

It has been pointed out in Section III-9 that the peak in elastic or total cross section is shifted with respect to the position of the maximum of the resonant amplitude. This shift will be present also in production experiments and it will depend on the energy dependence of the function

$f(M_{12}^2)$ in Eq. (4.22). Let us now compare the two matrix elements for production and formation experiments. The energy dependence of $\Gamma$ is still given by Eq. (3.43) and the quantity $(E_R - E)/(\Gamma/2)$ will again be replaced by $\varepsilon$ as in Eq. (3.45). The matrix element (4.21) will now be:

$$T_\beta = \frac{C\sqrt{\Gamma_\beta/\Gamma}}{\varepsilon - i} = \frac{2C\sqrt{x_\beta}/\sqrt{\Gamma}}{\varepsilon - i} \tag{4.23}$$

which is different from Eq. (3.44) in the factor $(\Gamma)^{-\frac{1}{2}}$. If we now assume that the particle pair $m_1 + m_2$ is always in a resonant state, the distribution of the invariant mass squared $(M_{12}^2 = E^2)$ of the pair $m_1 + m_2$ will deviate from $f(M_{12}^2)$ by the factor $|T_\beta|^2$. So we get

$$F(M_{12}^2) = f(M_{12}^2)|T_\beta|^2 = f(M_{12}^2)\frac{A(E_R + E)}{\varepsilon^2 + 1}\frac{D_l(qr)}{\Gamma_R(qr)^{2l+1}} \tag{4.24}$$

where for $\Gamma$ we have used expressions (3.43), $A$ is a normalization constant. Usually the resonant amplitude is normalized to one at the resonant energy $|T_\beta|^2 = 1$ for $M_{12} = M_R$ so that $A \propto \Gamma/2E_R[(qr)^{2l+1}/D_l(qr)]_R$. It is evident from Eq. (4.24) that the peak of $F(M_{12}^2)$ will be shifted to lower masses, because of the factor $(D_l/q)^{2l+1}$, if the function $f(M_{12}^2)$ does not have a stronger $q$ dependence. Comparing Eq. (4.24) with Eq. (3.48) we can conclude: (a) in formation experiments the peak is shifted to lower mass, and (b) in production experiments the peak can be shifted to lower or higher masses depending on the factor $[f(M_{12}^2)D_l(qr)^{2l+1}]$. As an example, in Figure 19 we plot the production of $\Delta(1236)$ at 1.0 GeV/c incident $\pi^-$ momentum, using phase space for $f(M_{12}^2)$ and a radius of interaction of 2 fermi. In this case the peak is shifted to lower mass; in fact it appears at $M = 1220$ MeV. Note that the apparent width is $\Gamma_a = 108$ MeV and of course it is dependent on $f(M_{12}^2)$. A comparison of Figures 8, 10, and 19 illustrates the fact that resonance parameters might not be as expected from the experimental data.

### B. Modification of Dalitz Plot and Mass Distributions

The presence of a resonance in a three-body final state will modify the Dalitz plot of Figure 17, producing a band of higher intensity along the line corresponding to the value of $M_{12}^2 = E_R^2$, with a width corresponding to the resonance width. If no other amplitude describing final-state interactions is present, the projection of the Dalitz plot onto the

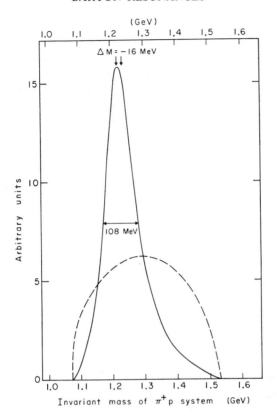

FIG. 19. Calculated invariant mass distribution for the production of $\Delta(1236)$. The assumptions made are: (1) the three-body final state can be described by phase space, (2) in all the events $\Delta(1236) \rightarrow \pi^+ + p$ is produced. The Breit-Wigner form used is defined in the text, and a radius of interaction of 2 fermis has been used. The resonance parameters used were $M_R = 1236$ MeV and $\Gamma_R = 126$ MeV. $\Delta M$ indicates the displacement of the peak and $\Gamma_a = 108$ MeV the apparent width of the resonance at half maximum. $(---)\pi^+ + p \rightarrow \pi^+ + p + \pi^0.$ ($\longrightarrow$) $\pi^+ + p \rightarrow \Delta(1236) + \pi^0.$ The incident momentum used was $p_{\pi^+} = 1.0$ GeV/c.

$M_{12}^2$ axis will be described by Eq. (4.24). In general, not all the events will contribute to the resonance region; in this case

$$F(M_{12}^2) = f(M_{12}^2)(1 - x) + xf(M_{12}^2)|T_\beta|^2 \qquad (4.25)$$

is a more appropriate form to use in order to fit the experimental distribution. Here $x$ is the percentage of final state decaying through the resonance. A densely populated band in the Dalitz plot will obviously affect the projections onto the other axes, therefore the $F(M_{13}^2)$ and $F(M_{23}^2)$ distributions will also deviate from phase space, as will be seen in Section VI-2 for production of $\Sigma(1385)$.

In general, for high energy incident particles, more than one resonance will be produced in the final state. In this case, assuming no interference effects between the various matrix elements, a more general form of Eq. (4.25) is

$$F(M_{12}^2) = f(M_{12}^2)\{x_1 \, |T_1|^2 + x_2 \, |T_2|^2 + \cdots + (1 - \sum_i x_i)\} \quad (4.26)$$

where $x_i$ is the partial contribution to the total cross section of the resonance with matrix element $T_i$, and $\sum x_i \le 1$ is the total contribution of the resonances to the final distribution. Notice that $T_i$ is not necessarily a resonance in the $m_1 + m_2$ system, since reflections of resonances in the other mass combinations must also be taken into account. This expression is correct if each resonance falls in a different part of the Dalitz plot, so that there are no overlapping bands. The case of overlapping bands will be discussed in Section IV-6.

### 5. Production Mechanisms: s, t, u Channel Processes

Given a multibody final state, the simplest description of its characteristics is obtained by assuming a statistical distribution for any physical quantity (a momentum, an invariant mass, an angular distribution, etc.). This approach corresponds to the assumption in Eq. (4.1) that the transition probability is proportional to phase space, therefore $|M|^2$ is taken to be unity. This hypothesis has often been proved to be incorrect by the experiments performed up to now, especially for large incident momenta.

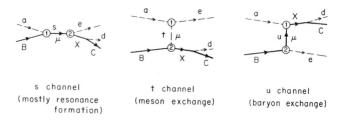

| s channel | t channel | u channel |
|---|---|---|
| (mostly resonance formation) | (meson exchange) | (baryon exchange) |

FIG. 20. Three possible types of diagrams for meson initiated reactions. The numbers in circles represent the vertex number used in Table IX.

In the previous section Eq. (4.22) shows that the distribution $f(M_{12}^2)$ (either phase space or the cross section for the production of the particular final state) has to be modified if one or more resonances is produced. A resonance, however, can be considered as any other particle, therefore the problem of a description of the production process is still present. This is again the problem of finding an expression for $|M|^2$ in Eq. (4.1).

The study of production mechanisms is outside the purpose of this article, therefore only general considerations will be made here. Let us consider, for example, the simple quasi-two-body reaction

$$a + B \to X + e \qquad\qquad (4.27)$$
$$\phantom{a + B \to } \hookrightarrow C + d$$

where $a$, $d$, and $e$ are mesons, and $B$ and $C$ are baryons. It is possible to draw at least three Feynman diagrams to describe this interaction, as seen in Figure 20. The line between the vertices 1 and 2 indicates that a particle of mass $\mu$ is exchanged between the two vertices; the variable characterizing the exchange is $s$, $t$, and $u$ in the three cases. For meson-originated reactions the three diagrams correspond to resonance formation in the $s$ channel, and to meson or baryon exchange in the $t$ or $u$ channel. If we indicate with $p$ and $q$ the four momenta, in the c.m. system for the initial and the final states, respectively, we have:

$$s = (p_a + p_B)^2 = (q_e + q_X)^2 = M_a^2 + M_B^2 + 2\,|\mathbf{q}|^2$$
$$t = (q_e - p_a)^2 = M_a^2 + M_e^2 - 2E_aE_e + 2\,|\mathbf{p}|\,|\mathbf{q}|\cos\theta_{ae} \quad (4.28)$$
$$u = (p_B - q_e)^2 = M_B^2 + M_e^2 - 2E_BE_e - 2\,|\mathbf{p}|\,|\mathbf{q}|\cos\theta_{ae}$$

where $|\mathbf{p}|$ and $|\mathbf{q}|$ are the three-dimensional momenta for the initial and final states, and $\theta_{ae}$ is the angle between the two mesons $a$ and $e$ in the c.m. of the $a + B$ system.

The quantum numbers of the exchanged particle must be such that the conservation laws are obeyed at each vertex, which gives selection rules on the quantum numbers of the exchanged particle. Table IX summarizes the possible production processes for some reactions. For each process, therefore, the interaction should be described by the sum of the amplitudes corresponding to each possible diagram, which is a very hard task.

However, as first pointed out by Chew and Low,[36] the matrix element for the process [Eq. (4.27)] includes a term describing a diagram which constitutes the major contribution in a certain energy region. In

## TABLE IX
### Allowed Intermediate States for Some Common Reactions

| Reaction | Quantum numbers of exchanged particle | | | | | |
| --- | --- | --- | --- | --- | --- | --- |
| | s channel | | t channel | | u channel | |
| | Vertex 1 | Vertex 2 | Vertex 1 | Vertex 2 | Vertex 1 | Vertex 2 |
| **(a) $\pi^- p \to \Delta^+(1236)\pi^-$** | | | | | | |
| $B$ | 1 | 1 | 0 | 0 | 1 | 1 |
| $S$ | 0 | 0 | 0 | 0 | 0 | 0 |
| $Q$ | 0 | 0 | 0 | 0 | +2 | +2 |
| $I$ | 1/2, 3/2 | 1/2, 3/2 | 0, 1, 2 | 1, 2 | 3/2 | 3/2 |
| $J^{PG}$ | Any | Any | $0^{2+}, 1^{-+}\dots$ | Any | Any | Any |
| Allowed states | $\begin{cases} n,\ N(1400),\ N(5112),\dots \\ \Delta(1690)\dots\Delta(1236), \end{cases}$ | | $\rho$ | | $\Delta(1236),\ \Delta(1690)\dots$ | |
| **(b) $\pi^- p \to \Delta^-(1236)\pi^+$** | | | | | | |
| $B$ | 1 | 1 | 0 | 0 | 1 | 1 |
| $S$ | 0 | 0 | 0 | 0 | 0 | 0 |
| $Q$ | 0 | 0 | +2 | +2 | 0 | 0 |
| $I$ | 1/2, 3/2 | 1/2, 3/2 | 2 | 2 | 1/2, 3/2 | 1/2, 3/2 |
| $J^{PG}$ | Any | Any | $0^{2+}, 1^{-+}\dots$ | Any | Any | Any |
| Allowed states | $\begin{cases} n,\ N(1400),\ N(1512)\dots \\ \Delta(1690)\dots\Delta(1236), \end{cases}$ | | None | | $n,\ N(1400),\ N(1512)\dots$ $\Delta(1236),\ \Delta(1690)\dots$ | |
| **(c) $K^- p \to \Lambda(1520)\pi^0$** | | | | | | |
| $B$ | 1 | 1 | 0 | 0 | 1 | 1 |
| $S$ | -1 | -1 | -1 | -1 | 0 | 0 |
| $Q$ | 0 | 0 | +1 | +1 | +1 | +1 |
| $I$ | 0, 1 | 1 | 1/2, 3/2 | 1/2 | 1/2 | 1/2, 3/2 |
| $J^{PG}$ | Any | Any | $0^{2+}, 1^{-+}\dots$ | Any | Any | Any |

Allowed states

| | {Σ, Σ(1385), Σ(1660), Σ(1765)}… | | K*(890), K*(1420) | | p, N(1400), N(1512)… | |
|---|---|---|---|---|---|---|
| (d) $pp \rightarrow \Delta^{++}(1236) + n$ | | | | | | |
| B | 2 | 2 | 0 | 0 | 0 | 0 |
| S | 0 | 0 | 0 | 0 | 0 | 0 |
| Q | +2 | +2 | −1 | −1 | +1 | +1 |
| I | 1 | 1, 2 | 1 | 1 | 1 | 1 |
| $J^{PG}$ | Any | Any | Any | Any | Any | Any |
| Allowed states | None | | $\pi, \rho, A_2$… | | Same as $t$ channel | |

this case the other diagrams can be ignored and the analysis of experimental data becomes easier. This leading term has the form

$$M(a\mu \to e) \frac{1}{\Delta^2 - \mu^2} M(B\mu \to X \to C + d) \qquad (4.29)$$

where $M$ denotes the amplitude for the specified process at each vertex, $1/(\Delta^2 - \mu^2)$ is a propagator, and $\Delta^2$ is the four-dimensional momentum carried by the particle of mass $\mu$. ($\Delta^2 = t$ for a $t$ channel exchange, $\Delta^2 = u$ for the $u$ channel, and $\Delta^2 = s$, total energy squared for the $s$ channel.) This term contains a singular point at $\Delta^2 = \mu^2$ which for $t$ or $u$ channel exchange always corresponds to unphysical production angles or to unphysical momenta, since the physical $\Delta^2$ is negative according to the definition [Eq. (4.28)]. For $s$ channel Eq. (4.29) can represent the contribution of a pole below threshold, like $\Lambda$, $\Sigma$, $\Sigma(1385)$ or a resonance, as in formation experiments. In the last case Eq. (4.29) is replaced by the Breit-Wigner amplitude of Section III-7. For $t$ or $u$ channel the extrapolation to the point of singularity has proved to be very difficult in practice; however, terms like Eq. (4.29) are still dominant in the physical region near the pole and the **T** matrix elements derived from such terms, with correction factors dependent on $\Delta^2$, are still expected to give the main feature of the reaction for $|\Delta^2| \lesssim \mu^2$. Many models have been suggested in order to replace the simple form [Eq. (4.29)] with a suitable form to be used in the physical region, and we refer the reader to the article by J. D. Jackson, which contains a comparison of the various models with experimental data.[37]

The inspection of Table IX shows that selection rules forbid certain diagrams—as $t$ channel in $\pi^- p \to \Delta^- \pi^+$, $s$ channel in $pp \to \Delta^{2+}n$ or the $u$ channel of this same reaction which turns out to be the same as the $t$ channel—or limit the number of possible intermediate states. Furthermore, for different incident energy regions or $\Delta^2$ values, different diagrams are the leading term of the matrix element; therefore, there is no single prescription on how to use a particular model. Let us now give a few simple examples.

### A. s Channel

From Table IX we see that the allowed states in $s$ channel are either resonances in the direct channel or poles below threshold, like $n$ in case ($a$), and $\Sigma$ and $\Sigma(1385)$ in case ($b$). If the energy region to be analyzed is such that direct resonances can be formed, often, these amplitudes are the most important and the others can be ignored. In this case the quasi-two-body final state can be studied according to the methods described in Section III for formation experiments. As an example reaction $c$ of Table IX

$$K^- + p \rightarrow \Lambda(1520) + \pi^0$$

has been already mentioned in Section III-18, its $s$ channel being dominated by $\Sigma(1765)$ formation for incident beam momentum in the 0.8–1.0 GeV region (see experimental data in Sect. VI-9). In this case, out of all the possible amplitudes listed in Table IX, it is sufficient to use only the one which describes formation of $\Sigma(1765)$. For different incident beam momenta, of course, the situation is different.

### B. $t$ Channel

A reaction dominated by meson exchange shows large production at small values of $t$, which corresponds to large production in the forward direction for the produced meson. A convenient way to detect such $t$ channel exchanges is to construct a scatter plot like the one in Figure 21, which is called a Chew-Low plot. The clustering of data at very low value of $|t|/\mu(<20)$ shows that a one pion exchange diagram is dominant in the reaction $\pi^- p \rightarrow p\pi^- \pi^0$ for a $\pi^- \pi^0$ invariant mass corresponding to $\rho$ production. These data are from Miller et al.[38] at a $\pi^-$ incident momentum of 2.7 GeV/c.

As a good example of a baryon resonance produced with very low momentum transfer, Figure 22 shows the results of an experiment done at CERN on the reaction

$$K^+ p \rightarrow \Delta^{2+}(1236) + K^0 \tag{4.30}$$
$$\phantom{K^+ p \rightarrow} \;\;\; \hookrightarrow \pi^+ p$$

at $p_K = 3.0$ GeV/c,[39] where the $\Delta(1236)$ is produced mainly at a very small angle with respect to the proton and, therefore, through $\rho$ or $A_2$ exchange. Figure 22a shows the Dalitz plot for reaction (4.30), which exhibits two bands or production of two resonances. Figures 22b and c show the angular distribution of the $\Delta(1236)$ and the $K^*(890)$. It is evident that both are produced at very small angle (very small $\Delta^2$) which is an indication that the reaction is dominated by meson exchange in the $t$ channel, specifically $\rho$ and/or $A_2$ exchange in the case of process (4.30).

When, as in this case, it is clear that the three-body final state is dominated by a particular process, it is possible to calculate an

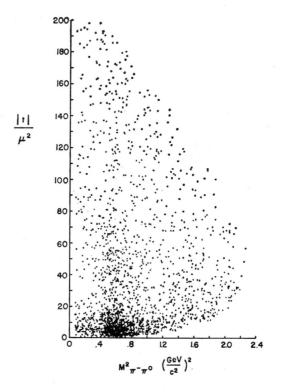

FIG. 21. Chew-Low plot for the reaction $\pi^- p \to p\pi^- \pi^\circ$ at $P_\pi = 2.7$ GeV/c.[38] It shows a concentration of events at low momentum transfer and at the invariant mass of the $\pi^- \pi^\circ$ system corresponding to $\rho$ meson production. This is a strong indication that the one pion exchange diagram dominates $\rho$ production.

expression for $F(M_{12}^2)$ of Eq. (4.22) instead of using the three-body phase space. The production and decay of $\Delta(1236)$ in reaction (4.30) have been successfully fitted using the Stodolsky and Sakurai model which considers $\rho$ exchange only.[40]

As another example, Figure 23 shows the experimental cross sections for the reaction $K^- p \to \Sigma(1385)^\pm \pi^\mp$, collected in a graph by Schlein.[41] As the energy increases, the production of negative $\Sigma(1385)$ diminishes at a faster rate than the production of the positive state. This last state, in fact, is produced through meson exchange, while no known meson can be exchanged for production of $\Sigma(1385)^-$. This is similar to the situations for reactions (a) and (b) of Table IX.

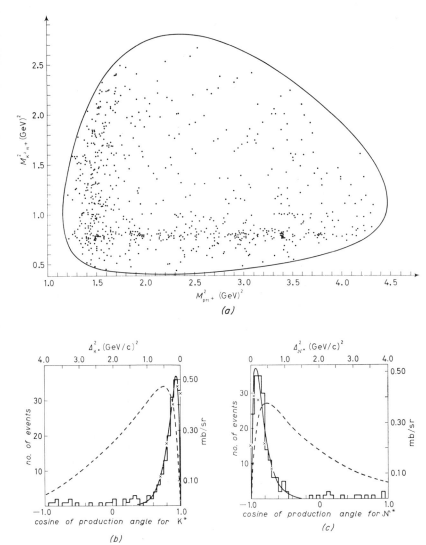

FIG. 22. Data on the reaction $K^+ + p \rightarrow K^0 p\pi^+$, at $P_K = 3.0$ GeV/c.[39] (a) Dalitz plot, which shows two resonant bands: $K^*$ and $\Delta(1236)$. (b) production angular distribution of $\Delta(1236)$ with respect to the $K^-$ meson, (c) production angular distribution of $K^*(890)$ with respect to the $K^-$ meson. Solid curves in (b) and (c) are calculated with the Stodolski-Sakurai model.[40]

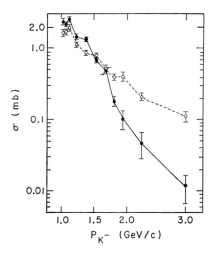

FIG. 23. Cross sections for $K^-p \to \Sigma(1385)^\pm + \pi^\mp$ as a function of laboratory $K^-$ beam momentum. Experimental data from various authors as collected
by Schlein.[41] The cross sections for the negative $\Sigma(1385)$ above 1.8 GeV/c is
smaller than for the positive state because no $t$ channel exchange is allowed for the
former state. The dashed and solid lines have been drawn through the points as a
guide. ($\bigcirc$)$\Sigma(1385)^+$. ($\bullet$)$\Sigma(1385)^-$.

### C. u Channel

A baryon exchange process will be characterized by a peak at small
values of $u$ or, according to Eq. (4.28), by a backward peak in the meson
production angular distribution. The dominance of $u$ channel exchange is expected to occur at high energy. For $K^-p \to \Sigma^-\pi^+$ at
3.0 GeV/c incident momentum, baryon exchange seems to dominate the
reaction.[42] Various channels in $\pi^+p$ interactions at 4.0 GeV/c show
backward peaking (or large $t$, which means small $u$), as can be seen in
Figure 24, taken from ref. 43.

### 6. Further Remarks on Production of Resonances

As we have seen so far, the position and the width of a resonance
found in a production experiment are dependent on the production
mechanism through the function $f(M_{12}^2)$ in Eq. (4.24). For different
incident beams ($\pi$, $K$) and for different momenta of the same beam,
the knowledge of $f(M_{12}^2)$ permits us to find the "true resonance parameters."

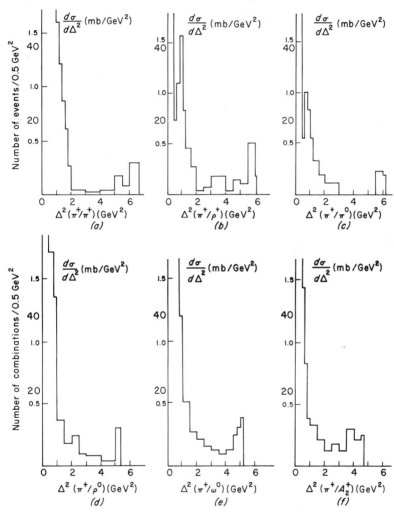

FIG. 24. The four-momentum transfer squared ($\Delta^2 = -t$) to the final meson is plotted for six different reactions in the $\pi^+ + p$ experiment of the German-British collaboration at 4.0 GeV/c.[43] Here small values of $u$ correspond to large values of $t$ (backward produced mesons). (a) $\pi^+ + p \rightarrow \pi^+ + p$; (b) $\pi^+ + p \rightarrow \rho^+ + p$; (c) $\pi^+ + p \rightarrow \pi^0\ N^{*++}$; (d) $\pi^+ + p \rightarrow \rho^0 + N^{*++}$; (e) $\pi^+ + p \rightarrow \omega^0 + N^{*++}$; (f) $\pi^+ + p \rightarrow A_2^+ + p$.

In addition to the production mechanism, other distortive effects can arise from different phenomena and again alter the resonance parameters. We will briefly review some of these effects; however, in baryon resonances they are seldom large enough to produce bumps which simulate resonances. For meson resonances the situation is, of course, different, and we refer the reader to the review article by A. H. Rosenfeld for a discussion of the so-called "kinematical effects."[44]

### A. Interference Effects between Overlapping Bands

Dalitz has discussed this point extensively.[12] For a three-body final state, the following situation may exist

$$m + B \to \begin{cases} A + e \\ m_1 + D^* \\ m_2 + B^* \end{cases} \to A + m_1 + m_2 \qquad \begin{matrix} (4.31a) \\ (4.31b) \\ (4.31c) \end{matrix}$$

i.e., three different resonances can be produced (capital letters indicate baryons; small letters indicate mesons) so each particle in the final state is shared by two different resonances. The Dalitz plot of this reaction will present three bands, which, depending on the total c.m. energy, may or may not overlap in some regions. If they overlap, Eq. (4.26) is not correct; instead the amplitudes corresponding to each resonance have to be added coherently to give the total amplitude which, once squared, will contain interference terms of the type Re $T_A^* T_{D^*}$, Re $T_A^* T_{B^*}$, etc.

Dalitz and Miller[45] have discussed the case of $K^- p \to \Lambda \pi^+ \pi^-$, with overlapping $\Sigma(1385)^\pm$ bands for $K^-$ momentum of 750 and 850 MeV/c. In this case the two pions have to obey Bose statistics, therefore the total wave function has to be even for interchange of the two pions. Since the $\Sigma(1385)$ is quite broad, the interference effects can also distort the resonance shape, the width might appear broader or narrower, and the position of the peak can be displaced. If possible, the best way to determine resonance parameters is to use experiments with total c.m. energy such as to avoid overlapping bands. The Dalitz and Miller method to describe this problem, however, turns out to be very useful to extract information on the parity of a resonance decaying into a three-body final state, as we will discuss in Section IV-7.

As an example of overlapping resonance bands, Figure 25 shows the data of Conforto et al.[46] for the reaction $\bar{p}p \to K_1^0 K^\pm \pi^\mp$ at rest. In this case three meson states can be formed, $K^*$, $\bar{K}^*$, and $A_2$, and each band crosses the other two.

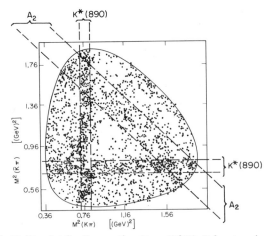

FIG. 25. Dalitz plot for the reaction $\bar{p}p \to K_1^0 K^{\pm} \pi^{\mp}$ for stopping antiprotons. Data is from Conforto et al.[46] Three resonance bands clearly cross in three points, therefore interference effects should be taken into account as discussed in the text.

### B. Interference with Background

To simplify the problem, let us assume that only the resonance $B^*$ in a $P_3$ state can be produced in the three-body final state [Eq. (4.31)] and that only one background amplitude, $S_1$, is present in the $A + m_1$ system. We can analyze the $A + m_1$ invariant mass plot or the angular distribution of $A$ measured in the $B^*$ rest frame. Apart from all the kinematical factors (including phase space) it will be, from Tables V and VII

$$F(M_{12}^2) \sim |S_1|^2 + 2\,|P_3|^2 \tag{4.32a}$$

$$\frac{d\sigma}{d\Omega}(\cos\theta) \sim |S_1|^2 + 2\,|P_3|^2 + 4\,\mathrm{Re}\,(S_1^* P_3)\cos\theta + |P_3|^2(3\cos^2\theta - 1)$$

$$\tag{4.32b}$$

For a constant value of $S_1$ through the resonant region of $M_{12}^2$, the total intensity [Eq. (4.32a)] will just be larger by the amount of $|S_1|^2$, but the form of the peak is the same as for $S_1 = 0$. If $S_1$ varies, however, it will produce a displacement of the resonance peak to the right (the left) for increasing (decreasing) magnitude of $S_1$. For a background of 5%, $|S_1|^2/|P_3|^2 = 0.053$ and we could hardly notice any effect at all.

The angular distribution, however, will be affected even by this small background; in fact, it corresponds to an amplitude ratio $|S_1|/|P_3| = \sqrt{0.053} = 0.23$, therefore the asymmetry in the distribution [Eq. (4.32b)] can be quite large. The forward–backward asymmetry is given by

$$\frac{F - B}{F + B} = \frac{\text{Re } S_1{}^*P_3}{|S_1|^2/2 + |P_3|^2} \tag{4.33}$$

Figure 26 shows the calculated asymmetry [Eq. (4.33)] as a function of $\epsilon = 2(E_R - E)/\Gamma$, for constant value of $S_1$ and for three different orientations of this background amplitude. $P_3$, of course, is rapidly moving, according to the Breit-Wigner formula [Eq. (3.40)]. As we can see, the asymmetry produced by 5% intensity background is quite large. In order to find the magnitude and orientation of $S_1$, one should study the asymmetry [Eq. (4.33)] across the resonance band. If $S_1$ is also energy-dependent through the resonant region, the situation gets rather complicated, and the use of Eq. (4.32) and a more complicated expression for the baryon polarization as a means to measure the spin-parity state

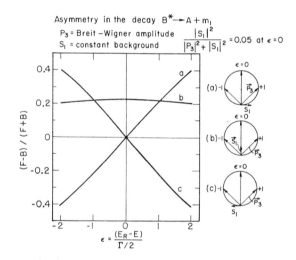

FIG. 26. Plot showing how a small background added to a resonance in a production experiment can alter the decay of the resonance itself. In this case $B^*$ is a resonance in a $P_3$ state, while the background is the $A + m_1$ system, in an $S$ wave. The forward–backward asymmetry in the decay of the resonance is shown for three different orientations of the background amplitude, $S_1$.

of the resonance $B^*$ is not likely to succeed. The situation gets worse if the background is larger and if more than one background amplitude is present.

The analysis here is more complicated than in formation experiments (where at least for the elastic channel we know how to parameterize the background), because the production mechanism in general is not known; therefore Eq. (4.32b) can be used in a very small production angle interval as a guarantee that whatever variations are observed do not depend on the production mechanism. This restriction, of course, cuts down the available data for the analysis. Jackson[47] and other authors have suggested models to fit the production and decay of resonances simultaneously in processes like Eq. (4.31).

### 7. Spin and Parity Determination of Baryon Resonances in Production Experiments

Some baryon resonances [$\Sigma(1385)$, $\Xi(1520)$, etc.] can only be made in production experiments, therefore the partial wave analysis described in Section III is not useful to measure spin and parity of these resonances. In production reaction we have the following chain of processes

$$m_1 + N \rightarrow Y^* + m_2 \qquad (4.34a)$$

$$Y^* \rightarrow Y + m_3 \qquad (4.34b)$$

$$Y \rightarrow B + m_4 \qquad (4.34c)$$

where $m$ stands for meson, $N$ for nucleon, $Y(Y^*)$ for hyperon of spin $\frac{1}{2}$ and $B$ for a nucleon (if $Y$ has strangeness $S = -1$) or a hyperon (if $Y$ has $S = -2$). The first two processes are described by strong interactions; the third one is a weak decay which, to be useful, must not conserve parity. In order to be able to measure the spin of the $Y^*$ produced in reaction (4.34), the following must be true:

1. The background amplitude must be very small so that the resonant amplitude is the only important one and none of the interference effects discussed in the previous section can influence the decay. As can be seen in Figure 26, even a few per cent of background can invalidate the analysis in certain situations.

2. The $Y^*$ must live for a sufficiently long time so that the interactions between the $Y^*$ decay products and $m_2$ are negligible.

Stapp,[48] Gatto and Stapp,[49] and Capps[50] described the formalism which can be used to find the $J^P$ assignment of $Y^*$ in a chain of reactions like Eq. (4.34) for $J \leq \frac{3}{2}$, and subsequently the method has been generalized to any spin by Byers and Fenster.[51] This last method, known as the "moments method," has the advantage of extracting all the possible information contained in the data and imposes no conditions on the production angles used; therefore, all the data are useful. This method has been formulated for decays of $Y^* \rightarrow Y + m$, where $Y$ is a spin $\frac{1}{2}$ hyperon and $m$ is a spin 0 meson. It has been extended to cases $Y^* \rightarrow (\frac{3}{2}, 0)$ by Shafer[52] and to the case of a meson resonance $M \rightarrow (0, 1)$ by Chung.[53]

In general, the production of a $Y^*$ is expected to result in an anisotropic spin distribution for the final state. This distribution is described by a density matrix given by

$$\rho = \frac{1}{2J + 1} \sum \sum (2L + 1) t_L^{M*} T_L^M$$

The $T_L^M$ are the spin operators, called spherical tensors, which form a complete orthogonal set of matrices and have the same form in spin space that $Y_L^M$ spherical harmonics have in coordinate space. The general method consists of studying the coefficient $t_L^{M*}$ of these spherical tensors which can be obtained from the experimental data, i.e., the angular distributions and the polarization of the decay hyperon in some specified rest frame.

The general method of Byers and Fenster will not be discussed here since it is not too intuitive, but we refer the reader to the original article or to the review articles by Dalitz[12] or Tripp.[54] We will, however, describe in physical terms the simpler situations of $J \leq \frac{3}{2}$ according to the description of Stapp and Gatto,[48,49] and how this description has been used by Shafer et al.[55] to determine the spin and parity of $\Sigma(1385)$.

### A. Spin $\frac{1}{2}$

Let us consider a sample of $Y^*$ of spin $\frac{1}{2}$ with polarization along the normal. In Figure 27 the incident meson (a $K^-$ for example) is taken to be along the $x$ axis and the $z$ axis is the normal to the $Y^*$ production plane, in the c.m. of the reaction.

The relative $Y^* Y$ parity can be negative or positive, which gives two possible angular momentum states, $S_{1/2}$ or $P_{1/2}$, for the decay (4.34b). There are two quantities we can measure: (a) The angular distribution of $Y$ with respect to the normal, $\cos \chi = (\mathbf{Y} \cdot \mathbf{n})$, and (b) $\alpha_Y \mathbf{P}_Y$: the

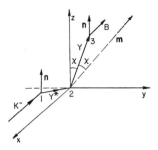

Fig. 27. The coordinate system used for the spin-parity analysis mentioned in the text. The magic direction is taken to be at an angle with the $z$ axis twice as large as the angle of the hyperon $Y$, in the $Y^*$ rest frame. The $1, 2, 3$ refer to the three successive Lorentz transformations carried out: ($1$) the $Y^*$ direction is in the $Kp$ c.m. ($K^-p \rightarrow Y^* + \pi_1$), ($2$) the $Y$ direction is in the $Y^*$ rest frame ($Y^* \rightarrow Y + \pi_2$), ($3$) the $B$ direction is in the $Y$ rest frame ($Y \rightarrow B + \pi_3$). $\mathbf{m}$ = magic direction. $\mathbf{n}$ = normal to production plane.

polarization of $Y$ times the decay asymmetry parameter for the decay (4.34c), which must not conserve parity and must be a mixture of $S$ and $P$ waves in order to have $\alpha_Y \neq 0$ (see Table I for definition and measured values of $\alpha_Y$). The component of $\alpha_Y \mathbf{P}_Y$ with respect to $\mathbf{n}$ (or any other axis) is simply obtained from

$$f_n(\chi) = \alpha_Y(\mathbf{P}_Y(\chi)\cdot\mathbf{n}) = \frac{3}{N_{ev}} \sum_{i=1}^{N_{ev}} \cos \widehat{(\mathbf{B}\cdot\mathbf{n})}_i \qquad (4.35)$$

where $\widehat{(\mathbf{B}\cdot\mathbf{n})}$ represents the angle of the decay baryon in (4.34c) (taken in the $Y$ rest frame) and the normal $\mathbf{n}$ (or any other axis), for a given value of $\cos \chi = (\mathbf{Y}\cdot\mathbf{n})$ (taken in the $Y^*$ rest frame). For $J = \frac{1}{2}$ the angular distribution $(\mathbf{Y}\cdot\mathbf{n})$ is supposed to be isotropic and does not give information on the parity of $Y^*$. The polarization instead contains the parity information. For negative $(YY^*)$ parity [$S$ wave decay in Eq. (4.34b)], $\mathbf{P}_Y$ will be the same as $\mathbf{P}_{Y^*}$, directed along the normal. For positive $(YY^*)$ parity [$P$ wave decay in Eq. (4.34c)], $\mathbf{P}_Y$ will retain the magnitude of $\mathbf{P}_{Y^*}$ but, as can easily be proved, along a new direction, called the magic direction $\mathbf{m}$ (see Fig. 27), defined as $\mathbf{m} = 2(\mathbf{n}\cdot\mathbf{Y})\mathbf{Y} - \mathbf{n}$, in the $Y^*$ rest frame. In other words, the parity is negative if the polarization is maximum along the normal and positive if the polarization is maximum along the magic direction.

## B. Spin $\frac{3}{2}$

In this case there are two tests: (a) Stapp[48] has pointed out that the hyperon $Y$ of reaction (4.34b) may go preferentially along the normal and that this effect is larger for $Y^*$ produced around 90°, therefore the distribution of $\cos \chi$ is not isotropic, but contains a $\cos^2 \chi$ term; (b) the polarization direction is neither the normal nor the magic direction, but has a different form which is predictable. The following equations, taken from Shafer et al.,[55] summarize the situation for $J = \frac{1}{2}$ and $\frac{3}{2}$, with $f_k(\chi)$ defined in Eq. (4.35).

| $k$ = normal | $k$ = magic | $f_k(\chi)$ | |
|---|---|---|---|
| $S_{\frac{1}{2}}$ | $P_{\frac{1}{2}}$ | $1$ | (4.36a) |
| $P_{\frac{1}{2}}$ | $S_{\frac{1}{2}}$ | $-1 + 2\cos^2 \chi$ | (4.36b) |
| $P_{\frac{3}{2}}^{\pm}$ | $D_{\frac{3}{2}}^{\pm}$ | $1 - \cos^2 \chi$ | (4.36c) |
| $P_{\frac{1}{2}}^{\pm}$ | $D_{\frac{1}{2}}^{\pm}$ | $-1 + 5\cos^2 \chi$ | (4.36d) |
| $D_{\frac{3}{2}}^{\pm}$ | $P_{\frac{3}{2}}^{\pm}$ | $-1 + 3\cos^2 \chi - 2\cos^4 \chi$ | (4.36e) |
| $D_{\frac{1}{2}}^{\pm}$ | $P_{\frac{1}{2}}^{\pm}$ | $1 - 15\cos^2 \chi + 18\cos^4 \chi$ | (4.36f) |

From the above equations it is clear that the experimental distributions of $f_n(\chi)$ and $f_m(\chi)$ are sufficient to determine spin and parity of the hyperon $Y^*$. We will see the application to $\Sigma(1385)$ in Section VI-2.

## C. Study of the Properties of the Dalitz Plot

The parity of a resonance which decays into three particles, two of which are pions, can in certain situations be determined by the analysis of the Dalitz plot of the three particles in the final state. The presence of the two pions, which must obey Bose statistics, permits one to use symmetry arguments concerning the matrix elements of the final state as first discussed by Dalitz and Miller.[45] Let us describe briefly two cases in which this type of analysis has been used. Consider the following chain of reactions

$$K^- + p \rightarrow \Sigma^+(1660) + \pi^- \qquad (4.37)$$
$$\Sigma^+(1660) \rightarrow \Sigma^- \pi^+ \pi^+ \qquad (4.37a)$$
$$\rightarrow \Lambda \pi^+ \pi^\circ \qquad (4.37b)$$

*1.* In the $\Sigma^- \pi^+ \pi^+$ decay of $\Sigma(1660)$, the $\pi^+ \pi^+$ system has to obey Bose statistics, therefore the system of two identical particles has to

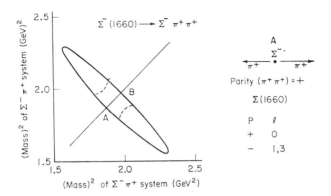

FIG. 28. Dalitz plot for $\Sigma^- \pi^+ \pi^+$ of a total mass of 1660 MeV. Properties of the Dalitz plot in a region close to $A$ can be used to study the parity of $\Sigma(1660)$. A depletion is expected at $A$ for negative parity.

have an overall parity $+$. Since its isotopic spin state is $I = 2$, its angular momentum state must be even. This fact has some implications at point $A$ of the Dalitz plot in Figure 28. In fact, at this point the $\Sigma^-$ is at rest in the c.m. so its angular momentum state, with respect to the $\pi^+ \pi^+$ system, can only be in an $S$ wave, which implies a positive parity for $\Sigma(1660)$. If the parity of $\Sigma(1660)$ is negative, there will be a depletion at point $A$ (due to centrifugal barrier). In practice, the situation is more complicated by the presence of the decay through $\Lambda(1405) + \pi$ and the presence of background. Furthermore, the statistics required for one to look at only a very small region of the Dalitz plot are very large. However, definite predictions can be made for certain angular distributions, and in Section VI-8 we will see the application to experimental data.

2. In the second case, the symmetry arguments used regard the overlapping bands of the Dalitz plot and are discussed in ref. 24, to which paper we refer the reader for details. At this energy the two decays $\Sigma^+(1660) \rightarrow \Sigma(1385)_0^+ + \pi_+^0$ are allowed, and the two $\Sigma(1385)$ bands overlap in the center of the Dalitz plot. Again, depletion or enhancement at point $A$ of Figure 28 would suggest negative or positive parity for $\Sigma(1660)$. Point $B$ gives information on the $I$ spin of the initial state. The experimental data, however, did not show a large decay of $\Sigma(1660)$ in this channel, therefore this method has not given any results for this decay mode. It is possible, however, to apply this method to

other resonances where a similar chain of reactions occurs and the kinematics allows overlapping bands in the Dalitz plot.

## V. Baryon Resonances with Zero Strangeness ($Y = 1$)

### A. Introduction

All the baryon resonances with strangeness 0 have been discovered in formation experiments. They appeared first as bumps in total cross-section experiments. Subsequent analysis of elastic and charge-exchange differential cross section and polarization data were necessary in order to determine their properties. Phase-shift and partial-wave analyses have provided quantum number assignment for the resonances with mass below 2.2 GeV.

Since the discovery of $\Delta(1238)$ as a bump in the $\pi^+ p$ total cross section, 14 more resonances and 9 possible ones have been added to the family of pion–nucleon resonances. In this section we will review the analysis of experimental data which showed the existence of these resonances.

### 1. Survey of Experimental Data

A first general indication of the resonant states present in the $\pi p$ system is given by the total cross sections for $\pi^\pm p$ interactions which are shown in Figure 11 up to a total c.m. energy of 2500 MeV. Figure 29 shows the two isospin states. The $\pi^+ p$ state is pure $I = \frac{3}{2}$, while $\pi^- p$ is a mixture of the two $I$-spin states, whose relative proportions are given by the Clebsch-Gordon coefficients. One gets

$$\sigma(\pi^- p) = \tfrac{1}{3}\sigma(I = \tfrac{3}{2}) + \tfrac{2}{3}\sigma(I = \tfrac{1}{2})$$
$$\sigma(\pi^+ p) = \sigma(I = \tfrac{3}{2})$$

The bumps and shoulders which turned out to contain resonances are indicated by arrows. [This plot is taken from Diddens et al.[18]] The region above 2.5 GeV kinetic energy will be discussed in Section V-8.

Experimentally, pion–nucleon scattering can be divided into four regions.

*1.* Below 300 MeV kinetic energy of the incident pion ($M_{\pi p} < 1300$ MeV), where inelastic scattering is unimportant. Good data are available; phase shift analyses have been completed and are relatively well understood in terms of partial wave dispersion relations.[56] The most

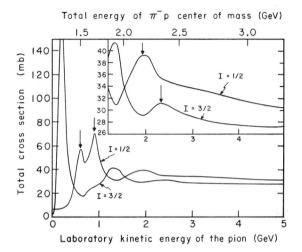

Fig. 29. The $\pi N$ total cross section in the two isotopic spin states. For pion energy greater than 1.2 GeV, the cross sections are also shown magnified. The arrows indicate bumps and shoulders which turned out to be resonance. (Plot taken from ref. 18.) For total energy above 2.4 GeV, more recent data are shown in Fig. 51.

recent phase shifts and collection of data can be found in Roper et al.[57]

2. The region above 300 MeV up to $T_\pi \approx 1000$ MeV ($M\pi p \approx 1740$ MeV), where a large amount of data is available which have been extensively analyzed in recent years.

3. The region 1.0–2.0 GeV ($M_{\pi p} < 2.2$ GeV), where only recently good experimental data have been obtained. Complete phase shift analyses have been extended to this region and some partial wave analyses of the expansion coefficients of differential cross sections and polarization have been made. However, the density of data points is still not good enough to allow definite conclusions on the behavior of the various amplitudes.

4. The region above 2.0 GeV where, besides total cross section and $\pi^-p$ elastic scattering at 180°, the experimental data are still too scarce to clarify the situation.

The analysis of regions (2) and (3) above will be discussed in Section V-2. The data for this analysis come from $\pi p$ scattering. The photoproduction data have not been completely analyzed yet, although many $\gamma p$ and $\gamma d$ experiments have been performed in this

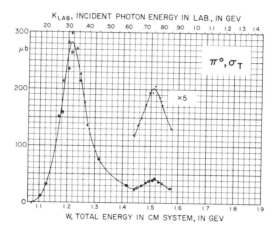

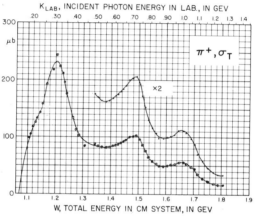

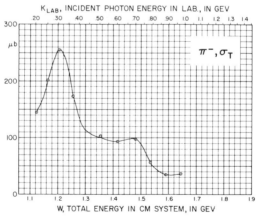

FIG. 30. Total cross sections for (a) $\gamma p \to \pi^0 p$, (b) $\gamma p \to \pi^+ n$, and (c) $\gamma n \to \pi^+ p$. These curves were obtained by Beale et al.[58] through integration of the differential cross sections fitted with Moravicsik's model.[59]

energy region. A good collection of data has been made by Beale et al.[58]

In Figure 30 the total cross section data for (a) $\gamma p \to \pi^\circ p$, (b) $\gamma p \to \pi^+ n$, and (c) $\gamma n \to \pi^- p$ are reported. These graphs are model dependent since they have been obtained by Beale et al.[58] through a fit to the differential cross sections of the above reactions at various energies. The model used is the one suggested by Moravcsik,[59] which includes a one-pion-exchange amplitude and a resonant amplitude.

Many experiments on $\pi^+ p$ elastic scattering, $\pi^- p$ elastic and charge exchange have been done since the first accelerators made pion beams available. Good polarization measurements of the recoiling proton in elastic scattering, however, were not made until recently and, as we have seen in Section III-17, they are essential to resolve the Minami ambiguity. The polarization of the recoil neutron in charge exchange has not been measured yet and it turns out to be necessary to resolve the differences between the various phase shift analyses. Figure 31 shows what data is presently available for the phase shift analysis as collected by Johnson and Steiner.[60a] Each vertical line represents the momentum at which measurements have been done for the indicated quantity. Lists of references can be found in ref. 60b.

Out of this multitude of measurements, we report only a few representative distributions. Figure 32 shows the total elastic cross sections for $\pi^\pm p$ scattering. Figure 33 shows the coefficients of a Legendre polynomial expansion of the $\pi^- p \to \pi^\circ n$ differential cross section.[61] Both Figures 32 and 33 show that some resonant phenomena are present at $T_\pi \approx 600$ and $T_\pi \approx 900$ MeV. In Figure 33 the coefficient $C_5$ suggests the presence of a large $D_5 F_5$ interference, according to Table V, in the $\pi p$ amplitudes around $T_\pi \approx 900$ MeV ($M_{\pi p} \approx 1700$ MeV). All the data have been analyzed together to find the two isotopic spin amplitudes. The $I = \frac{1}{2}$ amplitude contributes to the $\pi^- p$ and charge exchange data and not to the $\pi^+ p$ data.

## 2. Phase Shift Analysis of $\pi p$ Scattering

Various groups have been working on phase shift analysis of all available data in the 300–1000 MeV region ($M_{\pi p} < 1740$ MeV). As has been pointed out in Section III-17, measurements of the recoiling nucleon polarization are not enough to solve all the ambiguities connected with the parameterization given by Eqs. (3.21), (3.23), and (3.24), but additional assumptions on the energy dependence of the phase

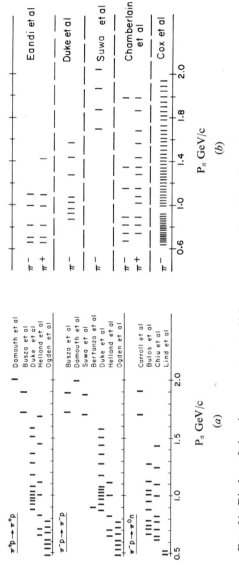

Fig. 31. Display of the pion momenta at which measurements have been done: (a) of $\pi-N$ $d\sigma/d\Omega$ differential cross sections, (b) of $\pi-N$ proton polarizations. The names at right identify the articles whose references can be found in ref. 60b.

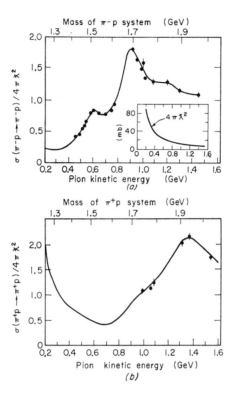

FIG. 32. Plot of experimental data on $\pi^{\pm}p$ elastic cross sections, as collected by Auvil and Lovelace[63] up to 2 GeV total c.m. energy. The curves are hand drawn through the experimental points. Below 1.0 GeV a few points are plotted, above 1.0 GeV all experimental points are plotted. (a) Plot of $\sigma_e(\pi^- p)/4\pi\lambda^2$, (b) plot of $\sigma_e(\pi^+ p)/4\pi\lambda^2$.

shifts have to be made. The approaches of the various groups to this problem have been different and we will try to summarize their work here.

*1.* Roper and collaborators[62] at Livermore have analyzed the data up to $T_\pi = 700$ MeV ($M_{\pi p} = 1570$ MeV), using an energy-dependent form for the phase shifts of the type

$$\delta_l = k^{2l+1} \sum_{n=0}^{l_{max}-l} a_n k^n$$

$$\gamma_l = (k - k_0)^{2l+1} \sum_{n=0}^{l_{max}-l} b_n k^n \tag{5.1}$$

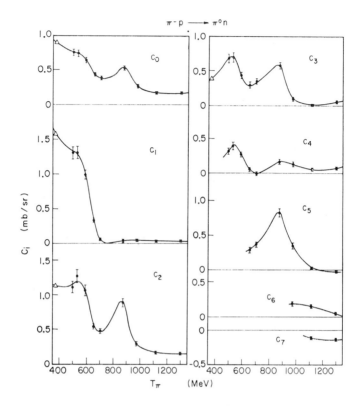

FIG. 33. Coefficients $C_l$ of the Legendre polynomial expansion

$$\frac{d\sigma}{d\Omega} (\pi^- p \to \pi^0 n) = \sum_l C_l P_l(\cos \theta)$$

$C_0$ represents $\sigma_{c.ex.}/4\pi$. The curves have been drawn through the points as a guide. Plot taken from Chiu et al.[61]

where $l_{max}$ is the maximum $l$ used in the fit, $k_0$ is the threshold for one pion production, and $\gamma_l$ is related to $\eta_l$ by $\eta_l = e^{-2\gamma_l}$. This form was used for the nonresonant amplitudes, whereas for the resonances Breit-Wigner amplitudes were used. In this way they found that the phase shift of the $P_{11}$ amplitude, which had the energy dependence (5.1), went through $90°$ at $M = 1485$ MeV. This is known as the Roper resonance, and subsequent analyses have confirmed its existence, as will be seen in Section V-3.

The set of $\eta_{l^\pm}$, $\delta_{l^\pm}$ obtained by this group should not be used quantitatively because the experimental data used in their analysis does not include recent polarization and charge-exchange measurements.

2. Collaborators at Imperial College and the University College of London and now CERN have analyzed experimental data up to $T_\pi = 1900$ MeV.[63] In various articles, Auvil, Lovelace, Donnachie, and Lea (ALDL) have developed a semiphenomenological technique which uses fits to partial-wave dispersion relations in addition to phase-shift analysis. In their recent articles they use theoretical predictions for all partial waves, errors are placed on these theoretical predictions and they are fitted at the same time as the phase shifts. In this way they get the energy dependence of the amplitudes from theory. The theoretical predictions use the dispersion–relation calculations of Donnachie and Hamilton.[64]

Figure 34 shows their latest results on phases and absorption parameters for the $P_{11}$, $D_{13}$, $D_{15}$, $F_{15}$, $S_{31}$, and $P_{33}$ amplitudes. The solid lines represent the dispersion relation predictions; the squares are the experimental phases and elasticities, results of the dispersion relation fit. All these amplitudes, except for $S_{31}$, have a phase shift going rapidly through 90° and the energy dependence expected for a resonance, as discussed in Section III-7. However, as discussed in Section III-8, the condition $\delta = 90°$ is not necessary in order to have a resonant state. The $S_{31}$ and other amplitudes also have a resonant behavior as shown by arrows in the Argand diagrams of Figure 35. These diagrams are drawn from plots into the ones of Figure 34, but do not show the experimental points, nor the energy dependence along each diagram, they only give the quantitative behavior. In the next section we will discuss the significance to attach to each of these possible resonant states.

3. Bransden, Moorhouse, and O'Donnel[65] use dispersion relations for the inverse partial wave amplitudes[66] in order to predict the energy dependence and therefore to choose between the various solutions of the fit to differential cross sections. Their parameterization is different from ALDL, but they also include some parameters in their theoretical prediction of the partial wave amplitudes. The solutions they obtain are in qualitative agreement with ALDL, however, they have not included recent experimental data, so their results should not be used quantitatively.

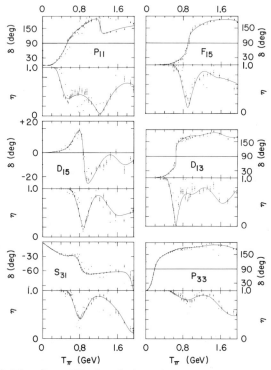

Fig. 34. The phase shifts δ and absorption parameters η for the $P_{11}$, $D_{13}$, $D_{15}$, $F_{15}$, $S_{31}$, and $P_{33}$ amplitudes. These are the solutions of the phase shift analysis of Donnachie et al.[63] (—) Dispersion relation predictions, (□) experimental phases and elasticities obtained by a dispersion relation fit, (○) results of Bareyre et al.[16]

4. Bareyre et al., at Saclay, have used a completely different approach.[16] For each energy, starting from a random set of phase shifts, they fit Eqs. (3.21)–(3.24) to the data, searching for the minimum $\chi^2$. They find that the solution is not unique, but if they require continuity of the solutions with energy, then the ambiguity is completely removed. The analysis, done at 23 different kinetic energies between 310 and 1560 MeV ($1320 < M_{\pi p} < 2022$ MeV), includes $S$ to $F$ waves up to $T_{\pi} = 650$ MeV; above this energy $G$ waves are also included. At each energy there were 28 or 32 parameters to fit (7 or 8 partial waves

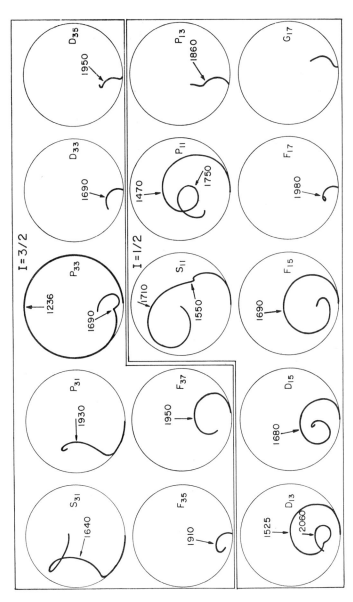

Fig. 35. Behavior of the partial wave amplitudes in $\pi$-$p$ elastic scattering, according to the latest solutions of Donnachie et al.[63] The coordinates for each circle are not shown, but they follow the notation of Figure 4. The energy dependence along each diagram is not shown. Arrows point to approximate positions of resonant states (in MeV), as quoted by the authors. The reader can find in Table II the list of confirmed resonant states and in the footnote of Table II a list of unconfirmed states.

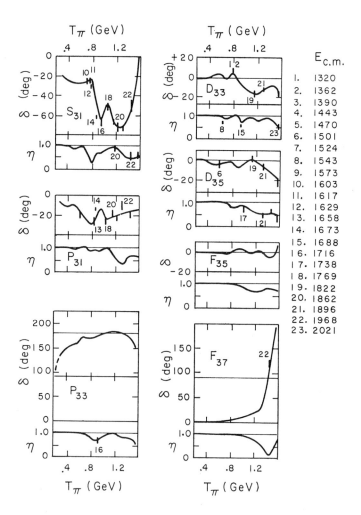

FIG. 36. The phase shifts δ and absorption parameters η up to the F partial wave for the I = 3/2 spin state of the πp system. These are the solutions of the analysis of Bareyre et al.[16] The curves are hand drawn by the authors. The experimental points shown are only the ones with large errors or which deviate from the curve. The energy corresponding to each point is shown at the right of the figure.

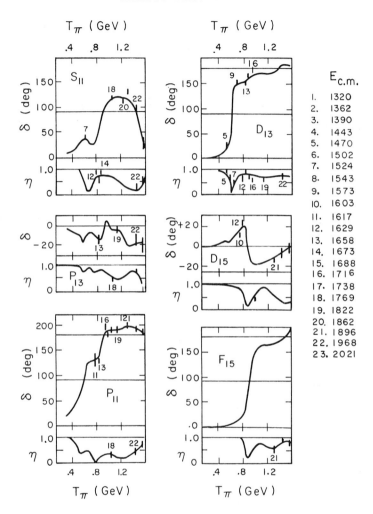

FIG. 37. The phase shifts δ and absorption parameters η up to the F partial wave, for the $I = \frac{1}{2}$ spin state of the $\pi p$ system. These are the solutions of the analysis of Bareyre et al.[16] See caption of Figure 36.

in two different $I$ spin states), and the average number of points used was 94. Figure 36 shows their final values of $\eta$ and $\delta$ of various partial waves for the isotopic spin $\frac{3}{2}$ state, and Figure 37 shows the results for $I = \frac{1}{2}$.

In Figures 36 and 37, six partial waves have a phase shift going through $90°$ ($P_{33}$, $F_{37}$, $S_{11}$, $D_{13}$, $P_{11}$, $F_{15}$), but when the amplitudes are plotted in the complex plane, three more amplitudes show a resonant behavior ($S_{31}$, $S_{11}$, $D_{15}$) according to the discussion of Sections III-7 and III-8. Figure 38 shows the Argand diagrams for some of these amplitudes. Note that most of them are not circular, which is an indication that background amplitudes are present and displace the resonant energy from the Re $T_e = 0$ point.

5. Cence[67] has published a set of phase shifts in the region of $T_\pi$ between 300 and 700 MeV ($M_{\pi p} < 1570$ MeV). Although he includes in the analysis all the recent data used by the authors of 2–4, he finds solutions which do not agree with any of the previous four groups. His set of phase shifts and absorption parameters do not show any resonances in this region except for the $P_{33}$ [$\Delta(1236)$]. The large bump in total cross section (Fig. 11) at $T_\pi = 600$ MeV ($M_{\pi p} = 1512$ MeV) is not due to a resonance according to this analysis since no one of the partial waves shows a resonant behavior in this region.

## 3. Results of Phase Shift Analyses

All the phase shift analyses, except Cence's, show the same qualitative behavior below $M = 1700$ MeV, even if quantitative differences are still present. Two bumps in total cross section (Figs. 11 and 29), known as the second and third resonance, have been resolved as containing three and four resonances, respectively. [Donnachie et al.[63] claim that seven resonances are present in the region of the third bump.] However, it should be emphasized that this multitude of resonances should be looked upon with some caution. There is still need of new, improved data before unique solutions and agreement between the various groups can be achieved.

Draxler and Huper[68] have checked the consistency of the phase-shift analysis of Bareyre et al. Cence, and Donnachie et al. with dispersion relations for the $\pi N$ scattering amplitude in the forward direction. They find that the agreement of the Saclay group analysis with prediction is good, but the analysis of Cence is clearly in disagreement with the prediction. The set of $\delta, \eta$ of Donnachie et al. was obtained by using dispersion relations and is clearly in agreement with the predictions. Höhler et al.[69] have done calculations of the same type for the forward-scattering amplitude in charge exchange. They found good agreement with experimental data in charge exchange,

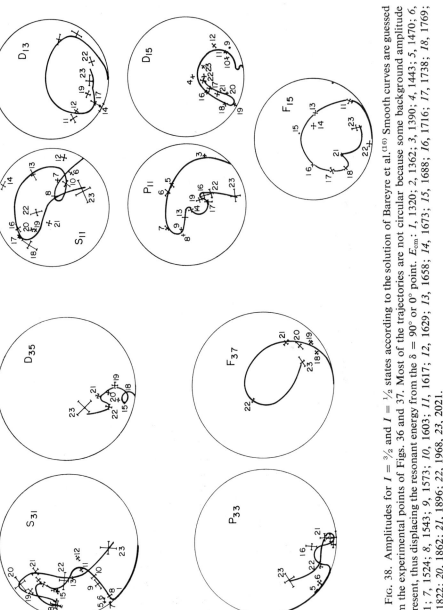

Fig. 38. Amplitudes for $I = \frac{3}{2}$ and $I = \frac{1}{2}$ states according to the solution of Bareyre et al.[16] Smooth curves are guessed from the experimental points of Figs. 36 and 37. Most of the trajectories are not circular because some background amplitude is present, thus displacing the resonant energy from the $\delta = 90°$ or $0°$ point. $E_{cm}$: $1$, $1320$; $2$, $1362$; $3$, $1390$; $4$, $1443$; $5$, $1470$; $6$, $1501$; $7$, $1524$; $8$, $1543$; $9$, $1573$; $10$, $1603$; $11$, $1617$; $12$, $1629$; $13$, $1658$; $14$, $1673$; $15$, $1688$; $16$, $1716$; $17$, $1738$; $18$, $1769$; $19$, $1822$; $20$, $1862$; $21$, $1896$; $22$, $1968$; $23$, $2021$.

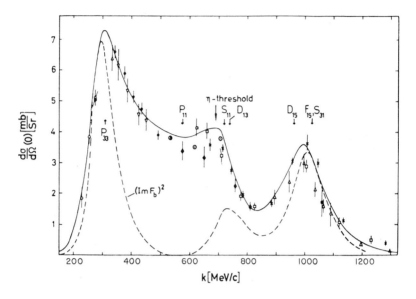

FIG. 39. Charge-exchange forward cross section. Plot for Höhler et al.[69] (——) prediction of dispersion relation, (– – –) contribution of the imaginary part. Data are from various experiments listed in ref. 69. (○) Values calculated from the phase-shift analysis of Bareyre et al.[16]

and also with the phase-shift analysis of Bareyre et al. Figure 39 shows the comparison of their calculations with experimental values.

The only solutions obtained using the most recent data displayed in Figure 31 are those reported in the latest papers by Bareyre et al.[16] and Donnachie et al.[63] Other groups are working on phase shift analysis and some new results will soon be available.[60] As of now, we will have to draw some conclusions on the present status of the baryonic resonances at the $\pi N$ system from the results reported in Figures 34 through 38. From these plots it is clear that two quite related problems arise: (*1*) deciding which amplitudes have a resonant behavior, and (*2*) extracting resonant parameters from them.

*1.* It is clear that the agreement between the two sets of phase shifts is not very good especially above $M \sim 1700$ MeV. Of the possible resonant states indicated with arrows in Figure 35, there are three states below 1750 MeV which do not seem to be confirmed by the Saclay solutions. Specifically $P_{33}$ ($M = 1690$, $\Gamma = 280$, $x_e = 0.10$),

$D_{33}$ (1690), 270, 0.14), and $P_{11}$ (1750, 350, 0.32), all of which have small elasticities. Above $M = 1750$ MeV, in addition to the well-established $F_{37}$ (1950), the CERN group claims six new resonances, all included in Table X, which do not seem to be confirmed by the Saclay results at this time. My feeling is that the data in this energy region are still too scarce to permit definite statements about resonant states with such small elasticities without the additional information coming from the inelastic channels.

TABLE X

Parameters of Resonances Found in Phase-Shift Analyses

| $2I, 2J$ | $J^P$ | $T_\pi,$ GeV | $P_\pi,$ GeV/c | $M,$ MeV | $\Gamma,$ MeV | $x$ | Groups |
|---|---|---|---|---|---|---|---|
| $S_{11}$ | $\frac{1}{2}^-$ | 0.65 | 0.77 | 1540 | 140 | 0.3 | $b, c, d$ |
| $S_{11}$ | $\frac{1}{2}^-$ | 0.92 | 1.05 | 1700 | 300 | 0.8 | $c, d$ |
| $P_{11}$ | $\frac{1}{2}^+$ | 0.53 | 0.66 | $\approx 1470$ | $\approx 200$ | 0.65 | $a, b, c, d$ |
| $D_{13}$ | $\frac{3}{2}^-$ | 0.62 | 0.75 | 1525 | 100 | 0.55 | $a, b, c, d$ |
| $D_{15}$ | $\frac{5}{2}^-$ | 0.87 | 1.00 | 1670 | 170 | 0.4 | $b, c, d$ |
| $F_{15}$ | $\frac{5}{2}^+$ | 0.90 | 1.03 | 1688 | 130 | 0.65 | $a, b, c, d$ |
| $S_{31}$ | $\frac{1}{2}^-$ | 0.81 | 0.94 | 1640 | 180 | 0.3 | $b, d$ |
| $P_{33}$ | $\frac{3}{2}^+$ | 0.195 | 0.304 | 1236 | 126 | 1.0 | $a, b, c, d, e$ |
| $F_{37}$ | $\frac{7}{2}^+$ | 1.41 | 1.54 | 1950 | 220 | 0.4 | $b, d$ |

Parameters of unconfirmed states

| $P_{11}$ | $\frac{1}{2}^+$ | 1.02 | 1.15 | 1750 | 330 | 0.32 | $b^b$ |
| $P_{13}$ | $\frac{3}{2}^+$ | 1.23 | 1.36 | 1860 | 300 | 0.21 | $b^c$ |
| $F_{17}$ | $\frac{7}{2}^+$ | 1.47 | 1.60 | 1980 | 220 | 0.13 | $b^c$ |
| $D_{13}$ | $\frac{3}{2}^-$ | 1.65 | 1.78 | 2060 | 290 | 0.26 | $b^c$ |
| $P_{33}$ | $\frac{3}{2}^+$ | 0.90 | 1.03 | 1690 | 280 | 0.10 | $b^b$ |
| $D_{33}$ | $\frac{3}{2}^-$ | 0.90 | 1.03 | 1690 | 270 | 0.14 | $b^a$ |
| $F_{35}$ | $\frac{5}{2}^+$ | 1.33 | 1.46 | 1910 | 350 | 0.16 | $b^a$ |
| $P_{31}$ | $\frac{1}{2}^+$ | 1.37 | 1.50 | 1930 | 340 | 0.3 | $b^b$ |
| $D_{35}$ | $\frac{5}{2}^-$ | 1.41 | 1.54 | 1950 | 310 | 0.15 | $b^c$ |

[a] Strong candidates.

[b] Less certain.

[c] Very weak evidence.

*2.* As discussed in Section III-8, some background in the same *IJP* state as the resonance can distort the circular behavior of the amplitude. Figures 35 and 38 show that only the $P_{33}$ amplitude has a circular behavior for a large energy interval. In this case the resonant parameters can be chosen as follows: the resonant mass $M$ is where $T_e(E)$ crosses the imaginary axis, $x_e$ is the diameter of the circle at this point, and the total width $\Gamma$ is given by the difference $E_1 - E_2$ of the two values $(\varepsilon = \pm 1)$ where $|\operatorname{Re} T(E)| = |\operatorname{Im} T(E)| = x/2$. For the $D_{13}$, $D_{15}$, and $F_{15}$ amplitudes with the present data, we can use this method as a first approximation. For the other amplitudes the background should be parameterized and the resonance parameters should be found according to the anlysis mentioned in Section III-8 which requires information on the inelastic channels. This type of analysis has been done only for the $S_{11}$, which will be discussed in Section V-4. Until a detailed analysis of this type is done, the *criterion of maximum velocity* could be used to choose the resonance energy $M$ [for a Breit-Wigner resonance it is easy to show that $M$ corresponds to the point of maximum variation for the amplitude [1]]. The value of $x_e$ in this case will be the diameter of the circle and $-\Gamma/2(+\Gamma/2)$ will be given by the energy corresponding to a quarter circle to the right (left) of the resonant energy. The only amplitude where this method could easily be applied is the $P_{11}$ which presents maximum velocity at $\approx M = 1420$ MeV for the Saclay solutions. This would correspond to the 180° point of a circle starting from a negative value of the real part of the amplitude, in agreement with Roper et al.,[57] who find that the $P_{11}$ starts off negative. Other experimental results on the $P_{11}$ state will be presented in Section V-7.

In conclusion, below $M = 2000$ MeV, the two analyses agree on the existence of the first nine resonances listed in Table X, although they do not agree on the parameters for each of these resonances. However, with the exception of the $P_{33}[\Delta(1236)]$, none of the amplitudes shows a circular behavior (indication of background under the resonant state), therefore better data and information on the inelastic channels are necessary in order to determine uniquely all the parameters of the resonances. The values reported in Table X are the most educated guesses which can be made at the present time. The second part of Table X shows the nine new states claimed by the CERN group with an attempt to classify them on their probability of survival (this classification is taken from ref. 1).

Finally the photoproduction data have been fitted by Ecklund and

Walker[70] according to a model suggested by Moravcsik,[59] as mentioned in Section V-1. The data show the presence of all the resonances of Table X (the $D_{15}$ formation is considerably suppressed) except for the $J = \frac{1}{2}$ states which are not detectable with the method employed (fit to Legendre polynomial coefficients which represent the interference terms of a one-pion exchange and resonant amplitudes).

### 4. Resonances in the $S_{11}$ State. $\eta$ Production Near Threshold

The $S_{11}$ amplitude of Figures 35 and 37 shows a peculiar behavior and requires further study in order to extract the resonance parameters. Michel[17] has suggested that its shape is due to the presence of two resonances, as we have listed in Table X, and that the resonance at $M = 1700$ MeV is a slowly varying background to the first resonance. He has, therefore, performed the analysis discussed in Section III-8 and obtained resonance parameters very close to the ones reported in Table X. In order to completely understand the behavior of this amplitude, more experimental data are necessary, since the various phase shift analyses do not agree on its shape. However, Michel's interpretation of the Saclay results[16] is very attractive, for the moment.

The $S_{11}$ resonance at $M = 1550$ MeV seems to be associated with the observed large cross section for $\pi p \to \eta n$ production near threshold ($E_T = 1488$ MeV, $T_\pi = 561$ MeV). Three experiments have been reported up to now in this energy region[71] and are in very good agreement with each other; in addition, the cross section for $\gamma p \to \eta p$ shows similar behavior,[72] therefore many authors have studied the connection between the resonance detected in elastic scattering and the $\eta n$ inelastic channel.

Davies and Moorhouse,[73] in a recent article, have explored the possibility that the large $\eta$ cross section is not connected with the $S_{11}$ resonance, but is produced by other amplitudes. However, after trying many different fits, they conclude that the present experimental data require that the $S_{11}$ decay through the $\eta n$ channel unless the normalization of the $\eta n$ cross sections up to $T_\pi = 700$ MeV is wrong by 15 or 20% and the angular distributions are wrong.

Let us now review the analyses the various authors have performed on the data.

1. Dobson[74] has performed a two-channel scattering length analysis on the $\pi p \to \eta n$ data and the elastic $\pi p$ data using ALDL[63]

and Cence's[67] phase shifts. The formalism of Section III-14 is used, zero effective range is assumed, and only $S$ wave is considered, therefore the scattering amplitudes are expressed by Eq. (3.95). Searching for zeros of the denominator $D(s)$, he finds that the ALDL phase shifts would require a Breit-Wigner type of resonance in the $\eta n$ channel with $M \sim 1510$ MeV, while the Cence phase shift would require a "virtual state" (at $M \sim 1460$ MeV). The difference between the two states has been discussed in Section III-16. His fit of the total $\eta n$ cross section, however, is not very good, as shown by the dashed line in Figure 40. It misses the lowest energy point, although the high energy points are in agreement with the data. As discussed by Davies and Moorhouse,[73] this is probably due to the fact that the zero-effective range approximation is not adequate to describe these data or that other partial waves play an important role in this energy region.

2. Ball[75] has constructed a dynamical model of the $\eta$-nucleon interaction which depends on only two parameters. His fit to the $\eta n$

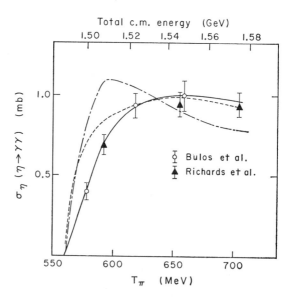

FIG. 40. The $\pi p \to \eta n$ total cross section with various fits: (–––) fit by Dobson,[74] (–·–) fit by Ball,[75] (——) fit by Hendry and Moorhouse[77] obtained with a method similar to Davies B (see text), but using older data.

cross section is shown in Figure 40 and it, too, misses the lowest energy points. This model would predict a pole of the $S$ matrix below the $\eta n$ threshold, but far from the physical sheet (at $M \sim 1460$ MeV) and it would be a "virtual state pole" according to the nomenclature of Fraser and Hendry,[30] discussed in Section III-16.

3. Uchiyama-Campbell and Logan[28] have introduced in their fit $P$ and $D$ waves in addition to the $S$ wave. They have used two methods of calculation which give similar results.

a. They fit only $\eta n$ with three Breit-Wigner amplitudes, (1) the $S$ wave resonance with only two open channels ($\pi p$ and $\eta n$) with $\Gamma_{\pi p}$, $\Gamma_{nn}$, $M_R$ as parameters; (2) the $P_{11}$ resonance chosen at $M = 1503$ MeV and $\Gamma = 308$ MeV (they show that the results are not sensitive to this choice) with $\Gamma_{nn}$ left as a parameter and other inelastic channels allowed; (3) the $D_{13}$ resonance at $M = 1531$ MeV and $\Gamma = 120$ MeV with $\Gamma_{nn}$ left as a parameter and still other inelastic channels allowed. They obtain two good fits of the $\eta n$ cross sections and angular distributions as shown in Figure 41. These two solutions are shown in Table XI with the symbols BWI

TABLE XI

Results of Various Fits to $\pi^- p \to \eta n$ Data[a]

| Parameter | Uchiyama BWI | Uchiyama BWII | Davies B | Davies C | Davies D |
|---|---|---|---|---|---|
| $E_R$ | 1557 | 1565 | 1507 | 1534 | 1506 |
| $\Gamma$ | 156 | 144 | 108 | 168 | 94 |
| $x_e$ | 0.71 | 0.29 | 0.31 | 0.43 | 0.41 |
| $x_{\eta n}$ | 0.29 | 0.71 | 0.69 | 0.45 | 0.43 |
| $\delta_\beta$ | | | $-25°$ | $-24°$ | $-18°$ |
| Channels for $S$ wave | 2 | 2 | 2 | 3 | 3 |
| Phase shifts used | Not fitted | Not fitted | Bareyre | Bareyre | Bransden I |
| Degrees of freedom[b] | 41 | 41 | 12 | 9 | 15 |
| $\chi^2$ | 33.7 | 31.1 | 28 | 7 | 6 |

[a] Only data of Bulos et al.[71a] and Richards et al.[71b] have been included in the fits.

[b] Uchiyama-Campbell and Logan[28] fit the angular distributions, while Davies and Moorhouse[73] fit the Legendre polynomial coefficients; therefore the number of experimental points used by the latter authors is smaller.

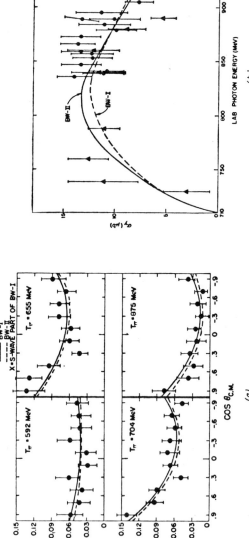

FIG. 41. (a) The curves represent the BWI (——) and BWII (– – –) fits of Uchiyama-Campbell and Logan[28] to total and differential cross section of $\pi p \to n\gamma$. (b) Fit of the above solutions to the $\gamma p \to \eta p$ data, when the $S_{11}$ resonance at $M \sim 1550$ MeV is allowed to decay in the $\gamma p$ channel ($x_{\gamma p} \sim 0.002$).[76]

and BWII. The total contribution of the $P_{11}$ and $D_{13}$ at the peak of the cross section turned out to be $\sim 4\%$. However, after the solutions are found they calculate the expected phase shifts assuming again only two channels in the $S$ wave and the agreement with the phase shifts reported by the various groups of Section V-2 is not very good. They also fit[76] the photoproduction data using these two solutions and adding a third channel $N(1560) \to \gamma p$, and find good agreement with the data, as shown in Figure 41$b$. The two solutions yield $x_{\gamma p} = 0.2\%$ or $x_{\gamma p} \sim 0.1\%$.

$b$. The $P_{11}$ and $D_{13}$ are expressed through Breit-Wigner amplitudes as before, while the $S_{11}$ amplitude is replaced by a two-channel effective range approximation. Using Eqs. (3.93) and (3.94), they obtain expressions like Eq. (3.95) for the $\mathbf{T}$ matrix elements, where $M_{ii}$ has to be replaced by $A_i = M_{ii} + R_{ii}(E - E_t)$, $E_t$ being the threshold energy, since Eq. (3.95) was obtained for zero effective range. The positions of the poles are found with a search for zeros of the denominator $D(s)$. With the usual $\chi^2$ minimization procedure they find three solutions, two being similar to BWI and BWII of Table XI and the third very close to the BWII. This coincidence of the solutions is very instructive, because it shows that for a pole above threshold (as their solutions indicate) the use of a Breit-Wigner parametrization or an effective range parameterization is equivalent.

4. Davies and Moorhouse[73] have fitted the $\eta n$ data and the $S_{11}$ phase shifts of $\pi p$ scattering at the same time in a unique fit. In the $\eta n$ channel they added to the $S$ wave a $D$ wave background produced by the $D_{13}$ resonance. Different models have been used to fit the data, but the only good fits obtained require that the $S_{11}$ resonance contributes at least 90% to the peak of the $\eta n$ cross section.

$a$. They have examined the possibility that the reduced $\mathbf{K}$ matrix below the $\eta$ threshold, $K_r$ with one less dimension as discussed in Section III-15, has a pole which produces the large $\eta n$ cross section. None of their fits is consistent with this hypothesis, therefore they exclude the possibility that a virtual bound state [like $\Lambda(1405)$] is at the origin of the effect.

$b$. They have tried to introduce a large $D$ wave contribution to the peak, but this turned out to be in disagreement with the behavior of the data at low energy, which show large $S$ wave production according to Jones et al.[71c]

*c.* They have finally used the **K** matrix formalism for the *S* wave and a Breit-Wigner amplitude for the *D* wave. The solution Davies B of Table XI was obtained assuming a two-channel *S* wave with nonzero effective range according to the formalism of Section III-14; however they do not make the assumption that the **R** matrix is diagonal. This model is similar to the one used by Uchiyama-Campbell and Logan.[28] The solution Davies B is very close to BWII which is in qualitative agreement with the Bareyre et al.[16] phase shifts. The confidence level of Davies B looks worse because the phase shifts have been fitted at the same time. Solutions C and D are obtained assuming a three-channel **K** matrix (the third channel includes all possible inelastic processes) so the **M** matrix of Eq. (3.94) is a 3 × 3 matrix, and the **R** matrix is taken to be a 2 × 2 matrix because the matrix elements for the third channel are assumed constant. The authors have also tried a three-channel fit of the $\eta n$ data and the Bareyre et al.[16] phase shifts assuming a large contribution of the *D* wave, but they did not obtain any good fits. In Table XI, the phase $\delta_B$ is the background phase to the resonance at $M \sim 1550$ MeV, as discussed in Section III-8. It is negative in all three fits, which means that the resonance circle starts off tangent to a straight line making a negative angle with the real axis, unlike Figure 9.

In conclusion, more data are necessary before the connection of the $S_{11}$ and the $\eta n$ channel is clarified, but this particular case illustrates quite well the difficulties encountered in analyzing many channels at the same time.

## 5. Use of Polarized Targets

A new technique recently introduced will help considerably in the analysis of nucleon resonances. The measure of the polarization of the recoil proton is very difficult, and this fact has delayed the understanding of $\pi p$ scattering for a long time. This new technique involves the use of a polarized target. As we have seen in Section III-3, the measure of the angular distribution of the recoil proton, $I(\theta)$, is sufficient to determine its polarization. In fact, according to Eq. (3.22),

$$I(\theta) = I_0(\theta)(1 + \mathbf{P}_0 \cdot \mathbf{P}_T)$$

where $I_0(\theta)$ and $\mathbf{P}_0$ are the differential cross section and the polarization, respectively, of the recoil proton for an unpolarized target, and $\mathbf{P}_T$ is the polarization of the target. By measuring a left–right asymmetry at a given angle $\theta$, we can obtain $P_0$ if $P_T$ is known:

$$\frac{I_L(\theta) - I_R(\theta)}{I_L(\theta) + I_R(\theta)} = P_0(\theta)P_T$$

Duke et al.,[78a] at Nimrod, have measured both $I_0(\theta)$ and $P_0(\theta)$ in the region between 1.56 and 2.02 GeV total c.m. energy for both $\pi^-$ and $\pi^+$ mesons ($0.8 < P_\pi < 1.7$ GeV/c). From these data, the spin and parity of the $\Delta(1920)$ were unambiguously assigned and were very recently confirmed by the phase-shift analyses of Figures 35 and 38.

Yokosawa et al.[79] at the ZGS in Argonne have measured both $I_0(\theta)$ and $P_0(\theta)$ at five different energies between 2.025 and 2.366 GeV total $\pi^-p$ energy ($1.7 < P_\pi < 2.5$ GeV/c). They have been able to establish the $J^P$ assignment of $N(2190)$.

Chamberlain et al.[80] at the Bevatron in Berkeley have done very precise polarization measurements of both $\pi^+p$ and $\pi^-p$ scattering from 1.48 to 2.82 GeV total c.m. energy ($0.67 \leq P_\pi \leq 3.75$ GeV/c) (see Fig. 31). These data, along with the data of Cox et al.[78b] of Figure 31, have been included in the phase-shift analysis of the Saclay[16] and CERN[63] groups and have made the extension of the analysis above $T_\pi = 1$ GeV possible.

### A. $\Delta(1920)$

Duke et al.[78a] have performed a partial wave analysis on their data which leads to an assignment $J^P = \frac{7}{2}^+$ for this resonance. It is useful to report their procedure here, even if phase-shift analyses have now confirmed this assignment. Figure 42 shows the coefficients of the Legendre polynomial expansion of differential cross section and polarization according to:

$$\left(\frac{d\sigma}{d\Omega}\right)^\pm = \sum_n C_n{}^\pm P_n(\cos\theta)$$

$$\frac{1}{\sin\theta}P_0\left(\frac{d\sigma}{d\Omega}\right)^\pm = \sum_n D_n{}^\pm P_n(\cos\theta)$$

The first expression follows our notation of Eq. (3.106), except for the $\lambda^2$ factor incorporated in the $C_n{}^\pm$, therefore Table V can be used to relate the coefficients $C_n{}^\pm$ with the various amplitudes, while the second

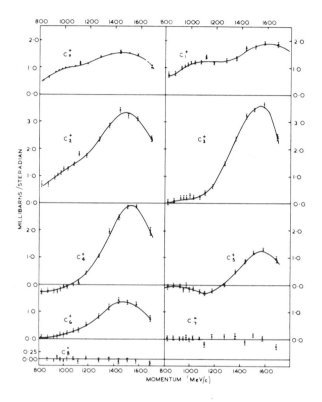

FIG. 42a. The coefficients at the Legendre polynomial expansion defined in the text from the experiment of Duke et al.[78a] Coefficients for $\pi^+ p$ differential cross section [points at 1.12, 1.44, and 1.69 GeV/c are taken from Helland et al.[81]].

expansion is different. The relevant coefficients for the discussion of these data are related to the amplitudes, up to $G_7$, as follows:

$$C_5/\lambda^2 = 14.3(F_5{}^*D_5) + 5.7(F_7{}^*D_5 + G_7{}^*F_5) + 6.6(G_7{}^*F_7)$$
$$C_6/\lambda^2 = 18.2(F_7{}^*F_5 + G_7{}^*D_5) + 3.0(|F_7|^2 + |G_7|^2)$$
$$C_7/\lambda^2 = 22.8(F_7{}^*G_7)$$
$$D_4/\lambda^2 = -12.9(F_5{}^*D_5) + 0.86(F_7{}^*D_5 - G_7{}^*F_5) - 22.6(G_7{}^*F_7)$$
$$D_5/\lambda^2 = 16.7(F_7{}^*F_5 - G_7{}^*D_5)$$

The first interesting feature which can be observed in Figure 42 is the behavior of the coefficient $C_5{}^-$ around the 1-GeV/c region. This is an

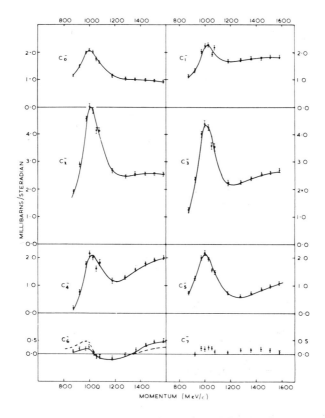

FIG. 42*b*. The coefficients at the Legendre polynomial expansion defined in the text from the experiment of Duke et al.[78a] Coefficients for $\pi^- p$ differential cross section.

indication of a large interference term ($F_5 F_5$) corresponding to two resonances at a very close mass in the $I = \frac{1}{2}$ isotopic spin state, since the $C^+$ coefficients do not show any particular structure in this energy region. (The $S_{31}$ at $M \sim 1700$ MeV is very difficult to detect with this method.) This has been the first indication of two very close resonances ($D_{15}$ and $F_{15}$) at $M \sim 1690$ MeV. The subsequent phase shift analysis of Bareyre et al.[16] confirmed this hypothesis.

The coefficients of the $\pi^+ p$ angular distributions as functions of the $\pi^-$ incident momentum clearly show the presence of $\Delta(1920)$. The $C_5{}^+$ and $C_6{}^+$ indicate that this resonance is either an $F_7$ state interfering with a $D_5$ background or a $G_7$ state interfering with an $F_5$ background.

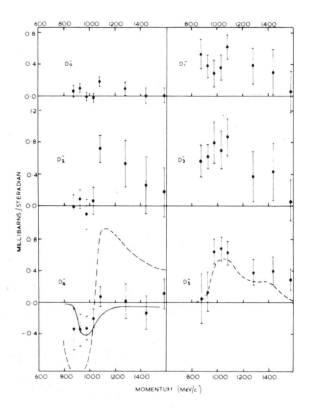

FIG. 42c. The coefficients at the Legendre polynomial expansion defined in the text from the experiment of Duke et al.[78a] Polarization coefficients for $\pi^- p$ scattering. These data show a large $D_5 F_5$ interference term in $\pi^- p$ data, effect of two resonances at $M \sim 1690$ MeV ($P_\pi = 1.0$ GeV/c), and the presence of $\Delta(1920)$ with $J^P = \frac{7}{2}^+$ in the $\pi^+ p$ data.

In fact, both the $F_5 D_5$ term and the $F_7 G_7$ term have to be small in order to reproduce the observed $C_6^+$ and $C_7^+$. The positive sign of the polarization coefficient $D_5^-$ resolves the ambiguity and establishes the $\Delta(1920)$ as an $F_7$ resonance ($J^P = \frac{7}{2}^+$) with $M = 1920$ MeV, $\Gamma = 170$ MeV, $x = 0.41$.

### B. N(2190)

Yokosawa et al.[79] have analyzed their data and all the data available between 1.4 and 2.5 GeV/c. Their analysis favors the assignment $J^P = \frac{7}{2}^-$ for $N(2190)$ through the study of the Legendre polynomial coefficients of the angular distributions and the coefficients of a Legendre function expansion of the polarization (3.106). These coefficients are related to the amplitudes as in Table VI. From the coefficients of the angular distribution they eliminate the possibility of $J > \frac{7}{2}$. From the sign of the $b_6$ coefficient they obtain the $G_7$ assignment for this resonant state. In addition, they attempt a phase-shift analysis, which is quite difficult because of the large energy steps of the existent data. However, using smoothness of amplitudes as a criterion as Bareyre et al.,[16] they obtain for $F_{17}$ and $G_{17}$ a set of solutions which show the two resonances at $M = 1920$ MeV and $M = 2190$ MeV.

Independent evidence on the parity of $N(2190)$ will be reported in Section V-9.

## 6. Inelastic Channels of Baryon States with Mass Below 2.2 GeV

Figures 43 and 44 show the cross sections for the reactions

$$\pi^- p \to \Lambda K^\circ$$
$$\pi^- p \to \Sigma^- K^+$$
$$\pi^- p \to \Sigma^\circ K^\circ$$

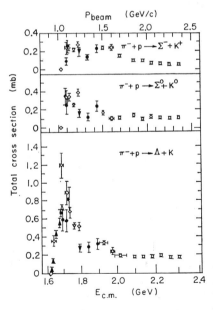

FIG. 43. Cross sections for associated production of strange particles up to 2.5 GeV total $\pi^- p$ energy, as collected by Schwartz.[82]

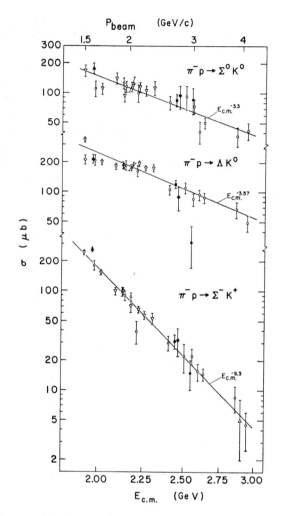

FIG. 44. Cross sections for associated production of strange particles up to $\pi^-$ incident energy of 4.0 GeV/c[82,83] (total c.m. energy of 3 GeV).

From threshold to $P_\pi = 2.4$ GeV/c ($M_{\pi p} < 2.5$ GeV) the data have been collected by Schwartz[82] (Fig. 43), and up to $P_\pi = 4$ GeV/c by Dahl et al.[83] (Fig. 44). The cross sections show a peculiar rise just above threshold and then a fall-off. The maximum corresponds to a total c.m. energy of 1700 MeV. Whether this behavior is due to a large $S$ wave production close to threshold or to resonant phenomena is not clear. From phase shift analysis we know that at least four resonant states are present in this region, however a complete partial wave analysis of the associated production data has not been done yet. In the region of $N(2190)$, Schwartz has analyzed the coefficients of the Legendre polynomial expansion and his results are consistent with a branching ratio for $N(2190) \rightarrow \Delta \bar{K}$ of less than 10%. The elasticity of all the resonances at and above $M = 1690$ MeV is small, therefore there might be some decay of these resonances in the $YK$ channels. It appears that further data and analyses are necessary before the decay into strange particles is understood.

The inelastic decay modes, involving decays into resonant states of lower mass or into multipion final states, like

$$N \text{ or } \Delta \rightarrow \Delta(1236) + \pi$$
$$\rightarrow N(1512) + \pi \text{ etc.} \qquad (5.2)$$
$$N \text{ or } \Delta \rightarrow N\pi\pi$$
$$\rightarrow N\pi\pi\pi \text{ etc.}$$

appear to be larger than the decays in strange particle channels. Figure 45 shows the cross sections for the three possible final states with two pions in the $\pi^-p$ interactions, as collected by Merlo and Valladas.[84] All three cross sections show structure in the 600- and 900-MeV regions, where, according to Figure 11 and Table X, at least six resonant states are present. The $P_{11}$, at about 430 MeV, seems to produce a shoulder in the $\pi^+\pi^-n$ cross section in the expected energy region.

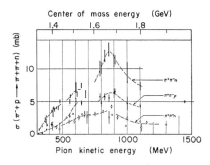

FIG. 45. Total cross sections of the reactions $\pi^-p \rightarrow \pi^0\pi^+n$, $\pi^-p \rightarrow \pi^0\pi^-p$, and $\pi^-p \rightarrow \pi^0\pi^0n$ plotted against incident pion kinetic energy by Merlo and Valladas.[84] The upper scale is the total c.m. energy for the $\pi^-p$ system.

A detailed partial wave analysis, as well as a break down into the various channels [Eq. (5.2)] has not been done yet on these data, because of the scarcity of the data and the complications involved in the analysis. The three-body final state $N\pi\pi$, in fact, presents many of the problems discussed in Section IV: (a) the Dalitz plot shows crossing resonance bands in the two $N\pi$ systems and $\pi\pi$ interactions, (b) Bose symmetrization has to be taken into account, and (c) partial wave analysis is difficult because of uncertainties in the resonance production in the final state and because many partial waves are involved in the initial state.

Figure 46 shows the cross sections for the $I = \frac{3}{2}$ inelastic processes, taken from Valladas review article.[85] The single pion production cross section $\pi^+ p \to \pi^+ \pi^\circ p$ shows an enhancement at the energy of the $S_{31}$ resonance (the shoulder in $\pi^+ p$ total cross section). Here also, even if the problem is simplified by the presence of only one $I$-spin state, the analysis of the data is far from complete.

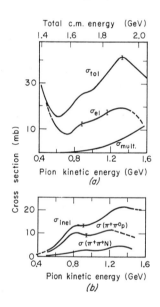

Fig. 46. Cross sections versus incident kinetic energy for $\pi^+ p$ interactions, as plotted by Valladas.[85] The upper scale is total c.m. energy. (a) Total elastic and multipion production cross sections. (b) Total inelastic cross section and the two partial cross sections with only one pion production.

Many groups are working on this problem at the present time, and it is hoped that the situation will be clarified soon.

### 7. Production of Baryon States with Mass Below 2.2 GeV

All the baryon states below $M = 2.2$ GeV have also been seen in production experiments, although in these experiments it is not possible to distinguish between the many states with $M \sim 1520$ MeV and $M \sim 1690$ MeV. However, $P_{11}$, the state at $M = 1470$ MeV, seems to be isolated from the $S_{11}$ and $D_{13}$ states, while this is not the case in total cross section experiments (Figs. 11 and 29).

Many experiments of the type

$$p + p \rightarrow p + X^+$$

where $X^+$ can be in an isotopic spin state $I = \frac{1}{2}$ or $\frac{3}{2}$, have been performed in various laboratories at many incident proton momenta.[86-88] In these experiments only the proton is detected in the final state (its momentum and angle are measured), therefore $X^+$ is the missing mass of the system.

Figure 47 illustrates the results of the experiment of Blair et al.[87] at four different incident proton momenta between 2.85 and 7.88 GeV/c. The cross section for $\Delta(1236)$ seems to diminish with increasing incident momentum and with increasing value of momentum transfer squared, $|t|$, defined in Section IV-5. The latter behavior is understood in terms of a one-pion exchange mechanism, as listed in Table IX, which predicts production at small values of $|t|$ as discussed in Section IV-5. For the other states the production mechanism is less clear.

Figure 48, taken from Anderson et al.,[88] shows the production of various states at two fixed values of $|t|$ [$|t| = 0.042$ (GeV/c)$^2$ and $|t| = 0.82$ (GeV/c)$^2$] for various incident proton momenta. Here again we see that the production cross section decreases for increasing proton momenta and increasing values of $|t|$. The total cross section for the various states is shown in Figure 49, which contains the data of refs. 87 and 88.

A very interesting phenomenon is observed by Gellert et al.,[89] who studied $p + p$ interactions in a hydrogen bubble chamber, and so were able to measure all the produced particles. At an incident momentum $P_p = 6.6$ GeV/c, they analyzed the following reaction,

$$p + p \rightarrow \Delta(1236)^{2+} + p + \pi^-$$

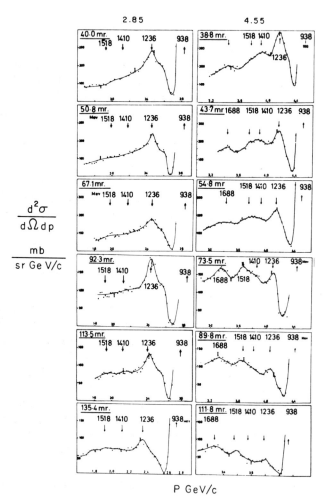

FIG. 47. Differential cross sections for the reaction $p + p \rightarrow p + X^+$, from Blair et al.[87] as function of the momentum of the outgoing proton. Each vertical column refers to the incident momentum shown at the top (in GeV/c). The laboratory scattering angle expressed in milliradians is shown in each graph. Arrows indicate the position of known resonances which can be produced in this experiment.

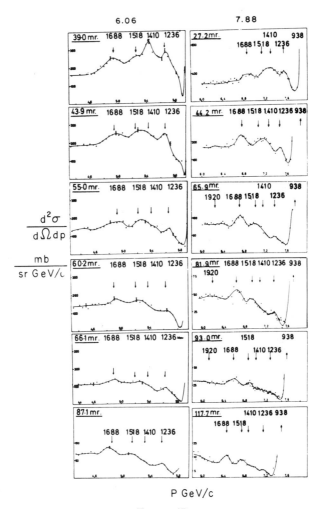

$$\frac{d^2\sigma}{d\Omega\,dp}$$

$$\frac{mb}{sr\ GeV/c}$$

P GeV/c

FIGURE 47

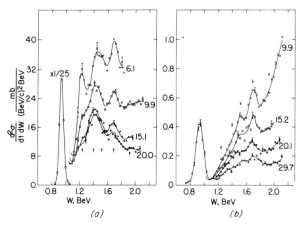

Fig. 48. Cross sections for the reaction $p + p \to p + X^+$, from Anderson et al.[88] as function of total energy for $X^+$. The values on the curves indicate the incident proton momentum in GeV/c. The arrows indicate, from left to right, the position of the baryon states $\Delta(1236)$, $N(1400)$, $N(1520)$, $N(1690)$, and $\Delta(1920)$. The two plots refer to different values of the momentum transfer (a) for $|t| = 0.042$ (GeV/c)$^2$, (b) for $|t| = 0.82$ (GeV/c)$^2$.

where the $\Delta^{++}$ is produced at very small angles and therefore this process can be described by the diagram of Figure 50a. The proton angular distribution at the upper vertex has been calculated assuming $\pi p$ elastic scattering on a real pion. Using the known phase shifts of $\pi p$ scattering, the authors have been able to predict all the coefficients of the Legendre polynomial expansion of the measured proton angular distribution, except for $A_0 = \sigma/4\pi\lambda^2$. The differential cross section is expressed as

$$\frac{d\sigma}{d\Omega} = \lambda^2 \sum_n A_n P_n = \frac{\sigma}{4\pi} \sum_n \frac{A_n}{A_0} P_n$$

Figure 50b shows the calculated coefficients $A_n/A_0$ compared with the experimental ones; the agreement is remarkable.

Gellert et al. have also studied the invariant mass of the $\Delta(1236)^{2+}\pi^-$ system. They find a large enhancement at a mass of $\sim 1450$ MeV in the events associated with the diagram of Figure 50a, but not in the other events. The enhancement appears to be larger at a very small momentum transfer, which corresponds to $\pi^- p \to \pi^- p$ diffraction scattering at the upper vertex of Figure 50a; therefore, the authors attribute the enhancement at $M \sim 1450$ MeV to a kinematical effect which is commonly

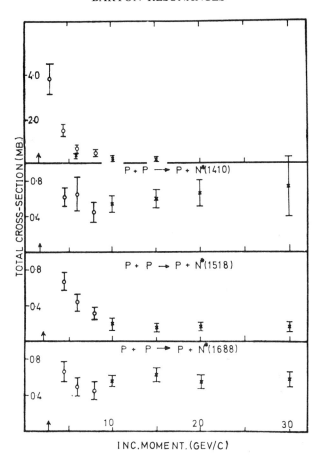

FIG. 49. Total cross section for the reaction $p + p \rightarrow p + N^{*+}$ as function of the incident momentum. The upper curve refers to production of $\Delta(1236)$. $\bar{\ominus}$ experimental points of Blair et al.[87] $\bar{\times}$ experimental points of Anderson et al.[88]

known as the "Deck Mechanism."[90] According to this model the $\Delta(1236)$ and the $\pi^-$ from the upper vertex tend to be peaked at low invariant mass. In the experiments of Blair et al.[87] and Anderson et al.[88] an enhancement at $M \sim 1400$ MeV has been observed as seen in Figure 47 and 48, but it disappears at large momentum transfer and the cross section for this enhancement seems to be very close to the one found by Gellert et al. At this point, then, it is questionable whether the

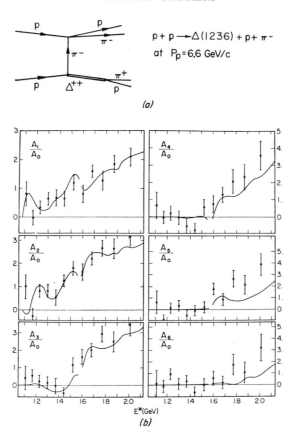

*(a)*

*(b)*

FIG. 50. Experimental results on $p + p \rightarrow \Delta(1236) + p + \pi^-$ of Gellert et al.[78] (a) Shows the diagram which has the major contributions to the reaction, and (b) shows the Legendre polynomial coefficients of the $\pi^- p \rightarrow \pi^- p$ differential cross section at the upper vertex. The curves represent the prediction of the phase shift analysis of $\pi p$ scattering.

$N(1400)$ observed in the missing mass type of experiments has to be identified with an inelastic channel of the $P_{11}$ resonance found in phase shift analyses or with a kinematical effect like the "Deck Mechanism." Further work has to be done on this model, and more experiments at different incident energies should be performed before any conclusion can be drawn on this subject.

## 8. Resonances with Mass Greater than 2.2 GeV

In Figures 11 and 29 we have seen an indication of an enhancement in the $\pi^+ p$ total cross section corresponding to a mass of 2400 MeV. Since then, other evidence has been added to the existence of this and other possible resonances, in photoproduction by Alvarez et al.,[91a] and in charge-exchange cross sections by Wahlig et al.[91b] The total cross sections have been measured with large accuracy by Criton et al.,[92] and more structure has appeared. Figure 51 shows the $I = \frac{3}{2}$ and $I = \frac{1}{2}$ total cross sections, as reported by Citron et al.[92] They show some structure, and the authors suggest that the following resonances are present in these data.

|  | Mass, MeV | Width, MeV | $\sigma_R$, mb | $(J + \frac{1}{2})x_e$ |
|---|---|---|---|---|
| $N^*$ | 2640 | 360 | 1.55 | 0.44 |
|  | 3020 | 400 | 0.15 | 0.055 |
| $\Delta$ | 2420 | 310 | 3.15 | 0.70 |
|  | 2840 | 400 | 0.77 | 0.26 |
|  | 3220 | 440 | 0.14 | 0.060 |

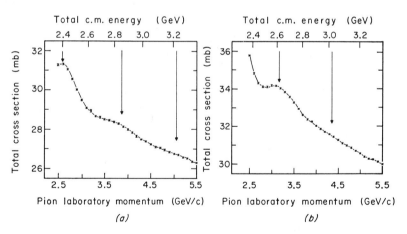

FIG. 51. The pion–proton total cross sections above 2.4 GeV/c,[92] (a) The $I = \frac{3}{2}$ cross section, (b) the $I = \frac{1}{2}$ cross section. Arrows indicate position of possible large mass resonances.

The contribution of a resonant state to the total cross section at the resonant energy is, according to Eq. (3.49),

$$\sigma_R = 4\pi\lambda^2(J + \tfrac{1}{2})x_e$$

The column on the right gives the product of spin factors and elasticities.

The charge-exchange data agree with this situation. Figure 52 shows the charge-exchange forward cross section from 1.5 to 1.8 GeV/c. This plot is taken from Höhler et al.[69] The arrows 2 through 5 refer to the position of the five higher mass resonances of the above table. The resonances $N(3020)$ and $\Delta(3220)$ are not evident in either Figures 51 or 52, and it is hoped a different kind of experiment will be used to ascertain their existence.

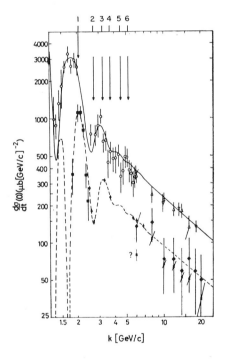

Fig. 52. Charge-exchange cross section (1.5–18 GeV/c). Plot from Höhler et al.[69] (——) predication of dispersion relation, (– – –) contribution of imaginary part. Data from various experiments listed in ref. 69. Arrows indicate the position of various resonances: $N(2190)$, $\Delta(2420)$, $N(2650)$, $\Delta(2850)$, $N(3020)$, and $\Delta(3220)$.

*9. Elastic Scattering at 180°*

The experimental differential cross section in the backward direction shows a sharp peak at 180°; this is true for $\pi^-p$ and $\pi^+p$ at 2 GeV/c and at higher energy. When the presence of only one resonance is assumed, the spin-flip and non-spin-flip amplitudes at 180° will be [see Eq. (3.23)]:

$$f(180°) = \lambda(J + \tfrac{1}{2})T_R P_l(-1) = \lambda(J + \tfrac{1}{2})[x_e/(\varepsilon - i)](-1)^l \quad (5.3)$$
$$g(180°) = 0$$

where we have used the relation $P_l(-1)^l = (-1)^l$, and, for the resonance, the Breit-Wigner amplitude of Eq. (3.41). This amplitude has the same sign as $(-1)^l$ up to the resonance energy and changes sign for $E > E_R$. If more than one resonance is present, the square of the sum of all the amplitudes will give the behavior of the cross section.

Kormanyos et al.,[93] at the ZGS, measured the cross section for $\pi^-p$ elastic scattering at 180° over the momentum range 1.6–3.5 GeV/c. Their data are shown in Figure 53a. The curve drawn on the data has been calculated by Dikmen[94] and assumes that only resonant amplitudes like Eq. (5.1) contribute to the cross section. The resonances used in the fit are the known resonances in this energy region from $\Delta(1920)$ to $\Delta(3220)$ and two additional ones according to the classification of Barger and Cline.[95] These authors suggest that all the known resonances except for the $S_{11}$ and $P_{11}$ states lie on three straight line trajectories [namely, they are recurrences of $N(938)$, $N(1525)$, and $\Delta(1236)$] in a Chew-Frautschi plot (Fig. 53b). In this way they assume the existence of two new states: $N(2200)$ and $N(2610)$. According to Eq. (5.3) the experimental data are sensitive only to the product $(J + \tfrac{1}{2})x_e$ $(-1)^l$ at the resonant energy; therefore, the assumption of Barger and Cline[95] would provide us with a value for $x_e$. The parameters used by Dikmen for the curve of Figure 53a are listed in Table XII; the values of $(J + \tfrac{1}{2})x_e$ are compared with the parameters obtained from other data.

Most of the values of $x_e$ for $M < 2.2$ GeV are poorly known, and above 2.2 GeV it is very hard to extract them from the total cross section data of Section V-8; therefore, I believe that all the conclusions from these data are speculative, except perhaps for the parities of $N(2190)$ and $\Delta(2410)$ which seem to be unambiguously determined. It should be mentioned, however, that Dikmen's fit was motivated by the explanation of these data, previously claimed by Barger and Cline,[95] by means

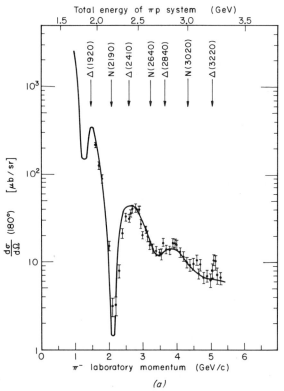

FIG. 53. $\pi^- p$ scattering at 180°. (*a*) Data of Kormanyos et al.[93] compared with the fits of Dikmen.[94] The curve is calculated using only the contribution of resonant amplitudes and the parity assignments according to the Regge recurrences scheme of Barger and Cline,[95] shown in (*b*).

of a sum of resonant amplitudes and a Regge trajectory exchange amplitude [Δ(1236) was assumed to be exchanged in the *u* channel in $\pi^- p$ scattering].

## 10. Conclusions on Y = 1 States

The phase shift analyses at low energy ($M_{\pi p} < 1750$ MeV) have shown that detailed analysis of experimental data is necessary in order to detect all the resonant states present, especially in the low partial waves. In fact, two peaks in total cross section data turned out to contain at least seven resonant states. These analyses have also shown that a large amount of data is necessary in order to understand the complexity of the $\pi p$ system.

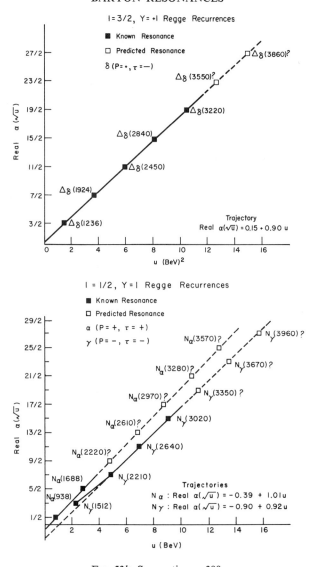

FIG. 53*b*. See caption p. 300

Figure 54 shows the established nucleonic resonances in a plot originally made by Tripp,[10] but brought up to date. It is possible that more accurate data above a mass of 1750 MeV and detailed analysis will populate this region with more resonances than are presently known. At high energy, however, the number of partial waves is large and the

TABLE XII

Parameters Used by Dikmen[94] to Fit the 180° Elastic Scattering

| State | $J^P$ | $x_e$ | $(J + \frac{1}{2})x_e$ | $[(J + \frac{1}{2})x_e]$ | $\Gamma$, MeV |
|---|---|---|---|---|---|
| $N(938)$ | $\frac{1}{2}^+$ | | | | |
| $N(1688)$ | $\frac{5}{2}^+$ | 0.6 | 1.8 | 1.95 [a] | 100 |
| $N(2200)$ | $(\frac{9}{2}^+)$ | 0.083 | 0.26 | — | 240 |
| $N(2610)$ | $(\frac{13}{2}^+)$ | 0.035 | 0.25 | — | 420 |
| $\Delta(1236)$ | $\frac{3}{2}^+$ | 1.0 | 2.0 | 2.0 [a] | 120 |
| $\Delta(1929)$ | $\frac{7}{2}^+$ | 0.46 | 1.84 | 2.0 [a] | 170 |
| $\Delta(2410)$ | $(\frac{11}{2}^+)$ | 0.163 | 0.78 | 0.70 [b] | 350 |
| $\Delta(2840)$ | $(\frac{15}{2}^+)$ | 0.061 | 0.49 | 0.26 [b] | 400 |
| $\Delta(3220)$ | $(\frac{19}{2}^+)$ | 0.025 | 0.25 | 0.060 [b] | 440 |
| $N(1512)$ | $\frac{3}{2}^-$ | 0.60 | 1.20 | 1.3 [a] | 120 |
| $N(2190)$ | $\frac{7}{2}^-$ | 0.20 | 0.80 | 1.2 [a] | 240 |
| $N(2640)$ | $(\frac{11}{2}^-)$ | 0.04 | 0.24 | 0.44 [b] | 350 |
| $N(3020)$ | $(\frac{15}{2}^-)$ | 0.002 | 0.016 | 0.055 [b] | 400 |
| $N(3350)$ | $(\frac{19}{2}^-)$ | 0.003 | 0.03 | — | 100 |

[a] Values taken from Table II.
[b] Values of Citron et al.[92] reported in Section V-8.

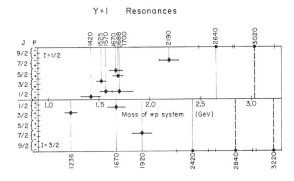

FIG. 54. Present spectroscopy of baryon resonances. The position along the vertical axis indicates the quantum numbers of the resonance. The mass and width of the resonance is indicated by the position and error flag along the horizontal axis. The quantum numbers of resonances above 2.4 GeV are not known at the present time.

elasticity of the resonances is low and, therefore, it will be difficult to analyze the data with the same methods used at low energy. Perhaps the study of inelastic channels, where a resonance can decay in a lower mass resonance, might help in clarifying the situation, if such decay modes turn out to be copious.

## VI. Baryon Resonances with Negative Strangeness ($Y = 0, -1$)

This section is a review of resonant states with baryon number $B = +1$ and negative strangeness $S = -1, -2$.

Most of these resonances have been discovered in production experiments and, in general, the analysis of the experimental data is different from that of nucleon resonances. However, as pointed out in Section IV-6, it is difficult to determine quantum numbers of resonant states in production experiments because the presence of very little background (as little as 5%) can produce difficulties in the uniqueness of the determination; therefore, accurate formation experiments are necessary. Of course, for $S = -2$ resonances this is not possible.

A peculiar characteristic of strange baryon states is that many two-body final states are open ($\bar{K}N$, $\Lambda\pi$, $\Sigma\pi$, $\Lambda\eta$) and when kinematics and isotopic spin conservation allow it, the resonance can decay in all these channels. In this case each channel provides information about the quantum numbers of the resonant state. This situation is different from $S = 0$ resonances where decays in the $N\eta$ and $YK$ channels are not large (with the exception of the $S_{11}$ resonance near the $N\eta$ threshold, discussed in Sect. V-4).

### 1. Survey of Experimental Data

There are many methods which can be used to detect resonant states with $S = -1$.

*a. Total cross section* experiments are useful as first exploratory means to find out which regions are interesting. However, accurate experiments have not been done until very recently. Figure 55 shows a collection of the measurements of $K^-p$ and $K^-d$ total cross sections made up to now.[96-101]

Chamberlain et al.[96] and Cook et al.[97] have performed experiments on total $K^-p$ cross sections at the Bevatron in 1961, which showed some structure in the 1 GeV/c region (total c.m. energy $M \sim 1820$ MeV)

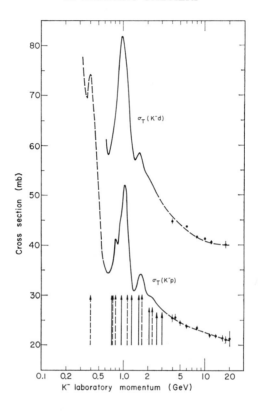

FIG. 55. The total cross section for $K^-p$ and $K^-d$ interactions from 0.1 to 20 GeV/c. The full line is hand drawn through the experimental points of refs. 98–100. (The errors are one to two times the width of the line.) The dashed curve is drawn in the regions where experimental errors are large. Some typical measurements are shown. Arrows show the position of known resonances with $I = 0$ (dashed arrows) and $I = 1$ (full arrows).

and in the 1.5 GeV/c region (c.m. energy $M \sim 2060$ MeV). However the $K^-d$ total cross section data were too scarce and the errors and energy resolution of the $K^-p$ data too large to study the detailed structure of these "bumps."

Cool et al. and Abrams et al.[98,99] at Brookhaven have recently performed an accurate measurement of the $K^-p$ and $K^-d$ total cross sections from 1.0 to 3.5 GeV/c incident $K^-$ momenta. The errors in these measurements are small and in Figure 55 they are of the order of the width of the line. Five new resonant states have been discovered in these data: $\Sigma(1915)$ and four more states with $M > 2.2$ GeV which will be discussed in Section VI-11.

Davies et al.,[100] at Nimrod, have also done a very accurate experiment in the 0.6–2.7 GeV/c region, thus increasing the region of high precision in Figure 55. By isolating the $I = 0$ from the $I = 1$ part of the cross section, as will be discussed in Section VI-6, these authors were able to discover a new $I = 0$ resonance at $M = 1695$ MeV ($P_K = 800$ MeV/c) which had escaped detection in all the previous experiments.

The total cross sections for $K^-p$ and $K^-d$ interactions have been measured up to $P_\pi = 20$ GeV/c in less precise experiments.[101]

b. *Formation experiments* turned out to be the most useful type of experiments to study spin and parity of resonant states. Partial wave analyses, according to Section III-17, can be performed on the data in order to identify the resonant amplitudes. $\Lambda(1520)$, $\Lambda(1675)$, $\Sigma(2035)$, and $\Lambda(2100)$ have been discovered with this method through the study of different two-body final states. As has been discussed in Section III-9, the enhancement in the total cross section for each channel is proportional to $x_\alpha x_\beta$ (where $\sum x_i = 1$). Therefore, if the elasticity for the resonance is small, the enhancement for each channel is small. The study of the differential cross sections is essential to the $J^P$ determination and the study of the interference terms between the various amplitudes is very useful to identify the resonant amplitude.

Figure 56 shows the total elastic cross section as a function of incident $K^-$ momentum as collected by Ferro-Luzzi.[102a] The cross section for the charge exchange reaction $K^-p \to \bar{K}^0n$ has been shown in Figure 2, which also shows $4\pi\lambda^2$ as function of incident momentum. Figures 57 and 58 show the total cross sections for the $\Lambda\pi$ and $\Sigma^\pm\pi^\mp$ channels. The positions of the known resonances are indicated by arrows.[102a]

c. *Production experiments* can, in certain circumstances, be the most favorable experiments to detect resonances. Resonances with small elasticities, $x_e$, might be coupled more strongly to the $\mu B$ channel (in a t channel production) of Figure 20 and therefore be more copiously produced in this type of experiment. This seems to be the case for the $\Sigma(1660)$, which will be discussed in Section VI-8. Resonances discovered in production experiments are: $\Sigma(1385)$, $\Lambda(1405)$, $\Sigma(1660)$, $\Sigma(1765)$, and, of course, all the $\Xi$ states. The study of spin parity of the resonant

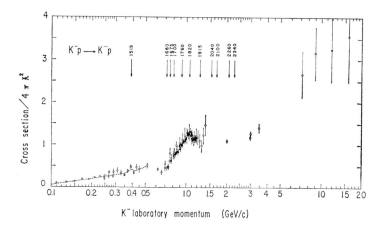

FIG. 56. Cross section, divided by $4\pi\lambda^2$ for $K^-p \to K^-p$ as a function of incident $K^-$ momentum as plotted by Ferro-Luzzi.[102a] The curves through the points represent the best solutions of the analyses of Kim[103] and Watson et al.[104] Arrows represent the position of known resonances.

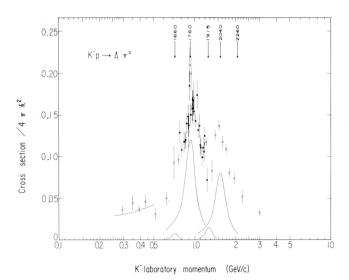

FIG. 57. The $\Lambda\pi$ total cross section, in units of $4\pi\lambda^2$, versus the momentum as plotted by Ferro-Luzzi.[102a] The positions of the known $I = 1$ resonances are indicated by arrows.

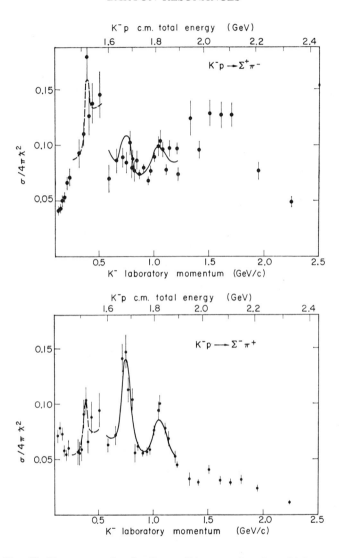

FIG. 58. The cross section for $K^-p \to \Sigma^\pm \pi^\mp$ as a function of laboratory $K^-$ momentum. The experimental points are: up to 0.3 GeV/c, Kim[103]; 0.25–0.51 GeV/c, Watson et al.[104]; 0.59–0.82, Rahm et al.[105]; 0.78–1.2, Armenteros et al.[106]; 1.2–1.7 GeV/c, Barbaro-Galtieri[107]; 1.80–1.95 GeV/c, Dauber et al.[108]; 2.24 GeV/c, London et al.[109] Dashed and full curves are fits of refs. 104 and 105, respectively.

states is complicated by the presence of background, as discussed in Sections IV-6 and IV-7.

## 2. $\Sigma(1385) \cdot P_{13}$

This was the first resonance discovered in a production experiment.[4] It appeared as a peak in the $\Lambda\pi$ invariant mass, which established the isotopic spin as $I = 1$, in the reaction $K^-p \to \Lambda\pi^+\pi^-$ at $P_K = 1.15$ GeV/c. Since then it has been detected also in pion- and antiproton-initiated reactions. Its main decay mode is $\Lambda\pi$, and the less frequent mode is $\Sigma\pi[(9 \pm 3)\%]$.

Although this resonance has been studied in many high statistics experiments, its mass and width are still not well measured (as for most of the baryon resonances); the values reported in Table II are averages of experiments in disagreement between themselves. As expected, there seems to be a definite electromagnetic mass difference between the two charge states $\Sigma^-(1385)$ and $\Sigma^+(1385)$. Figure 59, taken from ref. 1, shows the gaussian ideogram of the mass and width values obtained by the most accurate experiments, for the positive charge state. It shows that there is a large disagreement between the various experiments, all $Kp \to \Sigma(1385) + \pi$ in the momentum region $1.15 < P_K < 1.95$ GeV/c, probably due to interference effects of overlapping bands or background, as discussed in Section IV-6, or to experimental systematic errors.

The spin-parity assignment is $J^P = \frac{3}{2}^+$, with very little doubt about this assignment. It has been studied by various authors[110,111] with similar conclusions. The analysis of Shafer et al.[55] is based on larger statistics than the other analyses and give a satisfactory fit for $J^P = \frac{3}{2}^+$. Figure 60 shows the Dalitz plot of their data at $P_K = 1.22$ GeV/c. The two $\Sigma^\pm(1385)$ bands do not overlap and the background under the resonance peak is very small. We report here the analysis of these data with the simple method described in Section IV-7. The sequence of reactions is

$$K^-p \to \Sigma^\pm(1385)\pi^\mp$$

$$\Sigma^\pm(1385) \to \Lambda\pi^\pm$$

$$\Lambda \to p\pi^-$$

Figure 61a shows the distribution of $\mathbf{\Lambda \cdot n}$ which has a $(\mathbf{\Lambda \cdot n})^2$ behavior in agreement with the assignment $J \geq \frac{3}{2}$. The effect of the

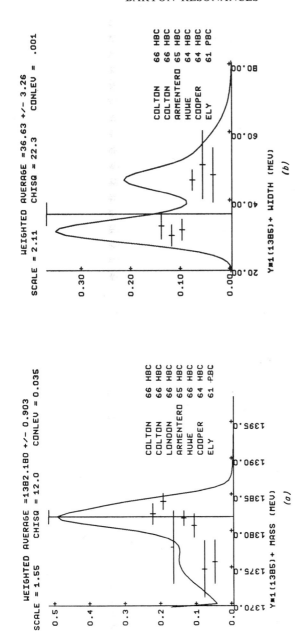

Fig. 59. Gaussian ideogram for (a) the mass of $\Sigma^+$(1385) and (b) the width of $\Sigma^+$(1385), taken from ref. 1. The name and year at the right of each value identifies the experiment which gave that value (references to be found in ref. 1). Each experimental value has been given an area inversely proportional to its error. The weighted average is represented by the vertical line and the $\chi^2$ that all measurements agree is reported on top of each ideogram. The symbol SCALE is $[\chi^2/(N-1)]^{1/2}$, where $N$ is the number of experiments. SCALE larger than 1 indicates disagreement between the various experiments.

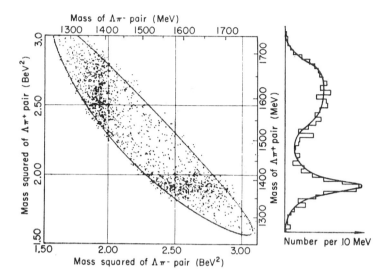

FIG. 60. Dalitz plot of $\Lambda\pi^+\pi^-$ events from $K^-p$ interaction at 1.22 GeV/c.[55] The projection of the plot onto the $\Lambda\pi^+$ mass axis is shown at the right. The curve represents the fit to the data with Breit-Wigner resonance amplitudes. It is evident that the wide bump at high mass is a reflection of $\Sigma^-$ (1385).

background on this distribution can be very large, as discussed in Section IV-6, where an $S_1$ background has been assumed to interfere with a $P_3$ resonance, but within errors no detectable asymmetry has been found in these data. Figures 61$b$ and $c$ show the distributions of $\alpha_\Lambda P_\Lambda N_\Lambda$ versus the angle of the $\Lambda$ with respect to the normal and the magic direction. Distribution $b$ is in agreement with a combination of Eqs. (4.36c) and (4.36d) and the distribution along the magic direction is in agreement with a combination of Eqs. (4.36e) and (4.36f), as expected for a $P_3$ assignment. $J = \frac{5}{2}$, however, cannot be excluded, and the overall confidence level for the $P_3$ state is $(CL)_{P3} = 0.23$, compared with $CL = 0.13$ for either a $D_5$ or an $F_5$ assignment. A successive analysis of these data and higher energy data[112] with the "moments method" of Byers and Fenster[51] gives the results summarized in Figure 62. The assignment $F_5$ is ruled out, while the $D_5$ is still possible at all except two momenta. Only $J^P = \frac{3}{2}^+$ gives a satisfactory fit everywhere. Malamud and Schlein[113] obtained similar conclusions from an analysis of the same reaction at $P_K = 1.45$ GeV/c.

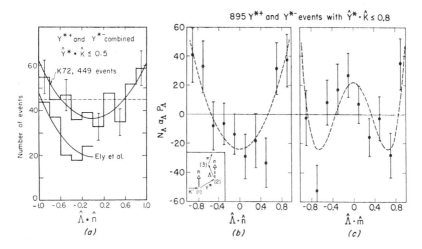

FIG. 61. The spin analysis of ref. 55 on the $\Sigma(1385) \rightarrow \Lambda\pi$ decay and polarization data. (a) Distribution of $\Lambda$ with respect to the normal to the production plane. Ely et al. refer to the results of the experiment of ref. 110. (b) Component of the $\Lambda$ polarization (multiplied by $N_\Lambda$ and the $\Lambda$ decay asymmetry) with respect to the normal and (c) $N_\Lambda \alpha_\Lambda P_\Lambda$ with respect to the magic direction plotted as functions of the $\Lambda$ direction. The small sketch at the lower left of $b$ indicates the reference systems as in Fig. 27.

## 3. $\Lambda(1405)S_{01}$

This resonance has been discovered in the four-body final state reaction $K^- + p \rightarrow \Sigma^\pm \pi^\mp \pi^+ \pi^-$ at $P_K = 1.15\ \text{GeV}/c$ by Alston et al.[114] and it has subsequently been produced in other $K^-p$ and $\pi p$ reactions. Its mass and width have not been measured with large precision yet, because of background difficulties due to production of the neutral $\Sigma(1385)$ which populates the lower part of the mass plot. Figure 63 shows one such invariant mass plot where $\Lambda(1405)$ is clearly produced.[115]

The spin-parity analysis of this state has not been carried out yet in production experiments, but its $J^P$ assignment comes from the study of $Kp$ interactions at low energy. In fact $\Lambda(1405)$ turns out to be a "virtual bound state" of the $Kp$ system, according to Dalitz notation for this type of pole, as discussed in Section III-16, and as will be shown in the next section.

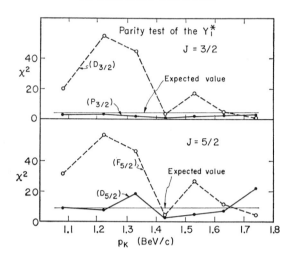

FIG. 62. Spin and parity tests of $\Sigma(1385)$ with the "method of moments,"[51] made by Shafer at al.,[112] are shown as a function of incident $K^-$ momentum. For $J = \frac{3}{2}$ the only parity state is $P$ state, for $J = \frac{5}{2}$ the $D_5$ state is not completely excluded by the data. The $P_{3/2}$ state, however, has a satisfactory fit at all momenta.

## 4. Analyses of Low Energy $K^-p$ Interactions

### A. Zero-Effective Range Analysis

The analysis of experimental data was first carried out using a zero-effective range expansion of the complex phase shifts according to the **K** matrix formalism discussed in Section III-13, the relation between complex phase shift $\Delta$ and the scattering length $A$ being

$$k \cot \Delta_I = 1/A_I = 1/(a_I + ib_I)$$

As in Eq. (3.69), the subscript $I$ refers to the isotopic spin state. Only $S$ waves have been considered up to $P_K = 270$ MeV/c, therefore the angular distributions for all the reactions are expected to be isotropic and no polarization of the outgoing baryons is expected, because it takes two partial waves to produce polarization, as seen in Table VI.

All the possible reactions in this energy region are listed in Eq. (3.68) in Section III-12. Apart from the $K^- - K^\circ$ mass difference and Coulomb scattering, a charge-independent formulation of the scattering amplitudes of these processes can easily be obtained from the two-channel **K** matrix formalism of Section III-13. The $\bar{K}N$ and $\Sigma\pi$ final

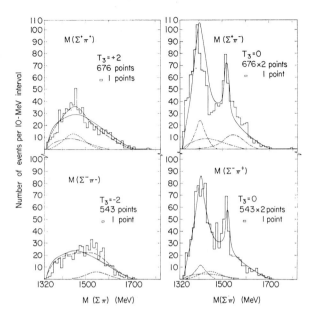

FIG. 63. Mass plot of $\Sigma\pi$ systems in the reactions $K^-p \rightarrow \Sigma^{\pm}\pi^{\mp}\pi^+\pi^-$ at 1.51 GeV/c incident momentum.[114] The left-hand plots are evidence that no isotopic spin 2 resonances are produced in the $\Sigma\pi$ system. The right-hand plots show large $\Lambda(1405)$ and $\Lambda(1520)$ production.

states contribute to both $I = 0$ and $I = 1$ amplitudes, and the $\Lambda\pi^\circ$ contributes only to the $I = 1$ amplitude. As seen in Section III-13, Eq. (3.88), the $I = 1$ state can also be reduced to a two-channel problem through the use of a submatrix. From Eqs. (3.80) and (3.82) the scattering amplitudes are

$$(T'_{11})_I = A_I/(1 - ikA_I)$$

$$(T'_{21})_I = N_I/(1 - ikA_I)$$

where $N_I$ is different for the different final states ($\Sigma\pi$, $\Lambda\pi$). The notation used here is the one used by Dalitz[24] and is as follows:

$$M_0 \text{ for } (\Sigma\pi)_{I=0}$$

$$M_1 \text{ for } (\Sigma\pi)_{I=1}$$

$$N_1 \text{ for } (\Lambda\pi)_{I=1}$$

Using this notation and taking into account the isotopic spin composition for each reaction, the cross sections for the processes (3.68a)–(3.68d) are:

$$\sigma_{K^- p} = 4\pi \left| \frac{\frac{1}{2}(A_1 + A_0) - ikA_0A_1}{(1 - ikA_0)(1 - ikA_1)} \right|^2$$

$$\sigma_{\bar{K}^0 n} = 4\pi \left| \frac{\frac{1}{2}(A_1 - A_0)}{(1 - ikA_0)(1 - ikA_1)} \right|^2$$

$$\sigma_{\Sigma^+ \pi^-} = \frac{4\pi q_\Sigma}{k} \left| \frac{1}{\sqrt{6}} \frac{M_0}{1 - ikA_0} + \frac{1}{2} \frac{M_1}{1 - ikA_1} \right|^2$$

$$\sigma_{\Sigma^- \pi^+} = \frac{4\pi q_\Sigma}{k} \left| \frac{1}{\sqrt{6}} \frac{M_0}{1 - ikA_0} - \frac{1}{2} \frac{M_1}{1 - ikA_1} \right|^2$$

$$\sigma(\Sigma^0 \pi^0) = \frac{4\pi q_\Sigma}{k} \left| \frac{1}{\sqrt{6}} \frac{M_0}{1 - ikA_0} \right|^2$$

$$\sigma(\Lambda \pi^0) = \frac{4\pi q_\Lambda}{k} \left| \frac{1}{\sqrt{2}} \frac{N_1}{1 - ikA_1} \right|^2$$

The introduction of Coulomb scattering and of the $K^- - K^0$ mass difference slightly modifies these equations, the most affected being $\sigma_{K^- p}$ where the Coulomb scattering contribution has to be taken into account. The reader can find these expressions in ref. 24. The final expressions have been fitted to the experimental data in order to find the six parameters: $a_0$, $b_0$, $a_1$, $b_1$, $\varepsilon$, and $\Phi$, with

$$\varepsilon = \frac{\sigma_\Lambda}{\sigma_{I=1}} = \frac{q_\Lambda |N_1|^2}{q_\Sigma |M_1|^2 + q_\Lambda |N_1|^2}$$

$$\Phi = \text{Arg}\left(\frac{M_0}{M_1}\right) + \text{Arg}\left(\frac{1 - ik_0 A_1}{1 - ik_0 A_0}\right)$$

where $\Phi$ is the phase between the two isotopic spin states of the $\Sigma\pi$ system, and the first term is called $\Phi_{th}$, the phase between the $I = 0$ and $I = 1$ amplitudes at the $\bar{K}^0 n$ threshold.

Humphrey and Ross[116] made the first attempt to solve these equations and found two solutions which fit the data quite well. Sakitt et al.,[117] with better statistics, have reduced the errors, but still find two solutions. Kim[103] has done a large statistics experiment and favors one solution over the other (see Table XIII).

TABLE XIII

The Various Solutions of Zero-Effective Range Fits to Low-Energy $K^-p$ Interactions

| | Kim I | Sakitt II | Kittel II, includes Sakitt's data | Tripp et al., at 400 MeV/c |
|---|---|---|---|---|
| $a_0$ | $-1.674 \pm 0.038$ | $-1.63$ | $-1.57 \pm 0.04$ | $-0.1 \pm 0.5$ |
| $b_0$ | $0.722 \pm 0.040$ | $0.51$ | $0.54 \pm 0.06$ | $3.1 \pm 0.8$ |
| $a_1$ | $-0.003 \pm 0.058$ | $-0.19$ | $-0.24 \pm 0.05$ | $0.02 \pm 0.1$ |
| $b_1$ | $0.688 \pm 0.033$ | $0.44$ | $0.43 \pm 0.05$ | $0.46 \pm 0.03$ |
| $\epsilon$ | $0.318 \pm 0.021$ | $0.31$ | $0.32 \pm 0.04$ | $0.29 \pm 0.03$ |
| $\gamma^a$ | $2.093 \pm 0.091$ | $2.11$ | | |
| $\Phi_{th}$ | $-53.8°$ | | $(-100 \pm 7)°^b$ | $(-104 \pm 7)°^c$ |

$^a$ $\gamma = \Gamma(K^-p \to \Sigma^-\pi^+)/\Gamma(K^-p \to \Sigma^+\pi^-)$.
$^b$ This angle is defined as $\Phi_{th}$-arctan $A_0/A_1$.
$^c$ This phase angle value is at 400 MeV/c.

Other data in the $\bar{K}^0n$ channel have been obtained by Kittel et al.[118]

Figures 64 and 65 show Kim's[103] fit to his experimental data. The $\Sigma\pi$ final states allow us to distinguish between the two solutions, since the interference term between the two $I$-spin amplitudes has a large contribution here. The $\Sigma^+/\Sigma^-$ ratio, in fact, is very sensitive to the phase difference $\Phi_{th}$ between the two $I$-spin amplitudes for the $\Sigma\pi$ reactions. The two solutions would correspond to $\Phi_{th} = -54°$ and $\Phi_{th} = +71°$.

A more direct way to distinguish between the two solutions is to study $K_2^0p$ interactions. Kadyk et al.[119] have studied the following reactions:

$$K_2^0 + p \to K_1^0 + p \quad 403 \text{ events}$$
$$\to \Lambda + \pi^+ \quad 481 \text{ events}$$
$$\to \Sigma^0 + \pi^+ \quad 332 \text{ events}$$

The quantity of interest is the ratio $R$

$$R = \frac{\sigma(K_1^0p)}{\sigma(\Lambda\pi^+) + 2\sigma(\Sigma^0\pi^+)} = \frac{\sigma(K_1^0p)}{\sigma(Y)}$$

which is very sensitive to the $I = 1$ scattering length of the $K^-p$ system. In fact, calling $\bar{A}_1$ this complex scattering length and $a_0$ and $a_1$ the

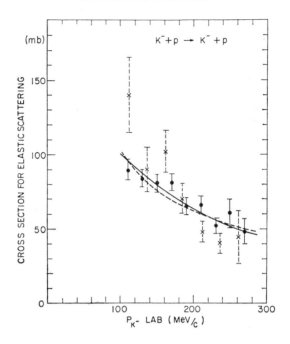

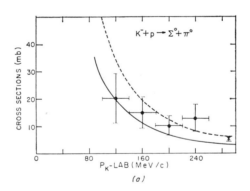

FIG. 64. The cross sections as function of laboratory momentum from Kim's experiment.[103] The plots shown are for the reactions $K^-p \to K^-p$, $K^-p \to \bar{K}^0 n$, $K^-p \to \Sigma^0\pi^0$, and $K^-p \to \Lambda\pi^0$. The curves represent the best fit to all the data: (———) solution I, (– – –) solution II. (●) Kim's data[103] and (×) Humphrey Ross data.[116]

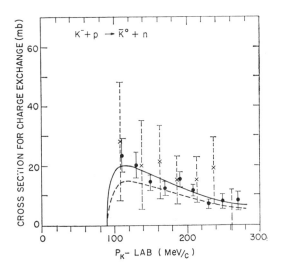

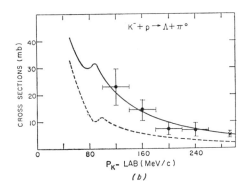

(b)

---

*real* scattering lengths for $I = 0, 1$ in the $K^+p$ system (there are no channels other than the elastic open at these energies), we have:

$$\sigma(K_1{}^0p) = \pi \left| \frac{1}{2} \left( \frac{a_0}{1 - ika_0} + \frac{a_1}{1 - ika_1} \right) - \frac{\overline{A}_1}{1 - ik\overline{A}_1} \right|^2$$

and

$$\sigma(Y) = \frac{2\pi}{k} \frac{\overline{b}}{|1 - ik\overline{A}_1|^2}$$

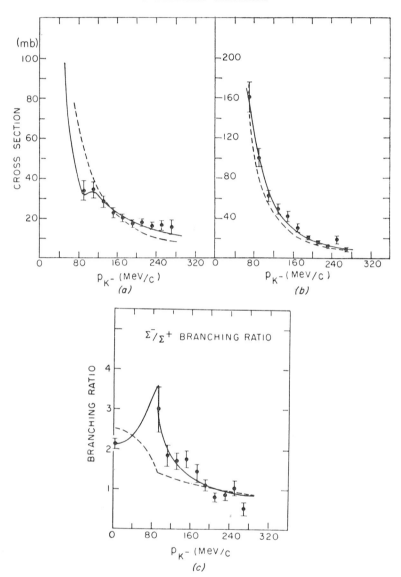

FIG. 65. The cross sections for (a) $K^-p \to \Sigma^+\pi^-$ and (b) $K^-p \to \Sigma^-\pi^+$ as obtained by Kim,[103] (c) shows the ratio of the cross sections as function of incident $K^-$ momentum. The two curves represent the two solutions obtained from the fit of all the data. (——) Solution I, preferred by this channel. (---) Solution II.

Using the values of $a_0$ and $a_1$ of Stenger et al.,[159] the solution labeled Kim I is the favored one for this analysis and it is also the one favored by Kim. Table XIII shows the solutions which seem to be closer to the $K_2^0 p$ experimental results, i.e., Kim I,[103] Sakit II,[117] Kittel II,[118] which includes the data of Sakitt, and Tripp et al.[104] This last solution comes from fitting the $K^- p$ data at momenta between 250 and 513 MeV/c where up to $D$ waves have been considered in the fit, because of formation of $\Lambda(1520)$, which will be discussed in Section VI-5. The parameters of this solution are at $P_k = 400$ MeV/c; the $A_0$ is considerably different at this energy, while the $A_1$ has not changed much.

The low momentum solutions of Table XIII show that the $I = 0$ scattering length requires the presence of a $\overline{K}N$ bound state in this isospin state according to the discussion of Section III-15. In fact $a$ is negative as expected, according to Eq. (3.102b), and the pole appears to be below threshold since $|a| < b$. Using Eq. (3.102), Dalitz et al.[27] have calculated the following mass and width, using Kim's solution,

$$M = 1419.5 \text{ MeV} \qquad \Gamma = 26.5 \text{ MeV}$$

Note that the values quoted by Kim (1410.7, 37.0) or other authors are different because they used an approximation of Eq. (3.102) which assumes $b \ll a$. This pole below threshold or "virtual bound state" has been identified with the $\Lambda(1405) \rightarrow \Sigma\pi$ discovered in production experiments, even though the mass and width of the two states do not seem to be in agreement. However, as Dalitz et al.[27] point out, the parameters derived from $K^- p$ scattering are subject to all the uncertainty associated with any extrapolation from the physical region to the resonance location. In addition, the introduction of an effective range in the whole analysis of $K^- p$ data turns out to produce different parameters for this resonant state, which are in better agreement with the parameters measured in production experiments.

### B. Effective Range Analysis

In his most recent paper, Kim[103] has used the multichannel effective range formalism of Ross and Shaw, discussed in Section III-14, to analyze his data, the data of Kadyk et al.[119] and of Watson et al.,[104] covering in this way the momentum region 0–550 MeV/c.

Using the **M** matrix formalism five parameters are needed to describe the $I = 0$ amplitudes and nine for the $I = 1$ amplitudes. Since the energy region to be analyzed is quite large $S$, $P_1$, $P_3$, and $D_3$ waves were used. (The subscript refers to $2J$.) The $S$ and $P_3$ waves required 14 parameters each, whereas the $P_1$, being small, was considered to have constant $\mathbf{M}$ matrix elements. The $D_3$ finally was described by four constant scattering length parameters in the $I = 1$ state and a Breitz-Wigner resonance for the $I = 0$ state. A total of 610 data points were fitted to a 44-parameter function and a $\chi^2$ of 580 was obtained. Figure 66 shows the fit to the elastic, charge exchange $\Sigma^{\pm}\pi^{\mp}$ data and to the ratio $R$ defined above. Figure 66$f$ shows the variation with energy of the scattering length parameters $a_I$ and $b_I$ for the $S$ wave, related to the $M_{ij}$ according to Eq. (3.97). The $I = 0$ parameters show a strong energy dependence above 200 MeV/c. Note however that the new values at $P_K = 0$ and $P_K = 400$ MeV/c are not different from the ones obtained with the zero-effective range analysis and reported in Table XIII.

For the $S$ wave in the $I = 0$ state a pole was found in the reduced $\mathbf{K}$ matrix for the $\Sigma\pi$ channel, according to Eq. (3.103). The mass and width for this resonance were

$$M = 1403 \pm 3 \text{ MeV} \qquad \Gamma = 50 \pm 5 \text{ MeV}$$

in agreement with the values found in production of $\Lambda(1405)$. As discussed in Sections III-15 and III-16 this resonance is called by Dalitz a "virtual bound state." In fact the pole occurs in the reduced $\mathbf{K}$ matrix, but does not occur in the whole $\mathbf{K}$ matrix. As shown in Figure 67$a$ the elements $\alpha,\gamma$ of the $\mathbf{K}$ matrix show a smooth energy dependence.

In the $P_{13}$ state a pole was found in the whole $\mathbf{K}$ matrix. As shown in Figure 67$d$ all three diagonal elements have a pole at the energy corresponding to the $\Sigma(1385)$ resonance. According to the discussion of Sections III-15 and III-16, this is a resonance of type ($b$); in fact the cross section has the shape of a Breit-Wigner resonance as can be seen in Figure 67$f$.

The other amplitudes turned out to be slowly varying with energy except for the $D_{03}$ resonant amplitude which gave parameters very similar to the ones obtained by the analysis of Watson et al.[104] which will be discussed in the next section.

## 5. $\Lambda(1520)D_{03}$

This resonance was discovered in an $H_2$ bubble chamber experiment in the study of $K^-p$ interactions at 400 MeV/c.[104] This has been

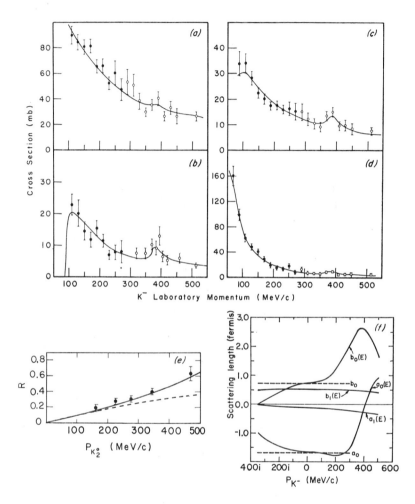

FIG. 66. Result of Kim's[103] fit of the $K^-p$ data in the 0–550 MeV/c momentum region. (●) Kim, (○) Watson et al. The effective range formalism of Section III was used. (a) $K^- + p \to K^- + p$; (b) $K^- + p \to \overline{K}^\circ + n$; (c) $K^- + p \to \Sigma^+ + \pi^-$; (d) $K^- + p \to \Sigma^- + \pi^+$. (a)–(d) show the total cross sections for the reactions specified. (e) shows the ratio $R$ $\{R = K_1^\circ p/[\Lambda\pi^+ + 2(\Sigma^\circ\pi^+)]\}$ measured by Kadyk et al.,[119] which allows one to choose between the Yang set (——) and the Fermi set (– – –) of the $I = 0$ $K^+n$ phase shifts of Stenger et al.[159] (f) $S$ wave scattering length parameters for the $I = 0,1$ states of the $S$ wave.

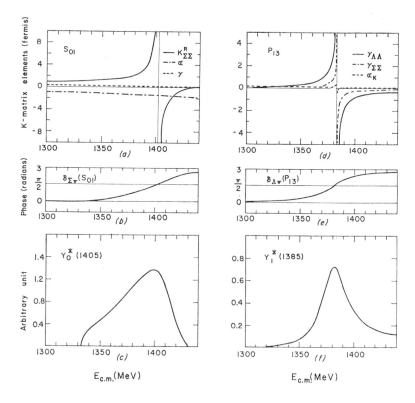

FIG. 67. Shows the results of Kim's effective range analysis, (a)–(c) for the
$\Lambda(1405)$ resonance and (d)–(e) for the $\Sigma(1385)$ resonance. (a) Plot of the reduced
**K** matrix for the $\Sigma\pi$ system in the $S_{01}$ wave as a function of total c.m.s. energy.
The diagonal elements of the **K** matrix ($\alpha$ and $\gamma$) are also shown. (b) Phase shift of
the $\Sigma\pi$ scattering. (c) Cross section for $\Sigma\pi$ production in arbitrary units. (d) Plot
of the diagonal elements of the **K** matrix for the $P_{13}$ wave. (e) Phase shift for the
$\Lambda\pi$ scattering. (f) $\Lambda\pi$ production cross section in arbitrary units.

the first experiment where information coming from all the channels has
been used to determine spin and parity of a resonance. In addition, this
experiment gave the first evidence for odd $KN\Sigma$ parity positive $\Sigma\Lambda$
parity.

Figure 68 shows the cross sections as function of incident $K^-$
momentum for all the allowed channels in this energy region, with the
exception of $\sigma(K^-p \to \Lambda\pi^0\pi^0)$ and $\sigma(K^-p \to \Sigma^\pm\pi^\mp\pi^0)$ which are very

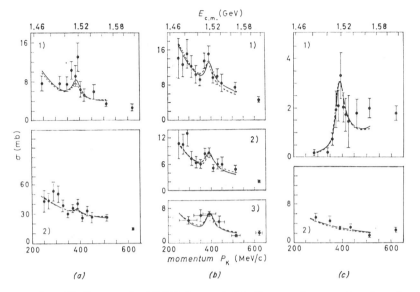

FIG. 68. Data on the $\Lambda(1520)$ from ref. 104. Cross sections as a function of momentum for (a) $K^-p$ charge exchange (1) and elastic scattering (2); (b) $\Sigma^+\pi^-$, $\Sigma^-\pi^+$, and $\Sigma^0\pi^0$ productions in the order; (c) $\Lambda\pi^+\pi^-$ (1) and $\Lambda\pi^0$ production (2). The solid line corresponds to the best fit of all cross sections, angular distributions, and polarizations to negative $KN\Sigma$ parity; the dashed lines correspond to the best fit for positive $KN\Sigma$ parity. Cross sections are not sensitive to the parity.

small.[104] In terms of isotopic spin the amplitudes for the various two-body channels can be written as

$$T_{K^-p} = \tfrac{1}{2}(T_0^{\bar{K}N} + T_1^{\bar{K}N})$$

$$T_{\bar{K}n} = \tfrac{1}{2}(T_0^{\bar{K}N} - T_1^{\bar{K}N})$$

$$T_{\Sigma^+\pi^-} = \frac{1}{\sqrt{2}}\left(\frac{1}{\sqrt{3}}T_0^{\Sigma\pi} - \frac{1}{\sqrt{2}}T_1^{\Sigma\pi}\right)$$

$$T_{\Sigma^-\pi^+} = \frac{1}{\sqrt{2}}\left(\frac{1}{\sqrt{3}}T_0^{\Sigma\pi} + \frac{1}{\sqrt{2}}T_1^{\Sigma\pi}\right) \qquad (6.1)$$

$$T_{\Sigma^0\pi^0} = \frac{1}{\sqrt{2}}\left(\frac{-1}{\sqrt{3}}T_0^{\Sigma\pi}\right)$$

$$T_{\Lambda\pi^0} = \frac{1}{\sqrt{2}}(T_1^{\Lambda\pi})$$

In addition to the isotopic spin decomposition, $S$, $P$, and $D$ waves were considered, and thus a total of six amplitudes were necessary to describe the states which are isotopic spin mixtures. All amplitudes, except for the $D_{03}$ which turned out to be resonant, have been expressed in terms of a constant scattering length according to Eqs. (3.70) and (3.72). For the $\bar{K}N$ channels:

$$(T_e)_{I,l} = (T_{\alpha\alpha})_{I,l} = \frac{k^{2l+1}A_{I,l}}{1 - ik^{2l+1}A_{I,l}} \tag{6.2}$$

where the $I$, $l$ indices refer to isotopic spin and orbital angular momentum, respectively. For the inelastic channels

$$(T_{\alpha\beta})_{I,l} = \left[\frac{k^{2l+1}b_{I,l}r_{\beta,I,l}}{(1 + k^{2l+1}b_{I,l})^2 + (k^{2l+1}a_{I,l})^2}\right]^{\frac{1}{2}} e^{i\phi_{\beta,I,l}} \tag{6.3}$$

where $r_{\beta,I,l}$ represents the fraction of the total reaction cross section which goes into the channel $\beta$ ($\sum_{i=1}^{Nch} r_i = 1$, to preserve unitarity) and $\phi_\beta$ is a phase angle which determines the position of the amplitude in the unitary circle of Figure 5. The amplitude $D_{03}$ was taken to be resonant, therefore it had the expression (3.44) of Section III-7.

Cross sections, angular distributions, and $\Sigma^+$ polarizations have been expressed in terms of the above amplitudes according to Eqs. (3.21) and (3.23). A total of 257 data points were fitted to a 34-parameters function and an overall $\chi^2$ of 221 was obtained. The angular distributions undergo very rapid changes with energy because the $\Lambda(1520)$ is a very narrow resonance. The data, therefore, were divided in very small energy intervals and the angular distributions were analyzed in terms of front–back and polar–equatorial ratios; Figures 69$a$ and 69$b$ show such ratios for the $\Sigma^\pm\pi^\mp$ data. Figure 69$c$ shows the evidence on the $\Sigma\Lambda$ parity. The polarization of the $\Sigma^+$ is very sensitive to this parity. The plotted values are the coefficients of the following expansion

$$I(\theta)P(\theta) = \sin\theta(B_0 + B_1\cos\theta + B_2\cos^2\theta)$$

and the two curves represent the best fits for the two opposite parities. It is clear that the negative $KN\Sigma$ parity is the only hypothesis that fits the data. The resonant parameters found from this fit are

$$
\begin{aligned}
M &= 1519\ \text{MeV} & \Gamma &= 16.4\ \text{MeV} \\
& & \Gamma_{\bar{K}N} &= 4.8\ \text{MeV} \\
& & \Gamma_{\Sigma\pi} &= 8.9\ \text{MeV} \\
& & \Gamma_{\Lambda\pi\pi} &= 2.7\ \text{MeV}
\end{aligned}
$$

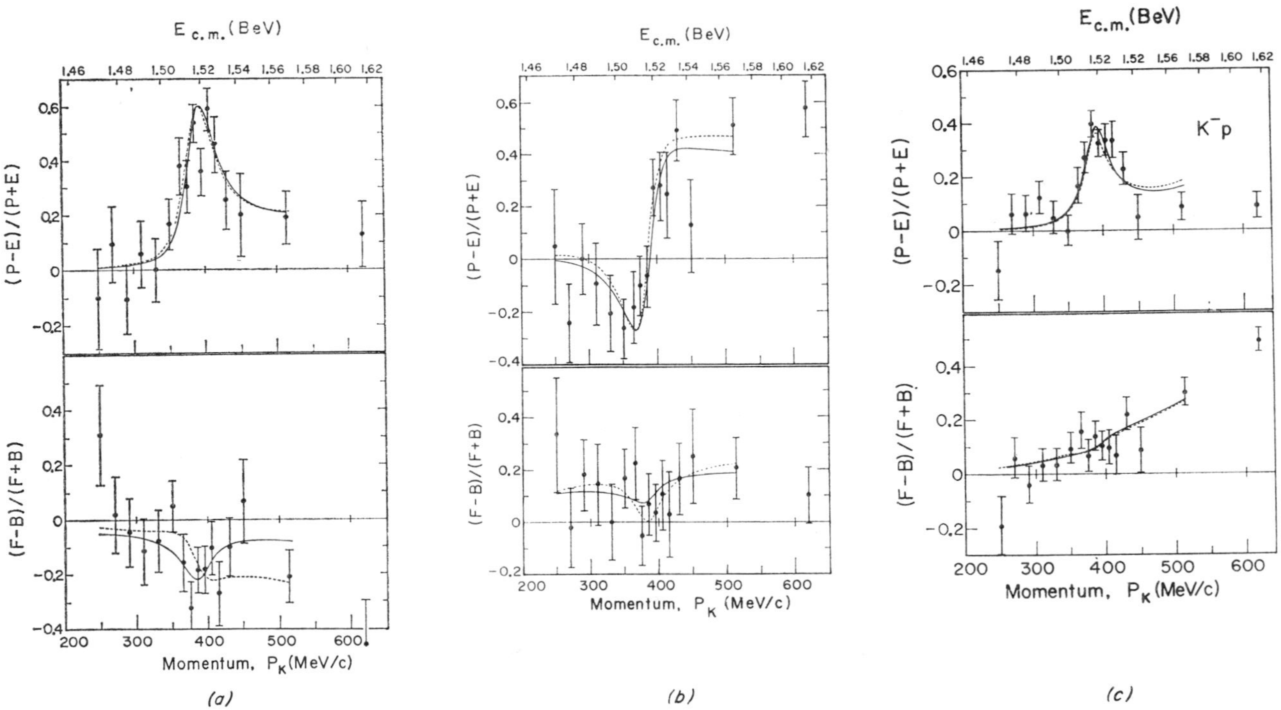

FIG. 69. Data of Watson et al.[104] Polar–equatorial and front–back ratios as a function of momentum, (a) for $\Sigma^+\pi^-$, (b) for $\Sigma^-\pi^+$. (c) Coefficients of the $I(\theta)P(\theta)$ expansion defined in the text. The solid curves correspond to negative $K N \Sigma$ parity, the dashed curves correspond to positive $K N \Sigma$ parity and clearly do not fit the data in (c).

$\Lambda(1520)$ has been detected in many production experiments and the branching ratios from these experiments seem to be in disagreement with the above values. Other formation experiments are in progress at the present time with much larger statistics than Watson et al.,[104] therefore it is possible that slightly different parameters from the above will be found. The branching ratios of Table II are the average of Watson et al.[104] and various production experiments (the references are listed in ref. 1).

### 6. Structure in Total Cross Section Data up to 2 GeV/c (M < 2.2 GeV)

As shown in Figure 55, rather precise cross-section measurements are available up to 3.5 GeV/c incident $K^-$ momentum.

The $K^-p$ system, however, is a mixture of $I = 0$ and $I = 1$ states; therefore, in order to isolate the two $I$-spin states, it is necessary to use the $K^-d$ cross sections and perform rather elaborate calculations, unlike the $\pi p$ system where one of the $I$-spin states ($\pi^+ p$) can be directly measured. At a particular center of mass energy

$$\sigma(I = 1) = \sigma(K^-d) + \sigma_G - \sigma(K^-p) = \sigma(K^-n) \qquad (6.4a)$$

$$\sigma(I = 0) = 3\sigma(K^-p) - \sigma(K^-d) - \sigma_G = 2\sigma(K^-p) - \sigma(K^-n) \quad (6.4b)$$

where $\sigma_G$ is the Glauber[120] screening correction

$$\sigma_G = \frac{\sigma(K^-p)\sigma(K^-n)}{8\pi a^2 + \pi/b^2}$$

Here $a$ characterizes the size of the $K^-N$ system and $b^{-1}$ the size of the deuteron. Lynch[121] uses $a^2 = 0.28$ fermi$^2$ and $b^2 = 0.0961$ fermi$^{-2}$ which corresponds to 395 mb for the denominator of the above expression. In addition to this correction the effect of the Fermi motion of the nucleons in the deuteron has to be taken into account. In fact, for a given incident momentum $P_K$, the measured cross section corresponds to a spectrum of total c.m. energies for the kaon–nucleon system. Consequently all the peaks appear to be broader. This effect can be taken into account with two different procedures. One can "smear out" the measured $K^-p$ cross section, and, using Eq. (6.4a) subtract it from the measured $\sigma(K^-d)$ in order to obtain $\sigma(K^-n)$, and then unfold the Fermi motion to obtain $\sigma(I = 1)$. This method has been used in refs. 98–100. Alternatively, one can directly unfold the $K^-d$ cross section and then use the measured $K^-p$ cross section in order to get $\sigma(I = 1)$. This last procedure has been used by Lynch.[121] The results of the two methods are in agreement.

Figure 70 shows the $I = 0$ and $I = 1$ part of the total cross sections up to 2.0 GeV/c, as obtained by Lynch[121] using both sets of data of refs. 98 and 100. The arrows show the position of the resonant states. Two new states are shown: $\Lambda(1700)$ and $\Sigma(1915)$. Also $\Sigma(1660)$, which had failed to appear in any elastic channel before, is evident in the $I = 1$ curve. Its elasticity is somewhat difficult to extract from here, because the lower part of the curve is missing and it is hard to evaluate the background. Davies et al.[100] estimate a "bump" of 1.5 mb which,

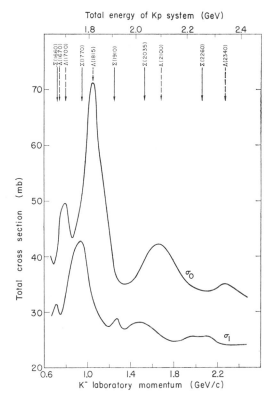

FIG. 70. Shape of the $I = 0$ and $I = 1$ components of the total cross section as calculated by Lynch,[121] using experimental data of Davies et al.[100] and Cool et al.[98] The arrows indicate the position of the resonances.

assuming $J = \frac{3}{2}$, leads to $x = 0.050$. Table XIV summarizes the positions and widths of the resonances as found by Davies et al.,[100] Cool et al.,[98] and Lynch,[121] who used the data of both experiments. The product $(J + \frac{1}{2})x_e$, calculated according to Eq. (3.49), is also given at the resonant energy.

### 7. $\Lambda\eta$ and $\Sigma\eta$ Reactions near Threshold

Berley et al.[122] at Brookhaven have measured the cross section for the reaction $K^-p \to \Lambda\eta$ from threshold to 200 MeV/c relative momentum in the $\eta$ c.m. Their results are shown in Figure 71. They have analyzed the data in terms of a constant $S$ wave scattering length or $P$ wave scattering length, according to the formalism discussed in Section III-13. For $S$ wave the $\sigma_{\Lambda\eta}$ is expressed by Eq. (3.87) multiplied by a parameter $r$ which measures the coupling to channels other than

TABLE XIV

Resonant States Present in Total Cross Section Data, up to $P_{K^-} = 2.0$ GeV/c

| Isospin | Symbol | Mass, MeV | Width, MeV | $4\pi\lambda^{2a}$, mb | $\sigma_R$, mb | $(J + \frac{1}{2})x$ | Ref. |
|---|---|---|---|---|---|---|---|
| 1 | $\Sigma(1660)$ | $1665 \pm 5$ | $30 \pm 15$ | 29.9 | 1.5 | 0.05 | 100 |
|   |   | 1662 | — |   |   | $\approx 0.2$ | 121 |
| 0 | $\Lambda(1700)$ | $1695 \pm 5$ | $40 \pm 7$ | 25.0 | 12.3 | 0.46 | 100 |
|   |   | 1695 | 50 |   |   | 0.5 | 121 |
| 1 | $\Sigma(1770)$ | $1768 \pm 5$ | $110 \pm 7$ | 19.4 | 21.8 | 1.12 | 100 |
|   |   | 1765 | 110 |   |   | 1.0 | 121 |
| 0 | $\Lambda(1820)$ | $1819 \pm 5$ | $75 \pm 7$ | 16.5 | 35.6 | 2.15 | 100 |
|   |   | 1819 | 80 |   |   | 2.36 | 121 |
| 1 | $\Sigma(1910)$ | $1905 \pm 5$ | $60 \pm 10$ | 12.9 | 2.4 | 0.18 | 100 |
|   |   | 1914 | $\approx 30$ |   |   | $\approx 0.4$ | 121 |
|   |   | $1915 \pm 20$ | 65 |   | 4.0 | 0.31 | 98 |
| 1 | $\Sigma(2035)$ | $2040 \pm 20$ | 150 | 9.83 | 6.0 | 0.62 | 98 |
|   |   | $2020 \pm 7$ | $130 \pm 10$ |   | 5.5 | 0.54 | 100 |
| 0 | $\Lambda(2100)$ | $2100 \pm 20$ | 160 | 8.68 | 10.8 | 1.15 | 98 |
|   |   | $2100 \pm 7$ | $140 \pm 15$ |   | 10.6 | 1.22 | 100 |

[a] This value corresponds to the nominal mass value in parentheses with the symbol.

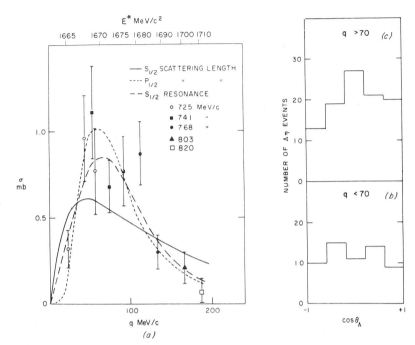

FIG. 71. (a) Cross section of $Kp \to \Lambda\eta$ as a function of the $\eta$ c.m.'s momentum [Berley et al.[(122)]]. (b) angular distributions for ($q < 70$) and (c) for ($q > 70$).

$K^-p$. The best fit is shown in Figure 71 with $B = (4 + 0.4i)F$ and $r = 0.9$. The sign of $c$ is not known, since the above cross section measures $|c|^2$ and $|d|^2$, if only one partial wave is present. The fit is not satisfactory and a $P$ wave scattering length fit has been tried which gives the best fit shown in Figure 71 with $B = (9.5 + 30.4i)F^3$ and $r = 0.3$. However, close to threshold the angular distribution observed is isotropic, contrary to the $P$ wave hypothesis.

The curve which seems to fit the data better is obtained with a Breit-Wigner amplitude for an $S$ wave resonance. The parameters obtained in this case are $M = 1675$ MeV, $\Gamma = 15$ MeV, and $x_{\bar{K}N}x_{\Lambda\eta} = 0.053$. Here again we have the same phenomenon as for the $\pi^-p \to n\eta$ cross section discussed in Section V-4. As seen there, the fits of Uchiyama-Campbell and Logan[(28)] with a Breit-Wigner resonance turned out to be identical to the ones done with an effective range

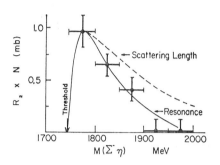

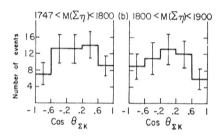

FIG. 72*a*. Data for the reaction $K^-p \to \Sigma^0\eta$ and $K^-n \to \Sigma^-\eta$. Data of Cline and Olson[123] in a deuterium experiment. $R_2$ is the number of $\Sigma^-\eta$ events divided by the number of events expected for the internal momentum distribution of the deuteron. $N$ is a normalization factor which contains an uncertainty that can produce a $\pm 0.3$ mb systematic error in the cross section. A constant $S$ wave scattering length $[B = (1 + i)$ fermi] has been used to calculate the cross section as well as a Breit-Wigner resonance, as shown.

approximation; it is possible that, here too, the introduction of an effective range would produce a good $S$ wave fit. This point has been discussed by Davies and Moorhouse[73] for the $\pi p \to n\eta$ data as discussed in Section V-4. In conclusion, the data at the present time are consistent with an $S$ wave resonance decaying through the $\Lambda\eta$ channel; however before accepting this interpretation, the other channels should be analyzed in detail to detect the presence of this resonance and to study further its quantum numbers.

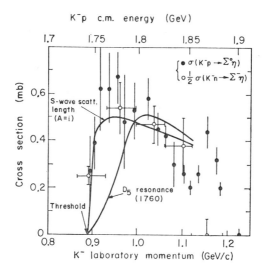

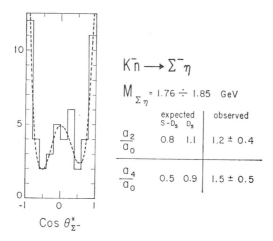

FIG. 72b. Data for the reaction $K^-p \rightarrow \Sigma^0\eta$ and $K^-n \rightarrow \Sigma^-\eta$. Data from CERN-Saclay-Heidelberg collaboration.[3] The upper graph shows the cross section as function of incident $K^-$ momentum. The lower graph shows the angular distribution for $K^-n \rightarrow \Sigma^-\eta$ in the indicated energy range. The $a_i$ are the coefficients of a Legendre polynomials expansion of $dq/d\Omega$, $S$ is a constant $S$ wave amplitude and $D_5$ is the resonant amplitude for $\Sigma(1765)$.

As for the $\Sigma\eta$ threshold effect, the situation has been summarized by Ferro-Luzzi[102a] at the Berkeley Conference on High Energy Physics. Figure 72 shows the situation. Cline and Olson[123] have fitted the cross section with a Breit Wigner amplitude for an $S$ wave resonance ($M = 1780$ MeV, $\Gamma = 100$ MeV) and with an $S$ wave zero-effective range approximation. The $S$-wave resonance seems to be in better agreement with the data and the $\Sigma$ production angular distribution seems to be isotropic as expected for $S$ wave. However, the data of the CERN, Heidelberg, Saclay collaboration,[3] as reported by Ferro-Luzzi,[102a] are in disagreement with Cline and Olson in that they show higher complexity than isotropy in the $\Sigma$ angular distribution, as seen in Figure 72b. This, according to the authors, is an indication that higher partial waves are involved in the process. A possible explanation given by this last group is that near 900 MeV/c besides an $S$ wave large scattering length effect, there might be a contribution from the $D_{15}$ resonance $\Sigma(1765)$. However, in their most recent report at the Heidelberg Conference,[102b] these authors[3] have presented new, improved data which show a value of $a_2$ at two standard deviations from zero and an $a_4$ consistent with zero. Before drawing any conclusions, it is clear that more work and more data are needed on this reaction.

## 8. Resonances in the 1660–1700 MeV Region

A resonance in this region was discovered in a production experiment[124] and in a formation experiment at Berkeley in 1962.[125] Since then, enhancements in this energy region have been detected and studied in both formation and production experiments. The fine structure of these enhancements and the quantum number assignments are not clear yet, but it is certain that at least three resonances are present. (1) The $\Lambda(1675)$ discussed in the preceding section, with a visible decay mode:

$$\Lambda(1675) \to \Lambda\eta$$

which appears to be an $S$ wave resonance.[122] (2) The $\Lambda(1700)$ discussed in Section VI-6 which has been seen in total cross section data[100a] and in the $\Sigma\pi$ final state[106] with branching ratios:

$$\Lambda(1700) \to \bar{K}N \qquad x_{\bar{K}N} = 0.25$$
$$\to \Sigma\pi \qquad x_{\Sigma\pi} = 0.46$$

There is a strong indication from the analysis of Armenteros et al.[106] which will be discussed in the next section, that its $J^P$ assignments are $J^P = \frac{3}{2}^-$. *(3)* An $I = 1$ resonance at about 1660 MeV which has been seen in formation experiments as decaying copiously in the $\Sigma\pi$ channel[106] (with $J^P = \frac{3}{2}^-$ preferred) and in production experiments decaying into $\Sigma\pi$ and through

$$\Sigma(1660) \to \Lambda(1405) + \pi$$

This last decay mode indicates quantum numbers $J^P = \frac{3}{2}^-$ (ref. 126).

*1. I = 0 State.* It is very unlikely, with the present experimental data, that these two resonant states are different decay modes of the same resonance. $\Lambda(1700)$ has a mass of $\sim 1695$ MeV (from Table XIV and ref. 106) which is only 20 MeV away from $\Lambda(1675)$; however, the analysis of Armenteros et al.[106] clearly shows that an orbital angular momentum of 2 is more appropriate to the $\Sigma\pi$ decay mode, which is in disagreement with the isotropy found in the $\Lambda\eta$ data of ref. 122.

*2. I = 1 State.* Here the situation is more complicated than in the $I = 0$ state, and it is possible that more than one particle in the $I = 1$ state is present. Results from formation and production experiments seem to be contradictory. Let us review the situation.

### A. Formation Experiments

The only two channels studied up to now are the $\Lambda\pi$ and $\Sigma\pi$ channels. The $\Lambda\pi$ channel shows a very small enhancement in this region ($x_e x_{\Lambda\pi} \sim 0.01$), therefore the treatment of the background is very critical for the $J^P$ assignment of the resonant amplitude. Two experiments have been performed in this channel. The data of Berley et al.[127] suggest a $\frac{3}{2}^-$ assignment, after certain assumptions on the background are made. Taher-Zadeh et al.[128] have studied $K^-n \to \Lambda\pi^-$ and suggested the opposite parity. Recently the UCLA group has reanalyzed the data of this experiment, introducing an additional background amplitude, a $D_{15}$ due to the presence of $\Sigma(1765)$ which they had not included in their first paper. With this different treatment of the background they seem to agree with the $\frac{3}{2}^-$ assignment.[129] The $\Sigma\pi$ channel has been studied by Armenteros et al.[106] who included the data of Rahm et al.[105] in their analysis above 800 MeV/c. The fit to the data will be discussed in the next section. Their results give a branching ratio for $\Sigma(1660) \to \Sigma\pi$ of $(67 \pm 10)\%$ and require a $J^P = \frac{3}{2}^-$ assignment for its quantum numbers.

## B. Production Experiments

A charged $\Sigma(1660)$ has been seen in $\Sigma\pi$ and $\Sigma\pi\pi$ final states. The latter reaction has been studied by various groups in order to measure the quantum numbers. As discussed in Section IV-7, some properties of the Dalitz plot can be used in order to find the parity of $\Sigma(1660)$. For incident $K^-$ momentum above 2.0 GeV/c, it seems to be produced peripherally through $K^*$ exchange in the $t$ channel, therefore as discussed in Section IV-5, a selection of the events at small momentum transfer considerably reduces the background. Four different groups have studied this reaction.[109,126,130,131] The data of ref. 126 are based on larger statistics than any of the other experiments and favor a $3/2^-$ assignment. Figure 73 shows these results: (a) shows the evidence for spin $3/2$. The Adair analysis[132] is carried out on the events produced in the small production angle interval indicated in the figure; the predicted distributions are calculated for three different $J$ assignments and $J = 3/2$ is in better agreement with the data. (b) The kinetic energy of the $\Sigma^-$ in the $\Sigma(1660)$ rest frame is shown, compared with the best fit to the data for negative parity and positive parity. The negative parity hypothesis assumes the following processes

$$\Sigma^+(1660) \to \Lambda(1405) + \pi^+ \to \Sigma^-\pi^+\pi^+$$
$$\to \Sigma(1385) + \pi \to \Sigma^-\pi^+\pi^+$$
$$\to (\Sigma^-\pi^+)\pi^+ \quad S \text{ wave background}$$

The contribution of the $\Sigma(1385)$ amplitude has been calculated using the $\Lambda\pi^+\pi^-$ decay of the $\Sigma(1660)$ and the known branching ratio of $\Sigma(1385)$ in the two channels.[1] For the positive parity the fit shown in Figure 74b requires a very large fraction of $\Sigma(1385) + \pi$ decay which is not in agreement with the observed $\Lambda\pi^+\pi^-$ decay mode; if the correct amount of $\Sigma(1385)$ is used, the positive parity fit would be worse.

Derrick et al.[133a] at 5.5 GeV/c incident $K^-$ momentum have reported an enhancement at a mass of 1680 MeV ($\Gamma = 120 \pm 30$ MeV) in the $\Lambda\pi^+$ channel which does not seem to be present in the $\Sigma^0\pi^+$ channel. The authors argue that this is an indication that this enhancement is different from the previously observed $\Sigma(1660)$. However, the branching ratio of $\Sigma(1660)$ into $\Sigma\pi$ and $\Lambda\pi$ from production experiments seems to be different at different energies (at 1.5 GeV/c Huwe[134] obtains $[\Sigma(1660) \to \Sigma\pi]/[\Sigma(1660) \to \Lambda\pi] = 6.8 \pm 3.0$; at 2.24 GeV/c London et al.[109] observe very little $\Sigma\pi$ decay mode as well as very little $\Lambda\pi$). The width seems to be inconsistent with previous

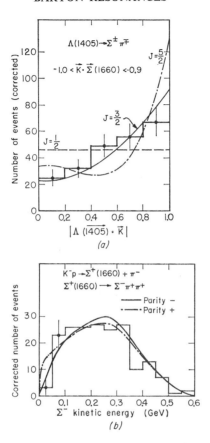

FIG. 73. The data of Eberhard et al.[126] on the $\Sigma(1660)$ decay into the $\Lambda(1405) + \pi$ channel; (a) shows the spin analysis $J = {}^3\!/_2$ is preferred over the other assignments, (b) the c.m. kinetic energy distribution of the $\Sigma^-$ indicates that negative parity is favored by the data.

measured values ($\Gamma \sim 50$ MeV), therefore this experiment adds to the confusion of the $I = 1$ state in this energy region unless a second $I = 1$ resonance is present which would explain many inconsistencies. Other confirmations of this effect are due to Colley et al.,[133b] who detect a similar effect at 6.0 GeV/c incident $K^-$ momentum, and Leitner et al.[133c] at $P_{K^-} = 4.6$ and 5.0 GeV/c. The combined data of the authors of refs. 133a and 133c are shown in Figure 74, which is taken from ref. 122b.

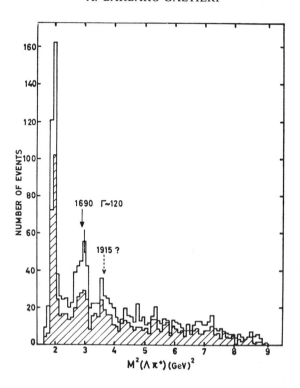

FIG. 74. The $\Lambda\pi^+$ invariant mass squared distribution in the reaction $K^-p \rightarrow \Lambda^0\pi^+\pi^-$ at 4.6, 5.0, and 5.5 GeV/c. Plots include data of Derrick et al.[133a] and Leitner et al.[133c]

In summary, total cross sections and formation experiments require the existence of a $\Sigma(1660)$ with parameters:

$$M \sim 1660 \text{ MeV} \quad \Gamma \sim 50 \text{ MeV} \quad x_{\bar{K}N} \sim 0.1$$
$$x_{\Sigma\pi} \sim 0.67 \quad (6.5)$$
$$x_{\Lambda\pi} \sim 0.1 \text{ or } 0.3$$

(The value of $x_{\Lambda\pi} \sim 0.3$ is from the authors of ref. 3, as reported in ref. 102a, and is somewhat in contradiction with ref. 127.) Production experiments, however, fail to be consistent with this situation because they show: (a) $\Sigma\pi$ branching ratio varying with energy [at 2.24 GeV/c London et al.[109] report 75% of $\Sigma(1660)$ decaying into $\Lambda(1405) + \pi$

and very little $\Sigma\pi$ decay mode, consistent with $(25 \pm 15\%)$]; (b) very large $\Lambda(1405) + \pi$ decay mode which has to be $\leq 13\%$ according to Eq. (6.5); (c) large production in the $\Lambda\pi$ channel at 5 GeV/c. The only common feature to the two types of experiments is the small coupling to the $\bar{K}N$ channel and the fact that the $J^P$ assignment is consistent with $\frac{3}{2}^-$ in both cases. We notice, however, that both large production of $\Sigma^+(1660) \rightarrow \Lambda(1405) + \pi^+$ and $\Sigma(1680) \rightarrow \Lambda\pi^+$ seem to be associated with a $K^*$ exchange diagram $(K^{*0}p \rightarrow \Sigma^+(1660))$].

It is clear, at this point, that more data and detailed analyses are needed to understand what is really happening in this energy region.

### 9. Resonant States in the 1765–1915 MeV Region

Two very close resonances, $\Sigma(1765)$ and $\Lambda(1820)$, of opposite $I$-spin and parity and same $J$, have been disentangled in a production experiment,[135] whereas this has been done in formation experiments for nucleonic resonances. In fact, the $\Sigma(1765)$ was detected in a reaction $K^-n \rightarrow K^-p\pi^-$ at 1.5 GeV/c $K^-$ incident momentum in the $K^-p$ invariant mass, shown in Figure 75. At this energy the production of $\Lambda(1820)$ was very small because the phase space available for it was negligible compared to that for $\Sigma(1765)$. The data on elastic $Kp$ scattering and charge exchange had suggested a $J = \frac{5}{2}$ assignment for both resonances and opposite parity states; the parity remained to be determined. This suggestion was made on the basis of a large $A_5$ coefficient present in the Legendre polynomial expansion of $Kp$ and $\bar{K}^0n$ differential cross sections. This could be explained only by the $D_{5/2}F_{5/2}$ interference term which appears in the $A_5$ coefficient. The parity assignments have now been established through the study of various channels.

*1.* The CERN–Heidelberg–Saclay collaboration has studied the decay of $\Sigma(1765)$ into $\Lambda(1520) + \pi$, which is a pure $I = 1$ state.[136] The cross section as a function of momentum is shown in Figure 76a. This is an example of a $\frac{5}{2}^-$ resonance decaying into a $\frac{3}{2}^-$ resonance and a pion, as discussed in Section III-18. The predicted angular distributions for various $J^P$ states are given in Table VIII. Here, the situation is particularly favorable because the $\Lambda(1520)$ is very narrow and so stands out clearly over the background. Figure 76b shows the production angular distribution, which favors the $\frac{5}{2}^-$ assignment for this resonance; the decay angular distribution of the $\Lambda(1520)$ into $\Sigma^\pm\pi^\mp$ supplies additional information that the $J^P$ assignment is $\frac{5}{2}^-$. The same analysis has been done by Fenster et al.[137] using the decay

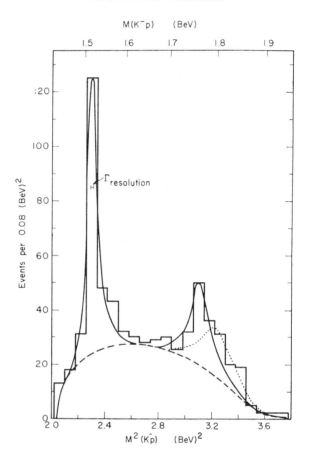

FIG. 75. Discovery of $\Sigma(1765)$ in a production experiment.[135] The two peaks correspond to $\Lambda(1520)$ and $\Sigma(1765)$. (——) A fit to the data assuming these two resonances, (- - -) phase space, ($\cdots$) the expected shape for production of $\Lambda(1820)$. (649 events).

$\Lambda(1520) \rightarrow K^- p$ and by Bell et al.[138] using the $\Lambda(1520) \rightarrow \Sigma^- \pi^+$ channel.

2. There is evidence[139,140] that this resonance decays into $\Sigma(1385) + \pi$, but the situation is more complicated than in the previous case, because the final state is not in a pure isospin state, and various channels have to be used to eliminate the background.

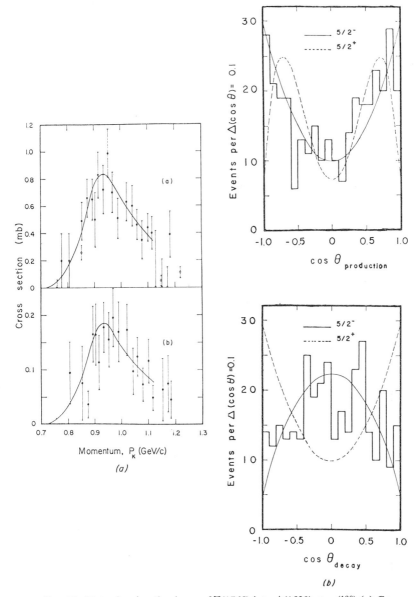

FIG. 76. Data showing the decay of $\Sigma(1765)$ into $\Lambda(1520) + \pi$.[136] (a) Cross section for $K^-p \to \Lambda(1520) + \pi$ as function of laboratory $K^-$ momentum, (b) production and decay angular distribution of $\Lambda(1520)$ and $\Lambda(1520) \to \Sigma^\pm \pi^\mp$. $J^P = \frac{5}{2}^-$ for $\Sigma(1765)$ is clearly preferred. (———) $\frac{5}{2}^-$, (———) $\frac{5}{2}^+$.

3. Another decay mode of $\Sigma(1765)$ studied is the decay into $\Lambda\pi$. We have already seen in Figure 57 that a large enhancement is present in the total cross section for $\Lambda\pi$ production.[102a] Figure 77 shows the results of the partial wave analysis of Smart et al.[141] The fit is done assuming some constant background for the states $P_3$, $S_1$, $P_1$ and a resonant amplitude for $D_3[\Sigma(1660)]$, $D_5[\Sigma(1765)]$, $F_5[\Sigma(1915)]$, and $F_7[\Sigma(2035)]$. The relations between amplitudes and Legendre polynomial coefficients follow the notation of Section III-17. Here again $\Sigma(1765)$ appears to have negative parity. It is possible to fit the coefficients $A_2$ and $A_3$ for opposite parity assignment of $\Sigma(1765)$, just by taking the opposite sign for the background amplitudes. However, in doing so, it is not possible to fit the polarization data at the same time, as can be seen in the $B_2$ and $B_3$ coefficients in Figure 77. This is a very good example of the Minami ambiguity, discussed in Section III-17.

4. The analysis of the *elastic channels* has been done by Gelfand et al.[142] and by Armenteros et al.[3] The two $I$-spin states $(0,1)$ are present here; therefore, all the resonant amplitudes have to be included

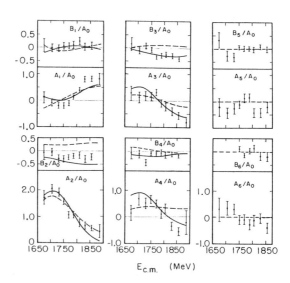

FIG. 77. Coefficients of the Legendre polynomial expansion, normalized to $A_0 = \sigma/4\pi\lambda^2$, of $I$ and $IP$ for the reaction $K^-p \rightarrow \Lambda\pi^-$. Data are from Smart et al.[141] Full lines represent the best fit for $J^P = \frac{5}{2}^-$ assignment to $\Sigma(1765)$, dashed lines represent the best fit for the opposite parity.

in the analysis. The data require the presence of a new $I = 0$ resonant state at $M = 1817$ MeV with a width of 97 MeV, a small elasticity ($x_e = 0.08$) and $J^P = \frac{5}{2}^-$ and an $F_{07}$ state at $M = 1864$ MeV, with $\Gamma = 34$ MeV and $x_e = 0.13$. The latter state is also required by Davies et al.[100] in order to fit the total cross section data. Figure 78 shows the fits of ref. 3 for both $K^-p$ and $\bar{K}^0N$ Legendre polynomial coefficients; the notation used is the one of Section III-17.

5. Finally, both $\Sigma^+\pi^-$ and $\Sigma^-\pi^+$ data have been analyzed by Armenteros et al.,[106] in the energy region $0.6 \leq P_K \leq 1.2$ GeV/c [including the data of Rahm et al.[105]]. Various quantum numbers have been tried for all the resonances in this region, including $S$ wave for $\Lambda(1700)$, however the best fits, shown in Figures 79 and 80, were obtained assuming a nonresonant background of the type $T = a + bP_K$ for the amplitudes $S_{01}, S_{11}, P_{01}, P_{11}, P_{03}, P_{13}$ and resonant Breit-Wigner amplitudes for all the other states (eight resonances included). Table XV

TABLE XV

Parameters of the Best Solution Obtained by Armenteros et al.[106] in the Analysis of $K^-p \to \Sigma^\pm\pi^\mp$ in the c.m. Energy Region 1600–1900 MeV. Quantities in Brackets Were Not Parameters of the Fit

| Resonant amplitudes | Mass, MeV | Width, MeV | Elasticity, $x_e$ | $\Sigma\pi$ branching ratio, $x_{\Sigma\pi}$ | $\Lambda\pi$ branching ratio, $x^f_{\Lambda\pi}$ | Reference for $x_{\Lambda\pi}$ |
|---|---|---|---|---|---|---|
| $D_{03}$ | $1682 \pm 2$ | $55 \pm 4$ | $[0.25]^a$ | $0.46 \pm 0.06$ | | |
| $D_{13}$ | $1665 \pm 2$ | $32 \pm 4$ | $[0.10]^a$ | $0.67 \pm 0.10$ | 0.06 or 0.32 | 3, 141 |
| $D_{05}$ | $1827 \pm 3$ | $75 \pm 9$ | $[0.08 \pm 0.01]^b$ | $0.29 \pm 0.08$ | | |
| $D_{15}$ | $[1760]^c$ | $[120]^c$ | $[0.45 \pm 0.02]^b$ | $0.01 \pm 0.006$ | $0.17 \pm 0.03$ | 3, 141, 143 |
| $F_{05}$ | $1813 \pm 2$ | $87 \pm 15$ | $[0.63 \pm 0.01]^b$ | $0.12 \pm 0.01$ | | |
| $F_{07}$ | $1864 \pm 2$ | $34 \pm 5$ | $[0.13 \pm 0.02]^b$ | $< 0.01$ | | |
| $F_{15}$ | $[1915]^a$ | $[65]^a$ | $[0.12]^b$ | $0.00 \pm 0.01$ | $0.20 \pm 0.05$ | 141 |
| $F_{17}$ | $[2040]^a$ | $[150]^a$ | $[0.25]^d$ | $[0.06]^e$ | 0.16 | 143 |
| $G_{07}$ | $[2100]^a$ | $[160]^a$ | $[0.25]^d$ | $[0.06]^e$ | | |

<sup></sup>$^a$ From total cross section data, see Table XIV.
$^b$ Elasticity taken from the partial-wave analysis of Armenteros et al.[3]
$^c$ This value comes from the analysis of $\Sigma(1765) \to \Lambda(1520) + \pi$, see refs. 136–138.
$^d$ From Wohl et al.[143]
$^e$ From Barbaro-Galtieri.[107]
$^f$ Masses and widths used for these fits are not always the same as the ones of columns 2 and 3.

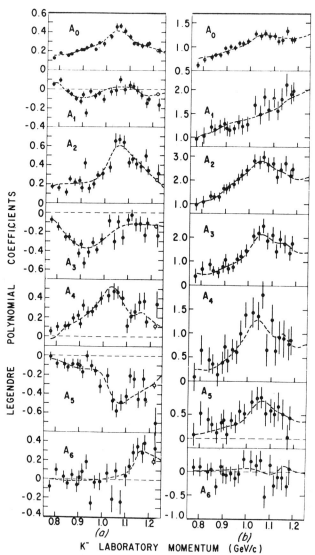

FIG. 78. Coefficients of the Legendre polynomial expansion of the differential cross section of elastic and charge exchange data[3] in the 1700–1915 MeV total c.m. energy. The dashed curves represent the fit of Armenteros et al.[3] which requires seven resonant states in this energy region [$\Sigma(1660)$, $\Lambda(1700)$, $\Sigma(1765)$, $\Lambda(1820)$, $\Lambda(1840)$, $\Lambda(1860)$, $\Sigma(1915)$]. (a) $K^-p \to \bar{K}^0 n$. (b) $K^-p \to K^-p$.

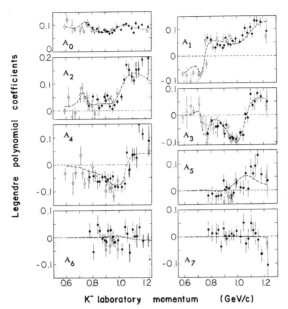

FIG. 79. Coefficients of the Legendre polynomial expansions for the reaction $K^-p \to \Sigma^+\pi^-$ taken from Armenteros et al.[106] The curves are the best fit to the data. The values of the parameters for the resonances are reported in Table XV.

is a summary of the parameters found in this fit, as well as elasticities and branching ratios in the $\Lambda\pi$ channel from ref. 3 and other experiments. Notice that the $D_{05}$ state, $\Lambda(1840)$, is again present in the $\Sigma\pi$ channel with a somewhat lower mass and with a branching ratio of 29% $\Sigma(1915)$ is not required by the data at all in the $\Sigma\pi$ channel. For these last two resonances, and for the $F_{07}$ found only in the elastic channel, it is evident that more experimental data are needed in order to ascertain their existence and properties.

## 10. $\Sigma(2035)$, $F_{17}$ and $\Lambda(2100)$, $G_{07}$

Evidence for structure at $P_K \sim 1.5$ GeV/c first appeared in a total cross section experiment performed by Cook et al.[97] in 1961. Since then new evidence has been collected.

A formation experiment in the 72-in. hydrogen bubble chamber at Berkeley has shown more detailed structure in the reactions $K^-p \to \Lambda\pi^0$

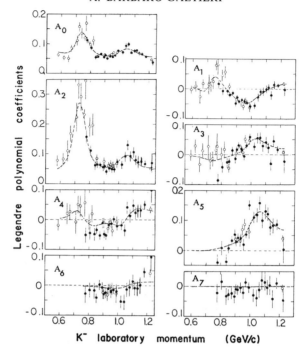

FIG. 80. Same as Fig. 79 for the reaction $K^-p \to \Sigma^-\pi^+$.

and $K^-p \to \bar{K}^0n$, which indicates the presence of two states of different isotopic spin.[145]

Production experiments have also detected the presence of these states: Böck et al.[146] have analyzed the invariant mass spectra of the final states produced in $\bar{p}p$ collisions at 5.7 GeV/c and found an enhancement at $M \sim 2100$ MeV with a width of 38 MeV (very narrow compared to the widths reported by others of $\sim 150$ MeV) decaying through the $\bar{K}N$ and $\bar{K}N\pi$ final states, as well as an enhancement at 2300 MeV. Blanpied et al.[147] in a photoproduction experiment have studied the reaction $\gamma p \to K^+ +$ missing mass ($MM$) and detected small enhancements at $MM \sim 2020$ MeV and $MM \sim 2245$ MeV.

Finally the new precise total cross section experiments of Cool et al.[98] and Davies et al.[100] have shown distinctly the presence of $\Sigma(2040)$ and $\Lambda(2100)$ with enhancements of 6 and 10 mb. respectively, and the parameters reported in Table XIV.

*Spin and parity determinations* are from the formation experiment of Wohl et al.[143] who measured the differential cross sections for $K^-p \to \bar{K}^0 n$ and $K^-p \to \Lambda\pi^0$ and the polarization as function of angle for the $\Lambda\pi^0$ reaction, in the region between 1.2 and 1.7 GeV/c $K^-$ momentum.

The evidence for the $IJ^P$ assignment is shown in Figures 81 and 82. The coefficients of the Legendre polynomial expansion of the differential cross section are shown as functions of the laboratory momentum. The expansion for the $\Lambda\pi^0$ reaction is the following:

$$\frac{d\sigma}{d\Omega}(\cos\theta) = \frac{\lambda^2}{2} \sum_{i=1}^{7} a_i P_i(\cos\theta)$$

which is in agreement with our convention, Eq. (3.106), except for a factor of $\frac{1}{2}$. With this convention $\sigma_e = 2\pi\lambda^2 a_0$. For the $\bar{K}^0 n$ reaction an extra $I$-spin factor has been added; therefore, $\sigma_e = \pi\lambda^2 a_0$.

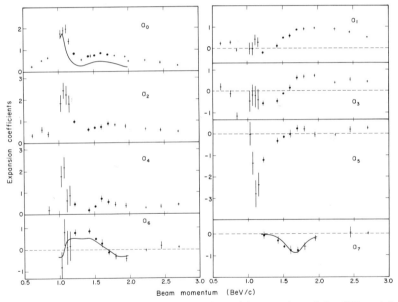

FIG. 81. Coefficients of Legendre polynomial expansion of the differential cross section for the reaction $K^-p \to \bar{K}^0 n$. Data are from Wohl et al.[143] The $J^P$ assignment of $\Sigma(2035)$ at $P_K = 1.53$ GeV/c and $\Lambda(2100)$ at $P_K = 1.68$ GeV/c turn out to be $J^P = \frac{7}{2}^+$ and $J^P = \frac{7}{2}^-$, respectively. The coefficients of interest are

$$a_6 = 18.18(D_5^*G_7 + F_5^*F_7) + 3.03(|F_7|^2 + |G_7|^2)$$
$$a_7 = 22.84(F_7^*G_7)$$

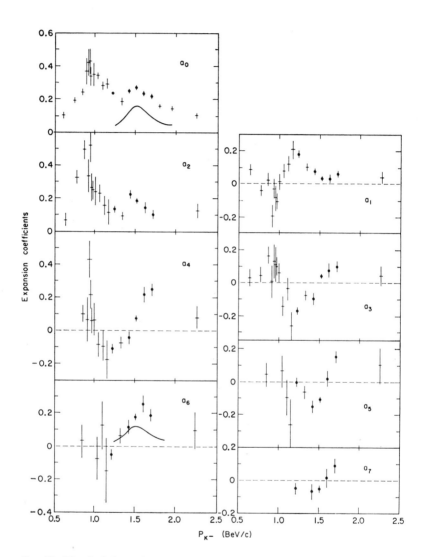

FIG. 82. The $\Lambda\pi^0$ data of Wohl et al.[143] Only $\Sigma(2035)$ is present in these data.
(See caption of Fig. 81.)

Figure 81 shows the coefficients for the $\bar{K}^0 n$ reaction. First of all, the coefficients with $i > 7$ are consistent with zero (they have not been plotted) which is an indication, from inspection of Table V, that partial waves higher than $G_7$ are not present. The shape of the $a_7$ coefficient, therefore, can be explained only by a strong interference term of the type $F_7 G_7$ which reaches a maximum and goes to zero rapidly. This would be the case if both $F_7$ and $G_7$ were resonant amplitudes. The curve in Figure 81 has been calculated with this assumption. The statement is supported by the behavior of the $a_6$ coefficient: the curve of Figure 81 has been obtained adding to the $F_7$ and $G_7$ amplitudes the only two $J = \frac{5}{2}$ resonances known at that time [the $D_{15}$, $\Sigma(1765)$ and the $F_{05}$, $\Lambda(1820)$]. The curve under $a_0$ is the contribution of these four resonant states alone.

Figure 82 shows the $\Lambda \pi^0$ data. The $a_7$ coefficient here does not show the presence of two resonant states, but perhaps the interference with a small background of some higher partial wave. The $a_6$ coefficient, however, is consistent with a $J = \frac{7}{2}$ resonance added to an interference term with a $J = \frac{5}{2}$ resonance. This gives the $I$ spin assignment for $\Sigma(2035)$, but it is not sufficient to assign the parity. The $\Lambda$ polarization coefficients, not shown, give the conclusive evidence for the $F_{7/2}$ assignment to this state. The branching ratios of both resonances have been reported in Table XV.

Other channels show these resonances: in a formation experiment the $\Sigma \pi$ channel[107] requires the presence of both resonances; in production experiments the $\Sigma \pi \pi$ channel shows the presence of $\Sigma(2035)$[126] and the $\bar{K} N$ and $\bar{K} N \pi$ channels[146] show the presence of $\Lambda(2100)$.

## 11. Structure in Total Cross Section Data above 2 GeV/c ($M > 2.2$ GeV)

As seen in Section VI-1 precise total cross-section measurements have been made up to 3.5 GeV/c.[99] Figure 83 shows the cross sections for the two $I$-spin states which have been calculated by Abrams et al.[99]

| $I$ | Symbol | Mass, MeV | Width, MeV | $\sigma_R$, mb | $(J + \frac{1}{2})x$ |
|---|---|---|---|---|---|
| 1 | $\Sigma(2260)$ | $2260 \pm 20$ | 180 | 3.0 | 0.45 |
| 0 | $\Lambda(2340)$ | $2340 \pm 20$ | 105 | 3.0 | 0.51 |
| 1 | $\Sigma(2455)$ | $2455 \pm 10$ | 140 | 1.3 | 0.25 |
| 1 | $\Sigma(2600)$ | $2595 \pm 10$ | 140 | 1.1 | 0.25 |

with the same method described in Section VI-6. The arrows correspond
to the new resonant states found by the authors in these data and the
data of ref. 98.

The first three states have also been found in the experiment performed at the Rutherford Laboratory,[100] with parameters very close to
the above. $\Sigma(2600)$ was outside the energy region of this last experiment.

There is very little information on the formation of these resonances. The only reported experiment which seems to observe some
strong $J = \frac{9}{2}$ amplitude variations is by Dauber et al.,[108] who studied
the reaction $K^- p \rightarrow \Sigma^- \pi^+$ around the 2.1 GeV/c energy region.

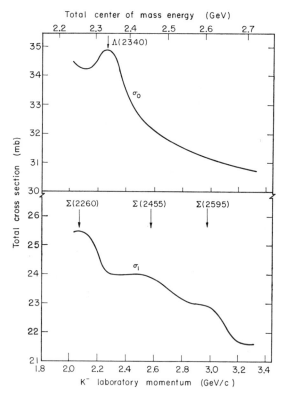

FIG. 83. The cross sections for the two $I$ spin states $I = 0.1$ in the momentum
region 1.8–3.4 GeV/c. Arrows indicate positions of "bumps" which the authors
[Abrams et al.[99]] fit with the resonance parameters reported in the text.

From production experiments the only information collected so far is by Bock et al.[146] who see an enhancement in the $\bar{K}N$ and $\bar{K}N\pi$ invariant mass plot from their $\bar{p}p$ experiment at a mass $M \sim 2300$ MeV, and by Blanpied et al.,[147] who observe an enhancement at $\sim 2245$ MeV.

The data on these last four resonant states, therefore, are too scarce to permit any study of their properties and here, as in the high-energy $\pi p$ resonant states, we hope that some cleaner way to detect these states is possible.

## 12. Conclusions on Y = 0 Resonances

Figure 84 shows the spectroscopy of the $Y = 0$ resonant states found up to now. The particles with measured quantum numbers are located in correspondence to their $J^P$ assignment, the others are only represented by a vertical line corresponding to their mass. At the present time 12 resonant states are established with their quantum numbers; four more still require some investigation to ascertain their existence and quantum numbers. One feature of this plot is that [with the exception of $\Lambda(1675)$] the $J^P$ assignment increases with the mass of the particle. This is due to the type of analysis (partial wave analysis) performed on the data which tends to enhance the particles with large $J$ (study of larger partial waves, with the lower ones assumed to be

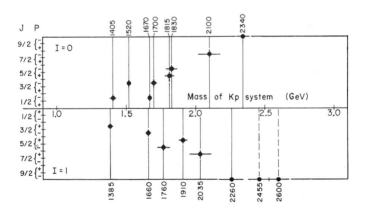

FIG. 84. Spectroscopy of hyperon resonances, $Y = 2$. The position along the vertical axis indicates the quantum numbers of the resonance. The mass and width of the resonance is indicated by the position and error flag along the horizontal axis.

constant or with linear momentum dependence). When more detailed analyses, phase shift analyses like the ones performed on $\pi p$ data, are done on the strange particle final states, it is possible that new structure will appear.

### 13. Particles with Strangeness $-2$ ($Y = -1$)

Three resonant states with $S = -2$ have been detected up to now, and, except for $\Xi(1530)$, not much is known about their properties.

#### A. $\Xi(1530)\ J^P = \frac{3}{2}^+$

It has been discovered in the study of the reaction

$$K^-p \to \Xi\pi K \tag{6.6}$$

by the UCLA group[148] and the Brookhaven group.[149] The only allowed decay mode through strong interactions for this resonant state is $\Xi\pi$, therefore this is the only channel which can be studied to determine its quantum numbers. Schlein et al.,[150] who studied reaction (6.6) at $P_K = 1.8$ and $1.95$ GeV/c, had a clean sample of $\Xi(1530)$ and were able to determine its spin and parity using the Byers and Fenster[51] method discussed in Section IV-7. Figure 85 shows their Dalitz plot for reaction (6.6) and the distribution of the $\Xi^-\pi^+$ invariant mass. The background to the resonance is about 5% but it does not invalidate the spin parity analysis. In fact the authors, within statistics, were not able to detect any differences between the various subsets of events across the resonance, which should reveal any interference effects due to the background, as discussed in Section IV-6. The positive parity assigned to this resonance depends on the assumption that the $\Xi\Lambda$ parity, which has not been directly measured yet, is positive as for the $\Sigma$ and the other baryons which are part of the $SU(3)$ octet with $J^P = \frac{1}{2}^+$. Similar analysis has also been done by Shafer et al.,[151] with the same conclusions on the $J^P$ assignment for this resonance.

#### B. $\Xi(1815)$ and $\Xi(1930)$

The data on these two resonant states are scarce, and therefore no definite statements about branching ratios and quantum numbers can be made at this time. $\Xi(1815)$ was first detected in the $\Xi(1520)\pi$ final state and in the $\Lambda K$ final state by Smith et al.,[152] while Badier et al.[153] have detected $\Xi(1915)$. Figure 86 shows the Dalitz plot and the projections for the reaction $K^-p \to \Xi(1520)\pi K$ taken from Smith et

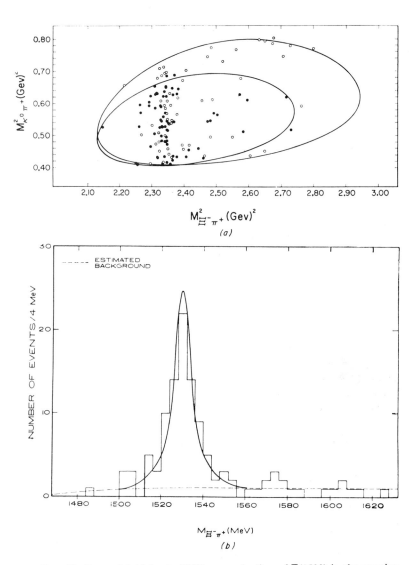

FIG. 85. Data of Schlein et al.[150] on production of $\Xi(1530)$ in the reaction $K^-p \rightarrow \Xi^-\pi^+K^0$ at 1.8 and 1.95 GeV/c (128 events). (a) Dalitz plot. (●) 1.80 GeV/c, (○) 1.95 GeV/c. (b) The distribution of the invariant mass of the $\Xi^-\pi^+$ system. (---) estimated background.

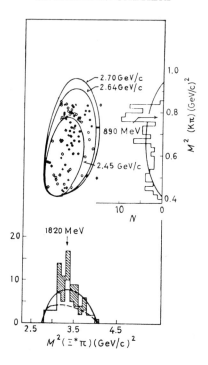

FIG. 86. Data of Smith et al.[152] on the production of $\Xi(1815)$ in the reaction $K^-p \to \Xi(1530)\pi K$. Different symbols in the Dalitz plot refer to different charges in the final state. In the $M^2(\Xi^*\pi)$ projection, the shaded histogram represents events in the $K^*(890)$ region.

al.[152] The production of $\Xi(1815)$ is clearly not a statistical fluctuation. For the $\Lambda \bar{K}$ channel, the data of Badier et al.,[153] are shown in Figure 87. The production of $\Xi(1815)$ and $\Xi(1930)$ is evident (although not too strong for the latter) in the projection of the invariant mass squared of the $\Lambda \bar{K}$ system. The presence of this decay mode assigns the isotopic spin of both resonances to be $I = \frac{1}{2}$.

The best estimates for the branching ratios of these two resonances in the various channels are reported in Table II. As for the quantum numbers, only $\Xi(1815)$ has been studied and it turns out that the assignments of $\frac{1}{2}^\pm$ and $\frac{3}{2}^-$ are equally probable. This result comes from the study of the $\Xi(1815) \to \Xi(1530) + \pi$ channel. The background present is quite large and the amount of statistics is small.[154]

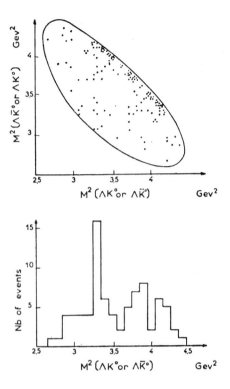

FIG. 87. Data of Badier et al.[153] on the production of $\Xi(1815)$ and $\Xi(1930)$ in the reaction $K^- p \to \Lambda K^0 \bar{K}^0$ at $P_K = 3.0$ GeV/c. The diagonal band in the Dalitz plot represents $\varphi$ meson production $(K_1^0 K_2^0)$. The projection on the $\Lambda K^0$ or $\Lambda \bar{K}^0$ axis contains only events outside the $\varphi$ band.

## VII. Baryon Systems with Positive Strangeness ($Y = 2$)

The $K^+$-nucleon system has hypercharge 2 and positive strangeness. Although many experiments have been done using $K^+$ mesons as bombarding beams, "peaks" and "bumps" have appeared only recently. In fact, although the first resonant state with negative strangeness [$\Sigma(1385)$] was discovered in 1960,[4] structure was not detected in the $K^+ p$ system until 1966, with the precise total cross section measurements of Cool et al.[155]

What is so surprising about these enhancements? The main reason for excitement at this discovery was the fact that the symmetry scheme $SU(3)$ which classifies all the baryon and meson states known up to now in octets, nonets, and decuplets, requires the use of higher representations to accommodate the $B = 1$, $Y = 2$ states. In fact, such a state with $I = 0$ belongs to a $\overline{10}$ representation and an $I = 1$ state would belong to a 27 representation. If such "bumps" turn out to be resonances, $SU(3)$ predicts the existence of other resonant states in order to complete these multiplets (none have as yet been detected).

Let us now review the situation.

### 1. Structure in the $K^+N$ Total Cross Sections

Very precise measurements of the $K^+p$ and $K^+d$ total cross sections have been made by Cool et al.[155a] and Abrams et al.[155b] at the AGS in the 0.85–3.5 GeV/c incident momentum region. Figures 88 and 89 show their data, taken from ref. 155, together with all the measurements made by other authors. Recently Bugg et al. have extended the cross section measurements down to 650 MeV/c.[100]

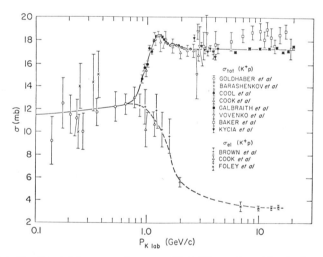

FIG. 88. $K^+p$ total cross section up to 20 GeV/c, as plotted by Cool et al.[155a] The reader is referred to their article for the references of the experiments listed in the figure. The dashed curve represents the elastic cross section $K^+p \rightarrow K^+p$. This curve is hand drawn through the data.

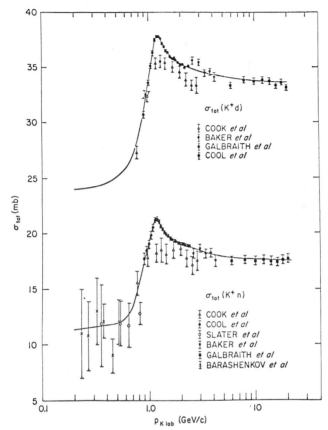

FIG. 89. Total cross section for $K^+d$ and $K^+n$ as plotted by Cool et al.[155a] The references for the experimental points reported in this graph can be found in ref. 155.

The $K^+p$ system is in a pure $I = 1$ state, while the $K^+d$ system is a mixture of the $I = 0$ and the $I = 1$ isotopic spin states. The cross section for $K^+d$ interactions in terms of isotopic spin states is

$$(K^+d) = \tfrac{1}{2}[\sigma(I = 0) + 3\sigma(I = 1)] - \sigma_G$$

where $\sigma_G$ is the Glauber correction[120] and the two $I$-spin states can be isolated with the same procedures described in Section VI-6. They are

$$\sigma(I = 1) = \sigma(K^+p)$$
$$\sigma(I = 0) = 2\sigma(K^+d) - 3\sigma(K^+p) + 2\sigma_G$$

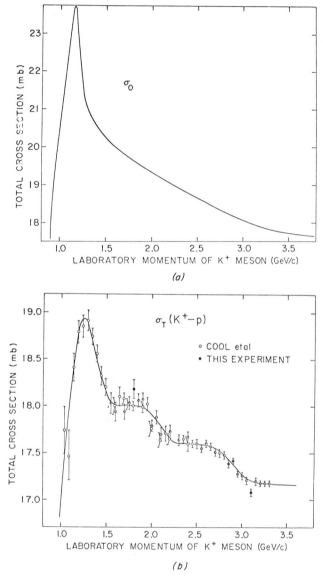

Fig. 90. The total cross section for the two isotopic spin states in $K^+$ interactions, above 0.9 GeV/c. Plot taken from ref. 155b. (a) The calculated $I = 0$ cross section, (b) the measured $I = 1$ total cross section. The experimental points of Cool et al.

These cross sections above 0.9 GeV/c incident $K^+$ momentum are shown in Figure 90, taken from ref. 155b. If all the peaks seen in total cross sections are due to resonances, they would have the following properties

|       | $I$ | $P_K$, GeV/c | Mass, MeV | Width, MeV | $\sigma_R$, mb | $(J + \frac{1}{2})x$ |
|-------|-----|--------------|-----------|------------|----------------|----------------------|
| $Z_0$ | 0   | 1.15         | 1863 ± 20 | 150        | 8              | 0.55                 |
| $Z_1$ | 1   | 1.25         | 1910 ± 20 | 180        | 4              | 0.31                 |
| $Z_1$ | 1   | 1.89         | 2190 ± 10 | 120        | 0.20           | 0.03                 |
| $Z_1$ | 1   | 2.70         | 2505 ± 10 | 120        | 0.20           | 0.04                 |

In order to determine whether these peaks are due to resonances or to some effect of a different type, it is necessary to study in detail the elastic and inelastic channels in the energy region of each peak. If it turns out that the "bump" is produced by one particular amplitude, in a definite $J^P$ state and with a resonant behavior according to the discussions of Section III-7, then the "bump" has to be explained with the existence of such a resonance.

As we will see in the next two sections, there is not enough data at the moment to carry out such a study. Only $Z_1(1910)$ has been investigated, and there is no indication at the present time that the peak is produced by a resonance.

## 2. Study of Elastic Channels

The threshold for pion production in the $K^+p$ interaction is at 520 MeV/c, and since there are no hyperons with positive strangeness only the $K^+p$ elastic channel is open up to this energy. Figure 88 shows the behavior of the elastic cross section, which departs from the total cross section only above 600 MeV/c. With the presently available data it appears that the $I = 1$ elastic cross section does not show any structure in the region of $Z_1(1910)$.

The phase shift analysis of Goldhaber et al.[156] up to 642 MeV/c shows that only an $S$ wave amplitude is necessary to fit the data and that the cross section from Eqs. (3.25) and (3.26) can be expressed as

$$\sigma = 4\pi\lambda^2 \sin^2 \delta_1$$

where $\delta_1$ decreases almost linearly down to $-36.2°$ at 642 MeV/c. At 780 MeV/c some $P$ and $D$ wave contributions have to be introduced.[157] Lea et al.[158] have performed a phase shift analysis in the range 140–1500 MeV/c, using all the available data on total cross sections [including all the BNL measurements[155]], differential cross sections, inelastic and elastic cross sections, and proton polarization. They also used the calculated values for the real parts of the forward scattering amplitude by evaluating a dispersion relation for $K^+p$ forward scattering. Three partial waves ($S$, $P$, $D$) with five amplitudes were included in the analysis and a simple energy dependence for $\eta_J$ and $\delta_J$ (which required a maximum of six parameters for each amplitude) was used. It turned out that the available data is too scarce to permit any definite set of phase shifts. The authors list 24 possible sets which have a good fit ($\chi^2/N_{DF} < 2.0$, where $N_{DF}$ is the number of degree of freedom, $N_{DF} \sim 330$). These 24 solutions are divided into four groups according to the general behavior of the amplitudes. Two of these groups favor a resonant behavior for the $P_{11}$ amplitude at an energy above 1.5 GeV/c, but none shows resonancelike behavior at 1.25 GeV/c where the total cross section shows the bump called $Z_1$ (1910). Figure 91 shows the best solutions of groups I, II, and IV, along with the predicted proton polarization at two different $K^+p$ momenta. It is clear that more data are necessary and that polarization measurements could help considerably in narrowing down the possible solutions.

*The elastic scattering in the $I = 0$ state* has been studied up to 810 MeV/c by Stenger et al.[159] This isotopic spin state is experimentally difficult to study because the reactions $K^+n \rightarrow K^+n$ or $K^+n \rightarrow K^0p$ take place on the neutron which is bound in the deuteron. Furthermore, the $K^+n$ is a mixture of $I = 1$ and $I = 0$ isotopic spin states, therefore the $I = 1$ elastic channel has to be used in order to obtain the $I = 0$ state. Stenger et al.[159] have performed a phase shift analysis up to 810 MeV/c and found that $S$, $P$, and $D$ waves are appreciable at 530 MeV/c and increase with incident momenta.

Above 810 MeV/c no data are available at the present time to study the elastic channel in the energy range of $Z_0(1863)$. Preliminary data of Hirata et al.[160] show that some of the enhancement in total cross section might be due to the rise of the elastic cross section.

An attempt to extract information on the behavior of the amplitude in the $Z_0(1863)$ energy region from the available data has been made by Carter.[161] In his paper the imaginary part of the forward scattering

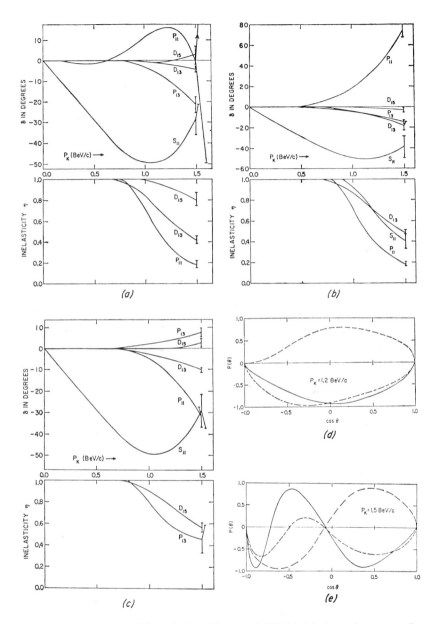

FIG. 91. Phase shift analysis of Lea et al.[158] (a)–(c) show three sets of solutions. (d) and (e) show the predicted proton recoil polarizations for the three above sets of phase shifts at two different $K^+$ momenta. (——) solutions of group I (a), (—·—) group II (b), (–––) group IV (c).

amplitude is calculated from the measured total cross sections in both isotopic spin states, and the real parts of these amplitudes are then calculated using the dispersion relations as given by Lusignoli et al.[162] The amplitudes for the two $I$-spin states so obtained contain contributions from all the partial waves present in this energy region. The $I = 1$ amplitude does not show any rapid variation of phase, which could indicate the resonant behavior of some partial wave, whereas this seems to be the case for the $I = 0$ amplitude. From the plot of the real and imaginary parts of the $I = 0$ amplitude as a function of c.m. momentum, the author evaluates the background as a smooth curve and finds that the remaining amplitude plotted in an Argand diagram has the characteristic behavior of a resonance with the mass and width of $Z_0(1863)$. If the elastic scattering data confirm this behavior for some of the partial waves, then the existence of $Z_0(1863)$ has to be accepted.

### 3. Study of Inelastic Channels

Bland et al.[163] have studied the inelastic $K^+p$ interactions between 860 and 1580 MeV/c, which is the region of the first "bump" seen in the total cross section. Figure 92 shows the cross sections for the various final states. The reaction studied was $K^+p \to K^0p\pi^+$ and the quasi two-body final states

$$K^+p \to K^0\Delta^{++}(1236)$$

$$\to K^{*+}(891) + p$$

account for almost all the events. The total cross section for single pion production $KN\pi$ is shown in Figure 92, as well as the cross section for two-pion production. The reaction $K^+p \to K\Delta(1236)$ appears to be responsible for the peak in total cross section, therefore the analysis of this channel should shed light on the nature of the bump called $Z_1(1910)$.

Bland et al.[163] have studied the production and decay of $\Delta(1236)$ and found that no partial wave can be singled out to explain the bump in the cross section, but both $P_{11}$ and $P_{13}$ waves in the $K^+p$ system seem to be responsible for this behavior. The coefficients of the Legendre polynomial expansion of the $\Delta$ production angular distribution (with respect to the incident proton direction in the c.m.)

$$\left(\frac{d\sigma}{d\Omega}\right)_\Delta = \sum_l A_l P_l(\cos\theta)$$

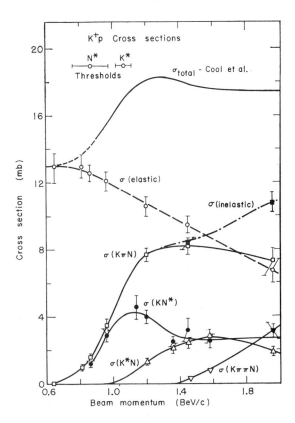

FIG. 92. Cross sections for all the channels, elastic and inelastic, in the region of the bump of Cool et al. in $I = 1$ state.[163] The curves are hand drawn through the points to guide the eye.

are shown in Figure 93. The behavior of the odd coefficients, which contain the interference between the $P_{11}$ and $P_{13}$ waves, indicates that the phase of these partial waves does not change throughout the peak region, and neither of the two shows a resonant behavior. The fall-off of the cross sections after the 1.2 GeV/c bump can be explained with the fact that both $P$ waves reach the unitary limit around the "bump" region and then fall off like $4\pi\lambda^2$.

In conclusion, according to the authors, most of the features of the $K\Delta$ channel can be explained with the $\rho$ exchange model of Stodolsky and Sakurai[40] (with the $P_{11}$ and $P_{13}$ waves larger than predicted by

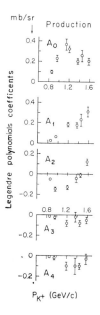

FIG. 93. Legendre polynomial coefficients for the expansion of the differential cross section of $K^+p \to K^0\Delta(1236)^{++}$. Data are from Bland et al.[163]

this model), and no resonant behavior can be detected with the present data.

As for the $I = 0$ bump, there are no data in the inelastic channels at the present time, but a $\Delta K$ final state cannot explain the peak, since it is forbidden by $I$-spin conservation.

### 4. Search for $Y = 2$ Resonances in Production Experiments

Various experiments have been done with $K^+$ mesons interacting on protons and no resonances in the $KN$ or $KN\pi$ systems have been detected up to now. The $I = 1$ effect at 1910 MeV is clearly inelastic, as seen in the previous sections. Shen et al.,[164] at $P_K = 4.6$ GeV/c, have investigated the $KN\pi$ invariant mass in the four- and five-body final states and have not detected any resonant state at the expected masses. The upper limit of the cross section for production of such resonances is between 30 and 7 $\mu$b, depending on the reaction studied.

The $I = 0$ bump in total cross section might be related to the elastic channel, so $K^+n$ final states have been investigated and again have failed to show any resonant effect. The data of Dodd et al.[165] at 3.0 GeV/c and of Ferro-Luzzi et al.[39] at the same momentum, also did not show any $Y = 2$ resonances in either $KN$ or $KN\pi$ final states.

### 5. Conclusions on $Y = 2$ Systems

As discussed in the previous sections, four bumps have appeared in total cross-section data in the $Y = 2$ system. However, formation and production experiments have not been able yet to explain the nature of these bumps.

The $Z_1(1910)$ is the only one studied in some detail and it does not seem to have a resonant origin. For the other bumps the only evidence against a resonant interpretation comes from production experiments where they did not appear as resonances. Before drawing any conclusion on the four bumps, it is clear that more data are needed.

### VIII. Classification of Baryon States in $SU(3)$ Supermultiplets

Now that we have reviewed the present knowledge on baryon states, it would be natural to review the situation on the classification of these states. We will only briefly compare the experimental properties of the known baryons with the predictions of $SU(3)$, the classification scheme proposed by Gell-Mann[166] and Ne'eman[167] based on unitary symmetry. Gell-Mann called it the "eightfold way."

As we have seen in Section I, particles occur in isotopic spin multiplets, whose members are distinguished only by the $z$ component of the isotopic spin and have the same properties with respect to strong interactions. Their properties with respect to weak and electromagnetic interactions, however, can be different; in fact there is a mass difference (of the order of 10 MeV or less) of electromagnetic origin between the members of the same multiplet.

We have also seen in Section I that each particle has some quantum numbers related to its space–time properties: its spin $J$, its parity $P$, and its mass $M$ (and width if it is unstable). The "eightfold way" derives from the observation that there are eight baryons, stable with respect to strong interactions, whose spin and parity are $\frac{1}{2}^+$—the nucleons, the $\Lambda$, the $\Sigma$'s, and the $\Xi$'s (only for the $\Xi$ the parity has not been measured yet)—and whose masses are close together, all lying within 20% of their common mean mass. This observation led to investigation of the possibility that strong interactions are approximately symmetric under a group larger than the isotopic spin group and that the particles can be classified in supermultiplets, larger than the isotopic spin multiplets. In this scheme the eight baryons form an octet which is an irreducible representation of this higher symmetry group. The symmetry, however, is not exact, because the masses of the eight baryons are not identical, but a symmetry-breaking interaction exists which produces the observed mass splitting of about 20%.

We refer the reader to the original articles,[168] or to the many review articles[169] written on the subject, for the theory connected to the $SU(3)$ symmetry scheme. We will report here only the formulas necessary to compare the experimental data with the predictions for the known singlets, octets, and decuplets. At the present time there is no need for higher representations, since all known baryon resonances could be accommodated in the 1, 8, and 10 representations. This, of course, will not be true if the $K^+N$ bumps of Section VII turn out to be due to resonances.

### 1. Mass Formulas and Decay Rate Calculations

#### A. Mass Formulas

The medium-strong interactions are supposed to be responsible for the mass splitting of the members of a supermultiplet. The Gell-Mann–Okubo (GMO) mass formula has been derived with the assumption that the symmetry is broken by a medium-strong interaction in such a way that the isospin $I$ and the hypercharge $Y$ are still conserved. In first order perturbation theory, one gets

$$M = a + bY + c[I(I + 1) - (Y^2/4)] \qquad (8.1)$$

where $a$, $b$, $c$ are constants and $Y$ and $I$ are hypercharge and $I$-spin of the particle in consideration. Table XVI shows the comparison of the prediction of this formula and the experimental values of the masses for the $\frac{1}{2}^+$ octet of stable baryons and the $\frac{3}{2}^+$ decuplet.

For the octet the formula has three parameters so it leads to the relation

$$2(N + )\Xi = 3\Lambda + \Sigma \qquad (8.2)$$

where the particle symbol indicates the corresponding particle mass. For the decuplet the hypercharge $I$-spin relation is such that Eq. (8.1)

TABLE XVI

Test of the Gell-Mann–Okubo Formula for the Two Best-Known Baryon
Supermultiplets

(a) $\frac{1}{2}^+$ Octet

GMO formula: $2(N + \Xi) = 3\Lambda + \Sigma$

| Y | I | Particle | Input, MeV | Predicted, MeV | Observed, MeV |
|---|---|---|---|---|---|
| 1 | $\frac{1}{2}$ | $N$ | 939 | | |
| 0 | 0 | $\Lambda$ | 1115 | | |
| 0 | 1 | $\Sigma$ | 1193 | | |
| $-1$ | $\frac{1}{2}$ | $\Xi$ | | $1330 \pm 1$ | $1317 \pm 1$ |

(b) $\frac{3}{2}^+$ Decuplet

GMO formula: $\Delta - \Sigma - \Xi = \Xi - \Omega^-$

| Y | I | Particle | Input, MeV | Predicted, MeV | Observed, MeV |
|---|---|---|---|---|---|
| 1 | $\frac{3}{2}$ | $\Delta$ | 1236 | | |
| 0 | 1 | $\Sigma$ | 1383 | | |
| $-1$ | $\frac{1}{2}$ | $\Xi^*$ | | 1530 | $1530 \pm 1$ |
| $-2$ | 0 | $\Omega^-$ | | 1677 | $1675 \pm 3$ |

leads to a particularly simple form, called the "equal spacing rule":

$$\Delta - \Sigma = \Sigma - \Xi = \Xi - \Omega \tag{8.3}$$

where again the particle symbol indicates the corresponding particle
mass. Notice, however, that the decuplet is now made up of unstable
particles (except for the $\Omega$), therefore the main symbol should be
followed by the mass of the state.

If, instead of the medium-strong interactions, the electromagnetic
interactions are considered in such a way that $I_z$ and $Y$ are conserved,
one can derive a relationship between the mass differences of the
members of the isomultiplets which belong to the same octet. The
following relation has been obtained by Coleman and Glashow[170]:

$$\Xi^- - \Xi^0 = \Sigma^- - \Sigma^+ - (n - p) \tag{8.4}$$

By inspection of Table I it is easy to calculate that this is equivalent to:

$$6.5 \pm 0.2 = 6.68 \pm 0.11 \text{ MeV}$$

which shows that Eq. (8.4) is remarkably well satisfied.

The derivation of the GMO formula [Eq. (8.1)] neglects the possibility of mixing between different unitary multiplets of the same spin parity, mixing due to other symmetry-breaking interactions. This mixing has been discussed for meson octets and singlets,[171] but it can be extended to baryon octets. If we call $\Lambda'$ a unitary singlet with the same $J^P$ assignment as $N$, $\Sigma$, $\Lambda$, and $\Xi$, the mixing of the two isosinglets $\Lambda$ and $\Lambda'$ can be expressed in terms of an angle $\theta$, defined as follows:

$$\langle 8| = \langle \Lambda'| \sin \theta + \langle \Lambda| \cos \theta$$
$$\langle 1| = \langle \Lambda'| \cos \theta - \langle \Lambda| \sin \theta \tag{8.5}$$

where $\langle 8|$ and $\langle 1|$ represent the pure octet and singlet states and $\langle \Lambda|$ and $\langle \Lambda'|$ represent the physical states. The angle $\theta$ can be expressed as a function of measurable quantities, specifically masses. By applying the mass operator to both Eqs. (8.5), one obtains for the angle $\theta$:

$$\sin^2 \theta = (\Lambda - M_8)/(\Lambda - \Lambda') \tag{8.6a}$$

with $M_8$ easily obtained from Eq. (8.2) to be

$$M_8 = [2(N + \Xi) - \Sigma]/3 \tag{8.6b}$$

Equation (8.6a) was first derived by Glashow and Socolow[172] for mesons, and it was obtained by applying the mass-squared operator to Eqs. (8.5). (For mesons the mass formula seems to work better with mass squared instead of mass, but there is no justification for this difference.) If there is mixing, Eqs. (8.6) have to be used to calculate the value of the mixing angle $\theta$ for the set of nine particles; in this case the mass formula is not a check of $SU(3)$ any more, but the decay rates still offer a good test.

### B. Decay Rates

In the unitary symmetry model of strong interactions there are some very definite predictions of the relations between the different meson–baryon coupling constants. These relations can be checked experimentally by comparing the various decay rates of the members of a supermultiplet into mesons and baryons, which belong to other supermultiplets.

For the members of a decuplet decaying into a baryon (member of the $\frac{1}{2}^+$ octet) and a meson (member of the pseudoscalar octet), the expression used by Tripp et al.[173] to compare partial widths is the following

$$\Gamma = C^2 g^2 B_l(q)(M_N/M_R)q \qquad (8.7)$$

where $C$ is the appropriate $SU(3)$ Clebsch-Gordon coefficient, which can be found in de Swart's Tables,[174] $g^2$ is related to the only coupling constant which appears for a decuplet decaying into a baryon and a meson (members of octets); $B_l(q)$ is the barrier factor discussed in Section III-7 and with the form given in Eqs. (3.42); $q$ is the momentum of the decay particles, which is the phase space factor; $M_R$ is the mass of the resonant state, and $M_N$ is the mass of the nucleon which has been introduced only to make $g^2$ dimensionless and of the order of unity.

For the members of an octet decaying into a baryon belonging to an octet and a pseudoscalar meson, two types of coupling are possible; therefore, the partial width [Eq. (8.7)] is now:

$$= (Cg_d + C'g_f)^2 B_l(q)(M_N/M_R)q \qquad (8.8)$$

where $C$ and $C'$ are the Clebsch-Gordon coefficients[174] for the two couplings $g_d$ and $g_f$. This notation used by Tripp et al.[173] is related to Gell-Mann's[166] $\alpha = D/(F + D)$ through the relation

$$\alpha^{-1} = \frac{F + D}{D} = 1 + \sqrt{5}\, g_f/3g_d$$

We now have a basis for making a comparison of $SU(3)$ predictions with experimental results. Tripp et al.[173] have recently made this comparison using the most recent data available, so we will follow their calculations. Most of the parameters used for masses and decay rates are the ones reported in Tables II and III, with more recent data (published and unpublished) for which we refer the reader to ref. 173.

## 2. Decuplets

There are two possible decuplets at the present time: a $\frac{3}{2}^+$ and a $\frac{7}{2}^+$. The $\frac{7}{2}^+$ decuplet could be the recurrence of the $\frac{3}{2}^+$ since it has the same parity and obeys the $\Delta J = 2$ rule expected for the Regge recurrence of a resonance.

### A. $\frac{3}{2}^+$ Decuplet

The mass formula is very well satisfied, as seen in Table XVI. The discovery in 1964 of the strangeness $= -3$ state of this decuplet, the $\Omega^-$, has been perhaps the largest success of $SU(3)$, which predicted the existence of this stable baryon in 1962.

Equation (8.7) can be used to test the $SU(3)$ predictions for the partial decay rates. Tripp et al.[173] have suggested a very straightforward method to check the consistency of the various experimental results. It consists of plotting the value of $g^2$ for each decay rate, which, if $SU(3)$ gives the correct prediction, should be the same for all decays of the members of the same decuplet. Figure 94a shows the values of $g^2$ calculated for the $\frac{3}{2}^+$ decuplet. The major discrepancy lies in the values of $g^2$ for $\Delta(1236) \to N\pi$ and $\Lambda\Xi(1530) \to \Xi\pi$, which differ by a factor of 2 (i.e., they are three standard deviations apart).

### B. $\frac{7}{2}^+$ Decuplet

The mass formula cannot be checked here, because only two members of this decuplet have been detected as yet. Figure 94b shows

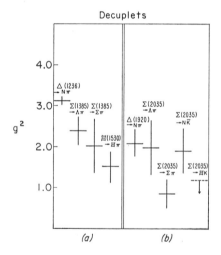

Fig. 94. The coupling constants calculated from the partial width for decay modes of the members of the same decuplet. (a) for the $\frac{3}{2}^+$ decuplet, (b) for the $\frac{7}{2}^+$ decuplet. Each decuplet should have a unique value of the coupling constant, since all the $SU(3)$ and kinematical factors have been introduced in the calculation of $g^2$ (see text for the definitions of $g^2$). Plot taken from Tripp et al.[173]

the calculated values of $g^2$ for the measured decay rates. It is interesting to notice that the $g^2$ value found for this decuplet ($\sim 2$) is not far from the one found for the $\frac{3}{2}^+$ decuplet.

### 3. Octets and Singlets

The basic octet of $J^P = \frac{1}{2}^+$ baryons obeys the mass formula (8.2) within 1%, as can be seen in Table XVI. Many other octets have been suggested in the literature, the difficulties of assignments arising from the difficulties encountered in the measurements of spin and parity of the resonances, especially the $\Xi$ states. Only the $\Xi(1530)$ quantum numbers have been established and the $S = -2$ system in general has been poorly studied, as seen in Section VI-13. Recently Goldberg et al.[175] have discussed some possible octets of $J^P = \frac{3}{2}^-$ and $\frac{5}{2}^+$. Tripp et al.,[173] with more recent data, have discussed the $\frac{1}{2}^-$, $\frac{3}{2}^+$, $\frac{5}{2}^-$, and $\frac{5}{2}^+$, and we report their conclusions here.

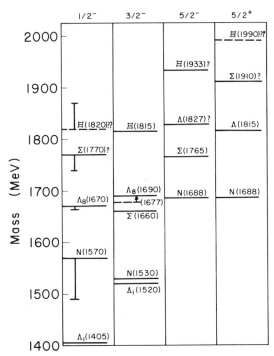

FIG. 95. Mass spectroscopy of four proposed octets.[173] The short horizontal lines in the $\frac{1}{2}^-$ octet correspond to the baryon-$\eta$ thresholds.

## A. $\frac{1}{2}^-$ States

There are some states with $J^P = \frac{1}{2}^-$ : $\Lambda(1405)$, $\Lambda(1670)$, $N(1570)$, and the possible $\Sigma(1770)$ discussed in Section VI-7. If $\Lambda(1405)$ were a singlet, then the other states together with a $\Xi(1820)$ could fill an octet of $\eta$-baryon resonances. Figure 95 shows this nonet of particles, the short horizontal line indicating the threshold for the $\eta$-baryon corresponding to each state. $\Xi(1820)$ would be below threshold for $\pi\Xi$ decay.

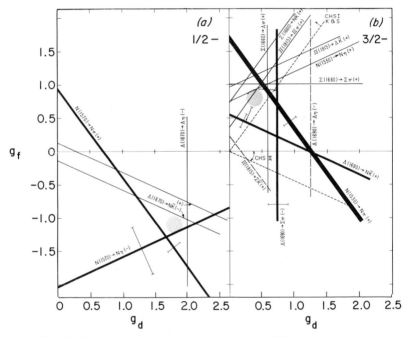

FIG. 96. Plot of $g_f$ vs. $g_d$ for the proposed octets.[173] The heavy lines refer to decay rates measured with an error of about 25% (indicated by the error bars), medium lines refer to decay rates with larger errors (the error bars shown an error of 50%), light lines refer to decay rates with uncertainties of a factor two or more. Long dashed lines indicate upper limits. The shaded area in each figure shows the approximate values of $g_f$ and $g_d$ which seem to be in better agreement with all the experimental partial widths of that octet.

It is not clear if the detected $\Xi(1820)$ is part of this octet, however it has been considered part of the $3/2^-$ octet, as we will see later.

As for the decay rates, again we report the calculations of Tripp et al.[173] Using expression (8.8) to relate the partial widths to the coupling constants, they plot $g_f$ vs. $g_d$. In such a plot each experimental value of $\Gamma$ yields a straight line which is symmetric with respect to the origin since it carries a sign ambiguity corresponding to the two $\pm(\Gamma)^{1/2}$ possibilities. Tripp et al. plot the straight line which is in best agreement with the lines of the other decay rates of the same octet. Agreement between members of the same octet is indicated by a common value of $g_d$ and $g_f$, therefore by a common intersection point for all the lines of the plot. Figure 96a shows $g_f$ vs. $g_d$ for the measured decay rates of $\Lambda(1670)$ and $N(1570)$. The lines seem to cross in the region $g_d = 1.8$ and $g_f = -1.1$. However, these values of the coupling constants predict a width $\Gamma = 250$ MeV for the decay $\Lambda(1670) \rightarrow \Sigma\pi$ which is in contra-

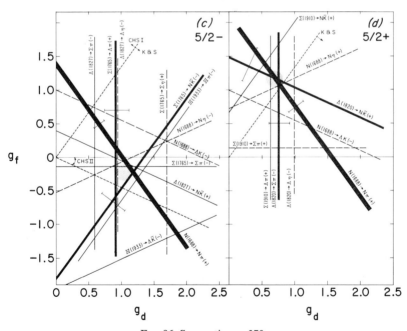

FIG. 96. See caption p. 370.

diction with the total width of 18 MeV observed by Berley et al.[122] So the decay rate predictions of "unbroken $SU(3)$" do not seem to be in agreement with experiment for the octet suggested here.

### B. $\frac{3}{2}^-$ States

Figure 95 shows the states which could belong to this nonet. The mass of the isosinglet $M_8 = 1677$ MeV predicted by the mass formula (8.2) does not seem to be in agreement with the experimental value of the mass for $\Lambda(1700)$. However, if a compromise mass of 1690 MeV is used for this resonance [see Table XV, where Armenteros et al.[106] report a mass of $1682 \pm 2$ MeV], using Eqs. (8.6) a mixing angle of $-16°$ between $\Lambda(1520)$ and $\Lambda(1690)$ would account for the discrepancy.

Figure 96b shows the $g_f$ vs. $g_d$ plot for the measured decay rates of the members of this octet. A common acceptable point of intersection seems to be at $g_f = 0.8$ and $g_d = 0.4$. For $\Lambda(1690)$ the lines plotted assume no mixing with $\Lambda(1520)$, but once the mixing is introduced the lines tend to move closer to the intersection point as indicated by the two wavy lines which show the displacement due to assumption of no mixing. The major discrepancy here is due to the absence of $\Xi(1815) \rightarrow \Sigma\bar{K}$, but the experimental data on this state are very scarce, its quantum numbers have not been established, and therefore it could be a member of a different octet.

### C. $\frac{5}{2}^-$ States

There are only two established states in this octet and no candidate for a singlet state has been detected yet. Using $\Xi(1933)$ as the possible $\Xi$ member of the octet, Tripp et al.[173] calculate the mass of the possible isosinglet member of the octet to be at 1827 MeV. This is the same mass at which Armenteros et al.[106] detected a new $D_{05}$ state in their analysis of the $K^-p \rightarrow \Sigma^\pm\pi^\mp$ data (see Table XV).

The decay rates for this octet are shown in Figure 96c. A reasonably satisfactory intersection point occurs at $g_f = -0.2$ and $g_d = 1.05$. Here again the $\Xi(1933)$ decay rates show the largest disagreement and here again the same comment made for $\Xi(1815)$ is valid.

### D. $\frac{5}{2}^+$ States

Only $N(1688)$ and $\Lambda(1815)$ have these established quantum numbers. If $\Sigma(1910)$ were included here, then a $\Xi(1990)$ would be expected to complete the octet; again if there is no singlet state with $J^P = \frac{5}{2}^+$

and if there is no mixing between this isosinglet and the isosinglet member of the octet.

As for the decay rates, apart from $\Sigma(1910) \rightarrow \Sigma\pi$, they seem to be in agreement and cross at $g_f = 1.15$ and $g_d = 0.7$. Here the big discrepancy lies in the $\Sigma(1910) \rightarrow \Sigma\pi$ decay which is found to be $\sim 100$ times smaller than expected. But again, the quantum numbers of this state have not been measured yet.

## 4. Conclusions

The experimental parameters—mass and partial widths for the baryon resonances of known $J^P$—seem mostly to be in remarkable agreement with $SU(3)$.

The mass formula works reasonably well for all conjectured decuplets and octets (the $\frac{3}{2}^-$ octet seems to need a mixing angle of $16°$).

The decay rates have been calculated assuming exact symmetry and part of the discrepancies could be attributed to the necessity of introducing a "symmetry breaking" interaction as for the mass formula. Some large discrepancies have been observed, most of them, however, involve states whose experimental knowledge is still very scarce.

### Acknowledgments

I wish to thank Professor Luis W. Alvarez for his encouragement and support during this work. I thank also the many friends who read parts of the manuscript and gave me suggestions for improvement, in particular Dr. Janos Kirz, Miss Maxine Matison, Dr. Alberto Pignotti, and Professor Gordon Shaw. Finally, I thank Professors Robert D. Tripp and Arthur H. Rosenfeld for many useful discussions.

### References

1. A. H. Rosenfeld, N. Barash-Schmidt, A. Barbaro-Galtieri, L. R. Price, M. Roos, P. Soding, W. J. Willis, and C. G. Wohl, *Rev. Mod. Phys.*, **40**, 77 (1968); *Rev. Mod. Phys.*, **39**, 1 (1967).
2. The reader can find more extensive discussion of quantum numbers and conservation laws in *An Introduction to Elementary Particles*, W. S. C. Williams, Academic Press, New York, 1961.

3. R. Armenteros, M. Ferro-Luzzi, D. W. G. Leith, R. Levi-Setti, A. Minten, R. D. Tripp, H. Filthuth, V. Hepp, E. Kluge, H. Schneider, R. Barloutaud, P. Gianet, J. Meyer, and J. P. Porte, *Nucl. Phys.*, **B3**, 592 (1967).
4. M. Alston, L. W. Alvarez, P. Eberhard, M. L. Good, W. Graziano, H. K. Ticho, and S. G. Wojcicki, *Phys. Rev. Letters*, **5**, 520 (1960).
5. N. F. Mott and H. S. W. Massey, *Theory of Atomic Collisions*, 2nd ed., Oxford University Press, London, 1949.
6. W. S. C. Williams, ref. 2, ch. 8.
7. Roger G. Newton, *Scattering Theory of Waves and Particles*, McGraw-Hill, New York, 1966.
8. J. Ashkin, *Nuovo Cimento, Suppl.*, **14**, 221 (1959).
9. J. V. Lepore, *Phys. Rev.*, **79**, 137 (1950).
10. R. D. Tripp, *Baryon Resonances*, lectures delivered at the International School of Physics, Enrico Fermi, XXXIII Course, Strong Interactions, Academic Press, New York, 1966, p. 70.
11. E. P. Wigner, *Phys. Rev.*, **98**, 145 (1955).
12. R. H. Dalitz, *Ann. Rev. Nucl. Sci.*, **13**, 339 (1963).
13. J. M. Blatt and V. F. Weisskopf, *Theoretical Nuclear Physics*, Wiley, New York, 1952.
14. W. Layson, *Nuovo Cimento*, **27**, 724 (1954).
15. J. M. McKinley, *Rev. Mod. Phys.*, **35**, 788 (1963).
16. P. Bareyre, C. Brickman, A. V. Stirling, and G. Villet, *Phys. Letters*, **18**, 342 (1965); P. Bareyre, C. Brickman, and G. Villet, *Phys. Rev.*, **165**, 1730 (1968).
17. C. Michael, *Phys. Letters*, **21**, 93 (1963).
18. A. N. Diddens, E. W. Jenkins, T. F. Kycia, and K. F. Riley, *Phys. Rev. Letters*, **10**, 262 (1963).
19. J. S. Schwinger, *Phys. Rev.*, **72**, 742 (1947); H. A. Bethe, *Phys. Rev.*, **76**, 38 (1949).
20. M. H. MacGregor, M. J. Moravcsik, and H. P. Stapp, *Ann. Rev. Nucl. Sci.*, **10**, 291 (1960).
21. J. D. Jackson, D. G. Ravenhall, and H. W. Wyld, Jr., *Nuovo Cimento*, **9**, 834 (1958); see also J. D. Jackson and H. Wyld, *Nuovo Cimento*, **13**, 84 (1959).
22. R. Dalitz and S. Tuan, *Phys. Rev. Letters*, **2**, 445 (1959); R. Dalitz and S. Tuan, *Ann. Phys.*, **8**, 100 (1959).
23. R. Dalitz and S. Tuan, *Ann. Phys.*, **10**, 307 (1960); R. H. Dalitz, *Phys. Rev. Letters*, **6**, 239 (1961); R. H. Dalitz, *Rev. Mod. Phys.*, **33**, 471 (1961).
24. R. H. Dalitz, *Strange Particles and Strong Interactions*, Oxford University Press, London, 1962.
25. M. H. Ross and G. L. Shaw, *Phys. Rev.*, **115**, 1773 (1959); *Ann. Phys.*, **9**, 391 (1960).
26. M. H. Ross and G. L. Shaw, *Ann. Phys.*, **13**, 147 (1961); *Phys. Rev.*, **126**, 806, 814 (1962).
27. R. H. Dalitz, T. C. Wong, and G. Rajasekaran, *Phys. Rev.*, **153**, 1617 (1967).
28. F. Uchiyama-Campbell and R. K. Logan, *Phys. Rev.*, **149**, 1220 (1966).
29. G. F. Chew, "Resonances, Particles and Poles from the Experimenter's Point of View," Lawrence Radiation Laboratory Report, UCRL-16983 (1966).
30. W. R. Frazer and A. W. Hendry, *Phys. Rev.*, **134**, B1307 (1964).

31. S. Minami, *Progr. Theoret. Phys.* (*Kyoto*), **11**, 213 (1954).
32. See, for example, R. P. Feynman, *Theory of Fundamental Processes*, W. A. Benjamin, New York, 1962.
33. R. H. Dalitz, *Phil. Mag.*, **44**, 1068 (1953); see also E. Fabri, *Nuovo Cimento, Suppl.*, **12**, 205 (1959).
34. P. Srivastava and G. Sudarshan, *Phys. Rev.*, **110**, 765 (1958).
35. See, for example, J. D. Jackson, *Nuovo Cimento*, **34**, 1644 (1964).
36. G. F. Chew and F. E. Low, *Phys. Rev.*, **113**, 1640 (1959).
37. J. D. Jackson, "Periferal Collisions at Intermediate Energies," in *Proc. Intern. Conf. High Energy Physics, 13th*, Berkeley, University of California Press, 1967, p. 149.
38. D. H. Miller, L. Gutay, P. B. Johnson, F. J. Loeffler, R. L. McIlwain, R. J. Sprafka, and R. B. Willmann, *Phys. Rev.*, **153**, 1423 (1967).
39. M. Ferro-Luzzi, R. George, Y. Goldschmidt-Clermont, V. P. Henri, B. Jongejans, D. W. G. Leith, G. R. Lynch, F. Muller, and J. M. Perreau, *Nuovo Cimento*, **36**, 1101 (1965).
40. L. Stodolsky and J. J. Sakurai, *Phys. Rev. Letters*, **11**, 90 (1963).
41. P. E. Schlein, in "Baryon Exchange and Production of $J \geq \frac{3}{2}$ Baryons," *Lectures in Theoretical Physics*, Vol. 8b, University of Colorado Press, Boulder, Colorado, 1966, p. 111.
42. J. Badier, M. Demoulin, J. Goldberg, B. P. Gregory, C. Pelletier, A. Rougue, M. Ville, R. Barloutaud, A. Leveque, C. Louedec, J. Meyer, P. Schlein, A. Verglas, D. J. Holthuizen, W. Hoagland, J. C. Kluyver, and A. G. Tenner, Reports CEA-N532 (1965) and CEA-R3037 (1966).
43. Aachen, Berlin, Birmingham, Bonn, Hamburg, London (IC), Munchen collaboration, *Phys. Rev.*, **138**, B897 (1965).
44. A. H. Rosenfeld, *Proc. Intern. Conf. Elementary Particles Suppl.*, Oxford (1965).
45. R. H. Dalitz and D. H. Miller, *Phys. Rev. Letters*, **6**, 562 (1961).
46. B. Conforto, B. Maréchal, L. Montanet, M. Tomas, C. D'Anlau, A. Astier, J. Cohen-Ganouna, M. Della Negra, M. Baubillier, J. Duboc, F. James, M. Goldberg, and D. Spencer, *Nucl. Phys.*, **B3**, 468 (1967).
47. J. D. Jackson, *Rev. Mod. Phys.*, **37**, 484 (1965).
48. H. P. Stapp, Lawrence Radiation Laboratory Report UCRL-9526, December 1960, unpublished.
49. R. Gatto and H. P. Stapp, *Phys. Rev.*, **121**, 1553 (1961).
50. R. Capps, *Phys. Rev.*, **122**, 929 (1961).
51. N. Byers and S. Fenster, *Phys. Rev. Letters*, **11**, 52 (1963).
52. J. B. Shafer, *Phys. Rev.*, **139**, B607 (1965).
53. S. U. Chung, *Phys. Rev.*, **138**, B1541 (1965).
54. R. D. Tripp, *Ann. Rev. Nucl. Sci.*, **15**, 325 (1965).
55. J. B. Shafer, J. J. Murray, and D. O. Huwe, *Phys. Rev. Letters*, **10**, 179 (1963).
56. A. Donnachie, J. Hamilton, and A. T. Lea, *Phys. Rev.*, **135**, B515 (1964).
57. L. D. Roper, R. B. Wright, and B. T. Feld, *Phys. Rev.*, **138**, B190 (1965).
58. J. T. Beale, S. D. Ecklund, and R. L. Walker, "Pion Photoproduction Data Below 1.5 GeV," California Institute of Technology Report CTSL 42, Calt-68-108 (1966).

59. M. J. Moravcsik, *Phys. Rev.*, **104**, 1451 (1956).

60a. C. H. Johnson and H. Steiner, "Pion-Proton Elastic Scattering: Low Energy Experiments and Phase Shift Analysis," presented at the Irvine Conference on Pion Nucleon Scattering, Lawrence Radiation Laboratory Report UCRL 18001 (1967).

60b. C. H. Johnson, thesis, UCRL 17683 (1967).

61. C. B. Chiu, R. D. Eandi, A. C. Helmholz, R. W. Kenney, B. J. Moyer, J. A. Poirier, W. B. Richards, R. J. Cence, V. Z. Peterson, N. K. Sehgal, and V. J. Stenger, *Phys. Rev.* **156**, 1415 (1967).

62. L. D. Roper, *Phys. Rev. Letters*, **12**, 340 (1964); L. D. Roper and R. W. Wright, *Phys. Rev.*, **138**, B921 (1965).

63. P. Auvil and C. Lovelace, *Nuovo Cimento*, **33**, 473 (1964); P. Auvil, C. Lovelace, A. Donnachie, and A. T. Lea, *Phys. Letters*, **12**, 76 (1964); A. Donnachie, A. T. Lea, and C. Lovelace, *Phys. Letters*, **19**, 146 (1965); A. Donnachie, R. G. Kirsopp, and C. Lovelace, *Phys. Letters*, **26B**, 161 (1968).

64. A. Donnachie and J. Hamilton, *Phys. Rev.*, **138**, B678 (1965).

65. B. H. Bransden, R. G. Moorhouse, and P. J. O'Donnell, *Phys. Rev.*, **139**, B1566 (1965); B. H. Bransden, R. G. Moorhouse, and P. J. O'Donnell, *Phys. Letters*, **11**, 339 (1964); B. H. Bransden and P. J. O'Donnell, *Phys. Letters*, **19**, 420 (1965).

66. J. W. Moffat, *Phys. Rev.*, **121**, 926 (1961).

67. R. Cence, *Phys. Letters*, **20**, 306 (1966).

68. K. Draxler and R. Huper, *Phys. Letters*, **20**, 199 (1966).

69. G. Höhler, J. Baacke, and R. Strauss, *Phys. Letters*, **21**, 223 (1966), and references therein.

70. S. D. Ecklund and R. L. Walker, *Phys. Rev.*, **159**, 1195 (1967).

71a. F. Bulos et al., *Phys. Rev. Letters*, **13**, 486 (1964).

71b. W. B. Richards, C. B. Chiu, R. D. Eandi, A. C. Helmholz, R. W. Kenney, B. J. Moyer, and J. A. Poirier, *Phys. Rev. Letters*, **16**, 1221 (1966).

71c. W. G. Jones, D. M. Binnie, A. Duane, J. P. Horsey, D. C. Mason, J. A. Newth, I. V. Rahman, J. Walters, N. Horwitz, and P. Palit, *Phys. Letters*, **23**, 597 (1966).

72a. C. Bacci, G. Penso, G. Salvini, C. Mencuccini, and V. Silvestrini, *Phys. Rev. Letters*, **16**, 157 (1966).

72b. R. Prepost, D. Lundquist, and D. Quinn, *Phys. Rev. Letters*, **18**, 82 (1967).

73. A. T. Davies and R. G. Moorhouse, in "$S_{1/2}$ and $D^{3}_{/2}N^*$ Resonant States and their $N\pi$ and $N\eta$ Decay Modes," Rutherford Laboratory preprint RPP/A8, December 1966.

74. P. N. Dobson, *Phys. Rev.*, **146**, 1022 (1966).

75. J. S. Ball, *Phys. Rev.*, **149**, 1191 (1966).

76. F. Uchiyama-Campbell and R. K. Logan, *Phys. Rev.*, **153**, 1634 (1967).

77. A. W. Hendry and R. G. Moorhouse, *Phys. Letters*, **18**, 171 (1965).

78a. P. J. Duke, D. P. Jones, M. A. R. Kemp, P. G. Murphy, J. D. Prentice, J. J. Thresher, H. H. Atkinson, C. R. Cox, and K. S. Heard, *Phys. Rev. Letters*, **15**, 468 (1965).

78b. C. R. Cox, K. S. Heard, J. C. Sleeman, P. J. Duke, R. E. Hill, W. R.

Holley, D. P. Jones, F. C. Shoemaker, J. J. Thresher, and J. B. Warren, Rutherford Report No. RHEL/M137 (1967).

79. A. Yokosawa, S. Suwa, R. E. Hill, R. J. Esterling, and N. E. Booth, *Phys. Rev. Letters*, **16**, 714 (1966).

80. O. Chamberlain, M. J. Hansroul, C. H. Johnson, P. D. Grannis, L. E. Holloway, L. Valentin, P. R. Robrish, and H. M. Steiner, *Phys. Rev. Letters*, **17**, 975 (1966).

81. J. A. Helland, C. D. Wood, T. J. Devlin, D. E. Hagge, M. J. Longo, B. J. Moyer, and V. Perez-Mendez, *Phys. Rev.*, **134**, B1079 (1964).

82. J. A. Schwartz, "Associated Production from 1.5 to 2.4 BeV/c," Ph.D. thesis, Lawrence Radiation Laboratory Report UCRL-11360, 1964.

83. O. I. Dahl, L. M. Hardy, R. I. Hess, J. Kirz, D. H. Miller, and J. A. Schwartz, *Phys. Rev.*, **163**, 1430 (1967).

84. J. P. Merlo and G. Valladas, *Proc. Roy. Soc.* (*London*), **A289**, 489 (1966).

85. G. Valladas, "Analysis of the Reaction $\pi p \to \pi\pi N$ below 1 GeV," Saclay preprint; presented at the Conference on High Energy Physics, 13th, Berkeley, 1966.

86a. G. Bellettini, G. Cocconi, A. N. Diddens, E. Lillethun, J. P. Scanlow, A. M. Shapiro, and A. M. Wetherell, *Phys. Letters*, **18**, 167 (1965).

86b. C. M. Ankenbrandt, A. R. Clyde, B. Cork, D. Keefe, L. T. Kerth, W. M. Layson, and W. A. Wenzel, *Nuovo Cimento*, **34**, 1052 (1965).

87. I. M. Blair, A. E. Taylor, W. S. Chapman, P. I. P. Kalmus, J. Litt, M. C. Miller, D. B. Scott, H. J. Sherman, A. Astbury, and T. G. Walker, *Phys. Rev. Letters*, **17**, 789 (1966).

88. E. W. Anderson, E. J. Bleser, G. B. Collins, T. Fujii, J. Menes, F. Turkot, R. A. Carrigan, Jr., R. M. Eldelstein, N. C. Hien, T. J. McMahon, and I. Nadelhaft, *Phys. Rev. Letters*, **16**, 855 (1966).

89. E. Gellert, G. A. Smith, S. Wojcicki, E. Colton, P. E. Schlein, and H. K. Ticho, *Phys. Rev. Letters*, **17**, 884 (1966).

90. R. T. Deck, *Phys. Rev. Letters*, **13**, 169 (1964); U. Maor and T. A. O'Halloran, *Phys. Letters*, **15**, 281 (1965).

91a. R. Alvarez, Z. Bar-Yam, W. Kern, D. Luckey, L. S. Osborne, S. Tazzari, and R. Fessel, *Phys. Rev. Letters*, **12**, 710 (1964).

91b. M. A. Wahlig, I. Mannelli, L. Sodickson, O. Fackler, C. Ward, T. Kan, and E. Shibata, *Phys. Rev. Letters*, **13**, 103 (1964).

92. A. Citron, W. Galbraith, T. F. Kycia, B. A. Leontic, R. H. Philips, and A. Rousset, *Phys. Rev. Letters*, **13**, 205 (1964); A. Citron, W. Galbraith, B. A. Leontic, R. H. Philips, A. Rousset, and P. H. Sharp, *Phys. Rev.*, **144**, 1101 (1966).

93. S. W. Kormanyos, A. D. Krisch, J. R. O'Fallon, K. Ruddick, and L. G. Ratner, *Phys. Rev. Letters*, **16**, 709 (1966).

94. F. N. Dikmen, *Phys. Rev. Letters*, **18**, 798 (1967).

95. V. Barger and D. Cline, *Phys. Rev. Letters*, **16** (1966).

96. O. Chamberlain, K. M. Crowe, D. Keefe, L. T. Kerth, A. Lemonick, T. Maung, and Z. F. Zipf, *Phys. Rev.*, **125**, 1696 (1962).

97. V. Cook, B. Cork, T. F. Hoang, D. Keefe, L. T. Kerth, W. A. Wenzel, and T. F. Zipf, *Phys. Rev.*, **123**, 320 (1961).
98. R. L. Cool, G. Giacomelli, T. F. Kycia, B. A. Leontic, K. K. Li, A. Lundby, and J. Teiger, *Phys. Rev. Letters*, **16**, 1228 (1966).
99. R. J. Abrams, R. L. Cool, G. Giacomelli, T. F. Kycia, B. A. Leontic, K. K. Li, and D. N. Michael, *Phys. Rev. Letters*, **19**, 678 (1967).
100. J. D. Davies, J. D. Dowell, P. M. Hattersley, R. J. Homer, A. W. O'Dell, A. A. Carter, K. F. Riley, R. J. Tapper, D. V. Bugg, R. S. Gilmore, K. M. Knight, D. C. Salter, G. H. Stafford, and E. J. N. Wilson, *Phys. Rev. Letters*, **18**, 62 (1967); and by the same authors in Rutherford Laboratory Report RPP/H/31 (1967).
101a. A. N. Diddens, E. W. Jenkins, T. F. Kycia, and K. T. Riley, *Phys. Rev.*, **132**, 2721 (1963).
101b. W. F. Baker, E. W. Jenkins, T. F. Kycia, R. H. Phillips, A. L. Read, K. F. Riley, and H. Ruderman, *Proc. Intern. Conf. Elementary Particles*, Sienna, 634 (1963).
101c. W. Galbraith, E. W. Jenkins, T. F. Kycia, B. A. Leontic, R. H. Philipps, A. L. Read, and R. Rubinstein, *Phys. Rev.*, **138**, B913 (1965).
102a. M. Ferro-Luzzi, "Baryon Resonances with $S \neq 0$," in *Proc. Intern. Conf. High Energy Physics, 13th*, Berkeley, University of California Press, 1967, p. 183.
102b. J. Meyer, "Baryonic Resonances with $S \neq 0$," in *Proc. Heidelberg Intern. Conf. Elementary Particles*, North-Holland Publ. Co., 1968.
103. J. K. Kim, *Phys. Rev. Letters*, **14**, 29 (1965); "Low Energy $K^- p$ Interactions and Interpretation of the 1405 MeV $Y^*_0$ Resonance as a $K^- N$ Bound State," Ph.D. thesis, Columbia University, Nevis Laboratories report Nevis-149, May 1966; J. K. Kim, *Phys. Rev. Letters*, **19**, 1074 (1967).
104. M. B. Watson, M. Ferro-Luzzi, and R. D. Tripp, *Phys. Rev.*, **131**, 2248 (1963).
105. D. Rahm et al., "$\Sigma$ Production in $K^- p$ interactions from 600 to 820 MeV/c," *Proc. Intern. Conf. High Energy Physics, 13th*, Berkeley (1966); included in M. Ferro-Luzzi, rapporteur's talk, University of California Press, 1967, p. 183.
106. R. Armenteros, M. Ferro-Luzzi, D. W. G. Leith, R. Levi-Setti, A. Minten, R. D. Tripp, H. Filthuth, V. Hepp, E. Kluge, H. Schneider, R. Barloutaud, P. Granet, J. Meyer, and J. P. Porte, *Phys. Letters*, **24B**, 198 (1967).
107. A. Barbaro-Galtieri, Lawrence Radiation Laboratory at Berkeley, unpublished data.
108. P. M. Dauber, P. E. Schlein, W. A. Slater, D. H. Stork, and H. K. Ticho, *Phys. Letters*, **23**, 154 (1966).
109. G. W. London, R. R. Rau, N. P. Samios, S. S. Yamamoto, M. Goldberg, S. Lichtman, M. Primer, and J. Leitner, *Phys. Rev.*, **143**, 1034 (1966).
110. R. P. Ely, S. Y. Fung, G. Gidal, Y. L. Pan, W. M. Powell, and H. S. White, *Phys. Rev. Letters*, **7**, 461 (1961).
111. L. Bertanza, V. Brisson, P. L. Connolly, E. L. Hart, I. S. Mittra, G. C. Moneti, R. R. Rau, N. P. Samios, I. O. Skillicorn, S. S. Yamamoto, M. Goldberg, J. Leitner, S. Lichtman, and J. Westgard, *Phys. Rev. Letters*, **10**, 176 (1963).

112. J. B. Shafer and D. O. Huwe, *Phys. Rev.*, **134**, B1372 (1964).
113. E. Malamud and P. E. Schlein, *Phys. Letters*, **10**, 145 (1964).
114. M. H. Alston, L. W. Alvarez, P. Eberhard, M. L. Good, W. Graziano, H. K. Ticho, and S. G. Wojcicki, *Phys. Rev. Letters*, **6**, 698 (1961).
115. M. H. Alston, A. Barbaro-Galtieri, A. H. Rosenfeld, and S. G. Wojcicki, *Phys. Review*, **134**, B1289 (1964).
116. W. E. Humphrey and R. R. Ross, *Phys. Rev.*, **127**, 1305 (1962).
117. M. Sakitt, T. B. Day, R. G. Glasser, N. Seeman, J. Friedman, W. E. Humphrey, and R. R. Ross, *Phys. Rev.*, **139**, B719 (1965).
118. W. Kittel, G. Otter, and I. Wacek, *Phys. Letters*, **21**, 349 (1966).
119. J. A. Kadyk, Y. Oren, G. Goldhaber, S. Goldhaber, and G. H. Trilling, *Phys. Rev. Letters*, **17**, 599 (1966).
120. R. J. Glauber, *Phys. Rev.*, **100**, 242 (1955); also V. Franco and R. J. Glauber, *Phys. Rev.*, **142**, 1195 (1966).
121. G. Lynch, "$\bar{K}N$ Total Cross Sections from 0.65 to 2.48 GeV/c," Alvarez Memo 600, Lawrence Radiation Laboratory, September 1966, unpublished.
122. D. Berley, P. L. Connolly, E. L. Hart, D. C. Rahm, D. L. Stonehill, B. Thevenet, W. J. Willis, and S. S. Yamamoto, *Phys. Rev. Letters*, **15**, 641 (1965).
123. D. Cline and M. Olson, *Phys. Letters*, **25B**, 41 (1967).
124. L. W. Alvarez, M. H. Alston, M. Ferro-Luzzi, D. O. Huwe, G. R. Kalbfleisch, D. H. Miller, J. J. Murray, A. H. Rosenfeld, J. B. Shafer, F. T. Solmitz, and S. G. Wojcicki, *Phys. Rev. Letters*, **10**, 184 (1963).
125. P. L. Bastien and J. P. Berge, *Phys. Rev. Letters*, **10**, 188 (1963).
126. P. Eberhard, M. Pripstein, F. T. Shively, U. E. Kruse, and W. P. Swanson, Lawrence Radiation Laboratory preprint, UCRL (17590), to be published.
127. D. Berley, P. L. Connolly, E. L. Hart, D. C. Rahm, D. L. Stonehill, B. Thevenet, W. J. Willis, and S. S. Yamamoto, "Quantum Numbers of the $Y*_1(1660)$," *Proc. Intern. Conf. High Energy Physics, 12th* (Dubna 1964), Vol. 1, Atomizdat, Moscow, 1966, p. 565.
128. M. Taher-Zadeh, D. J. Prowse, P. E. Schlein, W. E. Slater, D. H. Stork, and H. K. Ticho, *Phys. Rev. Letters*, **11**, 470 (1963).
129. P. E. Schlein and P. G. Trippe, UCLA Memo 1016.
130. A. Leveque et al., French-British collaboration, *Phys. Letters*, **18**, 69 (1965).
131. W. E. Slater, P. M. Dauber, P. E. Schlein, D. H. Stork, and H. K. Ticho, *Bull. Am. Phys. Soc.*, **10**, 1196 (1965).
132. R. K. Adair, *Phys. Rev.*, **100**, 1540 (1955).
133. M. Derrick, T. Fields, J. Loken, R. Ammar, R. E. P. Davis, W. Kropac, J. Mott, and F. Schweingruber, *Phys. Rev. Letters*, **18**, 266 (1967).
134. D. O. Huwe, Lawrence Radiation Laboratory Report UCRL-11291.
135. A. Barbaro-Galtieri, A. Husein, and R. D. Tripp, *Phys. Letters*, **6**, 296 (1963).
136. R. Armenteros, M. Ferro-Luzzi, D. W. G. Leith, R. Levi-Setti, A. Minten, R. D. Tripp, H. Filthuth, V. Hepp, E. Kluge, H. Schneider, R. Barloutaud, P. Granet, J. Meyer, and J. P. Porte, *Phys. Letters*, **19**, 338 (1965).
137. S. Fenster, N. M. Gelfand, D. Harmsen, R. Levi-Setti, M. Raymund, J. Doede, and W. Manner, *Phys. Rev. Letters*, **17**, 841 (1966).

138. R. B. Bell, R. W. Birge, Y. Pan, and R. T. Pu, *Phys. Rev. Letters*, **16**, 203 (1966).

139. R. W. Birge, R. P. Ely, G. E. Kalmus, A. Kernan, J. Louie, J. S. Sahouria, and W. M. Smart, "Spin and Parity of the $Y*_0(1815)$ and $Y*_1(1765)$," *Proc. Athens Conf. Resonant Particles, 1965*, Ohio University Press, 1965, p. 296.

140. R. Armenteros, M. Ferro-Luzzi, D. W. G. Leith, R. Levi-Setti, A. Minten, R. D. Tripp, H. Filthuth, V. Hepp, F. Kluge, H. Schneider, R. Barloutaud, P. Granet, J. Meyer, and J. P. Porte, *Zeit. Phys.*, **202**, 486 (1967).

141. W. M. Smart, A. Kernan, G. E. Kalmus, and R. P. Ely, *Phys. Rev. Letters*, **17**, 556 (1966).

142. N. Gelfand, D. Harmsen, R. Levi-Setti, M. Raymund, J. Doede, and W. Männer, *Phys. Rev. Letters*, **17**, 1224 (1966).

143. C. W. Wohl, F. T. Solmitz, and M. L. Stevenson, *Phys. Rev. Letters*, **17**, 107 (1966).

144. R. P. Uhlig, G. R. Charlton, P. E. Condon, R. G. Glasser, G. B. Yodh, and N. Seeman, *Phys. Rev.*, **155**, 1448 (1967).

145. C. Wohl, F. T. Solmitz, and M. L. Stevenson, *Bull. Am. Phys. Soc.*, **10**, 529 (1965).

146. R. K. Bock, W. A. Cooper, B. R. French, J. B. Kinson, R. Levi-Setti, D. Revel, B. Tallini, and S. Zylberajch, *Phys. Letters*, **17**, 166 (1965).

147. W. A. Blanpied, J. S. Greenberg, V. W. Hughes, P. Kitching, D. C. Lu, and R. C. Minehart, *Phys. Rev. Letters*, **14**, 741 (1965).

148. G. M. Pjerrou, O. J. Prowse, P. Schlein, W. E. Slater, D. H. Stork, and H. K. Ticho, *Phys. Rev. Letters*, **9**, 114 (1962).

149. L. Bertanza, V. Brisson, P. L. Connally, E. L. Hart, I. S. Mittra, G. C. Moneti, R. R. Rau, N. P. Samios, I. D. Skillikorn, S. S. Yamamoto, M. Goldberg, L. Gray, J. Leitner, S. Lichtman, and J. Westgard, *Phys. Rev. Letters*, **9**, 180 (1962).

150. P. E. Schlein, D. D. Carmony, G. M. Pjerrou, W. E. Slater, D. H. Stork, and H. K. Ticho, *Phys. Rev. Letters*, **11**, 167 (1963).

151. J. B. Shafer, J. Lindsey, J. Murray, and G. Smith, *Phys. Rev.*, **142**, 883 (1966).

152. G. A. Smith, J. S. Lindsey, J. J. Murray, J. Button-Shafer, A. Barbaro-Galtieri, O. I. Dahl, P. Eberhard, W. E. Humphrey, G. R. Kalbfleisch, R. R. Ross, F. T. Shively, and R. D. Tripp, *Phys. Rev. Letters*, **13**, 61 (1964).

153. J. Badier, M. Demoulin, J. Goldberg, B. P. Gregory, C. Pelletier, A. Rougue, M. Ville, R. Barloutaud, A. Leveque, C. Louedec, J. Meyer, P. Schlein, A. Verglas, D. J. Holthuizen, W. Hoogland, and A. G. Tenner, *Phys. Letters*, **16**, 171 (1965).

154. D. Merrill, "Decay Properties of the $\Xi$ Hyperon," Ph.D. thesis, Lawrence Radiation Laboratory Report UCRL-16455 (1966).

155a. R. L. Cool, G. Giacomelli, T. F. Kycia, B. A. Leontic, K. K. Li, A. Lundby, and J. G. Teiger, *Phys. Rev. Letters*, **17**, 102 (1966).

155b. R. J. Abrams, R. L. Cool, G. Giacomelli, T. F. Kycia, B. A. Leontic, K. K. Li, and D. N. Michael, *Phys. Rev. Letters*, **19**, 259 (1967).

156. S. Goldhaber, W. Chinowsky, G. Goldhaber, W. Lee, T. O'Halloran, T. Stubbs, G. M. Pjerrou, D. H. Stock, and H. K. Ticho, *Phys. Rev. Letters*, **9**, 135 (1962).

157. S. Focardi, A. Mingurzzi-Ranzi, L. Monari, G. Saltini, P. Serra, T. A. Filippas, and V. P. Henri, *Phys. Letters*, **24B**, 314 (1967).

158. A. T. Lea, B. R. Martin, and G. C. Oades, *Phys. Rev.*, **165**, 1770 (1968).

159. V. J. Stenger, W. E. Slater, D. H. Stork, H. K. Ticho, G. Goldhaber, and S. Goldhaber, *Phys. Rev.*, **134**, B1111 (1964).

160. A. Hirata, R. Bland, J. L. Brown, G. Goldhaber, S. Goldhaber, and G. H. Trilling, work in progress; reported by G. Goldhaber at the IV Coral Gables Conference, "Symmetry Principles at High Energy," Perlmutter and Kursunoglu, 1967, p. 191.

161. A. A. Carter, *Phys. Rev. Letters*, **18**, 801 (1967).

162. M. Lusignoli, M. Restignoli, G. Violini, and G. A. Snow, *Nuovo Cimento*, **45**, 792 (1966).

163. R. W. Bland, M. G. Bowler, J. L. Brown, G. Goldhaber, S. Goldhaber, V. H. Seeger, and G. H. Trilling, *Phys. Rev. Letters*, **18**, 1077 (1967).

164. B. C. Shen, I. Butterworth, C. Fu, G. Goldhaber, S. Goldhaber, S. L. Hagopian, and G. H. Trilling, "$K^+$ Interactions at 4.6 GeV/c and Evidence for a $K^*(1320)$ Resonance," presented at the 13th International Conference on High Energy Physics, Berkeley, 1966.

165. W. P. Dodd, R. B. Palmer, and N. P. Samios, *Bull. Am. Phys. Soc.*, **12**, 46 (1967).

166. M. Gell-Mann, "The Eightfold Way: A Theory of Strong Interaction Symmetry," California Institute of Technology, Synchrotron Laboratory Report CTSL-20 (1961).

167. Y. Ne'eman, *Nucl. Phys.*, **26**, 222 (1962).

168. M. Gell-Mann and Y. Ne'eman, in "The Eightfold Way" published in the series "Frontier in Physics," Benjamin, New York, 1964.

169. See, for example, S. Coleman, "An Introduction to Unitary Symmetry," lectures delivered at the 1966 International School "Ettore Maiorana," published in "Strong and Weak Interactions Present Problems," A. Zichichi, Ed., Academic Press, New York, 1966.

170. S. Coleman and S. L. Glashow, *Phys. Rev. Letters*, **6**, 423 (1961).

171. J. J. Sakurai, *Phys. Rev. Letters*, **9**, 472 (1962).

172. S. L. Glashow and R. H. Socolow, *Phys. Rev. Letters*, **15**, 329 (1966).

173. R. D. Tripp, D. W. G. Leith, A. Minten, R. Armenteros, M. Ferro-Luzzi, R. Levi-Setti, H. Filthuth, V. Hepp, E. Kluge, H. Schneider, R. Barloutaud, P. Granet, J. Meyer, and J. P. Porte, *Nucl. Phys.*, **B3**, 10 (1967).

174. J. J. de Swart, *Rev. Mod. Phys.*, **35**, 916 (1963).

175. M. Goldberg, J. Leitner, R. Musto, and L. O'Raifeartaigh, *Nuovo Cimento*, **45**, 169 (1966).

# Current Algebra, Part I. Application to Weak Decays

V. S. MATHUR

*Department of Physics and Astronomy, University of Rochester,
Rochester, New York*


L. K. PANDIT

*Tata Institute of Fundamental Research, Bombay, India*

**Contents**

# I. Introduction

Symmetries have always played a major role in organizing the physical data. In particle physics, the role of the space–time as well as the internal symmetries has been all the more important in view of the lack of any fundamental dynamical approach to the interactions of the hadrons. The isospin symmetry group $SU_2(I)$ is the oldest and the best-established group of internal symmetry of the strong interactions. The generalization of this symmetry group, required to incorporate the strangeness (or the hypercharge) quantum number, to the rank-two unitary unimodular group in three dimensions $SU(3)$ has met with a great deal of success. Higher symmetry groups such as $SU_3 \otimes SU_3$, $SU_6$, $\tilde{U}_{12}$ and their noncompact generalizations have also been considered with varying degrees of success.

The role of a symmetry group, such as the $SU(3)$ group, is twofold. First, it provides us with a classification scheme for the various particle states according to specific irreducible representations, thereby introducing an order into the ever-increasing proliferation of the particles as the experimentally available energies go up. Second, it provides an ordering of the various kinds of interactions of the particles by allowing the specification of their tensor structures, thus leading to various relations between masses, decay widths, and scattering amplitudes. Such "sum rules" do not require any detailed dynamics, but are essentially the outcome of the underlying group theoretical structure.

Equally important with the concept of group symmetry is the notion of symmetry breaking, since most symmetries are only approximate. The simplest isospin symmetry group, $SU_2$, is known to be only approximately valid, being broken by the electromagnetic interactions, so that one expects that the breaking effects are even more important as one considers higher symmetries. However, a properly founded dynamical treatment of the symmetry breaking is difficult, and until recently one had to be content with incorporating these effects on a purely phenomenological basis. Of course, the notion of the group is still important, even though the symmetry is approximate, since it has been found that all phenomenological symmetry-breaking interactions can be considered rather well as belonging to a simple irreducible representation of the group. For example, ascribing the $SU(3)$ symmetry breaking to the simple octet transformation property is enough to obtain the well known Gell-Mann–Okubo mass formula obeyed very well by the experimentally measured masses of the hadrons.

To be able to understand the working of the symmetry and its breaking at a deeper level, it is clearly necessary to inject some dynamics into the group theoretical structure. A framework for such a study has been proposed recently by Gell-Mann.[1] The idea proposed by Gell-Mann is that the algebraic structure underlying the group is more basic than the group symmetry itself, and that even though the symmetry may be broken, the commutation relations between the generators defining the algebra continue to hold as equal time commutators. In the symmetry limit, the generators of the group commute with the Hamiltonian of the system and are thus time independent. When the symmetry is broken, i.e., when the generators no longer commute with the Hamiltonian, the generators acquire a time dependence governed by the dynamics of the system. The assumption that this time dependence is such that the commutation relations continue to hold at equal times is a dynamical statement.

This idea acquires a richer physical content when the generators can be identified with "charges" of physical currents, such as the various types of weak and electromagnetic currents. The algebra being nonlinear in structure provides a means for setting the relative scales of the various physical currents. Further, by relating the matrix elements of these currents between strong interaction states to one another, one obtains a variety of "sum rules" which go beyond the results obtained from symmetry schemes.

The $SU_3 \otimes SU_3$ algebra generated by the space integrals ("charges") of the time components of the eight vector and the eight axial-vector current densities involved in the weak and the electromagnetic interactions has proved particularly useful, and much of the recent work uses this algebra. In practice, a particularly simple way of writing the equal time commutators forming the algebra is to build the "charges" according to the fundamental representation of the group, i.e., according to the quark model. One then uses the canonical commutation relation between quark fields to set up the algebra. Using the quark model as a guide, one may also write equal time-commutation relations between charges and current densities using the canonical commutation relation between quark fields. We would like to emphasize that although the equal time commutation relations are written using the quark model, one assumes that the same relations hold for the physical charges and currents even when the group symmetry is absent.

The general procedure for exploiting the commutation relations entails taking the matrix elements of the commutators between appropriate states and inserting a complete set of intermediate states. To write the matrix elements of the axial charges, a very useful concept is that of the partially conserved axial vector current (PCAC) first introduced[2] by Nambu and by Gell-Mann and Lévy. This hypothesis allows one to relate the matrix elements of axial charges to the corresponding ones of pseudoscalar meson field operators, which are quite often known from the data on the strong interaction processes involving these mesons. Much more is known about the matrix elements of the vector charges. For those charges that are either the diagonal conserved quantities or the conserved generators of the $SU(2)$ symmetry, the matrix elements are, of course, known directly.

The exact sum rule thus involves an infinite series of terms corresponding to the intermediate states. It is possible to cast the sum rule in a Lorentz covariant form so that one can evaluate the series in any convenient Lorentz frame; however, the number of intermediate states required for practical calculations for an approximate saturation of the sum rule, i.e., the rate of convergence of the series, depends on the particular Lorentz frame employed. Fubini and Furlan have made a very important contribution by showing that the convergence is fastest in the frame in which the momentum is infinite, so that the contribution of a small number of low-lying states provides an approximate saturation of the sum rule.

In many applications the retention of the low-lying single-particle intermediate states in the $p \to \infty$ frame leads to very interesting sum rules which can be tested experimentally. In some cases it is also possible to relate the leftover continuum contribution coming from the intermediate states to known scattering amplitudes by the use of the PCAC hypothesis. Since the PCAC hypothesis provides significant information about the mass shell, i.e., in the limit of the four-momentum of the pion extrapolated to zero, the scattering amplitudes that one has to deal with are the unphysical "soft-pion" amplitudes. Thus one is led to "exact" sum rules, of which the Adler-Weisberger sum rule[3] is a famous example. For comparison of such sum rules with experiments one hopes that soft-pion extrapolation is essentially smooth and does not alter the matrix elements appreciably.

Closely related to the method of employing infinite momentum frame is the technique of soft pions first introduced by Nambu and collaborators. Inasmuch as one finally encounters soft-pion matrix elements by the use of the PCAC hypothesis, one might as well assume in problems involving the pions that they are soft right from the beginning. This technique is of considerable generality since it provides, through the use of the equal time-commutation relations and PCAC hypothesis, a relation between any arbitrary matrix element involving pions to another related matrix element of a process with one or more pions less. The latter matrix element may describe a physical process leading to a sum rule; for instance, one can relate $K_{l3}$ to $K_{l2}$ decay or $K_{3\pi}$ to $K_{2\pi}$ decay, etc. Alternatively, if the matrix element for lesser number of pions is not physical, one can exploit internal symmetry groups like $SU(3)$ at this stage to obtain sum rules for the original matrix elements. For example, one may obtain sum rules for nonleptonic decays in this way. The great importance of the method of soft pions stems, however, from the fact that the entire calculation can be made manifestly covariant, and one can establish contact with dispersion relations.

Thus the algebra of currents, PCAC hypothesis, and the soft-pion extrapolation technique lead to many interesting results. The applications[4] of these techniques to the weak decays form the basis of the present paper. We have covered only some of the basic applications to the problems involved in weak decays. We have made no attempt to present an exhaustive coverage of the growing literature in this field, but rather have deemed it fitting to give considerable emphasis to the arguments and calculational details involved. We believe we are addressing ourselves to the student who wants to learn the calculational techniques involved in this subject in some detail.

## II. Equal Time-Commutation Relations

We shall follow the proposal of Gell-Mann[1] that the algebraic structure underlying an internal symmetry group is more basic than the group symmetry itself. Thus the chiral $SU(3) \otimes SU(3)$ group may not be a symmetry group of hadrons in nature, but we shall assume that the algebra defined by the equal time-commutation relations between the generators is still valid. Let $v_b^a$ and $a_b^a$ denote the generators of the $U(3) \times U(3)$ group where $a$, $b$ ($= 1, 2, 3$) are the $SU(3)$ tensor indices. Let us first discuss the case when the group is assumed to be a symmetry group. The generators then commute with the Hamiltonian of the system and are therefore conserved time-independent quantities; they satisfy the algebra:

$$[v_b^a, v_d^c] = \delta_d^a v_b^c - \delta_b^c v_d^a \qquad (2.1.1)$$

$$[v_b^a, a_d^c] = \delta_d^a a_b^c - \delta_b^c a_d^a \qquad (2.1.2)$$

$$[a_b^a, a_d^c] = \delta_d^a v_b^c - \delta_b^c v_d^a \qquad (2.1.3)$$

We may interpret the generators as the charges associated with the octets of conserved vector and axial-vector current densities, $V_{\mu b}^a$ and $A_{\mu b}^a$, respectively, so that we express

$$v_b^a = -i \int d^3x [V_4(x)]_b^a \qquad (2.2.1)$$

$$a_b^a = -i \int d^3x [A_4(x)]_b^a \qquad (2.2.2)$$

The simplest way to check this interpretation is to write the vector and the axial-vector current densities in terms of the basic quark fields

$$[V_\mu(x)]_b^a = i\bar{\psi}_b(x)\gamma_\mu\psi^a(x) \qquad (2.3.1)$$

$$[A_\mu(x)]_b^a = i\bar{\psi}_b(x)\gamma_\mu\gamma_5\psi^a(x) \qquad (2.3.2)$$

where $\psi(x)$ is the field operator of the quark fields. Then using the canonical anticommutation relations for the quark fields

$$\{\psi^a(x), \psi_b^+(x')\}_{x_0 = x_0'} = \delta_b^a \delta^3(\mathbf{x} - \mathbf{x'}) \qquad (2.4)$$

one easily verifies that the algebra of Eqs. 2.1.1. results. Of course, using certain other models also it is possible to obtain the same commutation relations [Eqs. (2.1)].

If, however, the group is not a symmetry group, the generators do not generally commute with the Hamiltonian of the system and the corresponding currents are not conserved. If we assume that isospin $SU(2)$ is a good symmetry of the system, the generators $v_j^i$ $(i, j = 1, 2)$ would still commute with the Hamiltonian. The rest of the generators or charges [Eqs. (2.2)] are no longer conserved quantities and are time dependent. We shall now make the dynamical assumption that Eqs. (2.1) continue to hold as equal time-commutation relations:

$$[v_b^a(t), \quad v_d^c(t)] = \delta_d^a v_b^c(t) - \delta_b^c v_d^a(t) \tag{2.5.1}$$

$$[v_b^a(t), \quad a_d^c(t)] = \delta_d^a a_b^c(t) - \delta_b^c a_d^a(t) \tag{2.5.2}$$

$$[a_b^a(t), \quad a_d^c(t)] = \delta_d^a v_b^c(t) - \delta_b^c v_d^a(t) \tag{2.5.3}$$

Of course for charges [Eqs. (2.2)] obtained on the basis of the quark model [Eqs. (2.3)] the Eqs. (2.5) are certainly satisfied because of the equal time-anticommutation relation [Eq. (2.4)]. The basic assumption involved lies, then, in the assertion that even for the charges given in terms of the physical vector and axial-vector current densities, we have the equal time-commutation relations given by Eqs. (2.5).

For convenience we may identify our terminology in terms of the alternative and frequently used notation:

$$
\begin{aligned}
Q &= v_1^1 \\
Y &= -v_3^3 \\
I_3 &= \tfrac{1}{2}(v_1^1 - v_2^2) \\
I_+ &= v_1^2, \quad I_- = v_2^1 \\
K_+ &= v_1^3, \quad K_- = v_3^1 \\
L_+ &= v_2^3, \quad L_- = v_3^2
\end{aligned}
\tag{2.6}
$$

The correspondence with Gell-Mann's notation[1] is

$$
\begin{aligned}
v_1^2 &= F_1 + iF_2, \quad v_2^1 = F_1 - iF_2, \quad I_3 \equiv \tfrac{1}{2}(v_1^1 - v_2^2) = F_3, \\
v_1^3 &= F_4 + iF_5, \quad v_3^1 = F_4 - iF_5 \\
v_2^3 &= F_6 + iF_7, \quad v_3^2 = F_6 - iF_7 \\
v_3^3 &= -(2/\sqrt{3})F_8
\end{aligned}
\tag{2.7}
$$

The axial charges $F_i^5$ and $a_b^a$ in the two notations are similarly related. For future use we may identify, in our notation, the isovector current density

$$J_\mu^{(V)} = \tfrac{1}{2}(V_{\mu 1}^{\ \ 1} - V_{\mu 2}^{\ \ 2}) \tag{2.8}$$

and the isoscalar current density

$$J_\mu^{(S)} = -\tfrac{1}{2}V_{\mu 3}^{\ \ 3} \tag{2.9}$$

so that the total electromagnetic current density is

$$J_\mu = J_\mu^{(V)} + J_\mu^{(S)} = V_{\mu 1}^{\ \ 1} \tag{2.10}$$

We shall also use equal time-commutation relations between the charges and the vector and the axial-vector current densities. We assume, as before, that these equal time-commutation relations are the ones suggested by the quark model. Using the canonical commutation relations for the quark fields given in Eq. (2.4), we obtain:

$$\begin{aligned}
\{v_b^a(t), \quad [V_\mu(x)]_d^c\}_{x_0 = t} &= \delta_d^a[V_\mu(x)]_b^c - \delta_b^c[V_\mu(x)]_d^a \\
\{v_b^a(t), \quad [A_\mu(x)]_d^c\}_{x_0 = t} &= \delta_d^a[A_\mu(x)]_b^c - \delta_b^c[A_\mu(x)]_d^a \\
\{a_b^a(t), \quad [V_\mu(x)]_d^c\}_{x_0 = t} &= \delta_d^a[A_\mu(x)]_b^c - \delta_b^c[A_\mu(x)]_d^a \\
\{a_b^a(t), \quad [A_\mu(x)]_d^c\}_{x_0 = t} &= \delta_d^a[V_\mu(x)]_b^c - \delta_b^c[V_\mu(x)]_d^a
\end{aligned} \tag{2.11}$$

We wish to emphasize that the equal time-commutation relations [Eqs. (2.5)] among the physical charges, and the relations [Eqs. (2.11)] between the physical charges and the physical vector and axial-vector currents are basic assumptions of dynamical content. We have obtained these relations only in the quark model and have assumed that the structure of the equal time commutators from the quark model as a guide are true quite generally. We may mention here that it is also possible to derive the equal time-commutation relations in some other field theory models, notably the $\sigma$ model generalized to $SU(3)$.

We shall not employ in this article equal time-commutation relations of current densities with themselves. These commutation relations generally require a much more careful analysis. It was pointed out by Schwinger[5] that in a local quantum-field theory the fourth component of the electromagnetic current cannot commute with the spatial components of the same current, contrary to the model of Eqs. (2.3). In order to avoid the contradiction one has to exercise a great deal of caution.

## III. PCAC

### 1. The PCAC Hypothesis for the Hypercharge-Preserving Axial-Vector Currents

In 1958, Goldberger and Treiman[6] obtained a remarkable formula for the decay parameter of the charged pion which agrees rather well with experiments. Unfortunately, the formula was derived under somewhat questionable assumptions within the framework of dispersion theory. It was later suggested by Nambu[2] and in a series of papers by Gell-Mann and collaborators[2,7] that it was possible to derive the Goldberger-Treiman formula quite simply if one assumed that the axial-vector current is partially conserved. Specifically, it was assumed that the divergence of the hypercharge-conserving axial-vector current is proportional to the renormalized pion-field operator:

$$\partial_\mu A_{\mu b}^a = (C_\pi/\sqrt{2})\pi_b^a, \quad (a, b = 1, 2) \tag{3.1}$$

where $C_\pi$ is the proportional constant. The matrix elements of the axial-vector current and those of the pion field operator can then be related. From Lorentz invariance and other symmetry considerations, we may write, for instance

$$\langle p(p_2)|\, A_{\mu 1}^2(0)\, |n(p_1)\rangle$$

$$= \sqrt{\frac{M_n M_p}{p_{10}p_{20}V^2}}\, \bar{u}_p(p_2)\{iG_1(q^2)\gamma_\mu\gamma_5 + G_2(q^2)q_\mu\gamma_5\}u_n(p_1) \tag{3.2}$$

$$\langle 0|\, A_{\mu 1}^2(0)\, |\pi^-(k)\rangle = (1/\sqrt{2k_0 V})\, if_\pi k_\mu \tag{3.3}$$

where $q = p_1 - p_2$, $G_1(q^2)$, and $G_2(q^2)$ are the usual axial-vector and induced pseudoscalar form factors (real from considerations of time reversal), and $f_\pi$ is the (real) pion-decay constant. Taking the divergence of Eq. (3.2) and using the hypothesis Eq. (3.1), we obtain

$$\sqrt{\frac{M_n M_p}{p_{10}p_{20}V^2}}\, i\{(M_p + M_n)G_1(q^2) + q^2 G_2(q^2)\}\bar{u}_p(p_2)\gamma_5 u_n(p_1)$$

$$= (C_\pi/\sqrt{2}) < p(p_2)|\, \pi_1^2(0)\, |n(p_1)\rangle \tag{3.4}$$

Now using the field equation

$$(-\Box + M_\pi^2)\pi_1^2(x) = -j_1^2(x)$$

we have for the matrix element on the right-hand side of Eq. (3.4):

$$\langle p(p_2)| \pi_1^2(0) |n(p)\rangle$$

$$= -\frac{1}{q^2 + M_\pi^2} \langle p(p_2)| j_1^2(0) |n(p_1)\rangle$$

$$= -\sqrt{\frac{M_n M_p}{p_{10} p_{20} V^2}} \frac{1}{q^2 + M_\pi^2} \sqrt{2} \, G_{NN\pi} K_{NN\pi}(q^2) \bar{u}_p(p_2) i\gamma_5 u_n(p_1) \quad (3.5)$$

Here $K_{NN\pi}(q^2)$ is the (real) form factor for the $NN\pi$ vertex, and from the conventional definition of the renormalized coupling constant $\sqrt{2} \, G_{NN\pi}$ it is normalized to unity at $q^2 = -M_\pi^2$

$$K_{NN\pi}(-M_\pi^2) = 1 \quad (3.6)$$

From Eqs. (3.4) and (3.5), we obtain

$$2MG_1(q^2) + q^2 G_2(q^2) = -C_\pi \frac{G_{NN\pi}}{q^2 + M_\pi^2} K_{NN\pi}(q^2) \quad (3.7)$$

It is simple to see that if one writes, for instance, the dispersion relations for $G_1(q^2)$ and $G_2(q^2)$, the pion pole contributes only to $G_2(q^2)$. Furthermore $G_2(q^2)$ is well behaved at $q^2 = 0$, so that we obtain from Eq. (3.7) for $q^2 = 0$ the result

$$C_\pi = -2Mg_A M_\pi^2 / G_{NN\pi} K_{NN\pi}(0) \quad (3.8)$$

where $g_A \equiv G_1(0)$ is the Gamow-Teller axial-vector coupling constant.

The pion-decay constant $f_\pi$ can similarly be related to $C_\pi$. Taking the divergence of Eq. (3.3) and using PCAC Eq. (3.1), we obtain

$$C_\pi/\sqrt{2} \langle 0| \pi_1^2(0) |\pi^-(k)\rangle = 1/\sqrt{2k_0 V} f_\pi M_\pi^2 \quad (3.9)$$

Since

$$\langle 0| \pi_1^2(x) |\pi^-(k)\rangle = 1/\sqrt{2k_0 V} e^{ik\cdot x} \quad (3.10)$$

is the wave function of the pion by definition, one obtains

$$C_\pi = \sqrt{2} f_\pi M_\pi^2 \quad (3.11)$$

From Eqs. (3.8) and (3.11), we get the Goldberger-Treiman formula

$$f_\pi = -\sqrt{2} \, Mg_A / G_{NN\pi} K_{NN\pi}(0) \quad (3.12)$$

To be able to check Eq. (3.12), we assume that the pionic form factor for the $NN\pi$ vertex $K_{NN\pi}(q^2)$ has a gentle variation when continued from

$q^2 = -M_\pi^2$ to $q^2 = 0$.* Thus, taking $K_{NN\pi}(0) \sim 1$, $g_A = 1.18$, and $G_{NN\pi}^2/4\pi = 14.6$, we obtain from Eq. (3.12)

$$|f_\pi| = 115.7 \text{ MeV} \tag{3.13}$$

to be compared with the value of 133 MeV obtained† from the experimental decay rate $\pi_{\mu 2}$. The Goldberger-Treiman relation is therefore valid to about 13%.

In the literature there is an alternative way in which the hypothesis of PCAC is formulated which is more natural in a dispersion theoretic treatment. Here one assumes that the matrix element of the divergence of the axial-vector current satisfies an unsubtracted dispersion relation, and is dominantly given by the pion pole. We shall illustrate this hypothesis by deriving the equivalent Goldberger-Treiman relation in this formulation. From Eq. (3.2) we have

$$\langle p(p_2)| \, \partial_\mu A_{\mu 1}^2(0) \, |n(p_1)\rangle$$
$$= \sqrt{M_n M_p/p_{10} p_{20} V^2} \; G(q^2)\bar{u}_p(p_2)i\gamma_5 u_n(p_1) \tag{3.14}$$

where

$$G(q^2) = (M_p + M_n)G_1(q^2) + q^2 G_2(q^2)$$

According to the PCAC hypothesis we assume that $G(q^2)$ satisfies an unsubtracted dispersion relation, i.e.,

$$G(q^2) = \frac{1}{\pi} \int \frac{\text{Im } G(q'^2) \, dg'^2}{q'^2 - q^2 - i\varepsilon} \tag{3.15}$$

The contribution to the absorptive part of $G(q'^2)$ can be seen quite easily to come from the pion pole at $q'^2 = -M_\pi^2$, and the continuum starting at the three pion threshold $q'^2 = -(3M_\pi)^2$. We shall neglect the contributions from the continuum, in accordance with the hypothesis, hoping that this is small. The pole contribution can be easily calculated in the standard manner. For completeness, however, we shall give the relevant steps below.

* This hypothesis of gentleness is what gives a physical meaning to PCAC.
† In obtaining $|f_\pi| = 133$ MeV we have used the formula

$$\Gamma(\pi^+ \to \mu^+ \nu) = (G^2/8\pi) \cos^2 \theta_A m_\pi m_\mu^2 [1 - (m_\mu^2/m_\pi^2)]^2 f_\pi^2$$

and taken the Cabibbo factor $\sin \theta_A \simeq 0.268$.

Contracting the proton state by LSZ technique (see Appendix III), we obtain on dropping the term proportional to delta $fn$

$$\langle p(p_2)| \; \partial_\mu A_{\mu 1}^2(0) \; |n(p_1)\rangle = -i \int d^4x e^{-ip_2 \cdot x} \sqrt{\frac{M_p}{p_{20}V}} \; \bar{u}_p(p_2)$$
$$\times \; \langle 0| \; \Theta(x_0)[j_{\bar{p}}(x), \; \partial_\mu A_{\mu 1}^2(0)] \; |n(p_1)\rangle \quad (3.16)$$

The absorptive part of the matrix element [Eq. (3.16)] is then given by

$$\text{Abs} \; \langle p(p_2)| \; \partial_\mu A_{\mu 1}^2(0) \; |n(p_1)\rangle = -\tfrac{1}{2} \int d^4x e^{-ip_2 \cdot x} \sqrt{\frac{M_p}{p_{20}V}} \; \bar{u}_p(p_2)$$
$$\times \; \langle 0| \; [j_{\bar{p}}(x), \; \partial_\mu A_{\mu 1}^2(0)] \; |n(p_1)\rangle \quad (3.17)$$

Inserting a complete set of states now, and retaining only the pion state, we obtain

$$\text{Abs} \; \langle p(p_2)| \; \partial_\mu A_{\mu 1}^2(0) \; |n(p_1)\rangle$$
$$= \tfrac{1}{2} \sqrt{\frac{M_p}{p_{20}V}} \; \bar{u}_p(p_2) \sum_k (2\pi)^4 \delta^4(p_1 - p_2 - k)$$
$$\times \; \langle 0| \; \partial_\mu A_{\mu 1}^2(0) \; |\pi(k)\rangle \langle \pi(k)| \; j_{\bar{p}}(0) \; |n(p_1)\rangle \quad (3.18)$$

where use has been made of space–time translation. The matrix elements occuring in Eq. (3.18) can now be written as

$$\langle 0| \; \partial_\mu A_{\mu 1}^2(0) \; |\pi(k)\rangle = 1/\sqrt{2k_0 V} f_\pi M_\pi^2 \quad (3.19)$$

$$\langle \pi(k)| \; j_{\bar{p}}(0) \; |n(p_1)\rangle = \sqrt{2} \; G_{NN\pi} i\gamma_5 u_n(p_1) \sqrt{\frac{M_n}{p_{10}V}} \frac{1}{\sqrt{2k_0 V}} \quad (3.20)$$

Replacing $\sum_k \rightarrow (V/(2\pi)^3) \int d^3k$ and using the fact that $\int (d^3k/2k_0) = \int_{k_0 > 0} d^4k\delta(k^2 + M_\pi^2)$, one obtains from Eqs. (3.14), and (3.18)–(3.20) the result

$$\text{Im} \; G(q^2) = \pi\sqrt{2} f_\pi M_\pi^2 G_{NN\pi}\delta(q^2 + M_\pi^2) \quad (3.21)$$

From the dispersion relation [Eq. (3.15)], one then obtains

$$G(q^2) = 2MG_1(q^2) + q^2 G_2(q^2) = -\sqrt{2} f_\pi M_\pi^2 G_{NN\pi}/(q^2 + M_\pi^2) \quad (3.22)$$

which is identical to Eq. (3.7) with Eq. (3.11) if $K_{NN\pi}$ is set equal to unity, that is, at or near the pion pole position, where the relations are exact. $K_{NN\pi}(q^2)$ does not appear in Eq. (3.22) because the intermediate pion is on the mass shell in the dispersion treatment, so that what should appear in Eq. (3.20), for instance, is $K_{NN\pi}(k^2) = K_{NN\pi}(-M_\pi^2) = 1$.

It should be emphasized that the nature of the approximation in the two statements of the PCAC discussed above is quite different. It has been argued by Zimmerman and Haag and Nishijima[8] that the field theoretic statement [Eq. (3.1)] is merely a statement of the fact that any local operator having a nonzero matrix element between the one pion and the vacuum states can be defined to be the pion field operator. The approximation in this version then appears in the assumption of gentleness in the behavior of some relevant physical quantities when extrapolated from $q^2 = -M_\pi^2$ down to $q^2 = 0$, e.g., our confidence in the Goldberger-Treiman relation depends on the assumption that the $NN\pi$ vertex pionic form factor $K_{NN\pi}(q^2)$ does not change appreciably in this extrapolation, so that $K_{NN\pi}(0) \simeq K_{NN\pi}(-M_\pi^2) = 1$. In the dispersion theoretic version of PCAC, on the other hand, granting the assumption of an unsubtracted dispersion relation for the matrix element of the divergence of the axial-vector current, the result [Eq. (3.22)] is approximate to the extent that the $3\pi$ and higher cuts can be neglected. Although the two versions of the PCAC hypothesis appear somewhat different, they have led to very similar physical results. At the pion pole position $(q = M_\pi^2)$ both forms give identical results. At $q^2 = 0$, the correction due to $3\pi$ and higher cuts in the second form of PCAC would measure the deviation from unity of the factor $K_{NN\pi}(0)$ appearing in the first form.

Throughout this chapter we shall use the PCAC hypothesis as given by Eq. (3.1). The constant of proportionality $C_\pi$ can be evaluated from either Eq. (3.8) or Eq. (3.11). We shall choose to use Eq. (3.11) for this purpose, since the relation given by Eq. (3.8) requires a knowledge of the extrapolated $NN\pi$ vertex function. Using the experimental information on the $\pi_{\mu 2}$ decay rate we obtain

$$\left| \frac{C_\pi}{\sqrt{2} M_\pi^2} \right| = 0.95 \, M_\pi \qquad (3.23)$$

Thus Eq. (3.1) with $C_\pi$ given by Eq. (3.23) will form the basis of our PCAC hypothesis.

## 2. The PCAC Hypothesis for the Hypercharge-Changing Axial-Vector Currents

The success of the PCAC hypothesis for the hypercharge preserving axial-vector current makes it tempting to propose a similar hypothesis for the hypercharge-changing axial-vector currents also. One would then like to identify the divergence of such a current with the renormalized kaon field:

$$\partial_\mu A_{\mu3}^a = C_K K_3^a \quad (a = 1, 2) \tag{3.24}$$

One can now obtain the corresponding Goldberger-Treiman relation connecting the $K_{\mu2}$ decay constant $f_K$ with the Garnow-Teller axial-vector coupling constant $g_A^\Lambda$ for the $\Lambda$ $\beta$-decay. Proceeding as before one obtains the two relations for $C_K$:

$$C_K = -\frac{(M_\Lambda + M_N)g_A^\Lambda}{G_{\Lambda NK} K_{\Lambda NK}(0)} M_K^2 \tag{3.25}$$

and

$$C_K = f_K M_K^2 \tag{3.26}$$

so that the desired relation is

$$f_K = -(M_\Lambda + M_N)g_A^\Lambda / G_{\Lambda NK} K_{\Lambda NK}(0) \tag{3.27}$$

Here the extrapolation in the vertex function is much larger than before; we make the crude approximation $K_{\Lambda NK}(0) \approx K_{\Lambda NK}(-M_K^2) = 1$. In comparing Eq. (3.27) with the experiments there are further difficulties. At present the values of $g_A^\Lambda$ and $G_{\Lambda NK}$ are not known very well experimentally. To make crude estimates, if one assumes the $SU(3)$ symmetry and, further, that the $d/f$ ratio for the weak axial-vector interaction is the same as the $d/f$ ratio for the strong interactions, one obtains

$$g_A^\Lambda / G_{\Lambda NK} = 1/\sqrt{2} \, g_A / G_{NN\pi} \tag{3.28}$$

From Eqs. (3.27) and (3.28), one gets

$$|f_K| = 126.5 \text{ MeV} \tag{3.29}$$

to be compared with the value $f_K = 131.7$ MeV obtained from the experimental rate for $K_{\mu2}$ decay (with $\sin \theta_A = 0.268$).

The dispersion-theoretic interpretation of the PCAC hypothesis for the hypercharge-changing axial-vector current would be to assume that the matrix element of the divergence of this current satisfies an unsubtracted dispersion relation dominated by the $K$ pole. The large extrapolation in the kaon mass that we encountered in the Goldberger-Treiman relation [Eq. (3.27)] derived from the field theoretic version of the PCAC hypothesis, corresponds here to the somewhat dubious neglect of the continuum-state contribution to the dispersion integral which has a threshold rather close to the $K$ pole. However, if estimates based on $S\bar{U}(3)$ considerations* are any guide, the PCAC hypothesis for the hypercharge-changing currents works mysteriously well, at least for the Goldberger-Treiman relation.

As before, we shall employ the kaon PCAC in the form of Eq. (3.24) with $C_K$ given by Eq. (3.26), so that from the known $K_{l2}$ decay rate:

$$\left|\frac{C_K}{M_K^2}\right| = 0.94 \, M_\pi \qquad (3.30)$$

## 3. Consistency Conditions on Strong Interactions

In this section, following Adler,[9,10] we will obtain some further consequences of the PCAC hypothesis. Adler pointed out that, in addition to giving relations connecting weak and strong interactions, the PCAC hypothesis also leads to consistency relations involving strong interactions alone. We present these calculations in some detail to show how the PCAC hypothesis can lead to the so-called "soft pion" relations, a concept first introduced and studied by Nambu and Lurie[11] and Nambu and Schrauner[12] and which has played a central role in recent work using current algebra.

It will be convenient here to follow the field-theory notation so that we may rewrite the PCAC Eq. (3.1) as

$$\partial_\mu(A_\mu)_i = (C_\pi/2)\pi_i \quad i = 1, 2, 3 \qquad (3.31)$$

Taking the matrix element between $N$ and $\pi N$ states, we obtain

$$\langle \pi_j(q)N(p_2)| \, \partial_\mu[A_\mu(x)]_i \, |N(p_1)\rangle = (C_\pi/2)\langle \pi_j(q)N(p_2)| \, \pi_i(x) \, |N(p_1)\rangle \qquad (3.32)$$

Defining

$$k \equiv p_2 + q - p_1 \qquad (3.33)$$

and using translational invariance, we obtain

$$-ik_\mu\langle \pi_j(q)N(p_2)| \, [A_\mu(x)]_i \, |N(p_1)\rangle$$
$$= -\frac{C_\pi}{2} \frac{1}{k^2 + M_\pi^2} \langle \pi_j(q)N(p_2)| \, J_\pi^i(x) \, |N(p_1)\rangle \qquad (3.34)$$

The matrix element on the right-hand side of Eq. (3.34) just represents the $T$ matrix element for the scattering process

$$\pi_i(k) + N(p_1) \to \pi_j(q) + N(p_2) \qquad (3.35)$$

* On the basis of the exact $SU(3)$ symmetry, of course the PCAC hypothesis for the hypercharge-changing and the hypercharge-preserving axial-vector currents will have the same level of confidence.

Since we have, by LSZ contraction:

$$\langle \pi_j(q)N(p_2)|\pi_i(k)N(p_1)\rangle$$

$$= -i\int d^4x\, e^{ikx}\langle \pi_j(q)N(p_2)|\,[J_\pi(x)]_i\,|N(p_1)\rangle$$

$$= -(2\pi)^4 i\,\delta^4(p_1 + k - p_2 - q)\langle \pi_j(q)N(p_2)|\,[J_\pi(0)]_i\,|N(p_1)\rangle \quad (3.36)$$

An interesting situation arises if we consider the nonphysical limit $k \to 0$ in Eq. (3.34), i.e., if we regard the initial pion to be "soft" with zero momentum and zero energy. The right-hand side of Eq. (3.34) is nonzero, but the left-hand side seems to vanish except in the event that the matrix element $\langle \pi_j(q)N(p_2)|\,[A_\mu(x)]_i\,|N(p_1)\rangle$ is singular at $k_\mu = 0$. It is not very difficult to see that such a singularity arises only in those cases where this matrix element is dominated by single-particle intermediate states degenerate in mass with the initial or final baryon. In these Born contributions the propagator corresponding to the single nucleon line is given by $1/[(p_1 + k)^2 + M^2]$ or $1/[(p_2 - k)^2 + M^2]$, both of which have a pole at $k \to 0$. Thus in the limit $k \to 0$, the left-hand side of Eq. (3.34) picks up contributions only from Born diagrams illustrated in Figure 1.

Using standard Feynman rules for writing the contributions from Born diagrams, we obtain

$$\langle \pi_j(q)N(p_2)|\,[A_\mu(0)]_i\,|N(p_1)\rangle$$

$$= \left(\frac{M}{p_{10}}\frac{M}{p_{20}}\frac{1}{2q_0}\frac{1}{2k_0}\frac{1}{V^4}\right)^{1/2}$$

$$\times \left\{ -G_{NN\pi}g_A(\tau_j\tau_i/2)\bar{u}(p_2)\gamma_5\frac{-i(p_1 + k)\cdot\gamma + M}{(p_1 + k)^2 + M^2}\,\gamma_5 u(p_1)\right.$$

$$\left. -G_{NN\pi}g_A(\tau_i\tau_j/2)\bar{u}(p_2)\gamma_\mu\gamma_5\frac{-i(p_2 - k)\cdot\gamma + M}{(p_2 - k)^2 + M^2}\,\gamma_5 u(p_1)\right\} \quad (3.37)$$

One finally obtains, after some simple and straightforward algebra,

$$\lim_{k\to 0}\{-ik_\mu\langle \pi_j(q)N(p_2)|\,[A_\mu(0)]_i\,|N(p_1)\rangle\}\sqrt{2k_0 V}$$

$$= \left(\frac{M}{p_{10}}\frac{M}{p_{20}}\frac{1}{2q_0}\frac{1}{V^3}\right)^{1/2}G_{NN\pi}$$

$$\times g_A\left\{\delta_{ij}\bar{u}(p_2)u(p_1) - \tfrac{1}{2}\bar{u}(p_2)(i\gamma\cdot k)\left(\frac{\tau_j\tau_i}{\nu_B - \nu} - \frac{\tau_i\tau_j}{\nu_B + \nu}\right)u(p_1)\right\}$$

$$(3.38)$$

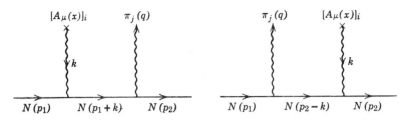

FIGURE 1

where

$$\nu = -(p_1 + p_2)\cdot k/2M$$
$$\nu_B = q\cdot k/2M \tag{3.39}$$

are the usual pion–nucleon scattering energy and momentum transfer variables. From Eqs. (3.34) and (3.38) we obtain, on using the value of $C_\pi$ given by Eq. (3.8),

$$\lim_{k\to 0} \langle \pi_j(q)N(p_2)|\,(J_\pi(0))_i\,|N(p_1)\rangle \sqrt{2k_0 V}$$

$$= \frac{G^2_{NN\pi}K_{NN\pi}(0)}{M}\left(\frac{M^2}{p_{10}p_{20}}\frac{1}{2q_0 V^3}\right)^{1/2}$$

$$\times \left\{ \delta_{ij}\bar{u}(p_2)u(p_1) - \tfrac{1}{2}\bar{u}(p_2)(i\gamma\cdot k)\left(\frac{\tau_j\tau_i}{\nu_B - \nu} - \frac{\tau_i\tau_j}{\nu_B + \nu}\right)u(p_1)\right\} \tag{3.40}$$

We may express the $T$ matrix for $\pi$-$N$ scattering in the usual form

$$\langle \pi_j(q)N(p_2)|\,[J_\pi(0)]_i\,|N(p_1)\rangle$$

$$\equiv \left(\sqrt{\frac{M^2}{p_{10}p_{20}}\frac{1}{2q_0}\frac{1}{2k_0}\frac{1}{V^4}}\right)^{1/2}\bar{u}(p_2)M_{ij}u(p_1) \tag{3.41}$$

where

$$M_{ij} = A_{ij}(\nu, \nu_B, k^2) - i(\gamma\cdot k)B_{ij}(\nu, \nu_B, k^2) \tag{3.42}$$

From Eqs. (3.40)–(3.42) one then obtains

$$A_{ij}(\nu = 0, \nu_B = 0, k^2 = 0) = [G^2_{NN\pi}K_{NN\pi}(0)/M]\,\delta_{ij} \tag{3.43}$$

Decomposing now $A_{ij}$ into the symmetric and antisymmetric isospin parts

$$A_{ij} = A^{(+)}\delta_{ij} + A^{(-)}\tfrac{1}{2}[\tau_i, \tau_j] \tag{3.44}$$

we get the following consistency conditions:

$$\frac{A^{(+)}(v = 0, v_B = 0, k^2 = 0)}{K_{NN\pi}(0)} = \frac{G^2_{NN\pi}}{M} \tag{3.45}$$

$$A^{(-)}(v = 0, v_B = 0, k^2 = 0) = 0 \tag{3.46}$$

Note that Eq. (3.46) is automatically satisfied due to the crossing symmetry of $A^{(-)}$. We know that for $q \to -q$, $k \to -k$, and $i$ and $j$ interchanged, the $\pi$-$N$ scattering amplitude must be the same, i.e.,

$$A_{ij}(v, v_B, k^2) = A_{ij}(-v, v_B, k^2) \tag{3.47}$$

so that for $k \to 0$, we must have $A_{ij}$ symmetric in $i$ and $j$. Equation (3.45) is, however, a nontrivial consequence of the PCAC hypothesis.

In order to compare Eq. (3.45) with experiments, one has to first obtain the $\pi$-$N$ scattering amplitude $A^+(v = 0, v_B = 0, k^2 = 0)$. One can do this in two steps. (1) From the physical $\pi$-$N$ scattering amplitude one can analytically continue to the unphysical point $v = 0$, $v_B = 0$, $k^2 = -M^2_\pi$ using, for instance, a dispersion relation for fixed momentum transfer subtracted at threshold, the subtraction constant being evaluated from the known $\pi$-$N$ scattering lengths. (2) The extrapolation of the amplitude from $v = 0$, $v_B = 0$, $k^2 = -M^2_\pi$ to the required point $v = 0$, $v_B = 0$, $k^2 = 0$ may be estimated by means of some models. Adler finds that step 2 is fortunately a negligible effect, and the main result comes from step 1, through the contribution of the $p$ waves to the subtraction constant. Adler has analyzed the continuation (step 1) from several viewpoints, and finds that the consistency condition [Eq. (3.45)] is satisfied to better than 10%.

In conclusion, we would like to mention that Adler's result can be regarded as a generalization of the work of Nambu and Lurié and Nambu and Schrauner, who worked with conserved axial-vector currents. For such currents, the associated "charge" (chirality) is a conserved quantum number, and Nambu et al. show that this conservation law demands specific relations between a given process and another with an extra "soft" pion.

Finally, conditions analogous to Eq. (3.45) can also be obtained for $\pi$-$\pi$ scattering, $\Lambda$-$\pi$ scattering, etc., but the experimental situation at the present time does not warrant a detailed investigation here.

## IV. The Fubini-Furlan Method and the Adler-Weisberger Sum Rule

### 1. The Technique of the Algebra of Currents

Although the equal time-commutation relations of vector and axial-vector charges had been known for some time, the technique for deriving sum rules relating various physical quantities was only recently developed by Fubini and Furlan.[13] Their main aim was to give a method of obtaining renormalization ratios between the bare and the dressed coupling constants and, in general, to obtain the effects of a broken symmetry generated by currents and charges. Although many refinements of the original method have been made by various authors[14] since then, we shall first describe the earlier formulation because of its simple intuitive appeal.

The method can be very simply described. One starts with a suitable equal-time commutator between some charges, specified in a particular Lorentz frame, and sandwiches it between states of suitable particles. Insertion of a complete set of intermediate states then essentially leads to the sum rule. It is necessary, of course, to specify the state of motion of the relevant particles in this Lorentz frame. It is in this connection that Fubini and Furlan made the important observation that the best sum rules are obtained when the particle momenta are infinite. It is important to note that the separation of the contribution from the intermediate states according to the number of particles is not a relativistic-invariant procedure; hence the importance of the frame chosen. In the infinite-momentum frame the sum converges fastest and the contribution coming from the single-particle intermediate states dominates. Advantages of this way of obtaining sum rules have been further discussed and clarified by Dashen and Gell-Mann.[15] A very important feature is that, for the integrated charges and currents (which do not change the momentum) occurring in the commutator, the invariant momentum transfer between the initial or final and the intermediate states is fixed and equal to zero. In any other frame this variable would vary with the changing mass of the intermediate states and the role of the different intermediate states would not be comparable in a meaningful way, so that the convergence of the resulting sum cannot even be reasonably discussed. The use of infinite momentum for obtaining sum rules has been put in a more satisfying covariant dispersion theoretic form in the refinements mentioned above. The two approaches are equivalent and the question of convergence of the sum in the first formulation becomes that of the convergence of a dispersion integral in the second.

In this section we shall illustrate in some detail the methods employed in obtaining sum rules from the algebra of currents. In particular we derive in Sections IV-2 to IV-4 the Adler-Weisberger[16] sum rule in various ways using somewhat different techniques.

## 2. Derivation of the A-W Sum Rule by the Infinite-Momentum Method

We first illustrate the original method of Fubini and Furlan by deriving the Adler-Weisberger sum rule[16] for the renormalization of the axial-vector $\beta$-decay coupling constant. Clearly we should start out with a commutator involving suitable axial-vector "charges," remembering that the axial-vector current density $(A_\mu)_2^1$ is involved in the $\beta$ decay of neutron to proton. We shall start with the commutator:

$$[a_1^2(t), a_2^1(t)] = v_1^1 - v_2^2 = 2I_3 \tag{4.1}$$

and take its matrix element between single-proton states with a given spin-quantum number and momenta $\mathbf{p}$ and $\mathbf{p}'$. Since we use states normalized as $\langle \mathbf{p}|\mathbf{p}'\rangle = \delta^3(\mathbf{p} - \mathbf{p}')$, the right-hand side of Eq. (4.1) then gives simply

$$\langle p(\mathbf{p}')| \, 2I_3 \, |p(\mathbf{p})\rangle = \delta^3(\mathbf{p} - \mathbf{p}') \tag{4.2}$$

In the matrix element of the commutator on the left-hand side of Eq. (4.1) we insert a complete set of states:

$$\langle p(\mathbf{p}')| \, [a_1^2(t), a_2^1(t)] \, |p(\mathbf{p})\rangle = \sum_j [\langle \, p(\mathbf{p}')| \, a_1^2(t) \, |j\rangle\langle j| \, a_2^1(t) \, |p(\mathbf{p})\rangle$$
$$- \langle p(\mathbf{p}')| \, a_2^1(t) \, |j\rangle\langle j| \, a_1^2(t) \, |p(\mathbf{p})\rangle \tag{4.3}$$

In the sum over the intermediate states, we first isolate the single-particle contribution. Since the operator $a_2^1$ decreases charge by one unit, whereas $a_1^2$ increases it, only the former acting on a proton state can lead to a single particle state, namely that of a neutron. Thus, the only single-particle contribution to Eq. (4.3) denoted here by $S$, is

$$S = \sum \int V \frac{d^3k}{(2\pi)^3} \langle p(\mathbf{p}^1)| \, a_1^2(t) \, |n(k, r)\rangle\langle n(k, r)| \, a_2^1(t) \, |p(\mathbf{p})\rangle \tag{4.4}$$

where $r$ denotes the spin state and $k$ the momentum of the intermediate neutron. In order to obtain the $n$-$p$ matrix element of $a_1^2(t)$, let us consider the matrix element of the corresponding axial vector current density $[A_\mu(x)]_1^2$:

$$\langle p(\mathbf{p}')| A_{\mu_1}^2(0) |n(\mathbf{k})\rangle$$

$$= \sqrt{\frac{M_N^2}{p_0' k_0 V^2}} \, \bar{u}_p(\mathbf{p}')[G_1(q^2)i\gamma_\mu\gamma_5 + G_2(q^2)q_\mu\gamma_5]u_n(\mathbf{k}) \qquad (4.5)$$

where we have denoted $k\text{-}p'$ by $q$. It is the constant

$$g_A = G_1(0) \qquad (4.6)$$

called the renormalization factor of the axial-vector coupling constant of the $\beta$ decay of the neutron, that we aim to calculate. By the definition, Eq. (2.4), of $a_1^2$ we then find:

$$\langle p(\mathbf{p}')| a_1^2(t) |n(\mathbf{k})\rangle = -i \int_{X_0 = t} d^3x \langle p(\mathbf{p}')| A_{4_1}^2(0) |n(\mathbf{k})\rangle e^{i(k - p')\cdot\kappa}$$

$$= -i(2\pi)^3 \delta^3(\mathbf{p}' - \mathbf{p}) \langle p(\mathbf{p}') |A_{4_1}^2(0) |n(\mathbf{k})\rangle \qquad (4.7)$$

Because of the $\delta$-function, $\mathbf{p}' = \mathbf{k}$, and since we assume here (charge independence) that $M_n = M_p = M$, we have also $p_0' = k_0$, so that $q = 0$. Thus, only that part of the right-hand side of Eq. (4.5) which contains $G_1(0)$ contributes to Eq. (4.7), and we have

$$\langle p(\mathbf{p}')| a_1^2(t) |n(\mathbf{k})\rangle = (2\pi)^3 \left(\frac{M_N}{Vk_0}\right) \delta^3(\mathbf{p}' - \mathbf{k}) g_A \bar{u}_p(\mathbf{p}')\gamma_4\gamma_5 u_n(\mathbf{k}) \quad (4.8)$$

Similarly,

$$\langle n(\mathbf{k})| a_2^1(t) |p(\mathbf{p})\rangle = (2\pi)^3 \left(\frac{M_N}{Vp_0}\right) \delta^3(\mathbf{p}' - \mathbf{k}) g_A \bar{u}_n(\mathbf{k})\gamma_4\gamma_5 u_p(\mathbf{p}) \quad (4.9)$$

Substituting these last two expressions in Eq. (4.4), we find simply:

$$S = (2\pi)^3 \delta^3(\mathbf{p}' - \mathbf{p}) \frac{1}{v} \frac{M_N^2}{p_0^2} g_A^2 \bar{u}_p(\mathbf{p})\gamma_4\gamma_5 \frac{-i\gamma\cdot p + M_N}{2M_N} \gamma_4\gamma_5 u_p(\mathbf{p})$$

$$= \delta^3(\mathbf{p}' - \mathbf{p}) g_A^2 \left(1 - \frac{M_N^2}{p_0^2}\right) \qquad (4.10)$$

It is interesting already at this stage to compare with the situation that obtains in the limit of the chiral $SU(3) \times SU(3)$ symmetry generated by the $a$'s and the $v$'s. In the symmetry limit these charges are constants in time and in particular the axial vector currents are conserved. The generator $a$ acting on the nucleon will not lead to any multiparticle state. Since, assuming no parity doubling for the baryons, the nucleon mass is zero in the symmetry limit, we obtain the result $g_A = 1$.

Next, we have to calculate the multiparticle (or the "continuum") contribution to Eq. (4.3). A little ingenuity must be used here, in order to relate this contribution to $\pi$-$N$ reaction amplitudes via PCAC. We proceed to recast the relevant matrix elements as follows. Since

$$\langle j(p_j)|\, a_2^1(t)\, |p(\mathbf{p})\rangle = e^{i(p_{j0}-p_0)t}\langle j(p_j)|\, a_2^1(0)\, |p(\mathbf{p})\rangle \qquad (4.11)$$

we may write

$$\langle j|\, a_2^1(t)\, |p(\mathbf{p})\rangle$$

$$= \langle j|\, \frac{d}{dt} a_2^1(t)\, |p(\mathbf{p})\rangle \, \frac{1}{i(p_{j0}-p_0)}$$

$$= \langle j|\, \int_{x_0=t} d^3x\, \partial_4[A_4(x)]_2^1\, |p(\mathbf{p})\rangle \, \frac{1}{i(p_{j0}-p_0)}$$

$$= \langle j|\, \int_{x_0=t} d^3x\, \partial_\mu[A_\mu(x)]_2^1\, |p(\mathbf{p})\rangle \, \frac{1}{i(p_{j0}-p_0)}$$

$$= \frac{C_\pi}{\sqrt{2}} \langle j|\, \int_{x_0=t} d^3x\, \pi^+(x)\, |p(\mathbf{p})\rangle \, \frac{1}{i(p_{j0}-p_0)}$$

$$= (2\pi)^3 \delta^3(\mathbf{p}_j - \mathbf{p})\langle j|\, \pi^+(0)\, |p(\mathbf{p})\rangle e^{i(p_{j0}-p_0)t} \, \frac{1}{i(p_{j0}-p_0)} \qquad (4.12)$$

where at the next to last step we have used PCAC, introducing thereby the pion field $\pi^+(x)$. The continuum contribution to Eq. (4.3), denoted from now on by $C$, can thus be written as:

$$C = \sum_j \frac{C_\pi^2}{2} (2\pi)^6 \delta^3(\mathbf{p}_j - \mathbf{p})\delta^3(\mathbf{p}_j - \mathbf{p}') \, \frac{1}{(p_{j0}-p_0)^2}$$

$$\times [\langle p(\mathbf{p}')|\, \pi^-(0)\, |j\rangle\langle j|\, \pi^+(0)\, |p(\mathbf{p})\rangle$$

$$\qquad - \langle p(\mathbf{p}')|\, \pi^+(0)\, |j\rangle\langle j|\, \pi^-(0)\, |p(\mathbf{p})\rangle] \qquad (4.13)$$

The states $j$ are the continuum states starting out from the least massive state of a pion and a nucleon. For the summation over $j$ we use the order:

$$\sum_j = \int \frac{V\, d^3p_j}{(2\pi)^3} \int_{M_N+M_\pi}^{\infty} dW \sum_{j(\text{INT})} \delta(W - M_j) \qquad (4.14)$$

where $j$(INT) stands for the "internal variables" of the system with invariant mass $M_j$ and total momentum $\mathbf{p}_j$. We may then write

$$C = (2\pi)^3 V \frac{C_\pi^2}{2} \delta^3(\mathbf{p} - \mathbf{p}') \int_{M_N + M_\pi}^{\infty} dW \sum_{j(\text{INT})} \delta(W - M_j)$$

$$\times \left[ \langle \mathbf{p}' | J_\pi(0) | j \rangle \langle j | J_{\pi+}(0) | \mathbf{p} \rangle - \langle \mathbf{p}' | J_{\pi+}(0) | j \rangle \langle j | J_{\pi-}(0) | \mathbf{p} \rangle \right]$$

$$\times \frac{1}{(p_{j0} - p_0)^2 [(p - p_j)^2 + M_\pi^2]^2} \qquad (4.15)$$

where we have introduced the notation:

$$(M_\pi^2 - \square)\pi(x) = -J_\pi(x) \qquad (4.16)$$

Thus putting Eqs. (4.2), (4.10) and (4.15) in the matrix element of Eq. (4.1) in question, we obtain the sum rule:

$$1 = \left(1 - \frac{M_N^2}{p_0^2}\right) g_A^2 + V(2\pi)^3 \frac{C_\pi^2}{2}$$

$$\times \int_{M_N + M_\pi}^{\infty} dW \sum_{j(\text{INT})} \frac{\delta(W - M_j)[R_j^- - R_j^+]M_N M_j}{p_0 p_{j0}(p_{j0} - p_0)^2 [(p - p_j)^2 + M_\pi^2]^2} \qquad (4.17)$$

where we have put

$$R_j^\mp = \frac{p_0}{M_N} \frac{p_{j0}}{M_j} |\langle j | J_{\pi\pm}(0) | p(\mathbf{p}) \rangle|^2 \qquad (4.18)$$

In Eq. (4.17) we then have a momentum-dependent sum rule for $g_A$. It is here that we have to use the Fubini-Furlan prescription of taking the limit of *infinite momentum* to obtain the final sum rule. We shall assume that the summation and the limiting process can be interchanged. Before doing this, however, we have to make a side calculation needed to interpret the continuum contribution in terms of $\pi$-$N$ total cross sections. Consider, for instance, the amplitude for the process $i(\pi^- + p) \to f(j)$ using the LSZ contraction:

$$\langle j_{\text{out}} | \pi^-(q) p(p)_{\text{in}} \rangle$$

$$= \delta_{if} + i \int d^4x \frac{e^{iqx}}{\sqrt{2q_0 V}} (M_\pi^2 - \square) \langle j | \pi^+(x) | p \rangle$$

$$= \delta_{if} - (2\pi)^4 i \delta^4(p_j - p - q) \frac{1}{\sqrt{2q_0 V}} \langle j | J_{\pi^+}(0) | p(\mathbf{p}) \rangle \qquad (4.19)$$

Let us suppose in this section that we are considering the pion to have "zero mass," i.e., $q^2 = 0$. Then in the center of mass frame for the above reaction we have

$$\mathbf{q} + \mathbf{p} = \mathbf{p}_j = 0$$
$$q_0 + p_0 = W, \quad p_{j0} = M_j$$
$$q_0 = |\mathbf{q}| = (W^2 - M_N^2)/2W \tag{4.20}$$

and the initial flux is given by

$$\text{Flux} = \frac{1}{V} \left[ \frac{|\mathbf{q}|}{q_0} + \frac{|\mathbf{q}|}{p_0} \right] = \frac{1}{V} \frac{W}{p_0} \tag{4.21}$$

Hence the total $\pi$-$p$ cross section in the center of mass with total energy $W$ for the *initial* pion treated as a *zero-mass* particle is given by:

$$\sigma_p^{\pi^-}(W \cdot 0) = V^2 \frac{p_0}{W} \sum_j (2\pi)^4 \delta^4(p_j - p - q) \frac{1}{2q_0 V} |\langle j| J_{\pi^+}(0) |p(\mathbf{p})\rangle|^2$$

$$= V^2 \frac{p_0}{W} \int V \frac{d^3 p_j}{(2\pi)^3} \sum_{j(\text{INT})} (2\pi)^4 \delta^4(p_j - p - q) \frac{1}{2q_0 V}$$
$$\times |\langle j| J_{\pi^+}(0) |p\rangle|^2$$

$$= V^2 \frac{2\pi p_0}{W^2 - M_N^2} \sum_{j(\text{INT})} |\langle j| J_{\pi^+}(0) |p\rangle|^2 \delta(M_j - W)$$

$$= V^2 \frac{2\pi M_N}{W^2 - M_N^2} \sum_{j(\text{INT})} R_j^- \delta(M_j - W) \tag{4.22}$$

Let us now take the limit $p_0 \to \infty$ in sum rule of Eq. (4.17) and make use of Eq. (4.22). Then since

$$p_{j0} = [p_0^2 - M_N^2 + M_j^2]^{-1/2} \to p_0$$
$$\frac{1}{(p_0 - p_{j0})^2} = \frac{(p_0 + p_{j0})^2}{(p_0^2 - p_{j0}^2)^2} = \frac{(p_0 + p_{j0})^2}{(M_j^2 - M_N^2)^2} \to \frac{4p_0^2}{(M_j^2 - M_N^2)^2}$$

we find that, for $p_0 \to \infty$, the sum rule obtains the form

$$1 = g_A^2 + \frac{C_\pi^2}{M_\pi^4} \frac{1}{\pi}$$
$$\times \int_{M_\pi + M_N}^{\infty} dW \frac{W}{W^2 - M_N^2} [\sigma_p^{\pi^-}(W, 0) - \sigma_p^{\pi^+}(W, 0)] \tag{4.23}$$

using the value of $C_\pi^2/M_\pi^4 = g_A^2 4 M_N^2/[K_{NN\pi}(0)]^2 G_{NN\pi}^2$ from Eq. (3.8) we have finally the Adler-Weisberger sum rule:

$$1 - \frac{1}{g_A^2} = \frac{4M_N^2}{[K_{NN\pi}(0)G_{NN\pi}]^2} \frac{1}{\pi}$$

$$\times \int_{M_\pi + M_N}^{\infty} dW \frac{W}{W^2 - M_N^2} [\sigma_p^{\pi^+}(W, 0) - \sigma_p^{\pi^-}(W, 0)] \qquad (4.24)$$

which expresses the renormalization factor $g_A$ in terms of the total $\pi$-$p$ cross sections, but with the incident pion extrapolated to zero mass.

## 3. Dispersion-Theoretic Derivation of the A-W Sum Rule

We present in this section an alternative derivation of the Adler-Weisberger sum rule using dispersion theory.

We start again with the commutator given in Eq. (4.1), but expressed in a different form. For this purpose we define (suppressing the tensor indices for the moment):

$$a(\mathbf{k}, t) = -i \int_{X_0 = t} e^{i\mathbf{k}\cdot\mathbf{x}} A_4(x) \, d^3 x \qquad (4.25)$$

so that the matrix elements of our axial charges are obtained by taking the limit $\mathbf{k} \to 0$:

$$\langle i| a(t) |j\rangle = \lim_{\mathbf{k}\to 0} \langle i| a(\mathbf{k}, t) |j\rangle \qquad (4.26)$$

Now we may reexpress $a(\mathbf{k}, t)$ in the form:

$$a(\mathbf{k}, t) = -\int d^4 x\, \theta(x_0 - t)\, \partial_\mu[e^{ikx} A_\mu(x)], \quad k_0 = -i\varepsilon, \quad \varepsilon > 0 \qquad (4.27)$$

A negative imaginary $k_0$ ($k_0 = -i\varepsilon$, $\varepsilon \to 0^+$) is necessary so that on partial integration of the integral in Eq. (4.27) one obtains Eq. (4.25), with the $x_0 = \infty$ surface term vanishing automatically. Carrying through the differentiation in Eq. (4.27) we find

$$a(\mathbf{k}, t) = -\int d^4 x\, e^{ikx} \theta(x_0 - t)\, \partial_\mu A_\mu(x) - ik\mu$$

$$\times \int d^4 x\, e^{ikx} \theta(x_0 - t) A_\mu(x), \quad k_0 = -i\varepsilon, \quad \varepsilon \to 0^+ \qquad (4.28)$$

Using translational invariance in time and integrating by parts, we obtain for the matrix elements of the second term in the limit $\mathbf{k} \to 0$:

$$\lim_{\mathbf{k} \to 0} [-ik_\mu \int d^4x\theta(x_0 - t) e^{ikx} e^{i(E_i - E_j)x_0}\langle i| A_\mu(\mathbf{x}, 0) |j\rangle]$$

$$= \frac{-k_0 \int d^3x \, e^{i\mathbf{k}\cdot\mathbf{x}} \, e^{i(E_i - E_j - k_0)t}\langle i| A_0(\mathbf{x}, 0) |j\rangle}{E_i - E_j - k_0} \tag{4.29}$$

Since at the end we have to use $k_0 = -i\varepsilon \to 0$, it is clear that this term gives a nonvanishing result only when the states $|i\rangle$ and $|j\rangle$ are *exactly degenerate*. We shall adopt the artifice of introducing fictitious mass differences even in situations of such a degeneracy, and of taking the degeneracy limit at the very end (see the next section for a discussion on this point). With this proviso, we can then write

$$a(t) \doteq \lim_{\mathbf{k} \to 0} \left[ -\int d^4x \, e^{ikx}\theta(x_0 - t) \, \partial_\mu A_\mu(x) \right]$$

$$(k_0 = -i\varepsilon, \quad \varepsilon \to 0^+) \tag{4.30}$$

where the symbol $\doteq$ instead of $=$ has been put in to emphasize the above understanding. It is important to note that in the limiting procedures to be employed $\mathbf{k} \to 0$ first and only at the end does $k_0 \to 0$.

Similarly, we may also write the alternative expression:

$$a(t) = \lim_{\mathbf{k} \to 0} \int \{d^4x\theta(t - x_0) \, \partial_\mu[e^{ikx}A_\mu(x)]\}$$

$$\doteq \lim_{\mathbf{k} \to 0} \int [d^4x\theta(t - x_0) \, e^{ikx} \, \partial_\mu A_\mu(x)], \quad k_0 = i\varepsilon, \quad \varepsilon \to 0^+ \tag{4.31}$$

Let us then recast the matrix element between single-proton state of the commutation relation of Eq. (4.1), using the last two equations in the following manner:

$$\langle\mathbf{p}'| 2I_3 |\mathbf{p}\rangle = -\int d^4x \int d^4y \, e^{-\varepsilon(x_0 - y_0)}\theta(x_0 - t)\theta(t - y_0)$$

$$\times \langle\mathbf{p}'| [\partial_\mu A_{\mu 1}^2(x), \partial_\nu A_{\nu 2}^1(y)] |\mathbf{p}\rangle, \quad \varepsilon \to 0^+ \tag{4.32}$$

Notice the use of both the forms of Eqs. (4.30) and (4.31), which allows to go to the following simpler expression involving only one $\theta$ function. For this we introduce new variables:

$$\xi = (x + y)/2, \quad \eta = (x - y)/2$$

and use translational invariance, so that the right-hand side of Eq. (4.32) becomes:

$$
-2^4 \int\int d^4\xi\, d^4\eta\, e^{-2\varepsilon\eta_0}\theta(\xi_0 + \eta_0 - t)\theta(-\xi_0 + \eta_0 + t)\, e^{-i\xi\cdot(p'-p)}
$$
$$
\times \langle p'|\, [\partial_\mu A_{\mu 1}^2(\eta),\, \partial_\nu A_{\nu 2}^1(-\eta)]\, |p\rangle
$$
$$
= -2^4(2\pi)^3\delta^3(\mathbf{p} - \mathbf{p}') \int d^4\eta\, e^{-2\varepsilon\eta_0} \int d\xi_0 \theta(\xi_0 + \eta_0 - t)
$$
$$
\times \theta(-\xi_0 + \eta_0 + t)\langle p'|\, [\partial_\mu A_{\mu 1}^2(\eta),\, \partial_\nu A_{\nu 2}^1(-\eta)]\, |p\rangle \qquad (4.33)
$$

Since the two $\theta$ functions enforce the conditions $t - \eta_0 < \xi_0 < t + \eta_0$ we have

$$
\int d\xi_0 \theta(\xi_0 + \eta_0 - t)\theta(-\xi_0 + \eta_0 + t) = \int_{t-\eta_0}^{t+\eta_0} d\xi_0 = 2\eta_0
$$

so that from Eqs. (4.32) and (4.33), we have (on putting $\eta = z/2$)

$$
\langle p'|\, 2I_3\, |p\rangle = -(2\pi)^3\, \delta^3(\mathbf{p} - \mathbf{p}') \int d^4z z_0 \theta(z_0)\, e^{-\varepsilon z_0}
$$
$$
\times \langle p'|\int \partial_\mu A_{\mu 1}^2\left(\frac{z}{2}\right),\, \partial_\nu A_{\nu 2}^1\left(-\frac{z}{2}\right) |p\rangle
$$
$$
= -(2\pi)^3\, \frac{C_\pi^2}{2}\, \delta^3(\mathbf{p} - \mathbf{p}') \int d^4z z_0\theta(z_0)\, e^{-\varepsilon z_0}
$$
$$
\times \langle p'|\left[\pi^-\left(\frac{z}{2}\right),\, \pi^+\left(-\frac{z}{2}\right)\right] |p\rangle \qquad (4.34)
$$

where at the last step we have introduced the pion field operators via PCAC.

Let us introduce a function

$$
F(q) = \frac{p_0}{M_p}\int d^4z\, e^{-iq\cdot z}\, e^{-\varepsilon z_0}\langle p|\,\theta(z_0)\left[\pi^-\left(\frac{z}{2}\right),\, \pi^+\left(-\frac{z}{2}\right)\right] |p\rangle \qquad (4.35)
$$

which, being invariant, depends on the invariant variables $\nu$ and $q^2$

$$
F(q) = F(\nu, q^2)
$$

where

$$
\nu = -\frac{p\cdot q}{M_p} \qquad (4.36)
$$

Further, since $F$ is a Fourier transform of a causal commutator we may treat it by standard dispersion theoretic methods. In terms of this function we may write our relation of Eq. (4.34) in the form (removing the $\delta$ functions from both sides):

$$1 = i(2\pi)^3 \frac{C_\pi^2}{2} \frac{M_p}{p_0} \lim_{q \to 0} \left[\frac{\partial}{\partial q_0} F(q)\right]$$

$$= i(2\pi)^3 \frac{C_\pi^2}{2} \lim_{v \to 0} \left[\frac{\partial}{\partial v} F(v, 0)\right] \tag{4.37}$$

We may at this state absorb the factor $e^{-\varepsilon z_0}$ into the exponential involving $q$ in Eq. (4.35). This means that in the limit $q \to 0$ we must first take $\mathbf{q} \to 0$ and only then can we let $q_0 \to 0$, since the limit $\varepsilon \to 0$ must be taken only at the end. We shall assume that $F(v, 0)$ satisfies an unsubtracted dispersion relation

$$F(v, 0) = \frac{1}{\pi} \int \frac{\text{Abs } F(v', 0) \, dv'}{v' - v - i\delta} \tag{4.38}$$

The absorptive part of $F$ is given in the standard manner by

$$\text{Abs } F = \frac{p_0}{M_p} \frac{1}{2i} \int d^4z \, e^{-iq \cdot z} \langle p(p)| \left[\pi^-\left(\frac{z}{2}\right), \pi^+\left(-\frac{z}{2}\right)\right] |p(p)\rangle$$

$$= \frac{2\pi^4}{2i} \frac{p_0}{M_p} \sum_j [\delta^4(p_j - p - q)\langle p(p)| \pi^-(0) |j\rangle\langle j| \pi^+(0) |p(p)\rangle$$

$$- \delta^4(p_j - p + q)\langle p(p)| \pi^+(0) |j\rangle\langle j| \pi^-(0) |p(p)\rangle] \tag{4.39}$$

The only single-particle contribution, namely that due to a neutron state, comes from the first term and is given by

$$S = \frac{p_0}{M_p} \frac{(2\pi)^4}{2i} \sum_{\text{spin }(n)} \int_{(p_{n0} > 0)} \frac{V}{(2\pi)^3} d^4 p_n (2p_{n0}) \delta(p_n^2 + M_n^2)$$

$$\times \delta^4(p_n - p - q)\langle p(p)| \pi^-(0) |n\rangle\langle n| \pi^+(0) |p(p)\rangle$$

$$= \frac{\pi}{iV} \frac{1}{2M_p^2} \frac{G_{NN\pi}^2 K_{NN\pi}^2(0)}{M_\pi^4} (M_n - M_p)^2 \delta\left(v - \frac{M_n^2 - M_p^2}{2M_p}\right) \tag{4.40}$$

In obtaining the above result, we use for the matrix element expressions of the form:

$$\langle p(p)| \pi^+(0) |n(p_n)\rangle|_{p_n = p - q, \, q^2 = 0} = -\sqrt{\frac{M_p M_n}{p_0 p_{n0} V^2}} \, \bar{u}_p i\gamma_5 u_n \frac{\sqrt{2} \, G_{NN\pi} K_{NN\pi}(0)}{M_\pi^2}$$

The continuum contribution to Abs $F$ in Eq. (4.39) can be calculated as for the case of the standard forward pion–nucleon scattering dispersion relation[17] in terms of the total $\pi$-$N$ cross sections. Here, since $q^2 = 0$, the pion will be of "zero mass." We shall thus obtain for the $F(\nu, 0)$, the dispersion representation:

$$F(\nu, 0) = \frac{1}{iV} \frac{1}{2M_p^2} \frac{G_{NN\pi}^2 K_{NN\pi}^2(0)}{M_\pi^4} (M_n - M_p)^2 \frac{1}{\dfrac{M_n^2 - M_p^2}{2M_p} - \nu}$$
$$+ \frac{1}{\pi i V} \frac{1}{M_\pi^4} \int_{M_\pi + \frac{M_\pi^2}{2M_p}}^{\infty} d\nu' \frac{\nu'[\sigma_p^{\pi-}(\nu', 0) - \sigma_p^{\pi+}(\nu', 0)]}{\nu' - \nu} \quad (4.41)$$

From Eq. (4.41) and (4.37) and using the value of $C_\pi^2/M_\pi^4$ given in Eq. (3.8), we then obtain

$$1 = g_A^2 + \frac{C_\pi^2}{M_\pi^4} \frac{1}{2\pi} \int_{M_\pi + \frac{M_\pi^2}{2M_p}}^{\infty} d\nu \frac{1}{\nu} [\sigma_p^{\pi-}(\nu, 0) - \sigma_p^{\pi+}(\nu, 0)] \quad (4.42)$$

This is exactly the sum rule of Eq. (4.23), when we put $M_n = M_p = M_N$ and note that $W^2 = M_p^2 + 2M_p\nu$.

## 4. General Technique for Low-Energy Theorems and the A-W Relation

We shall now discuss a general technique for deriving sum rules. This approach has been discussed chiefly by Alessandrini, Bég, and Brown[14d] and by Weisberger,[16] and has been extended to multiple pion problems by Weinberg.[14l] Here we shall illustrate this technique by deriving the Adler-Weisberger sum rule once again.

Consider the Fourier transform of the matrix element of the time-ordered product of two axial-vector current densities.

$$R_{\mu\nu} = \int d^4x \, e^{-iq\cdot x} \langle p| \, T[A_{\mu 1}^2(x) A_{\nu 2}^1(0)] \, |p\rangle \quad (4.43)$$

We restrict ourselves here to the case when the initial and final proton states have the same four momentum. From Eq. (4.43) we obtain on partial integrations the following fundamental identities

$$_\mu R_{\mu\nu} = -i \int d^4x \, e^{-iqx} \{\langle p| \, T[\partial_\mu A_{\mu 1}^2(x) A_{\nu 2}^1(0)] \, |p\rangle$$
$$+ \langle p| \, \delta(x_0)[A_{01}^2(x), A_{\nu 2}^1(0)] \, |p\rangle\} \quad (4.44)$$

$$q_\mu q_\nu R_{\mu\nu} = \int d^4x \, e^{iq\cdot x} \{\langle p| \, T[\partial_\mu A_{\mu 1}^2(0)\partial_\nu A_{\nu 2}^1(x)] \, |p\rangle$$
$$- \langle p| \, \delta(x_0)[\partial_\mu A_{\mu 1}^2(0), A_{02}^1(x)] \, |p\rangle$$
$$- iq_\nu \langle p| \, \delta(x_0)[A_{01}^2(0), A_{\nu 2}^1(x)] \, |p\rangle\} \quad (4.45)$$

The important point to note is the emergence in Eqs. (4.44) and (4.45) of the equal time commutators [terms involving $\delta(x_0)$] through the time derivatives of the form

$$\partial_0 T[A_0(x)B(0)] = \partial_0\{\theta(x_0)A_0(x)B(0) + \theta(-x_0)B(0)A_0(x)\}$$
$$= \delta(x_0)[A_0(x), B(0)] + T[\partial_0 A_0(x), B(0)] \qquad (4.46)$$

Using the invariant variables $q^2$ and $\nu$ defined by

$$\nu = -p \cdot q/M_N \qquad (4.47)$$

we shall now show that the Adler-Weisberger sum rule can be obtained from Eq. (4.45) as a low-energy theorem in the limit $q^2 \to 0$, $\nu \to 0$. In fact for a fixed $q^2 = 0$, we shall study the behavior of the various terms in Eq. (4.45) as a function of $\nu$, retaining only the zeroth and first-order dependence on $\nu$.

The last term on the right-hand side of Eq. (4.45) can be easily calculated by using the equal time-commutation relation:

$$\delta(x_0)[A_{01}^2(0), A_{\nu 2}^1(x)] = [V_{\nu 1}^1(x) - V_{\nu 2}^2(x)]\delta^4(x) \qquad (4.48)$$

In case more singular terms (Schwinger terms) involving derivatives of $\delta$ functions are present in the right-hand side of Eq. (4.48), these will only generate a polynomial in $q$ in the third term on the right-hand side of Eq. (4.45) and hence will play no role when we go to the limit $q_\mu \to 0$. Thus we find easily

$$-iq_\nu \int d^4x\, e^{iq \cdot x}\langle p|\, \delta(x_0)[A_{01}^2(0), A_{\nu 1}^2(x)]\, |p\rangle = \frac{M_N}{p_0 V}(i\nu) \qquad (4.49)$$

Let us denote the second term on the right-hand side of Eq. (4.45) by $C$

$$C = -\int d^4x\, e^{iq \cdot x}\delta(x_0)\langle p|\, [\partial_\mu A_{\mu 1}^2(0), A_{02}^1(x)]\, |p\rangle \qquad (4.50)$$

and the first term on the right-hand side of Eq. (4.45) by $R(q^2, \nu)$:

$$R(q^2, \nu) = \int d^4x\, e^{iq \cdot x}\langle p|\, T[\partial_\mu A_{\mu 1}^2(0), \partial_\nu A_{\nu 2}^1(x)]\, |p\rangle \qquad (4.51)$$

We note that $C$ will be independent of $q$, since the equal-time commutator it involves is proportional to $\delta^3(x)$. Indeed it is clear from Eq. (4.45) that we must have

$$R(0, 0) = -C \qquad (4.52)$$

This follows from the fact that in the limit $q \to 0$, the term on the left-hand side of Eq. (4.45) goes to zero since $R_{\mu\nu}$ does not have (see also below) a double pole at $q = 0$, and the last term on the right-hand side of the same equation vanishes because of Eq. (4.49). Note in passing that if $C = 0$, Eq. (4.52) yields Adler's consistency condition [Eq. (3.45)] discussed in Section III. The numerical success of the consistency condition can then be taken as evidence that $C$ must be small. Alternatively, one can see that the equal time commutator contained in $C$ involves the commutation between the divergence of $A_{\mu 1}^{\,2}$ and $A_{0 2}^{\,1}$. On most reasonable models of field theory one expects such a commutator to be proportional to $m_\pi^2$, and therefore of the second order of smallness in the extrapolation to soft pions.

Equation (4.52) implies that for the calculation of $R(q^2 = 0, \nu)$ we need only retain terms proportional to $\nu$ since the terms constant in $\nu$ will cancel away from the Eq. (4.45). Before calculating $R(0, \nu)$ let us look at the "surface" term $q_\mu q_\nu R_{\mu\nu}$ on the left-hand side of Eq. (4.45). Observe that for $\nu \approx 0, q^2 = 0$ the only possible singular contribution to $R_{\mu\nu}$ can come from the one-neutron pole. The contributions coming from multiparticle intermediate states (cuts) to $R_{\mu\nu}$ are all finite in this limit and may therefore be dropped. However, the calculation of the pole contribution in the limit $q^2 \to 0$, $\nu \to 0$ itself presents some ambiguity. This can be seen as follows. If we take the neutron (pole) mass to be the same as the proton mass, one obtains for the neutron propagator a term proportional to $1/(q^2 + 2M\nu)$ so that $q_\mu q_\nu R_{\mu\nu}$ would be of first order in $\nu$ in the limit $q \to 0$. However, if we allow for the mass difference as is the case physically, the propagator behaves like a constant, so that $\lim_{q \to 0} (q_\mu q_\nu R_{\mu\nu})$ would be of second order of smallness in $\nu$. To resolve the apparent paradox, one observes that the Born term in $R(q^2, \nu)$ which also corresponds to the neutron pole suffers from the same ambiguity. Writing

$$R(q^2, \nu) = R_{\text{Born}}(q^2, \nu) + \tilde{R}(q^2, \nu) \qquad (4.53)$$

where $\tilde{R}(q^2, \nu)$ represents the contributions coming only from multiparticle intermediate states, it is now easy to verify that the surface term $q_\mu q_\nu R_{\mu\nu}$ and the Born term $R_{\text{Born}}$ in Eq. (4.53) taken together have a unique limit. The combination $q_\mu q_\nu R_{\mu\nu} - R_{\text{Born}}$ thus does not suffer from the ambiguity mentioned above. In Section IV-3 we used the prescription of taking the limit of mass degeneracy after the soft pion limit; it is clear from the discussion here that the final results do not depend on this prescription.

A straightforward calculation from Feynman diagrams yields

$$\lim_{q \to 0} (q_\mu q_\nu R_{\mu\nu} - R_{\text{Born}}) = (iM_N/p_0 V)g_A^2(-2M + \nu) \qquad (4.54)$$

Finally, we are left with the evaluation of the continuum contribution to $R(0, \nu)$. Using the PCAC hypothesis as given in Eq. (3.1), we can rewrite Eq. (4.51) as

$$R(q^2, \nu) = \frac{C_\pi^2}{2} \int d^4x \, e^{-iq \cdot x} \langle p| \, T[\pi_1^2(x), \pi_2^1(0)] \, |p\rangle \qquad (4.55)$$

By invariance arguments the spinor dependence on the right-hand side of Eq. (4.55) can only be in the form $\bar{u}(p)u(p)$ which by the normalization condition is unity. We may thus write

$$R(q^2, \nu) = (M_N/p_0 V)S(q^2, \nu)\bar{u}(p)u(p) = (M_N/p_0 V)S(q^2, \nu) \qquad (4.56)$$

Note now that the right-hand side of Eq. (4.55) is related to the forward scattering

$$\pi^-(q) + p(p) \to \pi^-(q) + p(p) \qquad (4.57)$$

The scattering amplitude for the process (4.57) is given by

$$T_p^{\pi^-}(\nu) = i \int d^4x \, e^{-iq \cdot x}(q^2 + M_\pi^2)^2 \langle p| \, T[\pi_1^2(x), \pi_2^1(0)] \, |p\rangle \qquad (4.58)$$

which by invariance arguments may be written as before in terms of the invariant scattering amplitude denoted by $F(\nu)$:

$$T_p^{\pi^-}(\nu) = (M_N/p_0 V)F_p^{\pi^-}(\nu, q^2) \qquad (4.59)$$

From Eqs. (4.55), (4.56), (4.58), and (4.59) we obtain the relation

$$S(q^2, \nu) = \frac{C_\pi^2}{2i} \frac{F_p^{\pi^-}(\nu, q^2)}{(q^2 + M_\pi^2)^2} \qquad (4.60)$$

so that for $q^2 = 0$, we get

$$R(0, \nu) = (M_N/p_0 V)(1/2i)(C_\pi^2/M_\pi^4)F_p^{\pi^-}(\nu) \qquad (4.61)$$

where $F_p^{\pi^-}(\nu)$ now describes the scattering of a "zero mass" pion. In general $F(\nu)$ contains terms even ($F^+$) and odd ($F^-$) under crossing symmetry $\nu \to -\nu$

$$F_p^{\pi^-}(\nu) = F^+(\nu) + F^-(\nu) \qquad (4.62)$$

Then

$$F_p^{\pi^+}(\nu) = F^+(\nu) - F^-(\nu) \qquad (4.63)$$

Since we are interested only in terms in Eq. (4.61) which are linear in $v$, $F^+(v)$ will not contribute. We now assume that $F^-(v)$ satisfies an unsubtracted dispersion relation:

$$F^-(v) = F_{\text{Born}}^-(v) + (1/\pi) \int dv' \operatorname{Im} F^-(v') \left( \frac{1}{v' - v} - \frac{1}{v' + v} \right) \quad (4.64)$$

Writing

$$R(0, v) = R^+(0, v) + R^-(0, v) \quad (4.65)$$

we obtain from Eqs. (4.61) and (4.64) the dispersion representation

$$\tilde{R}^-(0, v) = \frac{M_N}{p_0 V} \frac{1}{\pi i} \frac{C_\pi^2}{M_\pi^4} v \int \frac{dv'}{v'^2 - v^2} \operatorname{Im} F^-(v') \quad (4.66)$$

where $\tilde{R}$ has been defined in Eq. (4.53). Now from the optical theorem

$$\operatorname{Im} F^-(v) \equiv \tfrac{1}{2}[\operatorname{Im} F_p^{\pi^-}(v) - \operatorname{Im} F_p^{\pi^+}(v)] = (k/2)[\sigma_p^{\pi^-}(v, 0) - \sigma_p^{\pi^+}(v, 0)] \quad (4.67)$$

where $\sigma_p^{\pi^\pm}$ represents the total $\pi^+ p$ cross sections, and $k$ is the magnitude of the pion three-momentum in the laboratory frame so that $k = (v^2 - M^2)^{1/2}$. Thus, one finally obtains

$$\tilde{R}^-(0, v) = \frac{M_N}{p_0 V} \frac{C_\pi^2}{M_\pi^4} \frac{1}{2\pi i} v \int \frac{dv'}{v'^2 - v^2} k^1[\sigma_p^{\pi^-}(v', 0) - \sigma_p^{\pi^+}(v', 0)] \quad (4.68)$$

Using now Eqs. (4.49), (4.54), (4.65), and (4.68) in the identity Eq. (4.45) and equating terms linear in $v$, one obtains the Adler-Weisberger sum rule

$$g_A^2 = 1 - \frac{C_\pi^2}{2M_\pi^4} \frac{1}{\pi} \int_{M_\pi}^\infty \frac{k\,dv}{v^2} [\sigma_p^{\pi^-}(v,0) - \sigma_p^{\pi^+}(v, 0)] \quad (4.69)$$

If we eliminate $C_\pi$ by the relation Eq. (3.8), we obtain the sum-rule in the usual form

$$\frac{1}{g_A^2} = 1 + \frac{2M_N^2}{\pi G_{NN\pi}^2 K_{NN\pi}^2(0)} \int_{M_\pi}^\infty \frac{k\,dv}{v^2} [\sigma_p^{\pi^-}(v, 0) - \sigma_p^{\pi^+}(v, 0)] \quad (4.70)$$

Since for a soft pion $k \to v$, the sum rule given by Eq. (4.70) is identical to the form of Eq. (4.42). Note that the cross sections in the sum rule as we have derived refer to the case of a "zero-mass" pion. However, if one had chosen to use the PCAC as a pole-dominance hypothesis (see Sect.

III), one would obtain in the sum rule the physical cross sections instead.[18] A detailed derivation of this result has been given by Weisberger.[14e]

## 5. Numerical Results

Using the pion–nucleon total cross sections measured up to 5 BeV/c, and using the asymptotic form $\sigma_p^{\pi^-}(\nu) - \sigma_p^{\pi^+}(\nu) = 7.73$ mb $\times [k/(\text{BeV}/c)]^{-0.7}$ the sum rule for $g_A$ has been evaluated by Adler and Weisberger. The convergence of the sum rule is, of course, assured by the Pomeranchuk theorem. Weisberger has employed the form where no off-shell correction for the pion is required and the approximation is in neglecting the branch cuts and he obtains

$$|g_A| = 1.15 \tag{4.71}$$

In this evaluation $f_\pi$ from the Goldberger-Treiman relation has been used. If instead $f_\pi$ is used from the experimental decay rate of the pion, then

$$|g_A| = 1.21 \tag{4.72}$$

Adler has used the form of the sum rule in Eq. (4.24), and has attempted to make off-mass shell corrections based on some simple models for the scattering amplitudes. His evaluations give

$$|g_A| = 1.24 \tag{4.73}$$

In view of the approximations employed, the above values of $|g_A|$ must be considered to be in excellent agreement with the recent experimental value[19]

$$g_A = 1.18 \pm 0.025 \tag{4.74}$$

## V. The Semileptonic Decays of Hadrons

### 1. Introduction

In this section we shall describe some applications of the methods developed in the last two sections to the theory of semileptonic decays. The presently accepted form of the interaction responsible for these decays is the current–current type[20]:

$$H_w = \frac{G}{\sqrt{2}} J_\lambda^* l_\lambda + \text{h.c.} \tag{5.1}$$

where $l_\lambda$ stands for the leptonic current density

$$l_\lambda = i\bar{\nu}_{(e)}\gamma_\lambda(1 + \gamma_5)e + i\bar{\nu}_{(\mu)}\gamma_\lambda(1 + \gamma_5)\mu \tag{5.2}$$

and $J_\lambda$ is the hadronic current density

$$J_\lambda = \cos\theta_v V_{\lambda 1}^2 + \sin\theta_v V_{\lambda 1}^2 + \cos\theta_A A_{\lambda 1}^2 + \sin\theta_A A_{\lambda 1}^3 \tag{5.3}$$

In writing Eq. (5.3) we follow Cabibbo,[21] incorporating, however, the possibility that the Cabibbo angle $\theta$ may be different for the vector and axial-vector parts of the current. In this form of the theory, the weak coupling constant $G$, which is measured in the purely leptonic process of muon decay, appears modified by a factor $\cos\theta$ for the hypercharge preserving and the factor $\sin\theta$ for the hypercharge-changing semi-leptonic decays.

The crucial question which one has to examine immediately is the meaning of the relative strengths specified above in terms of the relative strengths of the various currents. The relative strengths of the coupling parameters get unambiguously defined in the following manner as proposed by Gell-Mann. The vector strangeness-preserving current densities $V_{\mu 2}^1$ and $V_{\mu 1}^2$ have their scales set by their identification as the charge-changing members of the isovector part of the electromagnetic current density of the hadrons denoted by $\frac{1}{2}(V_{\mu 1}^1 - V_{\mu 2}^2)$. The corresponding "charges" $I_+ = v_1^2, I_- = v_2^1$, and $I_3 = \frac{1}{2}(v_1^1 - v_2^2)$ satisfy, under equal time commutation, the algebra of the isospin group $SU_2(I)$. To the extent that the strong interactions are $SU_2(I)$ invariant ("charge independent") these three vector charges are constant in time and the corresponding vector-current densities are conserved (CVC) and the vector coupling constant for $\beta$ decay is

$$G_V = G \cos\theta_V \tag{5.4}$$

The scales of the hypercharge-changing vector current densities $V_{\mu 1}^3, V_{\mu 3}^1$ are now set by the assumption that their "charges" $v_1^3, v_3^1$ are the hyper-charge- and charge-changing generators of the $SU(3)$ group containing the above $SU_2(I)$ subgroup generated by the vector "charges" $v_1^2, v_2^1$, $\frac{1}{2}(v_1^1 - v_2^2)$ (see Sect. II for the commutation relations and identification with the physical quantum numbers). If the strong interactions are invariant under the $SU(3)$ group so generated, all the above vector "charges" will commute with the strong Hamiltonian and will thus be constant in time in the absence of any other interactions. The vector current densities $V_{\mu b}^{a}$ ($a, b = 1, 2, 3$) will then form an octet of conserved current densities. However, the $SU(3)$ symmetry is only approximate, and hence the current densities $V_{\mu 1}^{3}$, $V_{\mu 3}^{1}$ are *not* conserved, so that the hypercharge-changing semileptonic decay constant gets a renormalization effect changing its value from $G \sin \theta_V$. These operators have, however, the theorem of Ademollo and Gatto,[22] which states that this renormalization effect is of only the second order in the $SU_3$ symmetry breaking, and hence, presumably small. We shall give below a simple proof of this theorem following the Fubini-Furlan method. As the next step, the setting of scales of the axial-vector current densities is provided by the proposal of Gell-Mann[1] that the "axial charges" $a_b^a(t)$ along with the vector charges $v_b^a(t)$ generate under equal-time commutation the algebra of the chiral $SU_3 \otimes SU_3$ group, the commutation relations being the ones noted in Eq. (2.6). However, since the $SU_3 \otimes SU_3$ group is not a good symmetry,[1,23] the axial-vector current densities are *not* conserved, so that the axial-vector decay constants are changed by sizable strong interaction renormalization effects from the values $G \cos \theta_A$ and $G \sin \theta_A$. The renormalization of the hypercharge-preserving axial-vector constant has been calculated by Adler[3a] and Weisberger[3b] in the manner already discussed in Section IV. The calculation of the renormalization of the decay constants of hypercharge-changing axial-vector baryon decays has also been shown by various authors[24] and will be discussed below. We shall also discuss the various applications to the leptonic decays of the $K$ meson.

## 2. Renormalization of the Vector Decay Constants and the Ademollo-Gatto Theorem

If the $SU(3)$ symmetry were exact, the vector currents would be conserved, and the vector charges would be constant in time. However, in the presence of the $SU(3)$ breaking, which we treat *perturbatively*, this is no longer the case. Let the Hamiltonian, in the absence of the weak and the electromagnetic interactions, be written as

$$H = H_s + \lambda H_B \tag{5.6}$$

where $H_s$ is the $SU(3)$ symmetric part and $\lambda H_B$ is the part that breaks the symmetry down to the $SU_2(I) \otimes U_1(Y)$ level with a strength parameter $\lambda$. Then a matrix element of, for instance, the strangeness-changing vector charge $v_1^3(t)$ between two eigenstates $a$ and $b$ of $H$ can be written as

$$\langle b|\, v_1^3(t)\, |a\rangle = \frac{\langle b|\, [H, v_1^3(t)]\, |a\rangle}{E_b - E_a}$$

$$= \frac{\langle b|\, [H_s(t) + \lambda H_B(t), v_1^3(t)]\, |a\rangle}{E_b - E_a}$$

$$= \frac{\lambda \langle b|\, [H_B(t), v_1^3]\, |a\rangle}{E_b - E_a} \tag{5.7}$$

where $E_b$ and $E_a$ are the energy eigenvalues of the states $a$ and $b$, respectively. If the states $|a\rangle$ and $|b\rangle$ are single-particle states belonging to the same irreducible representation in the $SU(3)$ symmetry limit $\lambda \rightarrow 0$ (and $E_b \rightarrow E_a$) then in the broken symmetry situation the energy denominator $(E_b - E_a)$ is of the first order in $\lambda$ and so the matrix element $\langle b|\, v_1^3(t)\, |a\rangle$ is of the zeroth order in $\lambda$. If, on the other hand, the state $|b\rangle$ does *not* belong to the same irreducible representation as the state $|a\rangle$ in the symmetry limit, then the energy denominator $(E_b - E_a)$ is zero order in $\lambda$ and hence the matrix element $\langle b|\, v_1^3(t)\, |a\rangle$ is first order in $\lambda$.

Consider now the matrix element of the equal time commutator (see Sect. II-6)

$$[v_1^3(t), v_3^1(t)] = v_1^1 - v_3^3 = Q + Y \tag{5.8}$$

between the single-particle state $|a\rangle$ and insert a complete set of states on the left-hand side:

$$\sum_n [\langle a|\, v_1^3(t)\, |n\rangle\langle n|\, v_3^1(t)\, |a\rangle - \langle a|\, v_3^1(t)\, |n\rangle\langle n|\, v_1^3(t)\, |a\rangle] = \langle a|\, Q + Y|a\rangle \tag{5.9}$$

From the foregoing discussion it is clear that when $|n\rangle$ is a single particle intermediate state belonging to the same irreducible representation as $|a\rangle$ in the $SU_3$ limit, then in the presence of the symmetry breaking, its contribution to the left-hand side of Eq. (5.9) is first order. The contribution of all the *other* possible states $|n\rangle$ which is zero in the symmetry limit, is in the presence of the symmetry breaking of order $\lambda^2$. In the limit of *infinite* momentum of the state $a$, the former contribution (often called the "single-particle contribution" or the "pole contribution") is found to be exactly[13] $SU_3$ symmetry result, so that the correction to the symmetric result, given by the latter contribution (also called the "continuum" contribution) is then of only the *second order* in $\lambda$. This then is a simple way of rederiving the Ademollo-Gatto theorem.[22]

The detailed calculation of the $SU_3$ symmetry-breaking corrections to the strangeness-changing leptonic vector-decay constants can be carried through by the methods discussed in the last section. A calculation of this type has been done by Furlan, Lannoy, Rossetti, and Segre.[14b] A modified version following the general dispersion theoretic method discussed in Section IV will be discussed here. We define the amplitude in analogy with Eq. (4.43)

$$R_{\mu\nu} = \int d^4x \, e^{-iqx} \langle a(p)| \, T[V_{\mu1}^3(x), V_{\nu3}^1(0)] \, |a(p)\rangle \qquad (5.10)$$

and analogous to Eq. (4.45), we obtain

$$q_\mu q_\nu R_{\mu\nu} = \int d^4x \, e^{iqx} \{\langle a(p)| \, T[\partial_\mu V_{\mu1}^3(0), \partial_\nu V_{\nu3}^1(x)] \, |a(p)\rangle$$
$$- \langle a(p)| \, \delta(x_0)[\partial_\mu V_{\mu1}^3(0), V_{03}^1(x)] \, |a(p)\rangle$$
$$- iq_\nu \langle a(p)| \, \delta(x_0)[(V_0)_1^3(0), (V_\nu)_3^1(x)] \, |a(p)\rangle\} \qquad (5.11)$$

In the $SU(3)$ symmetry limit the divergences of the vector-current-densities in the first two terms on the right-hand side of Eq. (5.11) vanish. We may use now the commutation relation

$$\delta(x_0)[V_{01}^3(0), V_{\nu3}^1(x)] = \delta^4(x)[V_{\nu1}^1(x) - V_{\nu3}^3(x)] + \cdots \qquad (5.12)$$

where we have dropped the possible Schwinger terms as we shall work in the limit $q_\mu \to 0$. Then

$$\lim_{q\to0} q_\mu q_\nu R_{\mu\nu} = \lim_{q\to0} (-i)q_\nu \langle a(p)| \, V_{\nu1}^1(0) - V_{\nu3}^3(0) \, |a(p)\rangle$$

Let us be specific and consider the state $|a(p)\rangle$ to be a positive pion state $|\pi^+(p)\rangle$; then we define

$$\langle \pi^+(p')| \, V_{\nu1}^1(0) \, |\pi^+(p)\rangle = (1/\sqrt{4p_0'p_0V^2})(p + p')_\nu f_+^\pi(t) \qquad (5.13)$$

where $t = (p - p')^2$ and only one form factor $f_+$ enters since the electromagnetic current density $V_{\nu1}^1$ is conserved. Also, since the charge of the $\pi^+$ is $+1$, we may normalize $f_+(t)$ through the following steps:

$$\delta^3(\mathbf{p}' - \mathbf{p}) = \langle \pi^+(p')| \, Q = v_1^1(0) \, |\pi^+(p)\rangle$$
$$= \langle \pi^+(p')| \, -i \int_{x_0=0} d^3x V_{41}^1(x) \, |\pi^+(p)\rangle = f_+^\pi(0)\delta^3(\mathbf{p} - \mathbf{p}')$$

so that

$$f_+^\pi(0) = 1$$

The matrix element of $V_{v3}^3$ need not be considered here since the pion has zero value for the hypercharge $Y = -v_3^3$.

The left-hand side of Eq. (5.13) will have a nonzero contribution only, from an intermediate-state degenerate with the initial pion. The corresponding Born contribution to $R_{\mu v}$ from a $\bar{K}^0$ state may be calculated from the Feynmen diagram of Figure 2. We may define the matrix elements of the currents by:

$$\langle \pi^+(p')| \, V_{\mu\bar{1}}^3(0) \, |\bar{K}^0(p)\rangle$$

$$= \frac{1}{\sqrt{4p_0 p_0' V^2}} [f_+(t)(p + p')_\mu + f_-(t)(p - p')_\mu] \qquad (5.14)$$

We shall put $q^2 = 0$ and consider the variable $\nu = -(p \cdot q/M_\pi)$ as approaching zero. Then Eq. (5.13) gives, on comparing terms of order $\nu$, the result:

$$\frac{1}{M_K^2 - M_\pi^2 + 2M_\pi \nu} \{[f_+(0)]^2 (2M_\pi \nu)^2\} = f_+^\pi(0)(2M_\pi \nu) \qquad (5.15)$$

Note that since we are in the $SU_3$ limit, we must *first* take $M_K \to M_\pi$ and then $\nu \to 0$. We thus find the $SU(3)$ symmetry result

$$|f_+(0)|^2 = f_+^\pi(0) = 1 \qquad (5.16)$$

When we consider the situation of the broken $SU(3)$ symmetry, the one that really interests us here, then $M_\pi \neq M_K$ and to the first order in $\nu$ the left-hand side of Eq. (5.15) must be taken as vanishing. The amusing fact now is that since $\partial_\mu V_{\mu 1}^3 \neq 0$ any more, we must look for the single-particle contribution in the first term on the right-hand side of Eq. (5.11)

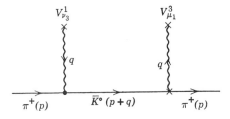

FIGURE 2

(we shall denote it by $R$) in the $\nu \to 0$ limit for $q^2 = 0$. It is this term that now gives the $SU(3)$ result. We find by calculation analogous to that above and remembering that from Eq. (5.14):

$$\langle \pi^+(p^1)| \; \partial_\mu V_{\mu1}^3(0) \; |\bar{K}^0(p)\rangle = \frac{i}{\sqrt{4p_0 p_0^1 V^2}} \, [f_+(t)(M_\pi^2 - M_k^2) + f_-(t)t]$$

the result

$$R^{\text{Born}} \, (\nu, q^2 = 0)$$

$$= \frac{-i}{2p_0 V} \, [f_+(0)]^2 (M_K^2 - M_\pi^2)^2 \, \frac{1}{M_K^2 - M_\pi^2 - 2M_\pi \nu}$$

$$= \frac{-i}{2p_0 V} \, [f_+(0)]^2 (M_K^2 - M_\pi^2) \left[ 1 + \frac{2M_\pi \nu}{M_K^2 - M_\pi^2} + O(\nu^2) \right] \qquad (5.17)$$

As pointed out in Section IV, the $\nu$ independent term of $R$ cancels against the second term on the right-hand side of Eq. (5.11). Comparing terms of order $\nu$ then we find

$$0 = -[f_+(0)]^2 2M_\pi \nu + \cdots + f_+^\pi(0) 2M_\pi \nu \qquad (5.18)$$

where the dots represent the multiparticle contributions to $R(\nu, 0)$ to order $\nu$. The point to note is that just retaining only the single-particle term in $R$, we again obtain the result of Eq. (5.16) that was obtained in the $SU(3)$ symmetry limit. Thus, even in the broken-symmetry situation we find that in the $q \to 0$ limit (or in the terminology of Sect. IV in the $p_z \to \infty$ limit) the single-particle contribution gives us the symmetry result, and the corrections due to the symmetry breaking which are of the second order in the symmetry-breaking parameter are given by the "multiparticle" or the continuum contribution.

The continuum contributions in the approximation of retaining only the two particle states of the lowest mass allowed, namely one pseudoscalar $(P)$ and one vector $(V)$ meson, have been estimated by Furlan et al.[14b] The contributions to $R$ are estimated by taking for the $\pi \to PV$ matrix elements of the divergence $\partial_\mu V_{\mu3}^1$ the perturbation-theoretic estimates corresponding to the Feynman diagrams of Figure 3. If $H_B(x)$ is the symmetry-breaking Hamiltonian density then we may take

$$\partial_\mu (V_\mu(x)_b^a = i[H_B(x), v_b^a(x_0)] \qquad (5.19)$$

For the above calculation these authors took the effective symmetry breaking as in the Gell-Mann–Okubo octet mass splitting and, for

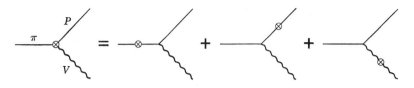

simplicity, considered its effect only on the single-particle lines of the diagram of Figure 3 as indicated by the crosses. They obtained the result:

$$|f_+(0)|^2/[f_+(0)]_{SU_3} \approx 1.067 \qquad (5.20)$$

Taking the experimental value[25] of $\sin \theta_V = 0.218 \pm 0.015$ they thus obtained for the renormalized value of $\sin \theta_V$ entering the $K_{l3}$ decay the value:

$$\sin \theta_V = (\sin \theta_V)_{\exp} \sqrt{1.067} = 0.223 \pm 0.015$$
$$\cos \theta_V = 0.975 + 0.003 \qquad (5.21)$$

With this value of $\cos \theta_V$, the comparison of the vector constants of the $\mu$ decay and the $\beta$ decay may be stated as follows:

$$G_v^\mu = (0.997 \pm 0.006)G_v^\beta \qquad (5.22)$$

This calculation is, of course, quite rough chiefly because of the neglect of the other possible intermediate states. The result is quite consistent with universality.

### 3. Renormalization of the Axial-Vector Decay Constants

The axial-vector currents, both strangeness-preserving and strangeness-changing, are nonconserved currents except in the limit of the apparently very badly broken chiral $SU_3 \otimes SU_3$ symmetry. One therefore expects large, strong interaction renormalization effects for the axial-vector decay constants. Experimentally, the neutron $\beta$-decay axial-vector coupling constant is however, found to be only about 1.2 times the vector coupling constant. This has led to the idea of the partially conserved axial-vector currents (PCAC) already discussed in Section III. Using PCAC along with the equal time commutator

$$[a_1^2(t), a_2^1(t)] = v_1^1 - v_2^2 = 2I_3 \qquad (5.25)$$

Adler and Weisberger[3] have made the successful calculation of the renormalization of the strangeness-preserving $\beta$-decay axial-vector coupling constant. This calculation has already been discussed in detail in Section IV. Similar calculations[24] of the renormalization of the strangeness-changing axial-vector decay constants will be discussed now. Here the presumably much more approximate kaon PCAC for the strangeness-changing axial-vector currents is employed in conjunction with the equal-time commutators:

$$[a_1^3(t), a_3^1(t)] = v_1^1 - v_3^3 = Q + Y \tag{5.26}$$

$$[a_2^3(t), a_3^2(t)] = v_2^2 - v_3^3 = \tfrac{3}{2}Y - I_3 \tag{5.27}$$

Consider, for example, the matrix element of Eq. (5.26) between single proton states and obtain the sum rule by the Fubini-Furlan-Adler-Weisberger method discussed in Section IV. The single particle intermediate states that must be separated from the continuum states are those of the $\Sigma^0$ and the $\Lambda^0$. The zero-momentum transfer matrix elements of the axial charges between the ("infinite momentum") states of the proton and of the $\Sigma^0$ and the $\Lambda$ introduce the axial-vector renormalization constants $g_A(\Sigma^0 \to p)$ and $q_A(\Lambda \to p)$

$$\langle p|\, A_{\mu 1}^3(0)\, |\Sigma^0\rangle = \sqrt{\frac{M_p M_\Sigma}{E_p E_\Sigma V^2}}\ \bar{u}_p[g_A(\Sigma^0 \to p)i\gamma_\mu\gamma_5]u_\Sigma \tag{5.28}$$

$$\langle p|\, A_{\mu 1}^3(0)\, |\Lambda\rangle = \sqrt{\frac{M_p M_\Lambda}{E_p E_\Lambda V^2}}\ \bar{u}_p[g_A(\Lambda \to p)i\gamma_\mu\gamma_5]u_\Lambda \tag{5.29}$$

The same constants also appear in the generalization of the Goldberger-Treiman relation with the kaon PCAC (of Sect. III). The sum rule, obtained in complete analogy with the Adler-Weisberger sum rule, reads as follows:

$$2 = [g_A(\Lambda \to p)]^2 + [g_A(\Sigma^0 \to p)]^2 + 2\left(\frac{C_K}{M_K^2}\right)^2 \frac{1}{\pi}$$
$$\times \int_{M_\pi + M_\Lambda}^{\infty} \frac{W dW}{W^2 - M_N^2}\, [\sigma_p^{K^-}(W, 0) - \sigma_p^{K^+}(W, 0)] \tag{5.30}$$

The notation is in obvious analogy with that introduced in Section IV. Here $\sigma_p^{K^-}(W, 0)$ stands, for example, for the total $K^-$-$p$ cross-section for a center of mass energy $W$ and with zero mass for the $K^-$. In the integral on the right of Eq. (5.30), the range $M\pi + M_\Lambda < W < M_k + M_N$ is below the threshold of $K^-p$ and is unphysical. In this region we have used $\sigma_p^K$ as a symbolic notation for $-(1/W^2 - M^2)\,\mathrm{Im}\, T(K^-p, 0)$, where $T(K^-p, 0)$ is the invariant amplitude for the forward $\bar{K}p$ scattering. Similarly, if we take the matrix element of Eq. (5.26) between single neutron states and that of Eq. (5.27) between single proton states, we can obtain the sum rules:

$$1 = [\Sigma g_A(^- \rightarrow n)]^2 + 2 \left(\frac{C_K}{M_K^2}\right)^2 \frac{1}{\pi}$$

$$\times \int_{M_\pi + M_\Lambda}^\infty \frac{W dW}{W^2 - M_N^2} [\sigma_n^{K^-}(W, 0) - \sigma_n^{K^+}(W, 0)] \qquad (5.31)$$

$$1 = [g_A(\Sigma^+ \rightarrow p)]^2 + 2 \left(\frac{C_K}{M_K^2}\right)^2 \frac{1}{\pi}$$

$$\times \int_{M_\pi + M_\Lambda}^\infty \frac{W dW}{W^2 - M_N^2} [\sigma_p^{\bar{K^0}}(W, 0) - \sigma_p^{K^0}(W, 0)] \qquad (5.32)$$

The evaluation of sum rules of Eqs. (5.30)–(5.32) is less reliable than the A-W sum rule. The reasons are, first, the extra complication due to the presence of the unphysical continuum region $M_\pi + M_\Lambda < W < M_K + M_N$ for the $\bar{K}N$ channel, second, the lack of a precise knowledge of the strong interaction coupling constants $G_{KN\Lambda}$ and $G_{KN\Sigma}$ entering through $C_K$, and third, the intrinsically more approximate nature of the kaon PCAC. The authors of ref. 24, therefore, have slightly different numerical evaluations of the various integrals in these sum rules. Their general results, however, agree.

The conclusions reached from these studies may be stated as follows. First, it is clear that the renormalizations are not so drastic as to allow the interpretation of the Cabibbo suppression factor $\sin \theta_A$ as a strong interaction renormalization effect of the strangeness-changing axial-vector coupling constants. Further, if one assumes that even though the $SU(3)$ symmetry is broken, the axial-vector currents and the single baryon states remain approximately as octets, and that the same $d/f$ ratio obtains for the pseudoscalar meson–baryon couplings as for the axial-vector currents (as implied by PCAC), then through a simultaneous use of all the sum rules of Eqs. (5.30)–(5.32), one can obtain an approximate value for $d/f$. The values found range from 1.7 to 3. The picture thus seems quite consistent with the Cabibbo theory. It is interesting that the kaon PCAC works so well here. This is perhaps due to the cancellation in the terms involving the integrals in the sum rules of the correction required in the numerator for the zero-mass cross sections and in the denominator due to the zero-momentum-transfer kaon–baryon coupling form factors. In any case, the conclusions here cannot be taken too literally in the quantitative sense.

## 4. The $K_{l3}$ Decays

A very interesting and early application of the algebra of currents and the soft-pion technique was made in relating the $K_{l3}$ and $K_{l2}$ form factors.[26] To introduce the relevant definitions, we note that the amplitude for the decay $K^+ \rightarrow \pi^0 l^+ \nu_l$ involves the matrix element of the strangeness-changing vector current density $V_{\mu 3}^1$:

$$\langle \pi^0(q)| \, V_{\mu 3}^1(0) \, |K^+(p)\rangle$$

$$= \frac{1}{\sqrt{4q_0 p_0 V^2}} [F_+(t)(p + q)_\mu + F_-(t)(p - q)_\mu] \qquad (5.33)$$

where the form factors $F_+$ and $F_-$ are (real, assuming $T$ invariance) invariant functions of $t = -(p - q)^2$. The $K^+ \rightarrow l^+ \nu_l$ decay, on the other hand, involves the matrix element of the axial-vector current density $A_{\mu 3}^1$:

$$\langle 0| \, A_{\mu 3}^1 \, |K^+(p)\rangle = \frac{i}{\sqrt{2p_0 V}} f_K p_\mu \qquad (5.34)$$

Here the decay constant $f_K$ is related to constant $C_K$ for the kaon PCAC (see Sect. III) by

$$f_K = C_K/M_K^2 \qquad (5.35)$$

Consider now the matrix element $\langle \pi^0(q)| \, v_3^1(0) \, |K^+(p)\rangle$, and contract the $\pi^0$ by the LSZ technique (see Appendix III):

$$\langle \pi^0(q)| \, v_3^1(0) \, |K^+(p)\rangle = i \int d^4x \, \frac{e^{-iq \cdot x}}{\sqrt{2q_0 V}} (q^2 + M_\pi^2)$$

$$\times \langle 0| \, \theta(x_0)[\pi^0(x), v_3^1(0)] \, |K^+(p)\rangle \qquad (5.36)$$

Using PCAC:

$$\partial_\mu(A_{\mu 1}^1 - A_{\mu 2}^2) = C_\pi \pi^0 \qquad (5.37)$$

and taking the soft-pion limit $q \rightarrow 0$ in the sense discussed in Section IV-2, we obtain

$$\lim_{q \to 0} \sqrt{2q_0 V} \, \langle \pi^0(q)| \, v_3^1(0) \, |K^+(p)\rangle$$

$$= -i \frac{M_\pi^2}{C_\pi} \langle 0| \, a_1^1(0) - a_2^2(0), v_3^1(0)] \, |K^+(p)\rangle$$

$$= i \frac{M_\pi^2}{C_\pi} \langle 0| \, a_3^1(0) \, |K^+(p)\rangle \qquad (5.38)$$

Using Eqs. (5.33) and (5.34) along with the definitions of Eqs. (2.3) and (2.4) we obtain from Eq. (5.38):

$$F_+(M_K^2) + F_-(M_K^2) = (M_\pi^2/C_\pi)f_K \qquad (5.39)$$

If we use $f_K \approx f_\pi \approx M_\pi$ (see Sect. III), and use for $|F_+(0)| =$ the $SU(3)$ symmetry value $1/\sqrt{2}$ (expected to be good in view of the Ademollo-Gatto theorem) and assume that $F_+$ and $F_-$ are constants, then we find for $\xi \equiv F_-/F_+$

$$|1 + \xi| \simeq 1 \qquad (5.40)$$

so that $\xi \approx 0$. Actually, the form factors may vary with $t$ and at the unphysical value $M_K^2$ of this variable, they may be quite different from those at $t = 0$.

Further extensions and modifications of the method outlined above with applications to the study of the $K_{l3}$ form factors, the $SU_3$ breaking effects on these form factors and the attendant renormalization of the Cabibbo angle $\theta_A$ have been made by many authors.[27] As an illustration we give below a treatment following a work of Furlan and Renner.[27] This will also serve to illustrate the use of PCAC in the form of "pole dominance." Consider the following equal-time commutator, the integrated form of which was used in obtaining Eq. (5.38)

$$\{a_1^{1-2}(0), [V_\mu(0)]_3^1\} = -[A_\mu(0)]_3^1 \qquad (5.39)$$

Taking the matrix element of this between the states $|K^+(p)\rangle$ and $|0\rangle$ and following the standard steps for converting the axial charges into integrals involving the corresponding divergences, we have

$$if_K p_\mu = \lim_{q \to 0} \sqrt{2p_0 V} \int d^4x\, e^{-iqx}\theta(x_0) \langle 0| \{\partial_\mu[A_\mu(x)_1^{1-2}], V_\mu(0)_3^1\} |K^+(p)\rangle$$
$$= \lim_{q \to 0} F_\mu(q \cdot p) \qquad (5.40)$$

Let us introduce the variable, $\nu = -p \cdot q/M_K$, $q^2$, and decompose $F_\mu$ as follows:

$$F_\mu(q^2, \nu) = q_\mu B(q^2, \nu) + p_\mu A(q^2, \nu) \qquad (5.41)$$

Assume that $A$ satisfies an unsubtracted dispersion relation in the variable $\nu$ for fixed $q^2$. We set $q^2 = 0$ and drop it from the arguments. Then from Eq. (5.40) we have

$$if_K = A(\nu = 0) = \frac{1}{\pi} \int \frac{\text{Abs } A(\nu')}{\nu'}\, d\nu' \qquad (5.42)$$

where the absorptive part of $A(\nu)$ is obtained by finding the terms containing $p_\mu$ in

$$\frac{i}{2}(2\pi)^4\sqrt{2p_0V}\sum_n \langle 0|\ [V_\mu(0)]_3^1\ |n\rangle\langle n|\ \partial_\mu A_{\mu 1}^{1-\frac{2}{3}}(0)\ |K^+(p)\rangle$$
$$\times\ \delta^4(p_n - p + q) \qquad (5.43)$$

Clearly the intermediate states $|n\rangle$ must have the quantum numbers $J^p = 1^-, 0^+$ and $Y = +1, I = \frac{1}{2}, I_3 = +\frac{1}{2}$. The scalar states ($J^p = 0^+$) will be denoted by $S$. For these we write:

$$\langle 0|\ V_\mu(0)_1^3\ |S(p)\rangle = \frac{1}{\sqrt{2p_{n0}V}}\ \phi_S(p_n)_\mu \qquad (5.44)$$

We shall now use PCAC in the pole-dominance form, which in the present context means that the matrix element of $\partial_\mu A_{\mu 1}^{1-\frac{2}{2}}$ between states $|S\rangle$ and $|K^+\rangle$ may be dispersed in the momentum transfer variable $q^2$ and only the $\pi^0$ pole retained, so that

$$\langle S(p - q)|\ \partial_\mu A_{\mu 1}^{1-\frac{2}{2}}(0)\ |K^+(p)\rangle$$
$$= \frac{\sqrt{2q_0V}\ \langle 0|\ \partial_\mu A_{\mu 1}^{1-\frac{2}{2}}(0)\ |\pi^0(q)\rangle\langle S(p - q)|\ j_{\pi 0}(0)\ |K^+(p)\rangle}{q^2 + M_\pi^2}$$
$$= \frac{\sqrt{2}\ M_\pi^2 f_\pi G(K^+ \to \pi^0 S)(4p_0 S_0 V^2)^{-1/2}}{q^2 + M_\pi^2} \qquad (5.45)$$

Here $G(K^+ \to \pi^0 S)$ is the indicated strong coupling constant (actually including the pionic form factor) defined by

$$\langle S|\ j_{\pi 0}(0)\ |K^+(p)\rangle = \frac{1}{\sqrt{4p_0 S_0 V^2}}\ G(K^+ \to \pi^0 S) \qquad (5.46)$$

We define similarly for the vector states $V$ with polarization $\varepsilon$

$$\langle 0|\ V_\mu(0)_3^1\ |V(\varepsilon, p_n)\rangle = \frac{i}{\sqrt{2p_{n0}V}}\ \varepsilon_\mu \phi_V \qquad (5.44.1)$$

$$\langle V(p_n)|\ \partial_\mu A_{\mu 1}^{1-\frac{2}{2}}(0)\ |K^+(p)\rangle$$
$$= \frac{i\sqrt{2}\ M_\pi^2 f_\pi G(K^+ \to \pi^0 V)\varepsilon^* \cdot (p - p_n)}{(q^2 + M_\pi^2)\sqrt{4p_{n0}p_0 V^2}} \qquad (5.44.2)$$

where we have put

$$\langle V(\varepsilon, p_n)|\ j_{\pi 0}(0)\ |K^+(p)\rangle = \frac{iG(K^+ \to \pi^0 V)\varepsilon^* \cdot (p - p_n)}{\sqrt{4p_{n0}p_0 V^2}} \qquad (5.47)$$

Putting everything together we finally get for the sum rule of Eq. (5.42):

$$\frac{f_K}{f_\pi} = -\sqrt{2} \int \frac{\rho_v(M^2)}{2M^2} \phi_v(M^2)G(K^+ \to \pi^0 V; M^2) \, dM^2$$

$$+ \sqrt{2} \int \frac{\rho_S(M^2)}{M^2 - M_K^2} \phi_S(M^2)G(K^+ \to \pi^0 S, M^2) \, dM^2 \qquad (5.48)$$

where $\rho_v(M^2)$ and $\rho_S(M^2)$ are the invariant mass-distribution functions for the vector and the scalar states.

Let us assume that the form factors $F_\pm$ introduced in Eq. (5.33) have similarly the (unsubtracted) dispersion representation:

$$F_+(t) = \tfrac{1}{2} \int \frac{\rho_v(M^2)}{M^2 - t} \phi_v(M^2)G(K^+ \to \pi^0 V; M^2) \, dM^2 \qquad (5.49)$$

$$F_-(t) = -\tfrac{1}{2}(M_K^2 - M_\pi^2) \int \frac{\rho_v(M^2)}{M^2(M^2 - t)} \phi_v(M^2)G(K^+ \to \pi^0 V; M^2)$$

$$\times \, dM^2 + - \int \frac{\rho_S(M^2)}{M^2 - t} \phi_S(M^2)G(K^+ \to \pi^0 S; M^2) \, dM^2 \quad (5.50)$$

From Eqs. (5.48)–(5.50), the earlier result of Eq. (5.39) by setting $M_2^\pi = 0, t = M_K^2$.

From this point one may make further hypotheses about dominance by vector states and scalar states seen experimentally, like the $K^*$ (890) and the rather evasive $\kappa$ (725).

If one assumes only the vector states are important, then without any further assumption about what these states are one finds the remarkable result

$$f_K/f_\pi = -\sqrt{2} F_+(0) \qquad (5.51)$$

Using the $SU(3)$ symmetry value $F_+(0) = -1/\sqrt{2}$, which we expect to be good even with the symmetry breaking because of the Ademollo-Gatto theorem, we find that $|f_K/f_\pi| \approx 1$. This implies using experimental $K_{12}$ and $\pi_{12}$ decay rates that $\tan \theta_A \approx 0.27$ to be compared with $\tan \theta_V \approx 0.22$.

If one starts with the commutator

$$[a_2^3, V_{\mu 3}^1] = A_{\mu 2}^1 \qquad (5.52)$$

sandwiched between $\langle 0|$ and $|\pi^+\rangle$ and uses $K^0$-PCAC as above, one would get, in the approximation of dominance of vector states alone, the result

$$f_\pi/f_K = f_K/f_\pi = -\sqrt{2} F_+(0) = 1$$

which is the $SU(3)$ symmetry result. Thus the scalar states bring in the violations of the $SU(3)$ symmetry.

To study the momentum transfer dependence of the form factors $F_+$ and $F_-$, Mathur, Pandit, and Marshak[27] have assumed that the $K^*$ (890) and $\kappa$ (725) poles dominate. To fix the residues at these poles, they contract the $K^+$ in Eqs. (5.46) and (5.47) and treat it as soft using PCAC both for the $\pi^0$ and the $K^+$. In this way $\phi_K$ is related to $G(K^+ \to \pi^0 \kappa)$ and $\phi_{K^*}$ to $G(K^+ \to \pi^0 K^*)$. The $G$'s are fixed from the measured widths of the $K^*$ and the $\kappa$. They find $F_+(0) \approx -0.67$. Also $F_-(0)$ which depends on the $\kappa$ is found to be $\simeq 0.09$ for a width of the $\kappa$ $\Gamma(\kappa) = 10$ MeV. Thus $\xi = F_-(0)/F_+(0) \approx -0.13$. The value of $\xi$ changes sign for $\Gamma(\kappa) \simeq 20$ MeV; becoming equal to $\approx 0.16$ for $\Gamma(\kappa) \approx 30$ MeV. The experimental situation[28] is unfortunately far from clear for any really meaningful comparisons.

## 5. The $K_{l4}$ Decays

A number of authors[14j,26a,29] have applied the soft-pion technique to the $K_{l4}$ decays: $K \to 2\pi l \nu$. The most successful treatment, which we shall discuss now, has been given by Weinberg. Since there are two pions in the final state satisfying Bose statistics for the physical process, it is clear that the approximation regarding the off-shell amplitude to sensibly represent the on-shell one requires that the off-shell amplitude should also satisfy Bose symmetry. For this purpose, following Weinberg, we contract both the pions together in a symmetrical fashion.

If we factor the $K_{l4}$ amplitude as usual into a leptonic part and a hadronic part, in principle both the vector and the axial-vector hadronic weak currents will contribute to the matrix element $\langle 2\pi | J_\mu | K \rangle$. However, since for the vector current

$$\langle \pi(q_1)\pi(q_2) | V_\mu | K(p) \rangle \propto \varepsilon_{\mu\nu\lambda\rho}(q_1)_\nu (q_2)_\lambda (p)_\rho$$

from general invariance arguments, in the soft-pion limit this matrix element will be of second order in smallness and hence may be neglected. The matrix element for the axial-vector current may be represented in terms of three form factors. As an illustration, consider the decay: $K^+ \to \pi^+ + \pi^- + e^+ + \nu$, so that we may write

$$\langle \pi^+(q_1)\pi^-(q_2) | (A_\lambda(0))_3^1 | K^+(p) \rangle = \frac{1}{\sqrt{8q_{10}q_{20}p_0 V^3}} \frac{i}{M_K}$$

$$\times [F_1(q_1 + q_2)_\lambda + F_2(q_1 - q_2) + F_3(p - q_1 - q_2)_\lambda] \qquad (5.53)$$

where the form factors $F_i$ are functions of the scalars in the problem. We have omitted the $SU(3)$ indices on $F_i$ for simplicity. To extrapolate both the pions "simultaneously" we first obtain an obvious extension of the general technique discussed in Section IV-4. If we define

$$
M_{\mu\nu\lambda} = (2p_0 V)^{1/2} \int d^4x \int d^4y \, e^{-iq_1 \cdot x} e^{-iq_2 \cdot y}
$$
$$
\times \langle 0| \, T\{[A_\mu(x)]_b^a [A_\nu(y)]_d^c [A_\lambda(0)]_m^l\} \, |K\rangle \qquad (5.54)
$$

then from the definition of the time-ordered product

$$
T[A(x)B(y)C(0)]
$$
$$
\begin{aligned}
&= \theta(x_0 - y_0)\theta(y_0)A(x)B(y)C(0) + \theta(x_0)\theta(-y_0)A(x)C(0)B(y) \\
&+ \theta(y_0 - x_0)\theta(x_0)B(y)A(x)C(0) + \theta(y_0)\theta(-x_0)B(y)C(0)A(x) \\
&+ \theta(-x_0)\theta(x_0 - y_0)C(0)A(x)B(y) \\
&+ \theta(-y_0)\theta(y_0 - x_0)C(0)B(y)A(x)
\end{aligned} \qquad (5.55)
$$

we obtain in a somewhat tedious but straightforward way the identity:

$$
(q_1)_\mu (q_2)_\nu M_{\mu\nu\lambda}
$$
$$
= (2p_0 V)^{1/2}(-i)^2 \int d^4x \int d^4y \, e^{-iq_1 \cdot x} e^{-iq_2 \cdot y}
$$
$$
\begin{aligned}
\times \, \{ & \langle 0| \, T[\partial_\mu A_\mu(x)]_b^a [\partial_\nu A_\nu(y)]_d^c [A_\lambda(0)]_m^l \, |K\rangle \\
&+ \delta(x_0)\langle 0| \, T\{[\partial_\nu A_\nu(y)]_d^c [A_0(x)_b^a, A_\lambda(0)_m^l]\} \, |K\rangle \\
&+ \delta(y_0)\langle 0| \, T\{[\partial_\mu A_\mu(x)]_b^a [A_0(y)_d^c, A_\lambda(0)_m^l]\} \, |K\rangle \\
&+ \tfrac{1}{2}\delta(x_0)\delta(y_0)\langle 0| \, \{A_0(x)_b^a, [A_0(y)_d^c, A_\lambda(0)_m^l]\} \, |K\rangle \\
&+ \tfrac{1}{2}\delta(x_0)\delta(y_0)\langle 0| \, \{A_0(y)_d^c, [A_0(x)_b^a, A_\lambda(0)_m^l]\} \, |K\rangle \\
&- (i/2)(q_1 - q_2)_\rho \delta(x_0 - y_0)\langle 0| \, T\{[A_0(x)_b^a, A_\rho(y)_d^c]A_\lambda(0)_m^l\} \, |K\rangle \\
&+ \delta(x_0 - y_0)\langle 0| \, T\{[A_0(x)_b^a, \partial_\nu A_\nu(y)_d^c]A_\lambda(0)_m^l\} \, |K\rangle \}
\end{aligned} \qquad (5.56)
$$

The first term on the right-hand side of Eq. (5.56) is proportional to the matrix element of Eq. (5.53), since using the LSZ reduction and PCAC we have in the limit $q_{1.2}^2 \to 0$

$$
\langle \pi_b^a(q_1)\pi_d^c(q_2)| \, A_\lambda(0)_m^l \, |K\rangle
$$
$$
= (i)^2 \frac{2M_\pi^4}{C_\pi^2} \int d^4x \int d^4y \, e^{-iq_1 \cdot x} e^{-iq_2 \cdot y}
$$
$$
\times \langle 0| \, T[\partial_\mu A_\mu(x)_b^a \partial_\nu A_\nu(y)_d^c A_\lambda(0)_m^l] \, |K\rangle \qquad (5.57)
$$

The rest of the terms (except the last one) on the right-hand side of Eq. (5.56) contain equal-time commutators which are given by

$$
\delta(x_0 - y_0)[A_0(x)_j^i, A_\rho(y)_i^k] = [\delta_i^i V_\rho(x)_j^k - \delta_j^k V_\rho(x)_i^i]\delta^4(x - y) \qquad (5.58)
$$

The use of Eq. (5.58) allows one to express the second and third terms on the right-hand side of Eq. (5.56) in terms of the $K_{l3}$ matrix elements defined by Eq. (5.33). The double commutators in the fourth and fifth terms may be easily evaluated using Eq. (5.58) and a similar commutator between $A_0$ and the vector current density. In the limit of $q_{1,2}^2 \to 0$ clearly these terms are proportional to the $K_{l2}$ matrix elements defined in Eq. (5.34). Using the equal time commutator Eq. (5.58) the sixth term on the right-hand side of Eq. (5.56) can be written as

$$\text{sixth term} = (i/2)(q_1 - q_2)_\rho M_{\rho\lambda}(2p_0 V)^{1/2} \qquad (5.59)$$

where

$$M_{\rho\lambda} = \int d^4x \, e^{-i(q_1 + q_2)\cdot x}\langle 0| \, T([\delta_d^a V_\rho(x)_b^c - \delta_b^c V_\rho(x)_d^a]A_\lambda(0)_m^l) \, |K\rangle \quad (5.60)$$

The last term in the right-hand side of Eq. (5.56) contains an equal-time commutator involving the divergence of the axial-vector current. The use of PCAC $\partial_\nu A_\nu(y)_d^c \propto m_\pi^2 \phi_\pi(y)_d^c$ for $c,d = 1,2$ suggests then that this equal time commutator will be proportional to $m_\pi^2$, so that the last term on the right-hand side of Eq. (5.56) would presumably be proportional to $m_\pi^2/m_K^2$ and hence negligible. Note, however, that the appearance of $\partial_\mu A_\mu(x)$ or $\partial_\nu A_\nu(y)$ in, e.g., the first term on the right-hand side of Eq. (5.56), does not, of course, imply that that term is also negligible; this is obviously because one has in this case a singularity, the pion pole, so that in the soft-pion limit one gets a factor $C_\pi/m_\pi^2$ which is independent of $m_\pi$. Finally, the left-hand side of Eq. (5.56) may be neglected in the soft-pion limit $q_{1,2} \to 0$. The identity [Eq. (5.56)] then provides a determination of the $K_{l4}$ matrix element in terms of $K_{l3}$ form factors, $K_{l2}$ decay constant, and the amplitude Eq. (5.60).

We now return to the study of the particular decay mode $K^+(p) \to \pi^+(q_1) + \pi^-(q_2) + e^+ + \nu$ as an illustration. In the limit of the soft pions, the above discussion reduces the identity [Eq. (5.56)] to the relation

$$\frac{C_\pi^2}{2M_\pi^4} (8p_0 q_{10} q_{20} V^3)^{1/2}\langle\pi^+(q_1)\pi^-(q_2)| \, A_\lambda(0)_3^1 \, |K^+(p)\rangle$$

$$- i \frac{C_\pi}{\sqrt{2M_\pi^2}} (4p_0 q_{10} V^2)^{1/2}\langle\pi^+(q_1)| \, V_\lambda(0)_3^2 \, |K^+(p)\rangle$$

$$- \tfrac{1}{2}(2p_0 V)^{1/2}\langle 0| \, A_\lambda(0)_3^1 \, |K^+(p)\rangle$$

$$+ \frac{i}{2}(q_1 - q_2)_\rho(2p_0 V)^{1/2}M_{\rho\lambda} = 0 \qquad (5.61)$$

where

$$M_{\rho\lambda} = \int d^4x \, e^{-i(q_1+q_2)\cdot x}\langle 0| \, T(V_\rho(x)_2^2 - V_\rho(x)_1^1, A_\lambda(0)_3^1] \, |K^+(p)\rangle \quad (5.62)$$

The $K_{l3}$ and $K_{l2}$ matrix elements appearing in Eq. (5.61) may be defined as follows from invariance considerations

$$\langle \pi^+(q_1)| \, V_\lambda(0)_3^2 \, |K^+(p)\rangle = \frac{1}{\sqrt{4q_{10}p_0V^2}} \, [F_+(K^+ \to \pi^+)(p_1 + q_1)_\lambda$$
$$+ \, F_-(K^+ \to \pi^+)(p - q_1)_\lambda] \quad (5.63)$$

$$\langle 0| \, A_\lambda(0)_3^1 \, |K^+(p)\rangle = \frac{1}{\sqrt{2p_0V}} \, if_K p_\lambda \quad (5.64)$$

We now turn to an evaluation of $M_{\rho\lambda}$ defined in Eq. (5.62) and use a method first suggested by Low, which exploits the fact that the vector current $V_\rho(x)_2^2 - V_\rho(x)_1^1$ appearing in Eq. (5.62) is conserved. It follows from Eq. (5.62) then that

$$(q_1 + q_2)_\rho M_{\rho\lambda} = -i \int d^4x \, e^{-i(q_1+q_2)\cdot x}$$
$$\times \, \langle 0| \, \delta(x_0)[V_0(x)_2^2 - V_0(x)_1^1, A_\lambda(0)_3^1] \, |K^+\rangle \quad (5.65)$$

Evaluating the equal-time commutator in Eq. (5.65) and using Eq. (5.64), we obtain

$$(q_1 + q_2)_\rho M_{\rho\lambda} = (f_K/\sqrt{2p_0V})p_\lambda \quad (5.66)$$

Writing

$$q_1 + q_2 = Q \quad (5.67)$$

we observe now that from invariance considerations $M\rho\lambda$ must be given by second-rank tensors constructed from the four momentum $p$ and $Q$, i.e.,

$$M_{\rho\lambda} = ap_\rho p_\lambda + bp_\rho Q_\lambda + cQ_\rho p_\lambda + dQ_\rho Q_\lambda + e \, \delta_{\rho\lambda} \quad (5.68)$$

where $a$, $b$, $c$, $d$, and $e$ are general functions of the scalars $p \cdot Q$ and $Q^2$. We are interested in evaluating $M_{\rho\lambda}$ in the soft-pion limit $Q \to 0$ and one has to be careful in taking the limit $Q \to 0$ since one or more of the form factors in Eq. (5.68) might have a pole at $Q = 0$. Indeed it is easy to see that such a case actually arises due to the $K$-meson pole in the expression [Eq. (5.62)]. The contribution of this pole can be easily written from Eq. (5.62) or equivalently from the Feynman diagram shown below,

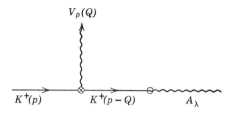

and is proportional to

$$(p - Q)_\lambda(2p - Q)_\rho \frac{1}{-2p\cdot Q + Q^2} \tag{5.69}$$

Also, it is easy to check that no other intermediate state gives rise to a propagator which blows up at $Q = 0$. Thus, for a study of the limit $Q \to 0$ we choose the explicit form of the expression [Eq. (5.68)] given by

$$M_{\rho\lambda} = \frac{C_1(p - Q)_\lambda(2p - Q)_\rho}{-2p\cdot Q + Q^2} + C_2\,\delta_{\lambda\rho} + C_3 p_\lambda p_\rho + 0(Q) \tag{5.70}$$

where the functions $C_1$, $C_2$, and $C_3$ now do not have a pole at $Q = 0$, and since they are functions of the scalars $p\cdot Q$ and $Q^2$, for $Q \to 0$ $C_i$ are essentially constants. Now using the condition [Eq. (5.66)] we evaluate the $C_i$'s to be

$$C_1 = -C_2 = -f_K/\sqrt{2p_0 V} \quad \text{and} \quad C_3 = 0 \tag{5.71}$$

so that finally in the soft-pion limit

$$M_{\rho\lambda} = \frac{f_K}{\sqrt{2p_0 V}}\left\{\frac{(p - Q)_\lambda(2p - Q)_\rho}{2p\cdot Q - Q^2} + \delta_{\lambda\rho} + 0(Q)\right\} \tag{5.72}$$

Eq. (5.61) with the help of Eqs. (5.53), (5.63), (5.64), and (5.72) may now be rewritten as

$$\frac{C_\pi^2}{2M_\pi^4}\frac{1}{M_K}[F_1(q_1 + q_2)_\lambda + F_2(q_1 - q_2)_\lambda + F_3(p - q_1 - q_2)_\lambda]$$

$$= \frac{C_\pi}{\sqrt{2}\,M_\pi^2}[F_+(K^+ \to \pi^+)(p + q_1)_\lambda + F_-(K^+ \to \pi^+)(p - q_1)_\lambda]$$

$$+ \tfrac{1}{2}f_K p_\lambda - \tfrac{1}{2}f_K\left[(p - q_1 - q_2)_\lambda\frac{p\cdot(q_1 - q_2)}{p\cdot(q_1 + q_2)} + (q_1 - q_2)_\lambda\right] \tag{5.73}$$

Comparing the coefficients of the terms $(q_1 + q_2)_\lambda$, $(q_1 - q_2)_\lambda$, and $(p - q_1 - q_2)_\lambda$, we obtain finally the $K_{l4}$ form factors in the decay $K^+ \to \pi^+ + \pi^- + e^+ + \nu$

$$F_1 = F_2 = A$$

$$F_3 = B \left\{ 1 + \frac{p \cdot (q_1 - q_2)}{p \cdot (q_1 + q_2)} \right\} \tag{5.74}$$

where

$$A = (\sqrt{2}\, M_\pi^2 / C_\pi) M_K F_+(K^+ \to \pi^+)$$

$$B = (\sqrt{2}\, M_\pi^2 / C_\pi) M_K \tfrac{1}{2}[F_+(K^+ \to \pi^+) + F_-(K^+ \to \pi^+)] \tag{5.75}$$

Using the experimental values of the $K_{l3}$ form factors, we obtain[14i]

$$|A| = 0.97 \pm 0.03 \qquad |B| = 1.75 \pm 0.33 \tag{5.76}$$

To compare the values [Eq. (5.74)] with the experiments, we first observe that for $K_{e4}$ decays, the term in Eq. (5.53) containing the form factor $F_3$ would be negligible. This is because by energy-momentum conservation $p - q_1 - q_2$ would be just the sum of the lepton four-momenta which when contracted with the lepton current would yield a term proportional to $m_e / m_K$ where $m_e$ is the mass of the electron. Only for $K_{\mu 4}$ decay will the $F_3$ term be important. Unfortunately at the present time very little experimental information exists on the $K_{\mu 4}$ to make any comparison. For the $F_1$ and $F_2$ form factors, the ratio of the phase-space averages has been measured for $K^+ \to \pi^+ + \pi^- + e^+ + \nu$ decay and found to be $\langle F_1 \rangle / \langle F_2 \rangle = 0.8 \pm 0.3$ in reasonable agreement with the calculated value given by Eq. (5.74). Also we may compute the rate for $K_{e4}$ decay using the calculated values of Eq. (5.74). For constant values of $F_1$ and $F_2$, the rate for $K_{e4}$ decay is given by

$$\Gamma = (1.67 F_1^2 + 0.32 F_2^2) \times 10^3 \text{ sec}^{-1} \tag{5.77}$$

with $F_1$ and $F_2$ given by Eq. (5.74). We obtain the predicted rate for $K^+ \to \pi^+ + \pi^- + e^+ + \nu$,

$$\Gamma = 1990 F_1^2 \text{ sec}^{-1} \simeq 1.87 \times 10^3 \text{ sec}^{-1} \tag{5.78}$$

to be compared with the experimental value $(2.9 \pm 0.6) \times 10^3 \text{ sec}^{-1}$.

For other $K_{e4}$ decays we can obtain the form factors in essentially the same way as discussed above for $K^+ \to \pi^+ + \pi^- + e^+ + \nu$. However, since the axial current in Eq. (5.53) transforms as an isospinor, we may use $SU(2)$ symmetry for this purpose. Note that $I = 2$ for the final $2\pi$ state is not allowed, since $A_\lambda$ transforms like $I = 1/2$. By Bose symmetry now the form factors $F_1$ and $F_2$ get contributions from the $I = 0$ and $I = 1$ states, respectively, of the final system of two pions. Using $SU(2)$ and Eq. (5.74), we then obtain the $F_1$ and $F_2$ form factors for the other $K_{l4}$ decay as follows: For $K^+ \to \pi^0 + \pi^0 + e^+ + \nu$

$$F_1 = A, F_2 = 0 \qquad (5.79)$$

for $K_2^0 \to \pi^- + \pi^0 + e^+ + \nu$

$$F_1 = 0, \ F_2 = A \qquad (5.80)$$

Note that isospin symmetry alone provides a relation between the various $K_{l4}$ decays:

$$\Gamma(K^+ \to \pi^+ + \pi^- + e^+ + \nu) = 2\Gamma(K^+ \to \pi^0 + \pi^0 + e^+ + \nu)$$
$$+ \ \Gamma(K^+ \to \pi^- + \pi^0 + e^+ + \nu) \qquad (5.81)$$

The equality of the form factors $F_1$ and $F_2$ obtained from current algebra for the decay $K^+ \to \pi^+ + \pi^- + e^+ + \nu$ given by Eq. (5.74) now leads to two relations:

$$\Gamma(K^+ \to 2\pi^0 + e^+ + \nu)/\Gamma(K^+ \to \pi^+ + \pi^- + e^+ + \nu) = 0.42$$
$$(5.82)$$

$$\Gamma(K_2^0 \to \pi^- + \pi^0 + e^+ + \nu)/\Gamma(K^+ \to \pi^+ + \pi^- + e^+ + \nu) = 0.16$$
$$(5.83)$$

Of course, only one of these is a new relation by virtue of Eq. (5.81). One has to await future experimental measurements to test these results.

## VI. Nonleptonic Decays

In this section, we consider the application of the techniques of current algebra to the seven hyperon decays:

$$\begin{aligned}
\Lambda_- : & \quad \Lambda \to p + \pi^- \\
\Lambda_0 : & \quad \Lambda \to n + \pi^0 \\
\Sigma_+^+ : & \quad \Sigma^+ \to n + \pi^+ \\
\Sigma_0^+ : & \quad \Sigma^+ \to p + \pi^0 \\
\Sigma_-^- : & \quad \Sigma^- \to n + \pi^- \\
\Xi_-^- : & \quad \Xi^- \to \Lambda + \pi^- \\
\Xi_0^0 : & \quad \Xi^0 \to \Lambda + \pi^0
\end{aligned} \qquad (6.1)$$

and to the $K$ meson decays:

$$K_{\pi 2}: \quad K \to 2\pi$$
$$K_{\pi 3}: \quad K \to 3\pi \tag{6.2}$$

## 1. Current–Current Interaction

We shall consider the nonleptonic weak Hamiltonian to be of the current × current form. Conventionally the nonleptonic Hamiltonian in the current × current form is written as:

$$H_w^{N,L} = \frac{G}{\sqrt{2}} \mathscr{J}_\mu^\dagger \mathscr{J}_\mu \tag{6.3}$$

where $G$ is the universal Fermi constant, $G = 1 \times 10^5/M_p^2$, $\sqrt{2}$ is a conventional factor, and $\mathscr{J}_\mu$ is the hadronic Cabibbo[21] current that transforms like an octet. $\mathscr{J}_\mu$ is assumed to be made up from charged currents only, both strangeness preserving and changing

$$\mathscr{J}_\mu = J_{\mu 2}^1 \cos \theta + J_{\mu 3}^1 \sin \theta \tag{6.4}$$

where

$$(J_\mu)_b^a = (V_\mu)_b^a + (A_\mu)_b^a \tag{6.5}$$

and $\theta$ is the Cabbibo angle, assumed to be the same for vector and axial-vector currents. Since under the $CP$ operation $\mathscr{J}_\mu \to \mathscr{J}_\mu^\dagger$ we choose the weak Hamiltonian in the symmetric form:

$$H_w^{N,L} = \frac{G}{\sqrt{2}} \tfrac{1}{2}\{\mathscr{J}_\mu^\dagger, \mathscr{J}_\mu\} \tag{6.6}$$

to obtain explicit $CP$ invariance.

Now since $\mathscr{J}_\mu$ and $\mathscr{J}_\mu^\dagger$ belong to the same octet of currents in the $SU(3)$ symmetry, the anticommutator in Eq. (6.6) can only belong to the completely symmetric representations in the direct product decomposition. This shows that $H_w$ can only transform as $\mathbf{1}$, $\mathbf{8}_s$, and $\mathbf{27}$. However, since $\mathbf{1}$ has only a strangeness-preserving term, for the strangeness-changing nonleptonic decays we are interested in $H_w$ can only transform as $\mathbf{8}_s$ and $\mathbf{27}$.

From Eqs. (6.4) and (6.6) we obtain:

$$H_w^{N,L} = (G/\sqrt{2})\tfrac{1}{2}[(J_{\mu 1}^2 J_{\mu 2}^1 + J_{\mu 2}^1 J_{\mu 1}^2) \cos^2 \theta$$
$$+ (J_{\mu 3}^1 J_{\mu 3}^1 + J_{\mu 3}^1 J_{\mu 1}^3) \sin^2 \theta$$
$$+ (J_{\mu 1}^2 J_{\mu 3}^1 + J_{\mu 3}^1 J_{\mu 1}^2 + \text{h.c.}) \sin \theta \cos \theta \tag{6.7}$$

The strangeness-changing part of the nonleptonic Hamiltonian is then given by the last term in Eq. (6.7). We shall designate this by just $H_w$:

$$H_w = (G/\sqrt{2})\tfrac{1}{2}(J_{\mu 1}^2 J_{\mu 3}^1 + J_{\mu 3}^1 J_{\mu 1}^2) \sin\theta \cos\theta + \text{h.c.} \qquad (6.8)$$

As mentioned, $H_w$ transforms as a combination of $8_s$ and $27$. If one wishes to express $H_w$ as a pure octet, it is easy to see that one would require the introduction of neutral currents.

### 2. Hyperon Decays: General Consideration

We would now like to derive the consequences of the Hamiltonian Eq. (6.8) for the nonleptonic hyperon decays [Eq. (6.1)]. To outline the technique, as an illustration consider the decay $\Lambda(p_1) \to p(p_2) + \pi^-(q)$. To first order in weak interactions, the matrix element for the decay is given by

$$\mathcal{M} = -i \int d^4x \, \langle p(p_2)\pi^-(q)| \, H_w(x) \, |\Lambda(p_1)\rangle$$

$$= -(2\pi)^4 i\delta^4(p_1 - p_2 - q)\frac{M}{\sqrt{2q_0 V}} \qquad (6.9)$$

where

$$M = (2q_0 V)^{1/2}\langle p(p_2)\pi^-(q)| \, H_w(0) \, |\Lambda(p_1)\rangle$$

Contracting $\pi^-$ by the standard technique of LSZ, we obtain

$$M = i \int d^4x \, e^{-iq\cdot x}(q^2 + M_\pi^2)\langle p(p_2)| \, T[\varphi_{\pi^-}(x)H_w(0)] \, |\Lambda(p_1)\rangle \quad (6.10)$$

Using PCAC Eq. (3.1) we obtain

$$M = \frac{i\sqrt{2}}{C_\pi} \int d^4x \, e^{-iq\cdot x}(q^2 + M_\pi^2)$$
$$\times \langle p(p_2)| \, T[\partial_\mu A_{\mu 1}^2(x)H_w(0)] \, |\Lambda(p_1)\rangle \qquad (6.11)$$

At this stage we employ the techniques of the algebra of currents to evaluate $M$. For this purpose consider the expression:

$$T_\mu = i \int d^4x \, e^{-iq\cdot x}\langle p(p_2)| \, T[A_\mu(x)_1^2 H_w(0)] \, |\Lambda(p_1)\rangle \qquad (6.12)$$

Multiplying both sides by $q_\mu$ and doing a partial integration, we obtain the identity

$$
q_\mu T_\mu = \int d^4x \, e^{-iq\cdot x} \langle p(p_2)| \, T[\partial_\mu A_\mu(x)_1^2, H_w(0)] \, |\Lambda(p_1)\rangle
$$
$$
+ \int d^4x \, e^{-iq\cdot x} \langle p(p_2)| \, \delta(x_0)[A_0(x)_1^2, H_w(0)] \, |\Lambda(p_1)\rangle \qquad (6.13)
$$

Taking the limit $q \to 0$ and using Eq. (6.10) and the definition [Eq. (2.4)] of the axial charge, we obtain

$$
M(0) = i \, \frac{\sqrt{2} \, M_\pi^2}{C_\pi} \, [\lim_{q \to 0} (q_\mu T_\mu) - \langle p(p_2)| \, [a_1^2(0), H_w(0)] \, |\Lambda(p_1)\rangle] \qquad (6.14)
$$

where $M(0)$ stands for the expression for the amplitude Eq. (6.10) when the pion four-momentum $q$ is extrapolated to be zero.

The surface term $\lim_{q \to 0}(q_\mu T_\mu)$ in Eq. (6.14) picks up contributions in the limit only from single-particle intermediate states degenerate in mass with either the initial or the final state. In actual calculations, however, it is easy to see that there is an ambiguity. One gets different answers for the surface term depending on whether one takes the mass-degeneracy limit first and then the limit $q \to 0$, or vice-versa. Fortunately, however, if one looks at the contribution to the left-hand side in Eq. (6.14) coming from the Born terms, one finds a similar ambiguity there, in such a way that the *totality* of the Born terms and surface terms has a *unique* limit. This point has been emphasized before in Section IV. To exhibit this feature explicitly, we may extract the Born terms (corresponding to the pole diagrams involving the $\Sigma^+$ and the $n$ states) and write the matrix element [Eq. (6.10)] on mass shell as

$$
M(q) = \tilde{M}(q) + M_B(q) \qquad (6.15)
$$

where $M_B(q)$ represents the on-shell Born amplitudes, and $\tilde{M}(q)$ is the continuum contribution. It follows from Eqs. (6.15) and (6.14) that

$$
\tilde{M}(0) = M(0) - M_B(0)
$$
$$
= \frac{i\sqrt{2} \, M_\pi^2}{C_\pi} \left[ \lim_{q \to 0} \left\{ q_\mu T_\mu + \frac{iC_\pi}{\sqrt{2} \, M_\pi^2} M_B(q) \right\} \right.
$$
$$
\left. - \langle p(p_2)| \, [a_1^2(0), H_w(0)] \, |\Lambda(p_1)\rangle \right] \qquad (6.16)
$$

As explained above, the expression in braces has a unique limit. In particular we will prefer to calculate it by assuming that the intermediate state mass is not degenerate with the initial or the final state (introduce a fictitious mass difference, if necessary, as in the case of the $n$ pole), and by taking the limit $q \to 0$ first (and only subsequently taking the mass-degeneracy limit). This procedure has the advantage that the surface term vanishes, and all the contribution to the braced term comes from the off-mass shell Born term which has to be calculated now in the same limiting procedure just obtained.

The equal-time commutator in Eq. (6.16) can be evaluated for the structure of the relevant weak Hamiltonian (6.8). Because of Eq. (6.6), it is easy to verify that

$$[a_j^i(0), H_w(0)] = [v_j^i(0), H_w(0)] \tag{6.17}$$

Thus the second term on the right-hand side of Eq. (6.16) becomes

$$\langle p(p_2)|\, [a_1^2(0), H_w(0)]\, |\Lambda(p_1)\rangle = \langle p(p_2)|\, [v_1^2(0), H_w(0)]\, |\Lambda(p_1)\rangle \tag{6.18}$$

Note that the vector charge $v_1^2 \equiv I_+$ is a generator of the $SU(2)$ group. If charge independence holds, we may rewrite Eq. (6.16) as

$$\langle p(p_2)|\, [a_1^2(0), H_w(0)]\, |\Lambda(p_1)\rangle = \langle n(p_2)|\, H_w(0)\, |\Lambda(p_1)\rangle \tag{6.19}$$

since $\qquad \langle p|\, v_1^2 = \langle n|\quad \text{and}\quad v_1^2\, |\Lambda\rangle = 0$

Hoping now, as usual, that the continuum contribution $\tilde{M}(q)$ to the decay amplitude has a gentle behavior on $q$, we may approximate

$$\tilde{M}(q) = \tilde{M}(0) \tag{6.20}$$

where $\tilde{M}(0)$ is given by Eq. (6.16). From Eq. (6.15) the total decay amplitude would then finally be given by

$$M(q) \sim \tilde{M}(0) + M_B(q) \tag{6.21}$$

We may now discuss the $s$-wave and the $p$-wave decays separately. Evidently, by conservation of the total angular momentum the only partial waves allowed in the final states of the decays are $l = 0$ and $l = 1$. It is easy to check that the $s$-wave decay is parity violating (p.v.) and the $p$-wave is parity conserving (p.c.). Using Eq. (6.6), we may now rewrite the Hamiltonian Eq. (6.8) as

$$H_w = H_w^{(\mathrm{p.v.})} + H_w^{(\mathrm{p.c.})} \tag{6.22}$$

where $H_w^{(p.v.)}$ contains terms of the type $V_\mu A_\mu$ or $A_\mu V_\mu$, and $H_w^{(p.c.)}$ has products like $V_\mu V_\mu$ or $A_\mu A_\mu$. Equation (6.17) can now be split into the following two equations:

$$[a_j^i(0), H_w^{(p.v.)}] = [v_j^i(0), H_w^{(p.c.)}] \qquad (6.23)$$

$$[a_j^i(0), H_w^{(p.c.)}] = [v_j^i(0), H_w^{(p.v.)}] \qquad (6.24)$$

Also note that in the explicit calculations for both $s$ waves and $p$ waves it is clear from Eq. (6.19) that we would encounter matrix elements of $H_w^{(p.c.)}$ and $H_w^{(p.v.)}$ between baryon states. The space–time structure of these matrix elements does not allow any simple calculation, so that following Suzuki[30a] and Sugawara[30b] we shall employ $SU(3)$ symmetry at this stage and express the individual matrix elements in terms of the reduced $SU(3)$ matrix elements. It should be noted that we are using a semidynamical approach since the dynamical content of Eqs. (6.23) and (6.24) is still being exploited. We therefore expect to get more information on the hyperon decays than from the use of $SU(3)$ symmetry alone. It is clear from the $\mathscr{C}$-parity arguments [see Eqs. (A.18) and (A.19) of Appendix IV] that whereas the matrix element of $H_w^{(p.c.)}$ between baryon states exists in the $SU(3)$ symmetry limit, the coupling of $H_w^{(p.v.)}$ to the baryons vanishes in this limit, i.e.,

$$\langle B' | H_w^{(p.v.)} | B \rangle = 0 \qquad (6.25)$$

Equation (6.25) will play a rather crucial role in our calculations.

From general invariance grounds, the decay amplitude $M$ may be written as

$$M = \sqrt{M_p M_\Lambda / E_p E_\Lambda V^2} \, i\bar{u}_p(p_2)\{A - B\gamma_5\}u_\Lambda(p_1) \qquad (6.26)$$

where $A$ and $B$ stand for the conventional (real) $s$- and $p$-wave amplitudes, respectively.

## 3. s-Wave Hyperon Decays[30a,30b]

In the $SU(3)$ limit there is no contribution from the Born terms to $s$ waves, since for these terms the weak vertex is the coupling of the parity-violating spurion (corresponding to $H_w^{(p.v.)}$) to baryons which vanish as shown in Eq. (6.25). Thus the Born term contributions are zero, both on shell and off shell. The only contribution to the decay amplitude [Eq. (6.21)] for $s$ waves then comes from the contribution of the equal time-commutator term in the expression [Eq. (6.16)] of $\tilde{M}(0)$. Thus, using Eq. (6.21)

$$M_s(\Lambda^0_-) = (-i\sqrt{2}\, M_\pi^2/C_\pi)\langle n(p_2)|\, H_w^{(\mathrm{p.c.})}\, |\Lambda(p_1)\rangle \qquad (6.27)$$

In the same manner, for the rest of the six decays [Eqs. (6.1)], it is easy to verify that

$$M_s(\Lambda^0_0) = +i(M_\pi^2/C_\pi)\langle n|\, H_w^{(\mathrm{p.c.})}\, |\Lambda\rangle$$
$$M_s(\Sigma^+_+) = -i(\sqrt{2}\, M_\pi^2/C_\pi)\{\langle p|\, H_w^{(\mathrm{p.c.})}\, |\Sigma^+\rangle + \sqrt{2}\langle n|\, H_w^{(\mathrm{p.c.})}\, |\Sigma^0\rangle\}$$
$$M_s(\Sigma^+_0) = +i(M_\pi^2/C_\pi)\langle p|\, H_w^{(\mathrm{p.c.})}\, |\Sigma^+\rangle$$
$$M_s(\Sigma^-_-) = +(2iM_\pi^2/C_\pi)\langle n|\, H_w^{(\mathrm{p.c.})}\, |\Sigma^0\rangle$$
$$M_s(\Xi^-_-) = (-i\sqrt{2}\, M_\pi^2/C_\pi)\langle \Lambda|\, H_w^{(\mathrm{p.c.})}\, |\Xi^0\rangle$$
$$M_s(\Xi^0_0) = +i(M_\pi^2/C_\pi)\langle \Lambda|\, H_w^{(\mathrm{p.c.})}\, |\Xi^0\rangle \qquad (6.28)$$

We may now express the baryon matrix elements

$$\langle B|\, H_w^{(\mathrm{p.c.})}\, |B'\rangle = \sqrt{M_B M_{B^1}/E_B E_{B^1} V^2}\, g(B' \to Bs)\bar{u}_B u_{B'} \qquad (6.29)$$

in terms of the (real) spurion couplings $g$ for the process indicated by the argument. Then from Eqs. (6.26) and (6.28), we get

$$A(\Lambda^0_-) = -\sqrt{2}\,(M_\pi^2/C_\pi)g(\Lambda \to ns)$$
$$A(\Lambda^0_0) = +(M_\pi^2/C_\pi)g(\Lambda \to ns)$$
$$A(\Sigma^+_+) = -\sqrt{2}\,(M_\pi^2/C_\pi)\{g(\Sigma^+ \to ps) + \sqrt{2}\,g(\Sigma^0 \to ns)\}$$
$$A(\Sigma^+_0) = (M_\pi^2/C_\pi)g(\Sigma^+ \to ps)$$
$$A(\Sigma^-_-) = 2(M_\pi^2/C_\pi)g(\Sigma^0 \to ns)$$
$$A(\Xi^-_-) = -\sqrt{2}\,(M_\pi^2/C_\pi)g(\Xi^0 \to \Lambda s)$$
$$A(\Xi^0_0) = +(M_\pi^2/C_\pi)g(\Xi^0 \to \Lambda s) \qquad (6.30)$$

Three sum rules follow immediately from Eq. (6.30):

$$\sqrt{2}\, A(\Lambda^0_0) + A(\Lambda^0_-) = 0 \qquad (6.31)$$

$$\sqrt{2}\, A(\Xi^0_0) + A(\Xi^-_-) = 0 \qquad (6.32)$$

$$A(\Sigma^-_-) + \sqrt{2}\, A(\Sigma^+_0) + A(\Sigma^+_+) = 0 \qquad (6.33)$$

Note that since the weak Hamiltonian Eq. (6.8) in general transforms like a mixture of an octet and a 27-plet, we have not assumed any octet dominance or $\Delta I = 1/2$ rule. It is therefore quite remarkable that Eqs. (6.31) and (6.32) are identical to the consequences of the $\Delta I = 1/2$ rule for the $\Lambda$ and $\Xi$ decays. Equation (6.33) differs from the usual $\Delta I = 1/2 \, \Sigma$ triangle in the sign of the term $\Sigma_+^+$. However, since $\Sigma_+^+$ decay is experimentally known to be predominantly a $p$-wave decay, the sign of term $A(\Sigma_+^+)$ is not known and will be very hard to measure. Hence the "pseudo" $\Sigma$ triangle (6.33) is practically indistinguishable from the normal $\Sigma$ triangle of the $\Delta I = 1/2$ rule.

To extract more information from Eq. (6.30), one may exploit the $SU(3)$ symmetry. Each of the matrix elements listed may be expressed in terms of three reduced matrix elements. Since seven decay amplitudes exist, we should get four sum rules, three of which obviously are given by Eqs. (6.31)–(6.33). In terms of the reduced matrix elements, the hitherto independent $s$-wave amplitudes are given by:

$$A(\Lambda_-^0) = (M_\pi^2/C_\pi)\{\sqrt{\tfrac{2}{3}}\,(d + 3f) + \tfrac{2}{15}\sqrt{15}\,a_{27}\} \qquad (6.34)$$

$$A(\Sigma_+^+) = (M_\pi^2/C_\pi)\tfrac{2}{3}\sqrt{10}\,a_{27} \qquad (6.35)$$

$$A(\Sigma_0^+) = (M_\pi^2/C_\pi)\{\sqrt{2}\,(d - f) - \tfrac{4}{15}\sqrt{5}\,a_{27}\} \qquad (6.36)$$

$$A(\Xi_-^-) = (M_\pi^2/C_\pi)\{\sqrt{\tfrac{2}{3}}\,(d - 3f) + \tfrac{2}{15}\sqrt{15}\,a_{27}\} \qquad (6.37)$$

where the octet part of the weak Hamiltonian gives rise to the two reduced matrix elements $d$ and $f$ and $a_{27}$ is the reduced matrix element arising from the part of the Hamiltonian that transforms like **27**. From Eqs. (6.34)–(6.37) we obtain

$$2A(\Xi_-^-) + A(\Lambda_-^0) = \sqrt{3}\,A(\Sigma_0^+) + \sqrt{\tfrac{3}{2}}\,A(\Sigma_+^+) \qquad (6.38)$$

This relation looks very similar to the Lee-Sugawara triangle, and differs from it by the addition of the last term on the right-hand side. However, since one knows experimentally that $A(\Sigma_+^+) \approx 0$ the "pseudo" Lee-Sugawara triangle [Eq. (6.38)] agrees rather well with the experiments.

If we further impose the assumption of octet dominance, i.e., we assume that $H_w$ transforms purely like an octet, we get an extra fifth relation from Eq. (6.35):

$$A(\Sigma_+^+) = 0 \qquad (6.39)$$

Note also that with octet dominance, the pseudo $\Sigma$ triangle (6.33) and the Lee-Sugawara triangle [Eq. (6.38)] both reduce to normal triangles because of Eq. (6.39).

## 4. p-Wave Hyperon Decays[31,32]

The p-wave decays are given by the parity-conserving part of the Hamiltonian. Using the commutation relation [Eq. (6.24)], the contribution of the continuum [Eq. (6.16)] to the p-wave matrix element of $\Lambda$ decay extrapolated to zero four-momentum of the pion is given by

$$\tilde{M}_p(0) = -M_B(0) - \frac{i\sqrt{2}\,M_{\frac{\pi}{2}}}{C_\pi} \langle n(p_2)|\, H_w^{(\text{p.v.})} \,|\Lambda(p_1)\rangle \qquad (6.40)$$

where we have ignored the surface term appearing in Eq. (6.16) following the procedure outlined before. Using $SU(3)$ symmetry, we find, because of Eq. (6.25), that the equal time-commutator term vanishes, so that

$$\tilde{M}_p(0) = -M_B(0) \qquad (6.41)$$

Finally, from Eq. (6.21) we obtain the matrix element for the p-wave $\Lambda_-^0$ decay:

$$M_p(\Lambda_-^0) = M_B(q) - M_B(0) \qquad (6.42)$$

where the Born terms have to be calculated from the pole terms (note only baryon poles contribute) in the matrix element given by Eq. (6.10). These pole terms for $\Lambda_-^0$ are given by the Feynman diagrams:

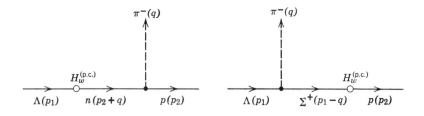

Using the conventional Feynman-Dyson rules, we get

$$M_B(q) = -\sqrt{\frac{M_\Lambda M_p}{p_{10}p_{20}V^2}} \left\{ \frac{G(n \to p\pi^-)g(\Lambda \to ns)}{M_n - M_\Lambda} \right.$$
$$\left. + \frac{G(\Lambda \to \Sigma^+\pi^-)g(\Sigma^+ \to ps)}{M_\Sigma - M_p} \right\}$$
$$\times \bar{u}_p(p_2)i\gamma_5 u_\Lambda(p_1) \qquad (6.43)$$

and

$$M_B(0) = -\sqrt{\frac{M_\Lambda M_p}{p_{10}p_{20}V^2}} \left\{ \frac{G(n \to p\pi^-)g(\Lambda \to ns)}{M_n + M_p} \right.$$

$$\left. + \frac{G(\Lambda \to \Sigma^+\pi^-)g(\Sigma^+ \to ps)}{M_\Sigma + M_\Lambda} \right\}$$

$$\times \bar{u}_p(p_2)i\gamma_5 u_\Lambda(p_1) \qquad (6.44)$$

where the $G$'s represent the strong vertices indicated and the $g$'s represent the coupling of the spurion $s$ corresponding to $H_w^{(\text{p.c.})}$ with the baryons as specified. Note that $M_B(0)$ is much smaller than $M_B(q)$ and may be neglected. This is a special feature of the $p$-wave decays and shows that the extrapolation of the Born terms off-mass shell to $q \to 0$ is not at all gentle. In contrast, for $s$ waves we had $M_B(q) = M_B(0)$, each being zero in the $SU(3)$ limit. Since for $p$ waves the extrapolation of the Born terms is quite bad now, it is just as well that we have given a special treatment to these terms right from the beginning. Note in this connection that in the calculation of the matrix element [Eq. (6.21)], the only object we extrapolated to $q \to 0$ was the part of the amplitude from which the Born terms have been subtracted. The contribution of the Born terms to the matrix element [Eq. (6.21)] is indeed calculated on the mass shell, a necessity for $p$ waves.

We thus obtain from Eq. (6.42),

$$M_p(\Lambda_-^0) \simeq M_B(q) \qquad (6.45)$$

where $M_B(q)$ is given by Eq. (6.43). The entire contribution to the $p$ wave matrix element thus comes from the baryon pole terms. For the other decays [Eqs. (6.1)], the $p$-wave amplitude is then given by the corresponding Born terms for baryon poles. Writing these explicitly, we obtain for the $p$-wave amplitude $B$ defined in Eq. (6.26), the following results:

$$B(\Lambda_-^0) = \left\{ \frac{g(\Lambda \to ns)G(n \to p\pi^-)}{M_N - M_\Lambda} + \frac{G(\Lambda \to \Sigma^+\pi^-)g(\Sigma^+ \to ps)}{M_\Sigma - M_N} \right\}$$

$$B(\Lambda_0^0) = \left\{ \frac{g(\Lambda \to ns)G(n \to n\pi^0)}{M_N - M_\Lambda} + \frac{G(\Lambda \to \Sigma^0\pi^0)g(\Sigma^0 \to ns)}{M_\Sigma - M_N} \right\}$$

$$B(\Sigma_+^+) = \left\{ \frac{g(\Sigma^+ \to ps)G(p \to n\pi^+)}{M_N - M_\Sigma} + \frac{G(\Sigma^+ \to \Lambda\pi^+)g(\Lambda \to ns)}{M_\Lambda - M_N} \right.$$

$$\left. + \frac{G(\Sigma^+ \to \Sigma^0\pi^+)g(\Sigma^0 \to ns)}{M_\Sigma - M_N} \right\}$$

$$B(\Sigma_0^+) = \frac{g(\Sigma^+ \to ps)G(p \to p\pi^0)}{M_N - M_\Sigma} + \frac{G(\Sigma^+ \to \Sigma^+\pi^0)g(\Sigma^+ \to ps)}{M_\Sigma - M_p}$$

$$B(\Sigma_-^-) = \frac{G(\Sigma^- \to \Sigma^0\pi^-)g(\Sigma^0 \to ns)}{M_\Sigma - M_N} + \frac{G(\Sigma^- \to \Lambda\pi^-)g(\Lambda \to ns)}{M_\Lambda - M_N}$$

$$B(\Xi_-^-) = \frac{g(\Xi^- \to \Sigma^-s)G(\Sigma^- \to \Lambda\pi^-)}{M_\Sigma - M_\Xi} + \frac{G(\Xi^- \to \Xi^0\pi^-)g(\Xi^0 \to \Lambda s)}{M_\Xi - M_\Lambda}$$

$$B(\Xi_0^0) = \frac{g(\Xi^0 \to \Sigma^0 s)G(\Sigma^0 \to \Lambda\pi^0)}{M_\Sigma - M_\Xi} + \frac{G(\Xi^0 \to \Xi^0\pi^0)g(\Xi^0 \to \Lambda s)}{M_\Xi - M_\Lambda} \qquad (6.46)$$

Note that the $g$'s which represent the couplings of the scalar spurion corresponding to $H_w^{(\text{p.c.})}$ with the baryons are precisely the couplings in terms of which we obtained the $s$-wave amplitudes Eq. (6.30). Using the experimental $s$-wave amplitudes as input and taking the coupling constants $G$'s from $SU(3)$ symmetry, one can compute the $p$-wave amplitudes in Eq. (6.46). Before doing this detailed experimental comparison, we would like to obtain sum rules, as in the case of the $s$ waves.

Although the sum rules can be discussed for the general structure of the weak Hamiltonian containing both **8** and **27**, we shall discuss here the simpler case and assume octet dominance. If we now assume $SU(3)$ symmetry, we may expand all the $G$'s in terms of the two ($D$ and $F$) $SU(3)$-invariant couplings and similarly the $g$'s in terms of the two invariants $d$ and $f$ already introduced in Eqs. (6.34)–(6.37). One thus has a total of four parameters. However, since the right-hand sides of Eqs. (6.46) involve only the homogenous terms of the type $Gg$, essentially one has only three parameters, because the overall multiplicative constant factor does not matter for linear sum rules. With seven decays and three parameters, one would expect four sum rules. Because of the assumption of octet dominance three of these sum rules have to coincide with the well-known $\Delta I = 1/2$ sum rules:

$$\sqrt{2}\, B(\Lambda_0^0) + B(\Lambda_-^0) = 0$$

$$\sqrt{2}\, B(\Xi_0^0) + B(\Xi_-^-) = 0$$

$$B(\Sigma_-^-) + \sqrt{2}\, B(\Sigma_0^+) - B(\Sigma_+^+) = 0 \qquad (6.47)$$

To obtain the fourth sum rule, we write explicitly the $SU(3)$-invariant structure of the amplitudes [Eqs. (6.46)] ($\delta m > 0$):

$$B(\Lambda_-^0) = (1/\delta m)\sqrt{\tfrac{2}{3}}\,\{2(D + F)(d + f) + (D - F)(d - f)\}$$
$$B(\Sigma_+^+) = -\tfrac{8}{3}(1/\delta m)Dd$$
$$B(\Sigma_0^+) = -\sqrt{2}\,(1/\delta m)(D - F)(d - f)$$
$$B(\Xi^-) = -(1/\delta m)\sqrt{\tfrac{2}{3}}\,\{(D + F)(d + f) + 2(D - F)(d - f)\} \quad (6.48)$$

where $D$ and $F$ represent the symmetrical and antisymmetrical couplings at the strong vertex, and $d$ and $f$ represent the same couplings for the spurion at the weak vertex already introduced in Eqs. (6.34)–(6.37). From Eq. (6.48), we obtain the extra sum rule:

$$2B(\Xi^-) + B(\Xi_-^0) = \sqrt{3}\,B(\Sigma_0^+) \quad (6.49)$$

which is the Lee-Sugawara triangle for $p$ waves. Experimentally there is good support for the sum rules given by Eqs. (6.47) and (6.49).

### 5. Numerical Calculation for s- and p-Wave Amplitudes

For purposes of numerical estimates of the amplitudes $A$ and $B$, we assume that the weak Hamiltonian transforms purely as an octet. For the strong couplings $D$ and $F$ which enter Eqs. (6.48) we take $D/F = 1.7$ with $(G_{NN\pi}^2/4\pi) = 14.6$ and use $SU(3)$ symmetry. The weak (parity-conserving) spurion couplings $d$ and $f$ are treated as adjustable parameters. For a value of $d/f = -0.75$ (Brown and Sommerfeld)[32] with $f = 130$ MeV sec$^{-1/2}$, the calculated values of the amplitudes $A$ and $B$ are exhibited in Table I. Comparison is made with the experimental values quoted by Birge.[33] The theoretical values agree reasonably with the experimental numbers for $s$-wave amplitudes. However, for $p$ waves

TABLE I

| Decay | s-Wave amplitude $A \times 10^5$ sec$^{-1/2}$ | | p-Wave amplitude $B \times 10^5$ sec$^{-1/2}$ | |
|---|---|---|---|---|
| | Theory | Experiment | Theory | Experiment |
| $\Lambda \to p\pi^-$ | 1.16 | $1.551 \pm 0.024$ | 5.66 | $11.045 \pm 0.475$ |
| $\Sigma^+ \to n\pi^+$ | 0 | $0.008 \pm 0.034$ | 6.20 | $19.081 \pm 0.347$ |
| $\Sigma^+ \to p\pi^0$ | $-1.62$ | $-1.558 \pm 0.142$ | 4.51 | $11.71 \pm 1.88$ |
| | | $-1.168 \pm 0.187$ | | $15.61 \pm 1.42$ |
| $\Sigma^- \to n\pi^-$ | 2.22 | $1.861 \pm 0.017$ | $-0.424$ | $-0.152 \pm 0.386$ |
| $\Xi^- \to \Lambda\pi^-$ | $-1.94$ | $-2.022 \pm 0.029$ | 3.38 | $6.628 \pm 0.574$ |

the calculated values are too small by a factor of at least 2. It is clear that it is not possible to fit both the $s$- and the $p$-wave amplitudes simultaneously.

It should be noted that whereas the sum rules derived in Sections IV-3 and IV-4 for $s$ and $p$ waves are separately in good agreement with experiments, the use of the same $d$ and $f$ values in obtaining the numerical values of the $A$ and $B$ amplitudes leads to a disagreement with the experimental data. So far it has not been possible to understand the reason for this discrepancy despite much effort in this direction. Among the many possible reasons that might hold a clue to this discrepancy are: (a) The use of the $SU(3)$ symmetry. It is known, for instance, that the $SU(3)$ value of the $\Lambda NK$ coupling[34] constant may be quite different from the value obtained by a dispersion theoretic estimate. (b) The extrapolation of the pion off the mass shell is well known not to be unique and the particular extrapolation we have performed may not be a good one.[35] We have already seen that the extrapolation of Born terms in the $p$-wave analysis is quite bad. (c) It is possible that the current × current form of the weak nonleptonic Hamiltonian may not be correct.[26a, 36, 37]

### 6. Nonleptonic Decays of the K meson: $K \to 3\pi$ [38]

Since the soft-pion technique with the current commutators and PCAC hypothesis can relate any arbitrary process involving pions to a corresponding one with at least one less pion, it is clear that one can obtain a relation between the $\tau$ and the $\Theta$ modes of the $K$-meson decays. A problem presents itself here however, since the $\tau$ decay mode involves three pions, and the question is which, if any, of the pions should one remove by the soft-pion technique. To appreciate the problem we shall first show that the result depends upon which of the pions is extrapolated to zero four-momentum.

For simplicity throughout this section we shall assume octet dominance in the weak Hamiltonian and neglect $CP$-violating effects.

Consider, for example, the decay $K_2^0 \to \pi^0\pi^+\pi^-$. The decay matrix element is given by

$$M(K_2^0 \to \pi^0\pi^+\pi^-)$$
$$= -i \int d^4x \langle \pi^0(q_1)\pi^+(q_2)\pi^-(q_3)| H_w(x) |K_2^0(q)\rangle$$
$$= -(2\pi)^4 i\delta^4(q - q_1 - q_2 - q_3)\langle \pi^0(q_1)\pi^+(q_2)\pi^-(q_3)| H_w(0) |K_2^0(q)\rangle$$
$$(6.50)$$

Contracting $\pi^0(q_1)$ from the final state by the well-known LSZ techniques, one gets

$$\langle \pi^0(q_1)\pi^+(q_2)\pi^-(q_3)| \, H_w(0) \, |K_2^0(q)\rangle = i \int d^4x \, e^{-iq \cdot x}(q_1^2 + M_\pi^2)$$

$$\times \, \langle \pi^+(q_2)\pi^-(q_3)| \, \theta(x_0)[\phi_{\pi^0}(x), H_w(0)] \, |K_2^0(q)\rangle \qquad (6.51)$$

Using PCAC Eq. (3.1) and carrying out the partial integration we get in the limit $q_1 \to 0$ the result

$$\langle \pi^0(0)\pi^+(q_2)\pi^-(q_3)| \, H_w(0) \, |K_2^0(q)\rangle$$

$$= -i(M_\pi^2/C_\pi)\langle \pi^+(q_2)\pi^-(q_3)| \, [a_1^1 - a_2^2, H_w(0)] \, |K_2^0(q)\rangle \qquad (6.52)$$

where for the axial charge $a_b^a$ we have used the definition in Eq. (2.2.2). Using now the equal time commutation relation [Eq. (6.17)] we obtain

$$[a_1^1 - a_2^2, H_w] = [v_1^1 - v_2^2, H_w] = [2I_3, H_w] \qquad (6.53)$$

so that from Eq. (6.52), the matrix element becomes

$$\langle \pi^0(0)\pi^+(q_2)\pi^-(q_3)| \, H_w(0) \, |K_2^0(q)\rangle$$

$$= -i(M_\pi^2/C_\pi)\langle \pi^+(q_2)\pi^-(q_3)| \, H_w(0) \, |K_1^0(q)\rangle \qquad (6.54)$$

In contrast, had we contracted one of the like pions $\pi^+$ or $\pi^-$ from the matrix element [Eq. (6.50)], we would have obtained,

$$\langle \pi^0(q_1)\pi^+(q_2)\pi^-(q_3)| \, H_w(0) \, |K_2^0(q)\rangle = i \int d^4x \, e^{-iq_3 \cdot x}(q_3^2 + M_2^\pi)$$

$$\times \, \langle \pi^0(q_1)\pi^+(q_2)| \, \theta(x_0)[\phi_{\pi^-}, H_w(0)] \, |K_2^0(q)\rangle \qquad (6.55)$$

Proceeding exactly as before, we get in the limit $q_3 \to 0$, the result

$$\langle \pi^0(q_1)\pi^+(q_2)\pi^-(0)| \, H_w(0) \, |K_2^0(q)\rangle$$

$$= -i(\sqrt{2} \, M_\pi^2/C_\pi)\langle \pi^0(q_1)\pi^+(q_2)| \, [a_1^2(0), H_w(0)] \, |K_2^0(q)\rangle \qquad (6.56)$$

With the assumption of octet dominance in the weak Hamiltonian the right-hand side of Eq. (6.56) must vanish, since the final state of $\pi^+\pi^0$ must be an $I = 2$ state by Bose statistics, and the equal-time commutator $[a_1^2, H_w] = [v_1^2, H_w]$ must belong to the same representation (i.e., $I = 1/2$) as $H_w$ itself, from $SU(2)$ symmetry considerations. Thus

$$\langle \pi^0(q_1)\pi^+(q_2)\pi^-(0)| \, H_w(0) \, |K_2^0(q)\rangle = 0 \qquad (6.57)$$

If we now believe, as usual, that extrapolation of pions off mass shell is a sufficiently smooth operation, we find that the two results, Eqs. (6.54) and (6.57), contradict each other.

To avoid the contradiction some prescriptions have been suggested in the literature. We shall follow here the technique suggested[38] by Hara and Nambu.

Since the $Q$ value and therefore the average energy available to the pions in $\tau$ decays is small in comparison with the mass of the pion, we may express the matrix element for the physical decay as a linear function of the pion energies. The matrix element can, however, only depend on the energy of the unlike pion. This is because the energy dependence of the like pions can only be proportional to the sum of the energies, which by energy conservation essentially reduces to the energy dependence of the unlike pion. If the like pions are identical, this result follows from Bose symmetry. For like pions of the type $\pi^+$ and $\pi^-$, this follows from the requirement of *CPT* invariance. Thus for the decay $K_2^0 \to \pi^0\pi^+\pi^-$, we may write

$$\langle \pi^0(q_1)\pi^+(q_2)\pi^-(q_3)|\ H_w(0)\ |K_2^0(q)\rangle = \alpha + \beta w_1 \qquad (6.58)$$

This linear dependence is also borne out well experimentally. For the unphysical amplitude when the four-momenta are arbitrary, we may similarly express the amplitude in terms of quadratic functions of the meson four-momenta, with the condition that at the physical limit the structure reduces to the form of Eq. (6.58). With energy–momentum conservation taken into account, one can construct six scalars if the mass-shell restriction for all the four mesons is dropped. With the constant term present in the matrix element, one may then write the general structure of the off-shell matrix element in terms of seven parameters. In the approximation of expressing the matrix element as quadratic functions of the meson four-momenta, the seven parameters are essentially constants, with the same values off shell as on shell. Since the matrix element should remain invariant under the interchange of like pions, as mentioned before, not all seven constants are independent. In fact, this requirement can be easily seen to impose two conditions, so that one may finally express the matrix element in terms of five unknown constants. For the decay $K_2^0 \to \pi^0\pi^+\pi^-$, we may then write for the off-shell matrix element,

$$\langle \pi^0(q_1)\pi^+(q_2)\pi^-(q_3)|\ H_w(0)\ |K_2^0(q)\rangle$$
$$= a_1 + a_2 q^2 + a_3[q_2^2 + q_3^2] + a_4 q_1^2 + a_5[q - q_1]^2 \qquad (6.59)$$

It is simple to check that with the mesons on mass shell, this structure indeed reduces to the form of Eq. (6.58).

The unknown constants $a_1 \ldots a_5$ may now be evaluated by using soft-pion relations of the type of Eqs. (6.54) and (6.57). Observe that by extrapolating different pions off mass shell in the matrix element Eq. (6.50), we obtain different conditions on the constants. The two relations Eqs. (6.54) and (6.57) are thus not contradictory, but supplement each other in the determination of the constants. We would like to emphasize that since the constants $a_1 \ldots a_5$ are the same off and on shell, an evaluation of these using off-shell relations would lead to an evaluation of the parameters $\alpha$ and $\beta$ for the physical matrix element Eq. (6.58).

The soft-pion ($q_3 \to 0$) relation given by Eq. (6.57) leads to the condition

$$a_1 + a_2 q^2 + (a_3 + a_4 + a_5)q_\pi^2 = 0 \qquad (6.60)$$

where we have put $q_1^2 = q_2^2 = q_\pi^2$. Thus

$$a_1 = 0$$
$$a_2 = 0$$
$$a_3 + a_4 + a_5 = 0 \qquad (6.61)$$

The second relation [Eq. (6.54)] for $q_1 \to 0$ leads to the result

$$a_1 + (a_2 + a_5)q^2 + 2a_3 q_\pi^2$$
$$= -i(M_\pi^2/C_\pi)\langle \pi^+(q_2)\pi^-(q_3)|\, H_w(0)\,|K_1^0(q)\rangle \qquad (6.62)$$

We then obtain on using Eq. (6.61),

$$-a_5 M_K^2 - 2a_3 M_\pi^2 = -i(M_\pi^2/C_\pi)\langle \pi^+ \pi^-|\, H_w(0)\,|K_1^0(q)\rangle \qquad (6.63)$$

Thus it seems we have four equations [Eqs. (6.61) and (6.63)] to solve for five constants. However, it is easy to see that one does have a fifth condition on the $K_2^0 \to \pi^0\pi^+\pi^-$ decay arising from the unphysical case when the kaon is off mass shell. Proceeding as before, one can check that

$$\langle \pi^0(q_1)\pi^+(q_2)\pi^-(q_3)|\, H_w(0)\,|K_1^0(0)\rangle = 0 \qquad (6.64)$$

This follows from the fact that in the octet dominance model we are using the weak Hamiltonian $H_w$ transforms as the sixth component (see Appendix IV), and the equal time commutator

$$[a_3^2 + a_2^3, (H_w)_3^2 + (H_w)_2^3] = 0 \qquad (6.65)$$

From Eqs. (6.59) and (6.64) we get the extra constraint

$$a_1 + (2a_3 + a_4 + a_5)q_\pi^2 = 0 \qquad (6.66)$$

We now obtain, from Eqs. (6.61), (6.63), and (6.66), the values of the constants

$$a_1 = a_2 = a_3 = 0$$

$$a_4 M_K^2 = -a_5 M_K^2 = -\frac{iM_\pi^2}{C_\pi} \langle \pi^+\pi^- | H_w(0) | K_1^0 \rangle \qquad (6.67)$$

The $K_2^0 \to \pi^0\pi^+\pi^-$ matrix element [Eq. (6.59)] on mass shell is then given in the rest frame of the $K$ meson as

$$\langle \pi^0\pi^+\pi^- | H_w(0) | K_2^0 \rangle = -i\frac{M_\pi^2}{C_\pi} \langle \pi^+\pi^- | H_w(0) | K_1^0 \rangle \left\{ 1 - \frac{2w_1}{M_K} \right\} \qquad (6.68)$$

Following the same technique the other $\tau$-decay amplitudes can be related to the $K_1^0 \to \pi^+\pi^-$ decay matrix element.

Phenomenologically, the $\tau$ decay amplitudes can be parameterized in the rest frame of the $K$ meson as

$$|\langle \pi^0\pi^+\pi^- | H_w(0) | K_2^0 \rangle|^2$$
$$= |\langle \pi^0\pi^+\pi^- | H_w(0) | K_2^0 \rangle_{\text{av}}|^2 \times \left\{ 1 + \frac{S(3T_0 - Q)}{Q} \right\} \qquad (6.69)$$

where $T_0$ is the kinetic energy of the odd pion $\pi^0$, and $Q$ stands for the $Q$ value of the decay. Also $S$ is the slope parameter which is known experimentally from the density distribution in the Dalitz plot. The average value of the matrix element in the right-hand side of Eq. (6.69) is the value of the matrix element for the average energy $T_0 = Q/3$ or $w_1 = M_K/3$. From Eq. (6.69), one then obtains

$$|\langle \pi^0\pi^+\pi^- | H_w(0) | K_2^0 \rangle_{\text{av}}| = \frac{M_\pi^2}{3C_\pi} |\langle \pi^+\pi^- | H_w(0) | K_1^0 \rangle| \qquad (6.70)$$

Similar relations can also be written for the other $\tau$ decays. One obtains in this way

$$(M_\pi^2/3C_\pi)|\langle \pi^+\pi^- | H_w(0) | K_1^0 \rangle| = |\langle \pi^0\pi^+\pi^- | H_w(0) | K_2^0 \rangle_{\text{av}}|$$
$$= \tfrac{1}{3}|\langle \pi^0\pi^0\pi^0 | H_w(0) | K_2^0 \rangle_{\text{av}}|$$
$$= \tfrac{1}{2}|\langle \pi^-\pi^+\pi^+ | H_w(0) | K^+ \rangle_{\text{av}}|$$
$$= |\langle \pi^+\pi^0\pi^0 | H_w(0) | K^+ \rangle_{\text{av}}| \qquad (6.71)$$

From experiments, one obtains (Hara and Nambu)[38]

$$(M_\pi^2/3C_\pi)|\langle\pi^+\pi^-|\ H_w(0)\ |K_1^0\rangle| = (0.81\ \pm\ 0.01)\ \times\ 10^{-6}$$
$$|\langle\pi^0\pi^+\pi^-|\ H_w(0)\ |K_2^0\rangle_{av}| = (0.89\ \pm\ 0.03)\ \times\ 10^{-6}$$
$$\tfrac{1}{3}|\langle\pi^0\pi^0\pi^0|\ H_w(0)\ |K_2^0\rangle_{av}| = (0.92\ \pm\ 0.05)\ \times\ 10^{-6}$$
$$\tfrac{1}{2}|\langle\pi^-\pi^+\pi^+|\ H_w(0)\ |K^+\rangle_{av}| = (0.96\ \pm\ 0.02)\ \times\ 10^{-6}$$
$$|\langle\pi^+\pi^0\pi^0|\ H_w(0)\ |K^+\rangle_{av}| = (0.94\ \pm\ 0.01)\ \times\ 10^{-6} \qquad (6.72)$$

Thus the agreement of relations [Eq. (6.71)] with experiments is very good.

Theoretically, the slope parameter $S$ in Eq. (6.69) is also predicted for the $\tau$ decays. From Eqs. (6.68) and (6.69), we obtain

$$S(K_2^0 \to \pi^0\pi^+\pi^-) \approx -4Q/M_{K^0}$$
$$S(K^+ \to \pi^-\pi^+\pi^+) \approx 2Q/M_{K^+}$$
$$S(K^+ \to \pi^+\pi^0\pi^0) \approx -4Q/M_{K^+} \qquad (6.73)$$

The comparison of these estimates with experimental values[26c,38] is shown below. Evidently the agreement is very good.

TABLE II

| $S$ | Theoretical values | Experimental values |
| --- | --- | --- |
| $S(K_2^0 \to \pi^0\pi^+\pi^-)$ | $-0.67$ | $-0.67 \pm 0.06$ |
| $S(K^+ \to \pi^-\pi^+\pi^+)$ | $0.30$ | $0.23 \pm 0.03$ |
| $S(K^+ \to \pi^+\pi^0\pi^0)$ | $-0.68$ | $-0.70 \pm 0.06$ |

## 7. Possible Dynamical Basis of $\Delta I = 1/2$ Rule[38a,39]

Suggestions have existed for some time that basically the non-leptonic Hamiltonian may have terms corresponding to both $\Delta I = 1/2$ and $\Delta I = 3/2$, and that somehow the dynamics of the nonleptonic decays tend to enhance the $\Delta I = 1/2$ part. In the terminology of $SU(3)$ one may hope to see the octet dominance of the nonleptonic weak Hamiltonian Eq. (6.8) emerge as a dynamical consequence. Such a situation would be quite attractive from the point of view of the current × current picture of weak interactions, built out of charged currents only. As mentioned earlier, to write a current × current nonleptonic Hamiltonian which transforms purely as an octet, one would have to include neutral currents, for which there seems to be no evidence from leptonic and semileptonic decays.

In this section we shall show how the techniques of current algebra indeed lead to an understanding of the dynamical enhancement of the $\Delta I = 1/2$ part of the weak nonleptonic Hamiltonian, at least in some nonleptonic decays. It is important to keep in mind that octet dominance is more restrictive than the $\Delta I = 1/2$ rule. Indeed, we shall see that in some cases where the enhancement of the $\Delta I = 1/2$ part of the weak Hamiltonian can be established, one cannot show octet dominance.

### A. $K \to 2\pi$

We shall first show that in the limit of the double soft-pion emission only the $\Delta I = 1/2$ part of the weak Hamiltonian contributes to $K \to 2\pi$ decays. As we have mentioned earlier, in problems involving more than one pion there are ambiguities which arise in the off-shell extrapolation, particularly from considerations of Bose statistics. We shall first follow the simple prescription of Suzuki[38a] and extrapolate the pions off shell one by one from a state of $2\pi$, which is explicitly symmetric in space. Consider, for example, the decay $K_1^0 \to \pi^+\pi^-$, for which we write the matrix element

$$M(q_1, q_2) = \frac{1}{\sqrt{2}} \langle \pi^+(q_1)\pi^-(q_2) + \pi^-(q_1)\pi^+(q_2)| H_w(0) |K_1^0\rangle \quad (6.74)$$

Using the standard procedure, we obtain in the limit $q_1 \to 0$, the result

$$M(0, q_2) = -i \frac{M_\pi^2}{C_\pi} \{\langle \pi^-(q_2)| [a_2^1(0), H_w(0)] |K_1^0\rangle$$
$$+ \langle \pi^+(q_2)| [a_1^2(0), H_w(0)] |K_1^0\rangle \quad (6.75)$$

where the $a$'s are the axial charges defined in Eq. (2.2.2). If we take $H_w$ as the current $\times$ current Hamiltonian containing both $\Delta I = 1/2$ and $3/2$ parts, we can use the equal time-commutation relation [Eq. (6.17)] to obtain

$$M(0, q_2) = (i\sqrt{2} M_\pi^2/C_\pi)\langle \pi^-(q_2)| H_w(0) |K^-\rangle \quad (6.76)$$

Contracting the $\pi^-(q_2)$ now and taking the limit $q_2 \to 0$, we obtain, following the same procedure as before, the result

$$M(0, 0) = -\sqrt{2} \left(\frac{M_\pi^2}{C_\pi}\right)^2 \langle 0| H_w(0) |K_1^0\rangle \quad (6.77)$$

Clearly only the $\Delta I = 1/2$ part of the Hamiltonian $H_w$ can lead to a nonvanishing contribution to Eq. (6.77). Since we expect Eq. (6.77) to be a reasonable approximation to the on-shell matrix element Eq. (6.74), we conclude that the contribution of the $\Delta I = 3/2$ part of $H_w$ to $K \rightarrow 2\pi$ amplitude must be small compared with the $\Delta I = 1/2$ part.

An alternative and perhaps better way of maintaining Bose symmetry is to contract both the pions simultaneously by a method due to Weinberg. If we define

$$T_{\mu\nu} = \int d^4x \, d^4y \, e^{-iq_1 \cdot x} \, e^{-iq_2 \cdot y} \langle 0| \, T(A_\mu(x)_2^1 A_\nu(y)_1^2 H_w(0) \, |K_1^0\rangle \quad (6.78)$$

then by multiplying with $q_{1\mu}$ and $q_{2\nu}$ and doing partial integrations, one obtains the identity:

$$M(q_1, q_2) = (2/C_\pi^2)(q_1^2 + M_\pi^2)(q_2^2 + M_\pi^2)$$

$$\times \left[ q_{1\mu} q_{2\nu} T_{\mu\nu} + \int d^4x \, d^4y \, e^{-iq_1 \cdot x} \, e^{-iq_2 \cdot y} \right.$$

$$\times \{\delta(x_0)\langle 0| \, T(\partial_\nu A_\nu(y)_1^2 [A_0(x)_2^1, H_w(0)]) \, |K_1^0\rangle$$

$$+ \, \delta(y_0)\langle 0| \, T(\partial_\mu A_\mu(x)_2^1 [A_0(y)_1^2, H_w(0)]) \, |K_1^0\rangle$$

$$+ \, \tfrac{1}{2}\delta(x_0)\delta(y_0)\langle 0| \, \{A_0(x)_2^1, [A_0(y)_1^2, H_w(0)]\} \, |K_1^0\rangle$$

$$+ \, \tfrac{1}{2}\delta(x_0)\delta(y_0)\langle 0|\{A_0(y)_1^2, [A_0(x)_2^1, H_w(0)]\} \, |K_1^0\rangle$$

$$- \, \frac{i}{2}(q_1 - q_2)_\mu \delta(x_0 - y_0)\langle 0| \, T\{[A_0(x)_2^1, A_\mu(y)_1^2] H_w(0)\} \, |K_1^0\rangle$$

$$+ \, \delta(x_0 - y_0)\langle 0| \, T\{[A_0(x)_2^1, \partial_\nu A_\nu(y)_1^2] H_w(0)\} \, |K_1^0\rangle\} \right] \quad (6.79)$$

Now letting $q_1, q_2 \rightarrow 0$, the first term on the right-hand side goes to zero. The second and the third terms on the right-hand side are proportional to the matrix element $\langle \pi| \, H_w \, |K\rangle$ which, in turn, we know is proportional to $\langle 0| \, H_w \, |K\rangle$ in the soft-pion limit. The fourth and fifth terms on the right-hand side are directly proportional to the matrix element $\langle 0| \, H_w \, |K\rangle$. The sixth term vanishes, since the matrix element can depend only on the four-momentum of $K_1^0$ from considerations of Lorentz invariance, and multiplication with the factor $(q_1 - q_2)_\mu$ gives a null result. Thus the first six terms on the right-hand side of Eq. (6.79) essentially give a contribution to $M(0, 0)$ which is proportional to the matrix element $\langle 0| \, H_w \, |K\rangle$, so that for this contribution one concludes that the $\Delta I = 3/2$ part of $H_w$ cannot contribute. All that remains to be shown is that the same conclusion also follows for the last term on the right-hand side of Eq. (6.79). This term contains an equal time commutator $\delta(x_0 - y_0)[A_0(x)_{\frac{1}{2}}^1, \partial_\nu A_\nu(y)_1^2]$. Since $\partial_\nu A_\nu$ is a pseudoscalar density, on the basis of the quark model the commutator can be calculated easily, and behaves like a member of the octet of scalar densities. Also note that we have here a $d$-type commutator; hence $\delta(x_0 - y_0)[A_0(x)_{\frac{1}{2}}^1, \partial_\nu A_{\nu 1}^2(y)]$ must transform like an object with $I = 0$. Thus the $\Delta I = 3/2$ part of $H_w$ cannot also contribute to the last term on the right-hand side of Eq. (6.79); note that this result depends on special models.

Since $K \to 3\pi$ is related to $K \to 2\pi$ (see Section V-6), it follows that the $\Delta I = 1/2$ part of the weak Hamiltonian also dominates the $K \to 3\pi$ decays.

### B. s-Wave Hyperon Decays

Using the current algebra techniques for the weak Hamiltonian Eq. (6.8) containing both an octet and a 27-plet part, we summarize for $s$-wave decays the following four sum rules [Eqs. (6.31)–(6.33) and (6.38)]:

$$\sqrt{2}\, A(\Lambda_0^0) + A(\Lambda_-^0) = 0$$
$$\sqrt{2}\, A(\Xi_0^0) + A(\Xi_-^-) = 0$$
$$A(\Sigma_-^-) + \sqrt{2}\, A(\Sigma_0^+) + A(\Sigma_+^+) = 0$$
$$2A(\Xi_-^-) + A(\Lambda_-^0) = \sqrt{3}\, A(\Sigma_0^+) + \sqrt{\tfrac{3}{2}}\, A(\Sigma_+^+) \qquad (6.80)$$

The first two relations are precisely the $\Delta I = 1/2$ results, and the last two which contain $\Sigma^-$ decays are different, as mentioned before. It is quite easy to see why only the $\Delta I = 1/2$ part of $H_w$ contributes to $\Lambda$ and $\Xi$ decays but not to $\Sigma$ decays. The contraction and off-shell extrapolation of the pion lead to the result that the $s$-wave amplitude is proportional to matrix elements of the type $\langle B' |\, H_w \,|B\rangle$. If now $B$ and $B'$ have isospins 0 and 1/2 or 1/2 and 0, respectively, then the $\Delta I = 3/2$ part of $H_w$ cannot contribute. This is clearly the case for the decays $\Lambda \to N\pi$ and $\Xi \to \Lambda\pi$, but not for the $\Sigma \to N\pi$ decays. Note here in passing that if there were a way of proving $A(\Sigma_+^+) = 0$ (not based on the assumption of octet dominance), all the four sum rules [Eq. (6.80)] would be consequences of octet dominance.

### C. p-Wave Hyperon Decays

Here no statement can be made about the $\Delta I = 1/2$ rule on the basis of the techniques of current algebra. The reason for this is because the $p$-wave amplitudes are essentially given by the baryon pole terms, (see Section V-4), and for all the decays there is at least one weak vertex of the type $\langle N| \ H_w \ |\Sigma\rangle$ or $\langle\Xi| \ H_w \ |\Sigma\rangle$ [see Eq. (6.46)] which would have contributions coming from the $\Delta I = 3/2$ part of $H_w$. In our treatment of $p$-wave decays we had assumed octet dominance right from the start. It is easy to check[39d] that if this assumption is relaxed, the current algebra techniques for the general current × current Hamiltonian containing both $\mathbf{8}_s$ and $\mathbf{27}$ parts yield two sum rules, which relate the deviations from the $\Delta I = 1/2$ results to those from the Lee-Sugawara triangle.

In conclusion we would like to briefly mention some attempts made on the basis of current algebra to estimate the absolute decay rate of the nonleptonic hyperon[40] and kaon decays.[41] Great interest attaches to this problem for the following reasons. The universality of the current–current interaction in the form proposed by Cabibbo has not yet been tested. The Cabibbo form of the current–current interaction would tend to supress the nonleptonic decay rate by a factor of $\sin^2 \theta$ and it is not clear whether this effect can be offset by a compensating enhancement of the relevant matrix elements.

To obtain the absolute decay rates, one can adopt the following procedure. One starts from the matrix elements given by Eqs. (6.28) and (6.46) for the hyperon decays and the expressions like Eq. (6.76) for the $K \rightarrow 2\pi$ decays, where one pion has been contracted and extrapolated to the soft limit. If we now insert a complete set of states in these matrix elements and confine ourselves to the contributions of only a few low-lying mass states, we can estimate these amplitudes in terms of integrals over the relevant form factors which are either known experimentally or may be suitably approximated. It is interesting that one does obtain reasonable results for the $s$-wave hyperon decays and $K \rightarrow 2\pi$ decays, despite the approximations used. For $p$ waves the situation is not so good, and this may be related to the troubles with the $p$-wave analysis mentioned before. A rather encouraging result[41] obtains in the case of $K^\pm \rightarrow \pi^\pm\pi^0$ decay, which we have seen in Section VI-7-A would vanish in the limit of both pions being soft. In the present case, when only one pion is soft, one does obtain a suppression of this decay mode in comparison to the other $K \rightarrow 2\pi$ decays by about the right order of magnitude. Although these calculations can at best be taken as qualitative indications, it is interesting that they are consistent with the concept of Cabibbo's form of universality.

## Acknowledgments

We would like to express our deep sense of appreciation to Professor R. E. Marshak for his advice and suggestions. We would also like to thank the members of the High Energy Group for many fruitful discussions. Finally, we are grateful to Mr. T. Becherrawy and Mrs. Y. W. Yang for their assistance.

## Appendix I

### A. Dirac Matrices, the Bilinear Covariants and CPT Transformations

We work in the metric such that $AB = A\mu B\mu = \mathbf{A} \cdot \mathbf{B} + A_4 B_4 = \mathbf{A} \cdot \mathbf{B} - A_0 B_0$. We shall use hermitian Dirac matrices $\gamma_\mu (\mu = 1\text{–}4)$ and

$$\gamma_5 = \gamma_1 \gamma_2 \gamma_3 \gamma_4 \tag{A.1}$$

with

$$\gamma_5^2 = 1 \tag{A.2}$$

The free-field Dirac equation reads

$$(\gamma_\mu \, \partial_\mu + m)\psi(x) = 0 \tag{A.3}$$

and in momentum space, for positive energy solution $\psi(x) \sim u(\mathbf{p}) \, e^{ip \cdot x}$, $(p^2 = -m^2)$

$$(i\gamma_\mu p_\mu + m)u(\mathbf{p}) = 0 \tag{A.4}$$

Defining

$$\bar{\psi}(x) = \psi^+(x)\gamma_4 \tag{A.5}$$

we have the adjoint equation

$$\partial_\mu \bar{\psi}(x)\gamma_\mu - m\bar{\psi}(x) = 0 \tag{A.6}$$

and

$$\bar{u}(p)(i\gamma_\mu p_\mu + m) = 0 \tag{A.7}$$

We shall use the invariant normalization for the (positive energy) spinors $u(p)$:

$$\bar{u}(p)u(p) = 1, \quad u^+(p)u(p) = \frac{p_0}{m} \tag{A.8}$$

The positive energy Casimir projection operator is then

$$\Lambda_+(\mathbf{p}) = (-i\gamma \cdot p + m)/2m \tag{A.9}$$

## B. Charge Conjugation C

Under the unitary transformation $C$ we have the following transformation properties

### 1. Spin 1/2

$$\psi(x) \rightarrow C\psi(x)C^{-1} = \mathscr{C}\bar{\psi}^T(x)$$
$$\bar{\psi}(x) \rightarrow C\bar{\psi}(x)C^{-1} = -\psi^T(x)\mathscr{C}$$

where

$$\mathscr{C}^{-1}\gamma_\mu\mathscr{C} = -\gamma_\mu^T, \quad \mathscr{C}^T = -\mathscr{C}, \quad \mathscr{C}^+ = \mathscr{C}^{-1}$$

$$|(\text{particle}) \, \mathbf{p}, r\rangle \rightarrow C \, |(\text{particle}) \, \mathbf{p}, r\rangle = |(\text{antiparticle}) \, \mathbf{p}, r\rangle$$

and

$$u_r(\mathbf{p}) = \mathscr{C}\bar{v}_r^T(\mathbf{p}) = u_r^C(p)$$

where $v(\mathbf{p})$ is the negative spinor of momentum $-\mathbf{p}$.

### 2. Spin 0

$$\phi(x) \rightarrow C\phi(x)C^{-1} = \phi^+(x)$$
$$C \, |\text{particle } p\rangle = |\text{antiparticle } p\rangle$$

### 3. Spin 1

$$A_\mu(x) \rightarrow CA_\mu(x)C^{-1} = \eta \begin{cases} A_\mu^+(x) & \text{for } \mu = 1, 2, 3 \\ -A_\mu^+(x) & \text{for } \mu = 4 \end{cases} \equiv \eta A_\mu^{\ddagger}(x)$$

where $\eta = -1$ for vector and $\eta = +1$ for axial vector. We have introduced the "double dagger" notation

$$A_\mu^{\ddagger} = A_\mu^+ \quad \text{for } \mu \neq 4$$
$$A_\mu^{\ddagger} = -A_\mu^+ \quad \text{for } \mu = 4$$

so that $A_\mu^{\ddagger}$ is a Lorentz four vector like $A_\mu$. Further

$$C \, |\text{particle } p \cdot \lambda\rangle = \eta \, |\text{particle } p \cdot \lambda\rangle$$

## C. Parity Transformation P

Under the unitary transformation $P$, the transform properties are as listed below:

### 1. Spin 1/2

$$\psi(x) \rightarrow P\psi(x)P^{-1} = \gamma_4\psi(-\mathbf{x}, x_0)$$
$$\bar{\psi}(x) \rightarrow P\bar{\psi}(x)P^{-1} = \bar{\psi}(-\mathbf{x}, x_0)\gamma_4$$

The state vector of a single spin 1/2 particle with momentum $\mathbf{p}$ and spin projection $r$ transforms as

$$|\mathbf{p}, r\rangle \to P \, | \, \mathbf{p}, r\rangle = | - \mathbf{p}, r\rangle$$

and

$$\gamma_4 u_r(\mathbf{p}) = u_r(-\mathbf{p})$$

2. Spin 0

$$\phi(x) \to P\phi(x)P^{-1} = \eta\phi(-\mathbf{x}, x_0)$$

where $\eta = -1$ for pseudoscalar field and $\eta = +1$ for scalar field and

$$P \, |\mathbf{p}\rangle = \eta \, |- \mathbf{p}\rangle$$

3. Spin 1

$$A_\mu(x) \to PA_\mu(x)P^{-1} = \eta \begin{cases} A_\mu(-\mathbf{x}, x_0), & \mu = 1, 2, 3 \\ -A_\mu(-\mathbf{x}, x_0), & \mu = 4 \end{cases}$$

where $\eta = -1$ for vector field and $\eta = +1$ for axial-vector field. For the corresponding single particle state vector with polarization state $\lambda$,

$$|\mathbf{p}, \lambda\rangle \to P \, |\mathbf{p}, \lambda\rangle = \eta \, |-\mathbf{p}, \lambda\rangle$$

and for the corresponding polarization vectors we have

$$\varepsilon_\mu^\lambda(\mathbf{p}) = \begin{cases} \varepsilon_\mu^{(\lambda)}(-\mathbf{p}), & \mu = 1, 2, 3 \\ -\varepsilon_\mu^{(\lambda)}(-\mathbf{p}), & \mu = 4 \end{cases}$$

### D. Time Reversal T

Under the *antiunitary* transformation $T$ we have

$$(\psi, \phi) \to (T\psi, T\phi) = (\psi, \phi)^*$$

$$T\lambda T^{-1} = \lambda^*$$

for any $c$ number $\lambda$. Also we have the following list of transformations:

### 1. Spin 1/2

$$T\psi(\mathbf{x}, x_0)T^{-1} = B\psi(\mathbf{x}, -x_0)$$

$$T\bar\psi(\mathbf{x}, x_0)T^{-1} = \bar\psi(\mathbf{x}, -x_0)B^{-1}$$

where

$$B\gamma_\mu B^{-1} = \gamma_\mu^* = \gamma_\mu^T; \qquad B^+ = B^{-1}, \quad B^T = -B$$

Since

$$\gamma_5 = \gamma_1\gamma_2\gamma_3\gamma_4, \quad B\gamma_r B^{-1} = \gamma_5^*$$

Also

$$Bu_r(\mathbf{p}) = u^*_{-r}(-\mathbf{p})$$

$$\bar{u}_r(\mathbf{p})B^{-1} = \bar{u}^*_{-r}(-\mathbf{p})$$

$$T\,|\mathbf{p}, r\rangle = |-\mathbf{p}, -r\rangle$$

## 2. Spin 0

$$T\phi(\mathbf{x}, x_0)T^{-1} = \eta\phi(\mathbf{x}, -x_0)$$

$$T\,|\,\mathbf{p}\rangle = \eta\,|-\mathbf{p}\rangle$$

where $\eta = -1$ for the pseudoscalar case and $\eta = +1$ for the scalar case.

## 3. Spin 1

$$TA_\mu(\mathbf{x}, x_0)T^{-1} = -A_\mu(\mathbf{x}, -x_0)$$

$$T\,|\mathbf{p}, \lambda\rangle = -|-\mathbf{p}, -\lambda\rangle \quad (\lambda = +1, 0, -1)$$

also

$$(\epsilon_\mu^{(\lambda)}(\mathbf{p}))^* = \epsilon_\mu^{(-\lambda)}(-\mathbf{p})$$

We shall define the standard Dirac bilinear covariants as the normal products:

$$J^i_{AB}(x) \equiv\, :\bar{\psi}_A(x)\mathcal{O}_i\psi_B(x):$$

with

$$\mathcal{O}^i = \mathbf{1},\, \gamma_\mu,\, \sigma_{\mu\nu} \equiv \frac{1}{2i}(\gamma_\mu\gamma_\nu - \gamma_\nu\gamma_\mu),\, i\gamma_\mu\gamma_5,\, \gamma_5$$

for the $i = S, V, T, A$, and $P$ covariants, respectively. The $C$, $P$, and $T$ transformation properties of these covariants are summarized in Table AI.

Let us remind ourselves that the invariance of the Lagrangian density under $T$ implies

$$T\mathscr{L}(\mathbf{x}, x_0)T^{-1} = \mathscr{L}(\mathbf{x}, -x_0)$$

We have made copious use of $T$ transformation properties for fixing the reality properties of the various coupling constants and form factors appearing in our matrix elements. For example, consider the matrix element

$$\langle p(\mathbf{p}_2, r_2)|\, A_\mu(0)\, |n(\mathbf{p}_1, r_1)\rangle = \bar{u}_p^{r_2}(\mathbf{p}_2)[F_1\gamma_\mu\gamma_5 + F_2(p_1 - p_2)_\mu\gamma_5]u_n^{r_1}(\mathbf{p}_1)$$

TABLE AI[a]

| Transformation | S<br>1 | V<br>$\gamma_\mu$ | T<br>$\dfrac{1}{2i}[\gamma_\mu, \gamma_\nu]$ | A<br>$i\gamma_\mu\gamma_5$ | P<br>$\gamma_5$ |
|---|---|---|---|---|---|
| C | $J^S_{BA}(x)$ | $-J^V_{BA}(x)$ | $-J^T_{BA}(x)$ | $J^A_{BA}(x)$ | $J^P_{BA}(x)$ |
| P | $J^S_{AB}(-\mathbf{x}, x_0)$ | $(-1)^n J^V_{AB}(-\mathbf{x}, x_0)$ | $(-1)^n J^T_{AB}(-\mathbf{x}, x_0)$ | $(-)^{n+1}J^A_{AB}(-\mathbf{x}, x_0)$ | $-J^P_{AB}(-\mathbf{x}, x_0)$ |
| T | $J^S_{AB}(\mathbf{x}, -x_0)$ | $J^V_{AB}(\mathbf{x}, -x_0)$ | $-J^T_{AB}(\mathbf{x}, -x_0)$ | $-J^A_{AB}(\mathbf{x}, -x_0)$ | $J^P_{AB}(\mathbf{x}, -x_0)$ |

[a] Transformation properties of the bilinear covariants under $C$, $P$, and $T$. $n$ stands for the number of $\gamma_k$ $(k = 1, 2, 3)$ appearing in the $\mathcal{O}^i$.

We have

$$
\begin{aligned}
\langle p(\mathbf{p}_2, r_2)| \, A_i(0) \, |n(\mathbf{p}_1, r_1)\rangle^* &= \langle p(\mathbf{p}_2, r_2)| \, T^{-1}TA_i(0) \, |n(\mathbf{p}_1, r_1)\rangle \\
&= \langle (\mathbf{p}_2, r_2)| \, T^{-1}[TA_i(0)T^{-1}]T \, |n(\mathbf{p}_1, r_1)\rangle \\
&= \langle p(\mathbf{p}_2, r_2)| \, T^{-1}[-A_i(0)]T \, |n(\mathbf{p}_1, r_1)\rangle \\
&= -\langle p(-\mathbf{p}_2, -r_2)| \, A_i(0) \, |n(-\mathbf{p}_1, r_1)\rangle \\
&= -\bar{u}_p^{-r_2}(-\mathbf{p}_2)[F_1\gamma_i\gamma_5 + F_2(-p_1 + p_2)_i\gamma_5] \\
&\qquad\qquad \times u_n^{-r_1}(-\mathbf{p}_1)
\end{aligned}
$$

Hence

$$
\begin{aligned}
\langle p(\mathbf{p}_2, r_2)| \, A_i(0) \, |n(\mathbf{p}_1, r_1)\rangle &\\
&= -\bar{u}_p^{-r_2*}(-\mathbf{p}_2)[F_1^*\gamma_i^*\gamma_5^* - F_2^*(p_1 - p_2)_i^*\gamma_5^*]u_n^{-r_1*}(-\mathbf{p}_1) \\
&= -\bar{u}_{p_2}^{r_2}(\mathbf{p}_2)B^{-1}[F_1^*\gamma_i^*\gamma_5^* - F_2^*(p_1 - p_2)_i\gamma_5^*]Bu_n^{r_1}(\mathbf{p}) \\
&= -\bar{u}_{p_2}^{r_2}(\mathbf{p}_2)[F_1^*\gamma_i\gamma_5 - F_2^*(p_1 - p_2)\gamma_5]u_n^{r_1}(\mathbf{p}_1)
\end{aligned}
$$

Therefore

$$
F_1^* = -F_1, \quad F_2^* = F_2
$$

## Appendix II

### A. The $SU_2$ and $SU_3$ Labeling of Particle States and Phase Conventions[42]

We shall denote a state belonging to the $N$-dimensional irreducible unitary representation of $SU_3$ by $|N; Y, I, I_3\rangle$ corresponding hypercharge value $Y$, isospin $I$, and third component of isospin $I_3$.

For relative phases between the states of a given isospin $SU_2$ multiplet we shall follow the standard Condon and Shortley phase convention:

$$
I_\pm \, |N; Y, I, I_3\rangle = +\sqrt{(I \mp I_3)(I \pm I_3 + 1)} \, |N; Y, I, I_3 \pm 1\rangle
$$

For relative phase between the different isomultiplets within a given $SU_3$ multiplet we shall use the following convention:

$$
\begin{aligned}
K_+ \, |N; &Y, I, I_3\rangle \\
&= k_+ \, |N; Y + 1, I + \tfrac{1}{2}, I_3 + \tfrac{1}{2}\rangle + k_- \, |N; Y + 1, I - \tfrac{1}{2}, I_3 + \tfrac{1}{2}\rangle
\end{aligned}
$$

with*

$$k_+ = (-)\left\{\frac{\begin{array}{c}[I + I_3 + 1][\frac{1}{3}(\lambda - \mu) + I + \frac{1}{2}Y + 1] \\ \times [\frac{1}{3}(\lambda + 2\mu) + I + \frac{1}{2}Y + 2][\frac{1}{3}(2\lambda + \mu) - I - \frac{1}{2}Y]\end{array}}{2(I + 1)(2I + 1)}\right\}^{1/2}$$

$$k_- = (-)\left\{\frac{\begin{array}{c}[I - I_3][\frac{1}{3}(\mu - \lambda) + I - \frac{1}{2}Y][\frac{1}{3}(\lambda + 2\mu) - I + \frac{1}{2}Y + 1] \\ \times [\frac{1}{3}(2\lambda + \mu) + I - \frac{1}{2}Y + 1]\end{array}}{2I(2I + 1)}\right\}^{1/2}$$

where the representation in the highest weight notation is represented by $(\lambda, \mu)$.

### 1. The Octet States

$$|\pi^+\rangle = M_1^2 |0\rangle = -|8; 0, 1, +1\rangle$$

$$|\pi^0\rangle = \frac{1}{\sqrt{2}}(M_1^1 - M_2^2)|0\rangle = |8; 0, 1, 0\rangle$$

$$|\pi^-\rangle = M_2^1 |0\rangle = |8; 0, 1, -1\rangle$$

$$|K^+\rangle = M_1^3 |0\rangle = |8; +1, \tfrac{1}{2}, +\tfrac{1}{2}\rangle$$

$$|K^0\rangle = M_2^3 |0\rangle = |8; +1, \tfrac{1}{2}, -\tfrac{1}{2}\rangle$$

$$|\bar{K}_0\rangle = M_3^2 |0\rangle = |8; -1, \tfrac{1}{2}, +\tfrac{1}{2}\rangle$$

$$|K^-\rangle = M_3^1 |0\rangle = -|8; -1, \tfrac{1}{2}, -\tfrac{1}{2}\rangle$$

$$|\eta^0\rangle = -\sqrt{\tfrac{3}{2}} M_3^3 |0\rangle = |8; 0, 0, 0\rangle$$

The traceless tensor $M_b^a$ stands for the tensor of the *creation* operators of the particle states indicated.

$$M_{b\,(\text{row})}^{a\,(\text{column})} |0\rangle$$

$$= \begin{bmatrix} \frac{1}{\sqrt{2}}|\pi^0\rangle + \frac{1}{\sqrt{6}}|\eta^0\rangle & |\pi^+\rangle & |K^+\rangle \\[2ex] |\pi^-\rangle & -\frac{1}{\sqrt{2}}|\pi^0\rangle + \frac{1}{\sqrt{6}}|\eta^0\rangle & |K^0\rangle \\[2ex] |K^-\rangle & |\bar{K}^0\rangle & -\sqrt{\frac{2}{3}}|\eta^0\rangle \end{bmatrix}$$

* Note the difference in signs from those in refs. 42 and 43.

For the vector meson octet replace

$$M \to V; \quad \pi \to \rho, \quad K \to K^*, \quad \eta \to \omega_8$$

For the baryon octet replace

$$M \to B; \quad \pi \to \Sigma, \quad K \to N, \quad \bar{K} \to \Xi, \quad \eta \to \Lambda$$

## 2. The Decuplet States

$$|N^{*++}\rangle = D_{111}|0\rangle = |10; 1, \tfrac{3}{2}, +\tfrac{3}{2}\rangle$$

$$|N^{*+}\rangle = \sqrt{3}\, D_{112}|0\rangle = |10; 1, \tfrac{3}{2}, \tfrac{1}{2}\rangle$$

$$|N^{*0}\rangle = \sqrt{3}\, D_{122}|0\rangle = |10; 1, \tfrac{3}{2}, -\tfrac{1}{2}\rangle$$

$$|N^{*-}\rangle = D_{222}|0\rangle = |10; 1, \tfrac{3}{2}, -\tfrac{3}{2}\rangle$$

$$|Y_1^{*+}\rangle = \sqrt{3}\, D_{113}|0\rangle = -|10; 0, 1, +1\rangle$$

$$|Y_1^{*0}\rangle = \sqrt{6}\, D_{123}|0\rangle = -|10; 0, 1, 0\rangle$$

$$|Y_1^{*-}\rangle = \sqrt{3}\, D_{223}|0\rangle = -|10; 0, 1, -1\rangle$$

$$|\Xi^{*0}\rangle = \sqrt{3}\, D_{133}|0\rangle = |10; -1, \tfrac{1}{2}, +\tfrac{1}{2}\rangle$$

$$|\Xi^{*-}\rangle = \sqrt{3}\, D_{233}|0\rangle = |10; -1, \tfrac{1}{2}, -\tfrac{1}{2}\rangle$$

$$|\Omega^-\rangle = D_{333}|0\rangle = -|10; -2, 0, 0\rangle$$

The completely symmetric tensor $D_{abc}$ is the tensor of *creation* operators as indicated.

## B. The Irreducible Tensor Operator

The set of operators $T^N_{Y,I,I_3}$ will denote the components of an $SU_3$ irreducible tensor operator of dimensionality $N$. They satisfy standard commutation relations with the generators; for example,

$$[I_\pm, T^N_{Y,I,I_3}] = +\sqrt{(I \mp I_3)(I \pm I_3 + 1)}\, T^N_{Y,I,I_3 \pm 1}$$

$$[K_+, T^N_{Y,I,I_3}] = k_+ T^N_{Y+1,I+\frac{1}{2},I_3+\frac{1}{2}} + k_- T^N_{Y+1,I-\frac{1}{2},I_3+\frac{1}{2}}$$

Thus, the pseudoscalar meson creation operators provide with the set of octet tensor operators:

$$(-(\pi^+)^\dagger, \pi^0, \pi^+; (K^+)^\dagger, (K^0)^\dagger; K^0, -K^+; \eta^0)$$

where $\pi^+(x)$ as operator creates a $\pi^-$ meson state and absorbs a $\pi^+$ meson state, etc.

Note, in passing, that the generators themselves form an irreducible octet tensor:

$$(-I_+, \sqrt{2}\, I_3, I_-;\; K_+, L_+;\; L_-, -K_-;\; \sqrt{\tfrac{3}{2}}\, Y)$$

### C. The Wigner-Eckart Theorem

For $SU(2)$ we have for the matrix element of any irreducible tensor operator $T_{l,m}$ (to be regarded as a creation operator acting to the right)

$$\langle I', I_3'|\, T_{l,m}\, |I, I_3\rangle = C^{I,l,I'}_{I_3,m,I_3'}\langle I' \| T_l \| I\rangle$$

where $C^{I,l,I'}_{I_3,m,I_3'}$ is the Clebsch-Gordon coefficient for the sum $I + l \rightarrow I'$.

Similarly denoting $(Y, I, I_3)$ values by $\nu$, we have for the $SU_3$ group the Wigner-Eckart theorem:

$$\langle N', \nu'|\, T_\mu^M\, |N, \nu\rangle = \sum_\gamma \begin{pmatrix} N & M & N'_\gamma \\ \nu & \mu & \nu' \end{pmatrix} \langle N' \| T^M \| N\rangle$$

where the index $\gamma$ distinguishes the multiple occurrences of the same representation in the product $N \otimes M$. The $SU_3$ Clebsch-Gordon coefficient $\begin{pmatrix} N & M & N' \\ \nu & \mu & \nu' \end{pmatrix}$ is as defined by de Swaart.[42]

## Appendix III

### The LSZ Contraction Formula

Consider the matrix element of an operator $J(y)$, of the form $\langle N_2\pi^+(q)\ \text{out}\ |\, J(y)\, |N_1\rangle$, where $N_1$ and $N_2$ stand, as an example, for nucleons, and $\pi(q)$ is a pion of momentum $q$. Then we may "contract" the pion and obtain the result

$$\langle N_2\pi^+(q)\ \text{out}\ |\, J(y)\, |N_1\rangle$$
$$= i \int d^4x\, \frac{e^{-iq.x}}{\sqrt{2q_0 V}} (q^2 + M_\pi^2)\langle N_2|\, \theta(x_0 - y_0)[(\pi^+(x))^\dagger, J(y)]\, |N_1\rangle$$

$$(A.10)$$

where $\pi^+(x)$ is field operator which asymptotically absorbs a $\pi^-$ or creates a $\pi^+$. This particular form of the reduction formula is the starting point of dispersion techniques, and will also be employed here.

Similarly, for the contraction of a $\pi^+$ pion on the right we would have

$$\langle N_2| \, J(y) \, |N_1\pi^+(q) \, \text{in}\rangle = i \int d^4x \, \frac{e^{iq\cdot x}}{\sqrt{2q_0 V}} (q^2 + M_\pi^2)$$

$$\times \langle N_2| \, \theta(y_0 - x_0)[J(y), \pi^+(x)] \, |N_1\rangle \quad \text{(A.11)}$$

Note that we have used translational operation in the form

$$\phi(x) = e^{-iP\cdot x}\phi(0) \, e^{iP\cdot x} \quad \text{(A.12)}$$

## Appendix IV

### 𝒞 Parity

This is a generalization[44] of the concept of charge-conjugation parity in the $SU(3)$ symmetry scheme. Consider a self-conjugate $SU(3)$ multiplet, an octet for simplicity. This could be, for example, an octet of mesons or of currents. If we designate the octet by the label $A_b^a$, the $\mathscr{C}$ parity for the octet (i.e., all the members of the octet) is defined as the phase factor which arises if one makes a transformation by the charge conjugation operator:

$$CA_b^a C^{-1} = \mathscr{C} A_a^b \quad \text{(A.13)}$$

For a given multiplet $A_b^a$, $\mathscr{C}$ parity can be easily fixed for the octet if one looks at the behavior under charge conjugation of the completely neutral member (charge $= 0$, strangeness $= 0$) of the octet. Then the known charge conjugation parity of this neutral member determines the $\mathscr{C}$ parity of the multiplet. For example, for the octet of $0^-$ mesons, since charge conjugation parity of $\pi^0$ is $+1$, $\mathscr{C}$ parity of $0^-$ mesons $= +1$. For the octets of self-conjugate $S$, $V$, $A$, $T$, and $P$, we know the behavior of the neutral members under charge conjugation (see Appendix I), namely

$$C \text{ parity of } S, A, P = +1$$

$$V, T = -1 \quad \text{(A.14)}$$

Hence,

$$\mathscr{C} \text{ parity of the octets: } S, A, P = +1$$

$$V, T = -1 \quad \text{(A.15)}$$

In the literature, one also speaks of octets of $S$ and $P$ with abnormal $C$ parity. The $C$ parity of the neutral members, and hence the $\mathscr{C}$ parity of such octets is then opposite to the one listed in Eqs. (A.14) and (A.15).

In the direct product of two selfconjugate octets $A_b^a$ and $B_d^c$ the symmetric and the antisymmetric terms again have a unique $\mathscr{C}$ parity. One can show for example that for the symmetric $\mathbf{8}_s$ and the antisymmetric $\mathbf{8}_a$, we have

$$\mathscr{C}[(A \otimes B)_{\mathbf{8}_s}] = \mathscr{C}(A)\mathscr{C}(B)$$

$$\mathscr{C}[(A \otimes B)_{\mathbf{8}_a}] = -\mathscr{C}(A)\mathscr{C}(B) \qquad (A.16)$$

*Proof*: Consider the symmetric and antisymmetric octets $S$ and $T$, respectively, occuring in the decomposition of the product of octets $A \otimes B$,

$$S_b^a = A_x^a B_b^x + A_b^x B_x^a - \tfrac{2}{3}\delta_b^a \langle AB \rangle$$

$$T_b^a = A_x^a B_b^x - A_b^x B_x^a \qquad (A.17)$$

From Eq. (A.13)

$$CS_b^a C^{-1}$$

$$= CA_x^a C^{-1} CB_b^x C^{-1} + CA_b^x C^{-1} CB_x^a C^{-1} - \tfrac{2}{3}\delta_b^a CA_x^c C^{-1} CB_c^x C^{-1}$$

$$= \mathscr{C}(A)\mathscr{C}(B)\{A_a^x B_x^b + A_x^b B_a^x - \tfrac{2}{3}\delta_a^b \langle AB \rangle\}$$

so that

$$CS_b^a C^{-1} = \mathscr{C}(A)\mathscr{C}(B)S_a^b$$

Similarly,

$$CT_b^a C^{-1} = -\mathscr{C}(A)\mathscr{C}(B)T_a^b$$

Equations (A.16) then follow immediately from definition Eq. (A.13).

Note that in the notation of Gell-Mann [see Eq. (2.7)], Eq. (A.13) implies for the second, fifth, and seventh components of an octet $\mathscr{C} = -C$, whereas for the rest $\mathscr{C} = +C$, where $C$ is the charge-conjugation parity of the neutral member.

The *importance* of the concept of $\mathscr{C}$ parity lies in the fact that for those reactions which conserve ordinary $C$ parity, the $SU(3)$ related processes must conserve $\mathscr{C}$ parity, if the symmetry is assumed good. For weak interactions which violate charge conjugation, we will use the spurion technique, whereby all internal quantum numbers will be conserved. The implications of $\mathscr{C}$ parity on weak interactions will now be discussed briefly.

If the nonleptonic weak Hamiltonian $H_w$ is of current $\times$ current type, properly symmetrized each current belonging to the same octet, then clearly symmetry demands that the Hamiltonian can transform* as $\mathbf{1}$, $\mathbf{8}_s$, or $\mathbf{27}$, which are the only symmetric representations in the product decomposition. If we now assume octet dominance, $H_w \sim \mathbf{8}_s$, the question arises, which component $\lambda_6$ or $\lambda_7$ of the $\mathbf{8}_s$ does $H_w$ transform like? The answer depends on considerations of $CP$ invariance.

### 1. Parity Conserving $H_w$

This is made out of the product of two vector currents or two axial-vector currents in a symmetrical manner ($\mathbf{8}_s$). Hence from Eqs. (A.15) and (A.16)

$$\mathscr{C}(H_w^{\text{p.c.}}) = +1 \tag{A.18}$$

Now if (a) $H_w^{\text{p.c.}} \sim \lambda_6$ ($\mathscr{C} = C$), since parity is even for $H_w^{\text{p.c.}}$ Eq. (A.18) implies that under $CP$, $H_w^{\text{p.c.}}$ is even; and if (b) $H_w^{\text{p.c.}} \sim \lambda_7$ ($\mathscr{C} = -C$), Eq. (A.18) implies similarly that $H_w^{\text{p.c.}}$ violates $CP$.

### 2. Parity-Violating $H_w$

This time the Hamiltonian is a symmetric combination of products of currents like $VA$ or $AV$. Hence from Eqs. (A.15) and (A.16),

$$\mathscr{C}(H_w^{\text{p.v.}}) = -1 \tag{A.19}$$

We consider the two possibilities again: (a) $H_w^{\text{p.v.}} \sim \lambda_6$ ($\mathscr{C} = C$). Eq. (A.19) then implies that $H_w^{\text{p.v.}}$ is even under $CP$ since parity is odd, (b) $H_w^{\text{p.v.}} \sim \lambda_7$ ($\mathscr{C} = -C$). Once again here $H_w^{\text{p.v.}}$ is odd under $CP$.

Thus if $CP$ is conserved in weak nonleptonic decays, the Hamiltonian must transform like the sixth member of the octet.

We can now show that[44] (1) if $H_w$ is of current $\times$ current type and transforms like an octet (octet dominance), conserving $CP$, and (2) if we assume generalized Bose statistics, then in the $SU(3)$ symmetry limit all $K \to 2\pi$ amplitudes vanish, and the $s$ wave amplitudes for nonleptonic hyperon decays satisfy the Lee-Sugawara triangle

$$A(\Lambda_-^0) + 2A(\Xi_-^-) = \sqrt{3}A(\Sigma_0^+) \tag{A.20}$$

---

* $H_w$ cannot $\sim \mathbf{1}$ since the Hamiltonian makes $\Delta S \neq 0$ transitions.

## References

1. M. Gell-Mann, *Phys. Rev.*, **125**, 1067 (1962); *Physics*, **1**, 63 (1964).
2. Y. Nambu, *Phys. Rev. Letters*, **4**, 380 (1960); M. Gell-Mann and M. Lévy, *Nuovo Cimento*, **16**, 705 (1960).
3. (a) S. L. Adler, *Phys. Rev. Letters*, **14**, 1051 (1965); (b) W. I. Weisberger, *Phys. Rev. Letters*, **14**, 1047 (1965).
4. For a general review and bibliography on the applications of current algebra see S. Fubini, lectures given at Cargese and Istanbul, 1966; G. Furlan and C. Rossetti, lectures given at the 1966 Bolaton Meeting; B. Renner, lectures given at the Rutherford Laboratory, 1966; J. S. Bell, Proceedings of the 1966 CERN School of Physics.
5. J. Schwinger, *Phys. Rev. Letters*, **3**, 296 (1959).
6. M. L. Goldberger and S. B. Treiman, *Phys. Rev.*, **109**, 193 (1958).
7. J. Bernstein, M. Gell-Mann, and W. Thirring, *Nuovo Cimento*, **16**, 560 (1960); J. Bernstein, S. Fubini, M. Gell-Mann, and W. Thirring, *Nuovo Cimento*, **17**, 757 (1960). See also Chou Kuang-Chao, *J. Exptl. Theoret. Phys. (USSR)*, **39**, 709 (1960); *Sov. Phys. JETP*, **12**, 492 (1962).
8. W. Zimmerman, *Nuovo Cimento*, **10**, 597 (1958); K. Nishijima, *Phys. Rev.*, **111**, 995 (1958); R. Haag, *Phys. Rev.*, **112**, 669 (1958).
9. S. L. Adler, *Phys. Rev.*, **137B**, 1022 (1965).
10. S. L. Adler, *Phys. Rev.*, **139B**, 1638 (1965).
11. Y. Nambu and D. Lurié, *Phys. Rev.*, **125**, 1429 (1962).
12. Y. Nambu and E. Schrauner, *Phys. Rev.*, **128**, 862 (1962).
13. S. Fubini and G. Furlan, *Physics*, **1**, 229 (1965).
14. (a) S. Fubini, G. Furlan, and C. Rossetti, *Nuovo Cimento*, **40**, 1171 (1965); (b) G. Furlan, F. Lannoy, C. Rossetti, and G. Segré, *Nuovo Cimento*, **38**, 1747; **40**, 597 (1965); (c) S. Okubo, *Nuovo Cimento*, **41**, 586 (1966); (d) V. A. Allessandrini, M. A. B. Bég, and L. S. Brown, *Phys. Rev.*, **144**, 1137 (1966); (e) W. I. Weisberger, *Phys. Rev.*, **143**, 1302 (1966); (f) S. L. Adler, *Phys. Rev.*, **140B**, 736 (1965); (g) S. Fubini, *Nuovo Cimento*, **43A**, 475 (1966); (h) R. Faustov, CERN preprint TH654 (1966); (i) S. Weinberg, *Phys. Rev. Letters*, **17**, 336 (1966) and erratum, **18**, 1178 (1967).
15. R. F. Dashen and M. Gell-Mann, *Proc. of the Third Coral Gables Conf. on Symmetry Principles at High Energy*, W. H. Freeman and Co., San Francisco, 1966.
16. S. L. Adler, *Phys. Rev. Letters*, **14**, 1051 (1965); ref. 14f.; W. I. Weisberger, *Phys. Rev. Letters*, **14**, 1047 (1965); ref. 14e.
17. G. F. Chew, M. L. Goldberger, F. Low, and Y. Nambu, *Phys. Rev.*, **106**, 1345 (1957).
18. B. Renner, *Phys. Letters*, **20**, 72 (1966).
19. C. P. Bhalla, *Phys. Letters*, **19**, 691 (1966).
20. E. C. G. Sudarshan and R. E. Marshak, *Proc. Padua-Venice Conf. Mesons and Newly Discovered Particles*, 1957; *Phys. Rev.*, **109**, 1860 (1958); R. P. Feynman and M. Gell-Mann, *Phys. Rev.*, **109**, 193 (1958); J. J. Sakurai, *Nuovo Cimento*, **7**, 649 (1958).
21. N. Cabibbo, *Phys. Rev. Letters*, **10**, 531 (1963).
22. M. Ademollo and R. Gatto, *Phys. Rev. Letters*, **13**, 264 (1965).

23. The chiral $SU(3) \otimes SU(3)$ symmetry group has also been studied by R. E. Marshak, N. Mukunda, and S. Okubo, *Phys. Rev.*, **137B**, 698 (1965).

24. L. K. Pandit and J. Schechter, *Phys. Letters*, **19**, 56 (1965); D. Amati, C. Bouchiat, and J. Nuyts, *Phys. Letters*, **19**, 59 (1965); A. Sato and S. Sasaki, *Progr. Theoret. Phys. (Kyoto)*, **35**, 335 (1966); C. A. Levinson and I. J. Muzinich, *Phys. Rev. Letters*, **15**, 715, E 842 (1965); W. I. Weisberger, ref. 14e.

25. N. Brene, L. Veje, M. Roos, and C. Cranström, *Phys. Rev.*, **149**, 1288 (1966).

26. (a) C. G. Callan and S. B. Treiman, *Phys. Rev. Letters*, **16**, 153 (1966); (b) V. S. Mathur, S. Okubo, and L. K. Pandit, *Phys. Rev. Letters*, **16**, 371, E601 (1966).

27. G. Furlan and B. Renner, *Nuovo Cimento*, **44**, 536 (1966); Riazuddin and Fayyazuddin, *Nuovo Cimento*, **44**, 546, (1966); R. Oehme, *Phys. Rev. Letters*, **16**, 215 (1966); V. S. Mathur, L. K. Pandit, and R. E. Marshak, *Phys. Rev. Letters*, **16**, 947 (1966).

28. G. Trilling, *Proc. Intern. Conf. Weak Interactions, Argonne*, 1965.

29. M. Suzuki, *Phys. Rev. Letters*, **16**, 212 (1966).

30. (a) M. Suzuki, *Phys. Rev. Letters*, **15**, 986 (1965); (b) H. Sugawara, *Phys. Rev. Letters*, **15**, 870, E997 (1965).

31. Y. Hara, Y. Nambu, and J. Schechter, *Phys. Rev. Letters*, **16**, 380 (1966).

32. L. S. Brown and C. M. Sommerfield, *Phys. Rev. Letters*, **16**, 751 (1966).

33. Data compiled by J. P. Birge, *Proc. Intern. Conf. High Energy Phys., 13th, Berkeley*, 1966.

34. See, e.g., M. Lusignoli, M. Restignoli, G. A. Snow, and G. Violini, *Phys. Letters*, **21**, 229 (1966).

35. V. S. Mathur, *Nuovo Cimento*, **50**, 661 (1967).

36. M. K. Gaillard, *Phys. Letters*, **20**, 533 (1966); Riazuddin and K. T. Manthappa, *Phys. Rev.*, **147**, 972 (1966); R. Gatto, M. Maiani, and G. Preparata, *Nuovo Cimento* **41**, 622 (1966).

37. K. Nishijima and L. J. Swank, *Phys. Rev.*, **146**, 1161 (1966); G. S. Guralnik, V. S. Mathur, and L. K. Pandit, Rochester preprint.

38. (a) M. Suzuki, *Phys. Rev.*, **144**, 1154 (1966); (b) Y. Hara and Y. Nambu, *Phys. Rev. Letters*, **16**, 875 (1966); (c) D. K. Elias and J. C. Taylor, *Nuovo Cimento*, **44**, 518 (1966); (d) S. K. Bose and S. N. Biswas, *Phys. Rev. Letters*, **16**, 330 (1966); (e) B. M. K. Nefkens, *Phys. Letters*, **22**, 94 (1966); (f) H. D. I. Abarbanel, *Phys. Rev.*, in press.

39. (a) W. Alles and R. Jengo, *Nuovo Cimento*, **42**, A419 (1966); (b) B. d'Espagnat and J. Iliopoulos, *Phys. Letters*, **21**, 232 (1966); (c) C. Bouchiat and P. Meyer, preprint; (d) Fayyazuddin and Riazuddin, *Nuovo Cimento*, **47**, 222 (1967).

40. Y. T. Chiu and J. Schechter, *Phys. Rev. Letters*, **16**, 1022 (1966); *Phys. Rev.*, **150**, 1201 (1966); S. N. Biswas, A. Kumar, and R. P. Saxena, *Phys. Rev. Letters*, **17**, 268 (1966); Y. Hara, ICTP preprint (1966).

41. E. Ferrari, V. S. Mathur, and L. K. Pandit, *Phys. Letters*, **21**, 560 (1966); S. N. Biswas and S. K. Bose, ICTP preprint (1966).

42. J. J. deSwaart, *Rev. Mod. Phys.*, **35**, 916 (1963).

43. L. C. Biedenharn, *Phys. Letters*, **3**, 69 and 254 (1962); *J. Math. Phys.*, **4**, 436 (1963).

44. M. Gell-Mann, *Phys. Rev. Letters*, **12**, 155 (1964).

# Nonleptonic Weak Interactions

S. P. ROSEN*

*Purdue University, Lafayette, Indiana*

S. PAKVASA†

*Syracuse University, Syracuse, New York*

## Contents

* Supported in part by the U.S. Air Force.
† Supported in part by the U.S. Atomic Energy Commission.

473

# I. General Aspects of Nonleptonic Decay

## 1. Introduction

For many years nuclear $\beta$ decay was regarded as the model for all weak interactions. It was distinguished from strong and electromagnetic interactions by the smallness of its coupling constant and by the radiation of excess energy as a charged lepton pair. Interactions conforming to this pattern, for example charged pion and $\mu$ meson decay, were recognized as weak, and those that did not were assumed to be either electromagnetic or strong.

When strange particles were discovered, this point of view resulted in a paradox. It was found that, after being produced in fast collisions between pions and nucleons, strange particles decayed into multipion or pion–nucleon final states. Since leptons and photons were not observed production and decay were taken to be similar processes, and their rates were expected to be comparable to each other. Instead, they differed by twelve orders of magnitude: production occurred within $10^{-22}$ sec of impact, and decay took place approximately $10^{-10}$ sec later.

Not unexpectedly, attempts were made to draw a parallel between this situation and similar ones in atomic and nuclear physics. For example, strange particles might have much greater spins than do pions and nucleons,[1] and their decay could be inhibited by a high centrifugal barrier coupled with a relatively low-energy release; their production, however, could take place at energies large enough to overcome the barrier. None of these attempts proved to be satisfactory, and the paradox was not resolved until the idea that the same interaction was responsible for both production and decay was given up.

In 1952, Pais[2] put forward the hypothesis now known as associated production. Up to that time, strange particles, for example the $\Lambda$ hyperon, were thought to be produced in reactions like

$$\pi^- + p \rightarrow \Lambda + \pi^0 \tag{1.1}$$

and their decay was envisaged as a kind of inverse process induced by strong interactions:

$$\Lambda \rightarrow \pi^- + (p' + \pi^0) \rightarrow \pi^- + p \tag{1.2}$$

Pais suggested that strange particles are produced not one at a time, as in Eq. (1.1), but in pairs:

$$\pi^- + p \rightarrow \Lambda + K^0 \tag{1.3}$$

The presence of the neutral $K$ meson in Eq. (1.3) prevented $\Lambda$ decay from being a strong inverse of production, and led to the conclusion that the two processes were completely independent of each other. From the observed rates, Pais identified production as a strong process and decay as a new type of weak interaction—one in which leptons play no part.

Implicit in the scheme of associated production was the idea that decay is inhibited by a selection rule. Its precise form came to light with the discovery of a new quantum number in 1953. In their attempts to extend the concept of isotopic spin to strange particles, Gell-Mann and Nishijima[3] found it necessary to introduce strangeness ($S$) into the formula

$$Q = T_3 + \tfrac{1}{2}(S + B) \tag{1.4}$$

relating electric charge ($Q$) to the third component of isotopic spin ($T_3$) and baryon number ($B$). They then generalized the charge independence of nuclear forces by requiring that strangeness be conserved in all strong interactions. Weak interactions are neither charge independent nor charge symmetric, and so they need not conserve strangeness. It is for this reason that decay of strange particles is slow.

The strangeness theory had hardly been confirmed by experiment before a new paradox appeared. Two mesons, known at the time as $\theta$ and $\tau$ were found to be very similar in all respects but one; the $\theta$ decayed into two pions and the $\tau$ into three. The simplest conclusion to be drawn from this was that the mesons were really two different decay modes of a single particle. However, it could be argued from the two- and three-pion configurations that the $\tau$ and $\theta$ had opposite parities.[4]

When several ingenious theories[5] had failed to explain this phenomenon, Lee and Yang[6] began to question the premise upon which they were based, namely the conservation of parity. From a survey of experimental data, they concluded that, while parity is conserved to a high degree of accuracy in strong and electromagnetic interactions, its conservation in weak ones was no more than an assumption. They therefore proposed three experiments to test the validity of this assumption: the angular distribution of electrons emitted from oriented $Co^{60}$ nuclei, a similar distribution in the $\pi-\mu-e$ sequence, and the up–down asymmetry of pions emitted in $\Lambda$ decay. The outcome of these experiments[7] is well known—parity is not necessarily conserved in any type of weak interaction, be it leptonic, semileptonic or nonleptonic. Consequently, the $\theta$ meson can be regarded as a parity-violating decay mode of the $K$ meson, and the $\tau$ as a parity conserving one.

Within a year of its discovery, parity nonconservation had led to a remarkable clarification of Fermi's original theory of $\beta$ decay.[8] Crucial to this development was the concept of a two-component neutrino,[9] according to which the neutral lepton is always created in one helicity state and its antiparticle in the opposite one. Under such conditions leptonic and semileptonic decays are symmetric neither with respect to the parity transformation $(P)$, nor with respect to charge conjugation $(C)$; they may, however, be invariant under the combined inversion $CP$.[10] Besides pointing toward $CP$ invariance as a substitute for parity conservation, the two-component neutrino was the cornerstone of the universal $V-A$ interaction,[11] the conserved vector current hypothesis,[12] and the current $\times$ current theory.[13]

The current $\times$ current theory has undergone some substantial modifications since 1958, but its basic hypothesis remains intact; namely, that all weak interactions, leptonic, semileptonic, and nonleptonic, are generated by the interaction of a charged current with itself. *CP* invariance, on the other hand, has fallen by the wayside; the observation in 1964 of the long-lived neutral *K* meson decaying into two pions[14] demonstrated that *CP* is not conserved. Although the magnitude of this effect is only about one-tenth of 1% in amplitude, the origin of *CP* violation still remains unknown.

By now it should be clear that the characteristic feature of non-leptonic decay is symmetry violation. Apart from Lorentz invariance and the conservation of electric charge and baryon number, the phenomenon appears to violate every symmetry that has been found to hold in strong interactions. It is natural, therefore, to inquire about the manner of these violations. For example, do the violations of strangeness and isotopic spin follow a definite pattern, or do they vary haphazardly from one decay mode to another? Is parity nonconservation a maximal effect, or merely a small correction? How is symmetry breaking in nonleptonic decay related to similar effects in other weak interactions?

Underlying these questions is the more fundamental one of whether or not symmetries play a significant role in the theory of weak interactions. A systematic pattern of violation would indicate that they do, whereas an unsystematic one would imply that they are merely incidental to the theory. Present evidence suggests a positive answer to our question, and it also provides us with a definite conception of what the role of symmetries is likely to be.

To illustrate this conception, let us consider the theory in which weak decays are generated by the self-coupling of a charged current:

$$H_{\text{Weak}} = (G/\sqrt{2})\{\mathcal{J}_\lambda, \mathcal{J}_\lambda^\dagger\}$$
$$\mathcal{J}_\lambda = J_\lambda + L_\lambda \tag{1.5}$$

The weak current $\mathcal{J}_\lambda$ consists of an hadronic part $J_\lambda$ and a leptonic one $L_\lambda$. Both of these terms are equal admixtures of vector and axial vector components, and therefore they have well-defined properties with respect to space–time transformations. In addition, the conserved vector current hypothesis[12] establishes a simple relationship between $V_\lambda$, the vector component of $J_\lambda$ and the electromagnetic current $J_\lambda^{(\text{em})}$; $J_\lambda^{(\text{em})}$ is known to behave in a well-defined way with respect to internal symmetries, and so $V_\lambda$ must do likewise. Similarly, the hypothesis of a partially conserved axial vector current,[15] from which stems the successful Goldberger-Treiman relation[16] for pion decay, relates the divergence of $A_\lambda$, the axial component of $J_\lambda$, to the meson field and thereby indicates specific symmetry properties for $A_\lambda$. Thus we see that, although weak interactions violate strong symmetries, the current × current theory requires them to do so in a definite way.

A simple and very powerful extension of these ideas is to identify $V_\lambda$ and $A_\lambda$ with elements of a Lie algebra.[17] The success obtained by Adler[18] and Weisberger[19] in calculating the renormalized axial vector coupling constant tends to confirm this identification, and it leads us to believe that symmetry is the matrix for a dynamical theory of weak interactions.

Nonleptonic decay is an ideal subject for such a theory. From the viewpoint of internal symmetries, most decay modes are different charge states of a few basic processes, and their amplitudes can be correlated by means of the transformation properties (selection rules) of the interaction Hamiltonian. These correlations are easily translated into observable relationships because the final state of decay, usually a two-body system, is characterized by a small number of parameters.

Once the consequence of selection rules has been established, it becomes possible to pinpoint dynamical effects. In the decay of the $\Sigma$ hyperon for example, the $\Delta T = 1/2$ rule predicts a triangular relation between the amplitudes for $\Sigma^+ \to p + \pi^0$, $\Sigma^+ \to n + \pi^+$, and $\Sigma^- \to n + \pi^-$ (see Sect. III), but it does not explain why the second and third decay modes show no visible effects of parity violation. In the case of $\Sigma^+ \to n + \pi^+$, this property can be derived from $SU(3)$ selection rules, but in the case of $\Sigma^- \to n + \pi^-$ it cannot. Therefore the absence of a maximal parity violation in $\Sigma^-$ decay must be regarded as a dynamical effect. In general, those properties of nonleptonic decay that cannot be derived from symmetry arguments constitute the definitive tests of dynamical theories.

The relationship between symmetry and dynamics assumes a more subtle form in the current × current theory. If the hadronic current is of the Cabibbo type, then the nonleptonic interaction

$$H_{NL} = (G/\sqrt{2})\{J_\lambda, J_\lambda^\dagger\} \tag{1.6}$$

has specific transformation properties in $SU(3)$, and these properties are sufficient to make a number of important predictions. Further dynamical assumptions, for example the partially conserved axial-vector current and quark model commutation rules, lead to other predictions which can also be interpreted along purely group-theoretical lines. In other words, many dynamical features of the current $\times$ current theory can be expressed as restrictions upon the $SU(3)$ behavior of $H_{NL}$ and its matrix elements.

In this review we shall describe the influence that symmetry has had upon the theory of nonleptonic decay. The remainder of this section is devoted to a discussion of parity, charge conjugation, and time reversal (Sect. I-2), and to the general influence of internal symmetries (Sect. I-3). The effect of isotopic spin upon meson decay is studied in Section II, and selection rules for baryon decay are examined in Section III. In Section IV we consider the current $\times$ current theory and other dynamical models.

## 2. Parity, Charge Conjugation, and Time Reversal

The importance of symmetries in elementary particle physics arises from the fact that they lead to conservation laws. Conservation laws, in turn, act as constraints upon the final state configuration in any process

$$A + B + \cdots \rightarrow \alpha + \beta + \cdots \tag{1.7}$$

In some cases, these constraints are sufficient to forbid a particular process, and in others they merely limit the range of available configurations. For example, the conservation of angular momentum and parity forbids the decay $\eta \rightarrow 2\pi$, but it requires only that the final state be a $P$ wave in $\rho \rightarrow 2\pi$.

When a symmetry is violated, two types of effect are possible: processes which would otherwise be forbidden can take place, and in processes which are not forbidden, the range of final-state configurations is enlarged. The enlargement gives rise to interference phenomena, and these provide the definitive tests of symmetry violation. The $\tau - \theta$ paradox, for example, was a strong indication that parity is not conserved by weak interactions, but the conclusive evidence came from the observation of interference effects in $Co^{60}$ $\beta$ decay.[20] Similarly, the occurrence of $K_L \rightarrow 2\pi$[14] might be due to a violation of charge conjugation invariance by electromagnetic interactions,[21] but a definite statement cannot be made until interference between states with opposite charge conjugation quantum numbers is observed.*

* Such an interference has been detected in $\eta \rightarrow \pi^+ \pi^- \pi^0$ by several groups,[22] but with rather low statistics. In an experiment carried out at CERN[23] with much higher statistics, no significant interference was detected. Thus, the experimental situation is not yet unambiguous.

## A. Parity Nonconservation

Because pions are pseudoscalar particles, the final state in $K \to 2\pi$ has parity $(-1)^J$, where $J$ is the spin of the $K$ meson. The $K$ meson is also pseudoscalar, and so its two-pion $(\theta)$ decay mode is a $O^- \to O^+$ transition. In $K \to 3\pi$, the parity of the final state is $(-1)^{l+L+1}$, where $l$ is the orbital angular momentum of two pions relative to their center of mass, and $L$ is that of the third pion. Because the vector sum of $l$ and $L$ must be zero, $l$ is equal to $L$, and the final state has negative parity. Thus, $K \to 2\pi$ is a pure parity-violating decay, and $K \to 3\pi$ is a pure parity-conserving one.

It is expected on general grounds that if meson decay violates parity, baryon decay will do likewise. The $\Lambda$ hyperon can dissociate strongly into a virtual proton–$K^-$ system, the $K^-$ then decays into two or three pions, and the extra pions are reabsorbed by strong interactions to yield

$$\Lambda \to p + \pi^- \tag{1.8}$$

Conversely, had parity violation first been discovered in baryon decay, it would have been expected to show up in meson decay through the $\tau$ and $\theta$ modes.

In transitions between one spin $1/2$ baryon and another, $\Lambda \to p + \pi^-$ for example, the conservation of angular momentum restricts the emitted pion to $S$- and $P$-wave channels. Parity is not conserved in the decay, and so neither channel need be closed. The interference between angular momentum states gives rise to three effects: an asymmetry in the angular distribution of the pion with respect to the spin of the $\Lambda$, a longitudinal polarization of the proton spin, and also a transverse one. In each case, the quantity measured is a pseudoscalar $\boldsymbol{\sigma}_\Lambda \cdot \hat{\mathbf{q}}$, $\boldsymbol{\sigma}_p \cdot \hat{\mathbf{p}}$, and $\boldsymbol{\sigma}_p \cdot \boldsymbol{\sigma}_\Lambda \times \hat{\mathbf{p}}$.

Parity is conserved in the strong reaction

$$\pi^- + p \to \Lambda + K^0 \tag{1.9}$$

and so the $\Lambda$ can be produced with its spin polarized only normal to the plane of production.* Therefore a correlation between pion momentum and the spin of the $\Lambda$ will show up as an up–down asymmetry of the decay pion with respect to the production plane. This is one of the tests

---

* The production plane is defined by the momenta $\boldsymbol{\pi}$, $\boldsymbol{\Lambda}$, of the incident pion and the $\Lambda$. Thus the normal is defined by $\boldsymbol{\pi} \times \boldsymbol{\Lambda}$, an axial vector, and the quantity $\boldsymbol{\sigma} \cdot \boldsymbol{\pi} \times \boldsymbol{\Lambda}$ is a scalar.

of parity nonconservation suggested by Lee and Yang.[6] The proton polarization is harder to detect, but it has been measured experimentally.

The magnitude of these effects can be calculated in terms of the amplitudes, $S$ and $P$, for decay into $S$- and $P$-wave final states.[24] In the rest-frame of $\Lambda$, the nonrelativistic transition matrix for Eq. (1.8) can be written as

$$M = S + P\boldsymbol{\sigma}\cdot\hat{\mathbf{p}} \qquad \hat{\mathbf{p}} = p/|\mathbf{p}| \qquad (1.10)$$

where $\mathbf{p}$ is the momentum of the proton, and $\boldsymbol{\sigma}$ denotes the usual Pauli matrices. If $\langle\boldsymbol{\sigma}_\Lambda\rangle$ and $\langle\boldsymbol{\sigma}_p\rangle$ denote polarization vectors of the parent $\Lambda$ and daughter proton, the differential transition probability is given by

$$dw = [\Gamma(\Lambda_-^0)/8\pi]\{[1 + \alpha\langle\boldsymbol{\sigma}_\Lambda\rangle\cdot\hat{\mathbf{p}}] + \langle\boldsymbol{\sigma}_p\rangle\cdot$$
$$[(\alpha + \langle\boldsymbol{\sigma}_\Lambda\rangle\cdot\hat{\mathbf{p}})\hat{\mathbf{p}} + \beta(\boldsymbol{\sigma}_\Lambda) \times \hat{\mathbf{p}} + \gamma(\hat{\mathbf{p}} \times (\langle\boldsymbol{\sigma}_\Lambda\rangle \times \hat{\mathbf{p}}))]\} \, d\Omega \quad (1.11)$$

In this formula, $\Gamma(\Lambda_-^0)$ is the rate for $\Lambda \to p + \pi^-$,

$$\Gamma(\Lambda_-^0) = (2pc/\hbar)(|S|^2 + |P|^2) \qquad (1.12)$$

where $p$ is the magnitude of the proton momentum; $d\Omega$ is an element of solid angle about the direction $\hat{\mathbf{p}}$, and

$$\alpha = \frac{2\,\mathrm{Re}\,(SP^*)}{|S|^2 + |P|^2} \qquad \beta = \frac{2\,\mathrm{Im}\,(SP^*)}{|S|^2 + |P|^2}$$
$$\gamma = \frac{|S|^2 - |P|^2}{|S|^2 + |P|^2} \qquad \alpha^2 + \beta^2 + \gamma^2 = 1 \qquad (1.13)$$

The up–down asymmetry of the pion is given by

$$(-\alpha\langle\overline{\boldsymbol{\sigma}_\Lambda}\rangle) \qquad (1.14)$$

and the polarization of the proton depends upon $\alpha$, $\beta$, $\gamma$. Notice that the signs of $\alpha$ and $\langle\boldsymbol{\sigma}_\Lambda\rangle$ cannot be separated from one another in Eq. (1.14). When the $\Lambda$ is unpolarized ($\langle\boldsymbol{\sigma}_\Lambda\rangle = 0$), the up–down asymmetry vanishes, but the proton has a longitudinal polarization equal to $\alpha$. This fact can be used to measure the sign of $\alpha$. Should the coefficient $\alpha$ vanish, then one of the amplitudes $S$ and $P$ must either vanish, or be 90° out of phase with the other. In the first case, the coefficient $\beta$ is zero, and the non-vanishing amplitude is determined by the sign of $\gamma$; in the second, the coefficient $\beta$ is nonzero. The significance of this possibility is discussed below.

## B. Time Reversal and CP

Ever since its discovery, parity nonconservation has been examined in the context of the $TCP$ theorem. This theorem is a consequence of the general assumptions usually made in quantized field theory,[25] and it asserts that any local interaction is invariant under the product, taken in any order, of space reflection ($P$), the time reversal ($T$), and charge conjugation ($C$). As far as is known at present, its most easily tested prediction, the equality of the masses and lifetimes of particle and antiparticle,[26] is consistent with experiment.[27]

Two conclusions can be drawn from $P$ nonconservation and the $TCP$ theorem. First, at least one of the operations, $C$ and $T$, must not be conserved; and second, if $T$ is conserved and $C$ is not, then the product $CP$ must also be conserved. Until 1964, there was no reason to doubt the second conclusion; no violation of $T$ had been observed, and the evidence from weak interactions, in particular the two-component neutrino, seemed to support $CP$ conservation. However, the decay of neutral $K$ mesons has shown it not to be valid.

According to the classic analysis of Gell-Mann and Pais,[28] the $K^0$ and its antiparticle, the $\bar{K}^0$, must be regarded for the purposes of decay as "particle mixtures":

$$K^0 = aK_S + bK_L$$
$$\bar{K}^0 = cK_S + dK_L$$
$$|a|^2 + |b|^2 = |c|^2 + |d|^2 = 1 \tag{1.15}$$

The suffixes $S$ and $L$ denote the fact that $K_S$ decays rapidly into two pions, and $K_L$ decays slowly into three[29]:

$$\Gamma(K_S \to 2\pi) = 1.24 \times 10^{10} \text{ sec}^{-1}$$
$$\Gamma(K_L \to 3\pi) = 0.72 \times 10^7 \text{ sec}^{-1} \tag{1.16}$$

A neutral two-pion system is always an even eigenstate of $CP$ and, from the structure of its Dalitz plot,[4] the three-pion system in $K_L$ decay, appears to be odd.* Therefore, if $CP$ is conserved, $K_S$ and $K_L$ are,

---

* From the Pauli principle, the angular momentum of two neutral pions with respect to their center of mass must be even, hence, $CP|2\pi^0\rangle = +|2\pi^0\rangle$. In a $\pi^+\pi^-$ system, $P$ interchanges the positions of the pions, and $C$ sends $\pi^\pm$ into $\pi^\mp$; therefore, $CP|\pi^+\pi^-\rangle = (-1)^l C|\pi^+\pi^-\rangle = (-1)^{2l}|\pi^+\pi^-\rangle = |\pi^+\pi^-\rangle$. A $3\pi^0$ system with zero angular momentum is odd under $P$ and even under $C$, i.e., $CP|3\pi^0\rangle = -|3\pi^0\rangle$. For $\pi^+\pi^-\pi^0$ it is necessary to appeal to the Dalitz plot. Let $l$ be the angular momentum of the $\pi^+\pi^-$ relative to its center of mass and let $L$ be that of

respectively, even and odd under $CP$,†

$$K_S \equiv K_1 = (1/\sqrt{2})(K^0 - \bar{K}^0)$$
$$K_L \equiv K_2 = (1/\sqrt{2})(K^0 + \bar{K}^0) \tag{1.17}$$

and the decay

$$K_L \not\to 2\pi \tag{1.18}$$

is forbidden.

Suppose now that a beam of $K^0$'s is produced in a reaction such as Eq. (1.9). Its $K_S$ component will effectively die out within $10^{-8}$ sec, and only the long-lived component will remain. At that point, the appearance of a $\pi^+\pi^-$ pair with the correct energy must be interpreted as coming from the decay $K_L \to \pi^+\pi^-$. Events like this were observed first by Christenson, Cronin, Fitch, and Turlay,[14] and subsequently by three other groups. They demonstrate that, barring unforeseen factors, $CP$ is not conserved, and that the size of the violation is measured by[30]:

$$|\eta_{+-}| = \sqrt{\Gamma(K_L \to \pi^+\pi^-)/\Gamma(K_S \to \pi^+\pi^-)} = (1.94 \pm 0.09) \times 10^{-3} \tag{1.19}$$

In principle, the violation of $CP$ can also be detected in the decay of the $\Lambda$ and other metastable baryons. If $CP$ were conserved in Eq. (1.8), and if final state interactions were ignored, the amplitudes $S$ and $P$ of the transition matrix [see Eq. (1.10)] would both be real. The coefficient $\beta$ [Eq. (1.13)] would then vanish, and the polarization of the daughter proton would have no component in the direction of $\langle \sigma_\Lambda \rangle \times \hat{p}$ [see Eq. (1.11)]. Final-state interactions introduce a slight phase difference between $S$ and $P$ and hence lead to a small value of $\beta$. Thus the observation of a large coefficient $\beta$ would imply a significant violation of $CP$. At present, the measured values of $\beta$ are small, and their accuracy is not sufficient to determine whether the effect is due solely to final-state interactions, or whether $CP$ is violated to the extent indicated by Eq. (1.19).

## C. Theories of CP Violation

As had been the case with the strange particle and $\tau - \theta$ paradoxes, the initial theories of $K_L \to 2\pi$ sought to preserve the hypothesis

---

the $\pi^0$, hence, $CP|\pi^+\pi^-\pi^0\rangle = (-1)^{2l}(-1)^{L+1}|\pi^+\pi^-\pi^0\rangle$. The distribution of events on the Dalitz plot indicates that in $K_L \to \pi^+\pi^-\pi^0$, the final state is dominated by configurations with $L = l = 0$ and has a small admixture of $L = l = 2$. Thus, $CP|\pi^+\pi^-\pi^0\rangle = -|\pi^+\pi^-\pi^0\rangle$.

† The sign convention used here is $CP: K^0 = -\bar{K}^0$.

that the effect appears to contradict. One[31] was based upon the idea of a long-range force similar to electromagnetic interactions. It would distinguish particle from antiparticle, but would couple to hypercharge instead of electric charge. Other theories[32] postulated new particles which either have very small mass, or are degenerate with $K$ mesons or pions. The failure of the rate for $K_L \to 2\pi$ to vary with the energy of the parent $K$ meson[14] rules out a long range force, and the observed interference[33] between $K_S \to 2\pi$ and $K_L \to 2\pi$ rules out new particles. Thus the experiment of Christenson, Cronin, Fitch, and Turlay[14] must be taken at face value—$CP$ is not conserved.

Exactly how the nonconservation comes about is not known. Some theories[32] are based upon a violation of $C$ in medium–strong or electromagnetic interactions,[21] and others presuppose that $CP$ is violated by an interaction whose strength is either slightly weaker than that of $CP$-conserving weak interactions, or very much weaker[34] (superweak). The choice between these two classes of theory depends upon the observation of $C$-violating decays such as $\pi^0 \to 3\gamma$ and $\eta \to \pi^0 e^+ e^-$, and interference effects such as an asymmetry between the $\pi^+$ and $\pi^-$ spectra in $\eta \to \pi^+ \pi^- \pi^0$.[21, 22] Within each class, however, the choice is more difficult because it depends upon rather uncertain estimates of the magnitude of various effects.

Some insight into this problem can be gained from the weak interactions themselves. If, for example, no $CP$-violating effects are found in leptonic decay, the violation in $K_L$ decay may be due either to a superweak interaction[34] with $\Delta S = 2$, or to a $\Delta S = -\Delta Q$ weak current which is 90° out of phase with the $\Delta S = +\Delta Q$ current.[35] Similarly, the branching ratios of $K_L \to 2\pi^0$ and $K_S \to 3\pi^0$ may determine whether or not a $C$-violating interaction conserves isotopic spin. Details of these and other arguments will be discussed in a later section.

## 3. Internal Symmetries

### A. Minimal Violation

Just as space–time symmetries give rise to conservation laws, so do the internal symmetries of strong interactions. These internal conservation laws have much the same effect as others, namely the constraint of physical phenomena, but they act upon charge states rather than spatial configurations. In the decay of the $N^*(1238)$ resonance for example, the conservation of isotopic spin determines the relative widths of $N^{*+}$ and

$N^{*0}$, while the conservation of angular momentum and parity requires each of the pion–nucleon final states to be a $P$ wave.

The breaking of internal symmetries by various interactions results in the relaxation of some constraints and the occurrence of forbidden processes. From the observed rates for these processes, it would appear that symmetries are broken not in a haphazard fashion, but in a gradual way. Unitary symmetry[36] is broken at the level of medium–strong interactions, charge independence is violated by electromagnetic interactions, and strangeness is conserved until weak interactions are encountered. In atomic and nuclear physics, situations like this often correspond to the progressive violation of a sequence of selection rules by higher order effects. It is attractive to consider internal symmetry breaking from a similar point of view.

All interactions conserve baryon number and electric charge, thus:

$$\Delta B = 0 \quad \text{and} \quad \Delta Q = 0 \tag{1.20}$$

are absolute selection rules. In addition, superstrong interactions are assumed to satisfy

$$\Delta F = 0 \qquad \Delta T = 0 \qquad \Delta T_3 = 0 \qquad \Delta S = 0 \tag{1.21}$$

where $F$ denotes unitary spin, $T$ is isotopic spin, and $T_3$ is its third component. Medium–strong interactions satisfy all but the first selection rule of Eq. (1.21) and electromagnetic ones obey only the last two. In the case of weak interactions, the unitary spin and isotopic spin selection rules are violated by all hadron decays, and the strangeness rule is violated by some semileptonic decays and all nonleptonic ones.

Next comes the question whether, when they are violated, the selection rules of Eq. (1.21) can be replaced by weaker ones. In electromagnetic interactions, isotopic spin can change by any of the amounts $\Delta T = 1, 2, 3, \ldots$. The principle of minimal coupling, however, requires that, to lowest order in the electronic charge $e$, the interaction be linear in the operator $Q$.[37] The Gell-Mann–Nishijima formula, Eq. (1.4), implies that $Q$ is an admixture of isoscalar and isovector parts, and so to first order in $e$, the selection rule

$$\Delta T \leq 1 \tag{1.22}$$

is obeyed. Similarly in weak interactions, strangeness can change by any amount, but the absence of decay modes like

$$\begin{aligned} \Xi &\to N + \pi, \quad N + e + \nu \\ \Omega &\to \Lambda + \pi, \quad \Lambda + e + \nu \end{aligned} \tag{1.23}$$

and the smallness of the $K_S$-$K_L$ mass difference[38] both indicate that the selection rule

$$\Delta S \leq 1 \tag{1.24}$$

holds to first order in the weak coupling constant. In each of these examples, the conservation laws of Eq. (1.21) are violated in a minimal fashion.

The same feature appears in the unitary symmetry scheme. Medium–strong interactions could transform according to the (8), (27), (64)... representations of $SU(3)$, but the success of the Gell-Mann–Okubo mass formula[39] indicates that they are dominated by the octet. In the same way, the Coleman-Glashow[40] sum rules for magnetic moments and electromagnetic mass differences are obtained by placing the electromagnetic current in an octet, which again is the lowest available representation. Thus it would appear that the selection rules associated with elementary particle interactions follow a simple pattern. The rules applicable to one level of strength differ from those of the preceding levels in the simplest possible way. We shall refer to this pattern as minimal violation.

### B. Selection Rules

Selection rules for weak interactions are derived from the Gell-Mann–Nishijima formula [Eq. (1.4)] and the empirical rule of Eq. (1.24). It is convenient to write the formula as

$$\Delta Q_h = \Delta Q_l = \Delta T_3 + \tfrac{1}{2}\Delta S + \tfrac{1}{2}\Delta B \tag{1.25}$$

where $\Delta Q_l$ is the charge carried off by leptons, and $\Delta Q_h$ is the difference in charge between the initial and final hadron states:

$$\Delta Q_h = (Q_h)_i - (Q_h)_f \tag{1.26}$$

The differences $\Delta S$, $\Delta T_3$, and $\Delta B$ are defined in the same way as $\Delta Q_h$. Because of the absolute conservation of baryon number, $\Delta B$ is always zero [Eq. (1.20)].

In semileptonic decay (e.g., $n, \Lambda \to p + e^- + \nu_e$), leptons carry off one unit of charge,

$$\Delta Q_l = -1 \tag{1.27}$$

and so the changes in $T_3$ and $S$ satisfy

$$\Delta_{Q_h} = -1 = \Delta T_3 + \tfrac{1}{2}\Delta S \tag{1.28}$$

When strangeness is conserved, as in nuclear $\beta$ decay, it follows that

$$\Delta T_3 = -1 \tag{1.29}$$

When strangeness is not conserved, it appears that $\Delta S$ and $\Delta Q_h$ are related by*

$$\Delta S = +\Delta Q_h \tag{1.30}$$

and hence

$$\Delta T_3 = -1/2 \tag{1.31}$$

The smallest changes of total isotopic spin consistent with Eqs. (1.29) and (1.31) are $\Delta T = 1$ and $1/2$, respectively. Therefore minimal violation leads to the selection rules[42, 43]

$$\begin{aligned} \Delta S = 0, \quad & \Delta T = 1 \\ \Delta S = 1, \quad & \Delta T = 1/2 \end{aligned} \tag{1.32}$$

for semileptonic decay. If the argument is extended to unitary symmetry, then both the strangeness-conserving current $J_\lambda^{(0)}$ and the strangeness-violating one $J_\lambda^{(1)}$ must be assigned to an octet; similarly in $SU(6)$, they must be placed in the (35)-dimensional representation. These higher symmetry assignments exclude currents with either $\Delta S = 2$ or $\Delta S = -\Delta Q_h$. They are consistent with present data on decay processes,[41] but have yet to be tested in neutrino reactions.†

In nonleptonic decay no charge is carried off by leptons, and therefore

$$\begin{aligned} \Delta Q_h = \Delta Q_l = 0 \\ \Delta T_3 + \tfrac{1}{2}\Delta S = 0 \end{aligned} \tag{1.33}$$

Since strangeness changes by one unit, it follows that[45]

$$\Delta S = \pm 1, \quad \Delta T_3 = +1/2 \tag{1.34}$$

Consequently the minimal change of total isotopic spin is

$$\Delta T = 1/2 \tag{1.35}$$

* The absence of $\Xi^- \rightarrow n + e^- + \bar{\nu}_e$ implies that $\Delta S \neq 2$, and the suppression of $\Sigma^+ \rightarrow n + l^+ + \nu$ and $K^+ \rightarrow 2\pi^+ + e^- + \bar{\nu}_e$ implies that $\Delta S \neq \Delta Q_h$. In $K^0 \rightarrow \pi^\pm + l^\pm + \nu$, the problem of $\Delta S = \pm Q_h$ is bound up with $CP$ violation, and no definite statement can be made at present. For a full discussion, see Willis.[41]

† M. M. Block[44] has proposed a number of interesting tests for the $\Delta S = \Delta Q_h$, $\Delta T = 1$, and $\Delta T = 1/2$ rules in energetic neutrino reactions.

The same argument leads to the octet rule[46] in $SU(3)$

$$\Delta F = (8) \tag{1.36}$$

and to the (35)-rule[47] in $SU(6)$

$$\Delta \tilde{F} = (35) \tag{1.37}$$

It is interesting to note that a minimal violation of the higher symmetries automatically yields a minimal violation of the lower ones: the (35)-rule implies the octet rule, and the octet rule implies $\Delta T = 1/2$.

Particles which undergo nonleptonic decay also take part in other symmetry-breaking interactions, and so these selection rules cannot hold exactly. Electromagnetic interactions, for example, do not conserve isotopic spin, and so they will induce $\Delta T = 3/2$ corrections to the $\Delta T = 1/2$ rule; however, these corrections are small, being of first, or higher, order in the fine structure constant $\alpha \equiv (e^2/\hbar c) \approx 1/137$. Similarly, deviations from the octet rule arise from medium–strong interactions, but they are also expected to be fairly small.*

Another possible source of corrections is the current × current theory itself. If the weak currents appearing in Eq. (1.6) have minimal transformation properties, then the $\Delta S = 1$ part of $H_{NL}$ does not. In isospace it behaves as an admixture of $\Delta T = 1/2$ and $3/2$, and in $SU(3)$ it is an admixture of $\Delta F = 8$ and 27. There are, however, a number of arguments which suggest that the $\Delta T = 3/2$ and the $\Delta F = 27$ components are suppressed by the dynamics of nonleptonic decay. Thus minimal violation may be an effective property of $H_{NL}$ even though it is not an intrinsic one.

### C. Shared Symmetries

In symmetry schemes higher than isotopic spin there exists the possibility that, although weak interactions are not invariant under all the transformations of the group, they may be invariant under some of them. When this happens, weak and strong interactions share certain symmetries in common,[48] and the consequences for the former interaction are not distorted by effects of the latter. To the extent that shared

---

* Medium–strong interactions are assumed to be an order of magnitude weaker than $SU(3)$-conserving interactions. Notice, however, that were it not for mass differences induced by medium–strong interactions, nonleptonic decay could not occur at all. The method by which $SU(3)$ breaking is taken into account is described in Section III.

symmetries reduce the degree of symmetry breaking in weak interactions, they may be regarded as a corollary of minimal violation.

Transformations cannot generate shared symmetries unless they always relate one charge-conserving process to another.[49] For example, charge symmetry,

$$p \leftrightarrow n, \qquad \Sigma^+ \leftrightarrow \Sigma^-, \qquad \pi^+ \leftrightarrow \pi^- \qquad (1.38)$$

which corresponds to the quantum number transformation

$$(T, T_3, S, B) \to (T, -T_3, S, B) \qquad (1.39)$$

can always be applied to strong interactions, but because it transforms $\Sigma^+ \to n + \pi^+$ into $\Sigma^- \to p + \pi^-$, it has no meaning for weak interactions. Another way of stating this result is to observe that the condition for charge conservation [Eq. (1.25)] is not invariant under Eq. (1.39) unless $\Delta T_3$ and $\Delta S$ are both zero. Thus shared symmetries for nonleptonic decay are generated only by those transformations that either commute, or anticommute with the charge operator.

In unitary symmetry, there are three transformations with the required property. The charge operator $Q$ can be identified with a generator of $SU(3)$,*

$$Q = -A_1{}^1 \equiv F_3 + \frac{1}{\sqrt{3}} F_8 \qquad (1.40)$$

and, since $R$ conjugation is defined by

$$R A_\nu{}^\mu R^{-1} = -A_\mu{}^\nu \qquad (1.41)$$

it anticommutes with $Q$. It follows from the commutation rules

$$[A_\nu{}^\mu, A_\beta{}^\alpha] = \delta_\nu{}^\alpha A_\beta{}^\mu - \delta_\beta{}^\mu A_\nu{}^\alpha \qquad (1.42)$$

that the $U$-spin operators[50]

$$\begin{aligned}
U_1 &= -\tfrac{1}{2}(A_2{}^3 + A_3{}^2) &&\equiv F_6 \\
U_2 &= (i/2)(A_2{}^3 - A_3{}^2) &&\equiv F_7 \qquad (1.43) \\
U_3 &= \tfrac{1}{2}(A_3{}^3 - A_2{}^2) &&\equiv \tfrac{1}{2}(\sqrt{3}F_8 - F_3)
\end{aligned}$$

---

* Two notations are currently used for the generators of $SU(3)$. One, $A_\nu{}^\mu$ ($\mu, \nu = 1, 2, 3$), is described by Okubo,[39] and the other, $F_i$ ($i = 1, \ldots, 8$), can be found in the papers of Gell-Mann.[36] Wherever possible, we shall describe quantities of physical interest in both of them.

commute with $Q$. Two particular $U$-spin transformations are applicable to weak interactions[51]:

$$T - L(1) \equiv \exp\left[i\pi(\tfrac{3}{2}Q - U_1)\right]$$
$$T - L(2) \equiv \exp\left[-i\pi U_2\right] \tag{1.44}$$

The first one requires that the weak Hamiltonian be symmetric under the interchange of the indices 2 and 3, and the second requires that it be antisymmetric.*

Electromagnetic interactions conserve $U$ spin,[50] and, provided that the photon is assigned odd $R$-conjugation parity, they are also $R$ invariant. It follows that if any one of these symmetries is satisfied by the basic weak interaction, its effects will be masked only by strong and medium–strong interactions. $R$ invariance is known not to be satisfied in strong interactions, and so it is unlikely to be a useful symmetry for weak decays. The $T - L$ symmetries are broken by medium–strong interactions, and so they may be expected to hold to the same extent as the octet rule.

### D. The Consequences of Selection Rules

The strangeness rule $\Delta S = 1$ serves to define the class of phenomena with which we shall be concerned. Decays that belong to this class, for example $\Lambda \to p + \pi^-$ and $K^+ \to \pi^+ + \pi^0$, are first-order effects of the nonleptonic weak interaction, and those that do not, for example $N^{*+} \to p + \pi^0$, $\eta \to \pi^+\pi^-\pi^0$, and $\Xi^- \to n + \pi^-$, are either strong interactions, electromagnetic ones, or second-order weak effects.

Because the particles belonging to an isotopic spin multiplet share a common strangeness quantum number, the $\Delta S = 1$ rule and charge conservation will usually allow more than one decay of the type $A \to B + \pi$, where $A$ denotes one isomultiplet and $B$ another. It follows that the decay modes of metastable baryons (see Table I) can be classified as different charge states of the transitions

$$\Lambda \to N + \pi, \qquad \Sigma \to N + \pi, \qquad \Xi \to \Lambda + \pi$$
$$\Omega \to \Xi + \pi, \qquad \Omega \to \Lambda + \bar{K} \tag{1.45}$$

---

* This statement can also be expressed as follows. An octet Hamiltonian for nonleptonic decay behaves, in general, as an admixture of the sixth and seventh components; $T - L\,(1)$ invariance restricts it to the sixth component, and $T - L\,(2)$ invariance to the seventh, [see Eq. (1.43)].

TABLE I
Principal Nonleptonic Decay Modes

| Particle | Mode | Partial rate, $10^{10}$ sec$^{-1}$ | Ref. | $Q$, MeV[52] | $P$, MeV/c[52] |
|---|---|---|---|---|---|
| $\Lambda$ | $p\pi^-$ | $0.262 \pm 0.028$ | 53 | 37.6 | 100.2 |
|  | $n\pi^0$ | $0.124 \pm 0.030$ |  | 40.9 | 103.7 |
| $\Sigma^+$ | $p\pi^0$ | $0.646 \pm 0.030$ | 53 | 116.2 | 189.0 |
|  | $n\pi^+$ | $0.584 \pm 0.030$ |  | 110.3 | 185.1 |
| $\Sigma^-$ | $n\pi^-$ | $0.606 \pm 0.015$ | 53 | 118.1 | 192.8 |
| $\Xi^0$ | $\Lambda\pi^0$ | $(0.345 \pm 0.048)$ | 53 | 63.9 | 134.8 |
|  | $p\pi^-$ |  |  | 236.5 | 298.7 |
| $\Xi^-$ | $\Lambda\pi^-$ | $(0.575 \pm 0.023)$ | 53 | 65.8 | 138.7 |
|  | $n\pi^-$ |  |  | 241.7 | 303.0 |
| $K^+$ | $\pi^+\pi^0$ | $(1.74 \pm 0.05) \times 10^{-3}$ | 29 | 219.2 | 205.2 |
|  | $\pi^+\pi^+\pi^-$ | $(4.50 \pm 0.09) \times 10^{-4}$ |  | 75.0 | 125.5 |
|  | $\pi^+\pi^0\pi^0$ | $(1.35 \pm 0.05) \times 10^{-4}$ |  | 84.3 | 133.0 |
| $K_S$ | $\pi^+\pi^-$ | $(0.798 \pm 0.025)$ | 29 | 218.5 | 206.0 |
|  | $\pi^0\pi^0$ | $(0.357 \pm 0.025)$ |  | 227.8 | 209.1 |
| $K_L$ | $3\pi^0$ | $(4.61 \pm 0.55) = 10^{-4}$ | 29 | 92.8 | 139.3 |
|  | $\pi^+\pi^-\pi^0$ | $(2.36 \pm 0.13) \times 10^{-4}$ |  | 83.6 | 132.8 |
|  | $\pi^+\pi^-$ | $(3.15 \pm 0.17) \times 10^{-6}$ |  | 218.5 | 206.0 |
|  | $\pi^0\pi^0$ | $\approx 6 \times 10^{-6} \times 10^{-6}$ |  |  |  |
| $\Omega^-$ | $\Xi^0\pi^-$ |  | 54 | 221 | 296 |
|  | $\Xi^-\pi^0$ | Total rate |  | 221 | 296 |
|  | $\Lambda K^-$ | $\approx 1$ |  | 66 | 216 |
|  | $\Xi^*\pi$ |  |  | $\sim 10$ | $\sim 50$ |

Similarly, meson decays are charge states of

$$K \to 2\pi \qquad K \to 3\pi \qquad (1.46)$$

From the viewpoint of unitary symmetry, the processes in Eqs. (1.45) and (1.46) are different isospin projections of transitions between $SU(3)$ multiplets*:

$$B \to B + M$$
$$D \to B + M \qquad (1.47)$$
$$M \to 2M, \qquad M \to 3M$$

* $B$ denotes the octet of $J = 1/2^+$ baryons, $M$ the octet of pseudoscalar mesons, and $D$ the decuplet of $J = 3/2^+$ baryon–meson resonances.

and from the viewpoint of $SU(6)$, they correspond to

$$(56) \rightarrow (56) + (35)$$
$$(35) \rightarrow 2(35), 3(35) \tag{1.48}$$

Thus we see that internal symmetries enable us to treat the decay modes of strange particles as special cases of a few basic transitions.

Isospin and unitary spin selection rules impose constraints upon nonleptonic decay and thereby correlate the amplitudes of various decay modes. In $\Lambda \rightarrow N + \pi$ for example, the final state may contain both $T = 1/2$ and $T = 3/2$ components; the $\Delta T = 1/2$ rule eliminates the $T = 3/2$ component and by doing so it predicts a definite ratio for the amplitudes of $\Lambda \rightarrow p + \pi^-$ and $\Lambda \rightarrow n + \pi^0$. Correlations such as this always take the form of linear sum rules, but their range in a given symmetry space is restricted to charge states of the same basic transition. As the symmetry progresses from isospin to $SU(6)$, the number of basic transitions decreases [compare Eqs. (1.45)–(1.48)] and the range of correlation widens. Thus isospin rules should correlate the decay modes of an isomultiplet (e.g., $\Sigma^+ \rightarrow p + \pi^0$, $\Sigma^\pm \rightarrow n + \pi^\pm$), $SU(3)$ rules should correlate the decay modes of a unitary multiplet (e.g., $\Sigma^+ \rightarrow p + \pi^0$, $\Lambda \rightarrow p + \pi^-$, $\Xi^- \rightarrow \Lambda + \pi^-$), and the rules of $SU(6)$ should relate the decays of $J = 1/2^+$ baryons to those of the $\Omega^-$.

The selection rules

$$\Delta T = 1/2 \qquad \Delta F = 8 \qquad \Delta \tilde{F} = 35 \tag{1.49}$$

exhibit this steadily increasing range and, in addition, they possess another important property. As shown above, they form a sequence in which each rule automatically implies the preceding one. Consequently we may expect that the sum rules predicted at each stage of the sequence will include those of the preceding stage and more besides.

We shall find that for baryons this expectation is under fulfilled in $SU(3)$ and over fulfilled in $SU(6)$. In other words, the octet rule by itself yields no predictions beyond those of $\Delta T = 1/2$, and the (35)-rule yields additional predictions which are not consistent with experimental data. To overcome these difficulties we shall have to use shared symmetries in $SU(3)$ and add a component of a representation higher than the (35) to the $SU(6)$ weak Hamiltonian. When this is done, we shall obtain sum rules which go beyond the $\Delta T = 1/2$ rule and which are in good agreement with experiment.

In the case of meson decay, the most important selection rules are those for isotopic spin. $SU(3)$ selection rules lead to some useful results for $K \to 2\pi$, but not for $K \to 3\pi$.

## II. Isotopic Spin in Meson Decay

As we saw in Section I, the decay of $K$ mesons has been responsible for two of the most important discoveries made in the past ten years. The coexistence of two-pion and three-pion decay channels provided the first indication that parity need not be conserved in weak interactions; and the observation of the long-lived neutral $K$ meson decaying into two pions demonstrated that $CP$ (or time-reversal) invariance is not an exact law of nature. In the present section, we analyze the properties of $K$ meson decay from a purely phenomenological point of view. We examine the charge space kinematics of the two- and three-pion channels and determine the consequences of isotopic spin selection rules. In particular, we discuss the connection between $CP$ violation and the breaking of the $\Delta T = 1/2$ rule.

### 1. The Two-Pion Channel

According to the generalized Pauli principle, the state vector for a system of $n$ pions must be symmetric under the exchange of all coordinates, charge space as well as configuration space, of any two pions. Because $K$ and $\pi$ mesons are pseudoscalar particles, the final state of $K \to 2\pi$ has zero orbital angular momentum and is therefore symmetric in configuration space; consequently it must also be symmetric in isospace. Pions being isovectors, the state of two pions with total isotopic spin $T = 1$ is antisymmetric, and the states with $T = 0$ and 2 are symmetric. The isospin channels open to $K \to 2\pi$ are therefore $T = 0$ and $T = 2$.

There are two decay modes for the neutral $K$ meson,

$$
\begin{aligned}
K^0 &\to \pi^+ + \pi^- \\
&\to \pi^0 + \pi^0
\end{aligned}
\tag{2.1}
$$

and one for the charged $K$,

$$
K^+ \to \pi^+ + \pi^0
\tag{2.2}
$$

In the final states of Eq. (2.1), the third component of total isotopic spin is zero, and therefore the neutral $K$ can decay into both the $T = 0$ and the $T = 2$ channels. By contrast, the charged $K$ is restricted to the $T = 2$ channel.

In general, the effective Hamiltonian for $K \rightarrow 2\pi$ transforms as an admixture of $\Delta T = 1/2$, $3/2$, and $5/2$. Because the $K$ meson is an isospinor, the $\Delta T = 1/2$ component of the Hamiltonian leads to the $T = 0$ decay channel, and the $\Delta T = 3/2$ and $5/2$ components both lead to the $T = 2$ channel. Therefore, if we impose the $\Delta T = 1/2$ rule, the $T = 2$ channel will be closed, and the decay of the charged $K$ meson will be forbidden; furthermore, the branching ratio in neutral $K$ decay will be fixed.

The observed rate for $K_S \rightarrow 2\pi$* is approximately 500 times as large as that for $K^+ \rightarrow 2\pi$, and the branching ratio of $\pi^+\pi^-$ and $2\pi^0$ decay modes is in reasonable agreement with the $\Delta T = 1/2$ rule prediction† (see Table I). Consequently, we may conclude that the effective Hamiltonian is dominated by a $\Delta T = 1/2$ component. The mere occurrence, however, of $K^+ \rightarrow 2\pi$ indicates that a component with $\Delta T \geq 3/2$ is present, and so we must consider the origin of such a component.

It is well known that the electromagnetic current, being an admixture of $\Delta T = 0$ and $\Delta T = 1$, can induce corrections of the type $\Delta T \geq 3/2$ to the $\Delta T = 1/2$ rule. If $K^+ \rightarrow \pi^+ + \pi^0$ is engendered by a combination of weak and second-order electromagnetic effects, its rate will be suppressed relative to $K_S \rightarrow 2\pi$ by a factor $\alpha^2$, where $\alpha$ is the fine structure constant. Such a suppression factor $[\alpha^2 = (1/137)^2 \approx 10^{-4}]$ yields a rate for $K^+ \rightarrow \pi^+ + \pi^0$ which is at least an order of magnitude smaller than the observed one. Thus, if we take the point of view that $K^+ \rightarrow \pi^+ + \pi^0$ represents an electromagnetic correction to weak interactions, we find that its rate appears to be enhanced rather than suppressed.

A way out of this paradox has been put forward by Cabibbo.[55] He has shown that in the limit of exact $SU(3)$ symmetry for strong interactions, the current × current theory together with octet dominance forbids $K_S \rightarrow 2\pi$. He then argues that the relatively large value for the ratio of rates $\Gamma(K^+ \rightarrow 2\pi)/\Gamma(K_S \rightarrow 2\pi)$ arises not from an enhancement of the charged $K$ decay, but from a suppression of the neutral $K$ decay. So far no successful quantitative estimate of the ratio of rates has been

---

* $K_S$ denotes the short-lived component of $K^0$.

† The branching ratio predicted by $\Delta T = 1/2$ will be calculated below.

made, and so Cabibbo's argument remains a qualitative one. It is also subject to criticism based upon $SU(3)$ considerations,[56] as will be seen in a subsequent section. Thus the decay mode $K^+ \to \pi^+ + \pi^0$ is still an unsolved problem.

Another puzzling deviation from the $\Delta T = 1/2$ rule has recently been found in the $CP$-violating decay $K_L \to 2\pi$. Two independent experiments[57] have shown that the branching ratio of $\pi^+\pi^-$ and $2\pi^0$ decay modes differs considerably from the value predicted by $\Delta T = 1/2$. Because the branching ratio in $K_S \to 2\pi$ is close to the $\Delta T = 1/2$ prediction, the experimental result for $K_L$ decay seems to rule out the possibility that $CP$ violation occurs in a superweak interaction with[34] $\Delta S = 2$; it also implies that the $CP$-violating interaction must contain a $\Delta T \geq 3/2$ component. Whether this component is much larger or much smaller than the $\Delta T = 1/2$ one is a question which cannot be decided on the basis of present experimental data. These uncertainties are further heightened by the fact that no significant violations of $CP$ have been observed in other weak decay processes.

### A. Phenomenological Analysis

To analyze $K \to 2\pi$ in terms of isotopic spin, we express the effective Hamiltonian as a sum of three terms,

$$H = H_{1/2} + H_{3/2} + H_{5/2} \qquad (2.3)$$

each of which corresponds to the value of $\Delta T$ indicated by the subscript.* The Wigner-Eckart theorem allows us to express the matrix element for the decay of an isospinor into a two-pion channel with definite isotopic spin in the form

$$\langle T, T_3 | H_{n/2} | 1/2, \lambda \rangle = C^T_{T_3\ 1/2\ \lambda}{}^{n/2\ 1/2} \langle T \| H_{n/2} \| 1/2 \rangle \quad (n = 1, 3, 5) \quad (2.4)$$

The dependence of this matrix element upon the quantum numbers $T_3$ and $\lambda$ appears in the Clebsch–Gordan coefficient, and so the reduced matrix element $\langle T \| H_{n/2} \| 1/2 \rangle$ is a factor common to both $K^+$ ($\lambda = 1/2$) and $K^0$ ($\lambda = -1/2$) decay amplitudes.

In terms of isospin eigenstates, a symmetric state of two pions takes the form

$$|\pi^\mu \pi^\nu\rangle = N_{\mu\nu} \sum_{T=0,2} C^T_{T_3\ \mu\ \nu}{}^{1\ 1} |T, T_3\rangle \qquad (2.5)$$

* Note that $\Delta T_3$ is always $\pm 1/2$.

where $N_{\mu\nu}$ is a normalization factor

$$
\begin{aligned}
N_{\mu\nu} &= \sqrt{2} \qquad \mu \neq \nu \\
&= 1 \qquad \mu = \nu
\end{aligned} \tag{2.6}
$$

Using Eqs. (2.4) and (2.5), we can write the amplitude for $K^\lambda \to \pi^\mu \pi^\nu$ as

$$
\langle \pi^\mu \pi^\nu | H | K^\lambda \rangle = N_{\mu\nu} \sum_{\substack{n=1,3,5 \\ T=0,2}} C^T_{T_3}{}^{1\ 1}_{\ \mu\ \nu} C^T_{T_3}{}^{n/2\ 1/2}_{1/2\ \lambda} \langle T \| H_{n/2} \| 1/2 \rangle \tag{2.7}
$$

In subsequent equations we denote the reduced matrix elements in Eq. (2.7) by

$$
\begin{aligned}
A_1 &= \langle 0 \| H_{1/2} \| 1/2 \rangle \\
A_n &= \langle 2 \| H_{n/2} \| 1/2 \rangle
\end{aligned} \tag{2.8}
$$

From Eqs. (2.7) and (2.8) we obtain the amplitudes for specific charge states of $K \to 2\pi$:

$$
\begin{aligned}
\langle \pi^+ \pi^- | H | K^0 \rangle &= (1/\sqrt{3})[A_1 e^{i\delta_0} + (1/\sqrt{2})(A_3 + A_5)e^{i\delta_2}] \\
\langle \pi^0 \pi^0 | H | K^0 \rangle &= (1/\sqrt{3})[-(1/\sqrt{2})A_1 e^{i\delta_0} + (A_3 + A_5)e^{i\delta_2}] \\
\langle \pi^+ \pi^0 | H | K^+ \rangle &= (1/\sqrt{3})(3/2 A_3 - A_5)e^{i\delta_2}
\end{aligned} \tag{2.9}
$$

The factors $e^{i\delta_0}$ and $e^{i\delta_2}$ represent the effects of final-state interactions; $\delta_0$ and $\delta_2$ are the $S$ wave $\pi$–$\pi$ scattering phase shifts for the $T = 0$ and $T = 2$ channels, respectively. The corresponding amplitudes for $\bar{K} \to 2\pi$ are obtained by substituting $-A_i^*$ for $A_i$ in Eq. (2.9); the minus sign appears as a consequence of our phase convention:

$$
\begin{aligned}
CP: K^0 &= -\bar{K}^0 \\
CP: K^+ &= -K^-
\end{aligned} \tag{2.10}
$$

It is convenient to define the short- and long-lived components of the neutral $K$ mesons as[58]

$$
\begin{aligned}
K_S &= (1/\sqrt{1 + |r|^2})[K^0 - r\bar{K}^0] \\
K_L &= (1/\sqrt{1 + |r|^2})[K^0 + r\bar{K}^0]
\end{aligned} \tag{2.11}
$$

The parameter $r$ is the ratio of off-diagonal elements in the $K^0 - \bar{K}^0$ mass matrix, and its deviation from unity

$$
\varepsilon = 1 - r \tag{2.12}
$$

is one measure of $CP$ violation. The amplitudes for $K_{S, L} \to 2\pi$ can now be written as

$$A(K_S \to \pi^+\pi^-) = \frac{1}{\sqrt{3(1 + |r|^2)}} \left\{ e^{i\delta_0}(2 \text{ Re } A_1) + \frac{e^{i\delta_2}}{\sqrt{2}} [2 \text{ Re } (A_3 + A_5)] \right.$$

$$\left. - \varepsilon \left[ A_1^* e^{i\delta_0} + \frac{1}{\sqrt{2}} (A_3^* + A_5^*)e^{i\delta_2} \right] \right\} \qquad (2.13)$$

$$A(K_S \to \pi^0\pi^0) = \frac{1}{\sqrt{3(1 + |r|^2)}} \left\{ -\frac{e^{i\delta_0}}{\sqrt{2}} (2 \text{ Re } A_1) \right.$$

$$+ e^{i\delta_2}[2 \text{ Re } (A_3 + A_5)]$$

$$\left. - \varepsilon \left[ -\frac{1}{\sqrt{2}} A_1^* e^{i\delta_0} + (A_3^* + A_5^*)e^{i\delta_2} \right\} \right] \qquad (2.14)$$

$$A(K_L \to \pi^+\pi^-) = \frac{1}{\sqrt{3(1 + |r|^2)}} \left\{ ie^{i\delta_0}(2 \text{ Im } A_1) \right.$$

$$+ \frac{ie^{i\delta_2}}{\sqrt{2}} [2 \text{ Im } (A_3 + A_5)]$$

$$\left. + \varepsilon \left[ A_1^* e^{i\delta_0} + \frac{1}{\sqrt{2}} (A_3^* + A_5^*)e^{i\delta_2} \right] \right\} \qquad (2.15)$$

$$A(K_L \to \pi^0\pi^0) = \frac{1}{\sqrt{3(1 + |r|^2)}} \left\{ -\frac{ie^{i\delta_0}}{\sqrt{2}} (2 \text{ Im } A_1) \right.$$

$$+ ie^{i\delta_2}[2 \text{ Im } (A_3 + A_5)]$$

$$\left. + \varepsilon \left[ \frac{-A_1^*}{\sqrt{2}} e^{i\delta_0} + (A_3^* + A_5^*)e^{i\delta_2} \right] \right\} \qquad (2.16)$$

### B. CP Conserved

If $CP$ invariance were an exact law of nature, then the parameter $\varepsilon$ [see Eq. (2.12)] would be zero, and the amplitudes $A_i$ ($i = 1, 3, 5$) would be real. The particles $K_S$ and $K_L$ would then be eigenstates of $CP$

$$K_S = (1/\sqrt{2})[K^0 - \bar{K}^0] \quad CP = +1$$

$$K_L = (1/\sqrt{2})[K^0 + \bar{K}^0] \quad CP = -1 \qquad (2.17)$$

[see Eqs. (2.10)–(2.12)], and the decay $K_L \to 2\pi$ would be forbidden. The occurrence of $K_L \to 2\pi$ indicates that $CP$ is not conserved; but, since the $CP$-violating amplitude is roughly 1000 times as small as the

*CP*-conserving one, we assume that *CP* invariance is a reasonable first-order approximation.

Under this assumption, our main interest lies in the relative rates for the decay modes of $K_S$ and $K^+$. If we assume that the $\Delta T = 1/2$ rule is valid, then the amplitudes $A_3$ and $A_5$ are both zero, and we find that

$$A(K_S \to \pi^+\pi^-) = -\sqrt{2}\, A(K_S \to \pi^0\pi^0) \qquad (2.18)$$

$$A(K^+ \to \pi^+\pi^0) = 0 \qquad (2.19)$$

Equation (2.18) predicts that the branching ratio in $K_S$ decay should be

$$B = \Gamma(K_S \to \pi^+\pi^-)/\Gamma(K_S \to \pi^0\pi^0) = 2 \qquad (2.20)$$

The experimental value for $B$, namely[29]

$$(B)_{\text{expt}} = 2.23 \pm 0.09 \qquad (2.21)$$

differs from the predicted value by about 10% and indicates a 5% deviation from $\Delta T = 1/2$ in the $K_S$ amplitudes. Similarly, the fact that the ratio

$$B^+ = \Gamma(K^+ \to \pi^+\pi^0)/[\Gamma(K_S \to \pi^+\pi^-) + \Gamma(K_S \to \pi^0\pi^0)] \qquad (2.22)$$

differs from zero,[29] i.e.,

$$(B^+)_{\text{expt}} = (1.50 \pm 0.07) \times 10^{-3} \qquad (2.23)$$

implies that there is a definite, though probably small, deviation from $\Delta T = 1/2$.

If this deviation occurs solely through a *CP*-conserving interaction with $\Delta T = 3/2$ (i.e., $A_5 = 0$), we obtain one sum rule among the three decay amplitudes[42, 59]:

$$A(K_S \to \pi^+\pi^-) + \sqrt{2}\, A(K_S \to \pi^0\pi^0) = 2A(K^+ \to \pi^+\pi^0) \qquad (2.24)$$

Because of the strong interaction phase factors in Eqs. (2.13)–(2.15), Eq. (2.24) is a sum rule for complex numbers and it represents a closed triangle in the Argand diagram. We can apply two crude tests to see whether the amplitudes are consistent with it.

One of the tests is the standard triangular inequality; from the data given in Table I, we see that the inequality is satisfied within experimental error. The second test arises from the fact that, when $A_5$ is set equal to zero, the observed value of $B^+$ [Eq. (2.23)] implies that the ratio

$$a = A_3/A_1 \qquad (2.25)$$

is a small number. To first order in $a$, we can set the following limits on the value of $B$ [Eq. (2.20)]:

$$[1 - \sqrt{24B^+} \mid \cos(\delta_2 - \delta_0)|] \leq B/2 \leq [1 + \sqrt{24B^+} \mid \cos(\delta_2 - \delta_0)|] \tag{2.26}$$

Not knowing the actual value of $(\delta_2 - \delta_0)$, we take the extremal limits of Eq. (2.26):

$$1.81 \leq B \leq 2.38 \tag{2.27}$$

We see from Eq. (2.21) that the measured branching ratio falls within this range; therefore, the assumption that $K \rightarrow 2\pi$ satisfies $\Delta T \leq 3/2$ is not inconsistent with the data.

If the violation of $\Delta T = 1/2$ takes place solely through a $\Delta T = 5/2$ interaction (i.e., $A_3 = 0$), then we obtain another sum rule for the amplitudes

$$A(K_S \rightarrow \pi^+\pi^-) + \sqrt{2}\, A(K_S \rightarrow \pi^0\pi^0) = -3A(K^+ \rightarrow \pi^+\pi^0) \tag{2.28}$$

and a new set of limits for $B$:

$$[1 - 3\sqrt{6B^+} \mid \cos(\delta_2 - \delta_0)|] \leq B/2 \leq [1 + 3\sqrt{6B^+} \mid \cos(\delta_2 - \delta_0)|] \tag{2.29}$$

The measured amplitudes satisfy the triangular inequalities implied by Eq. (2.28), and the extremal range for $B$, namely

$$1.43 \leq B \leq 2.57 \tag{2.30}$$

includes the observed value [Eq. (2.21)]. Thus it is not inconceivable that the selection rule for $K \rightarrow 2\pi$ is an admixture of $\Delta T = 1/2$ and $5/2$.

On grounds of simplicity, the possibility that $\Delta T = 1/2$ plus $5/2$ is not as attractive as the possibility that $\Delta T \leq 3/2$. The choice between them, however, can only be made by determining which of the sum rules in Eqs. (2.24) and (2.28) provides the better fit to the observed amplitudes. In turn this requires much more accurate data on the magnitudes and phases of the amplitudes, and a knowledge of the strong interaction parameters $\delta_0$ and $\delta_2$. Should it ultimately turn out that neither Eq. (2.24) nor Eq. (2.28) is satisfied, we will be forced to conclude that both $\Delta T = 3/2$ and $\Delta T = 5/2$ components are present in the effective Hamiltonian.

### C. The Violation of CP

We observed in the preceding section that the violation of the $\Delta T = 1/2$ rule is an effect of order $5\%$ in amplitude. The violation of CP is much smaller: if measured by the parameter

$$\eta_{+-} = A(K_L \to \pi^+\pi^-)/A(K_S \to \pi^0\pi^0) \qquad (2.31)$$

where[30]

$$|\eta_{+-}| = (1.94 \pm 0.09) \times 10^{-3} \qquad (2.32)$$

then it is an effect of order one-tenth of $1\%$. Such an effect is unlikely to distort the considerations of the preceding section.

A careful inspection of the amplitudes given in Eqs. (2.15) and (2.16) indicates that there are two possible sources for the decay $K_L \to 2\pi$. One is a direct CP violation in the weak interactions themselves, and the other is the parameter $\varepsilon$. In the case of a direct violation, the amplitudes $A_i$ ($i = 1, 2, 3$) must be complex, and $\varepsilon$ may be small. In the second case, $\varepsilon$ may be relatively large and the amplitudes $A_i$ need not be complex. There is, of course, an intermediate case in which both sources are equally important.

The parameter $\varepsilon$ is related to the off-diagonal elements in the $K^0 - \bar{K}^0$ mass matrix $M$,[58, 60] and it measures the deviation of their ratio from unity:

$$\varepsilon = 1 - (\langle K^0|M|\bar{K}^0\rangle/\langle \bar{K}^0|M|K^0\rangle) \qquad (2.33)$$

The matrix element $\langle K^0|M|\bar{K}^0\rangle$ is determined by the transition amplitudes for $K^0 \to \bar{K}^0$ and, from the smallness of the $K_L$–$K_S$ mass difference,[38] it is assumed to be of second order in the weak coupling constant $G$. Thus $\langle K^0|M|\bar{K}^0\rangle$ represents a sum over such second-order diagrams as

$$K^0 \underset{3\pi}{\overset{2\pi}{\diamond}} \bar{K}^0 \qquad (2.34)$$

and, if the $\Delta S = \Delta Q$ rule does not hold, it also includes contributions from[35]

$$K^0 \to \pi + \text{leptons} \to \bar{K}^0 \qquad (2.35)$$

If weak interactions conserve CP, $\langle K^0|M|\bar{K}^0\rangle$ and $\langle \bar{K}^0|M|K^0\rangle$ will be equal to one another unless there exists some other CP-violating interaction which has a strength no greater than $G^2$ and which changes strangeness by two units, i.e., $\Delta S = 2$.

Such a possibility has been considered by Wolfenstein.[34] He assumes that, because no $CP$-violating effects other than $K_L \rightarrow 2\pi$ have been observed, $CP$ is conserved in the usual weak interactions and violated in a superweak interaction $H_{SW}$ with strength $\approx \varepsilon \times G^2$ and $\Delta S = 2$. This interaction contributes to off-diagonal matrix elements via a diagram

$$K^0 \underline{\quad} \boxed{H_{SW}} \underline{\quad} \bar{K}^0 \qquad (2.36)$$

and it predicts that the amplitudes $A_i$ are real

$$A_i = A_i^* \qquad (2.37)$$

Inserting these results in the expressions of Eqs. (2.13)–(2.16), we obtain

$$\eta_{+-} = \eta_{00} = \varepsilon/(2 - \varepsilon) \approx \varepsilon/2 \qquad (2.38)$$

where $\eta_{+-}$ is given in Eq. (2.31) and $\eta_{00}$ is the corresponding ratio for $K_L \rightarrow 2\pi^0$:

$$\eta_{00} = A(K_L \rightarrow \pi^0\pi^0)/A(K_S \rightarrow \pi^0\pi^0) \qquad (2.39)$$

In two recent experiments,[57] the parameter $\eta_{00}$ has been found to have the following values

$$|\eta_{00}| = (4.9 \pm 0.5) \times 10^{-3}$$
$$|\eta_{00}| = \left(4.3^{+1.1}_{-0.8}\right) \times 10^{-3} \qquad (2.40)$$

These values are consistent within the limits of experimental error, and they are substantially different from the value of $\eta_{+-}$ in Eq. (2.32). Thus the major prediction of the superweak theory, namely Eq. (2.38), is inconsistent with the experimental data.

Let us now consider an alternative hypothesis, in which weak interactions exhibit a small violation of $CP$. We also assume that the $CP$-violating contributions of Eqs. (2.34) and (2.35) to the mass matrix tend to cancel one another and leave us with an extremely small value for $\varepsilon$, i.e.,

$$\varepsilon \approx 0 \qquad (2.41)$$

In this case the nonvanishing of $A(K_L \rightarrow 2\pi)$ is due to the amplitudes $A_i$ being complex. Now it can be seen from Eq. (2.9) that, apart from the strong interaction phase shifts, the relevant factor in the $K_L$ amplitude is the difference in phase between $A_1$ and $(A_3 + A_5)$. Because the relative phase of the states $|K^0\rangle$ and $|\bar{K}^0\rangle$ cannot be measured,[61] we may adopt a convention in which $A_1$ is real[58] and $(A_3 + A_5)$ is complex:

$$A_1 = A_1^* \qquad (A_3 + A_5) \equiv A_2 \neq A_2^* \qquad (2.42)$$

Notice that $A_2$ is the amplitude for decay into the $T = 2$ channel [see Eq. (2.8)].

From Eqs. (2.41) and (2.42) we obtain

$$\eta_{+-} = 1/2\varepsilon'[1 + \omega]^{-1} \qquad (2.43)$$

$$\eta_{00} = -\varepsilon'[1 - 2\omega]^{-1} \qquad (2.44)$$

where

$$\varepsilon' = (\sqrt{2}\,\mathrm{Im}\,A_2/A_1)e^{i(\pi/2 + \delta_2 - \delta_0)}$$

$$\sqrt{2}\,\omega = (\mathrm{Re}\,A_2/A_1)e^{i(\delta_2 - \delta_0)} \qquad (2.45)$$

The experimental values of $B$ and $B^+$ [Eqs. (2.20)–(2.23)] indicate that

$$|\omega| \approx 1/25 \qquad (2.46)$$

and so we may neglect this parameter. The resulting prediction for the ratio of $\eta_{+-}$ and $\eta_{00}$, namely

$$\eta_{+-} = 1/2\varepsilon'$$
$$\eta_{00} = -\varepsilon' = -2\eta_{+-} \qquad (2.47)$$

is in very good agreement with the observed ratio [Eqs. (2.32) and (2.40)]

$$|\eta_{00}/\eta_{+-}| \approx 2 - 3 \qquad (2.48)$$

To understand this result we note that, with our phase convention for $A_1$ [Eq. (2.42)], the decay $K_L \to 2\pi$ is forbidden when $\varepsilon$ and $A_2$ are both zero. Similarly, if $\varepsilon$ and $A_1$ were to vanish, the phase of $A_2$ could be taken as real, and the CP-violating decay would again be forbidden. It follows that the nonvanishing of $A(K_L \to 2\pi)$ in the case when $\varepsilon = 0$ is due to the accessibility of both the $T = 0$ and the $T = 2$ two-pion channels.

The predicted value for $\eta_{00}/\eta_{+-}$ [see Eq. (2.47)] reflects the fact that the CP-conserving decay, $K_S \to 2\pi$, is dominated by the $T = 0$ channel, and the CP-violating one, $K_L \to 2\pi$, by the $T = 2$ channel. In turn, this result implies that the violation of CP occurs in an interaction for which $\Delta T \geq 3/2$. This type of theory was first put forward by T. N. Truong[62] and has been discussed subsequently by D. Cline.[63]

Before we can accept the $\varepsilon \approx 0$ theory as the correct explanation for the experimental result of Eq. (2.48), we must consider another possibility. When $\varepsilon$ is nonzero and $|\omega|$ is much smaller than unity, the general expressions for $\eta_{+-}$ and $\eta_{00}$ are

$$\eta_{+-} = \tfrac{1}{2}(\varepsilon + \varepsilon')$$
$$\eta_{00} = \tfrac{1}{2}(\varepsilon - 2\varepsilon') \tag{2.49}$$

These parameters being complex numbers, the relationships implied by Eq. (2.49) can be represented by a triangle in the Argand diagram [the Wu-Yang triangle,[58] see Fig. 1]. It is not difficult to see that the ratio $|\eta_{00}/\eta_{+-}| \approx 2$ can be obtained in two ways: one is to set $\varepsilon \approx 0$, the case discussed above, and the other is to choose $\varepsilon \approx -4\varepsilon'$. The first possibility is known as the small solution and the second as the large solution.

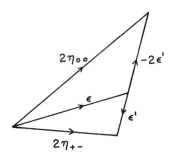

FIG. 1. The Wu-Yang triangle.

To distinguish the two solutions from each other, it is necessary to know the phases of $\eta_{+-}$ and $\eta_{00}$; the small solution implies that they are almost $180°$ out of phase (see Fig. 2), and the large one implies that they are almost in phase (see Fig. 3). In principle, the phases can be measured in regeneration experiments and by studying the time dependence of $K^0 \to 2\pi$ at times greater than $10^{-9}$ sec after birth.[64] In practice the regeneration method is subject to considerable uncertainty due to a lack of knowledge of the phase of the regeneration amplitude,[65] and the time dependence experiment is difficult to perform.

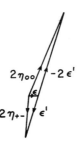

FIG. 2. The Wu-Yang triangle with $\varepsilon \approx 0$ (small solution).

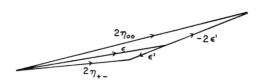

FIG. 3. The Wu-Yang triangle with $\varepsilon \approx -4\varepsilon'$ (large solution).

An alternative method for distinguishing the large and small solutions is to measure the real part of $\varepsilon$ directly. This can be done by studying the electron–positron asymmetry in $K_L \rightarrow \pi^{\pm} + e^{\mp} + \nu$.[66] However, this method is subject to some uncertainty caused by a possible violation of the $\Delta S = \Delta Q$ rule. We must therefore conclude that, at the present time, no choice can be made between the large and small solutions for $\varepsilon$.

We may summarize the situation of $CP$ violation by stating that the observed ratio of $|\eta_{00}/\eta_{+-}|$ rules out the superweak theory.[34] It is, however, consistent with the idea of a violation occuring in electromagnetic interactions[21] provided that the $CP$-violating current has an admixture of $\Delta T \geq 1$. Finally, we must point out that $CPT$ invariance has been assumed throughout our discussion.

### 2. The Three-Pion Channel

It is convenient to analyze the parity-conserving decays $K \rightarrow 3\pi$ in terms of the Dalitz plot.[4] This plot is based upon the property that in an equilateral triangle, the sum of the perpendicular distances from any point to each of the three sides is constant. Since the sum of kinetic energies of the three pions is also constant, we can identify the perpendicular distance from each side with the kinetic energy of a specific pion.

In this way, every point inside the triangle corresponds to an energy-conserving configuration of the final state. Conservation of linear momentum in the rest frame of the $K$ meson further restricts these points to lie within the inscribed circle.*

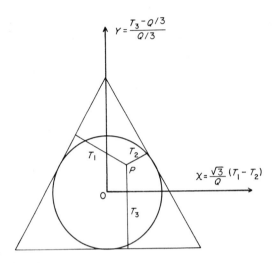

FIG. 4. The Dalitz Plot. $T_1$, $T_2$, and $T_3$ are the kinetic energies of the pions, $T_3$ being reserved for the unlike pion in $K^+ \to 3\pi$, and for the neutral pion in $K^0 \to \pi^+\pi^-\pi^0$. $Q$ is the energy release: $Q = M_K - m_1 - m_2 - m_3 \approx 80$ MeV.

The Cartesian coordinate system for the Dalitz plot is defined in Figure 4. In this system the volume element of phase space for $K \to 3\pi$ is just $dx\,dy$. Therefore, if the observed three-pion configurations are represented by points in a Dalitz plot, their density is directly proportional to the square modulus of the decay amplitude. If the amplitude varies with pion energy, the density will vary from one region of the plot to another; and if the amplitude is independent of energy, the density will be constant.

It has been found experimentally that the density deviates from being a constant by a small variation in the coordinate $y$ (see Fig. 4). Consequently the decay amplitude is of the form

$$A(K \to 3\pi) \propto (1 + \alpha y + \beta y^2) \qquad (2.50)$$

* Relativistic and electromagnetic mass-difference corrections lead to a slight distortion of the circle.

where $\alpha$ is the constant of the order $0.5^{(29)}$ and $\beta$ is smaller than $\alpha$ by at least one order of magnitude.[67] In view of this we shall ignore the quadratic term in the amplitude.

Along with the generalized Pauli principle, the dominance of the energy-independent term in Eq. (2.50) implies that the major component of the three-pion final state is totally symmetric in isospace. There are two such states, one with isotopic spin $T = 3$ and the other with $T = 1$. If the interaction Hamiltonian is such that $\Delta T \leq 3/2$, the $T = 3$ channel will be closed and if $5/2 \leq \Delta T \leq 7/2$, the $T = 1$ channel will be closed. In either case, we can predict the branching ratios for

$$K^+ \to \pi^+ + \pi^+ + \pi^- \qquad (\tau)$$
$$\to \pi^0 + \pi^0 + \pi^+ \qquad (\tau') \qquad\qquad (2.51.1)$$

and for

$$K^0 \to \pi^+ + \pi^- + \pi^0$$
$$\to 3\pi^0 \qquad\qquad (2.51.2)$$

To correlate the rates for $K^+$ and $K^0$ decay, however, we require a specific value for $\Delta T$, e.g., $\Delta T = 1/2$.

For the linear term of Eq. (2.50), the possible isospin states are $T = 1, 2$. Applying arguments similar to those used above, we can make predictions about the slope parameters $\alpha$ in each decay mode.

Whether or not $CP$ is conserved, both $K_S$ and $K_L$ can decay into three pions. A neutral three-pion state with zero angular momentum is an eigenstate of $CP$ with eigenvalue $(-1)^T$.* When $CP$ is conserved $K_S$ can decay into the $T = 0$ and 2 channels, and $K_L$ can decay into the $T = 1, 3$ channels; when $CP$ is violated, all four channels are open to both particles. It should be noted, however, that the specific mode $K_S \to 3\pi^0$ violates $CP$, and that all $K_S \to 3\pi$ decay modes are suppressed relative to $K_S \to 2\pi$ by their smaller phase-space volume.

### A. Phenomenological Analysis[68]

We shall approximate the decay amplitude by a linear function of the pion energies. In this approximation, the amplitude for

$$K^\rho \to \pi_1{}^\alpha + \pi_2{}^\beta + \pi_3{}^\gamma \qquad\qquad (2.52)$$

---

* The pion is pseudoscalar and has negative $G$ parity. Therefore, a $3\pi$ state with zero angular momentum has $GP = +1$. In the neutral state, $GP = CP(-1)^T$, and hence $CP = (-1)^T$.

is given by

$$A(\alpha\beta\gamma) = E(\alpha\beta\gamma)[1 + \sigma(\alpha\beta\gamma)(s_3 - s_0)] \qquad (2.53)$$

where $\alpha$, $\beta$, $\gamma$ denote the charges of the pions and

$$s_i = (K - k_i)^2$$

$$\sum_{i=1}^{3} s_i = 3s_0 = M_K^2 + \sum_{i=1}^{3} m_i^2 \qquad (2.54)$$

The variables $K$, $k_i$ represent the four-momenta of the $K$ meson and $i$th pion, respectively, and $M_K$ and $m_i$ are their masses. We reserve the indices 3 and $\gamma$ for the unlike pion in $\tau$ and $\tau'$ decay (e.g., the $\pi^-$ in $\tau$ decay) and for the $\pi^0$ in $K^0 \rightarrow \pi^+ + \pi^- + \pi^0$.

In suitable units, the decay rate is given by

$$\int |A(\alpha, \beta, \gamma)|^2 \, dy_3$$

$$= \left(\frac{1}{n!}\right) |E(\alpha, \beta, \gamma)|^2 \int [1 - 2M_K T_{max}\sigma(\alpha, \beta, \gamma)y_3] \, dy_3 \qquad (2.55)$$

where $n$ is the number of like pions in the final state, $y_3$ is the Dalitz plot variable (see Fig. 4 and note that $-1 \leq y_3 \leq +1$), and $T_{max}$ is the maximum kinetic energy of $\pi_3$, i.e.,

$$2M_K T_{max} = (M_K - m_3)^2 - (m_1 + m_2)^2 \qquad (2.56)$$

It follows that

$$\frac{1}{n!} |E(\alpha, \beta, \gamma)|^2 \approx \frac{\text{observed rate}}{\text{phase space volume}} = \Gamma(\alpha, \beta, \gamma)$$

$$\sigma(\alpha, \beta, \gamma) = -\frac{\text{observed slope}}{2M_K T_{max}} \qquad (2.57)$$

Although seven eigenstates of isotopic spin can be constructed from three pions, only four of them meet the requirements that (1) they be symmetric under the exchange of all coordinates of any two pions; and (2) that their dependence upon the variables $s_i$ be at most linear. Two other states are quadratic in the $s_i$; and one, with $T = 0$, is cubic. The states to be used in the linear approximation are

$$\Psi_1 = |1, T_z(S)\rangle$$
$$\Psi_1' = |1, T_z(L)\rangle$$
$$\Psi_2 = |2, T_z(L)\rangle$$
$$\Psi_3 = |3, T_z(S)\rangle \qquad (2.58)$$

where $|T, T_z(X)\rangle$ represents a state with isotopic spin $(T, T_z)$ which is either independent of $s_i$ ($X \equiv S$), or linearly dependent upon them ($X \equiv L$). The precise definition of $|T, T_z(X)\rangle$ can be found in Barton, Kacser, and Rosen.[68]

We denote the amplitude for the decay of the $K^+$ into the state of $\Psi_i$ by $a_i$, and the corresponding amplitude for $K^0$ by $b_i$. We may then write the amplitudes for the decay modes of Eq. (2.51) as

$$A(+ + -) = (1/\sqrt{15})[2a_1 + a_3] - (1/\sqrt{3})[a_1' + a_2](s_3 - s_0)$$

$$A(0\ 0\ +) = (1/\sqrt{15})[-a_1 + 2a_3] - (1/\sqrt{3})[a_1' - a_2](s_3 - s_0) \quad (2.59)$$

and

$$A(+ - 0) = (1/\sqrt{15})[b_1 + (\sqrt{3}/\sqrt{2})b_3] + (1/\sqrt{3})b_1'(s_3 - s_0)$$
$$+ (1/\sqrt{3})b_2(s_2 - s_1)$$

$$A(0\ 0\ 0) = (1/\sqrt{5})[-\sqrt{3}\ b_1 + \sqrt{2}\ b_3] \quad (2.60)$$

The corresponding amplitudes for $\bar{K}^0 \to 3\pi$ are obtained from Eq. (2.60) by substituting

$$b_T \to (-1)^{T+1}b_T{}^* \quad (2.61)$$

where the factor $(-1)^{T+1}$ arises from the $CP$ eigenvalue of the state $\Psi_T$ and our phase convention in Eq. (2.11).

If the final state in $K^+ \to 3\pi$ is pure $T = 1$, then the partial rates and slopes satisfy the relations

$$\Gamma(+ + -) = 4\Gamma(0\ 0\ +)$$
$$2\sigma(+ + -) = -\sigma(0\ 0\ +) \quad (2.62)$$

Similarly, if the final state in $K_L \to 3\pi$ is also $T = 1$, then the branching ratio is predicted to be

$$\Gamma_L(0\ 0\ 0) = 3/2\Gamma_L(+ - 0) \quad (2.63)$$

As can be seen from Tables II and III, the predictions in Eqs. (2.62) and (2.63) are in reasonable agreement with experimental data.

The $T = 1$ final state can be engendered by any interaction which contains an arbitrary admixture of $\Delta T = 1/2$ and $3/2$. Consequently, we cannot relate the properties of $K^+ \to 3\pi$ to those of $K_L \to 3\pi$ unless we

TABLE II
Data on $K \rightarrow 3\pi$[29]

| Mode | Phase space factor $\Phi$ | $\Gamma = \text{rate}/\Phi$, $10^6 \text{ sec}^{-1}$ | Slope $\sigma(\alpha\beta\gamma)(m_\pi{}^{-2})$ |
|---|---|---|---|
| $\pi^+\pi^+\pi^-$ | 1.0 | $4.50 \pm 0.09$ | $0.093 \pm 0.011$ |
| $\pi^0\pi^0\pi^+$ | 1.24 | $1.09 \pm 0.04$ | $-0.25 \pm 0.02$ |
| $\pi^+\pi^-\pi^0$ | 1.22 | $1.93 \pm 0.11$ | $-0.24 \pm 0.02$ |
| $\pi^0\pi^0\pi^0$ | 1.49 | $3.1 \pm 0.37$ | $0$ |

TABLE III
$\Delta T = 1/2$ in $K \rightarrow 3\pi$[29]

| Ratio | Expt. | Prediction |
|---|---|---|
| $\Gamma(+ - 0)/2\Gamma(0\,0\,+)$ | $0.89 \pm 0.07$ | 1 |
| $\Gamma(+ + -)/4\Gamma(0\,0\,+)$ | $1.03 \pm 0.04$ | 1 |
| $2\Gamma(0\,0\,0)/3\Gamma(+ - 0)$ | $1.07 \pm 0.13$ | 1 |
| $\sigma(0\,0\,+)/\sigma(+ + -)$ | $-2.7 \pm 0.4$ | $-2$ |
| $\sigma(0\,0\,+)/\sigma(+ - 0)$ | $1.0 \pm 0.11$ | 1 |

specify the admixture precisely. If we assume the $\Delta T = 1/2$ rule and $CP$ invariance, we find that

$$a_1 = \sqrt{2}\, b_1 = a_1^*$$
$$a_1' = \sqrt{2}\, b_1' = a_1'^* \qquad (2.64)$$

$$\Gamma(+ - 0) = 2\Gamma(0\,0\,+)$$
$$\sigma(+ - 0) = \sigma(0\,0\,+) \qquad (2.65)$$

Since Eq. (2.65) is in reasonable agreement with experiment (see Tables II and III), we may conclude that there are no serious deviations from $\Delta T = 1/2$ in $K \rightarrow 3\pi$.

As we remarked above, $CP$ invariance forbids $K_S \rightarrow 3\pi^0$, but it allows $K_S$ to decay into $\pi^+\pi^-\pi^0$ via the $T = 0$ and $T = 2$ channels. The $T = 0$ channel, being totally antisymmetric in isospin coordinates, is strongly inhibited by angular momentum barriers, and it does not appear in the linear approximation [see Eq. (2.58)]; the $T = 2$ channel is closed unless the interaction contains admixtures of $\Delta T \geq 3/2$. Thus $K_S \rightarrow 3\pi$ is effectively forbidden by $CP$ invariance and $\Delta T = 1/2$.

## B. The Violation of CP

It is a consequence of the $TCP$ theorem that the total rate for $K^+ \rightarrow 3\pi$ is equal to that for $K^- \rightarrow 3\pi$.[26,64,69]

$$\Gamma(+ + -) + \Gamma(0\,0\,+) = \Gamma(- - +) + \Gamma(0\,0\,-) \qquad (2.66)$$

The partial rates, however, will not be equal if $CP$ is not conserved.* Thus we expect that $\Gamma(+ + -)$ will differ from $\Gamma(- - +)$ and that $\Gamma(0\,0\,+)$ will differ from $\Gamma(0\,0\,+)$. If the parameter $\eta_{+-}$ is an accurate measure of the magnitude of $CP$ violation, the size of these differences, and of corresponding differences in the slope parameters will be about one-tenth of 1%.

In $K_S$ decay, the most immediate effect of $CP$ violation is the non-forbiddenness of the decay mode $K_S \rightarrow 3\pi^0$. This mode, however, is suppressed relative to $K_S \rightarrow 2\pi$ by its small phase space, and possibly by an additional factor of order $\eta_{+-}$ in amplitude. Thus it should be extremely hard to detect.

Other properties of $K_S \rightarrow 3\pi$ depend upon a model for $CP$ violation We may, for example, consider the superweak theory in which $\varepsilon \approx 10^{-2}$ to $10^{-3}$ and the amplitudes $b_T$ are real, or we may ignore the effect of $CP$ violation in the mass matrix (i.e., $\varepsilon = 0$) and take the amplitudes to be complex. To see what type of predictions these models yield, we shall assume in both cases that the $T = 1$ amplitude is dominant.

If terms linear in the $s_i$ are neglected, the $T = 1$ amplitudes for $K_S$ and $K_L$ decay become [see Eqs. (2.60) and (2.61)]

$$A_{\substack{S \\ L}}(+ - 0) = [1/\sqrt{15(1 + |r|^2)}][b_1 \mp (1 - \varepsilon)b_1{}^*]$$

$$A_{\substack{S \\ L}}(0\,0\,0) = -\sqrt{3/5(1 + |r|^2)}[b_1 \mp (1 - \varepsilon)b_1{}^*] \qquad (2.67)$$

Under these conditions the superweak model predicts that

$$A_S(+ - 0)/A_L(+ - 0) = A_S(0\,0\,0)/A_L(0\,0\,0) \approx \varepsilon/2 \qquad (2.68)$$

---

* In $K^\pm \rightarrow \pi^\pm + \pi^0$, $TCP$ is sufficient to prove that $\Gamma(K^+ \rightarrow \pi^+\pi^0) = \Gamma(K^- \rightarrow \pi^-\pi^0)$ because the two-pion charge states are unique.

Thus the ratio of $CP$-violating to $CP$-conserving decays is exactly the same in $K \to 3\pi$ as it is in $K \to 2\pi$.

The $\varepsilon = 0$ alternative yields

$$A_S(+ - 0)/A_L(+ - 0) = A_S(0\ 0\ 0)/A_L(0\ 0\ 0)$$
$$= i \operatorname{Im} b_1/\operatorname{Re} b_1 = \tan \Phi \qquad (2.69)$$

As pointed out by Cabibbo[70] and by Gaillard,[71] the magnitude of the angle $\Phi$ can be estimated from the $\Delta T = 1/2$ rule and the known rates for $K^+ \to \pi^0\pi^0\pi^+$. From the $\Delta T = 1/2$ rule [see Eqs. (2.59), (2.64), and (2.67)], it follows that

$$\Gamma_L(+ - 0)/\Gamma(0\ 0\ +) = 2 \cos^2 \Phi \qquad (2.70)$$

and from the rates given in Table II it turns out that

$$\cos \Phi = 0.94 \pm 0.05 \qquad (2.71)$$

This value is consistent with a small violation of $CP$ and sets an upper limit of $|\Phi| \lesssim 25°$. Thus

$$\Gamma(K_S \to 3\pi)/\Gamma(K_L \to 3\pi) < 0.2 \qquad (2.72)$$

If the $\Delta T = 1/2$ rule is broken, it may be possible for $\Gamma(K_S \to 3\pi)$ to be of the same order of magnitude as $\Gamma(K_L \to 3\pi)$.

## III. Selection Rules in Baryon Decay

### 1. Space–Time Interaction

The most general, relativistically covariant Hamiltonian for the decay

$$\alpha \to \beta + \pi \qquad (3.1)$$

of a $J = 1/2^+$ baryon includes both derivative and nonderivative coupling of the particle fields. Derivative coupling can be reduced to a nonderivative form by means of the Dirac equation, and so the *effective* Hamiltonian need include only one type of coupling.

In the nonderivative coupling scheme, the effective Hamiltonian is

$$H = i\overline{\Psi}_\beta (A + B\gamma_5)\Psi_\alpha \Phi_\pi{}^\dagger + i\overline{\Psi}_\alpha (-A^* + B^*\gamma_5)\Psi_\beta \Phi_\pi \qquad (3.2)$$

where $A$ and $B$ are the scalar and pseudoscalar coupling constants, respectively. Time reversal invariance* and the neglect of final-state interactions imply that $A$ and $B$ are real:

$$A = A^* \qquad B = B^* \qquad (3.3)$$

Because the pion is pseudoscalar, Eqs. (3.2) and (3.3) lead to "crossing" relations[51]

$$B(\alpha|\beta\pi) = +B(\beta|\alpha\pi^\dagger)$$
$$A(\alpha|\beta\pi) = -A(\beta|\alpha\pi^\dagger) \qquad (3.4)$$

where $B(\alpha|\beta\pi)$ denotes the parity-conserving ($P$-wave pion) amplitude for $\alpha \rightarrow \beta + \pi$, and $A(\alpha|\beta\pi)$ the parity-violating ($S$-wave pion) amplitude. Notice that Eq. (3.4) must be treated not as a precise equality, but rather as a "functional" equality; that is, the left-hand side is a function of the dynamical variables (mass, momentum, and spin) of $a$, $\beta$, and $\pi$, and apart from the indicated sign, the right-hand side is the same function with the variables of $\alpha$, $\beta$, $\pi$ replaced by those of $\beta$, $\alpha$, $\pi^\dagger$, respectively.

In the derivative coupling scheme the effective Hamiltonian is

$$H' = i\overline{\Psi}_\beta\gamma_\mu(A' + B'\gamma_5)\Psi_\alpha\partial_\mu\varphi^\dagger + i\overline{\Psi}_\alpha\gamma_\mu(A'^* + B'^*\gamma_5)\Psi_\beta\partial_\mu\varphi \quad (3.5)$$

Time reversal invariance, combined with the neglect of final-state interactions, implies that $A'$ and $B'$ are real and, hence, it yields another set of crossing relations[48]:

$$B(\alpha|\beta\pi) = +B(\beta|\alpha\pi^\dagger)$$
$$A(\alpha|\beta\pi) = +A(\beta|\alpha\pi^\dagger) \qquad (3.6)$$

The difference between Eqs. (3.4) and (3.6) arises from the fact that, when derivative coupling is reduced to a nonderivative form, the scalar and pseudoscalar coupling constants are given by

$$A'' = (m_\beta - m_\alpha)A'$$
$$B'' = (m_\beta + m_\alpha)B' \qquad (3.7)$$

$A''$ is antisymmetric under $m_\alpha \leftrightarrow m_\beta$ while $B''$ remains symmetric. It is precisely this antisymmetry that removes the negative sign in the functional equalities of Eq. (3.4) and gives rise to those in Eq. (3.6).

* At present no evidence exists for a significant violation of time reversal invariance in baryon decay. The interaction that gives rise to the $CP$-violating decay $K_L^0 \Rightarrow 2\pi$ will induce similar effects in $\alpha \Rightarrow \beta + \pi$, but they are expected to be of order $10^{-3}$ (see Sect. I-2-B) and will, therefore, be neglected in the present discussion.

That Eqs. (3.4) and (3.6) have different physical consequences becomes apparent when we make use of symmetry arguments. Consider, for example, the decay modes $\Xi^- \to \Lambda + \pi^-$ and $\Lambda \to p + \pi^-$. If $R$ conjugation* is a valid symmetry of strong and weak interactions, then

$$A(\Xi^-|\Lambda\pi^-) = A(p|\Lambda\pi^+)$$
$$B(\Xi^-|\Lambda\pi^-) = B(p|\Lambda\pi^+) \tag{3.8}$$

It follows from Eq. (3.4) that†

$$A(\Xi^-|\Lambda\pi^-) = A(\Lambda|p\pi^-)$$
$$B(\Xi^-|\Lambda\pi^-) = -B(\Lambda|p\pi^-) \tag{3.9}$$

and hence [72] that‡

$$\alpha_\Xi \approx -\alpha_\Lambda \tag{3.10}$$

By contrast, Eq. (3.6) implies

$$A(\Xi^-|\Lambda\pi^-) = -A(\Lambda|p\pi^-)$$
$$B(\Xi^-|\Lambda\pi^-) = -B(\Lambda|p\pi^-) \tag{3.11}$$

and hence

$$\alpha_\Xi \approx +\alpha_\Lambda \tag{3.12}$$

Thus the two types of coupling lead to different predictions, even though the same symmetry has been used.

If $R$ invariance is replaced in the above argument by invariance under the product $RP$ of $R$ conjugation and parity, then the nonderivative crossing relations predict $\alpha_\Xi \approx +\alpha_\Lambda$ and the derivative ones predict $\alpha_\Xi \approx -\alpha_\Lambda$. In other words, it is possible to derive the same prediction, say $\alpha_\Lambda \approx -\alpha_\Xi$, from both coupling schemes, provided that the symmetry argument is suitably modified when we pass from one scheme to the other. As a general rule, we can make the following statement: Predictions derived from an invariance principle $I$ in the nonderivative coupling scheme can be reproduced in the derivative coupling scheme provided that $I$ is replaced by $IP$.

It follows from this statement that before we can discuss the consequences of weak symmetries, we must make a definite assumption

* See Section I-3-C, Eq. (1.41), and following.
† We use a sign convention such that $(\pi^+)^\dagger = -\pi^\mp$, $(\pi^0)^\dagger = \pi^0$.
‡ As shown below, the coupling constant $A$ is proportional to the parameter $S$ of Eqs. (1.10)–(1.13) and $B$ is proportional to $P$.

about the space–time behavior of the effective Hamiltonian. Derivative coupling has the disadvantage that as a result of Eq. (3.7), the parity-violating amplitudes vanish in the limit of exact $SU(3)$ symmetry.* Nonderivative coupling, however, does not suffer from this disadvantage, and so we shall adopt it as the space–time structure of the *effective* Hamiltonian.

Having rejected the derivative coupling scheme on the basis of its behavior in the limit of exact $SU(3)$, we must now decide how to deal with symmetry-breaking effects in the nonderivative scheme. This is a very difficult problem, and as yet no satisfactory solution has been put forward; consequently, we can do no better than to adopt an *ad hoc* prescription. The simplest prescription, and the one most commonly found in the literature, is to assume that all symmetry predictions refer to the coupling constants $A$ and $B$ of Eq. (3.2). In this way, symmetry-breaking effects manifest themselves in kinematical factors which depend upon the masses of parent and daughter particles.

Because the $Q$ value of nonleptonic hyperon decay is small compared with the masses of parent and daughter baryons (see Table I), it is a reasonable approximation to take the nonrelativistic limit of Eq. (3.2). In the rest frame of the parent baryon, the transition matrix element for decay becomes†

$$M = \sqrt{(E_\beta + m_\beta)/(2E_\beta E_\pi)}\, u_\beta{}^\dagger [A + (B/E_\beta + m_\beta)\boldsymbol{\sigma}\cdot\mathbf{p}_\beta]u_\alpha \quad (3.13)$$

* In the limit of exact $SU(3)$, $\alpha$ and $\beta$, being members of the same octet, have equal masses; thus the coefficient $A''$ of Eq. (3.7) vanishes. It should be noted that even if $A''$ were not to vanish, the probability for $\alpha \Rightarrow \beta + \pi$ would be zero when $m_\alpha = m_\beta$ (and $m_\pi$ is not zero), because energy could not be conserved. The possibilities to be distinguished from each other are the vanishing of an amplitude in the symmetry limit, and the vanishing of a transition probability brought about by the failure of a kinematical constraint, namely energy conservation.

† We use a representation of the Dirac matrices in which

$$\gamma_k = -i\beta\alpha_k \quad (k = 1, 2, 3) \quad \gamma_4 = \beta$$

$$\beta = \begin{bmatrix} 1 & 0 \\ 0 & -1 \end{bmatrix} \qquad \alpha_k = \begin{bmatrix} 0 & \sigma_k \\ \sigma_k & 0 \end{bmatrix} \qquad \gamma_5 = \gamma_1\gamma_2\gamma_3\gamma_4 = -\begin{bmatrix} 0 & 1 \\ 1 & 0 \end{bmatrix}$$

The unit matrices are $(2 \times 2)$ matrices. The Dirac four-spinor has the general form

$$\Psi = \sqrt{\frac{E + m}{2E}} \begin{bmatrix} u \\ \dfrac{\sigma \cdot \mathbf{p}u}{E + m} \end{bmatrix}$$

where $u$ is a two-spinor.

where $\mathbf{p}_\beta$ is the three-momentum of the daughter baryon, and $E_\beta$ is its energy. $E_\pi$ is the energy of the pion. The decay rate and asymmetry parameters are then obtained from Eqs. (1.10)–(1.13) by means of the substitution:

$$S = A\sqrt{\hbar[(m_\alpha + m_\beta)^2 - m_\pi^2]/16\pi c m_\alpha^2}$$
$$P/S = B/A \sqrt{[m_\alpha - m_\beta)^2 - m_\pi^2]/[(m_\alpha + m_\beta)^2 - m_\pi^2]}$$
$$\approx (B/A)\tfrac{1}{2}(v/c)_\beta \qquad (3.14)$$

These equations enable us to see exactly how our prescription for dealing with symmetry-breaking effects comes into play. First there is the phase space factor

$$p_\beta = (1/2m_\alpha) \sqrt{\left\{ \begin{matrix} (m_\alpha^4 + m_\beta^4 + m_\pi^4) \\ -2(m_\alpha^2 + m_\beta^2 + m_\alpha^2 m_\pi^2 + m_\beta^2 m_\pi^2) \end{matrix} \right\}} \qquad (3.15)$$

which varies from one decay mode to another, and second there is the $(v/c)_\beta$ factor in Eq. (3.14) which affects both the rate and the asymmetry parameters.

In the case of the $\Omega^-$ particle, we write the effective Hamiltonian for the decay modes

$$\begin{aligned} \Omega^- &\to \Xi + \pi \\ &\to \Lambda + \bar{K} \end{aligned} \qquad (3.16)$$

in the form

$$H = (1/M)\overline{\Psi}(B + A\gamma_5)\psi_\lambda \delta_\lambda \varphi^+ + \text{h.c.} \qquad (3.17)$$

where $\psi_\lambda$ is a Rarita-Schwinger field representing the $J = 3/2^+$ baryon, and $\psi$ represents the $J = 1/2^+$ baryon. Because of the relatively small amount of energy released in Eq. (3.16), we shall usually ignore the parity-violating ($D$ wave) amplitude $A$, and consider only the parity-conserving ($P$ wave) amplitude $B$. For similar reasons we neglect all angular momentum states higher than the $S$ wave in

$$\Omega \to \Xi^* + \pi \qquad (3.18)$$

and write the effective Hamiltonian as

$$A'\bar{\psi}_\lambda \psi_\lambda' \varphi + \text{h.c.} \qquad (3.19)$$

The rates for $\Omega^-$ decay are given by

$$\begin{aligned} \Gamma(\Omega \to \Xi\pi) &= (1/12\pi\hbar)(|c\mathbf{p}|^3/M^3)[(p_0 + mc^2)|B|^2 + (p_0 - mc^2)|A|^2] \\ \Gamma(\Omega \to \Xi^*\pi) &= (1/2\pi\hbar)(m^*/M)[|c\mathbf{p}| \, |A'|^2] \end{aligned} \qquad (3.20)$$

where $M$, $m$, $m^*$ are the masses of $\Omega$, $\Xi$, $\Xi^*$, and $(\mathbf{p}, p_0)$ is the four-momentum of the daughter baryon.[73] As in the case of $J = 1/2^+$ hyperon decay, we take the predictions of selection rules to refer to $B$ and $A'$, and assume that symmetry-breaking effects enter through the kinematical factors.

## 2. The $\Delta T = 1/2$ Rule

The isospace behavior of the effective Hamiltonians in Eqs. (3.2), (3.17), and (3.19) is governed by the product of particle fields $\bar{\alpha}\beta\pi$. In general this product is an admixture of several isotopic spins, but by imposing a selection rule, we eliminate all but one of them.

### A. $\Lambda$ Decay

The $\Lambda$ hyperon has two decay modes

$$\Lambda \to p + \pi^-$$
$$\to n + \pi^0 \tag{3.21}$$

and the effective decay Hamiltonian behaves as

$$H_\Lambda = X_-(\bar{\Lambda}p\pi^-) + X_0(\bar{\Lambda}n\pi^0) + \text{h.c.} \tag{3.22}$$

where $X_-$ and $X_0$ are arbitrary constants. ($X \equiv A$ for parity-violating amplitudes and $X \equiv B$ for parity-conserving ones.) Since the $\Lambda$ has zero isotopic spin, $H_\Lambda$ is easily expressed in terms of isotopic spin eigenstates:

$$H_\Lambda = (X_1/\sqrt{3})(\sqrt{2}\,\bar{\Lambda}p\pi^- - \bar{\Lambda}n\pi^0)$$
$$+ (X_3/\sqrt{3})(\bar{\Lambda}p\pi^- + \sqrt{2}\,\bar{\Lambda}n\pi^0) \tag{3.23}$$

where $X_n$ is the amplitude for $\Delta T = n/2$ ($n = 1, 3$). The amplitudes for the decay modes in Eq. (3.21) can then be written as

$$\sqrt{3}\,X(\Lambda_-{}^0) = \sqrt{2}\,X_1 + X_3$$
$$\sqrt{3}\,X(\Lambda_0{}^0) = -X_1 + \sqrt{2}\,X_3 \qquad (X \equiv A, B) \tag{3.24}$$

where $X(\alpha_\mu{}^\lambda)$ denotes the amplitude for $\alpha^\lambda \to \beta + \pi^\mu$.

As it stands, Eq. (3.24) implies no relation between $\Lambda \to p + \pi^-$ and $\Lambda \to n + \pi^0$. If, however, we impose the $\Delta T = 1/2$ rule, then $X_3$ vanishes and we obtain a sum rule

$$\sqrt{2}\,X(\Lambda_-{}^0) + X(\Lambda_0{}^0) = 0 \qquad (X \equiv A, B) \tag{3.25}$$

To draw conclusions from this sum rule we note that the $n$–$p$ and $\pi^-$–$\pi^0$ mass differences are quite small in comparison with the neutron and pion rest masses; consequently we may treat the kinematical factors $\mathbf{p}_\beta$ and $(v/c)_\beta$ [see Eqs. (3.14) and (3.15)] for one decay as being equal to those for the other. We then conclude from Eq. (3.25) that if the $\Delta T = 1/2$ rule is valid, the partial rates in $\Lambda$ decay are in the ratio 2:1,

$$\Gamma(\Lambda_-{}^0) = 2\Gamma(\Lambda_0{}^0) \tag{3.26}$$

and that the asymmetry parameters [see Eq. (1.13)] are equal:

$$\alpha(\Lambda_-{}^0) = \alpha(\Lambda_0{}^0) = \alpha_\Lambda$$
$$\beta(\Lambda_-{}^0) = \beta(\Lambda_0{}^0) = \beta_\Lambda$$
$$\gamma(\Lambda_-{}^0) = \gamma(\Lambda_0{}^0) = \gamma_\Lambda \tag{3.27}$$

Experimentally, the ratio

$$B_\Lambda = \Gamma(\Lambda_-{}^0)/[\Gamma(\Lambda_-{}^0) + \Gamma(\Lambda_0{}^0)] \tag{3.28}$$

is found to be [53]

$$(B_\Lambda)_{\text{expt}} = 0.675 \pm 0.027 \tag{3.29}$$

and the ratio of asymmetry parameters is [74]

$$\alpha(\Lambda_0{}^0)/\alpha(\Lambda_-{}^0) = 1.10 \pm 0.27 \tag{3.30}$$

Both of these results are in good agreement with the predictions of Eqs. (3.26) and (3.27). The $\beta$ and $\gamma$ parameters in $\Lambda \to n + \pi^0$ have not yet been measured with sufficient accuracy to check the second and third lines of Eq. (3.27). However, Dalitz[75] used the data on $^4$He decay to show that $\gamma(\Lambda_-{}^0)$ and $\gamma(\Lambda_0{}^0)$ have the same sign. We note that experimental value [53]

$$\beta(\Lambda_-{}^0) = 0.18 \pm 0.24 \tag{3.31}$$

is consistent with zero and indicates that the violation of $CP$ is small.

### B. $\Xi$ and $\Omega$ Decay

The isospin analysis of $\Xi$ and $\Omega$ decay proceeds in exactly the same way as in $\Lambda$ decay, and the $\Delta T = 1/2$ rule gives rise to the following sum rules:

$$\sqrt{2}\, X(\Xi_0{}^0) - X(\Xi_-{}^-) = 0 \qquad (X \equiv A, B) \tag{3.33}$$

$$\sqrt{2}\, B(\Omega_0{}^-) + B(\Omega_-{}^-) = 0 \tag{3.34}$$

$$\sqrt{2}\, A'(\Omega_0{}^{*-}) + A'(\Omega_-{}^{*-}) = 0 \tag{3.35}$$

where $X(\Omega_\mu{}^-)$ is the amplitude for $\Omega \rightarrow \Xi\pi$ and $X(\Omega_\mu{}^{*-})$ is that for $\Omega \rightarrow \Xi^*\pi$. In line with the comments at the end of Section III-1, only the lowest angular momentum states in $\Omega$ decay have been considered.

Neglecting electromagnetic mass differences, we predict from Eq. (3.33) that the ratio of rates for $\Xi^-$ and $\Xi^0$ decay is 2:1,

$$B_\Xi = \Gamma(\Xi_-{}^-)/\Gamma(\Xi_0{}^0) = 2 \tag{3.36}$$

and that their decay parameters are equal, e.g.,

$$\alpha(\Xi_-{}^-) = \alpha(\Xi_0{}^0) = \alpha_\Xi \tag{3.37}$$

Experimentally the value of $B_\Xi$ is found to be[53]

$$B_\Xi = 1.66 \pm 0.23 \tag{3.38}$$

and the ratio of asymmetry parameters is[53]

$$\alpha(\Xi_-{}^-)/\alpha(\Xi_0{}^0) = 1.23 \pm 0.58 \tag{3.39}$$

In view of the difficulties involved in measuring the properties of $\Xi^0$ decay, these results cannot be regarded as a serious deviation from the predictions of $\Delta T = 1/2$.

Equations (3.34) and (3.35) lead to similar predictions for $\Omega$ decay, but present data is too meager for us to make a meaningful comparison. Notice that the $\Delta T = 1/2$ rule makes no prediction for $\Omega \rightarrow \Lambda + K^-$.

### C. $\Sigma$ Decay

The decay of the $\Sigma$ hyperon is more difficult to analyze than that of the $\Lambda$ hyperon. For one thing, the $\Sigma$ has unit isotopic spin rather than zero, and for another, there are, in addition to the observed decay modes

$$\Sigma^+ \rightarrow p + \pi^0$$
$$\rightarrow n + \pi^+$$
$$\Sigma^- \rightarrow n + \pi^- \tag{3.40}$$

two others

$$\Sigma^0 \rightarrow p + \pi^-$$
$$\rightarrow n + \pi^0 \tag{3.41}$$

which are allowed by energy conservation and the weak selection rules, but which are so much slower than the electromagnetic decay

$$\Sigma^0 \rightarrow \Lambda^0 + \gamma \tag{3.42}$$

as to be virtually unobservable. Consequently not all of the predictions of $\Delta T = 1/2$ can be tested in $\Sigma$ decay.

To construct the effective Hamiltonian, we couple the baryon and antibaryon fields to an intermediate isotopic spin $T = m/2$ ($m = 1, 3$), and then couple the intermediate state to the pion field to obtain a total isotopic spin $T = n/2$. If we restrict ourselves to the $\Delta T = 1/2$ we obtain two independent terms in the Hamiltonian

$$H_\Sigma = X_1 H(1, 1) + X_3 H(3, 1) \qquad (X \equiv A, B) \qquad (3.43)$$

where

$$H(m, n) = [\overline{\Sigma}N)_{m/2} \otimes \pi]_{n/2} \qquad (3.44)$$

Since there are five decay modes in Eqs. (3.40) and (3.41), $H_\Sigma$ gives rise to three sum rules. Two of them,

$$2X(\Sigma_0{}^0) - X(\Sigma_+{}^+) = X(\Sigma_-{}^-)$$
$$X(\Sigma_-{}^0) = X(\Sigma_0{}^+) \qquad (X \equiv A, B) \qquad (3.45)$$

involve amplitudes for both charged and neutral $\Sigma$ decay, and so they cannot be tested by direct experiment; however, the third sum rule[42]

$$\sqrt{2}\, X(\Sigma_0{}^+) + X(\Sigma_+{}^+) = X(\Sigma_-{}^-) \qquad (X \equiv A, B) \qquad (3.46)$$

applies only to charged $\Sigma$ decay, and so it can be tested directly.

To discuss the implications of Eq. (3.46), we neglect electromagnetic mass differences and assume that all $\Sigma$ decay modes have the same kinematical factors $\mathbf{p}_\beta$ and $(v/c)_\beta$ [see Eqs. (3.14) and (3.15)]. We may then interpret Eq. (3.46) as a sum rule for the parameters $S$ and $P$ as well as for $A$ and $B$.

If final-state interactions and small $CP$-violating effects are neglected, $S$ and $P$ are real parameters, and they can be used as Cartesian coordinates in a plane. In this plane, each decay mode

$$\Sigma^\lambda \to N + \pi^\mu \qquad (3.47)$$

is represented by a vector

$$\mathbf{M}_\mu{}^\lambda \equiv (S_\mu{}^\lambda, P_\mu{}^\lambda) \qquad (3.48)$$

whose norm, $(S^2 + P^2)$, is proportional to its decay rate, and whose inclination to the $S$ axis (see Fig. 5) is determined by the asymmetry parameters:

$$\alpha = 2SP/(S^2 + P^2) = \sin 2\theta$$
$$\gamma = (S^2 - P^2)/(S^2 + P^2) = \cos 2\theta \qquad (3.49)$$

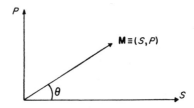

FIG. 5. The vectors $\mathbf{M}$ in the $S$–$P$ plane representing the amplitude for $\Sigma \rightarrow N + \pi$.

Equation (3.46), which can be rewritten as

$$\sqrt{2}\,\mathbf{M_0}^+ + \mathbf{M_+}^+ = \mathbf{M_-}^- \tag{3.50}$$

implies that the three vectors representing charged $\Sigma$ decay form a closed triangle. This triangle, known as the Gell-Mann–Rosenfeld triangle,[42] has two interesting properties. It is known from experiment that the three decay modes have approximately equal rates (see Table I). Consequently, the vectors have equal norms and the triangle must be right angled with $\mathbf{M_+}^+$ and $\mathbf{M_-}^-$ perpendicular to each other. It is also known that the asymmetry parameters $\alpha^\pm$ for $\Sigma^\pm \rightarrow n + \pi^\pm$ are close to zero and that the asymmetry parameter $\alpha^0$ for $\Sigma^+ \rightarrow p + \pi^0$ is almost one[76]

$$\alpha^0 = -0.960 \pm 0.067$$
$$\alpha^- = -0.017 \pm 0.042$$
$$\alpha^+ = 0.008 \pm 0.036 \tag{3.51}$$

Therefore the vector $\mathbf{M_+}^+$ must be parallel to one of the axes of the $S$–$P$ plane, and $\mathbf{M_-}^-$ must be parallel to the other (see Fig. 6). In other words the $\Delta T = 1/2$ rule, together with the experimental information

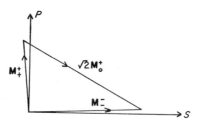

FIG. 6. The Gell-Mann-Rosenfeld triangle with the orientation of $M_+^+$ and $\mathbf{M_-}^-$ as indicated by experiment.

used so far, implies that one of the decays $\Sigma^{\pm} \to n + \pi^{\pm}$ is pure $S$ wave and the other pure $P$ wave.

One way of determining which decay is $S$ wave and which is $P$ wave is to measure the transverse polarization of the daughter neutron in the plane defined by its momentum and the spin of the parent $\Sigma$. This polarization depends upon the parameter $\gamma$ which takes a value of $+1$ for a pure $S$ wave decay and $-1$ for a pure $P$ wave decay [see Eq. (3.49)]. Experiments based upon this method[77] have shown that $\Sigma^{+} \to n + \pi^{+}$ is a pure $P$-wave decay. Thus we expect $\Sigma^{-} \to n + \pi^{-}$ to be pure $S$ wave, and the Gell-Mann–Rosenfeld triangle to be oriented as in Figure 6. It should be noted, however, that a direct measurement of the $\gamma$ parameter for $\Sigma^{-}$ decay has yet to be made.

An alternative method for determining the orbital angular momentum in $\Sigma^{\pm} \to n\pi^{\pm}$ is to determine the rates and spectra of the radiative decays $\Sigma^{\pm} \to n\pi^{\pm}\gamma$. Using a simple inner-bremsstrahlung model, Barshay, Nauenberg, and Schultz[78] have shown that these quantities depend upon the orbital angular momentum in the non-radiative decay. Experiments based upon this method[79] support the conclusion that $\Sigma^{+} \to n + \pi^{+}$ is $P$ wave and $\Sigma^{-} \to n + \pi^{-}$ is $S$ wave:

$$S_{+}^{+} = A(\Sigma_{+}^{+}) = 0$$
$$P_{-}^{-} = B(\Sigma_{-}^{-}) = 0 \tag{3.52}$$

### D. Pseudo $\Delta T = 1/2$ Rules

Although the observable properties of hyperon decay may depend upon the relative sign of $A$ and $B$ [see Eqs. (1.10), (3.14), and (3.15)], they do not depend upon the absolute signs of these amplitudes. In other words, decay rates and asymmetry parameters are invariant under the transformation

$$(A, B) \to (-A, -B) \tag{3.53}$$

From this it follows that the sum rule

$$X(\Lambda_{-}^{0}) = +\sqrt{2}\, X(\Lambda_{0}^{0}) \tag{3.54}$$

has exactly the same observable consequences as the $\Delta T = 1/2$ sum rule of Eq. (3.25). Moreover, Eq. (3.54) implies that the amplitude for $\Delta T = 3/2$ [see Eq. (3.24)] is both nonzero and much larger than the amplitude for $\Delta T = 1/2$. Therefore, the testable predictions of the

$\Delta T = 1/2$ rule in $\Lambda$ decay can be reproduced by an interaction which contains a nontrivial admixture of $\Delta T = 3/2$.[80]

It is not difficult to see that this result extends to all applications of the $\Delta T = 1/2$ rule. Given any sum rule predicted by $\Delta T = 1/2$, we can always construct another one with the same observable consequences by changing the sign of one amplitude. In $\Sigma$ decay, for example, the relations

$$\sqrt{2}\, \mathbf{M_0}^+ + \mathbf{M_+}^+ = -\mathbf{M_-}^- \qquad (3.55)$$

and

$$\sqrt{2}\, \mathbf{M_0}^+ - \mathbf{M_+}^+ = \mathbf{M_-}^- \qquad (3.56)$$

give rise to the same closed triangle as does the Gell-Mann–Rosenfeld relation [Eq. (3.50)]. We refer to such modified relations as "pseudo $\Delta T = 1/2$ rules" and note that they always imply a significant admixture of $\Delta T > 1/2$ in the effective Hamiltonian.

Since we cannot distinguish true $\Delta T = 1/2$ sum rules from pseudo $\Delta T = 1/2$ rules by studying the decay modes alone, we may ask whether there exists any method for distinguishing them from one another. To analyze this question, we consider the effective Hamiltonian of Eq. (3.22). It is easy to see that a change in the signs of $X_0$ and the neutron field,

$$X_0 \to -X_0 \qquad n \to -n \qquad (3.57)$$

leaves $H_\Lambda$ invariant.[81] Therefore, insofar as the transformation of Eq. (3.57) is permissible, the relative sign of $X_0$ and $X_-$ is not an observable quantity—a fact of which we are already aware. Now the charge independence of the strong interaction Hamiltonian $H_s$ serves to fix the relative phases of particle fields belonging to the same isomultiplet,* and so Eq. (3.57) cannot be applied to $H_s$. We may therefore conclude that the relative sign of $X_0$ and $X_-$ is observable, but only in processes for which strong interactions play an essential role.

Examples of this type of process are the nonmesonic decay of hypernuclei,

$$\Lambda + p \to n + p \qquad (3.58)$$

---

* In order to form isoscalars from strongly interacting fields, we must adopt some convention with regard to their behavior in isotopic spin space. For example, we may choose either $(p, n)$ or $(p, -n)$ as the components of an isodoublet, and, having made a choice, we must use it consistently.

and weak electromagnetic decays, e.g.,

$$\Sigma^+ \to p + \gamma \qquad (3.59)$$

Both can be envisaged as proceeding through virtual nonleptonic decays,[81] and their rates will depend upon such relative signs as that of $X_0$ and $X_-$. It is doubtful, however, whether calculations will be sufficiently reliable for us to determine relative signs in this way.

Another method based upon the same principle, namely interference between strong and weak interactions, has been proposed by Zakharov and Kaidalov.[82] They observe that when final-state interactions are taken into account, the parameter $\beta$ [see Eq. (1.13)] depends upon the isotopic spin of the final state. In $\Lambda$ decay, for example, the $\Delta T = 1/2$ rule requires the final state to be pure $T = 1/2$, and if $CP$ violation is neglected, the ratio of $\beta$ to $\alpha$ is

$$\beta/\alpha = \tan(\varphi_1 - \psi_1) \approx \tan 8^0 \qquad (3.60)$$

where $\varphi_k$ is the $S$-wave phase shift in the $T = k/2$ pion–nucleon channel and $\psi_k$ is the corresponding $P$-wave phase shift. The pseudo $\Delta T = 1/2$ rule, on the other hand, requires a specific admixture of $T = 1/2$ and $3/2$, and it gives

$$\beta/\alpha \approx \tan \tfrac{1}{3}(2\varphi_3 + \varphi_1 - 2\psi_3 - \psi_1) \approx 0 \qquad (3.61)$$

Thus by measuring $\beta/\alpha$ we can determine, at least in principle, whether or not the $\Delta T = 1/2$ rule holds. In practice, the interpretation of this measurement is rendered ambiguous by the fact that $CP$ is not exactly conserved.

Although it is virtually impossible to distinguish a true $\Delta T = 1/2$ rule from a pseudo one, the former has a distinct aesthetic advantage over the latter. Whereas the $\Delta T = 1/2$ rule is consistent with a large body of data in nonleptonic decay, the admixture of $\Delta T = 1/2$ and $3/2$ required for the pseudo $\Delta T = 1/2$ rule in one decay does not yield a pseudo $\Delta T = 1/2$ in all other decays. Therefore, if we were not to accept $\Delta T = 1/2$, we would have to use different admixtures of $\Delta T > 1/2$ to describe the decay properties of different hyperons—a situation too complicated to be very attractive. The only condition under which it might have any appeal would occur if we were forced into an admixture of $\Delta T > 1/2$ by some dynamical theory. As we shall see in a subsequent chapter, this condition arises in the current $\times$ current theory.

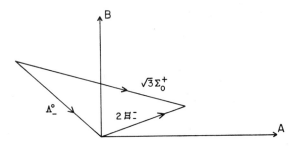

FIG. 7. The Lee-Sugawara triangle in the $A$-$B$ plane.

## 3. The Octet Rule

Aside from the $\Delta T = 1/2$ rule, the most interesting result to emerge from the application of the octet rule, $\Delta F = 8$, to nonleptonic hyperon decay is a relation

$$\sqrt{3}\, X(\Sigma_0{}^+) - X(\Lambda_-{}^0) = 2X(\Xi_-{}^-) \qquad (X \equiv A, B) \qquad (3.62)$$

amongst the amplitudes for $\Sigma^-$, $\Lambda^-$, and $\Xi$ decay. If the small violation of $CP$ is neglected, the amplitudes can be represented by vectors in a plane, and Eq. (3.62) then implies that these vectors should form a closed triangle (see Fig. 7). Experimental data indicate that the triangle does close within limits of about 10% (see Table IV).

TABLE IV
Decay Parameters[76]

| Decay mode | Asymmetry $\alpha$ | Amplitudes $\times$ $10^5$ sec$^{-1/2}$ | |
|---|---|---|---|
| | | $A/m_\pi$ | $B/m_\pi$ |
| $\Sigma_-{}^-$ | $-0.017 \pm 0.042$ | $1.861 \pm 0.017$ | $-0.152 + 0.386$ |
| $\Sigma_+{}^+$ | $0.008 \pm 0.036$ | $0.008 \pm 0.034$ | $19.08 \pm 0.35$ |
| $\Sigma^{0+a}$ | $-0.960 \pm 0.067$ | (a) $1.558 \pm 0.142$ | (a) $-11.71 \pm 1.88$ |
| | | (b) $1.168 \pm 0.187$ | (b) $-15.61 \pm 1.42$ |
| $\Lambda_-{}^0$ | $0.663 \pm 0.023$ | $-1.551 \pm 0.024$ | $-11.045 \pm 0.475$ |
| $\Xi_-{}^-$ | $-0.391 \pm 0.032$ | $2.022 \pm 0.029$ | $-6.628 \pm 0.574$ |

$^a$ In $\Sigma_0{}^+$ the amplitudes (a) correspond to $\gamma(\Sigma_0{}^+) > 0$, and the amplitudes (b) to $\gamma(\Sigma_0{}^+) < 0$.

Equation (3.62) was discovered simultaneously by B. W. Lee and H. Sugawara,[83] and it was subsequently derived in a variety of different ways by other authors.[84] Their methods can be divided into two broad classes, symmetrical and dynamic, and within each class there are significant differences of approach. Some authors, for example, use $R$ conjugation; others use $T$-$L$ symmetries, and still others consider dynamical models which have no apparent symmetry. That so many different arguments lead to the same result is, at first sight, quite puzzling.

The situation becomes even more puzzling when we observe that the $\Delta T = 1/2$ rule, by means of the relations (see Sect. III-2)

$$X(\Lambda_-^0) + \sqrt{2}\, X(\Lambda_0^0) = 0$$
$$X(\Xi_-^-) - \sqrt{2}\, X(\Xi_0^0) = 0 \qquad (X \equiv A, B)$$
$$\sqrt{2}\, X(\Sigma_0^+) + X(\Sigma_+^+) = X(\Sigma_-^-) \tag{3.63}$$

reduces the number of independent decay amplitudes* from seven to four. Now, the most general octet Hamiltonian contains five independent terms which give rise to observable decay modes, and so it does not predict any sum rules beyond those associated with $\Delta T = 1/2$. Furthermore, we might expect that, if we are to predict one more sum rule, Eq. (3.62) for example, then we must impose two constraints upon the Hamiltonian.

What is unusual about the Lee-Sugawara triangle, as we shall henceforth refer to Eq. (3.62), is that this expectation is not correct; it can, in fact, be derived from one constraint alone.[85] To prove this result, we shall show that the Lee-Sugawara triangle is an automatic consequence of any $SU(3)$ coupling scheme

$$[(\bar{B} \otimes B)_{(n)} \otimes M]_{(8)} \tag{3.64}$$

in which the intermediate representation $n$ is an octet or (27)-plet. Since the term obtained by taking $n$ to be a singlet does not contribute to observable decays, the only constraint needed is one between the terms in which $n$ is a decuplet ($n = 10$) or conjugate decuplet ($n = 10^*$). Once we know the explicit form of this constraint, we can enumerate the

---

* Each amplitude is, of course, an admixture of parity-conserving and parity-violating parts. Unless otherwise specified, statements about amplitudes refer to both parts separately.

symmetry arguments which give rise to it, and we can also explain why certain dynamical models predict the Lee-Sugawara triangle.

Another question to which we address ourselves is that of the maximal set of predictions that can be obtained from the octet rule and shared symmetries. In this connection we shall show that, while it is possible to predict the vanishing of $A(\Sigma_+{}^+)$, it is not possible to predict the vanishing of $B(\Sigma_-{}^-)$.[51]

### A. The Octet Hamiltonian

In tensor notation the octet of $J = 1/2^+$ baryons is represented by one traceless tensor $B_\nu{}^\mu$, the antibaryon octet by a second, $\bar{B}_\nu{}^\mu$, and the pseudoscalar meson octet by a third, $M_\nu{}^\mu$. Under charge conjugation these tensors behave according to the rules

$$CB_\nu{}^\mu C^{-1} = \bar{B}_\mu{}^\nu$$
$$CM_\nu{}^\mu C^{-1} = M_\mu{}^\nu \tag{3.65}$$

Their identification with particle fields is shown in Table V.

The effective Hamiltonian for nonleptonic hyperon decay transforms as an admixture of the octet components $H_2{}^3$ and $H_3{}^2$:

$$H_{NL} \sim aH_2{}^3 + bH_3{}^2 \tag{3.66}$$
$$\sim a'H_6 + b'H_7$$

TABLE V

Indentification of Baryons and Mesons with the Tensor Components of an Octet[51]

| Tensor | Baryon | Meson |
|--------|--------|-------|
| $D_1{}^3$ | $p$ | $K^+$ |
| $D_2{}^3$ | $n$ | $K^0$ |
| $-D_3{}^2$ | $\Xi^0$ | $-\bar{K}^0$ |
| $D_3{}^1$ | $\Xi^-$ | $K^-$ |
| $D_1{}^2$ | $\Sigma^+$ | $\pi^+$ |
| $\dfrac{1}{\sqrt{2}}(D_2{}^2 - D_1{}^1)$ | $\Sigma^0$ | $\pi^0$ |
| $-D_2{}^1$ | $\Sigma^-$ | $\pi^-$ |
| $-\dfrac{\sqrt{3}}{\sqrt{2}}D_3{}^3$ | $\Lambda^0$ | $\eta$ |

Note the traceless condition $D_1{}^1 + D_2{}^2 + D_3{}^3 = 0$

where time reversal invariance requires the coefficients $a$, $a'$ and $b$, $b'$ to be real. To construct such terms from the baryon and meson tensors, we use the coupling scheme of Eq. (3.64) and denote the $\bar{B} \otimes B$ intermediate representations by

$$(\bar{B} \cdot B) \quad F_v^{\ \mu} \quad D_v^{\ \mu} \quad [10]_{v\beta}^{\ \ \mu\alpha} \quad [10^*]_{v\beta}^{\ \ \mu\alpha} \quad [27]_{v\beta}^{\ \ \mu\alpha} \qquad (3.67)$$

for $n = 1, 8_F, 8_D, 10, 10^*$, and 27, respectively. The precise definition of these tensors is given by Rosen.[85] Although eight octets can be constructed from the terms of Eq. (3.67) and the meson tensor $M_v^{\ \mu}$, not all of them contribute to observable decay. Whenever $M_v^{\ \mu}$ carries an index equal to 3, it refers to either a $K$ or $\eta$ meson and implies such energetically forbidden processes as $p \to p + K^0$ or $\Sigma^+ \to p + \eta$. Neglecting such terms, we are left with five independent octets.

Because nonderivative coupling has been chosen for the space–time structure of the Hamiltonian (see Sect. III-1), the product of fields representing $Y \to B + \pi$ transforms under $CP$ according to

$$CP(\bar{B}_\alpha^{\ \mu} B_\beta^{\ \nu} M_\tau^{\ \rho})CP^{-1} = \varepsilon_x \bar{B}_v^{\ \beta} B_\mu^{\ \alpha} M_\rho^{\ \tau} \qquad (3.68)$$

The phase factor $\varepsilon_x$ depends upon the parity of the interaction:

$$\varepsilon_x = \begin{array}{l} +1 \text{ for parity conserving interactions} \quad X \approx B \\ -1 \text{ for parity violating interactions} \quad X \approx A \end{array} \qquad (3.69)$$

Using this result we can now write down the most general $CP$-conserving octet Hamiltonian for observable decays:

$$\begin{aligned}
H_{NL} = \sum_{X = A, B} \{ & f_x[(FM)_2^{\ 3} + \varepsilon_x(MF)_3^{\ 2}] + d_x[(DM)_2^{\ 3} + \varepsilon_x(MD)_3^{\ 2}] \\
& + (h_x + h_x')[[10]_2^{\ 3}M - \varepsilon_x[10^*]_3^{\ 2}M] \\
& + (h_x - h_x')[[10^*]_2^{\ 3}M - \varepsilon_x[10]_3^{\ 2}M] \\
& \qquad + k_x[[27]_2^{\ 3}M + \varepsilon_x[27]_3^{\ 2}M] \}
\end{aligned} \qquad (3.70)$$

where

$$\begin{aligned}
(PQ)_v^{\ \mu} &= P_\lambda^{\ \mu}Q_v^{\ \lambda} \\
[R]_v^{\ \mu}M &= [R]_{v\beta}^{\ \ \mu\alpha}M_\alpha^{\ \beta}
\end{aligned} \qquad (3.71)$$

### B. The L-S Constrained Hamiltonian

By means of the $\Delta T = 1/2$ prediction

$$X(\Sigma_0^{\ +}) = X(\Sigma_-^{\ 0})$$

[see Eq. (3.45)], we can rewrite the Lee-Sugawara triangle as

$$X(\tfrac{1}{2}[\sqrt{3}\,\Sigma^0 - \Lambda^0]|p\pi^-) = X(\Xi^-|\Lambda\pi^-) \qquad (3.72)$$

It follows that if an interaction is to predict the triangle, it must contain the terms

$$G_a \equiv \tfrac{1}{2}(\sqrt{3}\,\overline{\Sigma^0} - \overline{\Lambda})p \qquad G_b \equiv \overline{\Xi^-}\Lambda \qquad (3.73)$$

in the combination (see Table IV)

$$(G_a + G_b)\pi^- \equiv (G_a + G_b)M_2^{\ 1} \qquad (3.74)$$

Because the quantum numbers of $G_b$, $T = 1/2$, $Y = +1$, do not satisfy the relation $T = 1 + 1/2\,Y$, it follows that $G_b$ cannot appear in the decuplet $(\overline{B} \times B)_{(10)}$. The combination of $\overline{\Sigma^0}$ and $\Lambda$ appearing in $G_a$ is a $U$-spin singlet (see Table VI), and so $G_a$ has quantum numbers $U = 1/2$, $Q = +1$. Because these quantum numbers do not obey the relation $U = 1 + 1/2\,Q$, $G_a$ cannot appear in the conjugate decuplet $(B \times B)_{(10^*)}$. Therefore the Lee-Sugawara triangle requires at least one constraint upon the Hamiltonian, namely between the coupling constants $h_x$ and $h_x'$ of Eq. (3.70). This constraint turns out to be[85]

$$h_x' = 0 \qquad (X \equiv A, B) \qquad (3.75)$$

To show that no other constraints are needed, we note that the interactions depending upon the couplings $(\overline{B} \times B)_{(8)}$ and $(\overline{B} \times B)_{(27)}$ in Eq. (3.70) give rise to decays involving a negative pion via the terms

$$F_1^{\ 3}, \quad D_1^{\ 3}, \quad [27]_{2\ 1}^{3\ 2} \qquad (3.76)$$

It is not difficult to show that $G_a$ and $G_b$ appear with equal weights in each of these terms. Thus the condition of Eq. (3.74) is automatically satisfied and the Lee-Sugawara triangle follows.

TABLE VI
$U$ Spin Classification of Baryons[51]

| $U$ | $Q$ | $U_3 \to$ increasing |
|-----|-----|---------------------|
| 1/2 | +1 | $\Sigma^+$, $-p$ |
| 1 | 0 | $\Xi^0$, $-\tfrac{1}{2}(\Sigma^0 + \sqrt{3}\,\Lambda^0)$, $n$ |
| 0 | 0 | $\tfrac{1}{2}(\sqrt{3}\,\Sigma^0 - \Lambda^0)$ |
| 1/2 | −1 | $\Xi^-$, $-\Sigma^-$ |

We may now conclude that the Lee-Sugawara triangle is an automatic consequence of any octet Hamiltonian

$$H_{NL} = \sum_{(n)} g_n[(\bar{B} \times B)_{(n)} \times M]_8 \qquad (n = 1, \ldots, 27) \qquad (3.77)$$

which satisfies

$$g_{10} = g_{10*} \qquad (3.78)$$

Henceforth we shall refer to Eq. (3.78) [or, equivalently, Eq. (3.75)] as the $L$-$S$ constraint and to an octet Hamiltonian which satisfies it as an $L$-$S$ constrained Hamiltonian.

### C. The L-S Constraint and Shared Symmetries

As shown in Section I-3-C, there are two types of shared symmetry available in $SU(3)$. One, $R$ conjugation, is defined by*

$$R : Z_v{}^\mu \to Z_\mu{}^v \qquad (Z \equiv \bar{B}, B, M) \qquad (3.79)$$

and the other, the $T$-$L$ transformation, interchanges the $SU(3)$ indices 2 and 3:

$$2 \leftrightarrow 3 \qquad (3.80)$$

A given Hamiltonian may be symmetric under Eq. (3.80), or antisymmetric, or neither one nor the other. The symmetric case corresponds to $T$-$L(1)$ invariance, and the antisymmetric case to $T$-$L(2)$ invariance. In Gell-Mann's notation, $T$-$L(1)$ invariance is equivalent to the assumption that the Hamiltonian behaves as the sixth component of an octet, and $T$-$L(2)$ invariance is equivalent to assuming that it behaves as the seventh component:

$$\begin{aligned} T\text{-}L(1) &\equiv 2 \leftrightarrow 3 \text{ symmetry} &\equiv \lambda_6 \\ T\text{-}L(2) &\equiv 2 \leftrightarrow 3 \text{ antisymmetry} &\equiv \lambda_7 \end{aligned} \qquad (3.81)$$

In general, the $L$-$S$ constrained Hamiltonian has no definite symmetry. The $D$ and $F$ terms of Eq. (3.70) transform in opposite ways under $R$ conjugation and they are related by the $T$-$L$ transformation to unobservable interactions, e.g.,

$$(DM)_2{}^3 \to (DM)_3{}^2 \equiv D_\lambda{}^2 M_3{}^\lambda \qquad (3.82)$$

---

* In Eq. (27) of Section I-3-C, we defined the effect of $R$ conjugation upon the generators of $SU(3)$ by the equation $R : A_v{}^\mu \to -A_\mu{}^v$. While the negative sign must be used for *generators*, it is not necessary for octets of particles.

Nevertheless, the $L$-$S$ constraint is a necessary condition for certain weak symmetries.

It can be shown that the condition in Eq. (3.75) is satisfied by parity-conserving and parity-violating amplitudes simultaneously if the octet Hamiltonian satisfies any one of the following shared symmetries:

(*i*) $RP$ invariance;

(*ii*) $T$-$L(2) \times P$ invariance, which is equivalent to $T$-$L(1)$ invariance for parity-violating decay and $T$-$L(2)$ for parity-conserving decay; and

(*iii*) $R$ invariance plus $T$-$L(1)$ invariance.

The first of these symmetries must be rejected because it predicts the wrong relative sign for the asymmetry parameters in $\Lambda$ and $\Xi$ decay.* The second is not fully consistent with the Cabibbo current × current theory, which implies $T$-$L(1)$ invariance for both parity-conserving and parity-violating interactions; however, we shall show in a later chapter that, by combining the current × current theory with a dynamical pole model, we are led to precisely the situation described in symmetry (*ii*). In the case of the third symmetry, it must be borne in mind that $R$ invariance is not a valid symmetry of strong interactions, and that it can be applied to weak processes only when their dynamics conspire to make it an effective symmetry.

### D. Other Consequences of Shared Symmetries

Having seen how the Lee-Sugawara triangle can be derived, we may now ask whether these shared symmetry arguments have any other consequences.

It has already been shown that $R$ invariance and nonderivative coupling give rise to the relations between $\Xi$ and $\Lambda$ decay in Eq. (3.9). These relations predict the correct sign for $\alpha_\Xi \alpha_\Lambda$ and, when combined with the $\Delta T = 1/2$ and Lee-Sugawara sum rules, they reduce the number of independent decay amplitudes† from seven to two. Now the most general octet Hamiltonian that is both $R$-invariant and $T$-$L(1)$ invariant is given by Eq. (3.70) with the following coupling constants set equal to zero:

$$f_B = h_B = h_B' = 0$$
$$d_A = h_A' = k_A = 0 \qquad\qquad (3.83)$$

* See Section III-1.

† Here again we use the term amplitude to include both parity-conserving and parity-violating parts.

The number of independent terms remaining in the Hamiltonian is equal to the number of independent decay amplitudes, and so no more predictions can be deduced from $R$ invariance plus $T$-$L(1)$ invariance.

We now turn to symmetry $(ii)$. The most general octet Hamiltonian that is $T$-$L(2) \times P$ invariant is given by Eq. (3.70) with

$$k_x = h_x' = 0 \qquad (X \equiv A, B) \tag{3.84}$$

Since three independent terms are left in $H_{NL}$, and since there are three independent decay amplitudes, it follows that $T$-$L(2) \times P$ invariance has no consequences other than the Lee-Sugawara triangle.

If we combine $T$-$L(2) \times P$ invariance with $R$ invariance, we find that in addition to Eq. (3.84), the following coupling constants vanish in Eq. (3.70)

$$f_B = h_B = d_B = 0 \tag{3.85}$$

We are left with an effective Hamiltonian which contains one observable parity-conserving term, namely

$$d_B[(DM)_2{}^3 + (MD)_3{}^2] \tag{3.86}$$

and two parity-violating terms. Therefore, besides the $\Delta T = 1/2$ and Lee-Sugawara sum rules, we should obtain three more, two for parity-conserving amplitudes, and one for parity-violating amplitudes. $R$ invariance provides us with two sum rules, namely those in Eq. (3.9), and the third one follows from the observation that in the parity-conserving term of Eq. (3.86), the baryon-antibaryon system is coupled to an octet. The product of fields $\overline{\Sigma^+}n$ has isotopic spin $T = 3/2$ and cannot appear in an octet: therefore

$$B(\Sigma^+ | n\pi^+) = 0 \tag{3.87}$$

If, instead of $R$ invariance, we combine $T$-$L(2) \times P$ with $R'$ invariance, where

$$R' : Z_\nu{}^\mu \to -Z_\mu{}^\nu \qquad (Z \equiv \bar{B}, B, M) \tag{3.88}$$

we obtain an effective Hamiltonian with one parity-violating term:

$$d_A[(DM)_2{}^3 - (MD)_3{}^2] \tag{3.89}$$

and two parity-conserving ones. Again there are three additional sum rules, but in this case two of them refer to parity-violating decay. The predictions of $R'$ invariance are the same as $R$ invariance except that the signs in Eq. (3.9) are interchanged. The octet coupling of baryons and antibaryons in Eq. (3.89) implies that

$$A(\Sigma^+ | n\pi^+) = 0 \qquad (3.90)$$

Experimental evidence indicates that the amplitude for $\Sigma^+ \rightarrow n + \pi^+$ satisfies Eq. (3.90) rather than Eq. (3.89). Therefore $T\text{-}L(2) \times P$ invariance plus $R'$ invariance provides a better fit to the experimental data than does $T\text{-}L(2) \times P$ plus $R$ invariance.

Because there are no more shared symmetries available in $SU(3)$, we conclude that the results described above constitute a maximal set of predictions. Consequently we can make no more predictions for $J = 1/2^+$ baryon decay without introducing assumptions which go beyond the octet rule and shared symmetries. In particular we have not been able to derive results for $\Sigma^- \rightarrow n + \pi^-$ analogous to Eqs. (3.87) and (3.90) for $\Sigma^+ \rightarrow N + \pi^+$, and we cannot do so unless we make use of a dynamical model. Therefore, while we may regard the vanishing asymmetry parameter in $\Sigma^+ \rightarrow n + \pi^+$ as a consequence of symmetry, we must accept the vanishing asymmetry parameter in $\Sigma^- \rightarrow n + \pi^-$ as a dynamical effect.

In conclusion, we note that because the Kronecker product $10 \times 8 \times 8$ contains four octets, the octet rule yields no new predictions for $\Omega$ decay.

## 4. The (35)-Rule

Although $SU(6)^{(86)}$ cannot be an exact symmetry of strong interactions[87] in the same sense as $SU(3)$, it may be valid as an effective symmetry for three-point functions. For this reason we shall examine its consequences in hyperon decay.

With the usual assignments for baryons and mesons, the effective Hamiltonian for nonleptonic hyperon decay transforms as an admixture of the representations contained in the Kronecker product

$$\bar{B} \times B \times M = 56^* \times 56 \times 35 \qquad (3.91)$$

Apart from a singlet, the smallest representation in this product is the (35), and so we begin this discussion by assuming that the transformation properties of the Hamiltonian are dominated by the (35).

There are four independent (35)-plets contained in Eq. (3.91), but only two of them

$$H_1 = [(\bar{B} \times B)_{(35)} \times M]_{(35)}$$
$$H_2 = [(\bar{B} \times B)_{(405)} \times M]_{(35)} \qquad (3.92)$$

contribute to observable decays. Since the most general octet Hamiltonian contains five independent terms [Eq. (3.70)], it is clear that $\Delta\tilde{F} = 35$ will lead to stronger predictions than $\Delta F = 8$.

What we wish to show now is that these predictions are not consistent with experimental data. Before we do so, however, we must consider a difficulty associated with $P$-wave decay amplitudes. The subgroup $SU(2)_S$ which appears in the decomposition

$$SU(6)_S \supset SU(2)_S \times SU(3) \qquad (3.93)$$

pertains to the intrinsic spin of particles but not to their orbital angular momentum. Consequently the application of the theory to $S$-wave decay, in which no orbital angular momentum is involved, is quite straightforward, but its application to $P$-wave decay would appear to be ambiguous.

The underlying reason for this ambiguity is that, in its original form, $SU(6)$ is to be regarded as the static limit of a higher symmetry which combines Lorentz covariance and unitary symmetry in a nontrivial way. Now, the leading contributions to the parity-conserving ($P$-wave) interactions $\overline{\Psi}\gamma_5\Psi\Phi$ and $\overline{\Psi}\gamma_\mu\gamma_5\Psi\partial_\mu\Phi$ are proportional to $v/c$, [see Eq. (3.14)], whereas the parity-violating ($S$-wave) ones, $\overline{\Psi}\Psi\Phi$ and $\overline{\Psi}\gamma_\mu\Psi\delta_\mu\Phi$ are independent of $v/c$. Therefore the $P$-wave interactions vanish in the static limit, but the $S$-wave interactions do not. It follows that, if we are to extend the theory to the higher-wave decay, we must use a version of $SU(6)$ that is valid for nonzero velocities.

Such a version has been invented by several authors.[88] They observe that there exists a set of spin operators

$$\mathbf{W} \equiv (\gamma_4\sigma_x, \gamma_4\sigma_y, \sigma_z) \qquad (3.94)$$

which commute with the Dirac Hamiltonian of a particle moving freely in the $z$ direction. $W$ spin can be combined with unitary symmetry to form another $SU(6)$,

$$SU(6)_W \supset SU(2)_W \times SU(3) \qquad (3.95)$$

and this new group is applicable to phenomena involving one-dimensional motion (collinear processes). Since nonleptonic decay is, in the rest frame of the parent particle, a collinear process, we see that $SU(6)_W$ is the version of $SU(6)$ required for $P$-wave decay.

The groups $SU(6)_S$ and $SU(6)_W$ are both subgroups of $U(6, 6)$. Therefore if $U(6, 6)$ is taken as the relativistic generalization of static $SU(6)$, there will exist a definite connection between the intrinsic spin of elementary particles and their $W$ spin.[89] For the (35)-plet of mesons, the roles of pseudoscalar and vector particles are interchanged; the octet of pseudoscalars becomes the $W_3 = 0$ component of a $W = 1$ octet, and the $S_3 = 0$ component of the vector octet becomes an octet with $W = 0$. For baryons, however, $W$ spin is equal to intrinsic spin. In practical terms, this result implies that we can extract the consequences of $SU(6)_W$ for $P$-wave decay from the interactions of Eq. (3.92) by treating a $P$-wave pion as if it were a vector meson.

Having settled on this prescription, we now return to the (35)-rule. Because angular momentum is conserved in hyperon decay, the effective Hamiltonian transforms according to the (1, 8) component of the (35). In the coupling schemes of Eq. (3.92), this component consists of two types of interaction pertaining to $J = 1/2^+$ baryon decay: $S$-wave interactions behave like the term $\alpha^\dagger \beta \pi$ in which the intrinsic spins of baryon and antibaryon are coupled to zero; and $P$-wave interactions behave like $\alpha^\dagger \sigma \beta \cdot \rho$ in which the baryon and antibaryon spins are coupled to unity. Notice the phrase "behave like"; we use it to emphasize the point that our prescription for $P$-wave amplitudes is merely a convenient device and does not imply any correlation between $S$- and $P$-wave amplitudes.

The baryon–antibaryon coupling in a Hamiltonian constructed from $H_1$ and $H_2$ [see Eq. (3.92)],

$$H_{NL} = X_1 H_1 + X_2 H_2 \qquad (X \equiv A, B) \qquad (3.96)$$

is governed by the decomposition

$$(35) = (1, 8) + (3, 1 + 8)$$
$$(405) = (1, 1 + 8 + 27) + (3, 8 + 8 + 10 + 10^* + 27)$$
$$+ \text{ higher spins} \qquad (3.97)$$

Because there are no (10) and (10*) terms in the spin zero parts of Eq. (3.97) it follows that the $S$-wave amplitudes satisfy the Lee-Sugawara triangle for all values of $A_1$ and $A_2$.[90] In addition, they satisfy[90, 91]

$$\sqrt{3}\, A(\Sigma_-^-) = \sqrt{2}\, A(\Xi_-^-) \qquad (3.98)$$

Since the $S$-wave amplitude in $\Xi^-$ decay is large (see Table IV) and the asymmetry parameter in $\Sigma^-$ decay is small [see Eq. (3.51)], Eq. (3.98) requires $\Sigma^- \to n + \pi^-$ to be a pure $S$-wave decay:

$$B(\Sigma_-{}^-) = 0 \qquad (3.99)$$

It then follows from $\Delta T = 1/2$ that $\Sigma^+ \to n + \pi^+$ must be pure $P$ wave, i.e.,

$$A(\Sigma_+{}^+) = 0 \qquad (3.100)$$

Since $\overline{\Sigma^+}n$ has $T = 3/2$, Eq. (3.100) implies that

$$A_2 = 0 \qquad (3.101)$$

and hence that

$$A(\Lambda_-{}^0) = -A(\Xi_-{}^-) = -(\sqrt{3}/\sqrt{2})A(\Sigma_-{}^-) \qquad (3.102)$$

These results are in reasonable agreement with the data of Table IV, and so the (35)-rule appears to work quite well for $S$-wave hyperon decay.

The situation changes when we consider $P$-wave decay.[92, 93] The baryon–antibaryon system is coupled to an octet in $H_1$, and so the $B_1$ amplitudes automatically obey the Lee-Sugawara triangle. In $H_2$, however, the decuplet couplings [Eq. (3.97)] appear with a relative phase opposite from that required to yield the triangle [Eq. (3.78)]. Therefore, if the $P$-wave amplitudes are to satisfy Eq. (3.62), the coupling constant $B_2$ must vanish. Now the decay $\Sigma^+ \to n + \pi^+$ can arise only from $H_2$, and so the vanishing of $B_2$ implies that

$$B(\Sigma^+|n\pi^+) = 0 \qquad (3.103)$$

Equation (3.103) is not only at variance with the experimental data, but, when combined with Eq. (3.99), it predicts a vanishing asymmetry parameter for $\Sigma^+ \to p + \pi^0$ [see Eq. (3.63)]. Thus the (35)-rule is not consistent with the data on nonleptonic hyperon decay.

Another manifestation of this inconsistency shows up in the relative signs of the asymmetry parameters $\alpha_\Lambda$, $\alpha_0$, and $\alpha_\Xi$, for $\Lambda \to p + \pi^-$, $\Sigma^+ \to p + \pi^0$, and $\Xi^- \to \Lambda + \pi^-$, respectively.[90] It is known from experiment that these parameters satisfy

$$\alpha_\Lambda \alpha_0 < 0 \qquad \alpha_\Lambda \alpha_\Xi < 0 \qquad (3.104)$$

The amplitudes arising from the Hamiltonian of Eq. (3.96) are consistent with Eq. (3.104) only when $A_2 > 0$. Since $A(\Sigma_+{}^+)$ is proportional to $A_2$, it follows that the (35)-rule cannot yield the correct signs for $\alpha_0$, $\alpha_\Lambda$, $\alpha_\Xi$ and at the same time predict the $P$-wave nature of $\Sigma^+ \to n + \pi^+$. Moreover, this conclusion is valid whether or not we relax the condition ($B_2 = 0$) for the $P$-wave Lee-Sugawara triangle.

Although we are forced to give up the (35)-rule, we prefer not to relax the octet rule of $SU(3)$. Consequently we must add the $(1, 8)$ component of a higher $SU(6)$ representation to the effective Hamiltonian. Next to the (35), the lowest representations contained in the Kronecker product of Eq. (3.91) are the (189), (280), and (280*); however, it can be shown that the $(1, 8)$ components of these representations do nothing to remove the difficulties associated with $\Delta \bar{F} = 35$.[90] We therefore turn to the (405) representation[94, 95] and add the following two terms to the effective Hamiltonian of Eq. (3.96):

$$H_3 = [(\bar{B} \times B)_{(405)} \times M]_{(405)}$$
$$H_4 = [(\bar{B} \times B)_{(2695)} \times M]_{(405)} \tag{3.105}$$

It should be noted that the inclusion of these (405) terms is supported by theoretical arguments based upon the current $\times$ current theory, and by others based upon the existence of an intermediate vector boson.

When the terms arising from Eq. (3.105) are added to those in Eq. (3.96), the $S$-wave decay amplitudes will depend upon four independent coupling constants, and the P-wave amplitudes upon five. This number of constants is sufficient for us to fit the data on $J = 1/2^+$ baryon decay and to make the following predictions for $\Omega^-$ decay:*

$$\sqrt{2} A(\Omega_-^{*-}) = \sqrt{3} A(\Sigma_0^+) + 3A(\Lambda_-^0) + \sqrt{6} A(\Sigma_+^+)$$
$$13B(\Omega_-^{-}) = \sqrt{6} \{5\sqrt{6} B(\Lambda_-^0) + 4\sqrt{6} B(\Xi_-^{-}) - 7B(\Sigma_-^{-})$$
$$+ 5B(\Sigma_+^{+})\}$$
$$\sqrt{2} B(\Omega_K^-) = -\sqrt{3} \{4B(\Xi_-^{-}) + B(\Omega_-^{-})\} \tag{3.106}$$

It is interesting to note that we can apply the $T$-$L$ symmetries of $SU(3)$ to the $SU(6)$ amplitudes.[94] If the $S$-wave amplitudes are $T$-$L(1)$ invariant [see Eq. (3.81)], the constants associated with $H_2$ and $H_4$ [Eqs. (3.96) and (3.105)] are zero,[91, 94] and we obtain, in addition to the

---

* These sum rules are obtained from the decay amplitudes calculated by Pakvasa and Rosen.[94] Notice that the sign convention used in Eq. (3.106) is related to the one used by Pakvasa and Rosen[94] as follows:

$$(p, n, \Lambda) \to (p, n, \Lambda) \qquad (\Sigma, \Xi, \Omega) \to -(\Sigma, \Xi, \Omega)$$

Lee-Sugawara triangle, the prediction that $A(\Sigma_+{}^+)$ must vanish. If the $P$ waves are $T$-$L(2)$ invariant they will also satisfy the Lee-Sugawara triangle and one other sum rule. We shall take up $T$-$L(2)$ invariance for the $P$ waves later in connection with the pole model. $T$-$L(1)$ invariance leads to no useful results for $P$ waves.

Finally we note that the consequences of $T$-$L(1)$ invariance for $S$ waves can be reproduced by demanding that the effective Hamiltonian be symmetric under the exchange of $W$ spin and intrinsic spin.[92]

## 5. Special Coupling Schemes

As an alternative to the minimal selection rules described above, we may take a somewhat more phenomenological approach to the symmetry properties of the nonleptonic weak interaction. Several years ago, Pais[48] expressed the point of view that the vanishing asymmetry parameters in $\Sigma^\pm \to n + \pi^\pm$ are an important clue to the behavior of the Hamiltonian. Within the framework of global symmetry, his approach proved to be very successful, leading as it did to a derivation of the major properties of hyperon decay from the $\Delta T = 1/2$ rule and certain shared symmetries.[49] In $SU(3)$ we may adopt the same point of view by asking for the simplest coupling schemes in the effective Hamiltonian which give rise to the known properties of $\Sigma^\pm$ decay. The interesting question to explore is whether these coupling schemes lead to further predictions.[96]

Let us begin with $S$-wave decay. Because $\Sigma^+ n$ has $T = 3/2$, the simplest way of obtaining

$$A(\Sigma_+{}^+) = 0$$

is to couple the baryon–antibaryon system to an octet in the effective Hamiltonian:

$$H_A = \sum_{n=(8)...(27)} A_n[(B \times B)_{(8)} \times M]_{(n)} \qquad (3.107)$$

with no further assumptions about the transformation properties of $H_A$, we obtain two more sum rules, one for decays involving a negative pion,

$$(\sqrt{3}/\sqrt{2})A(\Sigma_-{}^-) - A(\Lambda_-{}^0) = 2A(\Xi_-{}^-) \qquad (3.108)$$

and the other for decays involving a neutral pion,

$$(\sqrt{3}/\sqrt{2})A(\Sigma_0{}^+) + A(\Lambda_0{}^0) = 2A(\Xi_0{}^0) \qquad (3.109)$$

Both of these sum rules are closely related to the Lee-Sugawara triangle [Eq. (3.62)], and the first one compares well with experimental data; a similar comparison for the second must await more accurate data on $\Xi^0 \to \Lambda + \pi^0$.

The underlying reason for the appearance of Eqs. (3.108) and (3.109) is that, once the charge of the pion is fixed, the important parameter in $H_A$ is the $F/D$ ratio of the $(\bar{B} \times B)$ octet rather than the overall transformation properties of the Hamiltonian. If this ratio is independent of pion charge, the $\Delta T = 3/2$ amplitudes for $\Lambda_-$, $\Xi_-$, and $\Sigma$ decay are proportional to one another, and when one vanishes the others do. No $\Delta T = 5/2$ amplitudes are present because the basic structure of $H_A$ is $8 \times 8$.

Because $n\pi^-$ has $T = 3/2$, the simplest way of obtaining

$$B(\Sigma_-{}^-) = 0$$

is to demand that the final state in parity-conserving decay be a pure octet. It then follows that, whatever the transformation properties of the Hamiltonian may be, the $P$-wave amplitudes in $\Lambda$ decay must satisfy the $\Delta T = 1/2$ rule, and in $\Sigma$ decay they satisfy

$$\sqrt{2}\, B(\Sigma_0{}^+) + B(\Sigma_+{}^+) = 0 \tag{3.110}$$

Predictions about $\Xi$ decay, however, cannot be made unless further assumptions are introduced.

One such assumption is suggested by the rough empirical result (see Table IV):

$$A(\Lambda_-{}^0) \approx -A(\Xi_-{}^-) \tag{3.111}$$

$$B(\Lambda_-{}^0) \approx +B(\Xi_-{}^-) \tag{3.112}$$

Equation (3.111) requires $H_A$ to be antisymmetric under $\bar{B} \leftrightarrow B$, and Eq. (3.112) requires the $P$-wave interaction to be symmetric under $\bar{B} \leftrightarrow B$. If this symmetry is coupled with our requirement of an octet final state in $P$-wave decay, the effective Hamiltonian is specified uniquely:

$$H_B = \bar{B}_\lambda{}^3 M_\mu{}^\lambda B_2{}^\mu + B_\lambda{}^3 M_\mu{}^\lambda \bar{B}_2{}^\mu \tag{3.113}$$

Moreover, it is a pure octet, and it yields one more prediction

$$\sqrt{3}\, B(\Lambda_-{}^0) = B(\Sigma_0{}^+) \tag{3.114}$$

When combined with Eq. (3.112), this prediction implies the Lee-Sugawara triangle.

It is interesting to note that if the interaction for the parity-violating meson decay, $K \to 2\pi$, is of the same form as $H_A$, namely

$$\sum_{n} g_n [(M \times M)_{(8)} \times M]_{(n)} \qquad (3.115)$$

then the $\Delta T = 5/2$ component is absent and we recover the sum rule of Eq. (2.24).

We shall see in a subsequent chapter that the coupling schemes described above are common to several dynamical models.

## IV. The Current × Current Interaction

In 1934, Fermi[8] proposed that the effective Hamiltonian density for nuclear $\beta$ decay be written as the product of a leptonic "current" $\bar{\psi}_e(x)\gamma_\lambda\psi_\nu(x)$ and a corresponding factor for nucleons. Twenty-five years later, after the discovery of parity nonconservation and the two-component neutrino, the only modification required in Fermi's Hamiltonian was the replacement of the operator $\gamma_\lambda$ by $1/\sqrt{2}\,\gamma_\lambda(1 + \gamma_5)$. Furthermore, the $V$–$A$ interaction[11]

$$(G/\sqrt{2})[\bar{\psi}_a\gamma_\lambda(1 + \gamma_5)\psi_b][\bar{\psi}_c\gamma_\lambda(1 + \gamma_5)\psi_d]$$
$$G = (1.01 \pm 0.01) \times 10^{-5} m_p^{-2} \qquad (4.1)$$

was found to provide an accurate description of the empirical properties of $\mu$-meson decay ($\mu^- \to e^- + \bar{\nu}_e + \nu_\mu$) and $\mu$ capture ($\mu^- + p \to n + \nu_\mu$) as well as those of $\beta$ decay.

To explain the universality of the coupling constant $G$, Feynman and Gell-Mann[11] envisaged the $V$–$A$ interaction as arising from the coupling of a charged current density with itself:

$$H_{\text{weak}}(x) = (G/\sqrt{2})\{j_\lambda(x), j_\lambda^+(x)\} \qquad (4.2)$$

The current $j_\lambda(x)$ is the sum of an hadronic term $J_\lambda(x)$ and a leptonic one $L_\lambda(x)$, and each term is an equal admixture of vector and axial vector components; for example,

$$J_\lambda(x) = V_\lambda(x) + A_\lambda(x) \qquad (4.3)$$

Drawing upon Fermi's original analogy with electromagnetic radiation, Feynman and Gell-Mann identified $V_\lambda(x)$ with the $T_3 = +1$ projection of the isovector electromagnetic current, and they noted that the ensuing conservation law,

$$\partial_\lambda V_\lambda(x) = 0 \qquad (4.4)$$

guaranteed the equality, within the limits of small electromagnetic corrections, of the vector coupling constants ($G^\mu$ and $G_v^\beta$) in $\mu$-meson decay and nuclear $\beta$ decay.

With the advent of unitary symmetry, Cabibbo[97] extended the conserved vector current hypothesis by assigning $V_\lambda$ to the same octet as the electromagnetic current. He wrote it in the form

$$V_\lambda = \cos \theta_V (V_\lambda)_1{}^2 + \sin \theta_V (V_\lambda)_1{}^3 \qquad (4.5)$$

and chose the value of $\theta_V$,

$$\theta_V \approx 0.26 \text{ radians} \qquad (4.6)$$

to allow for the suppression of strangeness changing semileptonic decay relative to nuclear $\beta$ decay. He also observed that the value of $\cos \theta_V$ might help to explain a small deviation from unity in the ratio

$$G_v^\beta / G^\mu \approx 0.98 \qquad (4.7)$$

Because the axial vector current engenders the decay modes $\pi^+ \rightarrow \mu^+ + \nu_\mu$ and $K^+ \rightarrow \mu^+ + \nu_\mu$, it must contain at least some admixture of the octet representation of $SU(3)$. Cabibbo assumed that it was pure octet,

$$A_\lambda = \cos \theta_A (A_\lambda)_1{}^2 + \sin \theta_A (A_\lambda)_1{}^3 \qquad (4.8)$$

and from the empirical ratio $\Gamma(\pi^+ \rightarrow \mu^+ \nu_\mu)/\Gamma(K^+ \rightarrow \mu^+ \nu_\mu)$ he found that

$$|\theta_A| \approx |\theta_V| \qquad (4.9)$$

Unlike the vector current $V_\lambda$, the axial vector current cannot be conserved: if it were, the leptonic decays of charged pseudoscalar mesons would not take place.[98] However, the success of the Goldberger-Treiman relation[16,99]

$$f_\pi = -\sqrt{2}\, G_A^\beta M_p m_\pi / g_{\pi NN} \qquad (4.10)$$

in correlating the pion decay constant $f_\pi$ with the renormalized axial vector coupling constant for neutron decay ($G_A^\beta$) gave rise to the hypothesis of a partially conserved axial vector current[15] (PCAC). According to this hypothesis, the divergence of $A_\lambda$ is proportional to the pseudoscalar meson field,

$$\partial_\lambda A_\lambda{}^\pi(x) = f_\pi m_\pi \varphi^\pi(x) \tag{4.11}$$

and its matrix elements between one-nucleon states vanish in the limit of infinite momentum transfer.

The next important development was the algebra of currents. Gell-Mann[17, 100] observed that if the vector currents $(V_\lambda)_j{}^k$ are constructed from quark[101] fields, the space integrals of their fourth components

$$\tilde{V}_j{}^k = -i \int (V_4(x))_j{}^k d^3x \tag{4.12}$$

can be regarded as the generators of $SU(3)$. He also pointed out that if the axial vector currents are constructed in the same way, their "charges"

$$\tilde{A}(t)_j{}^k = -i \int (A_4(x))_j{}^k d^3x \tag{4.13}$$

can be combined with the corresponding vector ones to form the generators of chiral $SU(3)^{(+)} \times SU(3)^{(-)}$:

$$2(Q_\pm)_j{}^k = \tilde{V}_j{}^k \pm \tilde{A}_j{}^k \tag{4.14}$$

$$[(Q_\pm)_j{}^k, (Q_\pm)_m{}^l] = \delta_j{}^l (Q_\pm)_m{}^k - \delta_m{}^k (Q_\pm)_j{}^l$$
$$[(Q_\pm)_j{}^k, (Q_\mp)_m{}^l] = 0 \tag{4.15}$$

It is important to note that for each value of $\lambda$, the current densities $(J_\lambda)_m{}^l$ [see Eq. (4.3)] commute with the generators $(Q_-)_j{}^k$ and behave as an octet with respect to the generators $\tilde{V}_j{}^k$ and $(Q_+)_j{}^k$. From this we conclude that, at equal times,

$$[(Q_+)_j{}^k, (J_\lambda)_m{}^l] = [\tilde{V}_j{}^k, (J_\lambda)_m{}^l]$$
$$= [\tilde{A}_j{}^k, (J_\lambda)_m{}^l]$$
$$= \delta_j{}^l (J_\lambda)_m{}^k - \delta_m{}^k (J_\lambda)_j{}^l \tag{4.16}$$

In 1965, Adler[18] and Weisberger[19] picked the commutator for two axial "charges" from Eqs. (4.14) and (4.15), and with the aid of

PCAC, they used it to compute the ratio $G_A^\beta/G_V^\beta$. The values they obtained

$$g_A \equiv |G_A^\beta/G_V^\beta| = 1.16$$
$$= 1.24 \tag{4.17}$$

compare well with the experimental value

$$(g_A)_{\text{expt}} = -1.18 \pm 0.02 \tag{4.18}$$

and provide strong support for the validity of the algebra of currents.

### 1. Symmetry Properties for Nonleptonic Decay

The current × current interaction of Eq. (4.2) gives rise to non-leptonic decay via a term

$$H_{NL}(x) = (G/\sqrt{2})\{J_\lambda(x), J_\lambda{}^+(x)\} \tag{4.19}$$

Consequently we may ask whether the properties of $J_\lambda(x)$ as determined from semileptonic decay have any influence upon the properties of non-leptonic decay.

We begin with the symmetry properties of $H_{NL}(x)$ and we assume that $J_\lambda(x)$ is constructed as in Eqs. (4.3), (4.5), (4.8), and that the octets $(V_\lambda)_m$, $(A_\lambda)_m$ are first-class currents*:

$$[(Z_\lambda)_m{}^l]^\dagger = (Z_\lambda)_l{}^m$$
$$CP(Z_\lambda)_m{}^l CP^{-1} = (Z_\lambda)_l{}^m \qquad (Z \equiv V, A) \tag{4.20}$$

It follows that the symmetrized product of Eq. (4.19) transforms as an admixture of the $SU(3)$ representations

$$1, 8, 27 \tag{4.21}$$

and that it is $CP$ invariant. In isospace, $H_{NL}(x)$ gives rise to transitions of the type

$$\Delta S = 0 \qquad \Delta T = 0, 1 \tag{4.22}$$

and

$$\Delta S = \pm 1 \qquad \Delta T = 1/2, 3/2 \tag{4.23}$$

There is some evidence that the $\Delta S = 0$ transitions have been detected in nuclei,[102] but we shall not consider them here. The $\Delta S = 1$ transi-

---

* Conserved vector currents must be first class, but for axial vector currents this is an extra assumption.

tions correspond, of course, to the decay modes discussed in preceding chapters.

In $U$-spin space, the $\Delta S = \pm 1$ component of $H_{NL}(x)$ behaves as a vector,

$$\Delta U = 1 \qquad \Delta U_3 = \pm 1 \qquad\qquad (4.24)$$

and its parity-conserving part is $T$-$L(1)$ invariant, i.e. symmetric under the exchange of $SU(3)$ indices 2 and 3:

$$\text{Symmetry under } 2 \leftrightarrow 3 \qquad\qquad (4.25)$$

Its parity-violating part will also be $T$-$L(1)$ invariant if the Cabibbo angles $\theta_V$ and $\theta_A$ are equal[56, 103] [see Eq. (4.9)]:

$$\theta_V = \theta_A = \theta \qquad\qquad (4.26)$$

The experimental data[41] being consistent with Eq. (4.26), we shall henceforth assume it to be correct.

### A. $K \rightarrow 2\pi$

The first important result to emerge from the symmetry properties of $H_{NL}$ was the fact that $K \rightarrow 2\pi$ is forbidden in the limit of exact $SU(3)$ for strong interactions and octet dominance for weak ones.[55, 104] This result can be extended to include the (27)-plet component of $H_{NL}$.[56, 105]

For our purposes it is sufficient to consider the hypothetical transition[104]

$$\text{Vacuum} \rightarrow K_1 \pi \pi \qquad\qquad (4.27)$$

whose matrix element is related to $\langle 2\pi | K_1 \rangle$ by crossing symmetry. In the limit of exact $SU(3)$, $K_1$ and $\pi$ are mass-degenerate members of the same octet, and the final state of Eq. (4.27) must satisfy the generalized Pauli principle for bosons. If we assume that the final state is pure $S$ wave (i.e., the effective Hamiltonian contains no derivative coupling), then it must be totally symmetric in unitary symmetry space.

Consider now the channel $K_1 \pi^0 \pi^0$. With our phase convention for mesons,

$$CP \, M_\nu{}^\mu \, CP^{-1} = -M_\mu{}^\nu \qquad\qquad (4.28)$$

$K_1$ is the $2 \leftrightarrow 3$ antisymmetric combination of the $U_3 = \pm 1$ components of a $U$-spin vector (compare Tables V and VI). In addition, $\pi^0$ is a linear combination of $\pi^{0\prime}$, the $U_3 = 0$ member of a triplet, and of $\eta^\prime$, a singlet.

Since $\pi^{0\prime}$ is antisymmetric with respect to $2 \leftrightarrow 3$ and $\eta'$ is symmetric, the states $K_1 \pi^{0\prime} \pi^{0\prime}$ and $K_1 \eta' \eta'$ are forbidden by the requirement in Eq. (4.25). The state $K_1 \pi^{0\prime} \eta'$ is allowed by Eq. (4.25), but forbidden by Eq. (4.24) and the generalized Pauli principle: $K_1$ and $\pi^{0\prime}$ are members of the same $U$-spin triplet $\pi'$, and any state $\pi_1' \pi_2' \eta'$ with $U = 1$ is necessarily antisymmetric under $\pi_1' \leftrightarrow \pi_2'$. It now follows that $K_1 \to \pi^0 \pi^0$ is forbidden.

If we assume that the final state of Eq. (4.27) is a pure octet, then $K^+ \to \pi^+ \pi^0$ is forbidden by the $\Delta T = 1/2$ rule; and the amplitude for $K_1 \to \pi^+ \pi^-$ is proportional to that for $K_1 \to \pi^0 \pi^0$ (see Sect. II). Since the latter amplitude is zero, the former must also be zero.

Another way of stating this argument is to note that the totally symmetric Kronecker product of three octets contains only one octet in its Clebsch-Gordan series. It can be shown[55, 104] that the component of this octet which meets the requirements of Eqs. (4.24) and (4.25) is an eigenstate of $CP$ with eigenvalue $-1$. Since $H_{NL}(x)$ conserves $CP$, the transition of Eq. (4.27) is forbidden. The same argument can be used to show that, when (27)-plet is admitted to the final state of Eq. (4.27), the transition is again forbidden.[56] Thus the current $\times$ current interaction forbids all $K \to 2\pi$ in the limit of exact $SU(3)$.

There are two sources of correction to this result, medium–strong interactions and electromagnetic ones. If the medium–strong Hamiltonian behaves as the $T = 0$ member of an octet, it can be written as a sum of two terms,

$$H_{MS} = H_3{}^3 = \tfrac{1}{2}(H_3{}^3 + H_2{}^2) + \tfrac{1}{2}(H_3{}^3 - H_2{}^2) \qquad (4.29)$$

the first of which has $U = 0$, and the second $U = 1$. In addition, the first term is symmetric under $2 \leftrightarrow 3$ and the second is antisymmetric. Thus the conditions stated in Eqs. (4.24) and (4.25) are not strictly satisfied in the presence of $H_{MS}$.

Once the $2 \leftrightarrow 3$ symmetry is relaxed, we can construct octet and (27)-plet final states for Eq. (4.27) which have $U = 1$ and $CP = +1$. Thus we may take the point of view that every mode of $K \to 2\pi$ represents a medium–strong correction to the current $\times$ current Hamiltonian, and that the smallness of the ratio $\Gamma(K^+ \to \pi^+ \pi^0)/\Gamma(K \to 2\pi)$ (see Sect. II) is due to a dynamical enhancement of the octet component in $H_{NL}(x)$.

Because the electromagnetic current is the $U = 0$ member of an octet, it does not upset the properties of $H_{NL}(x)$ given in Eqs. (4.24) and (4.25). Consequently, our initial argument for the vanishing of the amplitude $K_1 \to \pi^0 \pi^0$ remains valid in the presence of electromagnetic corrections. However, the arguments for the vanishing of other $K \to 2\pi$ amplitudes do break down, and both $K_1 \to \pi^+\pi^-$ and $K^+ \to \pi^+\pi^0$ may occur. As a result we may consider the $K^+ \to \pi^+\pi^0$ problem from another point of view.[55]

If we assume that the (27)-plet component of the current $\times$ current interaction makes no contribution to nonleptonic decay, $K_1 \to 2\pi$ may be treated as a medium–strong correction, and $K^+ \to \pi^+\pi^0$ must be regarded as an electromagnetic one. The ensuing suppression factors for these decays will then give rise to a ratio $\Gamma(K^+ \to 2\pi)/\Gamma(K_1 \to 2\pi)$ in the neighborhood of $10^{-2}$ to $10^{-3}$ (see Sect. II). As yet there exist no quantitative estimates which might enable us to choose between this point of view and the one expressed above.

It will be noted that our arguments appear to depend upon the use of nonderivative coupling in the effective Hamiltonian for $K \to 2\pi$. Had we used derivative coupling we would have been able to relax the requirement of total symmetry in $SU(3)$ space, and the arguments for the vanishing of $K \to 2\pi$ would break down. However, all decay amplitudes would then be proportional to the $K$–$\pi$ mass difference. Since this mass difference is a medium–strong effect, the qualitative results obtained above remain unchanged.

## B. Hyperon Decay

It is possible to construct an effective Hamiltonian for hyperon decay which meets all of the symmetry conditions, namely Eqs. (4.21), (4.24), and (4.25), imposed by the current $\times$ current interaction. Because of the negative sign in the nonderivative crossing relations of Eq. (3.4), such a Hamiltonian contains five parity-violating terms and eight parity-conserving ones. Since there are seven observable decays, we expect two sum rules for parity-violating amplitudes and none for parity conserving ones.

The octet terms in the parity violating Hamiltonian are given by Eq. (3.70) with two coupling constants set equal to zero:

$$h_A' = k_A = 0 \tag{4.30}$$

and the (27)-plet components are the $(T_2^{3\ 1} + T_2^{3\ 1})$ members of[56]

$$l_A\{[(\bar{B} \times B)_{(10)} + (\bar{B} \times B)_{(10^*)}] \times M\}_{(27)} \tag{4.31}$$

and

$$m_A[(\bar{B} \times B)_{27} \times M]_{27} \tag{4.32}$$

By direct calculation we obtain two sum rules from this Hamiltonian:

$$\Delta(\Lambda) + \Delta(\Xi) = 0$$
$$\sqrt{3}\,\Delta(\Sigma) - \Delta(\Lambda) = 2\Delta(LS) \tag{4.33}$$

where*

$$\Delta(\Lambda) = A(\Lambda_-{}^0) + \sqrt{2}\,A(\Lambda_0{}^0)$$
$$\Delta(\Xi) = A(\Xi_-{}^-) - \sqrt{2}\,A(\Xi_0{}^0)$$
$$\Delta(\Sigma) = A(\Sigma_0{}^+) + (1/\sqrt{2})A(\Sigma_+{}^+) - (1/\sqrt{2})A(\Sigma_-{}^-) \tag{4.34}$$

The first sum rule[106] in Eq. (4.33) relates the $T = 3/2$ amplitude in $\Lambda$ decay to the corresponding one in $\Xi$ decay; and the second sum rule[56] correlates the violation of the Lee-Sugawara triangle [Eq. (3.62)] with the violation of $\Delta T = 1/2$ in $\Lambda$ and $\Sigma$ decay. If we impose the $\Delta T = 1/2$ rule, we obtain four more sum rules,

$$\Delta(\Lambda) = \Delta(\Xi) = \Delta(\Sigma) = \Delta(LS) = 0 \tag{4.35}$$

To understand why this happens, we note that the combination of $\Delta T = 1/2$ and $T\text{-}L(1)$ invariance forces the effective Hamiltonian to transform as an octet[107] and reproduces the conditions under which Gell-Mann[104] derived the Lee-Sugawara triangle.

It is interesting to note that the sum rules of Eq. (4.33) can be derived for $P$-wave amplitudes from an octet plus (27)-plet Hamiltonian that is $T\text{-}L(2)$ invariant [i.e., antisymmetric under $2 \leftrightarrow 3$; see Eq. (3.81)].

### 2. The Use of Current Algebra

Following the success of the Adler-Weisberger calculation,[18,19] many authors[108] applied the methods of current algebra to a wide variety of phenomena. In particular, Sugawara[109] and Suzuki[110] showed that a number of interesting results could be obtained for non-leptonic hyperon decay. We now examine their approach.

The basic assumptions underlying the current algebra method are: (*a*) equal time commutation rules between currents [see Eqs. (4.12)–(4.16)]; (*b*) the PCAC hypothesis [see Eqs. (4.10) and (4.11)]; and (*c*) an unsubtracted disperson relation for decay amplitudes. It will also be assumed that the nonleptonic weak interaction is of the current $\times$ current form given in Eq. (4.19).

---

* As in preceding chapters, $A$ denotes a parity-violating amplitude, and $B$ a parity-conserving one.

By means of standard reduction techniques,[111] the matrix element for $\alpha \rightarrow \beta + \pi^{(k)}$ can be written as

$$\langle \beta \pi^{(k)} | H_{NL}(0) | \alpha \rangle = i \int d^4 x e^{iqx} (\square^2 + m_\pi^2) \theta(x_0) x \langle \beta | [\varphi^{(-k)}(x), H_{NL}(0)] | \alpha \rangle \tag{4.36}$$

where $k$ is an isotopic spin index for the pion, $q_\mu$ is its four-momentum, and $m$ its mass. With the pion taken off the mass shell and $\text{Im } q_0 > 0$, the right-hand side of Eq. (4.36) can be written as

$$i(m_\pi^2 - q^2) \int d^4 x e^{iqx} \theta(x_0) \langle \beta | [\varphi^{(-k)}(x), H_{NL}(0)] | \alpha \rangle \tag{4.37}$$

From PCAC [Eq. (4.11)] and an integration by parts, we obtain

$$\langle \beta \pi^{(k)} | H_{NL}(0) | \alpha \rangle$$
$$= iC(q^2 - m_\pi^2) \int d^4 x e^{iqx} \delta(x_0) \langle \beta | [A_4^{(-k)}(x), H_{NL}(0)] | \alpha \rangle$$
$$- C(q^2 - m_\pi^2) q_\mu \int d^4 x \theta(x_0) \langle \beta | [A_\mu^{(-k)}(x), H_{NL}(0)] | \alpha \rangle \tag{4.38}$$

where $C$ is the inverse of the factor $f_\pi m$ of Eq. (4.11).

In the limit as $q_\mu \rightarrow 0$, the second term will vanish unless the integral contains a pole[112] that behaves as $1/q$. For baryons, such a pole arises when a set of one-baryon intermediate states is inserted between the two operators in the commutator bracket.[112, 113] Now the matrix element of the parity-violating part of $H_{NL}(0)$ between one-baryon states vanishes because of $CP$ invariance and $T$-$L(1)$ invariance*: consequently the second term of Eq. (4.38) makes no contribution to parity-violating decay. By the same argument, the first term of Eq. (4.38) makes no contribution to parity-conserving decay. Therefore, in the limit $q_\mu \rightarrow 0$, the parity-violating amplitude for $a \rightarrow \beta + \pi$ is given by

$$\lim_{q_\mu \rightarrow 0} A(\alpha \rightarrow \beta + \pi) = Cm^2 \langle \beta | [\tilde{A}^{(-k)}, H_{NL}(0)] | \beta \rangle \tag{4.39}$$

and the parity-conserving one is given by a baryon pole model.[113]

If we assume that $A(\alpha \rightarrow \beta + \pi)$ is a slowly varying function of pion four-momentum, we can regard the right-hand side of Eq. (4.39) as an expression for the amplitude actually observed in experiments. The

* The argument is much the same as that for the vanishing of $K \rightarrow 2\pi$ in Section IV-2 above.

axial "charge" $\tilde{A}^{(-k)}$ is defined as in Eq. (4.13), with $(-k)$ representing its isotopic spin and $SU(3)$ coordinates. As a result of the current $\times$ current form of $H_{NL}(0)$, and of the chiral properties of the weak current [see Eqs. (4.16) and (4.19)], we can replace $\tilde{A}^{(-k)}$ by $\tilde{V}^{(-k)}$ in Eq. (4.39):

$$A(\alpha \to \beta + \pi) \approx Cm^2 \langle \beta | [\tilde{V}^{(-k)}, H_{NL}(0)] | \alpha \rangle \qquad (4.40)$$

Now, $\tilde{V}^{(-k)}$, being a generator of $SU(3)$, "rotates" each component of $H_{NL}(0)$ into another component of the same representation,

$$8 \to 8 \qquad 27 \to 27 \qquad (4.41)$$

but it does not introduce any new representations into the Hamiltonian. Therefore the expression for the parity violating amplitude in Eq. (4.40) corresponds to an effective Hamiltonian of the form*

$$\lambda[(\bar{B} \times B)_{(8)} \times M]_{(8)} + \mu[(\bar{B} \times B)_{(27)} \times M]_{(27)} \qquad (4.42)$$

Since the index $(-k)$ represents the isotopic spin coordinates of a pion, $\tilde{V}^{(-k)}$ is also a generator of the isotopic spin subgroup of $SU(3)$. Therefore, by the same argument as given above, the isospace structure of the effective Hamiltonian is

$$\lambda'[(\bar{B} \times B)_{1/2} \times M]_{1/2} + \mu'[(\bar{B} \times B)_{3/2} \times M]_{3/2} \qquad (4.43)$$

From this we can immediately conclude that the $\Lambda$- and $\Xi$-decay amplitudes must satisfy the $\Delta T = 1/2$ rule: $\bar{\Lambda}N$ and $\Xi\Lambda$ both have $T = 1/2$ and appear only in the first term of Eq. (4.43). Thus [see Eq. (4.34)]

$$\Delta(\Lambda) = \Delta(\Xi) = 0 \qquad (4.44)$$

It also happens that the $\Sigma$-decay amplitudes satisfy a "pseudo" $\Delta T = 1/2$ rule,

$$\sqrt{2}\, A(\Sigma_0{}^+) - A(\Sigma_+{}^+) = A(\Sigma_-{}^-) \qquad (4.45)$$

in which the sign of $A(\Sigma_+{}^+)$ is opposite from that required in the Gell-Mann–Rosenfeld triangle (see Sect. III). Since all the amplitudes for parity-violating decay must satisfy the general sum rules derived from the symmetry properties of $H_{NL}(0)$, we may combine Eqs. (4.44) and (4.45) with Eq. (4.33) to obtain

$$(\sqrt{3}/\sqrt{2})A(\Sigma_-{}^-) - A(\Lambda_-{}^0) = 2A(\Xi_-{}^-) \qquad (4.46)$$

* Note the limit $q \to 0$ requires the use of nonderivative coupling.

If $A(\Sigma_+{}^+)$ vanishes, then Eq. (4.45) is no different from the $\Delta T = 1/2$ rule, and Eq. (4.46) is identical with the Lee-Sugawara triangle [Eq. (3.62)]. In this connection it is worth noting that because $\overline{\Sigma^+}n$ has $T = 3/2$, the decay $\Sigma^+ \to n + \pi^+$ is engendered only by the (27)-plet term in Eq. (4.42), and by the $\Delta T = 3/2$ term of Eq. (4.43). Thus there exists a direct correspondence between the vanishing of $A(\Sigma_+{}^+)$ and the validity of octet and $\Delta T = 1/2$ rules in nonleptonic hyperon decay.

It is also worth noting that Eq. (4.40) leads to an expression of the form

$$\langle \beta | J_\lambda J_\lambda{}' | \alpha \rangle \tag{4.47}$$

for the parity-violating amplitudes. If a complete set of states is inserted between the two currents, $A(\alpha \to \beta + \pi)$ can then be expressed in terms of the form factors for semileptonic decay.[109] Recent calculations[114] indicate that when the intermediate states are restricted to the $J = 1/2^+$ octet and $J = 3/2^+$ decuplet, and when certain other assumptions are made, the estimated value of $A(\Sigma_+{}^+)$ is much smaller than that of other amplitudes. This result suggests that the octet component of $H_{NL}$ is enhanced relative to the (27)-plet component by the dynamics of weak interactions.

The current algebra method has also been applied to $K$-meson decay. By extracting all of the pions in $K \to 2\pi$ and $K \to 3\pi$ and setting their four-momenta equal to zero, Suzuki[115] reduced the relevant matrix elements to the form $\langle 0 | H_{NL}{}' | K \rangle$. Since the $K$ meson has $T = 1/2$, it follows that its decay satisfies an "effective" $\Delta T = 1/2$ rule. The reduction formula used by Suzuki was somewhat ambiguous,[116] but more careful treatments[117] lend support to his principal result.

When one pion is extracted from the $K \to 3\pi$ matrix element, it becomes possible to calculate the ratio of rates for $K \to 2\pi$ and $K \to 3\pi$[118] and to obtain information about the energy spectrum[119] of the $3\pi$ final state. To illustrate the argument, we note that the matrix element $\langle \pi^+\pi^-\pi^0 | H_{NL}(0) | K_2 \rangle$ reduces to $\langle \pi^-\pi^0 | [\tilde{A}^-(0), H_{NL}(0)] | K_2{}^0 \rangle$ after the $\pi^+$ is extracted and its four-momentum is set equal to zero. If the (27)-plet component of $H_{NL}(0)$ is neglected, then

$$[\tilde{A}^-(0), H_{NL}(0)] = 0 \tag{4.48}$$

and it follows that

$$\underset{q^+ \to 0}{\mathrm{Lim}} \ \langle \pi^+\pi^-\pi^0 | H_{NL}(0) | K_2{}^0 \rangle = 0 \tag{4.49}$$

If the matrix element is taken to be linear in pion energy (see Sect. II), then Eq. (4.49) implies that

$$[1 + \sigma(+ - 0)(s_3 - s_0)]|_{q^+ = 0} = 0 \qquad (4.50)$$

and leads to the prediction[119]

$$\sigma(+ - 0) = -0.25 m_\pi^{-2} \qquad (4.51)$$

It can be seen from Table III that this prediction is in excellent agreement with experiment. The slope parameters for the other modes of $K \to 3\pi$ can be obtained from Eq. (4.51) along with the $\Delta T = 1/2$ rule.

A different approach to the calculation of slope parameters has been taken by Abarbanel.[120] He expands the matrix element as a power series in the pion energies, treating all pions on an equal footing and keeping them on the mass shell. He then uses the conservation of the vector current and the commutation rules of Eqs. (4.12)–(4.16) to calculate the coefficient of the linear term. The resulting slope is very close to the value in Eq. (4.51).

## 3. The Pole Model for P-Wave Decay

As we pointed out above, the algebra of currents gives rise to a baryon pole model[113] for parity-conserving decay in the limit of zero pion four-momentum. Although the limiting procedure is not entirely unambiguous, it yields expressions for $P$-wave amplitudes which depend upon the same reduced matrix elements of $H_{NL}(0)$ as appear in the $S$-wave amplitudes. When these parameters are determined by fitting the data on $S$-wave decay, the resulting $P$-wave amplitudes are consistently smaller[121] than the empirical ones by a factor of order 2. However, off mass-shell effects and corrections due to the neglect of meson poles may help to remove this discrepancy.

It was first suggested by Feldman, Matthews, and Salam[122] that a good approximation for the nonleptonic decay amplitude may be obtained from its nearest singularities, namely those due to baryon and meson poles. Lee and Swift[123] subsequently showed that, in the context of a current × current theory with Cabibbo currents and octet dominance, the parity-violating poles are forbidden by $CP$ invariance. The underlying reason for this result is that a $CP$-invariant, parity-violating pole is $T$-$L(2)$ invariant, whereas the current × current theory requires it to be $T$-$L(1)$ invariant [see Eqs. (3.81) and (4.25)].

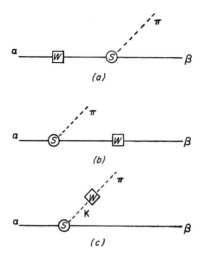

FIG. 8. Typical pole diagrams for $P$-wave hyperon decay.

The essential feature of the parity-conserving pole model is a symmetry flip, the pole itself is $T$-$L(1)$ invariant, but the effective amplitudes derived from it are $T$-$L(2)$ invariant [see Eq. (3.81)] in a particular limit.[124] If the (27)-plet part of the current × current interaction is neglected, the $P$-wave amplitudes must then satisfy the Lee-Sugawara triangle [Eq. (3.62) and Sect. III-3-C]; and if the (27)-plet baryon pole is retained, the $P$-wave amplitudes satisfy the same two sum rules as were derived for $S$ waves from the symmetry properties of $H_{NL}(x)$[125] [see Eqs. (4.33) and (4.34)]. We now turn to the proof of these statements.

Following Lee,[124] we write the effective Hamiltonian for the pole model as

$$H = H^{(0)} + H^{(1)} \tag{4.52}$$

where $H^{(0)}$ is the $SU(3)$ invariant free Hamiltonian for baryons and mesons, and $H^{(1)}$ contains the weak pole term, the strong $SU(3)$ invariant Yukawa coupling, and the mass breaking term. In the case of octet dominance, $H^{(1)}$ takes the form

$$
\begin{aligned}
H^{(1)} = {}& \Delta m \bar{B}(F_8 + \alpha D_8)B + f\bar{B}(F_6 + \beta D_6)B \\
& + g\bar{B}(F_k + \lambda D_k)\gamma_5 BM_k + \Delta\mu^2 M D_8 M + f'M D_6 M
\end{aligned} \tag{4.53}
$$

Here $f$ and $f'$ measure the strength of the weak transitons $B \rightarrow B'$ and $M \rightarrow M'$, respectively, and $g$ is the strong $SU(3)$ invariant coupling constant. We assume that $\Delta M \gg f$ and $\Delta \mu^2 \gg f'$.

The meson pole can be removed to first order in $f'$ by redefining the meson and baryon fields through an $SU(3)$ transformation

$$U = [1 + (i2/\sqrt{3})(f'/\Delta\mu^2)F_7] \qquad (4.54)$$

This transformation conserves charge and commutes with $CP$. In terms of the new fields, $H^{(0)}$ remains unchanged and $H^{(1)}$ is the same as before except that $f'$ is zero, and that $f$ and $\beta$ have been redefined. In a pure tadpole model,

$$f/\Delta m = f'/\Delta\mu^2 = \alpha/\beta \qquad (4.55)$$

the baryon pole is also transformed away, and all parity-conserving decays vanish.[126] Henceforth we shall assume that such is not the case, and that $f'$ can be taken to be zero.

We now apply an $SU(8)$ transformation,

$$V = 1 + (i2f/\Delta m)(aF_7 + bD_7) \qquad (4.56)$$

which commutes with charge and $CP$ to the baryon fields alone. By choosing the parameters $a$ and $b$ appropriately, we can remove the weak baryon pole in Eq. (4.53) and obtain an effective Hamiltonian for hyperon decay from the $SU(3)$ invariant baryon–meson interaction. In the limit of zero $\Sigma - \Lambda$ mass difference,

$$\delta \equiv (m_\Sigma - m_\Lambda)/m_\Xi - m_N) = 0 \qquad (4.57)$$

the parameter $\alpha$ in Eq. (4.53) vanishes and the appropriate values of $a$ and $b$ are

$$a = 1 \qquad b = \beta \qquad (4.58)$$

The effective decay Hamiltonian thus obtained,

$$H_{NL} = (i2fg/\sqrt{3}\Delta m)\bar{B}'[F_7 + \beta D_7, F_k + D_k]\gamma_5 B' M_k \qquad (4.59)$$

behaves as an octet, and it is $T$-$L(2)$ invariant [see Eq. (3.81)]. If a (27)-plet baryon pole is taken into account,[125] we must add a term $f\gamma\bar{B}\{F_6, F_Q\}B$ to Eq. (4.53) and a corresponding term $c\{F_7, F_Q\}$ to the transformation of Eq. (4.56). The resulting decay Hamiltonian is then an admixture of octet and (27)-plet, but it is still $T$-$L(2)$ invariant.

So far we have considered the limit of zero $\Sigma - \Lambda$ mass difference [Eq. (4.57)]. Now it is known that $\delta$, and hence $|\alpha|$ [see Eq. (4.53)], is a small parameter ($\delta \approx 0.3$), and that $\beta$ is also likely to be small. Thus we may expand $H^{(1)}$ as a power series in $\delta$, taking the pole parameters $\beta$ and $\gamma$ to be of order $\delta$. It then turns out[125] that the above results hold not only for the zero-order term, but also for the one linear in $\delta$. In particular, if octet dominance is assumed, the effective decay Hamiltonian is

$$H_{NL} = (i2fg/\sqrt{3}\,\Delta m)\bar{B}'[F_7 + (\beta - \alpha)D_7, F_k + \lambda D_k]\gamma_5 B' M_k \quad (4.60)$$

Should $\alpha$ and $\beta$ be exactly equal to one another, the baryon–antibaryon coupling in Eq. (4.60) is pure octet because $F_7$ is a generator of $SU(3)$. It then follows that the $P$-wave amplitude for $\Sigma^+ \to n + \pi^+$ will vanish. This result is independent of the presence of meson poles because they too give rise to octet $\bar{B}B$ coupling. Thus the vanishing of $B(\Sigma_+{}^+)$ represents a serious difficulty for pole models based upon a universal spurion. The same difficulty occurs when $\lambda$ is zero, i.e., when the meson–baryon interaction is pure $F$-type.

Finally, we wish to emphasize the parallel between parity-conserving and parity-violating decays. In the latter case, we obtain predictions of the current $\times$ current interaction alone, and in the former, we obtain the same predictions with the aid of a dynamical model.

### 4. SU(6) and the Current × Current Interaction

In $SU(6)$, $H_{NL}(x)$ [see Eq. (4.19)] is a symmetric product of two (35)-plets, and it can transform according to the representations (1), (35), (189), (405). $CP$ invariance and $T$-$L(1)$ invariance further restrict its behavior to the (35) and (405), and lead to two types of effective coupling.[127]

$$[(\bar{B} \times B)_{(n)} \times M]_{(n)} \qquad n = 35, 405 \qquad (4.61)$$

Because the spin zero part of (405) is an admixture of the $SU(3)$ singlet, octet, and (27)-plet, the couplings of Eq. (4.61) behave in $SU(3)$ space in exactly the manner described by Eq. (4.42). Hence we obtain the same sum rules for the parity-violating amplitudes of $J = 1/2^+$ baryon decay as were derived from current algebra [see Eqs. (4.44)–(4.46)]. In addition, we find that $\Omega^- \to \Xi^* + \pi$ satisfies the $\Delta T = 1/2$ rule, and that[128]

$$A(\Omega_-{}^{*-}) = \sqrt{3}\,A(\Sigma_+{}^+) + (\sqrt{3}/2)A(\Sigma_-{}^-) - (3/\sqrt{2})A(\Lambda_-{}^0) \quad (4.62)$$

If we impose the octet rule, then $A(\Sigma_+{}^+)$ vanishes, and if we impose the (35)-rule we obtain

$$A(\Xi_-{}^-) = -A(\Lambda_-{}^0) = \sqrt{3}\, A(\Sigma_0{}^+) = (1/2\sqrt{2})A(\Omega_-{}^{*-}) \quad (4.63)$$

The same results can also be obtained from the collinear subgroup $SU(3) \times SU(3)$ of $SU(6)$.

To deal with $P$-wave decay, we resort to a baryon pole model in $SU(6)_W$.[128] If members of the baryon (56)-plet with the same hypercharge are assumed to be mass degenerate, the effective Hamiltonian is $T$-$L(2)$ invariant [Eq. (3.81)]. The $\Omega$-decay amplitudes are found to satisfy the $\Delta T = 1/2$ rule, and the $J = 1/2^+$ baryon amplitudes satisfy the same sum rules as are given in Eq. (4.33). In addition, due to a peculiar admixture of $\Delta T = 1/2$ and $3/2$, the $\Sigma$-decay amplitudes satisfy the Gell-Mann–Rosenfeld triangle [Eq. (3.46)]. Other sum rules obtained are[128]

$$8\sqrt{3}\, B(\Xi_-{}^-) = (-5/\sqrt{2})B(\Sigma_+{}^+) + 3B(\Sigma_0{}^+) - 3\sqrt{3}\, B(\Lambda_-{}^0) \quad (4.64)$$

and

$$B(\Omega_-{}^-) = (\sqrt{3}/2)\{\sqrt{3}\, B(\Lambda_-{}^0) + (1/\sqrt{2})B(\Sigma_-{}^-)\}$$
$$B(\Omega_k{}^-) = 2B(\Sigma_+{}^+) \quad (4.65)$$

Equation (4.64) is satisfied to within about 15%, and Eq. (4.65) can be used to estimate the decay rate for the $\Omega$.[128, 129]

## 5. Other Dynamical Models

Although the combination of the current $\times$ current interaction and the algebra of currents leads to very good predictions for hyperon decay, it must be pointed out that other dynamical models yield much the same predictions. This is especially true of $S$-wave amplitudes; in the limit of octet dominance, the current algebra method gives rise to an effective Hamiltonian in which baryons and antibaryons are coupled to an octet [see Eq. (4.42)], and, as shown in Section III-5, this coupling scheme is sufficient to predict the Lee-Sugawara triangle [Eq. (3.62)] and the vanishing of $A(\Sigma_+{}^+)$. We shall see that the same coupling scheme appears in other dynamical models.

### A. Baryon Pole Model

The parity-conserving pole model has already been discussed in Section IV-4 above. We note here that the validity of such a model does not depend upon the existence of a current × current interaction, and that the property most responsible for its predictions, namely $T$-$L(1)$ invariance, is a consequence of $CP$ invariance alone.[130]

For $S$-wave decay, a $CP$-invariant baryon pole model is $T$-$L(2)$ invariant [see Eq. (3.81)]. If we neglect mass splittings in the baryon multiplet and assume that the weak pole transforms as a member of an octet, we can write the effective Hamiltonian in the form

$$(1/2M_0)\bar{B}\{F_7 + \beta D_7, F_k + \lambda D_k\}BM_k \qquad (4.66)$$

When the strong and weak vertices have the same $D/F$ ratio,[131] i.e.,

$$\beta = \lambda \qquad (4.67)$$

the anticommutator in Eq. (4.66) gives rise to a $\bar{B}B$ coupling which contains no decuplet terms; from the theorem proved in Section III-3-B, it then follows that the $S$-wave amplitudes will satisfy the Lee-Sugawara triangle [Eq. (3.62)]. Should it also happen that[131]

$$\beta = \lambda = \pm\sqrt{3} \qquad (4.68)$$

the $\bar{B}B$ coupling will be pure octet, and the $S$-wave amplitude for $\Sigma^+ \rightarrow n + \pi^+$ will vanish.

### B. The $K^*$-Pole Model for S Waves

The $K^*$-pole model has been proposed by several authors. Some of them[123,132] begin with the assumption that $S$-wave amplitudes are dominated by diagrams of the type

$$\begin{array}{l} \alpha \rightarrow \beta + K^* \\ \phantom{\alpha \rightarrow \beta +} \llcorner_{\!\!\rightarrow \pi} \end{array} \qquad (4.69)$$

(see Fig. 9), and others[133] derive the model by identifying the weak Hamiltonian with the divergence of an axial vector current. Because the transition

$$\Sigma^+ \rightarrow n + K^{*+} \qquad (4.70)$$

is superweak ($\Delta S = 2$), the $K^*$-pole model automatically implies that

$$A(\Sigma_+{}^+) = 0 \qquad (4.71)$$

In addition the strength of the $K^*$-$\pi$ junction obtained from hyperon decay is roughly consistent with that required for $K_1 \rightarrow 2\pi$.[132,134]

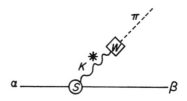

FIG. 9. The $K^*$-pole diagram for $S$-wave hyperon decay.

The effective Hamiltonian corresponding to Eq. (4.69) is given by

$$(1/M_0)g_{ijk}\bar{B}\gamma_\mu q_\mu(F_j + \lambda D_j)BM_k \qquad (4.72)$$

where $g_{ijk}$ is the coupling constant at the $K^*$–$\pi$ junction and $q_\mu$ is the four-momentum of the final state pion. By virtue of the Dirac equation, the operator $\gamma_\mu q_\mu$ can be replaced by the mass difference between parent and daughter baryon; and, if the Gell-Mann–Okubo mass formula holds, the effective Hamiltonian can be written as

$$(\Delta M/M_0)g_{ijk}\bar{B}[F_8 + \alpha D_8, F_j + \lambda D_j]BM_k \qquad (4.73)$$

Because $F_l$ is a generator of $SU(3)$, the $\bar{B}B$ coupling in Eq. (4.73) will be pure octet either when the strong baryon–vector-meson coupling is pure $F$-type ($\lambda = 0$), or when the $\Sigma$–$\Lambda$ mass difference is neglected ($\alpha = 0$). In both cases, we obtain the sum rules of Eqs. (3.108) and (3.109) irrespective of the transformation properties of the $K^*$–$\pi$ junction. However, we do not obtain the sum rules of Eq. (4.33) when the junction contains an admixture of the (27)-plet. Thus the $K^*$-pole model is equivalent to the current × current interaction only in the case of octet dominance.[135]

It is amusing to note that if the strong vector meson vertex were pure $D$ type, the sum rules of Eqs. (3.108) and (3.109) would hold in the limit of the Global Symmetry mass formula[136]:

$$m_\Lambda + 3m_\Sigma = 2(m_N + m_\Xi) \qquad (4.74)$$

### C. Quark Models

Two other models are based upon quarks. In one,[137] the weak Hamiltonian is constructed from scalar and pseudoscalar quark densities, and so it behaves as a member of an octet. If $CP$ invariance is assumed, the scalar density is $T$-$L(1)$ invariant and the pseudoscalar density is $T$-$L(2)$ invariant. The use of PCAC and current algebra leads to an effective $S$-wave interaction with octet $\bar{B}B$ coupling, and hence to the results described above. One feature of this model is that the scalar quark density can be placed in the same octet as the medium–strong mass splitting interaction; however, as noted in Section IV-5 above, this leads to serious difficulties for $P$-wave amplitudes.

The second quark model[138] makes use of the idea of additivity. Parity-violating hyperon decay[139] is envisaged as a process in which the strange quark $\lambda$ decays into a nonstrange quark $(n, p)$ plus a $\pi$ meson. Since the $\lambda$ cannot emit a $\pi^+$, the amplitude $A(\Sigma_+{}^+)$ vanishes; moreover, the $\bar{B}B$ coupling is again pure octet. Parity-conserving decays occur through a quark transition $\lambda \to n$ with the strong emission of a pion by a nonstrange quark. The final state is then pure octet and hence $B(\Sigma_-{}^-)$ vanishes; however it is found that $B(\Xi_-{}^-)$ also vanishes. A modification of this theory, in which baryon fields and the weak Hamiltonian density are assumed to obey certain equal time commutation rules,[138,140] appears to remove the difficulty associated with $\Xi$ decay; but it does not predict the vanishing of $B(\Sigma_-{}^-)$.

### D. Octet Enhancement

The common feature of the models discussed so far lies in their presupposition of a definite form for the weak interaction Hamiltonian. Some time ago, Nishijima[141] put forward the idea that although the fundamental weak interaction may include some components with $\Delta T = 1/2$ and others with $\Delta T \geq 3/2$, the dynamics of strong interactions may serve to enhance the former components and thereby lead to an "effective" $\Delta T = 1/2$ rule. Dashen, Frautschi, and Sharp[142] have shown that, within the framework of the bootstrap hypothesis, this type of enhancement does take place in the $S$-wave decay channel; they obtain an effective Hamiltonian with octet $\bar{B}B$ coupling and hence derive the sum rules found in other models. In the $P$-wave channel, however, they do not obtain octet enhancement, and when octet transformation properties are imposed upon their interaction, the resulting predictions are inconsistent with experiment.[143]

## V. Conclusions

We began this review by asserting that although strong interaction symmetries are violated by nonleptonic decay, they nevertheless play an essential role in the theory of this phenomenon. Our argument was based upon the observation that, within the hierarchy of elementary particle interactions, the symmetries applicable at one level of strength appear to be violated at the weaker levels in the simplest possible way. From this pattern of minimal violation (see Sect. I-3-A), we arrived at the selection rules $\Delta T = 1/2$, $\Delta F = 8$, $\Delta \tilde{F} = 35$ (Sect. I-3-B), and then we showed that both $\Delta T = 1/2$ and $\Delta F = 8$ are consistent with experimental data within limits of about 10% (Sects. II and III). The (35)-rule works well when applied to $S$-wave hyperon decay alone, but not when it is applied to $S$ and $P$ waves simultaneously.

To gain a deeper understanding of these selection rules we took the current $\times$ current interaction as the basis for a dynamical model. There are very good reasons for assigning minimal transformation properties to the weak current itself (Sect. IV), but in this case the part of the interaction responsible for nonleptonic decay does not transform in a minimal way. Nevertheless, when the apparatus of current algebra is employed, the $S$-wave amplitudes for $\Lambda$ and $\Xi$ decay obey the $\Delta T = 1/2$ rule, and the corresponding amplitudes for charged $\Sigma$ decay satisfy a "pseudo" $\Delta T = 1/2$ rule which is experimentally indistinguishable from the Gell-Mann–Rosenfeld sum rule. In a similar way, current algebra makes the idea of an "effective" $\Delta T = 1/2$ rule for $K$-meson decay plausible by relating all decay amplitudes to the matrix element $\langle 0|H_{NL}|K \rangle$ in the limit of zero pion mass.

It is also noteworthy that the parity-violating amplitudes $A(\Sigma_+{}^+)$ and $A(K^+|\pi + \pi^0)$ both turn out to be proportional to the admixture of $\Delta F = 27$ in the current $\times$ current interaction. As a result, the smallness of these amplitudes may be taken as a direct experimental indication that the (27)-plet is suppressed relative to the octet component of $H_{NL}$. Exactly how the dynamics of the current $\times$ current theory give rise to this suppression is not well understood at the present time. In the case of the hyperon decay some progress toward an understanding has been gained from attempts to calculate nonleptonic amplitudes in terms of semileptonic form factors,[114] but much work remains to be done. In the case of $K$-meson decay there are some unresolved ambiguities, and a convincing calculation of the rate $K^+ \rightarrow \pi^+\pi^0$ has yet to be carried out.

The origin of octet dominance for parity-conserving hyperon decay is another mystery. Current algebra gives rise to a pole model for these amplitudes, but it provides no hint with regard to the suppression of higher representations. Even more puzzling is the vanishing of the amplitude $B(\Sigma_-{}^-)$, or equivalently, the equality of the partial rates for charged $\Sigma$ decay. The effect bears no relation to the overall transformation properties of the Hamiltonian, and it is predicted by only one selection rule, namely the requirement that the final state be pure octet. It is not very clear, however, how such a final state is produced dynamically.

Whether the current $\times$ current theory is the correct dynamical model for nonleptonic decay is also an unresolved question. As shown in Section IV-5, there are other models which, in the limit of octet dominance, give rise to the same predictions as the current $\times$ current interaction. When octet dominance is relaxed, these models tend to differ in their predictions, and so the study of deviations from $\Delta T = 1/2$ and $\Delta F = 8$ may enable us to decide between them. To do this successfully, however, we will require empirical amplitudes which are accurate to 1% instead of 10%, and also a thorough understanding of the effects of medium–strong $SU(3)$ violating interactions. An alternate method may be the study of second-order effects, such as the $K_L$–$K_S$ mass difference[144] and weak electromagnetic phenomena, such as $\Sigma^+ \rightarrow p + \gamma$.[130]

Finally, there is the fundamental problem of $CP$ violation. If the rate for $K_L \rightarrow 2\pi$ is an accurate guide, the effect is of order one-tenth of 1% in amplitude, and it cannot be detected in baryon decay at present. Thus the study of $K$-meson decay is likely to be the most fruitful source of information. It remains to be seen whether the resolution of the $CP$ problem will be as elegant as was the resolution of parity violation, and whether it will clarify any of the problems discussed above.

## References

Despite the large number of papers included in the following list, it is likely that an equal number has been omitted. To the authors thus deprived of recognition, the present writers offer their apologies and the consolation that they are not alone.

1. E. Fermi and R. P. Feynman (private communication), as quoted in M. Gell-Mann and A. Pais, *Proceedings of 1954 Glasgow Conference on Nuclear and Meson Physics*, Pergamon, London, 1955, p. 342. This volume also contains a number of other papers of historical interest.
2. A. Pais, *Phys. Rev.*, **86**, 663 (1952); similar proposals were also put forward in Y. Nambu, K. Nishijima, and Y. Yamaguchi, *Progr. Theoret. Phys.* (*Kyoto*), **6**, 651 (1951); S. Oneda, *ibid.*, **6**, 633 (1951), and by R. P. Feynman, unpublished.

3. M. Gell-Mann, *Phys. Rev.*, **92**, 833 (1953); T. Nakano and K. Nishijima, *Progr. Theoret. Phys. (Kyoto)*, **10**, 581 (1953); K. Nishijima, *ibid.*, **13**, 285 (1955). An excellent review of these developments is given by M. Gell-Mann, *Nuovo Cimento Suppl. 2*, **4**, 848 (1956).

4. R. H. Dalitz, *Phil. Mag.*, **44**, 1068 (1953); *Phys. Rev.*, **94**, 1046 (1954); E. Fabri, *Nuovo Cimento*, **11**, 479 (1954).

5. T. D. Lee and J. Orear, *Phys. Rev.*, **100**, 932 (1955); T. D. Lee and C. N. Yang, *ibid.*, **102**, 290 (1956); S. Bludman, *ibid.*, **102**, 1420 (1956).

6. T. D. Lee and C. N. Yang, *Phys. Rev.*, **104**, 254 (1956).

7. (a) C. S. Wu, E. Ambler, R. W. Hayward, D. D. Hoppes, and R. P. Hudson, *Phys. Rev.*, **105**, 1413 (1957); (b) J. I. Freidman and V. L. Telegdi, *ibid.*, **105**, 1681 (1957); (c) R. L. Garwin, L. M. Lederman, and M. Weinrich, *ibid.*, **105**, 1415 (1957); (d) F. S. Crawford, M. Cresti, M. L. Good, K. Gottstein, E. M. Lyman, F. T. Solmitz, M. L. Stevenson, and H. K. Ticho, *ibid.*, **108**, 1102 (1957); (e) F. Eisner, R. Plano, A. Prodell, N. Samios, M. Schwartz, J. Steinberger, P. Bassi, V. Borelli, G. Puppi, G. Tanaka, P. Wotoschek, V. Zoboli, M. Conversi, P. Franzini, I. Mannelli, R. Santangelo, V. Silvestrini, D. A. Glaser, C. Graves, and M. L. Perl, *ibid.*, **108**, 1353 (1957).

8. E. Fermi, *Z. Physik*, **88**, 161 (1934).

9. (a) A. Salam, *Nuovo Cimento*, **5**, 299 (1957); (b) L. D. Landau, *Nuclear Physics*, **3**, 127 (1957); (c) T. D. Lee and C. N. Yang, *Phys. Rev.*, **105**, 1671 (1957).

10. See ref. 9b.

11. (a) E. C. G. Sudarshan and R. E. Marshak, *Proc. Padua-Venice Conf. on Mesons and Newly Discovered Particles, 1957*, 5; *Phys. Rev.*, **109**, 1860 (1958); (b) R. P. Feynman and M. Gell-Mann, *Phys. Rev.*, **109**, 193 (1958); (c) J. J. Sakurai, *Nuovo Cimento*, **7**, 649 (1958).

12. See Ref. 11b; S. Gerstein and Y. Zeldovich, *JETP USSR.*, **29**, 698 (1955); *Soviet Phys. JETP (English Transl.)*, **2**, 576 (1956).

13. See Ref. 11b.

14. J. H. Christenson, J. W. Cronin, V. L. Fitch, and R. Turlay, *Phys. Rev. Letters*, **13**, 138 (1964); A. Abashian, R. J. Abrams, P. W. Carpenter, G. P. Fisher, B. M. K. Nefkens, and J. H. Smith, *ibid.*, **13**, 243 (1964); W. Galbraith, G. Manning, A. E. Taylor, B. D. Jones, J. Malos, A. Astbury, N. H. Lipman, and T. G. Walker, *ibid.*, **14**, 383 (1965); X. de Bouard, D. Dekkers, B. Jordan, R. Mermod, T. R. Willitts, K. Winter, P. Scharff, L. Valentin, M. Vivargent, and M. Bott-Bodenhausen, *Physics Letters*, **15**, 58 (1965).

15. Y. Nambu, *Phys. Rev. Letters*, **4**, 380 (1960); M. Gell-Mann and M. Levy, *Nuovo Cimento*, **16**, 705 (1960).

16. M. L. Goldberger and S. B. Treiman, *Phys. Rev.*, **110**, 1178 (1958).

17. M. Gell-Mann, *Phys. Rev.*, **125**, 1067 (1962).

18. S. L. Adler, *Phys. Rev. Letters*, **14**, 1051 (1965).

19. W. I. Weisberger, *Phys. Rev. Letters*, **14**, 1047 (1965).

20. See Ref. 7a.

21. J. Bernstein, G. Feinberg, and T. D. Lee, *Phys. Rev.*, **139**, B1650 (1965); S. Barshay, *Phys. Rev. Letters*, **17**, 78 (1965); F. Salzman and G. Salzman, *ibid.*, **15**, 91 (1965).

22. C. Baltay, P. Franzini, J. Kim, L. Kirsch, D. Zanello, J. Lee-Franzini, R. Loveless, J. McFadyen, and H. Yarger, *Phys. Rev. Letters*, **16**, 1224 (1966); Columbia-Berkeley-Purdue-Wisconsin-Yale collaboration; *Phys. Rev.*, **149**, 1044 (1966).

23. A. M. Cnops, G. Finocchiaro, J. C. Lassalle, P. Mittner, P. Zanella, J. P. Duffey, B. Gobbi, M. A. Pouchon, and A. Muller, *Phys. Rev. Letters*, **22**, 546 (1966).

24. T. D. Lee and C. N. Yang, *Phys. Rev.*, **108**, 1645 (1957); R. Gatto, *Nucl. Phys.*, **5**, 183 (1958).

25. See, e.g., G. Luders, *Ann. Phys.* (*N.Y.*), **2**, 1 (1957).

26. T. D. Lee, R. Oehme, and C. N. Yang, *Phys. Rev.*, **106**, 340 (1957).

27. See, e.g., the discussion by T. D. Lee in *Proceedings Oxford International Conference on Elementary Particles*, Rutherford High Energy Laboratory, England, 1966, 230.

28. M. Gell-Mann and A. Pais, *Phys. Rev.*, **97**, 1387 (1955).

29. G. H. Trilling, *Proceedings International Conference on Weak Interactions*, Argonne National Laboratory Rept. No. ANL-7130, Argonne, Illinois, 1965, p. 115.

30. Data compiled by V. L. Fitch, *Proceedings of the XIIIth International Conference on High-Energy Physics*, University of California Press, Berkeley and Los Angeles, 1967, p. 63.

31. J. Bernstein, N. Cabibbo, and T. D. Lee, *Physics Letters*, **12**, 146 (1964); J. S. Bell and J. K. Perring, *Phys. Rev. Letters*, **13**, 348 (1964).

32. See the review by J. Prentki, *Proceedings Oxford International Conference on Elementary Particles*, Rutherford High Energy Laboratory, England, 1966, p. 47.

33. V. L. Fitch, R. F. Roth, J. S. Russ, and W. Vernon, *Phys. Rev. Letters*, **15**, 73 (1965).

34. L. Wolferstein, *Phys. Rev. Letters*, **13**, 562 (1964).

35. R. G. Sachs, *Phys. Rev. Letters*, **13**, 286 (1964).

36. See, e.g., M. Gell-Mann and Y. Ne'eman, *The Eightfold Way*, Benjamin, New York, 1964.

37. M. Gell-Mann, *Nuovo Cimento Suppl. 2*, **4**, 848 (1956).

38. O. Piccioni, *Proceedings International Conference on Weak Interactions*, Argonne National Laboratory Rept. No. ANL-7130, Argonne. Illinois, 1965, p. 230.

39. M. Gell-Mann, California Institute of Technology Synchrotron Laboratory Rept CTSL-20, 1961; S. Okubo, *Progr. Theoret. Phys.* (*Kyoto*), **27**, 949 (1962).

40. S. Coleman and S. L. Glashow, *Phys. Rev. Letters*, **6**, 423 (1961).

41. W. J. Willis, *Proceedings International Conference on Weak Interactions*, Argonne National Laboratory Rept. No. ANL-7130, Argonne, Illinois, 1965, p. 159.

42. M. Gell-Mann and A. H. Rosenfeld, *Ann. Rev. Nucl. Sci.*, **7**, 407 (1957).

43. S. Okubo, R. E. Marshak, E. C. G. Sudarshan, W. Teutch, and S. Weinberg, *Phys. Rev.*, **112**, 665 (1958).

44. M. M. Block, *Phys. Rev. Letters*, **12**, 262 (1964).

45. See Ref. 1.

46. K. Fujii and D. Ito, *Progr. Theoret. Phys. (Kyoto)*, **30**, 718 (1963).

47. S. P. Rosen, paper presented at Third Ann. Eastern United States Theoretical Physics Conference, University of Maryland, 1964.

48. S. B. Treiman, *Nuovo Cimento*, **15**, 916 (1960); A. Pais, *Phys. Rev.*, **122**, 317 (1961).

49. S. P. Rosen, *Phys. Rev. Letters*, **9**, 186 (1962).

50. N. Cabibbo and R. Gatto, *Nuovo Cimento*, **21**, 872 (1961); S. Meshkov, C. A. Levinson, and H. J. Lipkin, *Phys. Rev. Letters*, **10**, 361 (1963); S. P. Rosen, *ibid.*, **11**, 100 (1963).

51. S. P. Rosen, *Phys. Rev.*, **137**, B431 (1965).

52. Data taken from A. H. Rosenfeld, A. Barbaro-Galtieri, W. H. Barkas, P. L. Bastien, J. Kirz, and M. Roos, *Rev. Mod. Phys.*, **37**, 633 (1965).

53. N. P. Samios, *Proceedings International Conference on Weak Interactions*, Argonne National Laboratory Rept. No. 7130, Argonne, Illinois, 1965, p. 189.

54. J. Allison, University of Oxford preprint, 1966.

55. N. Cabibbo, *Phys. Rev. Letters*, **12**, 62 (1964).

56. S. P. Rosen, S. Pakvasa, and E. C. G. Sudarshan, *Phys. Rev.*, **146**, 1118 (1966).

57. J. M. Gaillard, F. Krienen, W. Galbraith, A. Hussri, M. R. Jane, N. H. Lipman, G. Manning, T. Ratcliffe, R. Day, A. G. Parham, B. T. Payne, A. C. Sherwood, H. Faissner, and H. Reithler, *Phys. Rev. Letters*, **18**, 20 (1967); J. W. Cronin, P. F. Kunz, W. S. Risk, and P. C. Wheeler, *ibid.*, **18**, 25 (1967).

58. T. T. Wu and C. N. Yang, *Phys. Rev. Letters*, **13**, 380 (1964).

59. E. C. G. Sudarshan, *Nuovo Cimento*, **41**, 282 (1966); T. Das and K. T. Mahanthappa, *ibid.*, **41**, 618 (1966).

60. T. D. Lee and L. Wolfenstein, *Phys. Rev.*, **138**, B1490 (1965).

61. T. D. Lee and C. S. Wu, *Ann. Rev. Nucl. Sci.*, **16**, 511 (1966).

62. T. N. Truong, *Phys. Rev. Letters*, **13**, 358a (1964).

63. D. Cline, University of Wisconsin preprint, 1967.

64. N. Byers, S. W. Macdowell, and C. N. Yang, *High Energy Physics and Elementary Particles*, International Atomic Energy Agency, Vienna, 1965, p. 953.

65. C. Rubbia and J. Steinberger, *Physics Letters*, **23**, 167 (1966).

66. T. N. Truong, *Argonne Symposium on CP Violation*, to be published as an Argonne Report in 1967.

67. See D. Amati, CERN Preprint (1966).

68. G. Barton, C. Kacser, and S. P. Rosen, *Phys. Rev.*, **139**, 783 (1963); S. Weinberg, *Phys. Rev. Letters*, **4**, 87, 585(E) (1960); R. F. Sawyer and K. C. Wali, *Nuovo Cimento*, **17**, 938 (1960).

69. T. D. Lee and C. S. Wu, *Ann. Rev. Nucl. Sci.*, **16**, 471 (1966).

70. N. Cabibbo, in *Symmetries in Elementary Particle Physics*, A. Zichichi, Ed., Academic Press, New York, 1965, p. 284.

71. M. K. Gaillard, *Nuovo Cimento*, **35**, 1225 (1965).

72. J. J. Sakurai, *Phys. Rev. Letters*, **7**, 426 (1961).

73. S. L. Glashow and R. Socolow, *Physics Letters*, **10**, 143 (1964).

74. B. Cork, L. Kerth, W. A. Wenzel, J. W. Cronin, and R. L. Cool, *Phys. Rev.*, **100**, 1000 (1960).
75. R. H. Dalitz, paper presented at International Conference on Weak Interactions, Brookhaven, 1963.
76. Data compiled by J. P. Berge, *Proceedings of the XIIIth International Conference on High-Energy Physics*, University of California Press, Berkeley and Los Angeles, 1967, p. 46.
77. D. Berley, S. Herzbach, R. Kofler, S. Yamamoto, W. Heintzelman, M. Schiff, J. Thompson, and W. Willis, *Phys. Rev. Letters,* **17**, 1071 (1966); D. Cline and J. Robinson, *Physics Letters*, **23**, 509 (1966); R. B. Willman and T. H. Groves, *Physics Letters*, **14**, 350 (1965).
78. S. Barshay, U. Nauenberg, and J. Schultz, *Phys. Rev. Letters*, **12**, 76, 156(E) (1964); R. D. Young, T. Sakuma, and M. Sugawara, *Phys. Rev.*, **145**, 1181 (1966); M. C. Li, *Phys. Rev.*, **141**, 1328 (1966).
79. M. Bazin, H. Blumfeld, U. Nauenberg, L. Seidlitz, R. J. Plano, S. Maratech, and P. Schmidt, *Phys. Rev.*, **140**, B1358 (1965).
80. S. Okubo, R. E. Marshak, and E. C. G. Sudarshan, *Phys. Rev.*, **113**, 944 (1958); R. H. Dalitz, *Rev. Mod. Phys.*, **31**, 823 (1959).
81. S. P. Rosen, *Phys. Rev. Letters*, **6**, 504 (1961); S. Hori, *Nucl. Phys.*, **17**, 227 (1960).
82. V. I. Zakharov and A. B. Kaidalov, *JETP Letters*, **3**, 300 (1966).
83. B. W. Lee, *Phys. Rev. Letters*, **12**, 83 (1964); H. Sugawara, *Progr. Thoeret. Phys.* (*Kyoto*), **31**, 213 (1964).
84. (a) M. Gell-Mann, *Phys. Rev. Letters*, **12**, 155 (1964); (b) B. Sakita, *ibid.*, **12**, 379 (1964); (c) S. P. Rosen, *ibid.*, **12**, 408 (1964); (d) S. Okubo, *Physics Letters*, **8**, 362 (1964); (e) Y. Hara, *Phys. Rev. Letters*, **12**, 378 (1964); (f) S. Coleman and S. L. Glashow, *Phys. Rev.*, **134**, B671 (1964).
85. S. P. Rosen, *Phys. Rev.*, **140**, B326 (1965).
86. B. Sakita, *Phys. Rev.*, **136**, B1756 (1964); F. Gursey and L. A. Radicati, *Phys. Rev. Letters*, **13**, 173 (1964); A. Pais, *ibid.*, **13**, 175 (1964); F. Gursey, A. Pais, and L. A. Radicati, *Phys. Rev. Letters*, **13**, 299 (1964).
87. See, e.g., the discussion in A. Pais, *Rev. Mod. Phys.*, **38**, 215 (1966).
88. (a) K. J. Barnes, P. Carruthers, and F. von Hippel, *Phys. Rev. Letters*, **14**, 82 (1965); (b) H. J. Lipkin and S. Meshkov, *ibid.*, **14**, 670 (1965).
89. See Ref. 88b.
90. S. P. Rosen and S. Pakvasa, *Phys. Rev. Letters*, **13**, 773 (1964).
91. M. Suzuki, *Physics Letters*, **14**, 64 (1965); G. Altarelli, F. Buccella, and R. Gatto, *ibid.*, **14**, 70 (1965); P. Babu, *Phys. Rev. Letters*, **14**, 166 (1965).
92. D. Horn, M. Kugler, H. J. Lipkin, S. Meshov, J. C. Carter, and J. J. Coyne, *Phys. Rev. Letters*, **14**, 717 (1965).
93. M. P. Khanna, *Phys. Rev. Letters*, **14**, 711 (1965); K. Kawarabayashi and R. White, *ibid.*, **14**, 527 (1965); R. Oehme, *Physics Letters*, **15**, 284 (1965); R. Gatto, L. Maiani, and G. Preparata, *Phys. Rev.*, **139**, B1294 (1965). These authors use $U(6,6)$ symmetry which for $P$ waves is identical to using the $SU(6)_W$ subgroup of $U(6,6)$.
94. S. Pakvasa and S. P. Rosen, *Phys. Rev.*, **147**, 1166 (1966).
95. C. Iso and M. Kato, *Nuovo Cimento*, **37**, 1735 (1965).

96. S. P. Rosen, *Phys. Rev.*, **143**, 138 (1966).

97. N. Cabibbo, *Phys. Rev. Letters*, **10**, 531 (1963).

98. J. C. Taylor, *Phys. Rev.*, **110**, 1216 (1958).

99. B. d'Espagnat, *Compt. Rend. Acad. Sci.*, **228**, 744 (1949).

100. M. Gell-Mann, *Physics*, **1**, 63 (1964).

101. M. Gell-Mann, *Physics Letters*, **8**, 214 (1964).

102. F. Boehm and E. Kankelheit, *Phys. Rev. Letters*, **14**, 312 (1965); P. Bock and H. Schopper, *Phys. Rev., Letters*, **16**, 284 (1965); Y. G. Abov, P. A. Krupchitsky, and Y. A. Oratovsky, *ibid.*, **12**, 25 (1964).

103. S. Coleman, S. L. Glashow, and B. W. Lee, *Ann. Phys. (N.Y.)*, **30**, 348 (1964).

104. See Ref. 84a.

105. K. Itabashi, *Phys. Rev.*, **136**, B221 (1964); see, however, footnote 16 in Ref. 56.

106. M. Suzuki, *Phys. Rev.*, **137**, B1062 (1965); see also D. Bailin, *Nuovo Cimento*, **38**, 1342 (1965).

107. S. P. Rosen, *Phys. Rev.*, **135**, B1041 (1964).

108. A large list of references is contained in B. Renner, Lectures on Current Algebras, Rutherford Laboratory Report RHEL/R 126, 1966.

109. H. Sugawara, *Phys. Rev. Letters*, **15**, 870, 997(E) (1965).

110. M. Suzuki, *Phys. Rev. Letters*, **15**, 986 (1965).

111. See, e.g., G. Barton, *Disperson Techniques in Field Theory*, Benjamin, New York, 1965.

112. Y. Nambu and E. Schrauner, *Phys. Rev.*, **128**, 862 (1962).

113. (a) Y. Hara, Y. Nambu, and J. Schechter, *Phys. Rev. Letters*, **16**, 380 (1966); (b) L. S. Brown and C. M. Sommerfield, *ibid.*, **16**, 751 (1966); (c) S. Badier and C. Bouchiat, *Physics Letters*, **20**, 529 (1966).

114. Y. T. Chiu and J. Schechter, *Phys. Rev. Letters*, **16**, 1022 (1966) and *Phys. Rev.*, **150**, 1201 (1966); Y. Hara, ICTP preprint (1966); see also S. N. Biswas, A. Kumar, and R. P. Saxena, *Phys. Rev. Letters*, **17**, 268 (1966).

115. (a) M. Suzuki, *Phys. Rev.*, **144**, 1154 (1966); (b) see also W. Alles and R. Jengo, *Nuovo Cimento*, **42A**, 419 (1966).

116. B. d'Espagnat and J. Iliopoulos, *Physics Letters*, **21**, 232 (1966).

117. C. Bouchiat and P. Meyer, *Physics Letters*, **22**, 198 (1966).

118. (a) See Ref. 115a; (b) C. G. Callan and S. B. Treiman, *Phys. Rev. Letters*, **16**, 153 (1966); (c) S. K. Bose and S. N. Biswas, *ibid.*, **16**, 330 (1966); (d) W. H. Carnahan, Western Reserve University preprint (1966); (e) Y. Hara and Y. Nambu, *Phys. Rev. Letters*, **16**, 875 (1966); (f) D. K. Elias and J. C. Taylor, *Nuovo Cimento*, **44A**, 518 (1966).

119. See Ref. 118e; Ref. 118f.

120. H. D. I. Abarbanel, *Phys. Rev.*, **153**, 1547 (1967).

121. See Ref. 113b.

122. G. Feldman, P. T. Matthews, and A. Salam, *Phys. Rev.*, **121**, 302 (1961); other papers on pole model are cited in S. Kawasaki, M. Imoto, and S. Furui, *Progr. Theoret. Phys. (Kyoto)*, **35**, 90 (1965).

123. B. W. Lee and A. R. Swift, *Phys. Rev.*, **136**, B228 (1964).

124. B. W. Lee, *Phys. Rev.*, **140**, B152 (1965).

125. S. Pakvasa, R. H. Graham, and S. P. Rosen, *Phys. Rev.*, **149**, 1200 (1966).

126. H. J. Lipkin, *Phys. Rev.*, **137**, B1561 (1965); see Ref. 84f.

127. M. Suzuki, *Phys. Rev.*, **140**, B1405 (1965).

128. A. P. Balachandran, M. G. Gundzik, and S. Pakvasa, *Phys. Rev.*, **153**, 1553 (1967).

129. Other estimates of decay rates of $\Omega^-$ are given by M. Suzuki, *Progr. Theoret. Phys. (Kyoto)*, **32**, 138 (1964); See Ref. 73; Ref. 94; Y. Hara, *Phys. Rev.*, **150**, 1175 (1966).

130. R. H. Graham and S. Pakvasa, *Phys. Rev.*, **140**, B1144 (1965).

131. S. Fenster and N. Panhcapakesan, Argonne National Laboratory preprint, 1967.

132. J. Schwinger, *Phys. Rev. Letters*, **12**, 630 (1964) and **13**, 355 (1964).

133. K. Nishijima and L. Swank, *Phys. Rev.*, **146**, 1161 (1966); G. S. Guralnik, V. S. Mathur, and L. K. Pandit, Rochester Preprint, 1966.

134. W. W. Wada, *Phys. Rev.*, **138**, B1488 (1965).

135. J. J. Sakurai, *Phys. Rev.*, **156**, 1508 (1967).

136. M. Gell-Mann, *Phys. Rev.*, **106**, 1296 (1957).

137. Riazuddin and K. T. Mahanthappa, *Phys. Rev.*, **147**, 972 (1966); M. K. Gaillard, *Phys. Letters*, **20**, 533 (1966).

138. A. M. Gleeson and S. Pakvasa, Syracuse Preprint, 1967.

139. F. C. Chan, *Nuovo Cimento*, **45**, 236 (1966).

140. For a different use of this commutator see Ref. 131, and M. C. Li, Institute for Advanced Study, Princeton Preprint, 1967.

141. E. McCliment and K. Nishijima, *Phys. Rev.*, **128**, 1970 (1962).

142. R. F. Dashen, S. Frautschi, and D. H. Sharp, *Phys. Rev. Letters*, **13**, 777 (1964).

143. R. F. Dashen, Y. Dothan, S. Frautschi, and D. H. Sharp, *Phys. Rev.*, **143**, 1185 (1966); B. Diu, H. R. Rubinstein, and R. P. Van Royen, *Nuovo Cimento*, **43A**, 961 (1966).

144. T. N. Truong, *Phys. Rev. Letters*, **17**, 1102 (1966); Riazuddin, V. S. Mathur, and L. K. Pandit, *ibid.*, **17**, 736 (1966).

# Broken Symmetries and the Goldstone Theorem

## G. S. GURALNIK

*Physics Department, Brown University, Providence, Rhode Island*

## C. R. HAGEN

*Physics Department, University of Rochester, Rochester, New York*

## T. W. B. KIBBLE

*Physics Department, Imperial College, London, England*

## Contents

## I. Introduction

The Goldstone theorem, because it makes an exact statement concerning the excitation spectrum of a physical system, occupies what is essentially a unique position in quantum field theory. Briefly stated, the theorem asserts that for systems in which the vacuum is not an eigenstate of a time-independent operator (in general, the integral of a local operator over a given spacelike surface), there must exist massless particle excitations. Physically such a statement is eminently plausible inasmuch as such massless particles (like the vacuum) can have zero energy and thus provide a mechanism whereby an arbitrarily large number of null eigenstates of the energy momentum four-vector can be constructed. Since these new "vacuum states" will not, in general, be eigenstates of the conserved operator, one can by this heuristic device produce what is generally referred to as a "broken symmetry." This approach is potentially useful since it provides a way in which one can obtain solutions possessing a lower symmetry than a given Lagrangian without the necessity of explicitly introducing a symmetry-breaking interaction. On the other hand, the price one pays for this apparent simplicity, aside from the problem of accommodating a massless particle within a given physical scheme, generally consists of a rather complicated set of dynamical constraints on the theory, which must be carefully handled in all perturbative calculations.

We initiate this study of broken symmetries in Section II with a presentation and comparison of a number of the presently known proofs of the Goldstone theorem. It is furthermore shown how so-called failures of the theorem can occur in acausal theories. The question of the existence of integral charge operators is discussed and related to the inequivalent representations which underlie all broken-symmetry theories.

Section III continues this line of development by a detailed consideration of relativistic theories in which one has the particularly simple situation in which the relevant conserved current is linear in one of the canonical variables. Although it is possible to illustrate a number of interesting aspects of broken symmetries within the framework of such models, unfortunately they invariably consist of generalizations of free fields (with a gauge variable) and the broken symmetry is consequently never observable.

In Section IV the connection between broken symmetries and gauge invariance is discussed within the context of electrodynamics as well as the more complicated non-Abelian gauge theories. In such cases it is demonstrated that for gauges which are not manifestly covariant, the Goldstone theorem need not apply and, furthermore, that the use of manifestly covariant formulations allows one only to infer the presence of unphysical zero-mass gauge modes. In addition, the problem of counting the number of distinct Goldstone bosons associated with the breaking of a group symmetry is considered.

The nonrelativistic applications of the Goldstone theorem are discussed in Section V in a manner which is intended to emphasize the correspondence to the relativistic case. The examples considered here are of particular interest since one has, in the domain of nonrelativistic quantum mechanics, the important advantage that there exist examples of physically interesting broken-symmetry theories which are amenable to calculation.

The corresponding relativistic case (in which the conserved current is bilinear in the canonical fields) is discussed in Section VI. A soluble model in two dimensions is considered with its four-dimensional counterpart. A relativistic analog of superconductivity is considered in perturbation theory, and nontrivial symmetry-breaking effects are displayed.

Finally, in Section VII, various versions of the scalar theory and the Lee model are considered with the inclusion of a symmetry-breaking effect. The high degree of solubility of these models, along with the fact that the symmetry-breaking effects are nontrivial, makes them particularly interesting. Although they are not fully relativistic, they have more elementary particle aspects than the usual nonrelativistic models and consequently are quite suggestive.

## II. The Goldstone Theorem

It is customary to begin any attempt to describe a physical situation within the framework of quantum field theory with the construction of a suitable interaction Lagrangian. In the event that there are several basic fields involved, this problem may often be simplified by a physical observation indicating a symmetry among these fields thereby restricting the choice of possible interaction terms to those particular combinations of fields which respect the symmetry. Frequently, however, the symmetry in question is not exact and it is consequently necessary to guess the form of the corrections to the symmetric interaction Lagrangian. This procedure is usually carried out under the assumption that the solutions of a given physical system will display the same degree of symmetry as the original Lagrangian. However, it has become evident (particularly in the domain of nonrelativistic quantum field theory) that the solutions to a set of field equations are often not unique and that perfectly acceptable solutions exist which have less symmetry than that displayed by the Lagrange function. Consequently, it might be possible to avoid the introduction of a symmetry-breaking interaction

Lagrangian and proceed instead by attempting to find an appropriate broken-symmetry solution to the symmetrical Lagrangian.

The reason this possibility even occurs is that, although the field equations and commutation relations respect the relevant invariance operation, under appropriate circumstances the states can be modified in such a way as to induce a breakdown of the symmetry. This is somewhat reminiscent of an interaction picture where the states are given in terms of the complete set $|a'\rangle$ of the symmetry-preserving Hamiltonian modified by exponential factors so as to form the new states

$$\left(\exp\left\{i\int_{t_0}^{t} dx\, H_{\text{s.b.}}(x)\right\}\right)_{+} |a'\rangle$$

In fact, however, the actual structure of the states involves a number of rather subtle problems (including, for example, the requirement that such a modification not affect the usual time independence of this complete set of states). Although the equations for the Green's functions of the broken symmetry case are functionally identical to the fully symmetric situation, nonetheless the possibility exists of asymmetric solutions as a consequence of the different boundary conditions which can be imposed on the solutions to the Green's function equations. In particular, the usual assumption that the state of lowest energy is an eigenstate of the group generators can be dropped in order to obtain asymmetric solutions. Although such an assumption is an external one, it is also quite natural, and dispensing with it often leads to constraints on the spectrum and parameters of the problem. The spectrum constraint is known as the Goldstone theorem[1] and requires that, under fairly general circumstances, the currents associated with the broken symmetry have zero-mass excitations. Insofar as the theorem is valid and the massless excitations are identifiable as physical particles, it is clear that these massless modes make it unlikely that the method of broken symmetries will be valid in the case of strongly interacting particles. A considerable amount of energy and ingenuity has been devoted to various attempts to avoid the consequences of the theorem for this reason. Indeed, until fairly recently, the apparent failure of the theorem in the case of certain many-body problems was frequently invoked to suggest a rather general breakdown of the theorem (which would, of course, greatly enhance the possibility of consistently applying the broken-symmetry approach to strong interactions).

The purpose of this section is to carefully state and prove the above-mentioned theorem. Having done this, the reason for any so-called failures will be clear. It will also follow that the only way to avoid the consequences of the theorem within the context of causal theories with conserved currents lies in the possibility that the predicted zero-mass modes need not be associated with physical particles, but may refer to decoupled nonphysical excitations. Unfortunately, however, such a decoupling cannot usually be demonstrated in the absence of a complete solution.

The next few paragraphs are devoted to what is essentially the classical proof of the Goldstone theorem with a clear statement concerning its domain of validity. We begin by emphasizing the important role of the causality condition in guaranteeing that commutators of the charge operator relevant to the broken symmetry are independent of the spacelike surface on which this charge is evaluated. This observation is essential to explain apparent failures of the theorem referred to above. In the process of developing these arguments, we shall observe that the integral charge cannot be well defined when the symmetry is broken. This is a fundamental aspect of the theory and is discussed in some detail. In particular, the exponentiated generators of the symmetry group are discussed. It is shown that the mappings they describe are to be interpreted in a limiting sense and that these operators serve to map from one representation of the commutation relations to another inequivalent representation in a manner consistent with the original field equations. Our treatment does not aspire to the degree of rigor which may be required by the most mathematically inclined. It is, however, basically correct, and, if desired, one may refine the arguments used here without encountering any fundamental difficulties. [An informative early discussion of these problems with greater emphasis on mathematical rigor may be found in a work by Streater.[2]]

We begin with the assumption that there exists a conserved current[3] $j^\mu(x)$, i.e.,

$$\partial_\mu j^\mu(x) = 0$$

Although for convenience we display only one spatial index and suppress all internal indices which label the current operator, there is no essential difficulty introduced by considering more complex operators. If, for example, Lorentz symmetry were to be broken, one would consider the operator

$$F^{\mu\nu\lambda}(x) = x^\mu T^{\nu\lambda}(x) - x^\nu T^{\mu\lambda}(x)$$

which obeys the differential conservation law

$$\partial_\lambda F^{\mu\nu\lambda}(x) = 0$$

Now let us consider any combination of operators $A$ of the field theory being considered. We emphasize that $A$ is not necessarily local and, indeed, it is sufficient for our purpose that $A$ exist only in a formal sense (provided that certain of its commutators are well defined). We define the generator[4,5]

$$Q_R(t) \equiv \int_{|\mathbf{x}| < R} d^3x \, j^0(\mathbf{x}, t)$$

and denote the surface of the sphere $|\mathbf{x}| = R$ as $\sigma(R)$. In order to incorporate the effect of current conservation, we consider the relation

$$\int_{|\mathbf{x}| < R} d^3x [\partial_\mu j^\mu(x), A] = 0$$

or

$$[\partial_0 Q_R(t), A] + \left[\int_{\sigma(R)} d\boldsymbol{\sigma} \cdot \mathbf{j}, A\right] = 0$$

If for some sufficiently large value of $R$ (say $L$), we find that

$$\left[\int_{\sigma(R > L)} d\boldsymbol{\sigma} \cdot \mathbf{j}, A\right] = 0 \tag{2.1}$$

it follows that

$$\partial_0 [Q_{R > L}(t), A] = 0$$

or

$$[Q_{R > L}(t), A] = B \tag{2.2}$$

with

$$dB/dt = 0$$

It might happen, of course, that these equations are only valid in the limit $R \to \infty$, in which case we find

$$\lim_{R \to \infty} \left[\int d\boldsymbol{\sigma} \cdot \mathbf{j}, A\right] = 0 \tag{2.3}$$

and thus

$$\lim_{R \to \infty} [Q_R(t), A] = B \tag{2.4}$$

with

$$dB/dt = 0$$

Note that, if we denote in the usual fashion

$$\lim_{R \to \infty} Q_R(t) = Q$$

Equation (2.4) becomes $[Q, A] = B$. Strictly speaking, however, though the commutator exists, we shall see that when the symmetry is broken, $Q$ does not and thus the limit Eq. (2.4) cannot be evaluated inside the commutator.

It should be pointed out that there are many theories in which Eq. (2.1) is valid for a large class of operators $A$. If we deal with a theory which is locally causal and $A$ is localized in a finite region of space time, Eq. (2.1) follows at once for sufficiently large $R$. If $A$ is not localized to a finite volume of space-time but has rapidly decreasing weights for large values of coordinates, Eq. (2.3) may still be valid in a causal theory. As we shall see in Section V, Eq. (2.3) is valid for non-relativistic problems involving rapidly decreasing potentials. How rapid this decrease must be depends explicitly on the structure of $j^k$ as well as the potential $V(r)$.

It is clear that the above remarks apply to a wide class of theories with no particular reference to symmetry breaking. We may now make the basic broken-symmetry assumption by setting

$$\langle 0|B|0\rangle \neq 0 \tag{2.5}$$

where $|0\rangle$ is a translationally invariant vacuum state. Before we prove the Goldstone theorem in the classical manner, we will examine some of the more general aspects of the very strong assumption (2.5). Through this study it will be much easier to make the connection to other forms of the proof. In particular, (2.5) implies that $|0\rangle$ cannot be an eigenstate of $Q$, and it follows from $\exp\{i\lambda Q\}|0\rangle \neq |0\rangle$ that $Q$ is not a unitary operator. In fact, as shown by Fabri and Picasso,[6] the operator $Q$ does not exist even in the sense of a weak limit. This follows from the observation that since $|0\rangle$ is translationally invariant, so is $Q|0\rangle$. Consequently,

$$\langle 0|QQ|0\rangle = \int d^3x \, \langle 0|j^0(x)Q|0\rangle$$

diverges unless $Q$ annihilates the vacuum. Since this is contrary to hypothesis, it follows that whenever the symmetry is broken, the associated generator does not exist. Such a result (which has been recognized in various forms since the early times of broken symmetries) is rarely, if ever, of any concern when doing general calculations with broken symmetries.[7] This is because $Q$ usually does not occur by itself, but only in commutators with some other operator. In that case, it is to be interpreted as the limiting form of (2.4) and no difficulty arises if $Q$ is sufficiently localizable and causal.

As a slight generalization of these statements, note that in a causal theory with any sufficiently localized operator $L$, the operator

$$\tilde{L}_R \equiv \exp\{i\eta Q_R(t)\} L \exp\{-i\eta Q_R(t)\}$$
$$= L + i\eta[Q_R(t), L] + \tfrac{1}{2}(i\eta)^2[Q_R(t), [Q_R(t), L]] + \cdots$$

considered term by term has no divergences in the limit $R \to \infty$ because of the assumed causality condition. We may assume that this power series expansion exists for sufficiently small $\eta$ and we shall formally denote $\lim_{R \to \infty} \tilde{L}_R$ as $e^{i\eta Q} L e^{-i\eta Q}$. From the exponential structure of the above transformation, it follows that, for the class of operators

$$\tilde{L}_R{}^i \equiv \exp\{i\eta Q_R(t)\} L^i \exp\{-i\eta Q_R(t)\}$$

we have for any matrix element

$$\langle a' | \tilde{L}_R{}^1 \tilde{L}_R{}^2 \ldots \tilde{L}_R{}^n | b' \rangle$$
$$= \langle a' | \exp\{i\eta Q_R(t) L^1 L^2 \ldots L^n \exp\{-i\eta Q_R(t)\} | b' \rangle$$

and so, to the extent that $\lim_{R \to \infty} \tilde{L}_R{}^i$ is well defined, so also is the limit of this matrix element as $R \to \infty$. This suggests that formally a new set of states $|\eta, a'\rangle \equiv \lim_{R \to \infty} \exp\{-i\eta Q_R(t)\} | a' \rangle$ be introduced.[8] This is a useful procedure and we shall outline its consequences here, noting however that some care must be exercised for this identification to be meaningful since the separation implied by the above equation is not mathematically well defined. As has been shown, the operator $e^{-i\eta Q}$ can only be given meaning when it appears in combination with $e^{i\eta Q}$. Indeed, in the following chapters it will be shown for several models that

$$\lim_{R \to \infty} \langle a' | e^{-i\eta Q_R(t)} | b' \rangle = 0$$

for all states $|a'\rangle$ and $|b'\rangle$. Consequently, $|\eta, a'\rangle$ is orthogonal to all members of the original Hilbert space and, if it were taken to be a member of the same space, it would necessarily be a null vector. This, of course, is inadmissible since then it would follow that all matrix elements of the form of (2.5) vanish.

We now are prepared to return to the proof of the Goldstone theorem which follows as a direct consequence of (2.4) upon imposition of (2.5). Taking the vacuum expectation and inserting a complete set of states, (2.4) becomes

$$\lim_{R \to \infty} \sum_n [\langle 0|Q_R(t)|n\rangle\langle n|A|0\rangle - \langle 0|A|n\rangle\langle n|Q_R(t)|0\rangle] = \langle 0|B|0\rangle \neq 0$$

The operator $j^0(x)$ is assumed to be local with the usual translational behavior

$$j^0(x) = e^{-iPx}j^0(0)e^{iPx}$$

and, further, it is assumed that $e^{iPx}|0\rangle = |0\rangle$. Thus, the preceding equation becomes

$$\lim_{R \to \infty} \sum_n \int_R d^3x [\langle 0|j^0(0)|n\rangle\langle n|A|0\rangle e^{ip_n x} - \langle 0|A|n\rangle\langle n|j^0(0)|0\rangle e^{-ip_n x}]$$

$$= \sum_n (2\pi)^3 \delta(\mathbf{p}_n)[\langle 0|j^0(0)|n\rangle\langle n|A|0\rangle e^{-ip_n^0 x^0}$$

$$- \langle 0|A|n\rangle\langle n|j^0(0)|0\rangle e^{ip_n^0 x^0}]$$

$$= \langle 0|B|0\rangle$$

Now this equation is valid for all times $x^0$ and, since $dB/dx^0 = 0$, it follows that the left-hand side of this equation must not depend on $x^0$. Clearly these conditions are consistent only if the left-hand side vanishes except for those states where $p_n^0|_{\mathbf{p}_n \to 0} = 0$. Furthermore, there must exist such states since the right-hand side does not vanish. Thus we have shown that if a symmetry is broken (in a "sufficiently" causal theory) there must be excitation modes in the spectrum of the generator of that symmetry whose energy vanishes in the limit that the momentum of these modes vanishes. The corresponding statement in the relativistic case is the assertion of the existence of zero mass particles. This is the celebrated Goldstone theorem. Note that the actual proof is quite trivial and the only real assumption, besides the translational behavior of the vacuum and current, has been that $dB/dt = 0$. It has been pointed out,[9] however, that this assumption could fail to hold in cases of some physical significance and was, indeed, the basis of some apparent breakdowns of the Goldstone theorem.

We have repeatedly emphasized above that if a symmetry is broken, the operator $e^{i\lambda Q}$ cannot be unitary. Now, having proved that the Goldstone theorem is applicable to causal theories, it is easy to exploit this result to demonstrate the converse statement, namely, that if $j^0(x)$ does not have a massless particle in its spectrum, the operator

$$U(\eta) = \lim_{R \to \infty} \exp\left\{ i\eta \int_R d^3x j^0(x, t) \right\}$$

$$= \lim_{R \to \infty} U_R(\eta, t)$$

is unitary. Since the exponential form guarantees that

$$U(\eta)U^+(\eta) = 1$$

and

$$U(\eta_1)U(\eta_2) = U(\eta_1 + \eta_2)$$

it is only necessary to demonstrate that

$$\lim_{R \to \infty} U_R(\eta, t)|0\rangle = |0\rangle$$

This, in turn, can be guaranteed if, for all Wightman functions, the relation

$$\lim_{R \to \infty} \langle 0|U_R(\eta, t)\phi_1(x_1)\phi_2(x_2)\ldots\phi_n(x_n)U_R^+(\eta, t)|0\rangle$$
$$= \langle 0|\phi_1(x_1)\phi_2(x_2)\ldots\phi_n(x_n)|0\rangle$$

is valid. The proof is performed by observing that if, for an operator $A$ of the form $\phi(x_1)\phi(x_2)\ldots\phi(x_n)$, it can be shown that

$$\frac{d}{d\eta}\langle 0|U(\eta)AU^+(\eta)|0\rangle = 0$$

for all $\lambda$, then

$$\langle 0|U(\eta)AU^+(\eta)|0\rangle = \langle 0|U(0)AU^+(0)|0\rangle$$
$$= \langle 0|A|0\rangle$$

which is the required result. Explicitly evaluating the derivative yields

$$\frac{d}{d\eta}\langle 0|U_R(\eta, t)AU_R^+(\eta, t)|0\rangle = i\langle 0|[Q_R(t), U_R(\eta, t)AU_R^+(\eta, t)]|0\rangle$$

$$(2.6)$$

Now, if $A$ is localized in a finite volume of space-time as is the case for $\phi(x_1)\phi(x_2)\ldots\phi(x_n)$ which is localized to a region of radius $L \le \sum_i [|x_i^0| + |\mathbf{x}_i|]$ it follows by causality that, for $R > L + |t|$

$$U_R(\eta, t)AU_R^+(\eta, t)$$

is independent of $t$ and $R$. By the same reasoning,

$$\frac{d}{d\eta}\langle 0|U_R(\eta, t)AU_R^+(\eta, t)|0\rangle\bigg|_{R > L+t}$$

is independent of $t$ and $R$. Consequently, the conditions required for the application of the Goldstone theorem to the right-hand side of

Eq. (2.6) are satisfied for sufficiently large $R$. Since by assumption no zero mass modes are present, it follows that this commutator vanishes and

$$\frac{d}{d\eta} \lim_{R \to \infty} \langle 0| U_R(\eta, t) A U_R^{+}(\eta, t)|0\rangle = 0$$

which demonstrates that

$$\langle 0| U(\eta) A U^{+}(\eta)|0\rangle = \langle 0|A|0\rangle$$

Thus, if $j^0(x)$ excites no massless modes, the transformation $U(\eta)$ is unitarily implementable.

What has been presented so far is the more or less traditional theoretical formulation of the Goldstone theorem. A reformulation in the mathematically more rigorous context of axiomatic quantum field theory has been given by Streater.[2] Kastler, Robinson, and Swieca[10] have also presented an axiomatic proof, which involves a reversal of the chain of argument. Without attempting to maintain their level of rigor we shall now present a version of their argument which displays in somewhat simpler form the underlying physical ideas. From this it will be clear that, despite the very different language used, the physical content of their proof is essentially the same as in the earlier and more straightforward proofs. It will also be apparent that the arguments can, with a little effort, be made fully rigorous.

Following their method in outline we shall show (without assuming the Goldstone theorem itself) that if a causal theory has a smallest mass different from zero and a conserved current $j^\mu(x)$ such that $\partial_\mu j^\mu(x) = 0$, then

$$\lim_{R \to \infty} \exp\left[i\eta Q_R(t)\right]$$

is a unitary operator. This statement is equivalent to the Goldstone theorem for, as shown in the preceding discussion, when the symmetry is broken (i.e., when $\langle 0|[Q, A]|0\rangle \neq 0$), the vacuum is not an eigenstate of $Q$ and hence $\exp[i\eta Q]$ is not unitary. Since it is assumed that $\partial_\mu j^\mu = 0$, it follows in that case that the lowest mass of the theory must vanish.

As before, let us choose an operator $A$ depending on strictly local operators "smeared" over a finite region of space-time. We may choose $A$ to be bounded. We shall only be interested in the part of $A$ which has vanishing vacuum expectation value, so we replace $A$ by

$$A - \langle 0|A|0\rangle$$

Now from $A$ we can form yet another operator $B$ which has the property that

$$\langle n|B|0\rangle = (1/E_n^2)\langle n|A|0\rangle \tag{2.7}$$

This is a sensible equation as, by assumption, $E_n$ can never vanish. Clearly one such operator [namely, $B = (1/H^2)A$] exists, although we shall need a somewhat more complicated structure for $B$. Once again all conclusions will be drawn from the usual Goldstone commutator

$$G_R \equiv \int_R d^3x \langle 0|[j^0(x), A]|0\rangle$$

We shall extract the spectral information that $\lim_{R\to\infty} G_R = 0$ if there are no massless modes in a much more complicated manner than before, even though no fewer assumptions are made. Straightforward manipulation and the use of Eq. (2.7) show that

$$G_R = \int_R d^3x \langle 0|[j^0(x)H^2B - BH^2j^0(x)]|0\rangle$$

$$= \int_R d^3x \langle 0|\big[[[j^0(x), H], H], B\big]|0\rangle$$

$$= -\partial_0^2 \int_R d^3x \langle 0|[j^0(x), B]|0\rangle$$

Now we are confronted with the classical Goldstone problem, namely, under what conditions does the fact that $\partial_\mu j^\mu(x) = 0$ insure that certain specific matrix elements of $Q = \lim_{R\to\infty} \int d^3x j^0(x, t)$ are independent of the time $t$. If $B$ were a localized operator, we would immediately have $\lim_{R\to\infty} G_R = 0$. However, assuming $A$ is localizable, $(1/H^2)A$ is not generally localizable. On the other hand, it is not difficult to construct from $A$ an operator $B$ which obeys Eq. (2.7) and is still sufficiently local for our purposes.

From the operator $A$ we use the unitary generators of time translation to form $A(x^0) = e^{iHx^0}Ae^{-iHx^0}$. In addition, a function $g(p^0)$ is defined so that, if $m$ is the smallest mass of the theory under consideration, $g(p^0) = 1/p_0^2$ if $|p^0| \geq m$ and, for $|p^0| \leq m$, $g(p^0)$ is chosen so as to be infinitely differentiable, even in $p^0$, and real. From this, the Fourier transform

$$g(x^0) = \int_{-\infty}^{\infty} \frac{dp^0}{2\pi} e^{-ip^0x^0} g(p^0)$$

is formed. Using the usual theorems of Fourier analysis, it follows that $g(x^0)$ decreases faster than any power of $1/x^0$ as $x^0 \to \infty$. Having made these definitions, we finally make the identification

$$B = \int_{-\infty}^{\infty} dx^0 g(x^0) A(x^0)$$

This is consistent with the previous assumptions about the behavior of $B$ since

$$\langle n|B|0 \rangle = \int_{-\infty}^{\infty} dx^0 g(x^0) \langle n|A(x^0)|0 \rangle$$

$$= \int_{-\infty}^{\infty} dx^0 \int_{-\infty}^{\infty} \frac{dp^0}{2\pi} g(p^0) e^{-i(p^0 - p^0{}_n)x^0} \langle n|A|0 \rangle$$

$$= \frac{1}{(p_n{}^0)^2} \langle n|A|0 \rangle$$

Because of current conservation, in order to demonstrate that

$$\lim_{R \to \infty} \langle 0|[Q_R(t), B]|0 \rangle$$

is independent of the time $t$, it is only necessary to show that

$$\lim_{R \to \infty} \langle 0| \left[ \int d^3x \, \boldsymbol{\nabla} \cdot \mathbf{j}(\mathbf{x}, t), B \right]|0 \rangle = 0$$

It is assumed that $A$ is confined to a space–time region of radius $L$ so that $A(t)$ is confined to a region of radius $L + |t|$. It is further convenient to decompose the function $g(x^0)$ into two continuous functions $g(x^0) = g_1{}^R(x^0) + g_2{}^R(x^0)$ so that $g_1(x^0) = 0$ if $|x^0| > R - L - |t|$ and where $g_2(x^0)$ has the property that, for each $n$,

$$\lim_{R \to \infty} (R - L - |t|)^n \|g_2{}^R\| = 0 \qquad (2.8)$$

where

$$\|g_2{}^R\| \equiv \int_{-\infty}^{\infty} dx^0 |g_2{}^R(x^0)|$$

Clearly, Eq. (2.8) is consistent with the extremely bounded behavior of $g(x^0)$ for large $x^0$. Now we find that

$$\lim_{R \to \infty} \left| \langle 0| \left[ \int_R d^3x \, \boldsymbol{\nabla} \cdot \mathbf{j}(\mathbf{x}, t), \int_{-\infty}^{\infty} dx^0 g(x^0) A(x^0) \right]|0 \rangle \right|$$

$$\leq \lim_{R \to \infty} 2\|g_2{}^R\| \, \|\langle 0| \int_R d^3x \, \boldsymbol{\nabla} \cdot \mathbf{j}\| \, \|A(x^0)\| \qquad (2.9)$$

Since $\|A(x^0)\| \equiv \sup \|A|a'\rangle\|$ is finite by assumption while we know that

$$\|g_2{}^R\| < 1/R^n \tag{2.10}$$

for any $n$ and large $R$, we will have the required result if it can be shown that $\|\langle 0| \int_R d^3x \boldsymbol{\nabla} \cdot \mathbf{j}\|$ is bounded by some power of $R$. It is quite easy to give an heuristic derivation of this. First, note that

$$\left\|\langle 0| \int_R d^3x \, \boldsymbol{\Delta} \cdot \mathbf{j}\right\| = \left|\langle 0| \int_R d^3x \, \boldsymbol{\nabla} \cdot \mathbf{j}(\mathbf{x}, t) \int_R d^3x' \, \boldsymbol{\nabla} \cdot \mathbf{j}(\mathbf{x}', t)|0\rangle\right|^{1/2}$$

Now, in this example, it is useful to introduce the type of smoothing function mentioned in reference (4) to make the identification

$$\int_R d^3x \, \boldsymbol{\nabla} \cdot \mathbf{j}(\mathbf{x}, t) \to \int_{-\infty}^{\infty} d^3x f_R(\mathbf{x}) \boldsymbol{\nabla} \cdot \mathbf{j}(\mathbf{x}, t)$$

We assume that $f_R(\mathbf{x})$ is differentiable and that $f_R(\mathbf{x}) = 0$ for $|\mathbf{x}| > R + \epsilon$ (see Fig. 1).

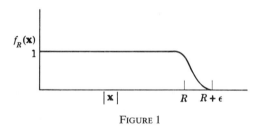

FIGURE 1

Using the fact that $\partial_\mu j^\mu(x) = 0$, the usual Lehmann representation shows that

$$\left\|\langle 0| \int_{-\infty}^{\infty} d^3x \, \boldsymbol{\nabla} \cdot \mathbf{j} f_R(\mathbf{x})\right\|$$
$$= \left|\int\int d^3x \, d^3x' f_R(\mathbf{x}) f_R(\mathbf{x}') \, \partial_0{}^2 \nabla^2 \Delta^{(+)}(x - x'; \kappa^2) B(\kappa) d\kappa^2\right|^{1/2}_{x^0 = x^{0'}}$$

In turn, we infer from this that

$$\left\|\langle 0| \int d^3x \, \boldsymbol{\nabla} \cdot \mathbf{j} f_R(\mathbf{x})\right\|$$
$$= \left|\frac{1}{2} \int \frac{d^3p}{(2\pi)^3} d^3x \, d^3x' e^{i\mathbf{p} \cdot (\mathbf{x} - \mathbf{x}')} \nabla f(\mathbf{x}) \cdot \nabla f(\mathbf{x}') \int d\kappa^2 \, (\mathbf{p}^2 + \kappa^2)^{1/2} B(\kappa)\right|^{1/2}$$

Since $f(\mathbf{x})$ is nonzero only for large values of $x \sim R$ as $R \to \infty$, the above integral only has contributions for $\mathbf{p}^2 \to 0$. Thus, we have

$$\left\| \langle 0| \int d^3x\, \boldsymbol{\nabla} \cdot \mathbf{j} f_R \right\| = \left| \frac{1}{2} \int d^3x (\boldsymbol{\nabla} f(x))^2 \int d\kappa^2\, \kappa B(\kappa) \right|^{\frac{1}{2}}$$

$$\sim \left[ \frac{2\pi R^2}{\epsilon} \int d\kappa^2\, \kappa B(\kappa) \right]^{\frac{1}{2}}$$

Assuming that $B(\kappa)$ is sufficiently bounded so the above integral exists and that $\epsilon \sim R$, we find $\| \langle 0| \int d^3x\, \boldsymbol{\nabla} \cdot \mathbf{j} f_R \| \sim R^{\frac{1}{2}}$. Inserting this into Eq. (2.9) and using Eq. (2.10), it follows that

$$\lim_{R \to \infty} \langle 0| \left[ \int_R d^3x\, \boldsymbol{\nabla} \cdot \mathbf{j}(\mathbf{x}, t), B \right] |0\rangle = 0$$

and, consequently, $\lim G_R = 0$. Thus, we have established that if $A$ is any localized operator and if the spectrum of the operator $j^0$ does not extend to zero, then

$$\langle 0| \left[ \int d^3x\, j^0(\mathbf{x}, t), B \right] |0\rangle = 0 \qquad (2.11)$$

in a causal theory. This is equivalent to the Goldstone theorem. Proceeding in exactly the same manner as before, it can be shown that the operator $\lim_{R \to \infty} \exp\{i\eta Q_R\}$ is unitary. Thus, through a somewhat more complicated (but basically identical) procedure, we have again established all the results proved with the classical formulation of the theorem.

To this point we have kept our discussion on a relatively abstract level and have not made direct contact with the local operators used for the quantitative calculations that have been performed in broken-symmetry theories. In these usually simple cases it is often assumed that $Q^i = \int d^3x\, j^{0i}(\mathbf{x}, t)$ are the generators of a Lie Group and that the local field operators $\phi^i(\mathbf{x}, t)$ form a representation of the group so that $i[Q^i, \phi^j(x)] = \sum f_{ijk} \phi^k(\mathbf{x}, t)$. The broken-symmetry assumption made is that

$$\langle 0|\phi^i(\mathbf{x}, t)|0\rangle = \langle 0|\phi^i(0)|0\rangle$$
$$= \eta^i \neq 0$$

for at least one $i$. The Goldstone theorem then asserts that there is a $\phi^i$ for which $\langle n|\phi^i|0\rangle \neq 0$ where $\langle n|$ is an excitation mode such that $\lim_{R \to 0} E_n(\mathbf{k}) = 0$. In a relativistic problem $E_n = (\mathbf{k}^2 + m^2)^{\frac{1}{2}}$ so one concludes that $m = 0$, that is, that massless particles with the quantum numbers of $\phi^l$ relative to the vacuum are present. In general, one would further anticipate that the propagator

$$G_{ll}(x, x') = i\langle 0|(\phi_l(x)\phi_l(x'))_+|0\rangle - i\langle 0|\phi_l(0)|0\rangle^2$$

has a pole in momentum space corresponding to this massless excitation. A third proof (historically, the second) of the Goldstone theorem, based on the occurrence of this pole at $p^2 = 0$ in the propagator, was given by Bludman and Klein.[11] Since its content is essentially the same as that of our previous proofs and it depends heavily on field theoretic detail not used there, we shall give it only cursory examination. It should be noted, however, that the methods used in deriving this theorem are very similar to those used in self-consistent calculation of Green's functions for broken-symmetry field theories. This will become apparent in Section VI.

Assume that the set of operators $\phi_i(\mathbf{x}, t)$ transform as an irreducible representation of the group generated by $Q_i$ and satisfy the field equation

$$(-\partial^2 + \mu_0{}^2)\phi_i = j_i + J_i$$

where $J_i$ is an external source. We assume that

$$\langle 0|\phi_i(\mathbf{x}, t)|0\rangle|_{J=0} = \eta_i \neq 0$$

so, for consistency, the above equation must satisfy the condition

$$\mu_0{}^2\langle 0|\phi_i|0\rangle|_{J=0} = \langle 0|j_i|0\rangle|_{J=0}$$

In addition, we define

$$\sum_\alpha [\lambda_\alpha Q_\alpha, \phi_j] = \sum_{\alpha,k} \lambda_\alpha f_{\alpha jk}\phi_k = \delta\phi_j$$

where $\lambda_\alpha$ is arbitrary. Applying this to the above field equation, we may write the vacuum expectation of the transformed equation as

$$\left[(-\partial^2 + \mu_0{}^2)\delta_{ij} - \frac{\delta\langle 0|j_i|0\rangle}{\delta\langle 0|\phi_j|0\rangle}\right]_{J=0} \langle 0|\delta\phi_j|0\rangle = 0$$

If $\langle 0|\delta\phi_j|0\rangle \neq 0$ for one index, $j'$ (in accord with the broken symmetry assumption), we must have

$$\mu_0{}^2\delta_{ij'} - \frac{\delta\langle 0|j_i|0\rangle}{\delta\langle 0|\phi_{j'}|0\rangle}\bigg|_{J=0} = 0 \qquad (2.12)$$

Now, using conventional techniques of quantum field theory, we find that the propagator of the field $\phi_i$ is given by

$$D_{ij}(x, x') = \frac{\delta\langle 0|\phi_i(x)|0\rangle}{\delta J_j(x')}\bigg|_{J=0}$$

which, in accord with the field equation, satisfies the momentum space equation

$$\left[\mu_0{}^2\delta_{ik} - \frac{\delta\langle 0|j_i|0\rangle}{\delta\langle 0|\phi_k|0\rangle}\right] D_{kl}(0) = \delta_{il} \qquad (2.13)$$

at $p^2 = 0$. Clearly, if $D_{kl}(p^2 \to 0) \to \infty$, as is the case if a zero mass excitation is present, then

$$\mu_0{}^2\delta_{ik} - \frac{\delta\langle 0|j_i|0\rangle}{\delta\langle 0|\phi_k|0\rangle} = 0 \qquad (2.14)$$

Thus Eqs. (2.12) and (2.14) are very similar and, in examining a particular problem we need only deduce from Eq. (2.12) when Eq. (2.14) is valid, to demonstrate the presence of a massless particle. The reader is referred to Bludman and Klein for examples.

Because the formulations discussed so far are not stated directly in terms of observable quantities but only vacuum expectations of operators, Streater[12] was led to formulate a corollary[13] of the Goldstone theorem in terms of the mass spectrum of the fields which form an irreducible representation of the group generated by $j^0{}_\alpha(x)$. For simplicity we confine ourselves to one conserved current $j^\mu(x)$ with time-independent charge operator $Q = \int d^3x\, j^0(x)$ and two fields, $\phi_1$ and $\phi_2$, such that $i[Q, \phi_1] = \phi_2$ and $i[Q, \phi_2] = -\phi_1$. With these assumptions it is possible to prove that if $\phi_1$ and $\phi_2$ excite particles of different mass $m_1$ and $m_2$, then $j^0(x)$ has a massless excitation in its spectrum. This can be directly generalized to show that if the two-point functions of $\phi_1$ and $\phi_2$ are not identical, then $j^0(x)$ excites a massless particle and, indeed, the same holds true if the whole excitation spectra of $\phi_1$ and $\phi_2$ are not identical. Starting with the proof for the two-point function, one notes

$$i[Q, \phi_1(x)\phi_2(x')] = \phi_2(x)\phi_2(x') - \phi_1(x)\phi_1(x')$$

from which it follows that

$$i\langle 0|[Q, \phi_1(x)\phi_2(x')]|0\rangle = \langle 0|\phi_2(x)\phi_2(x')|0\rangle - \langle 0|\phi_1(x)\phi_1(x')|0\rangle$$

Now, if for any value of $x$ and $x'$ the right-hand side does not vanish, it follows at once by the Goldstone theorem that $j^0(x)$ excites a massless particle. Further, it is clear that if the Lehmann spectral weights for the two Wightman functions on the right-hand side of the above equation are different for any value of the Lehmann weight parameter, then for some value of $x$ and $x'$ the right-hand side is nonvanishing and Streater's corollary follows. Note that the massless particle has the quantum numbers of $\phi_1 \phi_2$. The generalization of this is evident. Take any polynomial $\phi_{i_1} \phi_{i_2} \cdots \phi_{i_n}$ in the fields $\phi_1$ and $\phi_2$ and form

$$[Q, \phi_{i_1} \phi_{i_2} \cdots \phi_{i_n}] = \sum_{j=1}^{n} [Q, \phi_{i_j}] \phi_{i_1} \phi_{i_2} \cdots \phi_{i_{j-1}} \phi_{i_{j+1}} \cdots \phi_{i_n}$$

If

$$\langle 0 | [Q, \phi_{i_1} \phi_{i_2} \cdots \phi_{i_n}] | 0 \rangle \neq 0$$

it follows that $j^0(x)$ excites a massless particle and all the $n$th order Green's functions are not identical. Thus this corollary, which is easily generalized to include more complicated group structures, is clearly a straightforward application of the theorem as formulated in our previous discussions.

Finally, we wish to analyze in very direct terms the conditions under which the theorem need not apply. As stated previously, a manifestly Lorentz-invariant theory is locally causal, and there can be no failure of the theorem per se if the currents used to form the generators are actually conserved. We emphasize that this does not mean that the massless modes are physically observable. Thus, to see a failure we must examine theories which are not manifestly covariant. To indicate that the time component of a vector is now allowed to appear independently of whether or not the corresponding spatial components do, we introduce the vector $n^\mu = (0, 1)$. Then a straightforward analysis[14] with $\partial_\mu j^\mu(x) = 0$ shows that the Fourier transform of $\langle 0 | [j^\mu(x), \phi(0)] | 0 \rangle$ has the form

$$[A + B\epsilon(k^0)]k^\mu \delta(k^2) + Cn^\mu \delta(\mathbf{k})\delta(n \cdot k)$$
$$+ [k^\mu(n \cdot k) - n^\mu k^2]D + En^\mu \delta(n \cdot k)$$

where $A$ and $B$ are functions of $n \cdot k$, $E$ of $k^2$, and $D$ of both variables. If the term proportional to $k^\mu \delta(k^2)$ were the only one present, as in the case of manifestly covariant theories, the Goldstone theorem would hold and there would be no difficulties. Historically, the term proportional to $C$ was first held responsible for the nonrelativistic "failures" of the Goldstone theorem.[15] However, this is not the case, inasmuch as such a term represents an isolated state that might be interpreted as a transition between the various possible vacuum states which are implied by the broken symmetry. The fact that such a state is not a limit of a branch of the excitation spectrum as $\mathbf{k}$ tends to zero rules out this term as indicated by Eq. (2.4). That it is not relevant can be seen in a rather direct fashion by noting that, in general, the equation

$$\langle 0|[j^0(x), \phi(x')]|0\rangle|_{x^0 = x^{0'}} \sim \delta(\mathbf{x} - \mathbf{x}')$$

must be valid, but

$$\int dk \, e^{ik(x - x')} Cn^0 \delta(\mathbf{k}) \delta(n \cdot k)|_{x^0 = x^{0'}} = C$$

Thus the term proportional to $C$ does not have the correct structure and no escape from the Goldstone theorem can occur in this manner. The term proportional to $E$ has an unconventional spectral behavior but cannot be ruled out on general principles. Its presence, however, provides no contradiction to the assumptions of the theorem. The term proportional to $D$ is the important one inasmuch as it appears by explicit calculation in radiation gauge electrodynamics. It must be realized, however, that in no sense should it be related to the spurions of the type implied by $C$. Structures of the form $D \sim \delta(k^0)$ are unable to contribute, so they cannot be responsible for the nonvanishing of the Goldstone commutator. Consequently, if $D$ is to contribute and have a normal, well-defined spectral structure, we have

$$D(\mathbf{k} \to 0) \sim \int_{m^2 > 0} dm^2 \, \sigma(m^2) \delta(k_0^2 - m^2)$$

From this it follows at once that

$$\frac{d}{dt} \langle 0|\left[\int d^3x \, j^0(\mathbf{x}, t), \phi(x')\right]|0\rangle \neq 0$$

Thus the theory is not sufficiently causal to allow the term

$$\lim_{V \to \infty} \langle 0|\left[\int_{\sigma(V)} d\sigma_k \, j^{k0}(\mathbf{x}, t), \phi(x')\right]|0\rangle$$

to vanish and the assumptions used to prove the theorem are not valid. We will discuss this behavior in depth through several examples in the following sections.

## III. Naturally Occurring Broken Symmetries

In recent years a considerable insight into some of the more tractable problems associated with broken symmetries has been acquired through the study of theories which possess a rather remarkable set of gauge properties. Characteristic of such theories is their invariance under a class of $c$-number gauge transformations, the existence of which allows one to demonstrate the occurrence of a zero mass particle without any reference to a broken symmetry or the precise details of the dynamics. These massless quanta will generally be referred to in this work as naturally occurring[16,17] to distinguish them from their counterparts in theories which display a spontaneous breakdown of symmetry. Although the existence of zero mass particles in both types of theories may be inferred from a broken-symmetry condition, it can be shown that in the former case this approach invariably turns out to be merely another way of imposing a particular invariance property on the relevant Lagrangian. Since the usual procedure employed in broken-symmetry calculations appears to somewhat obscure the relative simplicity of systems whose massless boson excitation follows purely from gauge invariance arguments, it is our intention in the subsequent discussion of various field theoretical models to emphasize this crucial role of gauge invariance by displaying first the zero mass particle implied by the relevant Lagrangian and only then proceeding to demonstrate the possibility of constructing an associated broken symmetry. This procedure contrasts, of course, with that which has customarily been employed in the more conjectural domain of spontaneous symmetry breaking where one generally postulates at the outset a broken symmetry condition and subsequently deduces the associated zero mass particle implied by the Goldstone theorem. Since there is neither any *a priori* reason for assuming the internal consistency of these constraints expressing the spontaneous breaking of the symmetry (a point to be discussed more fully in Sect. VII) nor a dynamical mechanism for the massless boson, it is appropriate that this study of possible applications of the Goldstone theorem should begin with a consideration of massless particles of the naturally occurring variety. Despite the somewhat trivial nature of this type of broken symmetry, there is a considerable amount of contact with the features characteristic of the more general problem, while at the same time one has the advantage of being able to avoid some of the difficult consistency questions peculiar to spontaneous symmetry breaking.

In order to fix ideas more firmly, we consider as the simplest example of a naturally occurring massless particle a free spin-zero Hermitian field. We make use of the well-known result that a second-order differential equation can always be reduced to two first-order equations and thus describe this field by the vector $\phi^\mu(x)$ with the scalar $\phi(x)$. This leads to the Lagrangian density

$$\mathcal{L} = \phi^\mu \partial_\mu \phi + \tfrac{1}{2}\phi^\mu \phi_\mu - \tfrac{1}{2}\mu_0{}^2 \phi^2 \tag{3.1}$$

which for the case $\mu_0{}^2 = 0$ is readily seen to be invariant under the constant gauge transformation

$$\phi \to \phi + \eta \tag{3.2}$$

This invariance is, of course, equivalent to the local conservation law

$$\partial_\mu \phi^\mu = 0$$

a result which formally leads to the conclusion that the operator

$$Q = \int \phi^0(x)\, d^3x$$

is conserved and the generator of the transformation (3.2). It is indeed true that (3.2) is unitarily implementable in any finite volume $\Omega$ and that the operator

$$Q_\Omega = \int_\Omega \phi^0(x)\, d^3x$$

by virtue of the commutation relation

$$[\phi^0(x), \phi(x')]\delta(x^0 - x^{0'}) = -i\delta(x - x') \tag{3.3}$$

is the generator of Eq. (3.2) in $\Omega$, i.e.,

$$U_\Omega(\eta)\phi(x)U_\Omega{}^+(\eta) = \phi(x) + \eta$$

where

$$U_\Omega(\eta) = \exp\{i\eta Q_\Omega\}$$

The unitarity of the operator $U_\Omega(\eta)$ clearly implies the equivalence of the Hilbert spaces constructed on the two states $\langle 0|$ and $\langle 0|U_\Omega(\eta)$. To state this somewhat differently, since $\phi^0(x)$ and $\phi(x)$ are a complete set of operators, any state constructed from these operators and the state $\langle 0|U_\Omega(\eta)$ can be expanded in terms of the complete set of states generated by the same set of operators acting on the vacuum $\langle 0|$. Thus the set of states constructed on $\langle 0|U_\Omega(\eta)$ may be said to provide a representation of the canonical commutation relations which is fully equivalent to that constructed on $\langle 0|$. However, as has already been observed in the preceding chapter, in the limit $\Omega \to \infty$ such a result no longer obtains. This may be seen by a review of the simple calculation[18] performed in Section II of the norm of the state

$$|Q\rangle \equiv \lim_{\Omega \to \infty} Q_\Omega|0\rangle$$

Since $\lim_{\Omega \to \infty} Q_\Omega$ is translationally invariant, so also is $|Q\rangle$. Thus,

$$\langle Q|Q\rangle = \langle Q| \int_{\Omega \to \infty} \phi^0(x)\, d^3x|0\rangle$$
$$= \int d^3x \langle Q|\phi^0(0)|0\rangle$$

so that $\langle Q|Q\rangle$ is either zero or infinite. However, the first alternative implies

$$\int d^3x \phi^0(x)|0\rangle = 0$$

in contradiction with the canonical commutation relation (3.3), whereas the second implies that $\lim_{\Omega \to \infty} Q_\Omega$ cannot be defined on the vacuum. The net result of this discussion is that $U_{\Omega \to \infty}(\eta)$ does not exist and consequently the set of states constructed on $\langle 0|U_\infty(\eta)$ provides a representation of the canonical commutation relations which is inequivalent to that constructed on $\langle 0|$.

The inequivalence of these representations can be made somewhat more transparent by using the usual decomposition into creation and annihilation operators. Thus we write

$$\phi(x) = \int \frac{d^3k}{(2\pi)^{3/2}} \frac{1}{(2\omega)^{1/2}} [a(\mathbf{k})\, e^{ikx} + a^*(\mathbf{k})\, e^{-ikx}]$$
$$\phi^0(x) = -i \int \frac{d^3k}{(2\pi)^{1/2}} \left(\frac{\omega}{2}\right)^{1/2} [a(\mathbf{k})\, e^{ikx} - a^*(\mathbf{k})\, e^{-ikx}]$$
(3.4)

where $a(\mathbf{k})$ and $a^+(\mathbf{k})$ satisfy the usual commutation relations

$$[a(\mathbf{k}), a^*(\mathbf{k}')] = \delta(\mathbf{k} - \mathbf{k}')$$
$$[a(\mathbf{k}), a(\mathbf{k}')] = [a^*(\mathbf{k}), a^*(\mathbf{k}')] = 0$$
(3.5)

and we choose that representation of the commutation relations for which

$$a(\mathbf{k})|0\rangle = 0 \tag{3.6}$$

Since the field $\phi(x)$ has only a zero mass particle in its spectrum, the state formally defined by $\langle 0|U_\infty(\eta)$ can conveniently be viewed as a coherent superposition of states containing various numbers of zero-momentum, zero-energy quanta. In terms of the operators $a(\mathbf{k})$ and $a^*(\mathbf{k})$ these states can be written as

$$\langle a'| = \langle 0| \exp\{a'^*a(0) - a^*(0)a'\}$$

thereby implying the broken-symmetry conditions

$$\langle a'|a(\mathbf{k})|a'\rangle = a'\delta(\mathbf{k})$$
$$\langle a'|a^*(\mathbf{k})|a'\rangle = a'^*\delta(\mathbf{k})$$

One can see more precisely the necessary inequivalence of the Hilbert spaces based on $\langle 0|$ and $\langle a'|$ in the limit $\Omega \to \infty$ upon performing the quantization of $\phi(x)$ in a box of volume $\Omega$ rather than the infinite volume implied by Eqs. (3.4) and (3.5). Using the identity

$$e^{A+B} = e^A e^B e^{-\frac{1}{2}[A,B]}$$

for $[A, B]$ a $c$-number, it then follows that

$$\langle 0|a'\rangle = \exp\left[-\frac{1}{2}\frac{a'a'^*}{(2\pi)^3}\int_\Omega d^3x\right]$$

which clearly displays the orthogonality of the states $\langle 0|$ and $\langle a'|$ in the limit $\Omega \to \infty$. Since it requires only a trivial generalization to show that any state in the Hilbert space constructed on $\langle 0|$ is orthogonal to $\langle a'|$, one has the result that the Hilbert spaces corresponding to different values of $a'$ are all mutually orthogonal.

Having now displayed some of the mathematical complications associated with the implementation of the gauge group of the massless scalar field, it is well to emphasize here that the importance of the inequivalent representations of the canonical commutation relations is by no means confined to this particular example but is an essential ingredient of any broken symmetry, independent of whether it is of the naturally occurring or spontaneous variety. Since the basic characteristic of a broken symmetry is the noninvariance of the vacuum under the operations of the group, it follows in complete analogy to the massless scalar field that the generators of the group acting on the vacuum must lead to a state of infinite norm, i.e., they take one out of the original Hilbert space. Provided that these important features are kept in mind, it is instructive to formally construct, from the original vacuum, the new vacuum states

$$\langle \eta | = \langle 0 | U_\infty(\eta)$$

for which one derives the broken symmetry condition

$$\langle \eta | \phi(x) | \eta \rangle = \eta \tag{3.7}$$

The relation (3.7) may, of course, be viewed without any reference to an operator construction as a statement of the existence of other vacuum states $\langle \eta |$ (i.e., null eigenstates of $P^\mu$) for which Eq. (3.6) fails to hold. Thus the general characteristic of naturally occurring broken symmetries arises from the possibility of replacing Eq. (3.6) by

$$a(\mathbf{k}) | \eta \rangle = \eta | \eta \rangle \delta(\mathbf{k})(2\pi)^{3/2}(\tfrac{1}{2}\omega)^{1/2} \tag{3.8}$$

which by Eq. (3.4) insures that

$$\langle \eta | \phi(x) | \eta \rangle = \eta$$

Although the existence of such a representation is obviously in no way dependent upon the specific dynamics, the states $| \eta \rangle$ can be identified with the physical vacuum only for a special class of theories. Thus for the case of a free field whose equation of motion is of the form

$$(-\partial^2 + \mu_0{}^2)\phi(x) = 0$$

the consistency condition

$$\mu_0{}^2 \langle \eta | \phi(x) | \eta \rangle = 0$$

is clearly compatible with Eq. (3.7) only for the case of vanishing bare mass.

It may be somewhat instructive to consider at this point some general properties of the vacuum expectation values associated with this massless scalar field. Upon application of the field equations one is readily led to the conclusion that this theory is undefined only to the extent that it does not contain any prescription for the calculation of the expectation value of the field operator. Although the equations of motion and the canonical commutation relations enable one to express the time-ordered product of an arbitrary number of such operators in terms of the vacuum expectation value of $\phi(x)$, this latter number must remain completely undetermined. However, one can consistently choose it to be any real number merely by recognizing the fact that Eq. (3.8) defines an infinite number of inequivalent representations of the commutation relations, each of which corresponds to a different numerical value of $\langle 0|\phi(x)|0\rangle$. Although the class (3.8) by no means includes all possible representations,[19] it is sufficiently general to allow a complete discussion of the naturally occurring type of broken symmetry.

Thus far the only explicit example of a broken-symmetry theory which has been discussed in this section has consisted of a free field. However, it is not to be concluded from the considerable emphasis which it has received here that the free field is the only mathematically well-defined, broken-symmetry theory. In fact, of the two field equations

$$\partial_\mu \phi^\mu = 0 \tag{3.9}$$

$$\phi^\mu = -\partial^\mu \phi \tag{3.10}$$

implied by Eq. (3.1) only the first is relevant to the construction of the broken symmetry.[17] That this is indeed a sufficient condition becomes apparent upon recalling that the application of the Goldstone theorem requires only the existence of a conserved current such that the equal-time commutator of the fourth component with some other operator of the theory has a nonvanishing expectation value. Thus the conservation law [Eq. (3.9)] along with the commutation relation [Eq. (3.3)] immediately leads to the existence of a massless particle for any Lagrangian of the form

$$\mathscr{L} = \phi^\mu\,\partial_\mu\phi + \tfrac{1}{2}\phi^\mu\phi_\mu + \mathscr{L}'(\phi^\mu) \tag{3.11}$$

where $\mathscr{L}'(\phi^\mu)$ does not contain $\phi(x)$. To carry out the explicit construction one computes

$$\langle 0|[\phi^\mu(x), \phi(0)]|0\rangle$$

which is readily found from Eqs. (3.3) and (3.9) to have the form

$$-\partial^\mu \Delta(x, 0)$$

where

$$\Delta(x, \mu^2) = 2\pi \int \frac{dp}{(2\pi)^4}\, e^{ipx}\epsilon(p^0)\delta(p^2 + \mu^2)$$

A Goldstone theorem of this type is thus based on the elements $\phi^0$, $\phi$, and 1 of the canonical group. The essential point here which distinguishes this case from theories which display a spontaneous symmetry breakdown is that the commutator is proportional to unity (which necessarily has a nonvanishing expectation value) and therefore the consistency of requiring the nonvanishing of the equal time commutator is assured.

As an example of one of the simpler Lagrangians of the form of (3.11), we consider the system[17] described by

$$\mathcal{L} = \phi^\mu \, \partial_\mu \phi + \tfrac{1}{2}\phi^\mu \phi_\mu + \phi^{\mu\prime} \, \partial_\mu \phi^\prime + \tfrac{1}{2}\phi^{\mu\prime} \phi_\mu^\prime + \tfrac{1}{2}\mu_0^2\phi^{\prime 2} + \lambda\phi^\mu \phi_\mu^\prime$$

In addition to the conservation law $\partial_\mu \phi^\mu = 0$ implied by the invariance under

$$\phi \to \phi + \eta$$

one has the equations of motion

$$\phi^\mu = -\partial^\mu \phi - \lambda\phi^{\mu\prime}$$
$$\partial_\mu \phi^{\mu\prime} = -\mu_0^2\phi^\prime$$
$$\phi^{\mu\prime} = -\partial^\mu \phi^\prime - \lambda\phi^\mu$$

These can be readily shown to yield for the Green's functions

$$G(x) = i\langle 0|(\phi(x)\phi(0))_+|0\rangle$$
$$G^\prime(x) = i\langle 0|(\phi^\prime(x)\phi^\prime(0))_+|0\rangle$$

the momentum space representation

$$G(p) = \frac{1 - \lambda^2}{p^2} + \frac{\lambda^2}{p^2 + \mu_0^2}$$

$$G^\prime(p) = \frac{1}{p^2 + \mu_0^2} \tag{3.12}$$

thus explicitly confirming the existence of the massless particle implied by the invariance of the theory under $c$-number translation of $\phi(x)$.

It is clear from the form of Eq. (3.12) that the restriction $\lambda^2 \leq 1$ is essential to preserve the positive definite metric of the Hilbert space and that the limiting value $\lambda^2 = 1$ (corresponding to $Z = 0$) corresponds to the disappearance of the massless particle from the spectrum of $\phi(x)$. However, this latter limit is a rather delicate one, as is shown by a calculation of the two-point function of the field $\phi^{\mu}(x)$. One finds that the residue at the zero-mass pole of this latter function diverges as $(1 - \lambda^2)^{-1}$, a result which is in fact essential to the consistency of the canonical commutation relations. The fact that the massless particle appears in the spectrum of $\phi^{\mu}(x)$ rather than $\phi(x)$ in the limit is of some importance in itself if one considers the possibility of including less trivial interactions consistent with (3.11). If, for example, such couplings allow the $Z = 0$ limit, it is nonetheless true that $\phi^{\mu}$, in accord with the Goldstone theorem, will create massless quanta. Since it is $\phi^{\mu}$ rather than $\phi$ which appears in the coupling terms, these quanta will therefore be physical particles rather than mere gauge excitations. This result could be of some significance inasmuch as it suggests that one can anticipate considerable difficulty in attempting to decouple the unwanted massless particles which invariably occur in broken-symmetry models of elementary particles.

Because of the appreciable extent to which a number of soluble field theoretical examples of symmetry breaking have recently been investigated, we shall for the moment defer a discussion of some of the less trivial applications of naturally occurring zero mass particles in order to direct attention to these various models. It is our intent to show that, regardless of the context in which they have been considered, these models are all basically of the naturally occurring type. Although this may not be particularly obvious from an inspection of the relevant Lagrangian, it is useful to carry out this demonstration in order to sharpen the distinction between the two fundamental types of broken-symmetry theories.

One manner in which the relation of a broken-symmetry theory to the $c$-number translation group has been somewhat obscured is due to a frequently used, though basically irrelevant, increase in the number of degrees of freedom of the canonical fields. Thus, while it has been emphasized here that the existence of such a gauge group implies a Goldstone theorem based on the elements of the canonical group, this may be considerably less apparent if one constructs the argument using the conserved current operator implied by the introduction of additional degree of freedom. If, for example, one generalizes (3.1) with $\mu_0^2 = 0$ to the case of a free field described by $\phi_i(x)$ ($i = 1, 2$), the Lagrangian is invariant under

$$\phi(x) \rightarrow (1 + iq\delta\lambda)\phi(x) \tag{3.13}$$

the matrix $q$ in the two-dimensional charge space being given by

$$q = \begin{bmatrix} 0 & -i \\ i & 0 \end{bmatrix}$$

so that the operator

$$j^\mu = i\phi^\mu q\phi$$

is a conserved current. However, despite the fact that a consistent Goldstone theorem can be constructed using the equal-time commutator

$$\langle \eta | \left[ \int j^0(x')\, d^3x', \, \phi(x) \right] | \eta \rangle = q \langle \eta | \phi(x) | \eta \rangle$$
$$= q\eta \qquad (3.14)$$

it is somewhat misleading to assert that the symmetry generated by

$$Q = \int j^0(x)\, d^3x$$

has been broken. Though formally true, such a statement is merely a trivial consequence of the existence (in a finite volume) of a generator of the transformation

$$\phi \rightarrow \phi + \eta$$

This can be clarified (at the expense of some mathematical rigor) by using the ill-defined operators $U_\infty(\eta)$ relating the different vacuums to write Eq. (3.14) in the form

$$\langle 0 | U_\infty(\eta)[Q, \phi(x)]U_\infty{}^+(\eta)|0\rangle = \langle 0 | [Q, \phi(x)]|0\rangle$$
$$+ i\langle 0 | \left[ \int d^3x' \phi^0(x')q\eta, \, \phi(x) \right]|0\rangle$$
$$= q\eta + q\langle 0|\phi|0\rangle$$

a result which emphasizes the fact that the broken symmetry is supported by the generators $\phi^0$, $\phi$, and 1 of the canonical group rather than the corresponding elements of the gauge group of (3.13).

Another point which frequently leads to some confusion concerning broken-symmetry solutions in soluble models arises from the possibility that the invariances of a given Lagrangian under field translation may be considerably less than obvious. However, as has already been emphasized, this in no way alters the basic fact that the broken symmetry supported by such a system is of the naturally occurring variety. Perhaps the simplest example of a theory of this type (in which the invariance is only thinly disguised) is a slight variation of a model considered by Hellman and Roman.[20] It is described by the Lagrangian

$$\mathcal{L} = \phi^\mu \, \partial_\mu \phi + \tfrac{1}{2}\phi^\mu \phi_\mu - \tfrac{1}{2}\mu_0^2 \phi^2 - \tfrac{1}{2}g\phi q'\phi \tag{3.15}$$

where $\phi(x)$ is again a two-component Hermitian field and

$$q' = \begin{bmatrix} 0 & 1 \\ 1 & 0 \end{bmatrix}$$

Although this theory clearly does not possess an invariance under $\phi \to \phi + \eta$, the field equation

$$(-\partial^2 + \mu_0^2 + gq')\phi = 0 \tag{3.16}$$

shows that

$$\langle 0|\phi(x)|0\rangle \neq 0$$

is consistent provided that

$$\mu_0^4 = g^2 \tag{3.17}$$

This, of course, allows the two choices $\pm\mu_0^2$ for $g$, the significance of these roots being best displayed by a diagonalization of $q'$. Defining

$$\phi^{(+)} = (2)^{-\frac{1}{2}}(\phi_1 + \phi_2)$$
$$\phi^{(-)} = (2)^{-\frac{1}{2}}(\phi_1 - \phi_2)$$

the equation of motion [Eq. (3.16)] becomes

$$(-\partial^2 + \mu_0^2 \pm g)\phi^{(\pm)} = 0$$

a result which shows that the two values $\mu_0^2$ and $-\mu_0^2$ correspond respectively to the vanishing of the bare mass of the fields $\phi^{(-)}$ and $\phi^{(+)}$. Thus for the case $g = \mu_0^2$ the Lagrangian is invariant under

$$\phi^{(-)} \to \phi^{(-)} + \eta$$

and for $g = -\mu_0^2$ one has the corresponding invariance under

$$\phi^{(+)} \to \phi^{(+)} + \eta$$

This conclusion can, of course, be reached in a somewhat different manner by directly considering the change induced in the Lagrangian by

$$\phi_{1,2} \to \phi_{1,2} + \eta_{1,2}$$

Thus one finds

$$\delta\mathscr{L} = -\mu_0^2(\eta_1\phi_1 + \eta_2\phi_2 + \tfrac{1}{2}\eta_1^2 + \tfrac{1}{2}\eta_2^2) - g(\phi_1\eta_2 + \phi_2\eta_1 + \eta_1\eta_2)$$

which clearly vanishes for

$$\eta_1\mu_0^2 = -g\eta_2$$
$$\eta_2\mu_0^2 = -g\eta_1$$

whence

$$\mu_0^4 = g^2$$
$$\eta_1^2 = \eta_2^2$$

in agreement with Eq. (3.17).

It is, of course, possible to introduce some additional complexities into the two-field system described by (3.15) without in any way altering our general results. In particular one can consider a more general mass matrix and thus replace Eq. (3.15) by

$$\mathscr{L} = \phi^\mu \, \partial_\mu\phi + \tfrac{1}{2}\phi^\mu\phi_\mu - \tfrac{1}{2}g\phi q'\phi - \tfrac{1}{2}\mu_1^2\phi_1^2 - \tfrac{1}{2}\mu_2^2\phi_2^2 \quad (3.18)$$

In this case the field equations

$$(-\partial^2 + \mu_1^2)\phi_1 = -g\phi_2$$
$$(-\partial^2 + \mu_2^2)\phi_2 = -g\phi_1$$

imply that the condition

$$\langle 0|\phi_i(x)|0\rangle \neq 0$$

is consistent only for

$$\mu_1^2\mu_2^2 = g^2 \quad (3.19)$$

Although one could once again diagonalize the mass term in the Lagrangian, it is somewhat simpler in the present case to calculate the lowest order Green's function. For the field $\phi_1(x)$ one finds the momentum space representation

$$G^{-1}(p) = p^2 + \mu_1^2 - \frac{g^2}{p^2 + \mu_2^2}$$

which has zeros at

$$-p^2 = \frac{\mu_1^2 + \mu_2^2}{2} \pm \left[\left(\frac{\mu_1^2 - \mu_2^2}{2}\right)^2 + g^2\right]^{1/2}$$

Upon inclusion of the constraint (3.19) one finds that the propagator has a pole at zero as well as $\mu_1{}^2 + \mu_2{}^2$. Since the $\phi_i(x)$ are still free fields, however, it clearly must be possible to rewrite (3.18) as the sum of two free-particle Lagrangians of masses zero and $\mu_1{}^2 + \mu_2{}^2$ and to thus determine a conservation law corresponding to the zero mass particle. Choosing the root $g = \pm \mu_1 \mu_2$ of Eq. (3.19) and using the equations

$$\partial_\mu \phi_1{}^\mu = -\mu_1{}^2 \phi_1 - g\phi_2$$
$$\partial_\mu \phi_2{}^\mu = -\mu_2{}^2 \phi_2 - g\phi_1$$

one readily deduces that

$$\partial_\mu(\mu_2 \phi_1{}^\mu \mp \mu_1 \phi_2{}^\mu) = 0$$

thereby establishing the existence of the $c$-number translation group

$$\mu_2 \phi_1 \mp \mu_1 \phi_2 \rightarrow \mu_2 \phi_1 \mp \mu_1 \phi_2 + \eta$$

associated with the massless free field part of (3.18).

Although there is, in principle, no limit to the number of additional complexities one can introduce into the study of the broken symmetries associated with a finite number of coupled free fields, it is easy to convince oneself that there are no real conceptual advances to be derived from any of these generalizations. On the other hand, the case in which the number of such fields is allowed to become infinite, while not requiring any substantially new techniques, has been the subject of such considerable interest in this application as to merit a somewhat detailed discussion. We refer, of course, to the well-known Zachariasen model[21] which, despite its relatively simple structure, has in recent years proved to be an invaluable tool of the theoretical physicist in the testing of some of the new techniques employed in particle physics. Although this model was first discovered in the context of dispersion theory, it was subsequently shown by Thirring[22] that there is an alternative formulation within the framework of Lagrangian field theory, and it is, of course, this latter approach which provides the basis for a broken-symmetry application. It is to be emphasized at the outset that the Lagrangian of this theory includes only bilinear coupling terms and as such consists only of free fields. The fact that a nontrivial $S$-matrix can be defined for the Zachariasen model is a direct consequence of the introduction of a continuum of fields into the Lagrangian and therefore should not be taken to imply any deep physical content in the theory.

Although many authors have considered the model to provide a "reasonable" approximation to Yukawa and quartic boson interactions, this is a highly conjectural view and completely irrelevant to its application as a broken-symmetry theory. We shall therefore be content to show that the Zachariasen model can support a naturally occurring type of broken symmetry[23] at the same time completely avoiding any reference to its possible value as an approximation to a less trivial theory.

The Zachariasen model can be conveniently described as a theory in which the interaction of a $B$ particle with $A\bar{A}$ pairs is restricted by the important condition that the $A$ and $\bar{A}$ particles only be created in pairs. Because of this latter feature (i.e., the absence of an asymptotic condition for the $A$ particles), a Lagrangian formulation of the theory requires that $A\bar{A}$ pairs be described by a single field operator with a continuous mass parameter. This result is made more transparent upon observing that if one restricts a more conventional type of field theory which contains an $A$ particle in the manner described here, then the free Green's function $G_0(x)$ never appears alone but always in the combination $G_0^2(x)$. One thus need only refer to the identity

$$G_0^2(x, M_A) = \int_{4M_A^2}^{\infty} ds f^2(s) G_0(x, s) \qquad (3.20)$$

where

$$f^2(s) = \frac{1}{16\pi^2} \left(\frac{s - 4M_A^2}{s}\right)^{1/2}$$

and

$$G_0(p, s) = \frac{1}{p^2 + s}$$

to show the equivalence to a theory in which the interaction is mediated by a continuous mass field. It must be remarked that since $f^2(s)$ asymptotically approaches a constant, the integral in Eq. (3.20) does not really exist. However, this fact merely reflects the well-known, self-energy divergence and is completely irrelevant within the context of the present application. All the essential features of the model are retained upon replacing $f(s)$ by a function which vanishes sufficiently rapidly at infinity; we therefore freely assume such a regularization in the subsequent discussion.

One can now proceed to write the Lagrangian describing the interaction between the $B$ particle and the $A\bar{A}$ pairs [associated, respectively, with the fields $\phi(x)$ and $\phi(x, s)$] in the form

$$\mathscr{L} = \phi^\mu\, \partial_\mu\phi + \tfrac{1}{2}\phi^\mu\phi_\mu - \tfrac{1}{2}\mu_0{}^2\phi^2 + \int_{4M_A{}^2}^\infty ds\{\phi^\mu(s)\,\partial_\mu\phi(s) + \tfrac{1}{2}\phi^\mu(s)\phi_\mu(s)$$

$$- \tfrac{1}{2}s\phi^2(s)\} + g_0\phi \int_{4M_A{}^2}^\infty ds f(s)\phi(s) \tag{3.21}$$

The equations of motion implied by (3.21),

$$(-\partial^2 + \mu_0{}^2)\phi(x) = g_0 \int_{4M_A{}^2}^\infty ds f(s)\phi(x, s)$$

$$(-\partial^2 + s)\phi(x, s) = g_0 f(s)\phi(x)$$

together with the only nonvanishing equal-time commutation relations

$$[\partial_0\phi(x), \phi(x')] = -i\delta(\mathbf{x} - \mathbf{x}')$$
$$[\partial_0\phi(x, s), \phi(x', s')] = -i\delta(\mathbf{x} - \mathbf{x}')\delta(s - s')$$

yield a set of coupled integral equations for the Green's functions

$$G(x) = i\langle 0|(\phi(x)\phi(0))_+|0\rangle$$
$$G(x; s, s') = i\langle 0|(\phi(x, s)\phi(x', s'))_+|0\rangle$$

These integral equations can be solved by elementary techniques to yield the momentum space representation

$$G(p) = \left[p^2 + \mu_0{}^2 - g_0{}^2 \int_{4M_A{}^2}^\infty ds\, \frac{f^2(s)}{p^2 + s}\right]^{-1} \tag{3.22}$$

$$G(p; s, s') = \frac{\delta(s - s')}{p^2 + s} + g_0{}^2 \frac{f(s)}{p^2 + s}\, G(p)\, \frac{f(s')}{p^2 + s'}$$

Since it is usual to require the existence of a stable particle of mass $\mu$ in the theory, we set

$$\mu_0{}^2 = \mu^2 + g_0{}^2 \int_{4M_A{}^2}^\infty ds\, \frac{f^2(s)}{s - \mu^2} \tag{3.23}$$

which, upon insertion in Eq. (3.22), yields the once-subtracted form of the propagator

$$G(p) = (p^2 + \mu^2)^{-1} \left[1 + g_0{}^2 \int_{4M_A{}^2}^\infty ds\, \frac{f^2(s)}{(p^2 + s)(s - \mu^2)}\right]^{-1}$$

In addition to this formal mass renormalization procedure one can carry out the corresponding coupling constant renormalization by introducing the definitions

$$Z_3{}^{-1} = 1 + g_0{}^2 \int_{4M_A{}^2}^{\infty} ds \, \frac{f^2(s)}{(s - \mu^2)^2}$$

and

$$g^2 = Z_3 g_0{}^2$$

by means of which one writes the convenient alternative form for $G(p; s, s')$,

$$G(p; s, s') = \frac{\delta(s - s')}{p^2 + s} + \frac{g^2}{p^2 + \mu^2} \frac{f(s)}{p^2 + s}$$

$$\times \frac{1}{Z_3 + g^2 \displaystyle\int_{4M_A{}^2}^{\infty} ds \, \frac{f^2(s)}{(p^2 + s)(s - \mu^2)}} \frac{f(s')}{p^2 + s'}$$

Since the field $\phi(x, s)$ creates $A\bar{A}$ pairs, the $A\bar{A}$ scattering amplitude is readily extracted from $G(p; s, s')$ by straightforward techniques, thereby yielding the result

$$e^{i\delta} \sin \delta = \pi \frac{g^2}{p^2 + \mu^2} f^2(-p^2) \left[ Z_3 + g^2 \int_{4M_A{}^2}^{\infty} \frac{f^2(s) \, ds}{(p^2 + s)(s - \mu^2)} \right]^{-1}$$

$$= \pi \frac{g^2}{p^2 + \mu^2} f^2(-p^2) \left[ 1 - (p^2 + \mu^2) g^2 \int_{4M_A{}^2}^{\infty} ds \, \frac{f^2(s)}{(s - \mu^2)^2 (p^2 + s)} \right]^{-1}$$

which we note contains no reference whatever to unrenormalized quantities.

With this brief summary of the solution as obtained by direct application of the equations of motion, one can now proceed to examine the possibility of a broken symmetry approach to the model by imposing on the solution the constraint

$$\langle 0|\phi(x)|0 \rangle = \eta \neq 0$$

It follows immediately that the equations of motion require the consistency conditions

$$\mu_0{}^2 \langle 0|\phi(x)|0 \rangle = g_0 \int_{4M_A{}^2}^{\infty} ds f(s) \langle 0|\phi(x, s)|0 \rangle \tag{3.24}$$

$$s \langle 0|\phi(x, s)|0 \rangle = g_0 f(s) \langle 0|\phi(x)|0 \rangle \tag{3.25}$$

the first of which may be eliminated in favor of the equation

$$\mu_0{}^2 = g_0{}^2 \int_{4M_A{}^2}^{\infty} ds \frac{f^2(s)}{s} \, ds \tag{3.26}$$

Thus the broken symmetry implies a relation [Eq. (3.25)] between $\langle 0|\phi(x)|0\rangle$ and $\langle 0|\phi(x, s)|0\rangle$ as well as a condition [Eq. (3.26)] on the parameters of the theory. It is furthermore obvious upon comparison with Eq. (3.23) that the broken-symmetry solution of the model is merely a particular solution which is derivable from Eq. (3.22) by choosing the bare mass $\mu_0^2$ in accord with Eq. (3.26). The broken-symmetry condition serves only to ensure the existence of the required zero-mass particle and, as is invariably the case for a naturally occurring broken symmetry, the Green's functions [Eq. (3.22)] contain no reference to the broken-symmetry parameter $\eta$. The crucial point to be emphasized is that once the condition (3.26) is incorporated into the Lagrangian (by suitable choice of $\mu_0^2$ and/or $g_0^2$) there is no further physical content in the broken-symmetry condition. This situation is in sharp contrast to the case of spontaneous symmetry breaking where the constraints cannot merely be incorporated into the Lagrangian and subsequently ignored in all higher order calculations.

Before leaving the Zachariasen model in favor of more complex theories, it is well to display here the conservation law and associated gauge group which supports the broken symmetry. The conserved operator must clearly be of the form

$$\phi^\mu + g_0 \int_{4M_A^2}^\infty ds\alpha(s)\phi^\mu(x, s)$$

where $\alpha(s)$ is to be determined. Using the equations of motion one finds

$$\partial_\mu \left[\phi^\mu(x) + g_0 \int_{4M_A^2}^\infty ds\alpha(s)\phi^\mu(x, s)\right] = g_0 \int_{4M_A^2}^\infty [f(s) - s\alpha(s)]\phi(x, s)$$
$$- \phi(x)\left[\mu_0^2 - g_0^2 \int_{4M_A^2}^\infty f(s)\alpha(s)\, ds\right]$$

which by Eq. (3.26) vanishes for

$$\alpha(s) = (1/s)f(s)$$

It is now easy to show that the Lagrangian is invariant under the $c$-number gauge group

$$\phi(x) \rightarrow \phi(x) + \eta$$
$$\phi(x, s) \rightarrow \phi(x, s) + g_0(1/s)f(s)\eta$$

a result which could have been anticipated from Eq. (3.25).

For the sake of completeness it should perhaps be remarked that although we have considered here only one particular limit of the more general model discussed in Zachariasen's paper, no essentially new features emerge upon introduction of a direct coupling of the field $\phi(x, s)$ to itself. It has been pointed out that with this additional inter-action one can decrease $\mu_0{}^2$ to zero (thereby requiring also the vanishing of $g_0{}^2$) and consequently effect the decoupling of the massless boson even though the scattering amplitude fails to vanish.[24] Since, however, the massless particle in the limit refers to a free field, this is entirely equivalent to the statement that it is always possible to introduce extraneous massless free fields into any field theory. It does not provide any insight into the more interesting question of the possible decoupling of the massless quanta of a field with a nontrivial interaction. The results for the complete Zachariasen model therefore seem not to be of sufficient interest to warrant inclusion here.

Thus far the examples considered in this chapter have dealt exclusively with instructive, but essentially trivial, cases of broken-symmetry theories. In an effort to avoid leaving the reader with the impression that this exhausts the class of naturally occurring broken symmetries, we briefly discuss a somewhat more complex theory of the type suggested by (3.11).[17,20] The model consists of a pseudoscalar field $\phi(x)$ coupled to the pseudovector current of a Hermitian spinor field $\psi(x)$ and is described by the Lagrangian

$$\mathcal{L} = (i/2)\bar{\psi}\beta\gamma^\mu\,\partial_\mu\psi - (m/2)\bar{\psi}\beta\psi + \phi^\mu\,\partial_\mu\phi + \tfrac{1}{2}\phi^\mu\phi_\mu \\ + \tfrac{1}{2}g_0\bar{\psi}\beta\gamma_5\gamma_\mu\psi[\phi^\mu + \tfrac{1}{4}g_0\bar{\psi}\beta\gamma_5\,\partial^\mu\psi] \quad (3.27)$$

where the term quadratic in $g_0$ has been included in order to preserve equivalence with the well-known derivative coupling theory. Because of the translational invariance of (3.27) under

$$\phi(x) \rightarrow \phi(x) + \eta$$

it follows that one has the local conservation law

$$\partial_\mu\phi^\mu = 0 \qquad (3.28)$$

The remaining field equations implied by (3.27) are

$$\gamma^\mu[(1/i)\,\partial_\mu - g_0\,\gamma_5\,\partial_\mu\phi]\cdot\psi + m\psi = 0$$

$$\phi_\mu = -\,\partial_\mu\phi - g_0 j_{5\mu}$$

where a dot notation has been introduced to denote a symmetrical operator product and

$$j_5^\mu = \tfrac{1}{2}\bar\psi\beta\,\gamma_5\,\gamma^\mu\psi$$

It is now easy to verify that the condition

$$\langle 0|\phi(x)|0\rangle \neq 0$$

is consistent with the equations of motion without the introduction of any constraints upon the parameters of the system. From Eq. (3.28) one readily shows that the two-point function

$$G^\mu(x) = i\langle 0|(\phi^\mu(x)\phi(0))_+|0\rangle$$

has the form

$$G^\mu(x) = -\partial^\mu \int \frac{dp}{(2\pi)^4}\, e^{ipx}\, \frac{1}{p^2 - i\epsilon}$$

thereby demonstrating the existence of the zero-mass particle required by the Goldstone theorem which is based on the elements of the canonical group. It is to be noted that although the theory is soluble for the case $m = 0$ this point is entirely irrelevant to the present discussion. Indeed the interest of the model stems largely from the independence of the broken-symmetry aspects from the detailed dynamics.

The above discussion of the derivative coupling model has served to illustrate in a more concrete example our assertion concerning the occurrence of a zero-mass particle in theories of the type described by (3.11). The significance of this result becomes all the more remarkable when one realizes that upon leaving the rather limited domain of soluble field theories there exists no further class of field theories (other than the higher spin generalizations of the field translation group) which is known to admit such a precise statement concerning the physical mass spectrum. In this context it must be recalled that although it was long thought that the usual type of gauge invariance associated with electrodynamics implied the vanishing of the photon mass, this view has relatively recently been discredited.[25-27] It should, however, be noted that the objections raised against the massless photon do not apply to at least one type of electromagnetic coupling.[17] We refer to the spin 1 generalization of the field translation group which rigorously allows the conclusion of a vanishing photon mass. Such a theory is characterized by the fact that the coupling is mediated through the electromagnetic field tensor rather than the vector potential, so that one requires a Lagrangian of the form

$$\mathscr{L} = -\tfrac{1}{2}F^{\mu\nu}(\partial_\mu A_\nu - \partial_\nu A_\mu) + \tfrac{1}{4}F^{\mu\nu}F_{\mu\nu} + \mathscr{L}'(F^{\mu\nu})$$

Since $\mathscr{L}'(F^{\mu\nu})$ does not contain the vector potential $A^\mu$, one clearly has the local conservation law

$$\partial_\nu F^{\mu\nu} = 0 \qquad (3.29)$$

associated with the invariance of the Lagrangian under

$$A^\mu(x) \to A^\mu(x) + \eta^\mu \qquad (3.30)$$

for $\eta^\mu$ being arbitrary constants. As in the usual radiation gauge formulation one can take $A_k(x)$ to be transverse

$$\partial_k A_k = 0$$

so that using Eq. (3.29) leads to the result

$$\langle 0|[F^{\mu\nu}(x), A^\lambda(0)]|0\rangle$$

$$= a\left[g^{\mu\lambda}\,\partial^\nu - g^{\nu\lambda}\,\partial^\mu - \frac{n^\mu\,\partial^\nu - n^\nu\,\partial^\mu}{\nabla^2}(n\partial)\,\partial^\lambda\right]\Delta(x;0)$$

where $n^\mu = (\mathbf{0}, 1)$. From the commutation relation

$$[F_T{}^{0k}(x), A^l(x')] = i\left(\delta_{kl} - \frac{\partial_k\,\partial_l}{\nabla^2}\right)\delta(\mathbf{x} - \mathbf{x}')$$

for the transverse of $F^{0k}(x)$, one readily finds

$$a = 1$$

thereby establishing the existence of a massless photon solely from the invariance of $\mathscr{L}$ under the gauge transformation Eq. (3.30). It is clear from the brief discussion given here of electromagnetic couplings which are mediated entirely through the field tensor that theories of this type support a naturally occurring broken-symmetry condition of the form

$$\langle 0|A^\mu(x)|0\rangle \neq 0$$

One further notes that this does not require a nonvanishing $\mathscr{L}'(F^{\mu\nu})$ so that it applies equally well to the free field case ($\mathscr{L}' = 0$) and to a Pauli moment interaction ($\mathscr{L}' = \tfrac{1}{2}\lambda F^{\mu\nu}M_{\mu\nu}$).

Although the electromagnetic field in the context of broken symmetries merits a much more detailed consideration than that which has been given here, this properly belongs to a study of the usual gauge properties of electrodynamics and we consequently defer such a discussion to the following section.

## IV. Gauge Theories

As we have seen in Section II, any manifestly covariant broken-symmetry theory must exhibit massless particles in the spectrum of states associated with the corresponding current. There is, however, one class of relativistic theory which lacks manifest covariance and which may therefore escape the conclusions of the Goldstone theorem, namely gauge theories such as electrodynamics in the radiation gauge. This section is devoted to a discussion of a variety of broken-symmetry theories involving vector gauge fields.

If we wish to attribute any of the observed approximate symmetries of relativistic particle physics to spontaneous symmetry breaking, and at the same time avoid the appearance in the theory of unobserved massless particles, then there are really only two choices available. Either we couple in gauge fields, as described in this section, or we have to suppose that the massless particles required by the Goldstone theorem are in fact completely uncoupled, and therefore unobservable. In the latter case, however, the Hilbert space of the system may always be written as the direct product of a physical Hilbert space, free of massless particles, and a free-particle Fock space describing the Goldstone particles. The broken symmetry appears only in the latter, and no trace of it remains in the physical predictions of the theory, which must in fact exhibit complete symmetry.

There is another reason for considering the possible introduction of gauge fields. The success of the "gauge principle" in electrodynamics,[28] whereby the electromagnetic field is introduced in the course of extending the symmetry group from global to local transformations, and of its analog in gravitation,[29] led to the idea that other interactions might perhaps be understood in a similar fashion.[30] A major obstacle in the way of this hypothesis was the fact that the vector particles associated with the gauge fields are apparently required by the theory to be massless, like the photon and the graviton.

However, it was suggested some time ago by Anderson[31] that the two problems posed by the vanishing of the masses of the "Goldstone bosons" and the "Yang-Mills bosons" might in certain circumstances "cancel out." In fact, as we shall see explicitly below, in a theory with *both* gauge fields *and* symmetry breaking the two polarization states of the massless vector particles and the single state of the massless scalar may combine to yield the three states appropriate to a massive vector boson. This idea provides what is, at least at first sight, an extremely attractive escape from the problem of predicted but unobserved massless bosons. It has been discussed by Higgs,[32,33] Brout and Englert,[34] Guralnik, Hagen, and Kibble,[35] and Kibble.[36]

At least in the case of the electromagnetic field it is always possible to maintain manifest covariance, by using the Lorentz gauge and, for example, the Gupta-Bleuler formalism.[37] Then the Goldstone theorem certainly applies, and requires the existence of massless states. However, it says nothing about whether these states are physical, and indeed we shall see explicitly in cases discussed below that the corresponding massless fields are generally pure gauge parts whose matrix elements between physical states vanish identically. In the case of non-Abelian gauges, the Gupta-Bleuler formalism in inapplicable, but one can work in terms of Schwinger's extended-operator formalism,[38] with similar results.

Let us begin by examining the simplest possible model of a broken symmetry theory—a free massless scalar field described by the Lagrangian density

$$L = \phi^\mu \, \partial_\mu \phi + \tfrac{1}{2}\phi^\mu \phi_\mu \tag{4.1}$$

This Lagrangian is invariant under the field translations

$$\phi(x) \to \phi(x) + g\lambda \tag{4.2}$$

where $g$ is a positive coupling constant introduced for later convenience, and $\lambda$ is a real parameter. Obviously, $\langle\phi\rangle = \langle 0|\phi(x)|0\rangle$ cannot be invariant under (4.2), so this symmetry is always broken. As discussed in Section III, the various degenerate vacuums distinguished by different values of $\langle\phi\rangle$ belong to unitarily inequivalent (but physically indistinguishable) representations of the canonical commutation relations.

Now let us couple the conserved current $g\phi^\mu$ to a gauge vector field. We obtain[39]

$$L = -\tfrac{1}{2}F^{\mu\nu}(\partial_\mu A_\nu - \partial_\nu A_\mu) + \tfrac{1}{4}F^{\mu\nu}F_{\mu\nu} + \phi^\mu \, \partial_\mu \phi + \tfrac{1}{2}\phi^\mu \phi_\mu + g\phi^\mu A_\mu \tag{4.3}$$

which is invariant not only under Eq. (4.2), but also under the gauge transformations of the second kind,

$$\phi(x) \to \phi(x) + g\lambda(x)$$
$$A_\mu(x) \to A_\mu(x) + \partial_\mu\lambda(x)$$

(4.4)

Although this is an essentially trivial model, it will be helpful to analyze it in some detail in order to bring out a number of points of more general applicability, particularly in view of the fact that many other models reduce to this one in an appropriate linear approximation. In particular, we wish to discuss the relationship between the Lorentz gauge and Coulomb gauge methods.

In the Coulomb gauge we remove the arbitrariness corresponding to the transformations (4.4) by imposing on $A_\mu$ the condition $\partial_k A^k = 0$. This may be achieved, for example, by adding to the Lagrangian a Lagrange multiplier term

$$-C \, \partial_k A^k$$

(4.5)

The field equations are then

$$F_{\mu\nu} = \partial_\mu A_\nu - \partial_\nu A_\mu$$

(4.6)

$$\partial_\mu F^{\mu\nu} = -g\phi^\nu + \delta_k{}^\nu \, \partial^k C$$

(4.7)

$$\partial_k A^k = 0$$

(4.8)

$$\phi_\mu = -\partial_\mu\phi - gA_\mu$$

(4.9)

$$\partial_\mu\phi^\mu = 0$$

(4.10)

The independent dynamical variables are $\phi$ and $\phi^0$, and the two transverse components of each of $A_k$ and $F^{0k}$. The dependent variables are determined in terms of these by constraint equations. In particular, from Eqs. (4.6) and (4.7) one finds for $A_0$ and the longitudinal part of $F^{0k}$ the equations

$$-\nabla^2 A^0 = \partial_k F^{0k} = g\phi^0$$

(4.11)

Eliminating these variables, one finds the dynamical equations of motion

$$\partial_0 A_k{}^T = F_{0k}^T \qquad \partial_0 F^{0kT} = -\nabla^2 A^{kT} + g^2 A^{kT}$$

(4.12)

$$\partial_0 \phi = -\phi_0 + g^2(\nabla^2)^{-1}\phi_0 \qquad \partial_0\phi^0 = \nabla^2\phi$$

(4.13)

It follows that $A_k{}^T$, $F_{0k}^T$, and $\phi^0$ satisfy the Klein-Gordon equation for mass $g$. In fact, combining Eqs. (4.12) and (4.13), and introducing the new variables $V_k = A_k + g^{-1} \partial_k \phi$, we recover the standard equations describing a vector field of mass $g$. Note, however, that for $\phi$ we can only derive the equation

$$(-\partial^2 + g^2) \partial_\mu \phi = 0$$

One can verify these conclusions directly from the Lagrangian (4.3). Let us introduce in place of $A_\mu$ the new variables

$$V_\mu = A_\mu + g^{-1} \partial_\mu \phi \qquad (4.14)$$

Then Eq. (4.9) becomes an explicit solution for $\phi_\mu$,

$$\phi_\mu = -g V_\mu \qquad (4.15)$$

which may be used to eliminate $\phi_\mu$ from the Lagrangian, yielding

$$L = -\tfrac{1}{2} F^{\mu\nu} (\partial_\mu V_\nu - \partial_\nu V_\mu) + \tfrac{1}{4} F^{\mu\nu} F_{\mu\nu} - \tfrac{1}{2} g^2 V^\mu V_\mu$$
$$- C \partial_k (V^k - g^{-1} \partial^k \phi) \qquad (4.16)$$

The independent dynamical variables are now $V_k$ and all three components of $F^{0k}$. In this form it is clear that $V_\mu$ describes particles of spin one and mass $g$.

The Lagrangian (4.16) is still invariant under the transformations (4.2), though not of course under (4.4), but in a completely trivial way. In fact, from Eqs. (4.10) and (4.14) we see that $\phi$ is determined in terms of $V$ by the equation

$$\nabla^2 \phi = g \, \partial_k V^k \qquad (4.17)$$

and (4.2) represents merely the arbitrariness in the solution of this equation. (Explicit dependence on $x$ is ruled out by the requirement of translational invariance.) Note that the equation obtained by variation of $\phi$, namely

$$\nabla^2 C = 0$$

shows similarly that $C$ is at most a constant.

It is useful to reexamine the proof of the Goldstone theorem, in the context of this particular model, to see explicitly why it fails. The conserved current, whose integrated time component is the formal generator of the transformations (4.2) is simply $g\phi^\mu$. Thus the expectation value we have to consider in examining the proof of the theorem is

$$f^\mu(x) = -ig\langle [\phi^\mu(x), \phi(0)] \rangle \qquad (4.18)$$

By the canonical commutation relations, we have

$$\int d^3x f^0(\mathbf{x}, 0) = g$$

If this equation were true not only for $t = 0$, but for all times, then the Goldstone theorem would follow. However, reexpressing $f^\mu$ in terms of the vector field $V^\mu$, using Eqs. (4.15) and (4.17), we have

$$f^\mu(x) = +ig^3\langle[V^\mu(x), (\nabla^2)^{-1}\partial_k V^k]\rangle$$

But the commutator function of a free vector field has the form

$$i[V^\mu(x), V_\nu(y)] = (\delta_\nu{}^\mu - g^{-2}\partial^\mu\partial_\nu)\Delta(x - y; g^2)$$

Hence we find that $f^0$ has a causal structure,

$$f_0(x) = g\,\partial_0\Delta(x; g^2)$$

but that $f^k$ has not:

$$f_k(x) = g(1 - g^2/\nabla^2)\,\partial_k\Delta(x; g^2)$$

It is this nonlocal structure which makes the proof of the Goldstone theorem fail. We note that by explicit calculation one finds the time dependence

$$\int d^3x f^0(\mathbf{x}, t) = g\cos gt \qquad (4.19)$$

In any broken symmetry theory, the integral over all space of the current operator,

$$Q = \int d^3x j^0(x)$$

fails to exist. However, if we evaluate the commutator of $j^0$ with any local operator *before* doing the spatial integration, the result is always well defined. Formally, if the theory is manifestly covariant, the "operator" $Q$ is time independent, in the sense that all its commutators evaluated in this manner are time independent. However, in the same sense for our model it satisfies the equation

$$(\partial_0{}^2 + g^2)Q = 0$$

in agreement with Eq. (4.19). This was noted by Guralnik, Hagen, and Kibble.[35]

Now let us turn to the Lorentz gauge. We shall find it convenient to impose the Lorentz gauge condition by adding to the Lagrangian Eq. (4.3) a Lagrange multiplier term analogous to Eq. (4.5), namely,

$$-G\,\partial_\mu A^\mu + \tfrac{1}{2}\alpha GG \tag{4.20}$$

where $\alpha$ is an arbitrary constant introduced to allow direct comparison both with Schwinger's formalism[38] ($\alpha = 0$), and with the more conventional Fermi Lagrangian[37] ($\alpha = 1$). Note that in a second-order form Eq. (4.20) would correspond to a term

$$-(1/2\alpha)(\partial_\mu A^\mu)^2$$

The advantage of the first-order form lies precisely in the possibility of taking $\alpha = 0$.

With this addition to the Lagrangian, the only equations of motion which are changed are Eqs. (4.7) and (4.8) which are now replaced by

$$\partial_\mu F^{\mu\nu} = -g\phi^\nu + \partial^\nu G \tag{4.21}$$

and

$$\partial_\mu A^\mu = \alpha G \tag{4.22}$$

Note that from Eqs. (4.10) and (4.21), it follows that $G$ is a massless field,

$$\partial^2 G = 0 \tag{4.23}$$

The important difference between the Lorentz gauge and the Coulomb gauge derives from the fact that (4.20), unlike (4.5), contains a time derivative, so that $G$, unlike $C$, is formally a dynamical variable. The equations are no longer automatically equivalent to the gauge-invariant equations with $G = 0$, but have additional solutions with nonvanishing $G$ which must be eliminated by imposing some subsidiary condition on the physical states.

We note that the generator of the gauge transformations (4.4) is

$$G(\lambda) = \int d^3x[G(x)\,\partial_0\lambda(x) - \lambda(x)\,\partial_0 G(x)]$$

$$= \int d^3x[G\,\partial_0\lambda - \lambda(\partial_k F^{0k} - g\phi^0)] \tag{4.24}$$

There are two alternative procedures at this point. We can adopt either the Gupta-Bleuler formalism, or the extended-operator formalism of Schwinger. In the Gupta-Bleuler formalism, the fields are represented by operators in a Hilbert space with indefinite metric, and the subspace of physical states is selected by imposing on them the subsidiary condition

$$G^{(+)}(x)|\rangle = 0 \qquad (\partial_k F^{0k(+)} - g\phi^{0(+)})|\rangle = 0 \qquad (4.25)$$

where the superscript plus denotes the positive-frequency part. Equation (4.23) is essential here in allowing us to draw an invariant distinction between positive and negative frequencies.

On the other hand, in Schwinger's formalism the field variables are not represented in a Hilbert space, but in a more general functional space, and the physical states are distinguished by the requirement of gauge invariance,

$$G(\lambda)\Psi = 0$$

or equivalently

$$G\Psi = 0 \qquad (\partial_k F^{0k} - g\phi^0)\Psi = 0 \qquad (4.26)$$

We shall consider both these formalisms in the following.

The canonically conjugate pairs of field variables are now $(F^{0k}, A_k)$, $(G, A^0)$, and $(\phi, \phi^0)$. As before it is convenient to make a change of variables. We introduce a canonical transformation to the pairs $(F^{0k}, V_k)$, $(G, \chi^0)$, and $(\phi, \pi^0)$, where

$$
\begin{aligned}
V_k &= A_k + g^{-1}\,\partial_k\phi - g^{-2}\,\partial_k G \\
\chi^0 &= A^0 + g^{-2}\,\partial_k F^{0k} \\
\pi^0 &= \phi^0 - g^{-1}\,\partial_k F^{0k}
\end{aligned}
\qquad (4.27)
$$

To exhibit the Lagrangian in manifestly covariant form, it is convenient to introduce also the dependent variables $V_0$, $\chi^k$, $\pi^k$, so that we may write

$$
\begin{aligned}
L = &- \tfrac{1}{2}F^{\mu\nu}\,(\partial_\mu V_\nu - \partial_\nu V_\mu) + \tfrac{1}{4}F^{\mu\nu}F_{\mu\nu} - \tfrac{1}{2}g^2 V^\mu V_\mu \\
&+ \chi^\mu\,\partial_\mu G + \pi^\mu\,\partial_\mu\phi + \tfrac{1}{2}\pi^\mu\pi_\mu + g\pi^\mu\chi_\mu + \tfrac{1}{2}\alpha GG
\end{aligned}
$$

Here we clearly have a vector field $V_\mu$ describing particles of mass $g$, and two scalar fields. No coupling remains between the vector and scalar fields.

Let us first consider Schwinger's formalism, which in this case is somewhat simpler. To do this, we may adopt a representation in which states are labelled by the eigenvalues of, for example, $\phi$, $\chi^0$, and $V_k$, all at a given time $t$. On the space of functionals of these variables, the canonically conjugate fields are represented by functional differential operators, namely

$$\pi^0 = -i\frac{\delta}{\delta\phi'} \qquad G = i\frac{\delta}{\delta\chi^{0\prime}} \qquad F^{0k} = i\frac{\delta}{\delta V_{k'}}$$

The gauge-invariance requirements (4.26) become

$$G\Psi = 0 \qquad\quad \pi^0\Psi = 0$$

or

$$\frac{\delta}{\delta\chi_0'}\Psi = 0 \qquad\quad \frac{\delta}{\delta\phi'}\Psi = 0 \qquad\qquad (4.28)$$

They show that the physical states are in fact independent of the scalar fields $\chi_0'$ and $\phi'$, and may be represented by functionals of the vector field $V_k'$ alone. These states form a Hilbert space under the scalar product defined by functional integration over all functionals of $V_k'$. No massless particles remain among the physical states, in complete agreement with the results of the Coulomb gauge treatment.

In the formalism of Gupta and Bleuler, on the other hand, the fields are supposed to be represented in a Hilbert space with indefinite metric. The subspace of physical states is selected by imposing the subsidiary conditions

$$G^{(+)}\Psi = 0 \qquad\quad \pi^{0(+)}\Psi = 0 \qquad\qquad (4.29)$$

Here the scalar fields do not annihilate the physical states, but their matrix elements between pairs of physical states are nevertheless zero in virtue of Eq. (4.29). The large Hilbert space with indefinite metric may be written, because of the absence of coupling between the vector and scalar fields, as a direct product of a physical Hilbert space with positive definite metric (which is in fact the Fock space for the vector particles), and an unphysical Hilbert space describing the scalar particles. In this latter space, the subspace selected by the conditions (4.29) consists exclusively of states with zero norm with the sole exception of the vacuum state.

It is interesting to examine more closely the unphysical fields $\phi$ and $G$. The corresponding field equations are

$$\partial_\mu G = -g\pi_\mu \qquad \partial_\mu\phi = -\pi_\mu - g\chi_\mu$$
$$\partial_\mu\chi^\mu = \alpha G \qquad \partial_\mu\pi^\mu = 0 \qquad\qquad (4.30)$$

It follows that

$$\partial^2 G = 0 \qquad \partial^2 \phi = \alpha g G \qquad (4.31)$$

The massless particles required by the Goldstone theorem are described by the field $G$. In the special case $\alpha = 0$ there are two independent massless fields, corresponding to the fact that in that case the Lagrangian is also invariant (up to a divergence) under the transformation $G(x) \rightarrow G(x) + \lambda$, which is generated formally by the spatial integral of $A_0$ or $\chi_0$. In general, however, there is only one invariance, whose formal generator is the spatial integral of $g\phi^0$ or $g\pi^0$. Note that it is not the canonical conjugate $\phi$ of this density which describes the Goldstone bosons, but rather the field $G$ whose time derivative is $g\pi^0$. In fact the verification of the Goldstone theorem for this case rests on an examination of the commutator function $-ig[\pi_\mu, \phi] = i[\partial_\mu G, \phi]$, which must be nonzero and have a time-independent spatial integral.

The covariant commutation relations of the scalar fields are easy to derive from the equations of motion [Eqs. (4.30)] and the canonical commutation relations. We find that the mutual consistency of the subsidiary conditions [Eq. (4.28) or (4.29)] for different times is assured by the commutator

$$i[G(x), G(y)] = 0 \qquad (4.32)$$

The commutator function which is important for the discussion of the Goldstone theorem is

$$i[\phi(x), G(y)] = gD(x - y) = \frac{g}{2\pi} \epsilon(x^0 - y^0)\delta[(x - y)^2] \quad (4.33)$$

It is easily seen to have the requisite locality property, which ensures that

$$i \int d^3x [\partial_0 G(x), \phi(0)] = g \qquad (4.34)$$

Finally we note also that

$$i[\phi(x), \phi(y)] = D(x - y) - \alpha g^2 \left[\frac{\partial}{\partial m^2} \Delta(x - y; m^2)\right]_{m^2 = 0}$$

$$= \frac{1}{2\pi} \epsilon(x^0 - y^0)\{\delta[(x - y)^2] + \tfrac{1}{4}\alpha g^2 \theta[-(x - y)^2]\} \quad (4.35)$$

These covariant commutation relations are valid for both Schwinger's formalism and for that of Gupta and Bleuler. However, it is important to recall that they play significantly different roles in the two cases. In Schwinger's formalism they express the effect of reversing the order of a pair of functional differential operators. In that context their form is neither surprising nor troublesome. In the formalism of Gupta and Bleuler, however, they describe the commutation properties of Hilbert-space operators and are therefore required to satisfy rather more stringent requirements. In particular, let us take the vacuum expectation value of Eq. (4.35) and insert a complete set of states in the usual way. (Note that this operation has no meaning in Schwinger's formalism.) Denoting by $\rho_n$ the diagonal element, $\pm 1$, of the metric operator, we find

$$\sum_n \rho_n |\langle n|\phi(0)|0\rangle|^2 (2\pi)^4 \delta(p_n - k)$$

$$= \theta(k^0) 2\pi \delta(k^2) - \alpha g^2 \left[ \frac{\partial}{\partial m^2} \{\theta(k^0) 2\pi \delta(k^2 + m^2)\} \right.$$

$$\left. - \pi^2 ln\left(\frac{m^2}{M^2}\right) \delta(k) \right]_{m^2 = 0} \quad (4.36)$$

where $M$ is an arbitrary constant mass associated with the arbitrary constant in the field $\phi$. It is evident that unless $\alpha = 0$ the matrix elements of $\phi$ must be extremely singular. The type of structure which appears on the right-hand side of Eq. (4.36) can in fact be produced only by a cancellation between infinite positive and negative terms on the left-hand side. The root of this problem may be traced to Eq. (4.31). In momentum space, it is clear that the field $G$ is proportional to $\delta(k^2)$. Thus, in order to satisfy the second of this pair of equations, it is necessary that $\phi$ should be proportional to the derivative of the $\delta$ function, $\delta'(k^2)$. Now, the quantity which appears in the commutator function, namely the derivative with respect to $m^2$ of the odd function $\varepsilon(k^0)\delta(k^2 + m^2)$, evaluated at $m^2 = 0$, is a perfectly well-defined Lorentz-invariant distribution; however, the derivative of the even function $\delta(k^2 + m^2)$ is not, [40] but it is arbitrary to the extent of an additive multiple of the four-dimensional $\delta$ function. [This is represented in Eq. (4.36) by the arbitrariness in $M$.]

    These difficulties may be avoided either by using Schwinger's extended-operator formalism, in which Eq. (4.35) makes perfect sense but Eq. (4.36) cannot be written down, or alternatively by making the particular choice $\alpha = 0$, for which no problems arise. It is worth recalling that this is precisely the case for which the second-order form of the Lagrangian cannot be used.

Finally, before leaving this model we wish to point out that in the Gupta-Bleuler formalism it provides an example of the decoupling of the massless modes, leaving no trace of broken symmetry among the physical states. Here, the physical states are described by the vector field $V_\mu$, which is completely invariant under the symmetry transformations (4.2). In a sense, therefore, we have not so much broken the symmetry as eliminated it completely from the theory. As in the case of "naturally occurring" broken symmetries, the symmetry-breaking parameter is physically irrelevant.

As a rather less trivial example let us now consider the model of a self-interacting two-component scalar field

$$\phi = \begin{bmatrix} \phi_1 \\ \phi_2 \end{bmatrix}$$

described by the Lagrangian [41]

$$L = \phi^\mu \, \partial_\mu \phi + \tfrac{1}{2}\phi^\mu \phi_\mu - V(\phi\phi) \tag{4.37}$$

It is clearly invariant under the rotations

$$\phi \to e^{i\lambda q}\phi \tag{4.38}$$

where $q$ is the antisymmetric $2 \times 2$ matrix defined in Section III.

If $V$ has a maximum at $\phi\phi = 0$ and a minimum at some other value, e.g., if

$$V = -\tfrac{1}{2}a^2\phi\phi + \tfrac{1}{2}b^2(\tfrac{1}{2}\phi\phi)^2 \tag{4.39}$$

then we may expect that in the ground state the expectation value of $\phi$ will not be zero, but rather will approximate to the value at which $V$ has a minimum. Clearly, because of the invariance, there must be an infinitely degenerate set of ground states, with expectation values corresponding to all the points round the circle in the $\phi_1 - \phi_2$ space on which $V$ has its minimum value. From the equations of motion, and the requirement of translational invariance of the ground state, one easily derives the consistency requirement

$$\left\langle \frac{\partial V}{\partial \phi} \right\rangle = \langle \phi(\tfrac{1}{2}b^2\phi\phi - a^2) \rangle = 0 \tag{4.40}$$

which serves to fix the magnitude of $\langle\phi\rangle$. The various degenerate ground states are labeled by a phase angle $\alpha$, and characterized by the expectation values

$$\langle\phi\rangle = \eta = e^{i\alpha q}\eta_0 \tag{4.41}$$

where $\eta_0$ may be chosen to be, say,

$$\eta_0 = \begin{bmatrix} 0 \\ |\eta| \end{bmatrix} \tag{4.42}$$

with $|\eta|$ determined by Eq. (4.40). (By translational invariance, $\eta$ is of course independent of $x$.) In lowest order,

$$|\eta|^2 = 2a^2/b^2$$

The current corresponding to the invariance (4.38) is

$$j^\mu = i\phi^\mu q\phi \tag{4.43}$$

It satisfies

$$\partial_\mu j^\mu = 0 \tag{4.44}$$

Formally, the transformation between one member of the set of degenerate ground states and another is performed by the unitary operator

$$U(\lambda) = \exp\left\{ i\lambda \int d^3x j^0(x) \right\} \tag{4.45}$$

In fact, however, this integral does not converge to a well-defined operator in the limit of infinite volume, and the various degenerate ground states belong to unitarily inequivalent representations of the commutation relations (compare Section III).

The equations of motion obtained from the Lagrangian Eq. (4.37), with $V$ given by Eq. (4.39), are

$$\partial_\mu \phi = -\phi_\mu \tag{4.46}$$

$$\partial_\mu \phi^\mu = -\partial V/\partial \phi$$
$$= \phi(a^2 - \tfrac{1}{2}b^2\phi\phi) \tag{4.47}$$

To analyze the structure of the theory, it is useful to begin by making a linear approximation. We write $\phi = \eta + \phi'$, and retain only terms linear in $\phi'$ in the equations of motion. Then Eqs. (4.46) and (4.47) yield the equation

$$\partial^2 \phi' = b^2\eta(\eta\phi') \tag{4.48}$$

It is clear from the structure of the mass matrix $b^2\eta\eta$ that this theory describes two particles, one with mass zero, and the other with mass $m$ given by

$$m^2 = b^2\eta\eta = 2a^2$$

In higher approximations, there are, naturally, interactions between the two scalar fields, which will have the effect, among others, of renormalizing the mass of the massive mesons. However, we are assured by the Goldstone theorem that no such renormalization occurs for the massless mesons. These are the Goldstone particles, and their mass must remain zero. It should be noted that the value of $\eta$ must change in higher orders to take account more precisely of the consistency condition (4.40).

Now let us consider the effect of coupling the current [Eq. (4.43)] to the electromagnetic field. (We are now interpreting the two components of $\phi$ as the real components of a charged field.) The Lagrangian then takes the form

$$L = -\tfrac{1}{2}F^{\mu\nu}(\partial_\mu A_\nu - \partial_\nu A_\mu + \tfrac{1}{4}F^{\mu\nu}F_{\mu\nu} + \phi^\mu(\partial_\mu - ieqA_\mu)\phi$$
$$+\tfrac{1}{2}\phi^\mu\phi_\mu - V(\phi\phi) \tag{4.49}$$

As in our previous discussion of the simple free-field model, we could use either the Lorentz gauge or the Coulomb gauge to discuss this theory. However, since no new points of principle emerge from the use of the Lorentz gauge in this problem, we shall be content with the Coulomb gauge. Moreover, we shall not write explicitly the Langrange multiplier term analogous to Eq. (4.5).

The field equations derived from the Lagrangian Eq. (4.49) are

$$F_{\mu\nu} = \partial_\mu A_\nu - \partial_\nu A_\mu \tag{4.50}$$

$$\partial_\mu F^{\mu\nu} = ie\phi^\nu q\phi \tag{4.51}$$

$$\phi_\mu = -\partial_\mu\phi + ieA_\mu q\phi \tag{4.52}$$

$$(\partial_\mu - ieA_\mu q)\phi^\mu = -\partial V/\partial\phi$$
$$= \phi(a^2 - \tfrac{1}{2}b^2\phi\phi) \tag{4.53}$$

If we now make the same linearizing approximation as before, the last two equations become

$$\phi_\mu = -\partial_\mu\phi' + ieq\eta A_\mu \tag{4.54}$$

$$\partial_\mu\phi^\mu = b^2\eta(\eta\phi') \tag{4.55}$$

The components of these equations in the direction of $\eta$ are independent of $A_\mu$, and yield

$$(-\partial^2 + m^2)(\eta\phi') = 0 \tag{4.56}$$

with $m^2 = b^2|\eta|^2$ as before. Thus the massive scalar particles are unaffected by the coupling in of the electromagnetic field. To simplify the remaining equations, it is convenient to introduce the new variables

$$V_\mu = A_\mu + \frac{i}{e\eta\eta} \eta q \, \partial_\mu \phi' = -\frac{i}{e\eta\eta} \eta q \phi_\mu \qquad (4.57)$$

Then Eqs. (4.50) and (4.51) become

$$\begin{aligned} F_{\mu\nu} &= \partial_\mu V_\nu - \partial_\nu V_\mu \\ \partial_\mu F^{\mu\nu} &= M^2 V^\nu \end{aligned} \qquad (4.58)$$

with $M^2 = e^2|\eta|^2$. These are of course the standard equations describing a massive vector field. Thus we see that the massless Goldstone bosons have combined with the electromagnetic field to produce a massive vector field. No massless particles remain in the theory.

It is interesting to examine an alternative approach to this theory. This approach has the advantage of not being restricted to a perturbation treatment based on the linearized approximation, but correspondingly it has the defect of involving complicated algebraic transformations of the dynamical variables which are not obviously well-defined for operator fields.

We introduce the polar decomposition[42]

$$\phi = \begin{bmatrix} \rho \sin \theta \\ \rho \cos \theta \end{bmatrix} \qquad (4.59)$$

where the field $\rho$ has a nonvanishing expectation value, $\langle \rho(x) \rangle = |\eta|$. Then, ignoring problems of operator ordering (which may in fact be rather severe), we find that the Lagrangian Eq. (4.49) takes the form

$$\begin{aligned} L = -\tfrac{1}{2} F^{\mu\nu} (\partial_\mu A_\nu - \partial_\nu A_\mu + \tfrac{1}{4} F^{\mu\nu} F_{\mu\nu} + \rho^\mu \, \partial_\mu \rho \\ + \rho \sigma^\mu (\partial_\mu \theta - e A_\mu) + \tfrac{1}{2} \rho^\mu \rho_\mu + \tfrac{1}{2} \sigma^\mu \sigma_\mu - V(\rho^2) \end{aligned} \qquad (4.60)$$

where we have written

$$\begin{aligned} \rho^\mu &= \phi_1{}^\mu \sin \theta + \phi_2{}^\mu \cos \theta \\ \sigma^\mu &= \phi_1{}^\mu \cos \theta - \phi_2{}^\mu \sin \theta \end{aligned} \qquad (4.61)$$

We then introduce the new variables

$$V_\mu = A_\mu - (1/e) \, \partial_\mu \theta \qquad (4.62)$$

to which Eq. (4.57) is a linear approximation, and eliminate $\sigma^\mu$ using the relation

$$\sigma^\mu = e\rho V^\mu \tag{4.63}$$

This yields our final Lagrangian

$$L = -\tfrac{1}{2}F^{\mu\nu}\left(\partial_\mu V_\nu - \partial_\nu V_\mu + \tfrac{1}{4}F^{\mu\nu}F_{\mu\nu} - \tfrac{1}{2}e^2\rho^2 V^\mu V_\mu \right. \\ \left. + \rho^\mu\,\partial_\mu\rho + \tfrac{1}{2}\rho^\mu\rho_\mu - V(\rho^2) \right) \tag{4.64}$$

This Lagrangian evidently describes a scalar field $\rho$ and a vector field $V^\mu$ whose squared masses are determined in lowest approximation by the second derivative of $V(\rho^2)$ and by $e^2\langle\rho^2\rangle \approx e^2|\eta|^2$, respectively. Once again, we see that no massless particles remain in the theory—nor, of course, does any obvious trace of the broken symmetry.

That the Lagrangian (4.49) is really equivalent, in the quantized field theory, to (4.64) has been verified in low orders of perturbation theory by Higgs.[33] We conclude, therefore, that there is every indication that the exact theory, like its linearized approximation, is free of massless particles. Thus the coupling of the electromagnetic field to the current associated with the broken symmetry suffices to eliminate the massless Goldstone bosons.

We now turn to a very different class of theories, which involve only vector fields. It is instructive to examine the electromagnetic field itself from the point of view of broken symmetry, particularly in view of the relationship which has often been assumed between gauge invariance and the vanishing of the photon mass.[43,44]

Let us first recall that the Lagrangian (4.1) for the massless scalar field is invariant under the transformations (4.2), generated by the integrated time component of the conserved current $\phi^\mu$. The corresponding conserved quantity in the case of the free electromagnetic field is simply $F^{\mu\nu}$ itself. In view of Maxwell's equations, it satisfies the conservation law (for any constant $\eta_k$)

$$\partial_\mu(F^{\mu k}\eta_k) = 0 \tag{4.65}$$

From the canonical commutation relations

$$[F^{T0k}(\mathbf{x}, t), A_l(\mathbf{y}, t)] = i\left(\delta_l^{\,k} - \frac{\partial^k\,\partial_l}{\nabla^2}\right)\delta(\mathbf{x} - \mathbf{y}) \tag{4.66}$$

(where the superscript $T$ denotes the transverse part of a vector), we find

$$-i\int_V d^3x[(F^{0k}\eta_k)(\mathbf{x}, 0), A_l(0)] = \eta_l - \eta_k\int_{\sigma(V)} d\sigma^k\,\frac{x_l}{4\pi|\mathbf{x}|^3} = \tfrac{2}{3}\eta_l \tag{4.67}$$

Thus the integrated time component of (4.65) generates the constant field translations (or "constant gauge transformations")

$$A_k(x) \rightarrow A_k(x) + \tfrac{2}{3}\eta_k \tag{4.68}$$

which are the analog of (4.1).

In this free-field case, the integrated commutator (4.67) is actually independent of time, and there is no difficulty in applying the Goldstone theorem to deduce the existence of massless particles in the theory. However, it is clear that this result reflects only our choice of a free field and is essentially trivial.

A physically much more interesting model is interacting electrodynamics. We easily find that the continuity equation (4.65) may be generalized to[44]

$$\partial_\mu[(F^{\mu k} + ex^k j^\mu)\eta_k] = 0 \tag{4.69}$$

Using the general form of the two-point function for the electromagnetic field in the Coulomb gauge,

$$i\langle 0|A^\mu(x)A^\nu(0)|0\rangle - \frac{1}{4\pi|\mathbf{x}|}\,\delta(x^0)\delta_0{}^\mu\delta_0{}^\nu$$

$$= \left(g^{\mu\nu} - \frac{\delta_0{}^\mu\,\partial^\nu + \delta_0{}^\nu\,\partial^\mu}{\nabla^2}\,\partial_0 - \frac{\partial^\mu\,\partial^\nu}{\nabla^2}\right)\int_0^\infty dm^2\rho(m^2)\Delta^{(+)}(x;m^2)$$

we may verify that

$$\langle 0|[j^0(x), A^k(0)]|0\rangle = 0$$

for all values of $x^0$. This remarkable result, together with the canonical commutation relations (which of course remain valid in the interacting theory) enable us to derive the equal-time commutation relation

$$- i \int d^3x \langle 0|[(F^{0k} + ex^k j^0)(\mathbf{x}, 0)\eta_k, A_l(0)] = \tfrac{2}{3}\eta_l \tag{4.70}$$

Thus we see that the continuity equation (4.69) is still associated with the constant gauge transformations (4.68).

However, it is no longer true in general that the integral in Eq. (4.70) is independent of the time. Indeed, if we evaluate it explicitly for an arbitrary time difference $t$, we obtain the result

$$\tfrac{2}{3}\eta_l \int_0^\infty dm^2\rho(m^2)\cos(mt)$$

Thus the Goldstone theorem cannot be applied to deduce the existence of massless particles in the theory. Indeed, there is no contradiction in assuming that $\rho(m^2)$ vanishes for values of $m^2$ less than some finite threshold mass.

In the Lorentz gauge, of course, the Goldstone theorem must apply. In that case, the analogous continuity equation to Eq. (4.69) is

$$\partial_\mu[(\partial^\mu A^\nu + ex^\nu j^\mu)\eta_\nu] = 0 \tag{4.71}$$

In this case, the two-point function of the theory takes the form

$$i\langle 0|A^\mu(x)A^\nu(0)|0\rangle = \left(g^{\mu\nu} - \frac{\partial^\mu \partial^\nu}{\partial^2}\right)\left[Z_3\Delta^{(+)}(x;0)\right.$$
$$\left. + \int_0^\infty dm^2\rho(m^2)\Delta^{(+)}(x;m^2)\right] + \frac{\partial^\mu \partial^\nu}{\partial^2}\Delta^{(+)}(x;0)$$

in which we have explicitly separated out the contribution of the massless particles to the spectral function. It follows that

$$-i\int d^3x\langle 0|[(\partial^0 A^\nu + ex^\nu j^0)(x)\eta_\nu, A_\mu(0)]|0\rangle = \eta_\mu \tag{4.72}$$

independent of time. Thus the Goldstone theorem applies and there are massless particles in the theory. However, it is clear that (4.72) is independent of the value of $Z_3$ and, in particular, is perfectly consistent with the assumption that $Z_3 = 0$. The only term in the two-point function which is actually relevant is the longitudinal term which represents a pure gauge part. This again emphasizes the fact that the massless particles required to exist by the Goldstone theorem need have no connection with physical massless particles. They are pure gauge parts.

It is interesting to examine the special case of electrodynamics in two dimensions, when the electron mass is taken to be zero. As has been shown by Schwinger,[45] this theory is exactly soluble.

The field equations for the electromagnetic field in this model are

$$\partial_\nu F^{\mu\nu} = ej^\mu$$
$$F_{\mu\nu} = \partial_\mu A_\nu - \partial_\nu A_\mu \tag{4.73}$$

However, these are not really equations of motion for dynamical degrees of freedom of the system, for in two dimensions there are no independent degrees of freedom associated with the electromagnetic field. Indeed, if we choose the Coulomb gauge, then $A_1 = 0$, and $A_0$ is purely a constraint variable, given as an explicit function of the current by the equation

$$- \nabla^2 A^0 = ej^0 \qquad (4.74)$$

The electromagnetic field itself has only a single component

$$F_{01} = -\partial_1 A_0 = -F_{10}$$

It can be shown by careful evaluation of the relevant commutators[46] that in addition to these equations the current satisfies the condition

$$\varepsilon^{\mu\nu} \, \partial_\nu j_\mu = -\frac{e}{\pi} F_{01} = -\frac{e}{2\pi} \varepsilon^{\mu\nu} F_{\mu\nu}$$

where $\varepsilon^{\mu\nu}$ is the antisymmetric tensor with $\varepsilon^{01} = 1$. It follows that

$$(-\partial^2 + e^2/\pi)j^\mu = 0 \qquad (4.75)$$

Thus the excitations of vector type in the theory are massive. (It should be remarked in passing that there is no physical distinction between scalar and vector particles in two dimensions.)

This theory is interesting from the point of view of broken symmetries, because there exists a symmetry, namely, that under the chiral $(\gamma_5)$ gauge transformations of the massless fermion field, such that the corresponding current $\varepsilon^{\mu\nu}j_\nu$ is not conserved. It follows, of course, that it cannot support a Goldstone theorem. We also note that although the expression $F^{\mu 1} + ex^1 j^\mu$ does indeed obey a continuity equation, as in Eq. (4.69), its spatial integral

$$\int dx^1 (F^{01} + ex^1 j^0) \qquad (4.76)$$

does not generate a transformation analogous to Eq. (4.70).

In all these models, we see that the Goldstone theorem is essentially irrelevant to the question of whether or not the photon mass is zero. That is a dynamical question which cannot be answered on grounds of symmetry alone. Any attempt to apply the Goldstone theorem is defeated by the long-range character of the interaction, which ensures that the spatial integral of the time component of the appropriate current is not in fact time independent or, in the Lorentz gauge, by the fact that the resulting Goldstone bosons need have no connection with physical photons.

We now wish to return to models of the Goldstone type and consider the generalization to non-Abelian symmetry groups. Our aim will be to show that the earlier discussion of the Goldstone model may be extended to this case with essentially no change.

Let us consider an $n$-component real scalar field $\phi$ which transforms according to a given representation of a compact $g$-parameter Lie group $G$,

$$\phi \to e^{i\lambda \cdot T}\phi \qquad (4.77)$$

where

$$\lambda \cdot T = \lambda^A T_A$$

Here the $\lambda^A$ are $g$ real parameters, and the $T_A$ are $g$ real antisymmetric $n \times n$ matrices obeying the commutation relations of the Lie algebra of $G$,

$$[T_A, T_B] = T_C t^C_{AB}$$

These relations are satisfied in particular by the matrices

$$(t_A)^C_B = t^C_{AB}$$

of the adjoint representation.

We take as our Lagrangian an obvious generalization of (4.37),

$$L = \phi^\mu \, \partial_\mu \phi + \tfrac{1}{2}\phi^\mu \phi_\mu - V(\phi) \qquad (4.78)$$

in which, of course, $V(\phi)$ is assumed to be invariant under the transformations (4.77). However, we shall not in this case assume a particular form like Eq. (4.39).

From the invariance of the Lagrangian we may infer the existence of currents

$$j_A{}^\mu = -i\phi^\mu T_A \phi \qquad (4.79)$$

satisfying the continuity equations

$$\partial_\mu j_A{}^\mu = 0 \qquad (4.80)$$

Formally, the transformations (4.77) are generated by the integrated time components of these currents. However, as in Eq. (4.45), these operators do not in fact exist in the limit of infinite volume, except in the case where the symmetry is unbroken and the vacuum is invariant.

From the assumed translational invariance of the vacuum state, with the equations of motion

$$\begin{aligned} \partial_\mu \phi &= -\phi_\mu \\ \partial_\mu \phi^\mu &= -\partial V/\partial \phi \end{aligned} \qquad (4.81)$$

we obtain the consistency condition

$$\left\langle \frac{\partial V}{\partial \phi} \right\rangle = 0 \tag{4.82}$$

analogous to Eq. (4.40).

If $\langle \phi \rangle = \eta$ is a consistent broken-symmetry solution of Eq. (4.82), then so also is $\langle \phi \rangle = e^{i\lambda \cdot T} \eta$ for any $\lambda$. Thus, although $\langle \phi \rangle$ has $n$ components, and there are $n$ Eqs. (4.82), $\langle \phi \rangle$ is not completely determined, and these equations cannot all be independent. In fact, the number of algebraically independent equations is just the number of group invariants which can be constructed from the left-hand side of Eq. (4.82). Since these equations transform according to the same $n$-dimensional representation of $G$ as does $\langle \phi \rangle$, this number is equal to the number of group invariants constructible from $\langle \phi \rangle$. It has been called the *canonical number* $\nu$ by Bludman and Klein[47] and is completely determined by the representation to which $\phi$ belongs. We see, therefore, that there are just enough independent equations in (4.82) to fix the invariants formed from $\langle \phi \rangle$. Conceivably, there might be several distinct solutions for these invariants. However, for simplicity we shall assume that the solution is unique.

Let us now choose a particular canonical value of $\eta$, so that all other physically equivalent solutions of Eq. (4.82) may be written in the form $\langle \phi \rangle = e^{i\lambda \cdot T} \eta$. In general, not all values of the parameters $\lambda$ will yield distinct values of $\langle \phi \rangle$. For there may be a nontrivial subgroup $G^\eta$ of elements of $G$ which leave the canonical $\eta$ invariant,

$$e^{i\kappa \cdot T} \eta = \eta$$

This is the stability subgroup of $G$ at $\eta$. Let its dimension be $g - r$. Then every element of $G$ may be written in the form

$$e^{i\lambda \cdot T} = e^{i\mu \cdot T} e^{i\kappa \cdot T}$$

where $e^{i\kappa \cdot T}$ is an element of $G^\eta$, and the $r$ remaining parameters $\mu$ parameterize the factor space $G/G^\eta$. (This is the space of cosets of $G^\eta$, and is not in general a group.) Then

$$\langle \phi \rangle = e^{i\mu \cdot T} e^{i\kappa \cdot T} \eta = e^{i\mu \cdot T} \eta$$

so that these same parameters $\mu$ serve to label the various degenerate ground states distinguished by different values of $\langle \phi \rangle$. Moreover, distinct values of $\mu$ correspond to distinct values of $\langle \phi \rangle$, since otherwise the relevant group element should belong to $G^\eta$. (At any rate, this is true in the neighborhood of the identity. There could in fact be a discrete set of different values of $\mu$ corresponding to the same $\langle\phi\rangle$. However, this is irrelevant for our purposes.) The ground states therefore form an $r$-dimensional manifold. Since we have already seen that the $n$ components of $\langle\phi\rangle$ are restricted by $\nu$ conditions, we have the equality $r = n - \nu$.

To clarify the meaning of these numbers, it may be helpful to consider some simple examples. Let us take the group $G$ to be $SU(3)$. If $\phi$ belongs to the adjoint representation, then $n = g = 8$. By appropriate choice of axes, we can arrange that the only nonvanishing components of $\eta$ are $\eta_3$ and $\eta_8$, in the usual notation. Thus $\nu = 2$, corresponding to the fact that just two invariants can be formed from $\langle\phi\rangle$. Here the dimensionality of the manifold of equivalent values of $\langle\phi\rangle$ is $r = 6$. Moreover, $\eta$ is left invariant by a two-dimensional subgroup $U(1) \times U(1)$ of $G$, so that $g - r = 2$, as it should be.

As a second example, suppose that $\phi$ belongs to the fundamental three-dimensional representation of $G$. Since this representation is necessarily complex, while $n$ denotes the number of real components, we have $n = 6$. By appropriate choice of axes, $\eta$ may be brought to a form in which only one of its three components is nonzero, and this one is real. Thus $\nu = 1$, corresponding to the fact that only one group invariant can be formed from $\langle\phi\rangle$. It follows that $r = 5$. Moreover, $\eta$ is left invariant by a three-dimensional subgroup $SU(2)$ of $SU(3)$, so that $g - r = 3$.

It should be noted that when $\langle\phi\rangle = \eta$, the subgroup $G^\eta$ of transformations which leave $\eta$ unchanged is the subgroup of unbroken symmetry transformations. We have, therefore, $r$ broken components of the symmetry, and $g - r$ unbroken components. It will be convenient in the following discussion to distinguish these components by different types of indices. We shall use labels $I, J, \ldots = 1, \ldots, r$ for the parameters $\mu$ of the coset space $G/G^\eta$, and $P, Q, \ldots = r + 1, \ldots, g$ for the parameters $\kappa$ of the subgroup $G^\eta$ of unbroken symmetry transformations. By definition, we have

$$T_P\eta = 0 \qquad (4.83)$$

for these latter components. Thus $T_A\eta$ is nonzero only when $A$ is one of the first $r$ indices. Moreover, we can show that the $n \times r$ matrix

$$(T_I\eta)^a \qquad (4.84)$$

has its maximal rank $r$. For if not, it has an eigenvector $c^I$ with eigen-value zero, so that we can find a linear combination of the generators such that

$$c^I T_I \eta = 0$$

But then this linear combination $c^I T_I$ would have to belong to the subalgebra corresponding to $G^n$, which by definition it does not.

Now, to obtain a first approximation to the solution of the field equations [Eqs. (4.81)] we may, as in the Abelian case, make the substitution

$$\phi = \eta + \phi' \tag{4.85}$$

and retain only linear terms in $\phi'$. Defining the mass matrix

$$(m^2)_{ab} = \left( \frac{\partial^2 V}{\partial \phi^a \, \partial \phi^b} \right)_{\phi = \eta} \tag{4.86}$$

we then have

$$(-\partial^2 + m^2)\phi' = 0 \tag{4.87}$$

On grounds of stability it is reasonable to assume that $m^2$ has no negative eigenvalues. Moreover, since $V$ is an invariant, it is a function of the $\nu$ invariants which can be constructed from $\phi$. Therefore the rank of the matrix $m^2$ is at most equal to $\nu$. It could happen in special cases that the rank was in fact less than $\nu$, for example if $V$ were actually independent of certain of the invariants. However, we shall assume that this is not the case, and that $m^2$ has its maximal rank $\nu$. Thus we have $\nu$ massive fields, and $r = n - \nu$ massless ones, as one might expect from the fact that there are $r$ broken-symmetry components.

As in the case of the group parameters, it is now convenient to distinguish two sets of indices among the components of $\phi^a$. By an orthogonal transformation, we can arrange that $m^2$ consists of a non-singular $\nu \times \nu$ matrix surrounded by zeros. To match the decomposition of the indices labeling the group parameters, we shall use $i, j, \ldots = 1, \ldots, r$ for the indices corresponding to the subspace annihilated by $m^2$, and $p, q, \ldots = r + 1, \ldots, n$ for the indices of the orthogonal $\nu$-dimensional subspace on which $m^2$ is nonsingular.

Now, the invariance of $V$ requires that

$$\frac{\partial V}{\partial \phi} T_A \phi = 0$$

Hence, differentiating with respect to $\phi$ and setting $\phi = \eta$ we obtain

$$m^2 T_A \eta = 0$$

Using the coordinates we have chosen this equation may be written as

$$(T_I \eta)^p = 0 \tag{4.88}$$

Thus only the first $r$ components of $T_I \eta$ are different from zero. But, we showed earlier that the matrix (4.84) has rank $r$. Thus it follows that the $r \times r$ matrix

$$X_I{}^j = (T_I \eta)^j \tag{4.89}$$

is nonsingular. Moreover, from the antisymmetry of the matrices $T_I$ it follows that

$$\eta T_I \eta = \eta_j X_I{}^j = 0$$

whence

$$\eta_j = 0 \tag{4.90}$$

Thus the only nonvanishing components of $\eta$ are the $\nu$ components $\eta^p$ in the subspace on which $m^2$ is nonsingular.

Let us now examine the effect of coupling the conserved currents $j_A{}^\mu$ to a set of $g$ gauge vector fields $A_\mu{}^A$. We take in place of Eq. (4.78) the Lagrangian

$$L = -\tfrac{1}{2} F_A{}^{\mu\nu}(\partial_\mu A_\nu{}^A - \partial_\nu A_\mu{}^A - it_{BC}^A A_\mu{}^B A_\nu{}^C) + \tfrac{1}{4} F_A{}^{\mu\nu} F_{\mu\nu}^A$$
$$+ \phi^\mu(\partial_\mu - iA_\mu{}^A T_A)\phi + \tfrac{1}{2}\phi^\mu \phi_\mu - V(\phi) \tag{4.91}$$

We now make the same linearizing approximation as before, writing $\phi = \eta + \phi'$ and retaining only linear terms in the equations of motion, which thus reduce to

$$F_{\mu\nu}^A = \partial_\mu A_\nu{}^A - \partial_\nu A_\mu{}^A$$
$$\partial_\mu F_A^{\mu\nu} = i\phi^\nu T_A \eta$$
$$\phi_\mu = -\partial_\mu \phi' + iA_\mu{}^A T_A \eta$$
$$\partial_\mu \phi^\mu = -m^2 \phi'$$

with $m^2$ given as before by Eq. (4.86).

Using the fact that the only nonvanishing components of the matrix $(T_A \eta)^b$ are those of the nonsingular submatrix $X_I{}^j$, given by Eq. (4.89), we find that these equations separate into three distinct sets. For the vector fields $A_\mu{}^p$ corresponding to the $g - r$ unbroken components of the symmetry, we have simply the equations for free massless vector fields. Similarly, for the scalar fields $\phi^p$ corresponding to the subspace on which $m^2$ is nonsingular, we recover the corresponding members of the set of equations (4.87). Finally, for the first $r$ indices, it is convenient to introduce in place of $A^I$ and $\phi^i$ the new fields

$$V_\mu{}^I = A_\mu{}^I + i(X^{-1})_j{}^I \, \partial_\mu\phi^j$$

Then $\phi_\mu{}^j = X_I{}^j V_\mu{}^I$, and so the equations reduce to

$$\begin{aligned} F_{\mu\nu}^I &= \partial_\mu V_\nu{}^I - \partial_\nu V_\mu{}^I \\ \partial_\mu F_I{}^{\mu\nu} &= (M^2)_{IJ} V^{J\nu} \end{aligned} \tag{4.92}$$

where the vector-particle mass matrix

$$M^2 = - \tilde{X}X$$

is positive definite because of the nonsingularity of $X$. More explicitly, it is given by

$$(M^2)_{IJ} = - (T_I\eta)_j(T_J\eta)^j \tag{4.93}$$

We conclude therefore that at least in this linear approximation the effect of introducing vector gauge fields is to eliminate all the massless scalar particles from the theory. The $r$ massless scalar fields originally present combine with $r$ of the vector gauge fields to produce $r$ massive vector fields, with masses given in terms of the symmetry-breaking parameters $\eta$ by the eigenvalues of the mass matrix [Eq. (4.93)]. There remain in the theory $g - r$ massless vector fields, corresponding to the unbroken components of the symmetry group.

Finally, let us consider briefly the problem of going beyond the linear approximation. To do this, it is convenient, as in the Abelian gauge case, to adopt a polar decomposition of $\phi$, analogous to Eq. (4.59). We write

$$\phi = e^{i\theta \cdot T}\rho \tag{4.94}$$

where $\rho$ has only $\nu$ independent components $\rho^p$, while the $r$ variables $\theta = (\theta^I)$ correspond to the parameters $\mu$ of the coset space $G/G^n$.

We also introduce new fields related to $A_\mu{}^A$ and $F_A{}^{\mu\nu}$ by an operator gauge transformation determined by the variables $\theta$, namely

$$V_\mu{}^A = (e^{-i\theta \cdot t})_B{}^A A_\mu{}^B + \left(\frac{1 - e^{-i\theta \cdot t}}{i\theta \cdot t}\right)_I{}^A \partial_\mu\theta^I$$

and

$$G_A^{\mu\nu} = F_B^{\mu\nu}(e^{i\theta \cdot t})_A{}^B$$

Then, using the gauge invariance of the Lagrangian (4.91), we may write it as

$$L = -\tfrac{1}{2}G_A^{\mu\nu}(\partial_\mu V_\nu^A - \partial_\nu V_\mu^A - it_{AC}^B V_\mu^B V_\nu^C)$$
$$+ \tfrac{1}{4}G_A^{\mu\nu}G_{\mu\nu}^A + \rho^\mu(\partial_\mu - iV_\mu^A T_A)\rho$$
$$- \sigma^\mu V_\mu^A T_A \rho + \tfrac{1}{2}\rho^\mu \rho_\mu + \tfrac{1}{2}\sigma^\mu \sigma_\mu - V(\rho)$$

where we have written

$$\rho_p^{\;\mu} = (\phi^\mu e^{\theta \cdot T})_p$$
$$\sigma_i^{\;\mu} = (\phi^\mu e^{\theta \cdot T})_i$$

We may then eliminate the fields $\sigma^\mu$. Writing $\rho = \eta + \rho'$, we finally obtain

$$L = -\tfrac{1}{2}G_A^{\mu\nu}(\partial_\mu V_\nu^A - \partial_\nu V_\mu^A - it_{BC}^A V_\mu^B V_\nu^C)$$
$$+\tfrac{1}{4}G_A^{\mu\nu}G_{\mu\nu}^A + \rho^\mu \,\partial_\mu \rho' + \tfrac{1}{2}\rho^\mu \rho_\mu - V(\eta + \rho')$$
$$- i\rho^\mu T_A \rho' V_\mu^A + \tfrac{1}{2}[V_\mu^A T_A(\eta + \rho')]_j \, [V^{B\mu}T_B(\eta + \rho')]^j \quad (4.95)$$

Note that although the term

$$- i\rho^\mu T_A \eta V_\mu^A$$

vanishes identically in virtue of Eqs. (4.83) and (4.88), it is not generally true that the corresponding term involving $\rho'$, which we have included in Eq. (4.95), is necessarily zero.

The Lagrangian Eq. (4.95) clearly exhibits the same structure as its linearized approximation. There are $\nu$ massive scalar fields $\rho'$, with masses given in lowest order by the mass matrix (4.86). Of the vector fields, $r$ have a bare mass term in the Lagrangian, given by Eq. (4.93), while the remaining $g - r$ have only cubic or quartic interaction terms. There is, however, no guarantee in this case that the masses will remain unrenormalized, and it is quite conceivable that the physical particles corresponding to even these fields could be massive (just as there is no known requirement which forces the photon to have zero mass).

We see, therefore, that whether the broken symmetry group is Abelian or non-Abelian, the introduction of gauge vector fields serves to remove all the unwanted massless scalar particles from the theory. There remain $\nu$ massive scalar and $r$ massive vector fields, and also a number $g - r$ of massless vector fields, equal to the dimensionality of the subgroup of unbroken symmetry transformations. In particular, no such particles are left if all the components of the symmetry group are broken.

## V. Nonrelativistic Broken Symmetries

Broken symmetry theories (though not always recognized as such) have played a major role in our understanding of many phenomena in nonrelativistic physics, particularly ferromagnetism, superconductivity, and superfluidity. These theories can often be studied with much greater mathematical rigor than relativistic ones and, moreover, the physical significance of the mathematical formalism is often much clearer. It is therefore particularly valuable to study nonrelativistic broken-symmetry theories.

It will be useful to begin with some general remarks applicable to all broken-symmetry theories and later to concentrate on particular cases. We are in each case concerned with a theory whose basic equations of motion and commutation relations are invariant under some given group of transformations of the fundamental dynamical variables. So long as the total volume $\Omega$ of the system is finite, these transformations are induced by unitary operators of the form

$$U_\Omega(\eta) = \exp(i\eta Q_\Omega)$$

where the generator $Q_\Omega$ may be expressed either as an integral

$$Q_\Omega = \int_\Omega d^3x j^0(\mathbf{x}, t) \tag{5.1}$$

or a sum over lattice sites

$$Q_\Omega = \sum_{\mathbf{x} \in \Omega} j_{\mathbf{x}}^0(t) \tag{5.2}$$

where $j^0$ is an appropriately defined density. In either case it satisfies a conservation law

$$\frac{d}{dt} Q_\Omega = 0 \tag{5.3}$$

or, provided that $Q_\Omega$ is not explicitly time dependent,

$$[Q_\Omega, H_\Omega] = 0 \tag{5.4}$$

where $H_\Omega$ is the Hamiltonian in volume $\Omega$. The only case we shall be concerned with in which Eq. (5.4) does not hold is that of Galilean transformations. For the moment, however, we assume that Eq. (5.4) is satisfied.

We say that the symmetry is broken if, in the limit of infinite volume, the ground state is not itself invariant under these transformations. We may distinguish two classes of broken-symmetry theories. In the simpler case, of which the isotropic ferromagnet is a good example, the ground state $|0\rangle_\Omega$ in a finite volume $\Omega$ is already nonsymmetric. Then there must exist a set of states

$$|\eta\rangle_\Omega = U_\Omega^+(\eta)|0\rangle_\Omega \tag{5.5}$$

which, because of Eq. (5.4), are degenerate in energy with the ground state. However it may also happen that the ground state is completely symmetric in any finite volume, but that in the limit of infinite volume there is a degenerate set of ground states. We defer consideration of this case for the moment.

To show that the ground state $|0\rangle_\Omega$ is not invariant it is sufficient to find some operator $A$ whose ground-state expectation value is not invariant,

$$_\Omega\langle 0|U_\Omega(\eta)AU_\Omega^+(\eta)|0\rangle_\Omega \neq {}_\Omega\langle 0|A|0\rangle_\Omega$$

or, in infinitesimal form,

$$-i_\Omega\langle 0|[A, Q_\Omega]|0\rangle_\Omega = \bar{\eta} \neq 0 \tag{5.6}$$

In the ground state of a ferromagnet, for example, all the spins are aligned parallel to some given direction. The degenerate ground states, obtained by spin rotations, are characterized by different orientations of the overall magnetization vector. Here the operator $A$ may be chosen, for example, to be a component of the spin operator at a particular lattice site.

In any finite volume $\Omega$ the degenerate ground states $|0\rangle_\Omega$ are related by unitary transformations; however, it is easy to see that in the limit of infinite volume this can no longer be true. Suppose that there exist limiting states $|\eta\rangle$, related by unitary transformations,

$$|\eta\rangle = e^{i\eta Q}|0\rangle$$

with

$$Q = \int d^3x j^0(\mathbf{x}, t)$$

and that these states belong to the domain of definition of the operator $Q$. Then the scalar product $\langle 0|\eta\rangle$ must be a continuous, differentiable function of $\eta$. But

$$\frac{d}{d\eta} {}_\Omega\langle 0|\eta\rangle_\Omega = -i_\Omega\langle 0|Q_\Omega|\eta\rangle_\Omega$$
$$= -i\Omega_\Omega\langle 0|j^0(\mathbf{0}, t)|\eta\rangle_\Omega$$

by translational invariance. In the limit $\Omega \to \infty$ this expression in either zero (in which case all the states are identical) or infinite, which is impossible. What happens, in fact, is that the scalar products $_\Omega\langle 0|\eta\rangle_\Omega$ tend to zero as $\Omega \to \infty$. (We shall verify this statement in detail for specific examples later.) The limiting states $|\eta\rangle$ therefore constitute an uncountably infinite set of orthonormal states, which evidently cannot all belong to a single separable Hilbert space. Each of them actually belongs to a distinct unitarily inequivalent representation of the canonical commutation relations.

Let us now turn to the second class of broken-symmetry theories. These have the property that in any finite volume the degeneracy of the ground state is only approximate. That is to say, there is a unique nondegenerate ground state, but there are other states with only slightly larger energy which become degenerate with it in the limit of infinite volume. For example, the state of a crystal whose center of mass is localized to within some distance $R$ of the origin has slightly greater energy than the true ground state, but in the limit of infinite volume keeping the density fixed this energy difference tends to zero. Thus an infinite crystal has translationally noninvariant states degenerate with the ground state. Another example is provided by the condensed Bose gas. In any finite volume there is a unique nondegenerate ground state for any given particle number $N$. However in the limit of infinite volume keeping the density fixed, we find a degenerate set of ground states which may be labeled by the phase of the wave function. These states may be obtained as limits of finite volume states in which the total particle number is somewhat uncertain. However in the limit of infinite volume the particle density tends to a definite limit.

A very convenient way to treat such problems [see Bogoliubov[48]] is to add a small symmetry-breaking perturbation $\nu H_1$ to the Hamiltonian. [A recent discussion from a point of view similar to that adopted here has been given by Wagner.[49]] This is useful even in the first class of broken-symmetry theories if we want to discuss the effects of finite temperature. In a ferromagnet, for example, at finite temperature we should normally find a uniform population of all the degenerate ground states. It is, however, much more convenient for many purposes to deal with a state in which there is a definite magnetization direction. To achieve this we add a small external magnetic field. We then compute expectation values in an appropriate ensemble for volume $\Omega$,

$$\langle A\rangle_{\nu,\Omega} = \frac{\mathrm{tr}_\Omega\, A e^{-\beta(H+\nu H_1)}}{\mathrm{tr}_\Omega\, e^{-\beta(H+\nu H_1)}} \qquad (5.7)$$

where $\text{tr}_\Omega$ denotes the trace over the Hilbert space of states of the system in volume $\Omega$. Then we take the limit of infinite volume, and finally let $\nu \to 0$, obtaining

$$\langle A \rangle = \lim_{\nu \to 0} \lim_{\Omega \to \infty} \langle A \rangle_{\nu,\Omega} \qquad (5.8)$$

It is characteristic of broken symmetry theories that the order of these limits is not reversible. Indeed from the present point of view this may be taken as the definition of a broken symmetry. If we set $\nu = 0$ first we obtain for any $\Omega$ an ensemble in which all the degenerate ground states are equally populated. Thus the expectation values are fully symmetric under the transformations induced by the unitary operators $U_\Omega(\eta)$. This symmetry is naturally preserved in the infinite-volume limit. On the other hand, if we retain the symmetry-breaking interaction we find that for large $\Omega$ the energy differences it produces between the otherwise degenerate (or nearly degenerate) states are roughly proportional to $\Omega$. Thus for large $\Omega$ one particular member of the degenerate set will be much more heavily populated than any other. In the limit $\Omega \to \infty$ we select a single state. Thus the resulting expectation values will not be invariant under the transformations, and this noninvariance will persist even when we finally set $\nu = 0$.

This method can, of course, be used even at zero temperature. We introduce the interaction $\nu H_1$ which breaks the degeneracy of the ground states, or which artificially depresses the energy of the state we wish to select below that of the true ground state. Then in the limit of infinite volume a single member of the set of degenerate states is selected.

A very important question is the following. Are these various degenerate ground states in the infinite-volume limit *physically* equivalent or not? In other words, can we make a physical measurement which will distinguish between them? The answer to this question is closely bound up with measurement theory, and in fact depends on our choice of operators to represent observables. If we require that all observables should themselves be invariant under the group, then the answer must be that they are indistinguishable. But if we allow interactions with measuring apparatus which break the symmetry, then of course we can distinguish them. For example, it is usual to admit as observables operators which are not translationally invariant, but localized in some region of space. Naturally, the interaction with a measuring apparatus designed to measure such a quantity breaks the translational symmetry of the system, although viewed by an observer external to both system and apparatus there is complete translational symmetry. What we are measuring is of course position relative to the apparatus. In such a case, states distinguished only by the position of the center of mass are distinguishable. Similar remarks apply to the measurement of the magnetization direction of a ferromagnet and, less obviously perhaps, to the phase of a superfluid or superconductor. None of these quantities has any absolute significance, but all can be measured relative to an externally defined standard, provided that we allow interactions which break the appropriate symmetry. (The Josephson effect provides a possible realization of such a measuring device for a superconductor.)

It should be noted that if we allow symmetry-breaking interactions with external systems then these same interactions may be identified with the $\nu H_1$ above. An interaction which permits an observable distinction to be drawn between the degenerate ground states also provides a mechanism which can physically determine which ground state is selected by the system. Thus, for example, an external magnetic field can be used to measure the magnetization direction in a ferromagnet, and also to determine in advance along which direction the spins will align themselves. If such interactions are allowed, then the addition of a small symmetry-breaking interaction $\nu H_1$ is more than a mathematical device. It is a correct description of physical reality.

Now let us examine the application of the Goldstone theorem to nonrelativistic broken-symmetry theories. The theorem states that if there are no long-range interactions, then such a theory must possess excitation modes whose frequency tends to zero as $\mathbf{k} \to 0$. We shall follow in outline the method of Lange.[50] [See also Kibble.[51]]

We consider a particular "ground state" $|0\rangle_\Omega$, which need not in fact be the state of lowest energy, except in the infinite-volume limit. A similar discussion applies if we replace the expectation value in this state by an ensemble average of appropriate type.

We define the quantity

$$f_\Omega(\mathbf{k}, \omega) = -i \int_\Omega d^3x \int dt \, e^{-i\mathbf{k}\cdot\mathbf{x} + i\omega t} {}_\Omega\langle 0|[A, j^0(\mathbf{x}, t)]|0\rangle_\Omega \quad (5.9)$$

and its infinite-volume limit,

$$f(\mathbf{k}, \omega) = \lim_{\Omega \to \infty} f_\Omega(\mathbf{k}, \omega)$$

where $A$ is the operator in Eq. (5.6) whose ground-state expectation value is noninvariant. We assume that this operator is a quasi-local function of the dynamical variables at time $t = 0$. Let us suppose first that it is a completely local function, localized at the origin. Then Eq. (5.6) with the locality of the commutation relations would imply that

$$-i_\Omega \langle 0|[A, j^0(\mathbf{x}, 0)]|0\rangle_\Omega = \tilde{\eta}\delta(\mathbf{x}) \tag{5.10}$$

whence we obtain a sum rule

$$\int \frac{d\omega}{2\pi} f_\Omega(\mathbf{k}, \omega) = \tilde{\eta} \tag{5.11}$$

valid for all values of $\mathbf{k}$.

If $A$ is only approximately local, but depends on the field operators within some finite volume $V_0$, then the commutator in Eq. (5.10) is not proportional to a delta function. Nevertheless we still have

$$-i \int_V d^3x_\Omega \langle 0|[A, j^0(\mathbf{x}, 0)]|0\rangle_\Omega = \tilde{\eta} \tag{5.12}$$

for any volume $V$ containing $V_0$. In this case the integral in Eq. (5.11) is no longer independent of $\mathbf{k}$. However in the limit $\Omega \to \infty$ it is a continuous (indeed, entire) function of $\mathbf{k}$ satisfying the limiting condition

$$\lim_{\mathbf{k}\to 0} \int \frac{d\omega}{2\pi} f(\mathbf{k}, \omega) = \tilde{\eta} \tag{5.13}$$

which is in fact all we require. This is equivalent to the condition

$$\lim_{V\to\infty} \lim_{\Omega\to\infty} -i \int_V d^3x_\Omega \langle 0|[A, j^0(\mathbf{x}, 0)]|0\rangle_\Omega = \tilde{\eta} \tag{5.14}$$

This is the broken-symmetry condition in its weakest form and is sufficient to prove Eq. (5.13).

Equation (5.13), obtained by integrating over a large volume $V$ and taking the limit $V \to \infty$, should be carefully distinguished from the condition which results from integrating over the entire volume $\Omega$. Because of Eq. (5.3) this yields a time-independent result

$$-i \int_\Omega d^3x_\Omega \langle 0|[A, j^0(\mathbf{x}, t)]|0\rangle_\Omega = \tilde{\eta}$$

It follows that

$$\int \frac{d\omega}{2\pi} e^{-i\omega t} f_\Omega(\mathbf{0}, \omega) = \tilde{\eta}$$

whence

$$f_\Omega(\mathbf{0}, \omega) = 2\pi\tilde{\eta}\delta(\omega) \tag{5.15}$$

It is clear from the definition [Eq. (5.9)] that whenever $f_\Omega(\mathbf{k}, \omega) \neq 0$ there must be intermediate states of energy $\omega$ and momentum $\mathbf{k}$ (relative to the ground-state energy and momentum) which couple to the ground state via the operator $A$, and also via $j^0$. Thus from Eq. (5.15) we can conclude that for $\mathbf{k} = \mathbf{0}$ there are such states with $\omega = 0$. These are, however, simply the degenerate ground states $|\eta\rangle_\Omega$, and the fact that the energy of these "excitations" vanishes is simply a restatement of the broken-symmetry condition.

For example, for a ferromagnet the condition (5.15) tells us that no energy is required to rotate all the spins together. Clearly the rotated ground states may be regarded as formed from the original ground state by adding a number of $\mathbf{k} = \mathbf{0}$ spin waves. However the fact that $\omega = 0$ for these modes in fact tells us nothing about the physically interesting question of the frequency spectrum of long-wavelength spin waves.

These degenerate ground states may be eliminated from the problem by considering the limit of infinite total volume, $\Omega \to \infty$. For it is easy to see that they contribute to the sum over intermediate states in Eq. (5.9) only for the isolated value $\mathbf{k} = \mathbf{0}$. (This argument assumes translational invariance and requires modification when it is the translational symmetry itself that is being broken.) This contribution is proportional to a Kronecker delta $\delta_{\mathbf{k}\mathbf{0}}$ rather than to a Dirac delta function. Thus in Eq. (5.10) or Eq. (5.12) their contribution falls off like $\Omega^{-1}$ and vanishes in the limit $\Omega \to \infty$ [see Lange[50]].

In fact, in the infinite volume limit the degenerate ground states cannot be coupled to each other by any operator $A$, since they belong to quite distinct Hilbert spaces. Physically, in a ferromagnet for example, this is an expression of the fact that to go from one ground state to another in the case of infinite volume requires the flipping of an infinite number of spins. This cannot be achieved by operating with any finite operator.

Thus if we let $\Omega \to \infty$ then the condition (5.13) gives us genuine information about the frequency spectrum of long-wavelength excitations. The degenerate ground states are irrelevant. Let us then consider the expression (5.14). If we could show that it was time independent, then we could prove not only Eq. (5.15), but also the much more interesting result

$$\lim_{\mathbf{k} \to \mathbf{0}} f(\mathbf{k}, \omega) = 2\pi\tilde{\eta}\delta(\omega) \qquad (5.16)$$

This is the Goldstone theorem. It shows that there are excitations for which $\omega \to 0$ as $\mathbf{k} \to \mathbf{0}$.

To do this [see Lange[50]] it is sufficient to show that for all $n$

$$\lim_{\mathbf{k} \to 0} \int \frac{d\omega}{2\pi} \omega^n f(\mathbf{k}, \omega) = \bar{\eta}\delta_{n0} \qquad (5.17)$$

For $n = 0$ we already have the required result in Eq. (5.13). In many cases one can prove that $f$ (or some closely related function) must be positive. Then it is sufficient to prove Eq. (5.17) for one other value of $n$. For $n > 0$ it is equivalent to

$$i^{n+1} \lim_{V \to \infty} \int_V d^3x \langle 0 | \left[ A, \frac{d^n j^0}{dt^n}(\mathbf{x}, 0) \right] | 0 \rangle = 0 \qquad (5.18)$$

Now corresponding to the global conservation law [Eq. (5.3)] there must be a microscopic conservation law expressible in the form

$$\frac{d}{dt} \int_V d^3x j^0(\mathbf{x}, t) = -S_V(t) \qquad (5.19)$$

where $S_V$ is a surface integral over the bounding surface of $V$, or at any rate has contributions only from a small region close to this surface. Thus it is sufficient to show that

$$\lim_{V \to \infty} \langle 0 | [A, S_V(0)] | 0 \rangle = 0$$
$$\lim_{V \to \infty} \langle 0 | [A, [H, S_V(0)]] | 0 \rangle = 0 \qquad (5.20)$$

and so on. Often (as noted above) it is enough to prove one or two of these relations. The rest follow by positivity of the spectral function.

Since $A$ is assumed localized at or near the origin, and $S_V$ is localized on or near the boundary of $V$, the locality of the equal-time commutation relations will normally ensure that the first of these equations [Eqs. (5.20)] is satisfied. Whether the remaining equations are satisfied or not depends on the range of the interactions. If the interactions are of any given finite range $R$, then the commutator of $H$ with any given local function will depend on field operators only within a distance $R$ of the original point of localization. In that case it is clear that for every value of $n$ we can choose a volume large enough to make the multiple commutator vanish. In that case we have therefore established Eq. (5.16). An only slightly more complex argument serves to prove the same result for interactions which fall off exponentially with distance. However for those which fall off as an inverse power one must look at the magnitudes of the quantities involved in more detail. For this case a general discussion is rather difficult since as we shall see later the limiting power of $r$ is not the same in all cases but depends on the type of system being considered.

Let us then recapitulate the theorem briefly. In any broken symmetry theory with only short-range interactions there must be Goldstone excitations, whose frequency vanishes continuously ($\omega \rightarrow 0$) in the long-wavelength limit ($\mathbf{k} \rightarrow \mathbf{0}$). These may be pictured as space-dependent oscillations in the parameter which distinguishes the various degenerate ground states. (Recall that for finite volume the $\mathbf{k} = \mathbf{0}$ modes correspond to a constant change in this parameter.) However, when long-range interactions are present, the theorem does not follow, and indeed in practice, the introduction of long-range forces often serves to eliminate these zero-energy-gap modes. What precisely is meant by "long-range" and "short-range" is a question which can only be answered in the context of more specific theories.

Before turning to the discussion of the various examples of physical interest it may be helpful to consider a simple soluble model which serves to illustrate some of these ideas [see Kibble[51]]. This is, in essence, a nonrelativistic form of the Boulware-Gilbert model discussed in the preceding section, in which the electromagnetic field has been replaced by an instantaneous interaction. The model is described by the Hamiltonian

$$H = \tfrac{1}{2} \int d^3x [\pi^2 + (\nabla\phi)^2] + \tfrac{1}{2} \int d^3x \int d^3y \pi(\mathbf{x}) V(\mathbf{x} - \mathbf{y}) \pi(\mathbf{y}) \quad (5.21)$$

along with the canonical commutation relation

$$[\phi(\mathbf{x}, t), \pi(\mathbf{y}, t)] = i\delta(\mathbf{x} - \mathbf{y}) \quad (5.22)$$

It is invariant under the field translations

$$\phi(\mathbf{x}) \rightarrow \phi(\mathbf{x}) + \eta \quad (5.23)$$

which are generated in any volume $\Omega$ by the unitary operators

$$\exp\left[-i\eta \int_\Omega d^3x \pi(\mathbf{x})\right] \quad (5.24)$$

However, it is clear that the expectation value

$$\langle\phi\rangle = \langle 0|\phi(\mathbf{x}, t)|0\rangle \quad (5.25)$$

cannot be invariant under (5.23). We therefore have a broken symmetry of what we termed the "naturally occurring" type. There is a degenerate set of ground states labeled by different values of $\langle \phi \rangle$.

For this model $j^0 = -\pi$, and there is a microscopic conservation law of the form

$$-\dot{\pi} + \mathbf{\nabla} \cdot (\mathbf{\nabla} \phi) = 0 \tag{5.26}$$

so that the surface contribution defined in Eq. (5.15) is

$$S_V = \int_{\sigma(V)} d\boldsymbol{\sigma} \cdot \mathbf{\nabla} \phi \tag{5.27}$$

integrated over the boundary $\sigma(V)$ of $V$.

Equation (5.8) is, in this case, obtained simply by taking the expectation value of the canonical commutation relation (5.22). It is easy starting from this equation to follow through the discussion of the Goldstone theorem in detail. Instead of doing this, however, we shall simply solve the model and verify its conclusions.

Since we are interested in the limit of infinite volume, $\Omega \to \infty$, it will be convenient always to define Fourier components by

$$\phi_{\mathbf{k}} = \int_{\Omega} d^3x \phi(\mathbf{x}) \, e^{-i\mathbf{k}\cdot\mathbf{x}} \tag{5.28}$$

so that

$$\phi(\mathbf{x}) = \frac{1}{\Omega} \sum_{\mathbf{k}} \phi_{\mathbf{k}} \, e^{i\mathbf{k}\cdot\mathbf{x}} \to \int \frac{d^3k}{(2\pi)^3} \, \phi_{\mathbf{k}} \, e^{i\mathbf{k}\cdot\mathbf{x}}$$

Our Hamiltonian is then

$$H = \frac{1}{2\Omega} \sum_{\mathbf{k}} \{\mathbf{k}^2 \phi_{\mathbf{k}}{}^* \phi_{\mathbf{k}} + [1 + V_{\mathbf{k}}] \pi_{\mathbf{k}}{}^* \pi_{\mathbf{k}}\} \tag{5.29}$$

The transformations (5.23) affect only the $\mathbf{k} = \mathbf{0}$ component:

$$\phi_{\mathbf{k}} \to \phi_{\mathbf{k}} + \eta \Omega \delta_{\mathbf{k},0}$$

From the equations of motion

$$\dot{\pi}_{\mathbf{k}} = -\mathbf{k}^2 \phi_{\mathbf{k}}$$
$$\dot{\phi}_{\mathbf{k}} = [1 + V_{\mathbf{k}}] \pi_{\mathbf{k}}$$

it is clear that the excitation spectrum is

$$\omega^2 = \mathbf{k}^2 [1 + V_{\mathbf{k}}] \tag{5.30}$$

If $\Omega$ is finite then $V_0$ is finite. (We assume that the singularity at $\mathbf{x} = \mathbf{0}$, if any, is integrable.) Thus it follows that there is always a mode with $\omega = 0$ at $\mathbf{k} = \mathbf{0}$, in agreement with our earlier conclusion. In this mode $\pi_0 = 0$, so that the mode consists merely of a constant change in $\phi$, which is of course a transformation from one degenerate ground state to another.

What is really interesting, however, is not this single mode but the behavior of the modes near $\mathbf{k} = \mathbf{0}$ in the infinite volume limit. The condition that $\omega \to 0$ as $\mathbf{k} \to \mathbf{0}$ is clearly

$$\lim_{\mathbf{k} \to \mathbf{0}} \mathbf{k}^2 V_{\mathbf{k}} = 0 \tag{5.31}$$

which is satisfied if the potential falls off at large distances faster than $1/r$. For a Coulomb potential, however,

$$V(\mathbf{x}) = g^2/4\pi|\mathbf{x}|$$

we have

$$V_{\mathbf{k}} = g^2/\mathbf{k}^2$$

and therefore

$$\lim_{\mathbf{k} \to \mathbf{0}} \omega^2(\mathbf{k}) = g^2 \tag{5.32}$$

Thus we have verified the general conclusions reached in the discussion of the Goldstone theorem. When only short-range interactions are admitted, the frequency spectrum tends to zero in the limit of zero wave number. However in the presence of long-range interactions (meaning in this case a $1/r$ potential) there is a finite energy gap.

It is also worth noting that for stability the potential must satisfy the inequality

$$1 + V_{\mathbf{k}} \geq 0 \tag{5.33}$$

for all values of $\mathbf{k}$. This means, in effect, that the potential must be repulsive or at least not too strongly attractive. For example, if we choose a Yukawa potential

$$V(\mathbf{x}) = \gamma e^{-\mu|\mathbf{x}|}/4\pi|\mathbf{x}|$$

then condition (5.33) becomes

$$\gamma \geq -\mu^2 \tag{5.34}$$

It is interesting to note that in the limiting case $\gamma = -\mu^2$ we no longer have $\omega \sim k$ near $\mathbf{k} = \mathbf{0}$ but rather $\omega \sim k^2$. This is an illustration of the fact that although the Goldstone theorem can guarantee for us the existence of modes whose frequency tends to zero, it is not in itself sufficient to tell us the details of the frequency spectrum.

Now let us turn to what is in many ways the simplest of the non-relativistic broken-symmetry theories—the isotropic ferromagnet. This is the system which was chosen by Lange[50] to exemplify his discussion of the nonrelativistic Goldstone theorem. We shall use subscripts to label the lattice sites, and superscripts to denote vector components. In total volume $\Omega$ the Hamiltonian is

$$H = -\tfrac{1}{2} \sum_{\mathbf{x},\mathbf{y}\in\Omega} J_{\mathbf{x}-\mathbf{y}} \mathbf{S}_{\mathbf{x}} \cdot \mathbf{S}_{\mathbf{y}} \tag{5.35}$$

The commutation relations are

$$[S_{\mathbf{x}}^i(t), S_{\mathbf{y}}^j(t)] = i\delta_{\mathbf{x},\mathbf{y}}\epsilon^{ijk}S_{\mathbf{x}}^k(t) \tag{5.36}$$

This model is invariant under the spin rotations generated by the unitary operators

$$U_\Omega(\boldsymbol{\theta}) = \exp{(i\boldsymbol{\theta}\cdot\mathbf{S})}$$

where $\mathbf{S}$ is the total spin

$$\mathbf{S} = \sum_{\mathbf{x}\in\Omega} \mathbf{S}_{\mathbf{x}} \tag{5.37}$$

However the ground state is clearly not invariant under these transformations. The broken-symmetry condition is expressed by the fact that there is a nonvanishing total magnetization, so that

$$\langle \mathbf{S}_{\mathbf{x}} \rangle = {}_\Omega\langle 0|\mathbf{S}_{\mathbf{x}}(t)|0\rangle_\Omega = \mathbf{s} \neq \mathbf{0} \tag{5.38}$$

(The antiferromagnet requires a different treatment.) The other ground states degenerate with $|0\rangle_\Omega$ are obtained by spin rotations,

$$|\boldsymbol{\theta}\rangle_\Omega = U_\Omega(\boldsymbol{\theta})|0\rangle_\Omega \tag{5.39}$$

They are characterized by different orientations of $\mathbf{s}$ (whose length is of course fixed).

If we choose the direction of $\mathbf{s}$ to be the $z$ axis then the ground state is the one in which every spin has its maximum $z$ component, so that

$$S_{\mathbf{x}}^+|0\rangle_\Omega = 0 \tag{5.40}$$

where

$$S_{\mathbf{x}}^+ = S_{\mathbf{x}}^x + iS_{\mathbf{x}}^y \tag{5.41}$$

The corresponding ground-state energy is

$$E = {}_\Omega\langle 0|H|0\rangle_\Omega = -\tfrac{1}{2}s^2 \sum_{\mathbf{x},\mathbf{y}} J_{\mathbf{x}-\mathbf{y}}$$
$$= -\tfrac{1}{2}Ns^2\tilde{J}_0 \tag{5.42}$$

where $N$ is the total number of lattice sites and $\tilde{J}$ is the Fourier transform of $J$,

$$\tilde{J}_{\mathbf{k}} = \sum_{\mathbf{x}\in\Omega} J_{\mathbf{x}}\, e^{-i\mathbf{k}\cdot\mathbf{x}} \tag{5.43}$$

Now let us consider the limit of infinite volume $\Omega \to \infty$. We wish to show that in this limit the degenerate ground states are no longer related by unitary operators and in fact belong to distinct Hilbert spaces. To this end we evaluate the scalar product

$$_\Omega\langle 0|\boldsymbol{\theta}\rangle_\Omega = {}_\Omega\langle 0|\, e^{i\boldsymbol{\theta}\cdot\mathbf{S}}|0\rangle_\Omega \tag{5.44}$$

We have here the same factor for each lattice site. If we use the Euler-angle representation $(\phi, \theta, \psi)$ for $\boldsymbol{\theta}$, this factor is

$$D_{ss}^s(\phi, \theta, \psi) = e^{is\phi} \cos^{2s}\tfrac{1}{2}\theta\, e^{is\psi}$$

Hence

$$_\Omega\langle 0|\phi\theta\psi\rangle_\Omega = [e^{is(\phi+\psi)} \cos^{2s}\tfrac{1}{2}\theta]^N \tag{5.45}$$

which tends to zero as $N \to \infty$, unless $\theta = 0$. It follows immediately that in this limit the various ground states belong to different (orthogonal) Hilbert spaces, since they form an uncountably infinite set of orthonormal states and therefore cannot belong to a single separable Hilbert space.

From the Hamiltonian (5.35) and the commutation relations (5.36) we obtain the equations of motion

$$\dot{\mathbf{S}}_{\mathbf{x}} = \sum_{\mathbf{y}\in\Omega} J_{\mathbf{x}-\mathbf{y}}\mathbf{S}_{\mathbf{x}} \times \mathbf{S}_{\mathbf{y}} \tag{5.46}$$

In this particular case the densities corresponding to the group generators are in fact identical with the basic dynamical variables. Thus Eq. (5.46) plays a dual role. It is at the same time the fundamental equation of motion and also the microscopic conservation law. That it has the appropriate structure may be seen by summing over a finite volume $V$. We then obtain

$$\frac{d}{dt}\sum_{\mathbf{x}\in V} \mathbf{S}_{\mathbf{x}} = \sum_{\mathbf{x}\in V}\sum_{\mathbf{y}\in\Omega-V} J_{\mathbf{x}-\mathbf{y}}\mathbf{S}_{\mathbf{x}} \times \mathbf{S}_{\mathbf{y}} \tag{5.47}$$

The right-hand side of this equation is the surface term. Clearly if the interactions have a finite range $R$, which means that

$$J_{\mathbf{x}-\mathbf{y}} = 0 \qquad \text{if} \qquad |\mathbf{x} - \mathbf{y}| > R \qquad (5.48)$$

then it has contributions only from points within a distance $R$ of the boundary of $V$.

To discuss the application of the Goldstone theorem to this particular case we may define, as in Eq. (5.9), the expression

$$f_\Omega{}^{ij}(\mathbf{k}, \omega) = -i \sum_{\mathbf{x} \in \Omega} \int dt \, e^{i\mathbf{k} \cdot \mathbf{x} - i\omega t} {}_\Omega \langle 0|[S_0{}^i(0), S_\mathbf{x}{}^j(t)]|0\rangle_\Omega$$

The equal-time commutation relations (5.36), with the broken-symmetry condition (5.38), then yield the sum rule

$$\int \frac{d\omega}{2\pi} f_\Omega{}^{ij}(\mathbf{k}, \omega) = \epsilon^{ijk} s^k \qquad (5.49)$$

as the analog of Eq. (5.11). Moreover the conservation of total spin yields

$$f_\Omega{}^{ij}(\mathbf{0}, \omega) = 2\pi \epsilon^{ijk} s^k \delta(\omega) \qquad (5.50)$$

Like Eq. (5.15) this relation refers to transitions between different degenerate ground states. However if the forces are short-range then we can also prove that

$$\lim_{\mathbf{k} \to 0} f^{ij}(\mathbf{k}, \omega) = 2\pi \epsilon^{ijk} s^k \delta(\omega) \qquad (5.51)$$

which shows that the frequency of the spin waves tends to zero as $\mathbf{k} \to \mathbf{0}$. [This follows rigorously from the positivity of $if^{+-}$ with Eq. (5.52) below.]

It is interesting to verify this (well-known) conclusion directly, and also to investigate precisely what "short-range" means in this context. Let us for convenience take the $z$ axis in the direction of $s$. Using Eq. (5.41), we obtain from Eq. (5.46) the equation of motion

$$i\dot{S}_\mathbf{x}{}^+ = \sum_{\mathbf{y} \in \Omega} J_{\mathbf{x}-\mathbf{y}}(S_\mathbf{x}{}^+ S_\mathbf{y}{}^z - S_\mathbf{x}{}^z S_\mathbf{y}{}^+) \qquad (5.52)$$

Now to determine the spin-wave frequency spectrum let us linearize this equation by replacing $S^z$ by $s$. (Actually this linearization is unnecessary if we confine our attention to the states with single spin waves, which are in fact exact eigenstates of the Hamiltonian; however, it will simplify the discussion.) Then taking the Fourier transform we find for the frequency spectrum of $S^+$ the equation

$$\omega = s \sum_{\mathbf{x} \in \Omega} J_{\mathbf{x}}(1 - e^{-i\mathbf{k}\cdot\mathbf{x}})$$
$$= s[\tilde{J}_0 - \tilde{J}_{\mathbf{k}}] \tag{5.53}$$

When $\Omega$ is finite, it is immediately obvious that $\omega = 0$ for the isolated mode at $\mathbf{k} = \mathbf{0}$ which corresponds to a transition between one degenerate ground state and another. In the limit $\Omega \to \infty$ it is necessary to restrict $J_{\mathbf{x}}$ by the condition that $\tilde{J}_0$ be finite, which means that $J_{\mathbf{x}}$ must decrease at infinity at least like $1/r^{3+\epsilon}$. (Conventionally, of course, one considers only nearest-neighbor interactions, so that $J_{\mathbf{x}}$ is of strictly finite range.) Provided this condition is satisfied, it immediately follows that $\omega \to 0$ in the limit $\mathbf{k} \to \mathbf{0}$. Thus the frequency of the spin waves indeed tends to zero as the wave number tends to zero.

In the context of this model, therefore, the interaction is "short-range" if $J_{\mathbf{x}}$ behaves better than $1/r^3$ at large distances. In contrast to the previously considered example, the limiting case in which $J_{\mathbf{x}}$ behaves like $1/r^3$ does not lead to a finite frequency limit as $\mathbf{k} \to \mathbf{0}$, but rather to a more pathological theory in which $\omega$ is infinite for all values of $\mathbf{k}$. One could achieve a finite, but directionally dependent, limiting value of $\omega$ by allowing a directional dependence in $J_{\mathbf{x}}$. For example, if $J_{\mathbf{x}}$ behaves at large distances like $P_2(\cos \theta)/r^3$, then near $\mathbf{k} = \mathbf{0}$, $\omega$ is proportional to $P_2(\cos \theta)$. However, in all such cases the limiting value of $\omega$ is negative in some directions, which means that the ground state is not truly the state of lowest energy.

The stability criteria are also somewhat different in this model. From Eq. (5.40) it is clear that $S^+$ is the *annihilation* operator for spin waves. It should therefore have positive frequency, and indeed if it does not then there must exist states to which it can couple with energy lower than the ground state. Thus the stability condition is that

$$\tilde{J}_0 - \tilde{J}_{\mathbf{k}} \geq 0 \tag{5.54}$$

for all $\mathbf{k}$. This is satisfied in particular if

$$J_{\mathbf{x}} \geq 0$$

for all $\mathbf{x}$. (Note, however, that this latter condition is not necessary.)

In this model, violation of the stability condition (5.47) does not lead to $\omega$ becoming complex as it did in our previous model. If, for some specific value of $\mathbf{k}$, $\tilde{J}_\mathbf{k} > \tilde{J}_0$, then the addition of spin waves with this wave number will lower the energy. Hence the true ground state will be obtained essentially by adding in as many such spin waves as possible. The most important case is that of antiferromagnetism. Here, for a simple cubic lattice of lattice constant $a$ the relevant vector is the one with all three components equal to $\pi/a$. Addition of as many spin waves as possible with this wave number is equivalent to flipping over every alternate spin.

Now we turn to what is in many ways the most interesting of all nonrelativistic broken-symmetry theories—the Bose gas.

This system is described by the Hamiltonian

$$H = \frac{1}{2m} \int_\Omega d^3x \nabla\psi^* \cdot \nabla\psi + U \int_\Omega d^3x \psi^* \psi$$
$$+ \frac{1}{2} \int_\Omega d^3x \int_\Omega d^3y \psi^*(\mathbf{x})\psi^*(\mathbf{y}) V(\mathbf{x} - \mathbf{y})\psi(\mathbf{y})\psi(\mathbf{x}) \quad (5.55)$$

where $U$ is a constant external potential introduced mainly to allow us to treat the case of Coulomb interactions, with $U$ representing a uniform distribution of opposite charge. The canonical commutation relation is

$$[\psi(\mathbf{x}, t), \psi^*(\mathbf{y}, t)] = \delta(\mathbf{x} - \mathbf{y}) \quad (5.56)$$

This model is invariant under several different groups of transformations. Those we shall be concerned with are the following:

*a*. Phase transformations

$$\psi(\mathbf{x}) \rightarrow \psi(\mathbf{x})\, e^{i\lambda} \qquad \psi_\mathbf{k} \rightarrow \psi_\mathbf{k}\, e^{i\lambda} \quad (5.57)$$

These are induced by the unitary operators $e^{i\lambda N}$ with

$$N = \int_\Omega d^3x \psi^*(\mathbf{x})\psi(\mathbf{x}) = \frac{1}{\Omega} \sum_\mathbf{k} \psi_\mathbf{k}^*\psi_\mathbf{k} \quad (5.58)$$

*b*. Space translation

$$\psi(\mathbf{x}) \rightarrow \psi(\mathbf{x} + \mathbf{a}) \qquad \psi_\mathbf{k} \rightarrow \psi_\mathbf{k}\, e^{i\mathbf{k}\cdot\mathbf{a}} \quad (5.59)$$

These are induced by the unitary operators $e^{i\mathbf{a}\cdot\mathbf{P}}$, where

$$\mathbf{P} = -\frac{1}{2}i \int_\Omega d^3x [\psi^*(\nabla\psi) - (\nabla\psi^*)\psi]$$
$$\equiv \int_\Omega d^3x \mathbf{j}(\mathbf{x}) = \frac{1}{\Omega} \sum_\mathbf{k} \mathbf{k}\psi_\mathbf{k}^*\psi_\mathbf{k} \quad (5.60)$$

### c. Galilean transformations

For a system with a finite volume $\Omega$ the Galilean invariance group is, of course, discrete, because of the quantization of momentum. If $\Omega$ is a cube of edge $a$, then the allowable velocity vectors are those each of whose components is a multiple of $2\pi/am$. The transformations are

$$\psi(\mathbf{x}) \rightarrow \psi(\mathbf{x} - \mathbf{v}t)\, e^{im\mathbf{v}\cdot\mathbf{x} - i\frac{1}{2}m\mathbf{v}^2 t}$$
$$\psi_{\mathbf{k}} \rightarrow \psi_{\mathbf{k} - m\mathbf{v}}\, e^{i\frac{1}{2}m\mathbf{v}^2 t - i\mathbf{k}\cdot\mathbf{v}t} \tag{5.61}$$

They are induced by unitary operators $U_\Omega(\mathbf{v})$ which may be written in a purely formal sense as

$$U_\Omega(\mathbf{v}) = e^{i\mathbf{v}\cdot\mathbf{G}} \tag{5.62}$$

with

$$\mathbf{G} = m\int_\Omega d^3x\, \psi^*\mathbf{x}\psi - \mathbf{P}t \tag{5.63}$$

However, it should be noted that Eq. (5.62) does *not* define $U_\Omega(\mathbf{v})$ for all values of $\mathbf{v}$; for in a system with periodic boundary conditions $\mathbf{x}$ is only really defined modulo a translation of amount $a$ in any of the three coordinate directions. If we make a change $z \rightarrow z + a$ then $U_\Omega(\mathbf{v})$ changes by the amount $e^{iav_z Nm}$, which is equal to unity for the allowable values of $v_z$ (since the eigenvalues of $N$ are integers).

The operator $\mathbf{G}$ can of course be defined by making a specific choice of the range of $\mathbf{x}$ (say $-a/2$ to $a/2$ for each coordinate). But it is not time independent and does not represent a symmetry of the system. In fact, explicit calculation shows that, for example,

$$\frac{dG^z}{dt} = -ma\int_{z=a/2} dx\, dy\, j^z \tag{5.64}$$

Now let us examine the possibility of constructing a representation in which the expectation value $\langle\psi\rangle$ is nonzero. In one important respect the situation here is different from that in the relativistic models we have examined, for we have generally considered assigning a non-vanishing expectation value to an operator which transforms as a scalar under the Lorentz group. But $\psi$ does not transform according to a true representation of the Galilei group, but according to a projective representation. It would be natural to impose the requirement that the vacuum or ground state of our representation should be translationally invariant, so that $\langle\psi\rangle$ would necessarily be independent of $\mathbf{x}$ and $t$. However, if we can indeed construct such a representation then we can apply a Galilean transformation to it and obtain another representation in which $\langle\psi\rangle$ depends on $\mathbf{x}$ and $t$ via factors of the type that appear in Eq. (5.61). At first sight it would appear the ground state in such a representation could not be translationally invariant. In fact, however, it is essentially so in the limit of infinite volume, as we shall see.

The equation of motion obtained from the Hamiltonian (5.55) is

$$i\frac{\partial}{\partial t}\psi(\mathbf{x}) = -\frac{1}{2m}\nabla^2\psi(\mathbf{x}) + U\psi(\mathbf{x}) + \int_\Omega d^3y\,\psi^*(\mathbf{y})\psi(\mathbf{y})V(\mathbf{x}-\mathbf{y})\psi(\mathbf{x})$$

$$(5.65)$$

We now take the expectation value of this equation and make the approximation of replacing $\langle\psi^*\psi\psi\rangle$ by $\langle\psi^*\rangle\langle\psi\rangle\langle\psi\rangle$. Then, assuming the form

$$\langle\psi(\mathbf{x},t)\rangle = \alpha\,e^{i\mathbf{p}\cdot\mathbf{x}-iEt} \qquad (5.66)$$

or equivalently

$$\langle\psi_\mathbf{k}(t)\rangle = \alpha\Omega\delta_{\mathbf{k},\mathbf{p}}\,e^{-iEt} \qquad (5.67)$$

we obtain

$$E = \mathbf{p}^2/2m + E_0 \qquad (5.68)$$

with

$$E_0 = U + \alpha^*\alpha V_0 \qquad (5.69)$$

We note that to the same approximation we have used, the number density is

$$\langle n\rangle = \langle N\rangle/\Omega = \langle\psi^*\rangle\langle\psi\rangle = \alpha^*\alpha \qquad (5.70)$$

Hence $E_0$ is the potential energy due to the external potential and due to the uniform distribution of particles with density $\alpha^*\alpha$.

Thus if we can break the symmetry in this way, we find as usual a number of different "ground states" which are transformed into each other under the operations of the group. Since the Galilean transformations are explicitly time dependent, and do not commute with time translations, it is no longer true, however, that all our ground states are degenerate in energy.

The ground states are labeled by two parameters, the complex number $\alpha$ and the momentum vector $\mathbf{p}$ (which must form one of the allowed set of momentum vectors). It is interesting to see how these states are transformed under the various transformations we have considered. The magnitude of $\alpha$ is invariant under all of them. Galilean transformations, of course, change the value of $\mathbf{p}$ but leave $\alpha$ unaltered, whereas under the other two classes of transformations (and also under time translations) $\mathbf{p}$ does not change but the phase of $\alpha$ does. Under phase transformations $(A)$ we have

$$\alpha \to \alpha e^{i\lambda} \tag{5.71}$$

Under space translations

$$\alpha \to \alpha e^{i\mathbf{p} \cdot \mathbf{a}} \tag{5.72}$$

and finally under the time translation $t \to t + \tau$

$$\alpha \to \alpha e^{-iE\tau} \tag{5.73}$$

Thus for $\alpha \neq 0$ the phase symmetry and the Galilean symmetry are always broken. So is the space translation symmetry except in the case $\mathbf{p} = 0$. The time translation symmetry is broken unless $E = 0$.

Of course we have not yet established that representations with these properties exist at all. Let us consider first the case of the non-interacting Bose gas, for which $V(\mathbf{x}) = 0$. For convenience we shall also set $U = 0$. [This system has been studied in considerable detail by Araki and Woods.[52]] This noninteracting system has a further invariance, not shared by the interacting gas, under the constant field translations

$$\psi(\mathbf{x}) \to \psi(\mathbf{x}) + \alpha \tag{5.74}$$

or

$$\psi_{\mathbf{k}} \to \psi_{\mathbf{k}} + \alpha\Omega\delta_{\mathbf{k},0} \tag{5.75}$$

(We could also consider translations of any other Fourier component, but these other cases can be obtained by applying a Galilean transformation.) These transformations are generated by the unitary operators

$$U_\Omega(\alpha) = \exp \int_\Omega d^3x [\alpha\psi^*(\mathbf{x}) - \alpha^*\psi(\mathbf{x})] = \exp [\alpha\psi_0^* - \alpha^*\psi_0] \tag{5.76}$$

Now the vacuum state of the conventional Fock representation $|0\rangle_\Omega$ is defined by

$$\psi(\mathbf{x})|0\rangle_\Omega = 0 \tag{5.77}$$

Applying the operators (5.76) to this state we obtain a set of states

$$|\alpha\rangle_\Omega = U_\Omega(\alpha)|0\rangle_\Omega \tag{5.78}$$

characterized by the eigenvalue equations

$$\psi(\mathbf{x})|\alpha\rangle_\Omega = |\alpha\rangle_\Omega \alpha$$

or                                                                    (5.79)

$$\psi_{\mathbf{k}}|\alpha\rangle_\Omega = |\alpha\rangle_\Omega \alpha\Omega\delta_{\mathbf{k},0}$$

Using the operator identity

$$U_\Omega(\alpha) = \exp(\alpha\psi_0^*) \exp(-\alpha^*\psi_0) \exp(-\tfrac{1}{2}\Omega\alpha^*\alpha)$$

we can write these states in terms of more familiar ones. In fact,

$$|\alpha\rangle_\Omega = \sum |N\rangle_\Omega (N!)^{-\frac{1}{2}}(\Omega^{\frac{1}{2}}\alpha)^N \exp(-\tfrac{1}{2}\Omega\alpha^*\alpha) \qquad (5.80)$$

where $|N\rangle_\Omega$ is the $N$-particle ground state in volume $\Omega$,

$$|N\rangle_\Omega = (\Omega^{\frac{1}{2}}\psi_0^*)^N|0\rangle_\Omega (N!)^{-\frac{1}{2}}$$

Since these states contain only particles of zero momentum and energy, they are of course all degenerate with the vacuum state. The states $|\alpha\rangle_\Omega$ constitute the set of degenerate ground states associated with broken symmetry under the transformations (5.74).

We note that the scalar product of two such states is

$$_\Omega\langle\beta|\alpha\rangle_\Omega = \exp[\Omega(\beta^*\alpha - \tfrac{1}{2}\beta^*\beta - \tfrac{1}{2}\alpha^*\alpha)] \qquad (5.81)$$

For $\beta \neq \alpha$ this tends to zero as $\Omega \to \infty$. Hence we see that in the limit of infinite volume the states $|\alpha\rangle_\Omega$ go over into the ground states of a set of unitarily inequivalent representations. It is easy to characterize these representations, for they are clearly obtained from the Fock representation simply by a constant field translation. They may be realized in the Hilbert space of the infinite-volume Fock representation by operators of the form

$$\psi(\mathbf{x}) = \psi_F(\mathbf{x}) + \alpha \qquad (5.82)$$

where $\psi_F(\mathbf{x})$ is the field operator in the Fock representation. However, the transformation from $\psi_F$ to $\psi$ is not implementable by a unitary transformation.

The states $|\alpha\rangle_\Omega$ are of course invariant under space translations. However under the phase transformations generated by the number operator they transform according to

$$e^{i\lambda N}|\alpha\rangle_\Omega = |\alpha e^{i\lambda}\rangle_\Omega \qquad (5.83)$$

Thus the phase transformations cannot be unitarily implemented in any of these representations except the Fock representation.

By applying a Galilean transformation to the states $|\alpha\rangle_\Omega$ we obtain a set of states

$$|\alpha; \mathbf{v}\rangle_\Omega = U_\Omega(\mathbf{v})|\alpha\rangle_\Omega \tag{5.84}$$

characterized by the relations

$$
\begin{aligned}
\psi(\mathbf{x})|\alpha; \mathbf{v}\rangle_\Omega &= |\alpha; \mathbf{v}\rangle_\Omega \alpha e^{i m \mathbf{v} \cdot \mathbf{x} - i\frac{1}{2} m \mathbf{v}^2 t} \\
\psi_\mathbf{k}|\alpha; \mathbf{v}\rangle_\Omega &= |\alpha; \mathbf{v}\rangle_\Omega \alpha \Omega \delta_{\mathbf{k}, m\mathbf{v}} e^{-i\frac{1}{2} m \mathbf{v}^2 t}
\end{aligned}
\tag{5.85}
$$

Evidently, the state $|\alpha; \mathbf{v}\rangle_\Omega$ contains only particles of momentum $m\mathbf{v}$ and energy $\frac{1}{2}m\mathbf{v}^2$. However since it is not an eigenstate of the number operator it does not have definite total momentum or energy. Under space translations, for example, it transforms according to

$$e^{i\mathbf{a}\cdot\mathbf{P}}|\alpha; \mathbf{v}\rangle_\Omega = |\alpha e^{i m \mathbf{v} \cdot \mathbf{a}}; \mathbf{v}\rangle_\Omega \tag{5.86}$$

Hence in the infinite volume limit space translations are not unitarily implementable in these representations. Nor of course are time translations.

We note that the expectation value of the particle density $n = N/\Omega$ in one of the states $|\alpha\rangle_\Omega$ is

$$\langle n \rangle = {}_\Omega\langle\alpha|N|\alpha\rangle_\Omega/\Omega = \alpha^*\alpha \tag{5.87}$$

and that

$$\langle n^2\rangle - \langle n\rangle^2 = \alpha^*\alpha/\Omega$$

Hence in the limit $\Omega \to \infty$ the number density takes on the definite value $\alpha^*\alpha$. So too in the states $|\alpha; \mathbf{v}\rangle_\Omega$ do the momentum density and energy density.

So far this discussion has been mainly mathematical. A clearer idea of the physical significance of these representations may be gained from considering the problem of how we should describe an infinite Bose gas of finite density, whose states evidently do not belong to the Fock representation since the total particle number is infinite. To specify the representation completely it is sufficient to give the ground state expectation values of all quasi-local operators $A$ (those which can be written as limits of sequences of operators $A_\Omega$, with each $A_\Omega$ a function only of the field operators within $\Omega$). It is natural to start with the $N$-particle ground-state in volume $\Omega$, with $N = n\Omega$ and take the limit $\Omega \to \infty$. Thus we define[52]

$$\langle A \rangle_n = \lim_{\Omega \to \infty} {}_\Omega\langle n\Omega|A_\Omega|n\Omega\rangle_\Omega \tag{5.88}$$

This formula defines a representation of the commutation relations (5.56). It is, however, a reducible representation; that is to say there exist operators other than multiples of the identity which commute with every operator in the representation. To see this, we note that in the limit of infinite volume the addition or removal of any finite number of particles in the ground state makes no difference. Thus for example we arrive at the same value of $\langle A \rangle_n$ if we replace the states $|n\Omega\rangle_\Omega$ in Eq. (5.88) by

$$|n\Omega - 1\rangle_\Omega = (\psi_0/n^{1/2}\Omega)|n\Omega\rangle_\Omega$$

Hence if we define an operator $\phi$ by

$$\phi = \lim_{\Omega \to \infty} (\psi_0/n^{1/2}\Omega) \tag{5.89}$$

then we must have

$$\langle \phi^* A \phi \rangle_n = \langle A \rangle_n \tag{5.90}$$

It follows that the operator $\phi$ must be unitary, and must commute with every other operator. Hence the representation $\langle A \rangle_n$ is reducible, and can be decomposed into irreducible representations in each of which $\phi$ is represented by a number of modulus unity.

The explicit reduction may be accomplished by first noting that we can write instead of Eq. (5.88) the equation

$$\langle A \rangle_n = \lim_{\Omega \to \infty} \sum_N \frac{(n\Omega)^N}{N!} e^{-n\Omega} {}_\Omega\langle N|A_\Omega|N\rangle_\Omega \tag{5.91}$$

for, when $\Omega$ is large, the Poisson distribution here yields contributions significantly different from zero only for values of $N$ in the neighborhood of $n\Omega$ (within a range of order $(n\Omega)^{1/2}$). By the preceding argument, each of these gives in the limit the same contribution. Now we can reexpress the right-hand side of Eq. (5.91) in terms of the states $|\alpha\rangle_\Omega$ using the identity

$$\int \frac{d\theta}{2\pi} (|\alpha\rangle_{\Omega\Omega}\langle\alpha|)_{\alpha = n^{1/2}e^{i\theta}} = \sum_N |N\rangle_\Omega \frac{(n\Omega)^N}{N!} e^{-n\Omega} {}_\Omega\langle N| \tag{5.92}$$

(which is easy to verify by taking matrix elements). This yields the decomposition

$$\langle A \rangle_n = \int \frac{d\theta}{2\pi} \langle A \rangle_{n^{1/2}e^{i\theta}} \tag{5.93}$$

where

$$\langle A \rangle_\alpha = \lim_{\Omega \to \infty} {}_\Omega\langle \alpha | A_\Omega | \alpha \rangle_\Omega \tag{5.94}$$

Note that in these representations $\phi$ is represented simply by $e^{i\theta}$.

It should be noted that in the representation defined by $\langle A \rangle_n$, the phase transformations are unitarily implementable. In fact they are represented by rotations of $\theta$; however, this does not contradict our earlier discussion, since in the present case the degenerate ground states with definite values of $\theta$ are not normalizable states.

The representation described by the expectation value $\langle A \rangle_\alpha$ is of course that given by the operators (5.82). It is irreducible since the Fock representation is. Thus we have completed the reduction of the representation $\langle A \rangle_n$ into irreducible components.

If we were to consider as observables only operators invariant under the constant field-translations (5.74) then we should obtain exactly the same expectation values $\langle A \rangle_\alpha$ for any different values of $\alpha$. This is, however, too strong a restriction, for we clearly want to be able to regard the particle density as an observable. If we allow as observables operators which are not symmetric under these transformations but are nevertheless symmetric under the phase transformations (5.57), then we would still obtain the same expectation values by using the representation $\langle A \rangle_n$, or $\langle A \rangle_\alpha$ for any value of $\alpha$ satisfying $\alpha^*\alpha = n$. To this extent these representations are physically equivalent.

Is there then any physical sense in which we can distinguish between the various $\langle A \rangle_\alpha$ differing only in the phase of $\alpha$? For a ferromagnet, the analogous quantity is the magnetization direction, and it seems physically obvious that this *is* an observable, and that we should normally represent a ferromagnet by a state with definite magnetization direction, rather than by an ensemble with all possible magnetization directions. The particular direction is in this case selected by interaction with any small residual magnetic field. At first sight, it is much less clear that the phase of a condensed Bose gas should be treated as an observable. However, the difference between the two situations is more apparent than real. For any real Bose gas, there undoubtedly are interactions capable of changing the total particle number of our system by absorption, emission, or interchange with the surroundings. (Indeed, for a *photon* gas this is obvious, and there is surely no doubt that the phase of an electromagnetic wave has an observational significance.)

It is therefore perfectly reasonable to include a small external interaction term which breaks the number symmetry. As we shall see below, such a term can lead to a preferential selection of a state $|\alpha\rangle_\Omega$ with a particular phase. Of course, the absolute phase of our system has no physical significance. We can measure it only relative to some externally defined standard. But the same is equally true of magnetization direction.

In summary, if we do not accept the phase as an observable, we can choose it arbitrarily; if we do accept it, and allow symmetry-breaking interactions, then the phase will be determined by them. In either case, we can adequately describe the system by a state with well-defined phase.

Let us then examine the effect of including a small symmetry-breaking interaction of the form

$$\nu H_1 = -\nu \int_\Omega d^3x[\psi(\mathbf{x}) + \psi^*(\mathbf{x})] = -\nu(\psi_0 + \psi_0^*) \qquad (5.95)$$

One may regard the choice of real phase factor here analogous to the choice of the $z$ axis for the direction of the external magnetic field.

Since the interaction breaks the number symmetry, it is most convenient to discuss this problem using the grand canonical ensemble, in which the expectation value of any observable $A$ is given by

$$\langle A \rangle = \mathrm{tr}\,(\rho A) \qquad (5.96)$$

where $\rho$ is the density operator

$$\rho = \exp^{-\beta(H + \nu H_1 - \mu N)}/\mathrm{tr}\,[e^{-\beta(H + \nu H_1 - \mu N)}] \qquad (5.97)$$

Here $\beta = 1/kT$, $T$ is the temperature, and $\mu$ is the chemical potential. Because of the independence of the modes described by different values of $\mathbf{k}$ we can write

$$\rho = \Pi_{\mathbf{k}}\rho_{\mathbf{k}}$$

For any mode with $\mathbf{k} \neq \mathbf{0}$ the distribution is completely unaffected by the interaction term $\nu H_1$, and is given by

$$\rho_{\mathbf{k}} = [1 - e^{\beta(\mu - \mathbf{k}^2/2m)}]^{-1} \exp\left[\frac{\beta}{\Omega}\left(\mu - \frac{\mathbf{k}^2}{2m}\right)\psi_{\mathbf{k}}^*\psi_{\mathbf{k}}\right] \qquad (5.98)$$

(Recall that with our normalization the number operator for the mode $\mathbf{k}$ is $\psi_{\mathbf{k}}^*\psi_{\mathbf{k}}/\Omega$.) On the other hand, for the mode $\mathbf{k} = \mathbf{0}$ the only term in the energy is that arising from the interaction $\nu H_1$. Thus,

$$\rho_0 = c \exp \beta[(\mu/\Omega)\psi_0^*\psi_0 + \nu(\psi_0^* + \psi_0)]$$

where $c$ is a normalization constant. Recognizing that the effect of the term in $\nu$ is to translate the field operator, we can therefore write

$$\rho_0 = [1 - e^{\beta\mu}] \exp\left[\frac{\beta\mu}{\Omega}\left(\psi_0^* + \frac{\nu\Omega}{\mu}\right)\left(\psi_0 + \frac{\nu\Omega}{\mu}\right)\right] \qquad (5.99)$$

Thus the only effect of the interaction $\nu H_1$ is to translate $\psi_0$. All expectation values are obtainable from those in the ensemble with $\nu = 0$ by this translation. In particular we find

$$\langle \psi_0 \rangle = \langle \psi_0^* \rangle = -\nu\Omega/\mu \qquad (5.100)$$

or equivalently

$$\langle \psi(\mathbf{x}) \rangle = \langle \psi^*(\mathbf{x}) \rangle = -\nu/\mu \qquad (5.101)$$

and also

$$\langle \psi_0^*\psi_0 \rangle = \nu^2\Omega^2/\mu^2 + \Omega/(e^{-\beta\mu} - 1) \qquad (5.102)$$

Note that the mean value of the number density of particles in the ground state is

$$n_0 = \langle N_0 \rangle/\Omega = \langle \psi_0^*\psi_0 \rangle/\Omega^2 \qquad (5.103)$$

The chemical potential must of course be negative in order that the expectation value of the number of particles in each mode be positive. It is determined in terms of the mean value of the total number density by the implicit equation

$$n = \nu^2/\mu^2 + 1/\Omega(e^{-\beta\mu} - 1) + n(\beta, \mu) \qquad (5.104)$$

where $n(\beta, \mu)$ is the number density of particles in the excited states, given by

$$n(\beta, \mu) = \int \frac{d^3k}{(2\pi)^3} \frac{1}{\exp[\beta(\mathbf{k}^2/2m - \mu)] - 1} \qquad (5.105)$$

We note that for $\mu < 0$ each term on the right-hand side of Eq. (5.104) is a monotonically increasing function of $\mu$. Since the value of the right-hand side ranges from 0 at $\mu = -\infty$ to $+\infty$ at $\mu = 0$, there is therefore always a unique root for $\mu$.

Let us examine the limit $\Omega \to \infty$. Here we find very different behavior for $\nu = 0$ and $\nu \neq 0$. If $\nu = 0$ and

$$n > n_c(\beta) = n(\beta, 0) \qquad (5.106)$$

then $\mu \to 0$ and, in fact, for large $\Omega$,

$$\mu = -[\beta\Omega(n - n_c)]^{-1} \tag{5.107}$$

[Of course, if the inequality (5.106) is not satisfied the gas is not condensed and no problem arises.]

On the other hand, if $\nu \neq 0$, then it is clear that $\mu$ remains finite as $\Omega \to \infty$; for otherwise the first term in Eq. (5.104) becomes infinite, hence the second term is negligible and so in the limit

$$\mu = -\nu[n - n(\beta, \mu)]^{1/2} \tag{5.108}$$

or, for small $\nu$,

$$\mu \approx -\nu[n - n_c]^{1/2} \tag{5.109}$$

Thus from Eq. (5.87) we find the expectation value

$$\langle \psi(\mathbf{x}) \rangle = (n - n_c)^{1/2} \tag{5.110}$$

It is important to note that this expression is independent of $\nu$ for small $\nu$, and remains finite even in the limit $\nu \to 0$.

It is apparent that the limits $\nu \to 0$ and $\Omega \to \infty$ do not commute. By taking the limit $\Omega \to \infty$ first we have obtained a distribution which is just the usual one for the condensed Bose gas, but with the particles in the macroscopically occupied condensate being represented by the ground state $|\alpha\rangle$ with $\alpha = (n - n_c)^{1/2}$. We have, in fact, constructed an ensemble of states in the Hilbert space built on this particular ground state.

Let us now return to the problem of an interacting Bose gas described by the Hamiltonian (5.55).

From the Goldstone theorem we learn that if the potential is of sufficiently short range there must be a branch of the excitation spectrum which has zero energy gap. That the necessary short-range condition is satisfied, for potentials which fall off at infinity faster than Coulomb potential, has been proved by Swieca[53] on the basis of certain plausible assumptions about the behavior of the Green's functions. It is easy to verify the conclusion in the Bogoliubov approximation.[54]

In view of our discussion of the noninteracting Bose gas, it is reasonable to suppose that in the interacting case the condensed Bose gas should also be described (in the infinite volume limit) by an ensemble in a Hilbert space corresponding to a representation with $\langle \psi \rangle \neq 0$, and to treat $\psi - \langle \psi \rangle$ as small in comparison to $\langle \psi \rangle$.

From Eq. (5.66) we learn that the time dependence of $\langle\psi\rangle$ is given by

$$\langle\psi\rangle = \alpha e^{-iE_0 t} \qquad (5.111)$$

It is convenient to absorb this phase factor by writing

$$\psi(\mathbf{x}, t) = [\alpha + \psi'(\mathbf{x}, t)] e^{-iE_0 t} \qquad (5.112)$$

We now linearize the equation of motion [Eq. (5.65)] by substituting Eq. (5.112) and keeping only terms linear in $\psi'$. This yields in momentum space the equation

$$i\frac{\partial}{\partial t}\psi_{\mathbf{k}}' = (\mathbf{k}^2/2m)\,\psi_{\mathbf{k}}' + \alpha V_{\mathbf{k}}(\alpha^*\psi_{\mathbf{k}}' + \alpha\psi'^*_{-\mathbf{k}}) \qquad (5.113)$$

It follows that the excitation spectrum is given by

$$\omega^2 = \frac{\mathbf{k}^2}{2m}\left(\frac{\mathbf{k}^2}{2m} + 2\alpha^*\alpha V_{\mathbf{k}}\right) \qquad (5.114)$$

We note that $\omega \to 0$ as $\mathbf{k} \to \mathbf{0}$ provided that

$$\lim_{\mathbf{k}\to\mathbf{0}} \mathbf{k}^2 V_{\mathbf{k}} = 0 \qquad (5.115)$$

the same condition as in the case of the soluble model we discussed earlier [see Eq. (5.31)]. This is in conformity with the Goldstone theorem. There are modes with zero energy gap provided that the forces are of short range; specifically, provided that the potential falls off faster than $1/r$ at large distances. Note that the behavior of $\omega$ near $\mathbf{k} = \mathbf{0}$ is given by

$$\omega = c|\mathbf{k}| \qquad (5.116)$$

where $c$, the velocity of sound, is determined by the integral of the potential,

$$c^2 = (\alpha^*\alpha)V_0/m \qquad (5.117)$$

(It can be shown that this agrees with the classical formula.)

On the other hand, for a repulsive Coulomb potential,

$$V(\mathbf{x}) = e^2/4\pi|\mathbf{x}|$$
$$V_{\mathbf{k}} = e^2/\mathbf{k}^2$$

we find that as $\mathbf{k} \to \mathbf{0}$ the frequency tends to a finite plasma frequency,

$$\lim_{\mathbf{k}\to\mathbf{0}} \omega^2 = (\alpha^*\alpha)\,e^2/m = \omega_\rho{}^2 \qquad (5.118)$$

For long-range interactions we find an energy gap whose magnitude is determined by the strength of the potential and by the density.

An interesting fact which emerges from this model is that it is possible to have a number of distinct broken symmetries, all yielding the same Goldstone excitations. We recall that the Goldstone modes may be regarded as long-wavelength oscillations in the parameter which distinguishes the various degenerate ground states. In our case, the effects of both phase transformations and spatial translations as described by Eq. (5.83) and (5.86) are to change the phase of $\alpha$. It is therefore not surprising that the corresponding Goldstone modes are identical. On the other hand, the Galilean transformations change the value of the other symmetry-breaking parameter, $\mathbf{v}$. However, from Eq. (5.85) one sees that $m\mathbf{v}$ may be identified with the spatial gradient of the phase of $\langle \psi \rangle$. In fact, this is the conventional definition of the superfluid velocity. Thus an oscillation in $\mathbf{v}$ is actually no different from an oscillation in the phase of $\alpha$. Both, of course, represent phonons.

There is another situation in which translational symmetry is broken, namely, that of a crystal. In a finite volume the ground state $|0\rangle_\Omega$ of a crystal is translationally invariant, and, despite the periodic structure the particle density, for example, is completely uniform. However, it is obviously convenient for many purposes to consider a different type of state in which the particle density has the periodicity of the lattice. A state in which the atoms of the crystal are localized near a specific set of lattice points necessarily has some uncertainty in momentum, and therefore a higher energy than the ground state. However, we have seen in the previous example that it is possible in the infinite-volume limit to obtain a state which has definite values of both phase and number density, and in exactly the same way one can construct states with a definite center-of-mass and simultaneously definite momentum and energy density. Here too the Goldstone modes are phonons.

Finally we wish to consider a fermion gas. The system is described by a two-component field

$$\psi(\mathbf{x}) = \begin{bmatrix} \psi_1(\mathbf{x}) \\ \psi_2(\mathbf{x}) \end{bmatrix} \tag{5.119}$$

satisfying the canonical anticommutation relation

$$\{\psi_i(\mathbf{x}, t), \psi_j{}^*(\mathbf{y}, t)\} = \delta_{ij}\delta(\mathbf{x} - \mathbf{y}) \tag{5.120}$$

For simplicity we choose a spin-independent interaction, described by the Hamiltonian

$$H = \frac{1}{2m} \sum_i \int_\Omega d^3x \nabla \psi_i^* \nabla \psi_i + U \sum_i \int_\Omega d^3x \psi_i^* \psi_i$$

$$+ \frac{1}{2} \sum_{i,j} \int_\Omega d^3x \int_\Omega d^3y \psi_i^*(\mathbf{x})\psi_j^*(\mathbf{y}) V(\mathbf{x} - \mathbf{y})\psi_j(\mathbf{y})\psi_i(\mathbf{x}) \quad (5.121)$$

The corresponding equation of motion is

$$i\frac{\partial}{\partial t}\psi(\mathbf{x}) = -\frac{1}{2m}\nabla^2\psi(\mathbf{x}) + U\psi(\mathbf{x})$$

$$+ \int d^3y[\psi^*(\mathbf{y})\psi(\mathbf{y})]V(\mathbf{x} - \mathbf{y})\psi(\mathbf{x}) \quad (5.122)$$

This system possesses essentially the same symmetries as the boson gas. In particular, it is symmetric under the phase transformations generated by the total number operator

$$N = \int_\Omega d^3x \psi^*(\mathbf{x})\psi(\mathbf{x}) \quad (5.123)$$

In addition it is symmetric under spin rotations, generated by the total spin operators

$$\mathbf{S} = \frac{1}{2}\int_\Omega d^3x \psi^*(\mathbf{x})\boldsymbol{\sigma}\psi(\mathbf{x}) \quad (5.124)$$

We shall consider the possibility of breaking the phase symmetry corresponding to the conserved particle number, while maintaining the symmetry under spin rotations, as is done in the Bardeen–Cooper–Schrieffer model of superconductivity.[55] [This model has been discussed from the point of view of broken symmetry by Haag,[56] Ezawa,[57] and Emch and Guenin.[58]] To do this we look for a ground state in which the expectation value $\langle \psi\psi \rangle$ is nonvanishing. If this state is assumed translationally invariant, then

$$\langle \psi_i(\mathbf{x})\psi_j(\mathbf{y}) \rangle = f_{ij}(\mathbf{x} - \mathbf{y})$$

If, in addition, we impose the requirement of invariance under spin rotations, we must have

$$\langle \psi_i(\mathbf{x})\psi_j(\mathbf{y}) \rangle = \epsilon_{ij}f(\mathbf{x} - \mathbf{y}) \quad (5.125)$$

where

$$\epsilon = \begin{bmatrix} 0 & -1 \\ 1 & 0 \end{bmatrix}$$

Of course, $f(\mathbf{x})$ must be a function only of $|\mathbf{x}|$.

As before, if we can find one such state then we can find a whole family of them. In particular, by applying Galilean transformations, we would obtain translationally noninvariant states characterized by an overall velocity. However, for our purposes it will be sufficient to consider only one such state which for convenience we choose to be at rest.

In addition to Eq. (5.125) we shall also need

$$\langle \psi_i^*(\mathbf{x})\psi_j(\mathbf{y}) \rangle = \delta_{ij}g(\mathbf{x} - \mathbf{y}) \tag{5.126}$$

Note that

$$2g(\mathbf{0}) = n$$

the particle density.

If $V(\mathbf{x})$ is assumed to be of short range, then we know from the Goldstone theorem that there must be a branch of the excitation spectrum for which $\omega \to 0$ as $\mathbf{k} \to \mathbf{0}$. However, unlike the situation in the case of the boson gas which we considered earlier these modes are not the elementary quasi-particle excitations. Indeed if we make the linearizing approximation in Eq. (5.122) replacing

$$[\psi^*(\mathbf{y})\psi(\mathbf{y})]\psi(\mathbf{x})$$

by

$$2g(\mathbf{0})\psi(\mathbf{x}) - g(\mathbf{y} - \mathbf{x})\psi(\mathbf{y}) - f(\mathbf{y} - \mathbf{x})\epsilon\psi^*(\mathbf{y})$$

then we obtain an energy spectrum with a gap of the form

$$\omega^2 = \epsilon_\mathbf{k}^2 + \Delta_\mathbf{k}^2 \tag{5.127}$$

[see, for example, Valatin[59]].

In fact, the zero-energy-gap modes in this system are phononlike as before, and we must expect them to be excited only by bosonlike operators, constructed from pairs of fermi field operators, for example $\psi\psi$ or $\psi^*\psi$. The Goldstone theorem which establishes the existence of such modes rests on an examination of commutators of the form

$$[\psi^*\psi, \psi\epsilon\psi]$$

It therefore follows that these modes can be excited by the operators $\psi^*\psi$ or $\psi\epsilon\psi$. However, a direct verification of this conclusion by solving the equations of motion in an appropriate approximation would be too lengthy to include here. [In this connection see Gorkov[60] and Anderson.[61]]

## VI. Goldstone Bosons and Composite Fields

Until now our considerations have essentially been confined to examples of broken-symmetry theories in which the Goldstone bosons are directly associated with an elementary field operator obeying canonical commutation relations, rather than with the more complicated situation in which the field operator associated with the Goldstone particle is composite. However, the discussion in Section II demonstrated that in general we should anticipate that the Goldstone particle may be identifiable with a composite field and that this is particularly likely to be the case when the symmetry breaking is related to a physical attribute such as particle mass. However, it turns out as a practical matter that, as a consequence of divergences and fairly involved constraints, composite particle broken-symmetry theories are very difficult to handle in a consistent manner, even in the lowest orders of perturbation theory.

Because of these difficulties we choose to defer to a later point the examination of more realistic theories and shall begin this discussion by investigating the Thirring model (a soluble two-dimensional field theory), under the assumption that the vacuum expectation of the vector current $j^\mu$ associated with this model has a nonvanishing value. This problem has been considered previously[62] but, because of the imposition of certain arbitrary assumptions, only specialized and somewhat misleading solutions were obtained. Since the basic problem here is to maintain consistency with Lorentz invariance, it must be borne in mind that if a field $\phi$ carried intrinsic spin, it transforms under the generators of the Lorentz group $J^{\mu\nu}$ according to

$$-i[J^{\mu\nu}, \phi(x)] = (x^\mu\, \partial^\nu - x^\nu\, \partial^\mu)\phi(x) + \sigma^{\mu\nu}\phi(x)$$

where $\sigma^{\mu\nu}$ is a matrix associated with the spin of the field $\phi$. Thus in this case the requirement $\langle 0|\phi|0\rangle \neq 0$ becomes $\langle 0|[J^{\mu\nu}, \phi]|0\rangle \neq 0$ which, in turn, means that in general Lorentz invariance is broken. [Note that in the case $\phi^\lambda = j^\lambda$ we have $(\sigma^{\mu\nu})^{\lambda\sigma} = g^{\lambda\mu}g^{\nu\sigma} - g^{\lambda\nu}g^{\mu\sigma}$.] This procedure is thus obviously more likely to give nonsensical results than in the case of spinless fields. However, because of the special structure of the

Thirring model,[63] one is able to obtain meaningful and interesting results with this procedure, as we shall now demonstrate.

We take the Lagrangian to be

$$\mathscr{L} = (i/2)\psi\alpha^\mu \, \partial_\mu\psi + (\lambda/2)j^\mu j_\mu + j^\mu A_\mu \qquad (6.1)$$

where $\psi(x)$ is a Hermitian field and the Dirac algebra has the two-dimensional representation

$$\alpha^0 = -\alpha_0 = \begin{bmatrix} 1 & 0 \\ 0 & 1 \end{bmatrix}$$

$$\alpha^1 = \alpha_1 = \begin{bmatrix} 1 & 0 \\ 0 & -1 \end{bmatrix}$$

The current $j^\mu$ is defined so that

$$\frac{\delta j^\mu(x)}{\delta\psi(x)} = \alpha^\mu q\psi(x)$$

where we have introduced the usual matrix $q = \begin{bmatrix} 0 & -i \\ i & 0 \end{bmatrix}$ which acts in the internal charge space of the field $\psi$. It is to be emphasized that this implies $j^\mu(x) = \frac{1}{2}\psi(x)\alpha^\mu q\psi(x)$ only if such a quantity is well defined. Since this is not the case (as has frequently been observed in the literature), we note that the most general definition of $j^\mu(x)$ in the presence of the external source $A_\mu(x)$ is[64]

$$j^\mu(x) = \lim_{\mathbf{x}\to\mathbf{x}'} \frac{1}{2}\psi(x)\alpha^\mu q \exp\left\{ -iq \int_{x'}^{x} dx_\mu''[\xi A^\mu(x'') - \eta\gamma_5 A_5{}^\mu(x'') \right.$$
$$\left. + \lambda\xi j^\mu(x'') - \lambda\eta\gamma_5 j_5{}^\mu(x'')]\right\}\psi(x') \quad (6.2)$$

$\gamma_5$ being the pseudoscalar matrix $\alpha^0\alpha^1$ while $A_5{}^\mu$ and $j_5{}^\mu$ are defined by

$$A_5{}^\mu(x) = \epsilon^{\mu\nu}A_\nu(x)$$
$$j_5{}^\mu(x) = \epsilon^{\mu\nu}j_\nu(x)$$

where $\epsilon^{\mu\nu} = -\epsilon^{\nu\mu}$ and $\epsilon^{01} = +1$. It is understood that the limit is to be taken with $x^0 = x^{0'}$ subject to the condition $\xi + \eta = 1$ which is necessary for Lorentz invariance.[64] Returning to (6.1) and using the action principle, we find the field equation

$$\alpha^\mu\left(\frac{1}{i}\partial_\mu - qA_\mu - \lambda q j_\mu\right)\psi = 0 \qquad (6.3)$$

and the equal-time commutation relation

$$\{\psi(x), \psi(x')\} = \delta(\mathbf{x} - \mathbf{x}')$$

In the limit of vanishing source, it follows as a consequence of the solution of the detailed dynamics[64] that $\partial^2 j^\mu = 0$. This result would also follow from gauge invariance if the naive single-point description of the current operator were correct. Thus $j^\mu$ satisfies a massless free field equation invariant under the transformation

$$j^\mu(x) \rightarrow j^\mu(x) + \eta^\mu \qquad (6.4)$$

If $j^\mu(x)$ were an elementary field we could proceed directly as in the naturally occurring cases considered earlier. For example, Eq. (6.3) would appear to be invariant under the transformation (6.4) combined with the transformation

$$\psi(x) \rightarrow \exp\{i\lambda q\eta^\mu x_\mu\}\psi(x) \qquad (6.5)$$

and, if this were the case, it would be trivial to establish the consistency of the broken symmetry. In fact, however, the situation is far more complicated because of the composite field nature of $j^\mu(x)$. Thus a transformation of type (6.5), when fed into the definition of the current, as given by Eq. (6.2), will induce additional broken symmetry effects since $j^\mu(x)$ is not, in general, invariant under the transformation (6.5). Thus the consistency of the broken symmetry is not immediately evident.

We now consider this theory using a Green's function approach much like that used for more complicated problems. This discussion will rely heavily on techniques previously used to solve the model and the reader is consequently referred to these earlier works on the Thirring model for many of the details not supplied here.[63,64] We begin by considering the case $\lambda = 0$. Then, defining

$$G(x, x') = i\epsilon(x, x') \frac{\langle 0|(\psi(x)\psi(x'))_+|0\rangle_A}{\langle 0|0\rangle_A}$$

we find from Eq. (6.3) and the commutation relations that

$$\alpha^\mu\left(\frac{1}{i}\partial_\mu - qA_\mu\right)G(x, x') = \delta(x - x')$$

It follows that

$$G(x, x') = \tilde{G}_0(x - x')\exp\{iq[F(x) - F(x')]\} \qquad (6.6)$$

if

$$\alpha^\mu \frac{1}{i} \partial_\mu \tilde{G}_0(x - x') = \delta(x - x')$$

and

$$\alpha^\mu \partial_\mu F(x) = \alpha^\mu A_\mu(x)$$

The solutions to these equations are not unique and, indeed, if $\tilde{G}_0(x - x')$ satisfies the above equations, so does $\tilde{G}_0(x - x') + \text{constant}$. We thus write

$$\tilde{G}_0(x - x') = G_0(x - x') + \gamma$$

$\gamma$ being a constant matrix with $G_0(x)$ defined by

$$G_0(x) = i(\partial_0 - \alpha^1 \partial_1) D(x)$$

where $D(x)$ satisfies the equation

$$-\partial^2 D(x) = \delta(x)$$

subject to the usual causal boundary conditions. These same boundary conditions imply, however, a unique structure for $F(x)$, i.e.,

$$F(x) = -i \int dx' G_0(x - x') \alpha^\mu A_\mu(x')$$

The extra terms in $\tilde{G}_0(x - x')$ which are proportional to $q$ are associated with the broken symmetry and would normally be ruled out by requirements of Lorentz invariance. This can be seen explicitly by using the definition Eq. (6.2) of $j^\mu(x)$ and the result

$$G_0(x - x') = -\frac{\alpha^1}{2\pi} \frac{1}{\mathbf{x} - \mathbf{x}'} \qquad x^0 = x^{0'}$$

from which one infers

$$\begin{aligned}
\frac{\langle 0 | j^\mu(x) | 0 \rangle_A}{\langle 0 | 0 \rangle_A} &= \frac{i}{2} \lim_{\mathbf{x} \to \mathbf{x}'} \text{Tr} q \alpha^\mu G(x, x') \exp\left[-iq \int_{x'}^{x} dx_\mu{}''(\xi A^\mu - \eta \gamma_5 A_5{}^\mu)\right] \\
&= \frac{\langle 0 | j^\mu(x) | 0 \rangle_A}{\langle 0 | 0 \rangle_A}\bigg|_{\gamma = 0} + \eta^\mu
\end{aligned} \qquad (6.7)$$

where

$$\eta^\mu = \text{Tr} \frac{i}{2} q \alpha^\mu \gamma$$

and

$$\frac{\langle 0|j^\mu(x)|0\rangle_A}{\langle 0|0\rangle_A} = \int dx' D^{\mu\nu}(x - x') A_\nu(x')$$

The current correlation function $D^{\mu\nu}(x - x')$ has the structure

$$D^{\mu\nu}(x - x') = -\frac{1}{\pi} [\xi \epsilon^{\mu\sigma} \epsilon^{\nu\tau} + \eta g^{\mu\sigma} g^{\nu\tau}] \partial_\sigma \partial_\tau D(x - x')$$

It is noteworthy that the simplicity of this model, rather than any general principle, accounts for the fact that this function is independent of the external source.

Having determined the vacuum expectation value of $j^\mu(x)$ in the presence of a source, we may explicitly evaluate the function $\langle 0|0\rangle_A$ by using

$$\frac{1}{i} \frac{\delta}{\delta A_\mu(x)} \langle 0|0\rangle_A = \langle 0|j^\mu(x)|0\rangle_A$$

$$= \langle 0|0\rangle_A \left[ \eta^\mu + \int dx' D^{\mu\nu}(x - x') A_\nu(x') \right]$$

which upon integration yields

$$\langle 0|0\rangle_A = \exp\left\{ \frac{i}{2} \int dx dx' A_\mu(x) D^{\mu\nu}(x - x') A_\nu(x') + i \int \eta^\mu A_\nu(x) \, dx \right\} \quad (6.8)$$

In writing Eq. (6.8) we have included $\eta^\mu$ within the integral since it will be convenient for subsequent calculations to give $\eta^\mu$ a space–time behavior which allows one to freely carry out integration by parts. Such a procedure is admissible, provided that one ultimately proceeds to the limit $\eta^\mu = $ constant in the calculation of all matrix elements.

We are now equipped to consider broken symmetries in the fully interacting theory. To do this we observe that any matrix element $\langle a'|b'\rangle_{A,\lambda}$ in consequence of the action principle satisfies the relation

$$\frac{\delta}{\delta\lambda} \langle a'|b'\rangle_{A,\lambda} = -\frac{i}{2} \int dx \frac{\delta}{\delta A_\mu(x)} \frac{\delta}{\delta A^\mu(x)} \langle a'|b'\rangle_{A,\lambda}$$

or

$$\langle a'|b'\rangle_{A,\lambda} = \exp\left\{ -\frac{i\lambda}{2} \int dx \frac{\delta}{\delta A^\mu(x)} \frac{\delta}{\delta A_\mu(x)} \right\} \langle a'|b'\rangle_{A,0}$$

Thus, knowing the source dependence for $\lambda = 0$ makes it possible to find the matrix elements for the fully interacting theory. Referring to Eq. (6.8) we obtain

$$\langle 0|0 \rangle_{A,\lambda} = \exp\left\{ -\frac{i\lambda}{2} \int dx \, \frac{\delta}{\delta A^\mu(x)} \frac{\delta}{\delta A_\mu(x)} \right\} \exp\left\{ \frac{i}{2} \int A_\mu D^{\mu\nu} A_\nu \, dx \, dx' \right.$$
$$\left. + i \int \eta^\mu A_\mu \, dx \right\}$$

Using the commutation relation

$$\left[ \frac{\delta}{\delta A^\mu(x)}, A^\nu(x') \right] = \delta_\mu{}^\nu \delta(x - x')$$

the above expression is directly evaluated to yield

$$\langle 0|0 \rangle_{A,\lambda} = C \exp\left\{ i \int \eta^\mu A_\mu \, dx \right\} \exp\left\{ \frac{i}{2} \int (A_\mu + \lambda\eta_\mu) D_\lambda^{\mu\nu} (A_\nu + \lambda\eta_\nu) \right\} \quad (6.9)$$

where the constant $C$ is independent of $A^\mu$ and $\eta^\mu$ and so will not appear in any of the appropriately defined matrix elements of the theory. The current correlation function, including the effects of the interaction, is found to be[64]

$$D_\lambda^{\mu\nu}(x) = -\frac{1}{\pi} \left( \epsilon^{\mu\sigma} \epsilon^{\nu\tau} \frac{\xi}{1 + \lambda\xi/\pi} + g^{\mu\sigma} g^{\nu\tau} \frac{\eta}{1 - \lambda\eta/\pi} \right) \partial_\sigma \partial_\tau D(x)$$

From Eq. (6.9) we find directly

$$\frac{\langle 0|j^\mu(x)|0 \rangle_{0,\lambda}}{\langle 0|0 \rangle_{0,\lambda}} = \eta^\mu + \lambda \int D_\lambda^{\mu\nu}(x) \, dx \eta_\nu \quad (6.10)$$

Upon making the decomposition

$$\eta^\mu = \eta_1{}^\mu + \eta_2{}^\mu$$

where

$$\partial_\mu \eta_1{}^\mu = 0$$
$$\epsilon_{\mu\nu} \partial^\mu \eta_2{}^\nu = 0$$

one can readily evaluate the integral (6.10) to find in the limit $\eta^\mu = \text{constant}$

$$\frac{\langle 0|j^\mu|0 \rangle_{0,\lambda}}{\langle 0|0 \rangle_{0,\lambda}} = \eta_1{}^\mu \frac{1}{1 + \lambda\xi/\pi} + \eta_2{}^\mu \frac{1}{1 - \lambda\eta/\pi} \quad (6.11)$$

which clearly illustrates the renormalization of the symmetry-breaking parameters $\eta_1{}^\mu$ and $\eta_2{}^\mu$ induced by the interaction. Before discussing Eq. (6.11) any further, we calculate the remaining Green's functions in the presence of interaction. It is easily established that

$$G_{A,\lambda}(x_1, x_2, \ldots x_{2n}) = \frac{1}{\langle 0|0 \rangle_{A,\lambda}} \exp\left\{ -\frac{i\lambda}{2} \int dx \frac{\delta^2}{\delta A^\mu(x)\delta A_\mu(x)} \right\}$$

$$\times \langle 0|0 \rangle_A G_A(x_1, x_2, \ldots x_{2n})$$

where

$$G_A(x_1, x_2, \ldots x_{2n}) = \tilde{G}_0(x_1, x_2, \ldots x_{2n}) \exp\left\{ i \sum_{i=1}^{2n} q_i F(x_i) \right\}$$

$\tilde{G}_0(x_1, x_2, \ldots x_{2n})$ being the free field Green's function which satisfies the equation

$$\left( \alpha^\mu \frac{1}{i} \partial_\mu \right)_1 \tilde{G}_0(x_1, x_2, \ldots x_{2n}) = \sum_{i=2}^{2n} (-1)^i \delta(x_1 - x_i)$$

$$\times \tilde{G}_0(x_2, \ldots x_{i-1}, x_{i+1}, \ldots x_{2n})$$

and, as before,

$$F(x_i) = -i \int dx' G_0(x_i - x')\alpha^\mu A_\mu(x')$$

After a straightforward calculation it is found that

$$G_{A,\lambda}(x_1, x_2, \ldots x_{2n}) = \exp\left\{ i \sum_{i,j} q_i \int N_\mu(x' - x_i)[A^\mu(x' - x_i) + \lambda \eta^\mu] dx' \right\}$$

$$\times G_{0,\lambda}(x_1, x_2, \ldots x_{2n}) \quad (6.12)$$

where

$$G_{0,\lambda}(x_1, x_2, \ldots x_{2n}) = \tilde{G}_0(x_1, x_2, \ldots x_{2n}) \exp\left\{ i \frac{\lambda}{2} \sum_{i,j} q_i q_j D(x_i - x_j) \right.$$

$$\left. \times \left( \frac{1}{1 - \lambda\eta/\pi} - \frac{\gamma_{5i}\gamma_{5j}}{1 + \lambda\xi/\pi} \right) \right\}$$

and

$$N_\mu(x' - x_i) = \left( \frac{1}{1 - \lambda\eta/\pi} \partial_\mu - \frac{1}{1 + \lambda\xi/\pi} \epsilon_{\mu\nu}\gamma_5 \, \partial^\nu \right) D(x' - x_i)$$

From the form of Eq. (6.12) it is immediately evident that the broken symmetry does not affect the commutation relations of the current $j^\mu$ with the field $\psi$ and we have the usual results[64]

$$[j^0(x), \psi(x')] = -q \frac{1}{1 - \lambda\eta/\pi} \psi(x)\delta(\mathbf{x} - \mathbf{x}')$$

$$[j_5{}^0(x), \psi(x')] = -q \frac{1}{1 + \lambda\xi/\pi} \gamma_5\psi(x)\delta(\mathbf{x} - \mathbf{x}')$$

Having displayed the Fermi Green's functions, it is necessary to check the consistency of definition (6.2) with the result (6.11) through the use of Eq. (6.12). A straightforward calculation shows that the combination of Eq. (6.12) with Eq. (6.2) yields Eq. (6.10) so that no constraint whatever is placed on the theory for consistency of the broken symmetry. This is essentially the same situation as in naturally occurring broken symmetries and, indeed, it is clear that, because the dependence of the theory on the symmetry-breaking parameter [as exemplified by the Green's function (6.12)] is relatively simple, this theory is a natural although intrinsically more complex extension of the models discussed in Section III to composite particle field theories. We may now make contact in the case of the Thirring model with composite particle theories which do not support a broken symmetry in the free field limit by letting $\eta^\mu \to 0$ in such a way that $\langle 0|j^\mu|0\rangle_{A=0}$ does not vanish.[62] We then get a constraint on the coupling constant since this can only occur if

$$\lambda = \pi/\eta$$

or

$$\lambda = -\pi/\xi$$

These, however, are not very satisfactory solutions since pathological singularities are introduced into the Green's functions by such a choice.

In concluding this discussion of the Thirring model, it is amusing to make one further observation about the structure of this theory which will be of use in the consideration of the current–current model in four dimensions. In particular, we note that the equation for the Green's function $G(x - x')$ in the presence of the interaction and the source $A_\mu$ has the structure

$$\alpha^\mu \left[ \frac{1}{i} \partial_\mu - q\left(A_\mu + \lambda \frac{\langle 0|j_\mu|0\rangle}{\langle 0|0\rangle}\right) - \lambda q \frac{1}{i} \frac{\delta}{\delta A^\mu} \right] G = \delta(x - x')$$

which, in turn, may be written as

$$\alpha^\mu\left[\frac{1}{i}\,\partial_\mu - q\mathscr{A}_\mu(x)\right]G(x, x') + i\int \lambda q\alpha_\mu{}' D^{\mu\nu}(x - \xi)\,d\xi G(x, x'')$$
$$\times\ \Gamma_\nu(x'', x'''; \xi)G(x''', x')\,dx''\,dx''' = \delta(x - x') \quad (6.13)$$

where we have made the identifications

$$\mathscr{A}_\mu(x) \equiv A_\mu(x) + \lambda\,\frac{\langle 0|\,j_\mu(x)|0\rangle}{\langle 0|0\rangle}$$

$$'D^{\mu\nu}(x, x') \equiv \frac{\delta\mathscr{A}^\mu(x)}{\delta A_\nu(x')} = g^{\mu\nu}\delta(x - x') + \lambda D^{\mu\nu}_\lambda(x, x')$$

and

$$q\Gamma_\mu(x', x'; \xi) = -\frac{\delta}{\delta\mathscr{A}^\mu(\xi)}\,G^{-1}(x, x')$$

Equation (6.13) corresponds formally to the Green's function equation for electrodynamics in the presence of an external source. However, in this two-dimensional case, the analogy is purely formal since the singularities of $'D^{\mu\nu}(x, x')$ correspond to those of $D^{\mu\nu}_\lambda(x, x')$ and occur at zero mass while the boson in two-dimensional electrodynamics is massive. It is, of course, straightforward to check the consistency of Eq. (6.13) with previous forms displayed for this propagation function.

As the obvious generalization of the preceding discussion, we now consider broken-symmetry solutions of the current–current interaction in four dimensions. The natural procedure at this point would be to extend the Lagrangian (6.1) to four dimensions and to calculate the effect of the broken-symmetry condition on its solutions. This problem has been discussed in the literature[65,66] and solutions consistent with current conservation[66] have been presented. However, these solutions have been obtained in a fairly formal way without detailed reference to the definition of the current as the limit of field operators as was done for the Thirring model and as is also necessary here if $[j^0, j^k] \neq 0$ is to be consistent with the definition of $j^\mu(x)$. Such considerations are extremely difficult to handle in four dimensions since we anticipate that

$$j^\mu(x) = \lim_{\epsilon\to 0}\ \tfrac{1}{2}\psi(x + \epsilon)\exp\left\{i\lambda q\int_{x-\epsilon}^{x+\epsilon} dx_\mu{}''j^\mu(x'')\right\}q\,\alpha^\mu\psi(x - \epsilon)$$

and

$$\lim_{\epsilon\to 0}\psi(x + \epsilon)\psi(x - \epsilon)$$

is cubically divergent as $\varepsilon \to 0$, as opposed to the linear divergence in the case of one spatial dimension. Since it is probably desirable at this point to avoid detailed consideration of these problems, we shall first discuss the boson current–current interaction in four dimensions. One can readily show in this case that at equal times $[j^0, j^k] \neq 0$ even with a strictly local definition of the current. Consequently, for the level of rigor used here, it is not necessary to worry about the problems of Lorentz invariance, redefinition of the energy operator, etc., which occur when one is forced to define the current as a nonlocal limit. The Lagrangian is assumed to be

$$\mathscr{L} = \phi^\mu\, \partial_\mu\phi + \tfrac{1}{2}\phi^\mu\phi_\mu - \tfrac{1}{2}m^2\phi^2 - \tfrac{1}{2}g_0[i\phi q\phi^\mu][i\phi q\phi_\mu] + J^\mu i\phi q\phi_\mu \quad (6.14)$$

Here $J$ is an external source and the two component fields $\phi$ and $\phi^\mu$ are Hermitian and obey the usual equal–time commutation relation

$$[\phi^0(x), \phi(x')] = -i\delta(\mathbf{x} - \mathbf{x}')$$

Introducing the new operator

$$D'^\mu(j^\mu) = \partial^\mu + ig_0 q j^\mu - iqJ^\mu$$

(6.14) results in the field equations

$$D'^\mu(j^\mu)\phi = -\phi^\mu \quad (6.15)$$

$$D'^\mu(j^\mu)\phi_\mu + m^2\phi = 0 \quad (6.16)$$

It follows from these equations that the current $j^\mu(x) = i\phi(x)q\phi^\mu(x)$ is conserved in the case of vanishing source or if the source current is conserved. Combining Eqs. (6.15) and (6.16), we arrive at the familiar second-order field equation

$$[-D^\mu{}'(j^\mu)D_\mu{}'(j^\mu) + m^2]\phi = 0$$

In order to insure current conservation we tacitly assume here that $J^\mu(x)$ is confined to transverse sources. This actually entails no loss of generality in the final answer, but simplifies some calculations.

It is convenient to study the two boson propagators

$$G(x, x') = i\frac{\langle 0|(\phi(x)\phi(x'))_+|0\rangle}{\langle 0|0\rangle}$$

and

$$G^\mu(x, x') = i\frac{\langle 0|(\phi^\mu(x)\phi(x'))_+|0\rangle}{\langle 0|0\rangle}$$

which in consequence of the field equations, commutation relations, and action principle satisfy the equations

$$G^\mu(x, x') = D'^\mu\left(\frac{1}{i}\frac{\delta}{\delta J_\mu}\right)G(x, x') \tag{6.17}$$

$$D'^\mu\left(\frac{1}{i}\frac{\delta}{\delta J_\mu}\right)G_\mu(x, x') = \delta(x - x') - m^2 G(x, x') \tag{6.18}$$

These may be combined to yield the second-order form

$$\left[-D'^\mu\left(\frac{1}{i}\frac{\delta}{\delta J_\mu}\right)D_\mu'\left(\frac{1}{i}\frac{\delta}{\delta J_\mu}\right) + m^2\right]G(x, x') = \delta(x - x')$$

Following the technique outlined in our discussion of the Thirring model, we define a new conserved quantity

$$\mathscr{A}^\mu(x) = g_0\frac{\langle 0|j^\mu(x)|0\rangle}{\langle 0|0\rangle} - J^\mu(x)$$

$$\equiv g_0\eta^\mu(x) - J^\mu(x)$$

and the corresponding propagator function

$$D^{\mu\nu}(x, x') = \frac{\delta}{\delta J_\mu(x)}\mathscr{A}^\nu(x')$$

$$= -g^{\mu\nu}\delta(x - x') + g_0 G^{\mu\nu}(x, x')$$

where

$$G^{\mu\nu}(x, x') = i\frac{\langle 0|(j^\mu(x)j^\nu(x'))_+|0\rangle}{\langle 0|0\rangle} - \eta^\mu(x)\eta^\nu(x') + \frac{\langle 0\left|\frac{\delta j^\mu(x)}{\delta J_\nu(x')}\right|0\rangle}{\langle 0|0\rangle}$$

Then using the chain rule

$$\frac{\delta}{\delta J_\mu(x)} = \int\frac{\delta\mathscr{A}^\nu(x')}{\delta J_\mu(x)}\frac{\delta}{\delta\mathscr{A}^\nu(x')}dx'$$

$$= \int D^{\mu\nu}(x, x')\frac{\delta}{\delta\mathscr{A}^\nu(x')}dx'$$

one obtains

$$G^\mu(x, x') = -\left[\partial^\mu + iq\mathscr{A}^\mu + g_0 q\int D^{\mu\nu}(x, x'')\,dx''\frac{\delta}{\delta\mathscr{A}^\nu(x'')}\right]G(x, x')$$

and

$$\left[\partial^\mu + iq\mathcal{A}^\mu + g_0q \int D^{\mu\nu}(x, x'')\, dx'' \frac{\delta}{\delta\mathcal{A}^\nu(x'')}\right] G_\mu(x, x')$$
$$= \delta(x - x') - m^2 G(x, x')$$

Writing the Green's functions in this way serves to emphasize that upon replacement of $g_0$ by $e_0$ they become formally identical to the corresponding functions in electrodynamics.

Of course, to actually establish the equivalence of this theory to electrodynamics, we must demonstrate that the structure of $D^{\mu\nu}$ corresponds exactly to the photon propagator in electrodynamics with an appropriate identification of the renormalized charge and some choice of gauge. It is possible to establish this identification in general with $D$ describing a massless particle if the broken symmetry condition $\eta^\mu(x)|_{J=0} = \eta^\mu \neq 0$ is satisfied. We shall, for the sake of simplicity, examine only the lowest-order approximation in which $\delta G/\delta\mathcal{A}^\nu$ is neglected in the above equations. In this case we have

$$G^\mu(x, x') = -D^\mu(x)G(x, x')$$
$$D^\mu(x)G_\mu(x, x') + m^2G(x, x') = \delta(x - x')$$

which may be solved to yield

$$G = 1/(-D^\alpha D_\alpha + m^2) \tag{6.19}$$

and

$$G^\mu = -D^\mu[1/(-D^\alpha D_\alpha + m^2)] \tag{6.20}$$

where we have introduced the operator

$$D^\mu = \partial^\mu - iqJ^\mu(x) + ig_0q\eta^\mu(x)$$

It is now possible to determine the structure of $D^{\mu\nu}(x, x')$. To this end, note that since $j^\mu = i\phi q\phi^\mu$, it follows that

$$\eta^\mu = \frac{\langle 0|j^\mu(x)|0\rangle}{\langle 0|0\rangle} = \text{Tr}\, qG^\mu(x, x)$$

Using this result one obtains

$$\frac{1}{i}\frac{\delta}{\delta J_\nu(x')} D^\mu(x) = qD^{\mu\nu}(x, x')$$

so that differentiation of Eq. (6.19) yields

$$\frac{1}{i}\frac{\delta}{\delta J_\nu} G\bigg|_{J=0} = -D^{\nu\alpha}[GqG_\alpha + G_\alpha qG] \tag{6.21}$$

while differentiation of Eq. (6.20) now results in

$$\frac{1}{i} \frac{\delta}{\delta J_\nu} G_\mu \bigg|_{J=0} = -D^{\nu\alpha}\{g_{\alpha\mu}qG - D_\mu[GqG_\alpha + G_\alpha qG]\} \qquad (6.22)$$

Since

$$G^{\mu\nu}(x, x') = \operatorname{Tr} q \frac{\delta}{\delta J_\nu(x')} G^\mu(x, x)$$

Eq. (6.22) shows that

$$G_\mu{}^\nu = -iD^{\nu\alpha}[g_{\alpha\mu} \operatorname{Tr} G - \operatorname{Tr} D_\mu(GG_\alpha + G_\alpha G)]$$

which, when inserted into the equation

$$g_0{}^{-1}(D^{\mu\nu} + g^{\mu\nu}) = G^{\mu\nu}$$

with $J^\mu = 0$ yields

$$\int D^{\nu\alpha}(x - x'') \, dx''\{g_{\alpha\mu}\delta(x' - x'') + ig_0[g_{\alpha\mu}\delta(x' - x'') \operatorname{Tr} G(x'', x'')$$

$$+ \operatorname{Tr} G_\mu(x' - x'')G_\alpha(x'' - x') - \int \operatorname{Tr} [D_\mu(x' - x''')dx'''$$

$$G_\alpha(x''' - x'')G(x'' - x')]\} = -\delta_\mu{}^\nu\delta(x - x') \qquad (6.23)$$

If we introduce Fourier transforms so that

$$G(x - x') = \int \frac{dp}{(2\pi)^4} e^{ip(x - x')}G(p)$$

and, similarly for $D^{\nu\alpha}$, we find from Eq. (6.23) that

$$[D^{\alpha\mu}(k)]^{-1} = -g^{\alpha\mu} + \Pi'^{\alpha\mu}(k) \qquad (6.24)$$

where

$$\Pi'^{\alpha\mu}(k) \equiv -ig_0 \int \frac{dp}{(2\pi)^4} [g^{\alpha\mu} \operatorname{Tr} G(p) + \operatorname{Tr} \{G^\mu(p)G^\alpha(p + k)$$

$$- D^\mu(p)G^\alpha(p)G(p + k)\}] \qquad (6.25)$$

Up to this point, we have not specified that the symmetry be broken. We now make this requirement explicit by setting

$$\frac{\langle 0|j^\mu|0\rangle}{\langle 0|0\rangle}\bigg|_{J=0} = \eta^\mu \neq 0 \qquad (6.26)$$

We then find that

$$G(p)|_{J=0} = [(p^\alpha + g_0 q\eta^\alpha)(p_\alpha + g_0 q\eta_\alpha) + m^2]^{-1} \qquad (6.27)$$

which has the alternative expression

$$G(p) = \frac{p^2 + m^2 + g_0{}^2\eta^2 - 2g_0 q\eta p}{[p^2 + m^2 + g_0{}^2\eta^2]^2 - 4g_0{}^2(\eta p)^2} \tag{6.28}$$

The consistency of relation (6.26) with the Green's functions as given by Eqs. (6.27) and (6.28) requires that $\eta^\mu = \operatorname{Tr} q G^\mu(0)$ which is given explicitly by

$$\eta^\mu = -2ig_0\eta_v \int \frac{dp}{(2\pi)^4} \frac{g^{\mu v}(p^2 + m^2 + g_0{}^2\eta^2) - 2p^\mu p^2}{[p^2 + m^2 + g_0{}^2\eta^2]^2 - 4g_0{}^2(\eta p)^2} \tag{6.29}$$

Since the right-hand side of this equation is quadratically divergent, we must introduce a cutoff. Using a Euclidean cutoff, we find for large $\Lambda$ that Eq. (6.29) reduces to

$$\eta^\mu = g_0\Lambda^2(1/16\pi^2)\eta^\mu \tag{6.30}$$

or

$$1 = g_0{}^2\Lambda^2/16\pi^2 \tag{6.31}$$

Thus in this case, unlike the Thirring model, the consistency of the theory hinges upon placing a constraint on the parameters of the theory. That this constraint arises is due to the nonvanishing boson bare mass which makes it impossible for the free current to have massless excitations and, hence, a broken symmetry.

With this information we may carry out the inversion of Eq. (6.24). It is easily found by direct calculation that

$$\Pi'^{\alpha\mu}(0) = \frac{\partial}{\partial\eta_\alpha} \operatorname{Tr} q G^\mu(0) \tag{6.32}$$

It turns out that this equation is valid for all orders of perturbation theory and assures that $D^{\alpha\mu}(k)$ always has a pole at $k^2 = 0$. From the right-hand side of Eq. (6.30) with the use of Eq. (6.31), Eq. (6.32) becomes

$$\Pi'^{\alpha\mu}(0) = g^{\alpha\mu}$$

so that

$$[D^{\alpha\mu}(k)]^{-1} = [\Pi'^{\alpha\mu}(k) - \Pi'^{\alpha\mu}(0)]$$

Direct evaluation shows that

$$\Pi'^{\alpha\mu}(k) - \Pi'^{\alpha\mu}(0) = [g^{\alpha\mu}k^2 - k^\mu k^\alpha]\bar{I}'(k^2)$$

where $\bar{I}'(k^2)$ when evaluated, using a Euclidean cutoff, is given as

$$\bar{I}'(k^2) = \frac{1}{24}\left[\frac{g_0}{\pi^2}\ln\frac{\Lambda}{m} + \frac{g_0 k^2}{2}\int_{4m^2}^{\infty} d\kappa^2\,\frac{(1 - 4m^2/\kappa^2)^{3/2}}{\kappa^2(k^2 + \kappa^2 - i\epsilon)}\right]$$

From this we find that

$$D^{\alpha\mu}(k) = \frac{1}{k^2\bar{I}'(k^2)}\left[g^{\alpha\mu} - \frac{k^\alpha k^\mu}{k^2}\right]$$

Thus we may conclude that massless electrodynamics of a scalar field in the presence of a constant external field $A^\mu$ is reproduced if the identification $\alpha_0 = (24\pi^2)/\ln(\Lambda/m)$ is made. Consequently, the broken symmetry has no physically measurable effect and, although Lorentz symmetry is broken, the result has not been catastrophic for giving this theory physical meaning.

If one considers broken Lorentz symmetries of interactions with fewer invariance properties, the situation is very different. For example, in the case of a self-interacting vector meson field, $B^\mu$ with mass $\mu_0{}^2$ and an interaction of the form $g_0(B^\mu B_\mu)^2$ or a self-interacting Fermi field[67] $\psi$ with broken symmetry conditions $\langle 0|B^\mu|0\rangle \neq 0$, $\langle 0|\psi|0\rangle \neq 0$ one finds, using the same techniques as in the Goldstone model,[68] that the masses of the particles depend upon the Lorentz frame of the observation. Since this is not the basis for an acceptable theory within the scope of our present knowledge, one cannot take the broken symmetry seriously in these cases.

Since we have already verified that $j^\mu(x)$ excites a massless particle, we must verify that this particle contributes with the proper weight to the consistency of the Goldstone commutator, using our approximations in the current–current model. We start with the usual relation

$$-i[J^{\mu\nu}, j^\lambda(x)] = (x^\mu\,\partial^\nu - x^\nu\,\partial^\mu)j^\lambda(x) + g^{\mu\lambda}j^\nu(x) - g^{\lambda\nu}j^\mu(x) \quad (6.33)$$

where, in terms of the energy momentum tensor $T^{\mu\nu}(x)$,

$$J^{\mu\nu} = \int d^3x[x^\mu T^{0\nu}(x) - x^\nu T^{0\mu}(x)] \tag{6.34}$$

Upon taking the vacuum expectation of Eq. (6.33), we find that

$$-i\langle 0|[J^{\mu\nu}, j^\lambda(x)]|0\rangle = g^{\mu\lambda}\eta^\nu - g^{\lambda\nu}\eta^\mu \tag{6.35}$$

which serves to emphasize that the Goldstone theorem guarantees, independently of perturbation theory, the presence of a massless particle in the spectrum of $j^\lambda(x)$ and, hence, that the photon of this theory is massless. To ascertain that Eq. (6.35) is consistent with our solutions for this theory, we observe that because of Eq. (6.34) we need only to evaluate the quantity

$$C_\eta^{\mu\nu\lambda}(x' - x) \equiv i\langle 0|[T^{\mu\nu}(x'), j^\lambda(x)]|0\rangle$$

$C_\eta^{\mu\nu\lambda}$ being related in the usual manner to the function

$$T_\eta^{\mu\nu\lambda} = \frac{\delta}{\delta J^\lambda} \frac{\langle 0|T^{\mu\nu}|0\rangle}{\langle 0|0\rangle}\bigg|_{J=0}$$

To evaluate $T_\eta^{\mu\nu\lambda}$ explicitly, the energy-momentum tensor is observed to be

$$T^{\mu\nu} = \phi^\mu\phi^\nu - g_0 j^\mu j^\nu + J^\mu j^\nu + J^\nu j^\mu - \tfrac{1}{2}g^{\mu\nu}$$
$$\times [\phi^\alpha\phi_\alpha - g_0 j^\alpha j_\alpha + 2J^\alpha j_\alpha + m^2\phi^2]$$

Then, to the same order of approximation as in the Green's function calculations, we find

$$\frac{\langle 0|T^{\mu\nu}(x)|0\rangle}{\langle 0|0\rangle} = -ig_0 \operatorname{Tr} qG^\mu(x, x) \operatorname{Tr} qG^\nu(x, x) + iJ^\mu \operatorname{Tr} qG^\nu(x, x)$$
$$+ iJ^\nu \operatorname{Tr} qG^\mu(x, x) + \tfrac{1}{2}g^{\mu\nu}$$
$$\times [-ig_0 \operatorname{Tr} qG^\alpha(x, x) \operatorname{Tr} qG_\alpha(x, x) + 2iJ^\alpha \operatorname{Tr} qG_\alpha(x, x)]$$
$$+ \text{irrelevant terms}$$

It is straightforward but tedious to justify the neglect of the terms not explicitly displayed here and, indeed, the consistency of our result will indirectly confirm the validity of this procedure. From the above it follows that

$$T_\eta^{\mu\nu\lambda}(k) = \tfrac{1}{2}D^{\lambda\alpha}(k)\{-2\eta^\nu[\Pi_\alpha^{\prime\mu}(k) - \Pi_\alpha^{\prime\mu}(0)]$$
$$+ g^{\mu\nu}\eta_\beta[\Pi_\alpha^{\prime\beta}(k) - \Pi_\alpha^{\prime\beta}(0)] + (\mu \leftrightarrow \nu)\}$$

Using the forms previously derived for these functions and converting from the time-ordered product to the commutator form, we find

$$C_\eta^{\mu\nu\lambda}(k) = -2\pi i k^\lambda(\eta k)\left[g^{\mu\nu} - \frac{k^\mu\eta^\nu + \eta^\mu k^\nu}{\eta k}\right]\epsilon(k^0)\delta(k^2)$$

Using Eq. (6.34), it is finally verified that the approximations of this model are consistent with Eq. (6.35) with no further constraint on the theory.

Now we will use the same Green's function techniques[69] to consider a theory in which the symmetry-breaking parameter is a mass and, hence, appears in the solutions in a nontrivial physically significant way. We consider the Lagrangian of the Nambu–Jona-Lasinio theory[70]

$$\mathcal{L} = i\bar{\psi}\,\gamma^{\mu}\,\partial_{\mu}\psi + g_0[(\bar{\psi}\psi)^2 - (\bar{\psi}\gamma_5\tau_i\psi)^2] + \lambda_5{}^i i\bar{\psi}\gamma_5\tau_i\psi + S\bar{\psi}\psi \quad (6.36)$$

where $\lambda_5{}^i$ and $S$ are $c$-number sources. When the sources are turned off, we find from the usual invariance arguments that the axial current $j_{i5}^{\mu} = \bar{\psi}\,\gamma^{\mu}\gamma_5\tau_i\psi$ is conserved. We shall not concern ourselves here with the technically correct definition of the current obtained by separating points of the two fields involved in defining $j_{i5}^{\mu}$.

In the source-free limit it is usually argued that as a consequence of the chiral invariance associated with the vanishing of the bare mass term in Eq. (6.36), the physical mass of the particle excited by $\psi$ vanishes. However, such a statement can only be valid if the vacuum is required to be an eigenstate of the pseudoscalar charge operator

$$Q_{5i} = \int d^3x \, j_{i5}^0(x)$$

To see this, we examine the Goldstone commutator

$$[Q_5{}^i, i\bar{\psi}\gamma_5\tau_j\psi] = -2i\delta^i{}_j\bar{\psi}\psi$$

from which it follows that

$$\langle 0|[Q_5{}^i, i\bar{\psi}\gamma_5\tau_i\psi]|0\rangle = -2 \operatorname{Tr} G \quad (6.37)$$

where

$$G(x, x') = i\epsilon\,(x, x')\,\frac{\langle 0|(\psi(x)\bar{\psi}(x'))_+|0\rangle}{\langle 0|0\rangle}\bigg|_{\lambda = \lambda_5{}^i = 0}$$

According to the Lehmann representation

$$G(x - x') = \int \frac{dp}{(2\pi)^4}\, e^{ip(x-x')} \int_{-\infty}^{\infty} d\kappa\, \frac{A(\kappa)}{\gamma p + \kappa}$$

so

$$\operatorname{Tr} G(x, x) = 8 \int \frac{dp}{(2\pi)^4} \int_{-\infty}^{\infty} d\kappa\, \frac{\kappa A(\kappa)}{p^2 + \kappa^2}$$

Since $A(\kappa)$ generally has the structure

$$A(\kappa) = Z\delta(\kappa - m) + A'(\kappa)$$

one can obtain $\operatorname{Tr} G = 0$ if the renormalized mass vanishes and $A'(\kappa) = A'(-\kappa)$. On the other hand, we see that if $G$ is dominated by a single massive excitation such that

$$A(\kappa) = \delta(\kappa - m)$$

then

$$\text{Tr } G = 8 \int \frac{dp}{(2\pi)^4} \frac{m}{p^2 + m^2} \neq 0 \qquad (6.38)$$

and the vacuum is not an eigenstate of the chiral current $Q_5{}^i$. Of course, in practice Eq. (6.38) must be given meaning by the introduction of a cutoff and, therefore, we shall choose a simple Euclidean cutoff when this expression is to be explicitly evaluated. The condition described by Eq. (6.38) will be of prime concern in our analysis of the Lagrangian (6.36). Applying the Goldstone theorem to Eq. (6.37) combined with Eq. (6.38) illustrates that massless pseudoscalar bosons are excited by the "composite field operator" $i\bar{\psi}\gamma_5\tau_j\psi$.

Returning to more explicit considerations resulting from Eq. (6.36), we note that the field equations are

$$[i\gamma^\mu \, \partial_\mu + S + \lambda_5{}^i i\gamma_5\tau_i]\psi + 2g_0[(\bar{\psi}\psi)\psi - (\bar{\psi}\gamma_5\tau_i\psi)\gamma_5\tau^i\psi] = 0$$

and

$$-i \, \partial_\mu\bar{\psi}\gamma^\mu + \bar{\psi}S + \bar{\psi}i\gamma_5\tau_i\lambda_5{}^i + 2g_0[\bar{\psi}(\bar{\psi}\psi) - \bar{\psi}\gamma_5\tau^i(\bar{\psi}\gamma_5\tau^i\psi)] = 0$$

from which we find that $G$ in the presence of the sources satisfies the equation

$$\left\{ i\,\gamma^\mu \, \partial_\mu + 2ig_0[\text{Tr } G - \gamma_5\tau^i \text{ Tr } \gamma_5\tau_i G] + S + \lambda_5{}^i i\gamma_5\tau_i \right.$$
$$\left. + 2g_0\left[\frac{1}{i}\frac{\delta}{\delta S} + i\frac{\delta}{\delta\lambda_5{}^i}\gamma_5\tau^i\right] \right\}G(x, x') = \delta(x - x') \quad (6.39)$$

For the first approximation to $G$, we neglect the variational derivatives and make the identification

$$m = -2ig_0[\text{Tr } G - \gamma_5\tau^i \text{ Tr } \gamma_5\tau_i G] \qquad (6.40)$$

to find that

$$G = \left[\gamma^\mu \frac{1}{i} \partial_\mu + m - S - \lambda_5{}^i i\gamma_5\tau_i\right]^{-1} \qquad (6.41)$$

We now make the simplifying (but unnecessary) assumption that $m$ is pure scalar so that to this order $A(\kappa) = \delta(\kappa - m)$. Equation (6.40) with the sources off becomes, through the use of Eq. (6.41),

$$m = -2ig_0 \text{ Tr } G$$
$$= -16ig_0m \int \frac{dp}{(2\pi)^4} \frac{1}{p^2 + m^2}$$

and, since we assume $m$ to be nonvanishing, these lead to the constraint equation

$$
\begin{aligned}
1 &= -16ig_0 \int \frac{dp}{(2\pi)^4} \frac{1}{p^2 + m^2} \\
&= \frac{g_0}{\pi^2}\left[\Lambda^2 - m^2 \ln\left(1 + \frac{\Lambda^2}{m^2}\right)\right]
\end{aligned}
\tag{6.42}
$$

with $\Lambda$ as the usual Euclidean cutoff.

Now let us make a more careful analysis of Eq. (6.39) in order to see the role played by the Goldstone particle. We make the convenient definitions

$$
A_5{}^i = \lambda_5{}^i - 2g_0 \operatorname{Tr} \gamma_5\tau^i G
$$

and

$$
A = S + 2ig_0 \operatorname{Tr} G
$$

From these and the action principle it is possible to construct Green's functions involving four field operators. Those which are useful here are the meson propagators

$$
D_5{}^{ij}(x, x') = i\frac{\delta}{\delta\lambda_{5i}(x)} A_5{}^j(x')
\tag{6.43}
$$

and

$$
-iD(x, x') = \frac{1}{i}\frac{\delta}{\delta S(x)} A(x')
\tag{6.44}
$$

It is easily established that

$$
\frac{1}{i}\frac{\delta}{\delta\lambda_{5i}(x)} A(x') = \frac{1}{i}\frac{\delta}{\delta S(x)} A_5{}^i(x') = 0
$$

With these new functions and the chain rule for functional derivatives, Eq. (6.39) becomes

$$
\left\{\gamma^\mu\frac{1}{i}\partial_\mu + m - \lambda_5{}^i i\gamma_5\tau_i - S + 2ig_0\left[\gamma_5\tau_i D_5{}^{ij}\frac{1}{i}\frac{\delta}{\delta A_5{}^j} - D\frac{1}{i}\frac{\delta}{\delta A}\right]\right\}G = 1
$$

This equation formally has the same structure as the propagator for a fermion of bare mass $m$ interacting with a pseudoscalar isovector meson and a scalar meson. To establish equivalence to this order we must, of course, confirm that $D_5^{ij}$ and $D$ have the correct structure. The calculation is handled most easily by introducing the function

$$
G^i(x, x'; \xi) = \frac{1}{i}\frac{\delta}{\delta\lambda_{5i}(\xi)} G(x, x')
$$

so that

$$D_5^{ij}(\xi, \xi') = \delta^{ij}\delta(\xi - \xi') - 2g_0 i \operatorname{Tr} \gamma_5 \tau^j G^i(\xi', \xi'; \xi) \qquad (6.45)$$

since

$$G^i(x, x'; \xi) = -\int G(x, x'')\left[\frac{1}{i}\frac{\delta}{\delta\lambda_{5i}(\xi)}G^{-1}(x'', x''')\right]G(x''', x')\,dx''\,dx'''$$

We find from the approximation (6.41) with the use of Eq. (6.40) that

$$-G^i(\xi', \xi'; \xi) = G(\xi', \xi)\gamma_5\tau^i G(\xi, \xi') - \int G(\xi', \xi'')\,d\xi''$$

$$\times\{-2ig_0 \operatorname{Tr} G^i(\xi'', \xi''; \xi)$$

$$+ 2ig_0 \operatorname{Tr} (\gamma_5\tau_\alpha G^i(\xi'', \xi''; \xi))\gamma_5\tau_\alpha\}G(\xi'', \xi') \qquad (6.46)$$

Taking the trace of Eq. (6.46) on $\gamma_5\tau_j$ and inserting the results into Eq. (6.45), we find that, to this order

$$[D_5^{ij}(\xi, \xi')]^{-1} = \delta_{ij}\delta(\xi - \xi') + 2ig_0 \operatorname{Tr} G(\xi, \xi')\gamma_5\tau_j G(\xi', \xi)\gamma_5\tau_i \qquad (6.47)$$

It is of interest to note (as is easily shown) that to all orders we may write

$$[D_5^{ij}(\xi, \xi')]^{-1} = \delta_{ij}\delta(\xi - \xi') + 2ig_0\frac{1}{i}\frac{\delta}{\delta A_5^i(\xi)} \operatorname{Tr} \gamma_5\tau_j G(\xi', \xi')$$

With the sources off, Eq. (6.47) in momentum space becomes

$$[D_5^{ij}(k)]^{-1} = \delta_{ij} + 2ig_0 \int \frac{dp}{(2\pi)^4} \operatorname{Tr} G(p)\gamma_5\tau_j G(p + k)\gamma_5\tau_i$$

Using the consistency condition (6.42) to handle the most divergent part of the above integral, it follows that

$$D_5^{ij}(k) = \frac{1}{k^2 L}\frac{\delta^{ij}}{1 - \dfrac{k^2 g_0}{L2\pi^2}\displaystyle\int_{4m^2}^{\infty}\frac{d\kappa^2}{\kappa^2}\frac{(1 - 4m^2/\kappa^2)^{1/2}}{k^2 + \kappa^2}}$$

where

$$L = \frac{8g_0}{i}\int \frac{dp}{(2\pi)^4}\frac{1}{(p^2 + m^2)^2} = \frac{g_0}{\pi^2}\ln\frac{\Lambda}{m}$$

This form clearly displays the massless excitation. Further, we see that if we use an elementary particle interaction between a massless meson and a massive nucleon, the results are identical if one makes the identification

$$\frac{G^2}{2\pi^2} = \frac{g_0}{2\pi^2 L}$$

where $G$ is the renormalized meson–nucleon coupling constant.

Using essentially identical techniques, we find that for the scalar boson the propagator to this order is

$$D(\xi, \xi')^{-1} = \delta(\xi - \xi') - 2ig_0 \, \text{Tr} \, G(\xi, \xi')G(\xi', \xi) \qquad (6.48)$$

and, to all orders, is given as

$$D(\xi, \xi')^{-1} = \delta(\xi - \xi') - 2ig_0 i \frac{\delta}{\delta A(\xi)} G(\xi', \xi')$$

Explicit evaluation of Eq. (6.48) results in the momentum space representation

$$D(k) = \frac{1}{L(k^2 + 4m^2)} \frac{1}{1 - \dfrac{k^2}{L2\pi^2} \displaystyle\int_{4m^2}^{\infty} \dfrac{d\kappa^2}{\kappa^2} \dfrac{(1 - 4m^2/\kappa^2)^{1/2}}{k^2 + \kappa^2}}$$

so that the scalar particle of this theory has a mass $2m$.

It is to be noted that, in the case in which the symmetry is not broken, it is required that the pseudoscalar meson and scalar meson have the same mass. Indeed, the proof of this statement provides an interesting example of the "bad" behavior of the generator $Q_5{}^i$. If $|\pi\rangle$ is a state of a pseudoscalar meson such that $H|\pi\rangle = E|\pi\rangle$ ($H$ being the Hamiltonian) and $Q_5$ is assumed to be well defined and time independent, we see that the scalar particle state $Q_5|\pi\rangle$ has the same mass since

$$HQ_5|\pi\rangle = Q_5H|\pi\rangle$$
$$= EQ_5|\pi\rangle$$

That this does not follow here just confirms that the operator

$$Q_5{}^V = \int_V j_5{}^0(x) \, d^3x$$

does not exist in the limit $V \to \infty$. For finite volume, of course, we expect the matrix element of this operator to depend on $x^0$ and, hence, $[Q_5{}^V, H] \neq 0$.

It is of some interest to examine the other two-point functions of this theory. In particular, it is found that the matrix element

$$G_{ij}^{\mu\nu}(x, x') = i\langle 0|\,(j_{5i}^\mu j_{5j}^\nu)_+\,|0\rangle$$

has the Fourier transform

$$G_{ij}^{\mu\nu}(k) = i \int \frac{dp}{(2\pi)^4}\, \mathrm{Tr}\, \gamma^\mu\gamma_5\tau_i \frac{1}{\gamma p + m}\, \gamma^\nu\gamma_5\tau_j \frac{1}{\gamma(p+k) + m}$$
$$- 2\delta_{ij} \frac{m^2}{\pi^2} \ln \frac{\Lambda}{m} \frac{k^\mu k^\nu}{k^2}$$

which again exhibits the massless boson. Similarly, a straightforward calculation shows that

$$\langle 0|\, [\bar\psi(x)\, \gamma^\mu\gamma_5\tau_i\psi(x),\, i\psi(x')\gamma_5\tau_j\psi(x')]\,|0\rangle$$
$$= -2\pi \int \frac{dp}{(2\pi)^4}\, e^{ip(x-x')}\, \epsilon(p^0)\delta(p^2)2p^\mu\delta_{ij}\, \mathrm{Tr}\, G(x, x)$$

which is consistent with Eq. (6.37).

It is remarkable to note that in this model we have performed operations on a nonrenormalizable theory that have demonstrated its equivalence to a renormalizable theory. This peculiar result corresponds to the fact that different rearrangements of a power series expansion of such a divergent theory can lead to different answers. The broken-symmetry condition and the associated Green's function technique of solutions used here have served to pick out a particular familiar solution. As is well known, there may be other solutions.

It is of some interest to consider what happens to this model[69] in the presence of the electromagnetic interaction

$$\mathscr{L}_{\mathrm{int}}^{\mathrm{E.M.}} = e\bar\psi\, \gamma^\mu[(1 - \tau_3)/2]\psi A_\mu$$

A simple calculation shows that

$$\partial_\mu j_{5i}^\mu = e\epsilon_{3ij}A^\mu\bar\psi\, \gamma_\mu\gamma_5\tau_j\psi$$

so only $j_{53}^\mu$ is now conserved. Using the Goldstone theorem it is seen that the $\pi^0$ meson alone is required to remain massless if the fermion mass $m \neq 0$. The mass of the charged mesons may be calculated to second order in $e$ using the propagation functions derived as above as the $e = 0$ limit of the theory. These calculations are very tedious, but it is amusing to note the type of graphs that contribute. Using Eq. (6.47) we may give the pion propagator the pictorial representation

$$(D_5{}^{ij})^{-1} = 1 + \quad$$

where the solid lines are nucleon propagators $G$. This clearly points out the composite nature of the pion and shows that the electromagnetic mass splitting will be given as corrections to the nucleon bubble. The contributing terms are of the form

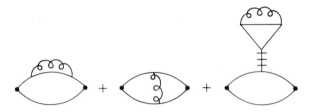

Here $\sim\!\!\diamond\!\!\diamond\!\!\diamond\!\!\sim$ represents the photon propagator while $+\!\!+\!\!+\!\!+\!\!+\!\!+$ is the propagator of the pseudoscalar meson. The structure of the corrections serves to emphasize the composite nature of the pion in this theory.

There are, of course, many other theories which have been considered in the context of nonsoluble relativistic broken symmetries but, for the most part, these theories are either modifications of the above theories or are much more complicated. In the latter category are the electrodynamics of Johnson, Baker, and Willey,[72] and the fundamental four-Fermi interactions of Heisenberg et al.[71] Within the framework of broken symmetries as discussed here, both of these theories appear to have serious faults. However, until such time as more complete solutions are presented, it is perhaps desirable to defer final judgment on the possible inconsistency of the broken-symmetry aspect of these theories.


## VII. Symmetry Breaking Effects in Some Noncovariant Field Theories

Despite the appreciable number of examples of relativistic theories displaying various forms of symmetry breakdown which have been presented in the preceding sections, none of the models considered can be described as being entirely satisfactory as a physically meaningful broken-symmetry theory of elementary particles. In particular, it has been noted that although the discussion of naturally occurring broken symmetries demonstrated how it may be possible in certain theories to solve the problem of how to consistently induce a nonvanishing expectation value for a certain field operator, one was nonetheless led to the conclusion that a symmetry breaking of this type is purely formal. Thus the fact that one can in such cases generate a nonvanishing vacuum expectation value for a field $\phi(x)$ has been seen to arise entirely from the cyclic (or ignorable) property of $\phi(x)$ and the consequent feature that $\phi(x)$ is undefined to within an additive constant. Since this ambiguity does not have any effect upon the (appropriately truncated) Green's functions, there can never be any observable consequence of choosing $\langle 0|\phi(x)|0 \rangle \neq 0$ regardless of how complex the interactions may be. This criticism, of course, does not apply to what we have called spontaneous symmetry breaking where the breakdown of symmetry will generally manifest itself in all measurement processes. On the other hand, theories of this latter type have a considerably less certain mathematical foundation, there being little basis for judging the consistency of constraints of the form (2.5).

This then naturally leads one to ask whether there is not a class of theories in which the desired features of mathematical tractability and physical nontriviality may be simultaneously realized. It has in fact recently been shown[73,74] that in the domain of nonrelativistic field theories there are a number of models which combine both of these attributes and we shall consequently devote the entirety of this chapter to a discussion of these rather remarkable theories.

In order to clarify the connection to our previous discussion as much as possible, we recall that the momentum space representation of the Hamiltonian for a simple scalar field has the form

$$H = \int d^3k \, \omega_k a^*(\mathbf{k}) a(\mathbf{k}) \tag{7.1}$$

where

$$\omega_k = (\mathbf{k}^2 + \mu^2)^{1/2}$$

It was shown in Section III that for such a system one can formally construct from the vacuum $\langle 0|$ the state

$$\begin{aligned}
\langle a'| &= \langle 0|U \\
&= \langle 0| \exp\{a'^*a(0) - a^*(0)a'\}
\end{aligned}$$

such that

$$\langle a'|a(\mathbf{k})|a'\rangle = a'\delta(\mathbf{k})$$

thus providing an inequivalent representation of the commutation relations by means of the improper unitary operator $U$. Now although it is readily shown in the case $\mu^2 = 0$ that it is consistent to take $\langle a'|$ to be a zero-energy eigenstate of the Hamiltonian (7.1), it is precisely the difficulty in generalizing this result to the interacting case which is responsible for the highly conjectural nature of most broken-symmetry theories. This problem can be avoided in the case of naturally occurring broken symmetries by virtue of the cyclic nature of the field $\phi(x)$ but only at the expense of accepting what is essentially a trivial type of symmetry breaking. It is easy to convince oneself that the problem is basically related to the fact that upon introducing a coupling of the field $\phi(x)$ of the form

$$J(x)\phi(x)$$

[where $J(x)$ is generally bilinear in the elementary field operators of the theory], it is not possible to solve the eigenvalue problem for those states containing an arbitrary number of massless bosons, and consequently one cannot retain the state $\langle a'|$ as a zero-energy eigenstate of $H$. Since this circumstance is a consequence of the fact that in a Lorentz-invariant theory $J$ will generally be capable of creating an arbitrarily large number of particles, it is clear that only when one gives up the requirement of relativistic covariance (and thereby the antiparticle concept) does it become possible to identify $\langle a'|$ with the state of lowest energy and at the same time produce a physically nontrivial effect.

The simplest example of a theory which is capable of displaying nontrivial symmetry-breaking effects is the well-known neutral scalar theory. In view of its unusually simple structure a detailed study of this model is quite feasible and at the same time can be expected to provide considerable insight into some aspects of broken symmetries. The relevant Hamiltonian is

$$H = mN^*N + \int d^3k\,\omega_k\,\theta^*(\mathbf{k})\theta(\mathbf{k}) - N^*N\int d^3k\,\alpha(|\mathbf{k}|)[\theta(\mathbf{k}) + \theta^*(\mathbf{k})]$$

where

$$\alpha(|\mathbf{k}|) = g_0\,\frac{u(|\mathbf{k}|)}{(2\pi)^{3/2}}\,\frac{1}{(2\omega)^{1/2}}$$

$u(|\mathbf{k}|)$ being the usual form factor inserted to guarantee the convergence of the theory. The commutation relations are taken to be of the form

$$\{N, N^*\} = 1 \tag{7.2}$$

$$[\theta(\mathbf{k}), \theta^*(\mathbf{k})] = \delta(\mathbf{k} - \mathbf{k}') \tag{7.3}$$

It is customary to choose that particular representation of the commutation relations defined by the requirement that the vacuum be annihilated by the operators $N$ and $\theta(\mathbf{k})$, i.e.,

$$N|0\rangle = 0 \tag{7.4}$$

$$\theta(\mathbf{k})|0\rangle = 0 \tag{7.5}$$

Because of the fact that the fermion field refers to only a single degree of freedom, it will turn out that there are no representations of Eq. (7.2) which are not unitarily equivalent to Eq. (7.4), and we shall consequently focus our attention entirely on the construction of representations of Eq. (7.3) other than that described by Eq. (7.5).

Let us assume for the moment the existence of a state $\langle\theta'|$ which is degenerate with the vacuum in the sense that $\langle\theta'|H = 0$ and such that it satisfies the condition

$$\langle\theta'|\theta(\mathbf{k})|\theta'\rangle \neq 0 \tag{7.6}$$

It follows from the equations of motion

$$i\frac{\partial\theta(\mathbf{k}, t)}{\partial t} = [\theta(\mathbf{k}), H] = \omega_k\theta(\mathbf{k}) - \alpha(|\mathbf{k}|)N^*N$$

$$i\frac{\partial N(t)}{\partial t} = [N, H] = mN - N\int d^3k\alpha(|\mathbf{k}|)[\theta(\mathbf{k}) + \theta^*(\mathbf{k})]$$

that Eq. (7.6) is consistent only if

$$\omega_k\langle\theta'|\theta(\mathbf{k})|\theta'\rangle = 0 \tag{7.7}$$

i.e., $\mu = 0$ and $\langle\theta'|\theta(\mathbf{k})|\theta'\rangle \sim \delta(\mathbf{k})$. Since $\theta'$ can be defined to be the constant of proportionality in this relation, it follows that in the limit of vanishing $\theta$ mass one can take

$$\langle\theta'|\theta(\mathbf{k})|\theta'\rangle = \theta'\delta(\mathbf{k}) \tag{7.8}$$

It is well to emphasize at this point that the theory we consider here is indeed intermediate in complexity between the naturally occurring and the spontaneous types of symmetry breaking. Thus by requiring $\alpha(0) \neq 0$ (which condition we shall impose throughout this section) the zero-momentum mode of the $\theta(\mathbf{k})$ field is not decoupled and $\theta(\mathbf{k}) \to \theta(\mathbf{k}) + \theta' \delta(\mathbf{k})$ is consequently not an invariance property of $H$. On the other hand, despite the nontrivial coupling of the zero-momentum mode, the constraint (7.8) is clearly consistent at the kinematical level and, in marked contrast to the cases considered in the preceding section, does not require any further constraints on the higher order vacuum expectation values. It is, of course, this latter circumstance which is responsible for the somewhat uncertain foundations of the usual theories of spontaneous symmetry breaking.

Here again it is possible to carry out the formal construction of $\langle \theta' |$ in terms of the usual improper transformation on $\langle \theta |$, i.e.,

$$\langle \theta' | = \langle 0 | U(\theta')$$
$$= \langle 0 | \exp \{ \theta'^* \theta(\mathbf{0}) - \theta^*(\mathbf{0}) \theta' \}$$

Despite the frequently mentioned fact that the operator $U(\theta')$ is not really well defined, one finds that in the calculation of all quantities of any possible physical interest one may conveniently ignore this slight subtlety. Thus for the present $U(\theta')$ will be freely employed as if it were an ordinary unitary operator with the implicit understanding that we shall subsequently return to reformulate the solution entirely in terms of the vacuum expectation values of the theory. Thus this discussion will consider $U(\theta')$ to be essentially only a heuristic tool which, though quite invaluable for purposes of displaying the physical content of the theory, can be entirely eliminated in the event that mathematical rigor may be preferred to simplicity of formulation.

In order to be able to discuss the effect of Eq. (7.8) on the solution it is necessary to briefly comment on the usual approach to the theory. The most direct treatment consists in defining the operator

$$U = \exp \left\{ -N^*N \int d^3k \, \frac{\alpha(|\mathbf{k}|)}{\omega_k} [\theta(\mathbf{k}) - \theta^*(\mathbf{k})] \right\}$$

which clearly generates the transformation.

$$\tilde{\theta}(\mathbf{k}) \equiv U\theta(\mathbf{k})U^* = \theta(\mathbf{k}) - \frac{\alpha(|\mathbf{k}|)}{\omega_k} N^*N \tag{7.9}$$

$$\tilde{N} \equiv UNU^* = \exp \left\{ \int d^3k \, \frac{\alpha(|\mathbf{k}|)}{\omega_k} [\theta(\mathbf{k}) - \theta^*(\mathbf{k})] \right\} N$$

In terms of the set (7.9) the Hamiltonian assumes the form

$$H = \left( m - \int d^3k \, \frac{\alpha^2(|\mathbf{k}|)}{\omega} \right) \tilde{N}^* \tilde{N} + \int d^3k \omega_k \hat{\theta}(\mathbf{k}) \hat{\theta}(\mathbf{k})$$

a result which immediately displays the well-known equivalence of the model to a theory describing uncoupled bosons and fermions of masses $\mu$ and

$$m - \int d^3k \, \frac{\alpha^2(|\mathbf{k}|)}{\omega_k}$$

respectively.

Although the above transformation appears at first sight to exhaust the entire physical content of the theory, there is one singular case which requires particular attention. This special circumstance occurs when $\alpha(0)$ is finite and $\omega(\mathbf{k} = 0) = 0$, i.e., in the case of a massless $\theta$ particle in the theory with a nonvanishing coupling of the zero-momentum mode of the field $\theta(\mathbf{k})$. In this case the transformation (7.9) clearly becomes singular and there arises the possibility of constructing additional solutions based on the inequivalent representations of the commutation relations.

Since our discussion of these additional representations has already remarked upon the consistency of the condition

$$\langle \theta' | \theta(\mathbf{k}) | \theta' \rangle = \theta' \delta(\mathbf{k}) \tag{7.10}$$

there remains only the task of demonstrating whether this constraint has a nontrivial effect upon the eigenvalue spectrum of the theory. To this end it is again convenient to refer to the operator $U(\theta')$ which, since it formally generates $c$-number translations on $\theta(\mathbf{k})$, can be used to provide a realization of Eq. (7.10). This result is made most transparent upon considering the vacuum expectation value

$$\langle \theta' | N(t) N^*(t') | \theta' \rangle$$

Now although one can (formally) show that the operator $U(\theta')$ in the case of a naturally occurring broken symmetry is time independent, it follows from the nontrivial coupling of $\theta(\mathbf{0})$ in this model that $U(\theta')$ cannot be assumed to be a constant of the motion. Thus we use the more explicit notation $U(\theta', t = 0)$ to denote the fact that we have chosen to construct the state $\langle \theta' |$ in terms of the operators $\theta(\mathbf{k}, t = 0)$ and $\theta^*(\mathbf{k}, t = 0)$. One thus has

$$\langle \theta' | N(t) N^*(t') | \theta' \rangle = \langle 0 | U(\theta', t = 0) \, e^{iHt} N(0) \, e^{-iH(t-t')}$$
$$\times \, N^*(0) \, e^{-iHt'} U^*(\theta', t = 0) | 0 \rangle$$
$$= \langle 0 | N(0) \, e^{-iH(N, \theta + \theta'\delta(\mathbf{k}))(t-t')} N^*(0) | 0 \rangle$$

where we have used the notation $H[N, \theta + \theta'\delta(\mathbf{k})]$ to indicate that in the expression for $H$ the operator $\theta(\mathbf{k})$ is to be replaced by $\theta(\mathbf{k}) + \theta'\delta(\mathbf{k})$. The above establishes the equivalence of the neutral scalar theory with the broken-symmetry condition (7.8) to a theory in which one chooses the usual representation

$$\theta(\mathbf{k}) | 0 \rangle = 0$$

of the commutation relation and incorporates the symmetry-breaking effect directly into the Hamiltonian. It is perhaps unnecessary to remark that the same calculations can be performed for the case of a naturally occurring broken symmetry with, however, the important modification that because of the cyclic nature of the zero mass field the Hamiltonian (and consequently all the Green's functions) of the model are invariant under this transformation.

Before going on to the next higher stage of complexity in theories which possess a nontrivial symmetry breaking, we shall provide a more rigorous derivation of the above results, thereby demonstrating the existence of the alternative approach alluded to earlier in this chapter. Thus we seek to verify for this model the statement that the operator $U(\theta', t)$ is indeed inessential for purposes of establishing the equivalence of the broken-symmetry condition to the c-number translation of $\theta(\mathbf{k})$ in the Hamiltonian. Since the net result of the replacement of $\theta(\mathbf{k})$ by $\theta(\mathbf{k}) + \theta'\delta(\mathbf{k})$ in the neutral scalar theory is the addition of the term

$$-2\alpha(0) \, N^*N \, \mathrm{Re} \, \theta'$$

it is to be shown directly from the equations for the Green's functions that the only nontrivial symmetry-breaking effect consists of a mass renormalization. Although it is also possible in some of the other soluble models which we shall discuss here to carry out the proof of equivalence by direct calculation, we shall only provide the alternative derivation in the neutral scalar case and refer the reader elsewhere for a discussion of additional examples.[73] However, it is well to emphasize at the outset the obvious impossibility of giving a completely general proof of this result, a circumstance which follows from the fact that there is no guarantee that the transformed Hamiltonian describes a meaningful theory except in the relatively few cases where an exact solution can be obtained for a wide class of inequivalent representations of the canonical commutation relations.

To carry out the proof for the neutral scalar theory we shall focus attention on the two-point function

$$G(t) = i\langle 0|(N(t)N^*(0))_+|0\rangle$$

the extension of this discussion to the most general vacuum expectation value being fairly straightforward. It is convenient to introduce a source function $J(\mathbf{k})$ by adding to the Hamiltonian the term

$$-\int d^3k[\theta(\mathbf{k}) + \theta^*(\mathbf{k})]J(\mathbf{k})$$

thereby enabling one to write the equation for $G(t)$ in terms of functional derivatives with respect to $J(\mathbf{k})$. We shall consider this source to be essentially an arbitrary function in the interval $(t_2, t_1)$ subject only to the condition that it vanishes at $t_1$ and $t_2$ $(t_1 > t_2)$. One then anticipates from our previous discussion that the physical vacuum $|\theta't_2\rangle$ at time $t_2$ is to be defined by

$$\theta(\mathbf{k}, t_2)|\theta't_2\rangle = \theta'\delta(\mathbf{k})|\theta't_2\rangle \qquad (7.11)$$

with the corresponding result

$$\langle\theta't_1|\theta^*(\mathbf{k}, t_1) = \theta'^*\delta(\mathbf{k})\langle\theta't_1| \qquad (7.12)$$

used to define the vacuum $\langle\theta't_1|$, after the source has been turned off. In fact Eqs. (7.11) and (7.12) need not be imposed as eigenvalue equations, since it is sufficient to merely impose the broken-symmetry condition in the weaker form

$$\langle\theta't_1|\theta(\mathbf{k}, t_2)|\theta't_2\rangle = \theta'\delta(\mathbf{k})\langle\theta't_1|\theta't_2\rangle \qquad (7.13)$$

$$\langle\theta't_1|\theta^*(\mathbf{k}, t_1)|\theta't_2\rangle = \theta'^*\delta(\mathbf{k})\langle\theta't_1|\theta't_2\rangle \qquad (7.14)$$

In the presence of the source $J(\mathbf{k})$ the appropriate Green's function $G(t)$ is

$$G(t, J) = i\frac{\langle\theta't_1|(N(t)N^*(0))_+|\theta't_2\rangle}{\langle\theta't_1|\theta't_2\rangle}$$

which, in terms of the amplitude

$$\langle \theta' t_1 | \theta' t_2 \rangle = e^{iw(J)}$$

satisfies the equation

$$e^{-iw(J)} \left[ m - i \frac{\partial}{\partial t} - \int d^3k \alpha(|\mathbf{k}|) \frac{1}{i} \frac{\delta}{\delta J(\mathbf{k})} \right] e^{wi(J)} G(t) = \delta(t)$$

In order to evaluate $w(J)$ we note that

$$\frac{\delta}{\delta J(\mathbf{k})} \langle \theta' t_1 | \theta' t_2 \rangle = i \langle \theta' t_1 | \theta(\mathbf{k}) + \theta^*(\mathbf{k}) | \theta' t_2 \rangle \tag{7.15}$$

Upon using the equation of motion

$$i \frac{\partial}{\partial t} \theta(\mathbf{k}) = \omega_k \theta(\mathbf{k}) - \alpha(|\mathbf{k}|) N^* N - J(\mathbf{k})$$

one easily deduces that

$$\frac{\langle \theta' t_1 | \theta(\mathbf{k}, t) | \theta' t_2 \rangle}{\langle \theta' t_1 | \theta' t_2 \rangle} = \theta' \delta(\mathbf{k}) + \int_{t_2}^{t_1} \mathcal{G}_r(\mathbf{k}, t - t') J(\mathbf{k}, t') \, dt'$$

where

$$\mathcal{G}_r(\mathbf{k}, t - t') = \int \frac{dE}{2\pi} e^{-iE(t-t')} \frac{1}{\omega_k - E - i\epsilon}$$
$$= i\theta_+(t - t_1) e^{-i\omega_k(t-t')}$$

and we have used Eq. (7.14). From the corresponding result for the matrix element of $\theta^*(\mathbf{k})$ one has the result

$$\frac{\langle \theta' t_1 | \theta(\mathbf{k}, t) + \theta^*(\mathbf{k}, t) | \theta' t_2 \rangle}{\langle \theta' t_1 | \theta' t_2 \rangle} = 2 \operatorname{Re} \theta' \delta(\mathbf{k}) + \int_{t_2}^{t_1} \mathcal{G}(\mathbf{k}, t - t') J(\mathbf{k}, t') \, dt'$$
$$\tag{7.16}$$

where

$$\mathcal{G}(\mathbf{k}, t) = \int \frac{dE}{2\pi} e^{-iEt} \left[ \frac{1}{\omega_k - E - i\epsilon} + \frac{1}{\omega_k + E - i\epsilon} \right]$$

One can thus integrate Eq. (7.15) to obtain the explicit expression for $w(J)$

$$w(J) = \frac{1}{2} \int d^3k \iint_{t_2}^{t_1} dt \, dt' J(\mathbf{k}, t) \mathcal{G}(\mathbf{k}, t - t') J(\mathbf{k}, t')$$
$$+ 2 \operatorname{Re} \theta' J(\mathbf{k} = 0, E = 0)$$

where

$$J(\mathbf{k}, E) = \int e^{iEt} J(\mathbf{k}, t)\, dt$$

To facilitate the solution of the integro-differential equation for $G(t, J)$ we introduce at this point the operator[75]

$$I(t) = \exp\left\{\int d^3k\, dE\, J(\mathbf{k}, E)(e^{-iEt} - 1); \frac{\delta}{\delta J(\mathbf{k}, E)}\right\}$$

where the semicolon indicates that in the expansion of $I(t)$ all variational derivatives appear to the right of all $J$'s. One can readily deduce from this definition the property

$$\frac{\delta}{\delta J(\mathbf{k}, t)} I(t') = I(t') \frac{\delta}{\delta J(\mathbf{k}, t + t')}$$

which leads to the alternative representation of $I(t)$

$$I(t) = \exp\left\{-it \int d^3k\, dE\, E\, J(\mathbf{k}, E) \frac{\delta}{\delta J(\mathbf{k}, E)}\right\}$$

Defining $I(t)G(t) \equiv \bar{G}(t)$ and taking the Fourier transform of equation for $G(t)$, there follows

$$e^{-iw(J)}\left[m - E + \int E'\, d^3k'\, dE'\, J(\mathbf{k}', E') \frac{\delta}{\delta J(\mathbf{k}', E')}\right.$$
$$\left. + \int d^3k'\, dE'\, \frac{\alpha(|\mathbf{k}'|)}{i} \frac{\delta}{\delta J(\mathbf{k}', E')}\right] e^{iw(J)}\bar{G}(E) = 1$$

from which one can immediately deduce the formal solution

$$G(E) = i\int_0^\infty dx\, e^{-ix(m - E)} \exp\left\{-ix \int E'\, d^3k'\, dE'\, J(\mathbf{k}', E') \frac{\delta}{\delta J(\mathbf{k}', E')}\right.$$
$$\left. + ix \int d^3k'\, dE'\, \alpha(|\mathbf{k}'|)\frac{1}{i} \frac{\delta}{\delta J(\mathbf{k}', E')}\right\} e^{iw(J)}\bigg|_{J = 0} \tag{7.17}$$

where we have observed that $\bar{G}(E; J = 0) = G(E; J = 0)$. One can now make use of the operator identity[75]

$$e^{A + B} = e^B \exp\left(A \frac{1 - e^{-\lambda}}{\lambda}\right)$$

$\lambda$ being a $c$-number defined by the commutator condition

$$[A, B] = -\lambda A$$

to rewrite Eq. (7.17) as

$$G(E) = i \int_0^\infty dx \, e^{-ix(m-E)} \exp \left\{ \int d^3k' \, dE' \frac{1 - e^{iE'x}}{-iE'} \right.$$

$$\left. \times \, \alpha(|\mathbf{k}'|) \frac{\delta}{\delta J(\mathbf{k}', E')} \right\} e^{iw(J)} \Bigg|_{J=0}$$

Using Eq. (7.16) one readily obtains the complete Green's function

$$G(E) = i \int_0^\infty dx \, e^{-ix(m-E-2\alpha(0)\,\mathrm{Re}\,\theta')} \exp \left\{ \frac{i}{2} \int \frac{d^3k' \, dE'}{2\pi} \frac{1 - \cos E'x}{E'^2} \right.$$

$$\left. \times \, \alpha^2(|\mathbf{k}'|) \left( \frac{1}{\omega' - E' - i\epsilon} + \frac{1}{\omega' + E' - i\epsilon} \right) \right\} \quad (7.18)$$

$$= i \int_0^\infty dx \, e^{-ix(m'-E)} \exp \left\{ - \int d^3k \, \alpha^2(|\mathbf{k}|) \frac{1 - e^{-i\omega x}}{\mathbf{k}^2} \right\}$$

where we have defined

$$m' = m - 2\alpha(0) \, \mathrm{Re} \, \theta' - \int d^3k \frac{\alpha^2(|\mathbf{k}|)}{|\mathbf{k}|}$$

It is now relatively straightforward to verify that the solution given by Eq. (7.18) has a simple pole at $E = m'$, a result which is in complete agreement with the somewhat more heuristic derivation of the symmetry-breaking effect quoted earlier in this chapter. Thus, in consequence of the fact that the quantity $\theta'$ appears only in the expression for $m'$ it follows that the symmetry-breaking effect consists entirely of a mass renormalization, thereby verifying the results of the more direct approach utilizing $U(\theta', t)$. It is also possible to extract from Eq. (7.18) some of the familiar properties of the neutral scalar theory which are customarily obtained by the somewhat less elegant approach in which one specifies the representation (7.5) at the outset and subsequently carries out the explicit construction of the single fermion state. In particular, the wave function renormalization constant $Z$ is found by inspection to be given by

$$Z = \exp \left[ - \int d^3k \frac{\alpha^2(|\mathbf{k}|)}{\mathbf{k}^2} \right] \quad (7.19)$$

It may be of interest to remark that this result can also be obtained directly by using the canonical variables defined by Eq. (7.9). Thus the definition

$$Z = |\langle 0|N|N \rangle|^2$$
$$= |\langle 0|N\tilde{N}^*|0 \rangle|^2$$

with the identity

$$e^{A+B} = e^A \, e^B \, e^{-\frac{1}{2}[A,B]}$$

for $[A,B]$ a $c$-number, immediately implies

$$Z = |\langle 0| \exp \left\{ - \int d^3k \, \frac{\alpha(|\mathbf{k}|)}{|\mathbf{k}|} \, [\theta(\mathbf{k}) - \theta^*(\mathbf{k})] \right\} |0\rangle |^2 \qquad (7.20)$$

$$= \exp \left[ - \int d^3k \, \frac{\alpha^2(|\mathbf{k}|)}{\mathbf{k}^2} \right]$$

in agreement with Eq. (7.19).

Before leaving this interesting model it would be well to comment in a more precise fashion upon the meaning we attach to the phrase "nontrivial symmetry breaking" within the context of this section. Thus we attempt to anticipate the possible objection that since the sole effect of the condition

$$\langle 0| \theta(\mathbf{k}) |0\rangle = \theta' \delta(\mathbf{k}) \qquad (7.21)$$

is to induce a mass renormalization term (which, of course, is not strictly speaking an observable quantity), the symmetry-breaking effect is in fact a trivial one. Without going into great detail on this point it is sufficient to note that a simple generalization of the neutral scalar theory shows that such an objection may be easily discounted. This can be accomplished by simply doubling the number of degrees of freedom of the $N$ field and replacing the interaction term in the Hamiltonian by

$$- N^* \tau_i N \int d^3k \alpha(|\mathbf{k}|)[\theta(\mathbf{k}) + \theta^*(\mathbf{k})] \qquad (7.22)$$

where $\tau_i$ is any one of the three Pauli spin matrices. Thus the fermion field in this variant of the model is described by two distinct operators $N_1$ and $N_2$ which for $\mu \neq 0$ are easily shown to possess identical excitation spectra. For vanishing $\theta$ mass it immediately follows in complete analogy to our previous discussion that one can consistently require

$$\langle 0| \theta(\mathbf{k}) |0\rangle \neq 0$$

In this case, however, one sees that the single fermion states are associated with the two eigenvalues

$$m \pm 2\alpha(0) \, \text{Re} \, \theta' - \int d^3k \, \frac{\alpha^2(|\mathbf{k}|)}{|\mathbf{k}|}$$

a result which clearly shows that for nonvanishing symmetry breaking one has an observable mass difference $4\alpha(0)$ Re $\theta'$ between the two single fermion states.

It is also interesting to note that this simple extension of the neutral scalar theory is particularly useful inasmuch as it actually requires one to break an invariance of the Hamiltonian in order to guarantee the consistency of Eq. (7.21). We refer to the fact that in the strict sense it is not entirely accurate in the case of the neutral scalar theory to refer to Eq. (7.21) as a broken-symmetry condition inasmuch as there is no invariance property which requires the vanishing of the expectation value of $\theta(\mathbf{k})$. On the other hand, it is clear that with the interaction term (7.22) the Hamiltonian is invariant under

$$\theta(\mathbf{k}) \to -\theta(\mathbf{k})$$
$$N \to -i\tau_j N \qquad j \neq i \tag{7.23}$$

a transformation which is effected by the operator

$$U = \exp\left\{i\frac{\pi}{2}N^*\tau_j N + i\pi \int \theta^*(\mathbf{k})\theta(\mathbf{k})\, d^3k\right\}$$

Since the requirement that the set of physical states in this extension of the neutral scalar theory fail to respect the invariance (7.23) may be imposed in the form (7.21), it is by no means inappropriate to designate this a broken-symmetry theory. It should be remarked that although the invariance property described by (7.23) represents a discrete symmetry of the Hamiltonian rather than the usual case of a continuous symmetry group, one can easily construct theories in which the symmetry breaking occurs in this latter type of invariance group by replacing (7.22) with an $SU_2$-invariant term describing the interaction of two fermions with a triplet of massless mesons. By requiring that one of the fields $\theta_i(\mathbf{k})$ satisfy a condition of the type (7.21) one can consistently break the $SU_2$ symmetry, but unfortunately the model is no longer exactly soluble for nonvanishing symmetry breaking. Thus, the fact that the preceding discussion has dealt with the breakdown of a discrete invariance group has not been motivated by any indication that the techniques described here cannot be applied to continuous groups but is rather a consequence of the fact that we lack sufficiently powerful mathematical tools to deal with these more complex theories.

There does exist, however, at least one well-known model with a continuous invariance group in which the solubility of the theory is not destroyed by imposing a condition of the type (7.21). This theory describes the interaction of a fixed fermion with a $\theta$ meson as described by the Hamiltonian

$$H = mN^*N + \int d^3k\omega_k\theta^*(\mathbf{k})\theta(\mathbf{k})$$

$$- \lambda \int d^3k\alpha(|\mathbf{k}|)\theta^*(\mathbf{k}) \int d^3k'\alpha(|\mathbf{k}'|)\theta(\mathbf{k}')N^*N \quad (7.24)$$

where $\alpha(|\mathbf{k}|)$ has the form

$$\alpha(|\mathbf{k}|) = \frac{u(|\mathbf{k}|)}{(2\omega_k)^{1/2}(2\pi)^{3/2}}$$

and the commutation relations are given by Eqs. (7.2) and (7.3).

It immediately follows from Eq. (7.24) that the operators

$$Q_N = N^*N$$

$$Q_\theta = \int d^3k\,\theta^*(\mathbf{k})\theta(\mathbf{k})$$

are separately conserved so that in the usual representation [Eq. (7.5)] of the commutation relations the set of physical states will be the eigenvectors of these two operators. However, we note that as in the neutral scalar theory there arises the possibility of having physically meaningful inequivalent representations in the event that $\mu = 0$. This is seen to be an immediate consequence of the fact that the condition which breaks the conservation law for the number of $\theta$ particles

$$\langle\theta'|\theta(\mathbf{k})|\theta'\rangle = \theta'\delta(\mathbf{k}) \quad (7.25)$$

is consistent with the equation of motion

$$\left(\omega - i\frac{\partial}{\partial t}\right)\theta(\mathbf{k}) = \lambda N^*N\alpha(|\mathbf{k}|)\int d^3k'\alpha(|\mathbf{k}'|)\theta(k')$$

if and only if the boson has vanishing mass. We again require that $\alpha(0) \neq 0$ so that the zero-momentum component of the field will have a nonvanishing coupling, thereby providing the basis for a nontrivial symmetry breaking. As in the neutral scalar theory we anticipate that the broken-symmetry condition may be eliminated by the replacement of $\theta(\mathbf{k})$ by $\theta(\mathbf{k}) + \theta'\delta(\mathbf{k})$ in the Hamiltonian. One thus obtains the equivalent description of this theory in terms of

$$H(\theta') = [m - \lambda\alpha^2(0)]N^*N + \int d^3k\omega\theta^*(\mathbf{k})\theta(\mathbf{k})$$

$$- \lambda \int d^3k\alpha(|\mathbf{k}|)\theta^*(\mathbf{k}) \int d^3k'\alpha(|\mathbf{k}'|)\theta(k')$$

$$- \lambda\alpha(0) \int d^3k\alpha(|\mathbf{k}|)[\theta'^*\theta(\mathbf{k}) + \theta^*(\mathbf{k})\theta']N^*N$$

and the usual representation Eq. (7.5) of the commutation relations. It is to be noted that the condition (7.25) leads to a mass renormalization of the $N$ field and has the further effect of introducing a Yukawa type coupling into the theory.

The physical content of the model can be conveniently displayed as in the neutral scalar theory by a canonical transformation

$$\tilde{\theta}(\mathbf{k}) = \theta(\mathbf{k}) - A(\mathbf{k})N^*N$$

$$\tilde{N} = \exp\left\{\int d^3k[A^*(\mathbf{k})\theta(\mathbf{k}) - A(\mathbf{k})\theta^*(\mathbf{k})]\right\}N \qquad (7.26)$$

where $A(\mathbf{k})$ is to be determined by the requirement that the Hamiltonian, when expressed in terms of the new variables (7.26), should have no terms linear in the meson field operators. This leads to the form

$$A(\mathbf{k}) = \frac{\lambda\alpha(0)\theta'\alpha(|\mathbf{k}|)/\omega}{1 - \lambda \int d^3k[\alpha^2(|\mathbf{k}|)/|\mathbf{k}|]}$$

and the Hamiltonian

$$H(\theta') = \left(m - \lambda\frac{\alpha^2(0)|\theta'|^2}{1 - \lambda \int d^3k[\alpha^2(|\mathbf{k}|)/|\mathbf{k}|]}\right)\tilde{N}^*\tilde{N}$$

$$+ \int d^3k\omega\tilde{\theta}^*(\mathbf{k})\tilde{\theta}(\mathbf{k}) - \lambda \int d^3k\alpha(|\mathbf{k}|)\tilde{\theta}^*(\mathbf{k}) \int d^3k'\alpha(|\mathbf{k}'|)\tilde{\theta}(\mathbf{k})$$

Although the symmetry breaking once again has only a mass renormalization effect on the physical spectrum, one can further anticipate that in this model the wave function renormalization constant also should depend upon $|\theta'|^2$. In particular, one readily infers from Eqs. (7.20) and (7.26) the result

$$Z = \exp\left[-\lambda^2\alpha^2(0)|\theta'|^2\left(1 - \lambda \int d^3k\frac{\alpha^2(|\mathbf{k}|)}{|\mathbf{k}|}\right)^{-2} \int d^3k \frac{\alpha^2(|\mathbf{k}|)}{|\mathbf{k}|^2}\right]$$

which differs from unity if, and only if, the symmetry-breaking parameter $|\theta'| \neq 0$.

In contrast to the case of the neutral scalar theory, the condition (7.25) in this model allows an immediate application of the Goldstone theorem. Thus we note that the commutator condition

$$\langle \theta' | [Q_\theta, \theta(\mathbf{k})] | \theta' \rangle = -\langle \theta' | \theta(\mathbf{k}) | \theta' \rangle$$
$$= -\theta' \delta(\mathbf{k})$$

shows directly the existence of a physical excitation with the quantum numbers of the $\theta$ particle which has zero energy and momentum. Since we have noted in detail some of the arguments which show the "nonexistence" of the operator $Q_\theta$ in the event that it fails to annihilate the vacuum, it is interesting to note that this result, while entirely correct, is quite harmless in the case under consideration. To see this we note that it is more convenient to discuss the operator $Q_\theta$ in terms of the usual representation (7.5). This, of course, requires that one transform $Q_\theta$ to the form

$$Q_\theta = \int d^3k\, \theta^*(\mathbf{k}) \theta(\mathbf{k}) + [\theta'^* \theta(0) + \theta^*(0)\theta'] + \theta'^* \theta' \delta(0)$$

which makes quite clear the nonexistence of $Q_\theta$ as a well-defined operator. Despite the fact that the models under consideration here are somewhat too simple to expect an exact analogy with the relativistic theories discussed in the preceding section, the above explanation of the divergences known to occur in the definition of the charge operator in a broken-symmetry theory is sufficiently model-independent to suggest that the nonexistence of such operators will cause no difficulty in a proper formulation of the theory. Not only do these infinities fail to represent any possible objection to the breaking of a symmetry, but they have been further seen to follow as an entirely natural consequence of the requirement that a given operator have a nonvanishing expectation value.

Although the preceding discussion of the direct interaction model has not proved the equivalence of the broken-symmetry condition to the replacement of $\theta(\mathbf{k})$ by $\theta(\mathbf{k}) + \theta' \delta(\mathbf{k})$, this can (by virtue of the solubility of the theory for all $\theta'$) be carried out by straightforward though laborious techniques.[73] If, however, we are to succeed in extending our results in the direction of more physically significant theories, it is necessary to allow the discussion of models whose mathematical structure is not quite so simple. Both the neutral scalar theory and the direct interaction model are mathematically tractable by virtue of the fact that the physical effect of the symmetry breaking consists entirely of a mass renormalization. In the more general case one finds that as soon as allowance is made for more complicated symmetry-breaking effects, the solubility of the theory is destroyed.

An outstanding example of such a theory which is soluble only for the usual representation of the canonical commutation relations is the Lee model.[76] The relevant Hamiltonian is

$$H = m_V V^*V + m_N N^*N + \int d^3k \omega_k \theta^*(\mathbf{k})\theta(\mathbf{k})$$
$$- \int d^3k \alpha(|\mathbf{k}|)[V^*N\theta(\mathbf{k}) + N^*V\theta^*(\mathbf{k})]$$

where the only nonvanishing canonical commutation relations are

$$\{V, V^*\} = 1$$
$$\{N, N^*\} = 1$$
$$[\theta(\mathbf{k}), \theta^*(\mathbf{k})] = \delta(\mathbf{k} - \mathbf{k}')$$

It is well known that there exist in this theory two conserved generators of gauge transformations

$$Q_1 = V^*V + N^*N$$
$$Q_2 = \int d^3k \theta^*(\mathbf{k})\theta(\mathbf{k}) - N^*N$$

corresponding, respectively, to the conservation of fermion number and the difference between the number of $\theta$ and $N$ particles. It is, of course, the existence of these two conservation laws which, in the usual representation of the commutation relations, is ultimately responsible for the solubility of the theory. Since in the customary approach to the Lee model one attempts to solve the eigenvalue problem sector by sector, the choice of representation must be specified at the outset, thereby requiring the adoption of a procedure which automatically dismisses the possibility of finding additional solutions of the theory. We shall, however, show that there can exist additional solutions for which the $\theta$ field has a nonvanishing vacuum expectation value.

It is clear that as in the direct interaction model a condition of the type

$$\langle \theta'|\theta(\mathbf{k})|\theta'\rangle = \theta'(\mathbf{k}) \tag{7.27}$$

corresponds to the breaking of the $\theta$–$N$ conservation law inasmuch as the consistency requirement

$$\langle \theta' | [\theta(\mathbf{k}), Q_2] | \theta' \rangle = \theta'(\mathbf{k})$$

implies that the vacuum $\langle \theta' |$ no longer is an eigenstate of the operator $Q_2$. Furthermore the time independence of $Q_2$ (which is, of course, unaltered by the broken symmetry) requires by the Goldstone theorem that $\theta(\mathbf{k})$ excite a zero-mass particle. Although allowance has been made in Eq. (7.27) for a result which is somewhat more general than Eq. (7.6), it is readily shown from the equation of motion

$$i \frac{\partial}{\partial t} \theta(\mathbf{k}, t) = [\theta(\mathbf{k}), H]$$
$$= \omega_k \theta(\mathbf{k}) - \alpha(|\mathbf{k}|)N^*N$$

and the condition

$$V | \theta' \rangle = N | \theta' \rangle = 0$$

that

$$\left( -i \frac{\partial}{\partial t} + \omega_k \right) \langle \theta' | \theta(\mathbf{k}) | \theta' \rangle = 0$$

which is consistent with the required time independence of $\theta'(\mathbf{k})$ only if $\omega_k \theta'(\mathbf{k}) = 0$. This clearly demands that $\mu$ vanish and $\theta'(\mathbf{k})$ be of the form $\theta' \delta(\mathbf{k})$, in complete analogy to the results obtained in the case of the somewhat simpler models which have been discussed. The fact that the consistency requirements on the symmetry-breaking condition can be satisfied entirely at the kinematical level without placing any further constraints on the theory thus allows one to infer immediately the internal consistency of Eq. (7.27). Strictly speaking the extension of our preceding results to the Lee model cannot be accomplished with the degree of rigor which characterized the discussion of the neutral scalar and direct interaction theories. This is a consequence of the fact that the Lee model is not soluble except in the usual representation of the commutation relations so that one cannot prove the existence of a well-defined solution in the case of a broken symmetry. On the other hand, the replacement of $\theta(\mathbf{k})$ by $\theta(\mathbf{k}) + \theta' \delta(\mathbf{k})$ can be formally shown to be equivalent to the broken-symmetry condition, and the Hamiltonian thereby generated

$$H(\theta') = H - \alpha(0)(V^*N\theta' + N^*V\theta'^*) \tag{7.28}$$

furthermore fails to suggest the occurrence of any pathological features in the theory. We shall therefore be content to assume that there is no essential difficulty in passing to the infinite volume limit in the commutators of the charge operator [which is, of course, essential in order to demonstrate the equivalence of the broken-symmetry condition to the replacement of $\theta(\mathbf{k})$ by $\theta(\mathbf{k}) + \theta'\delta(\mathbf{k})$]. Stated somewhat differently, the implementation of the transformation generated by the operator $Q_2$ in a finite volume can now be extended [in direct analogy to the discussion following Eq. (7.10)] to infinite volume by virtue of our assumption concerning the existence of meaningful solutions to the theory described by Eq. (7.28).

The breakdown of $Q_2$ conservation and the increased structural complexity of the model can be illustrated more forcefully by diagonalizing all the terms in $H(\theta')$ which are bilinear in the canonical fields. Thus we define the new operators $V'$ and $N'$ by the unitary transformation

$$\begin{bmatrix} V' \\ N' \end{bmatrix} = \begin{bmatrix} \cos\gamma & e^{-i\beta}\sin\gamma \\ -e^{i\beta}\sin\gamma & \cos\gamma \end{bmatrix} \begin{bmatrix} V \\ N \end{bmatrix}$$

which leads to a diagonal form of the mass matrix

$$\begin{bmatrix} m_V & -\alpha(0)\theta'^* \\ -\alpha(0)\theta' & m_N \end{bmatrix}$$

if one sets

$$\theta' = |\theta'|\, e^{i\beta}$$
$$\tan 2\gamma = \frac{2\alpha(0)|\theta'|}{m_N - m_V}$$

The eigenvalues are readily found to be

$$m_V' = \frac{m_N + m_V}{2} + \frac{m_V - m_N}{2}\left(1 + 4\frac{|\alpha(0)\theta'|_2}{(m_N - m_V)^2}\right)^{\frac{1}{2}}$$

$$m_N' = \frac{m_N + m_V}{2} + \frac{m_N - m_V}{2}\left(1 + 4\frac{|\alpha(0)\theta'|^2}{(m_N - m_V)^2}\right)^{\frac{1}{2}}$$

in terms of which one has

$$H(\theta') = m_V' V^{*'}V' + m_N' N^{*'}N' + \int d^3k\,\omega_k \theta^*(\mathbf{k})\theta(\mathbf{k})$$
$$- \cos^2\gamma \int d^3k\,\alpha(|\mathbf{k}|)[V^{*'}N'\theta(\mathbf{k}) + N^{*'}V'\theta^*(\mathbf{k})] \qquad (7.29)$$
$$+ \sin^2\gamma \int d^3k\,\alpha(|\mathbf{k}|)[V^{*'}N'\theta^*(\mathbf{k})\,e^{2i\beta} + N^{*'}V'\theta(\mathbf{k})\,e^{-2i\beta}]$$
$$- \sin\gamma\cos\gamma \int d^3k\,\alpha(|\mathbf{k}|)[V^{*'}V' - N^{*'}N'][e^{-i\beta}\theta(\mathbf{k}) + e^{i\beta}\theta^*(\mathbf{k})]$$

for the Hamiltonian of the broken-symmetry theory. It is to be noted that as a consequence of the breakdown of $Q_2$ conservation the additional processes $N \rightarrow V + \theta$, $N \rightarrow N + \theta$, and $V \rightarrow V + \theta$ are all allowed by Eq. (7.29) in addition to the usual transition $V \rightarrow N + \theta$ of the Lee model. Although the resultant theory is not soluble, it is clear that the broken-symmetry condition must imply a dependence of the $N$ and $V$ masses on the parameter $\theta'$, as can be readily verified in perturbation theory.

Although the only way in which one can generate nontrivial symmetry-breaking effects in the Lee model is accomplished by treating the $\theta$ meson as a Goldstone particle, it is instructive to carry out the analogous procedure for the fermions of the theory in order to illustrate the failure of such an approach for systems containing only a finite number of degrees of freedom. In order to carry out the construction it is essential to find a state which has the quantum numbers of the $N$ particle and is degenerate in energy with the vacuum. From the equation of motion

$$i\frac{\partial}{\partial t} N = [N, H]$$

$$= m_N N - \int d^3 k \alpha(|\mathbf{k}|) \theta^*(\mathbf{k}) V$$

one trivially calculates the two-point function

$$G(t) = i\epsilon(t)\langle 0| (N(t)N^*(0))_+ |0\rangle$$

in the usual representation of $N$, $V$, and $\theta(\mathbf{k})$ to have the form

$$G(t) = \theta_+(t) e^{-im_N t} \tag{7.30}$$

It is clear from Eq. (7.30) that the state $N^*(t)|0\rangle$ is time independent if, and only if, $m_N = 0$, for which case one is led to attempt a construction of a set of broken-symmetry states by defining

$$\langle N'| = \langle 0| \exp \{N'^* N - N^* N'\}$$

The parameters $N'$ and $N'^*$ are $c$-numbers which commute with boson field operators and anticommute with fermion operators, the only nonvanishing commutator containing $N'$ or $N'^*$ required by consistency to be nonzero being

$$\{N', N'^*\} = \xi^2$$

where $\xi$ is a real $c$-number. It is easy to show that $\langle N'|$ is a zero-energy eigenstate of $H$ (thereby allowing its identification as a vacuum state) and has the further property that

$$\theta(\mathbf{k})|N'\rangle = V|N'\rangle = 0$$

On the other hand, the fact that the $N$ field is associated with only a single degree of freedom means that, unlike the cases previously discussed, the operator

$$U = \exp\{N'^*N - N^*N'\}$$

is unitary.

By introduction of the parameter $\lambda$ one can calculate the operator

$$\tilde{N}(\lambda) = U(\lambda)NU^*(\lambda)$$

where

$$U(\lambda) = \exp\{\lambda(N'^*N - N^*N')\}$$

One readily verifies that $\tilde{N}(\lambda)$ satisfies the differential equation

$$\frac{\partial^2 \tilde{N}}{\partial \lambda^2} = -\xi^2 \tilde{N}$$

so that $\tilde{N} = \tilde{N}(\lambda = 1)$ has the form

$$\tilde{N} = N \cos \xi + N'(\sin \xi/\xi) \tag{7.31}$$

This result immediately leads to the broken-symmetry condition

$$\langle N'|N|N'\rangle = N'(\sin \xi/\xi)$$

which clearly displays the noninvariance of the new set of vacuum states $\langle N'|$ under gauge transformations on the fermion fields $N$ and $V$. It is to be noted that in consequence of the Fermi statistics the operator $U$ does not merely affect a $c$-number translation of the field and that the result [Eq. (7.31)] is entirely in accord with the canonical commutation relation

$$\{\tilde{N}, \tilde{N}^*\} = 1$$

Using the same technique as before, one can express the state $\langle N'|$ as a linear combination of the vacuum $\langle 0|$ and the single $N$ particle state $\langle 0|N$. Thus one readily derives the result[74]

$$\langle N'| = \langle 0|\cos\xi + \langle 0|N'N'^* \frac{1 - \cos\xi}{\xi^2} + \langle 0|N'^*N \frac{\sin\xi}{\xi} \tag{7.32}$$

Since each term on the right-hand side of Eq. (7.32) represents a zero-energy eigenstate of $H$, it is clear that any state $\langle N'|$ may be chosen as the physical vacuum. Thus in the usual way one can build up a complete Hilbert space constructed from this chosen vacuum state. The relation between the Hilbert spaces constructed from the different vacuums can be readily found in direct analogy to our earlier results. In particular one deduces that the effect of the broken-symmetry states can be entirely simulated by the replacement of $H$ by

$$UHU^* = H\left(N \cos \xi + N' \frac{\sin \xi}{\xi}, V, \theta\right)$$

$$= H(N, V, \theta) + 2 \sin^2 \xi/2 \int d^3k\alpha(|\mathbf{k}|)(V^*N\theta(\mathbf{k}) + N^*\theta^*(\mathbf{k})V)$$

$$- \frac{\sin \xi}{\xi} \int d^3k\alpha(|\mathbf{k}|)(V^*N'\theta(\mathbf{k}) + N'^*\theta^*(\mathbf{k})V)$$

where we have denoted the usual Hamiltonian of the Lee model by $H(N, V, \theta)$. It must be strongly emphasized, however, that because $U$ is a unitary operator this transformation must leave the eigenvalue spectrum of $H$ unaltered, a result which can be readily verified by direct calculation in the lowest sectors. Thus the sole effect of $U$ is to mix states of different fermion number, a circumstance which is in marked contrast with the case in which the Goldstone particle is the $\theta$ meson and the $c$-number translation of the $\theta$ field is effected by a nonunitary operator which generates inequivalent theories. In the latter case the symmetry breaking effected by the $\theta$ meson can change the basic physics of the model (even to the point of rendering the theory insoluble) whereas the symmetry breaking induced by a massless $N$ particle is entirely formal. This distinction is, of course, a consequence of the well-known fact that the inequivalent representations of the commutation relations can only occur in theories which possess an infinite number of degrees of freedom.

Since the models which we have considered here cannot be readily generalized to the relativistic case, it is well to conclude this section by briefly commenting upon the utility of the results which have been obtained. Certainly they must serve to dispel much of the pessimism which may have been generated in our discussion of physically trivial broken-symmetry theories with regard to the possibility of inducing real effects by means of a symmetry-breaking condition. On the other hand, a crucial ingredient in this consideration of static theories has been the exact solubility of the states containing no fermions but an arbitrary number of $\theta$ particles. Since it was precisely this feature which made possible the demonstration of the existence of additional vacuum states in the theory (corresponding to the inequivalent representations), it is clear that the attribute of partial solubility has been an indispensable tool throughout the present section. The fact that there is no Lorentz-invariant theory in which such a circumstance occurs appears, at first sight, to exclude the possibility of finding a correspondingly simple example in the relativistic domain. On the other hand, it is interesting to note that even in a covariant theory with a scalar zero-mass excitation (assuming one can establish the existence of such a particle) it might well be possible to proceed in a fashion somewhat analogous to that followed here. In particular the "in" and "out" field operators which create the zero-mass quanta can be used to assert the existence of additional zero-energy eigenstates of $P^\mu$ which are related to the vacuum by the usual improper operator transformation. Such a device enables one to anticipate the precise fashion in which a nontrivial broken-symmetry effect may arise from the noninvariance of a Lagrangian under translation of the boson field operator. By this heuristic argument the results of the present section are seen to imply the possibility of carrying out the construction of theories such as those proposed in Section VI with considerably greater confidence. At present, however, a more rigorous argument does not appear to lie within the realm of feasibility.

## VIII. Conclusion

In the preceding discussions we have attempted to outline in detail some of the most relevant and interesting aspects of the theory of broken symmetries. In so doing, it has been found that, under conditions met by manifestly covariant theories or nonrelativistic theories with sufficiently damped potentials, the Goldstone theorem is a rigorous result and the broken symmetry consequently requires the presence of a massless boson. On the other hand, we have also been able to supply interesting examples of acausal systems in which the "Goldstone bosons" become massive. Such theories might even be of physical relevance in the event that vector gauge fields of the type discussed in Section IV are found to have application to the real world. In addition, these examples serve to emphasize the fact that, in problems involving causal theories, there exists the possibility that the Goldstone bosons might completely decouple so as not to appear in any physically measurable amplitude.

In the case of nonrelativistic problems, we have been able to consider Hamiltonians which are physically significant and in which the broken symmetry plays a fundamental and understandable role. On the other hand, in the case of the corresponding relativistic problems, our success in practical terms has been rather limited even though it has been possible to demonstrate that broken symmetries actually occur in relativistic theories which possess a special type of gauge invariance. In such cases, the broken-symmetry argument makes no basic change in the physical content of the theory and is merely equivalent to the usual argument concerning the relation between gauge invariance and masslessness. Unfortunately, however, more complex and realistic, relativistic, broken-symmetry models can at present only be studied within the context of perturbation theory so that, despite the fact that a great deal is understood in general terms, the methods of broken symmetries have not thus far achieved any considerable success in the realm of relativistic particle physics.

### References

1. J. Goldstone, *Nuovo Cimento*, **19**, 154 (1961); Y. Nambu and G. Jona-Lasinio, *Phys. Rev.*, **122**, 345 (1961); J. Goldstone, A. Salam, and S. Weinberg, *Phys. Rev.*, **127**, 965 (1962); S. A. Bludman and A. Klein, *Phys. Rev.*, **131**, 2364 (1963).
2. R. F. Streater, *Proc. Roy. Soc. (London)*, **A287**, 510 (1965).
3. Of course, if the current is not conserved, the theorem is not valid. For a discussion which essentially makes this observation, see Lopuszanski and Reeh, *Phys. Rev.*, **140**, B926 (1965).

   The construction of bilinear currents in field theory is a major problem and must be approached through the use of limiting processes. Because of singularities, it can turn out that the current correctly constructed does not behave as expected from naive arguments. For example, in the Schwinger model [J. Schwinger, *Phys. Rev.*, **130**, 406 (1963)], which has formally conserved vector and axial-vector currents, it is seen upon solution of the field equations that the axial current is not conserved, a phenomenon which might also occur in more physical models. A model which supposedly exhibits this behavior has been presented by Th. A. J. Maris and G. Jacob, *Phys. Rev. Letters*, **17**, 1300 (1966). [See also Th. A. J. Maris, *Nuovo Cimento*, **45A**, 223

(1966).] However, it should be noted that in defining the current these authors omitted the exponential line integral factor which is required for gauge invariance.

4. To be more explicit, we may introduce a $C^\infty$ test function $f_R(x)$ which has the property that

$$f_R(\mathbf{x}) = 1 \qquad \text{if} \qquad |\mathbf{x}| \leq R$$

while

$$f_R(\mathbf{x}) = 0 \qquad \text{if} \qquad |\mathbf{x}| > R + \epsilon$$

and define

$$Q_R{}^i(t) = \int d^3x f_R(\mathbf{x}) j_i{}^0(\mathbf{x}, t)$$

5. We confine our considerations to charges that are integrals of local densities. For a discussion of charges not of this type, see, for example, A. Katz and Y. Frishman, *Nuovo Cimento*, **42A**, 1009 (1966).

6. E. Fabri and L. E. Picasso, *Phys. Rev. Letters*, **16**, 408 (1966).

7. In particular, the criticism made by P. Higgs, *Phys. Rev.*, **145**, 1156 (1966) of ref. 9 is not valid since the essential point of the latter paper was that the only measure of the time dependence of charges comes from the time dependence of the commutator $[Q(t), \phi(x)]$. This operator exists in a causal theory even when $Q(t)$ does not, as is the case if the symmetry is broken.

8. G. S. Guralnik, *Proc. Conf. Unified Field Theories*, Feldafing, Germany, July 1965.

9. G. S. Guralnik, C. R. Hagen, and T. W. B. Kibble, *Phys. Rev. Letters*, **13**, 585 (1964).

10. D. Kastler, D. Robinson, and A. Swieca, *Commun. Math. Phys.*, **2**, 108 (1966).

11. S. A. Bludman and A. Klein, *Phys. Rev.*, **131**, 2364 (1963).

12. R. F. Streater, *Phys. Rev. Letters*, **15**, 475 (1965).

13. G. S. Guralnik, *Nuovo Cimento*, **44**, 321 (1966); Y. Frishman and A. Katz, *Phys. Rev. Letters*, **16**, 370 (1966).

14. W. Gilbert, *Phys. Rev. Letters*, **12**, 713 (1964).

15. A. Klein and B. W. Lee, *Phys. Rev. Letters*, **12**, 266 (1964).

16. G. S. Guralnik, *Phys. Rev. Letters*, **13**, 295 (1964).

17. G. S. Guralnik and C. R. Hagen, *Nuovo Cimento*, **43A**, 1 (1966).

18. E. Fabri and L. E. Picasso, *Phys. Rev. Letters*, **16**, 408 (1966).

19. A somewhat more general discussion of inequivalent representations in the context of broken symmetries is given by H. Umezawa, Y. Takahashi, and S. Kamefuchi, *Ann. Phys. (N.Y.)*, **26**, 336 (1964); S. Kamefuchi and H. Umezawa, *Nuovo Cimento*, **31**, 429 (1964). See also G. Barton, *Introduction to Advanced Field Theory*, Wiley, New York, 1963.

20. W. S. Hellman and P. Roman, *Phys. Rev.*, **143**, 1247 (1964).

21. F. Zachariasen, *Phys. Rev.*, **121**, 1851 (1961).

22. W. Thirring, *Phys. Rev.*, **126**, 1209 (1962).

23. This application was first suggested in ref. 17. More detailed discussions have been given in refs. 20 and 24.

24. N. G. Deshpande and S. A. Bludman, *Phys. Rev.*, **146**, 1186 (1966).

25. J. Schwinger, *Phys. Rev.*, **125**, 397 (1962).

26. J. Schwinger, *Phys. Rev.*, **128**, 2425 (1962).

27. D. G. Boulware and W. Gilbert, *Phys. Rev.*, **126**, 1563 (1962).
28. See, for example, H. Weyl, *Gruppentheorie und Quantenmechanik*, 2nd ed., Hirzel, Leipzig, 1931, ch. 2, p. 89; and earlier references cited there.
29. R. Utiyama, *Phys. Rev.*, **101**, 1597 (1956); T. W. B. Kibble, *J. Math. Phys.*, **2**, 212 (1961).
30. A. Salam and J. C. Ward, *Nuovo Cimento*, **11**, 568 (1959); *Phys. Rev.*, **136**, B763 (1964); S. L. Glashow, *Nucl. Phys.*, **10**, 107 (1959); **22**, 579 (1961); M. Gell-Mann and S. L. Glashow, *Ann. Phys.* (*N.Y.*), **15**, 437 (1961); see also C. N. Yang and R. L. Mills, *Phys. Rev.*, **96**, 191 (1954).
31. P. W. Anderson, *Phys. Rev.*, **130**, 439 (1963).
32. P. W. Higgs, *Phys. Letters*, **12**, 132 (1964).
33. P. W. Higgs, *Phys. Rev.*, **145**, 1156 (1966).
34. R. Brout and F. Englert, *Phys. Rev. Letters*, **13**, 321 (1964).
35. G. S. Guralnik, C. R. Hagen, and T. W. B. Kibble, *Phys. Rev. Letters*, **13**, 585 (1964).
36. T. W. B. Kibble, *Phys. Rev.*, **155**, 1554 (1967).
37. See, for example, J. M. Jauch and F. Rohrlich, *The Theory of Photons and Electrons*, Addison-Wesley, Cambridge, Mass., 1955, ch. 2.
38. J. Schwinger, *Phys. Rev.*, **130**, 402 (1963).
39. This model has been discussed by D. G. Boulware and W. Gilbert, *Phys. Rev.*, **126**, 1563 (1962), and also in refs. 34 and 35.
40. L. Gårding and S. Lions, *Nuovo Cimento Suppl.*, **14**, 9 (1959).
41. This is essentially the original model of J. Goldstone, *Nuovo Cimento*, **19**, 154 (1961).
42. It should be noted that one cannot really ignore the fact that the ranges of the variables $\rho$ and $\theta$ do not extend over the whole real axis. This may give rise in particular to the phenomenon of "kinks." See D. Finkelstein, *J. Math. Phys.*, **7**, 1218 (1966); and earlier references cited there.
43. See J. D. Bjorken, *Ann. Phys.* (*N.Y.*), **24**, 174 (1963); I. Bialynicki-Birula, *Phys. Rev.*, **130**, 465 (1963); W. Heisenberg, *Rev. Mod. Phys.*, **29**, 269 (1957); G. S. Guralnik, *Phys. Rev.*, **136**, B1404, B1417 (1964).
44. G. S. Guralnik and C. R. Hagen, *Nuovo Cimento*, **43A**, 1 (1966).
45. J. Schwinger, *Phys. Rev.*, **128**, 2425 (1962).
46. L. S. Brown, *Nuovo Cimento*, **29**, 617 (1963).
47. S. A. Bludman and A. Klein, *Phys. Rev.*, **131**, 2364 (1963).
48. N. N. Bogoliubov, *Physica*, **26**, 1 (1960).
49. H. Wagner, *Z. Phys.*, **195**, 273 (1966).
50. R. Lange, *Phys. Rev. Letters*, **14**, 3 (65); *Phys. Rev.*, **146**, 301 (1966).
51. T. W. B. Kibble, *Proc. Intern. Conf. Elementary Particles*, Oxford, 1965, p. 19.
52. H. Araki and E. J. Woods, *J. Math. Phys.*, **4**, 637 (1963).
53. J. A. Swieca, *Comm. Math. Phys.*, **4**, 1 (1967).
54. N. N. Bogoliubov, *J. Phys. USSR*, **11**, 23 (1947).
55. J. Bardeen, L. N. Cooper, and J. R. Schrieffer, *Phys. Rev.*, **108**, 1175 (1957).
56. R. Haag, *Nuovo Cimento*, **25**, 287 (1962).
57. H. Ezawa, *J. Math. Phys.*, **5**, 1078 (1964).
58. G. Emch and M. Guenin, *J. Math. Phys.*, **7**, 915 (1966).
59. J. Valatin, *Nuovo Cimento*, **7**, 843 (1958).

60. L. P. Gorkov, *JETP* (*USSR*), **34**, 735 (1958); *Sov. Phys. JETP* (*Engl. Trans.*), **7**, 505 (1958).
61. P. W. Anderson, *Phys. Rev.*, **112**, 1900 (1958).
62. H. Leutwyler, *Helv. Phys. Acta*, **38**, 431 (1965); C. S. Lam, *Nuovo Cimento*, **34**, 637 (1964).
63. W. Thirring, *Ann. Phys.* (*N.Y.*), **3**, 91 (1958); V. Glaser, *Nuovo Cimento*, **9**, 990 (1958); F. Scarf, *Phys. Rev.*, **117**, 868 (1960); T. Pradhan, *Nucl. Phys.*, **9**, 124 (1958); K. Johnson, *Nuovo Cimento*, **20**, 773 (1961); C. Sommerfield, *Ann. Phys.* (*N.Y.*), **26**, 1 (1964).
64. C. R. Hagen, *Nuovo Cimento*, **51B**, 169 1967.
65. J. D. Bjorken, *Ann. Phys.*, (*N.Y.*), **24**, 174 (1963).
66. G. S. Guralnik, *Phys. Rev.*, **136**, B1404, B1417 (1964).
67. G. S. Guralnik and C. R. Hagen, *Nuovo Cimento*, **43A**, 1 (1966).
68. J. Goldstone, *Nuovo Cimento*, **19**, 154 (1961). See also Section IV of this article.
69. G. S. Guralnik, *Nuovo Cimento*, **36**, 1002 (1965).
70. Y. Nambu and G. Jona-Lasinio, *Phys. Rev.*, **122**, 345 (1961); G. Jona-Lasinio and Y. Nambu, *Phys. Rev.*, **124**, 246 (1961). This model has also been discussed in ref. 67, and by H. Umezawa, *Nuovo Cimento*, **40A**, 450 (1965).
71. H. P. Dürr, W. Heisenberg, H. Yamamoto, and K. Yamazaki, *Nuovo Cimento*, **38**, 1220 (1965), and many other related works of this group.
72. K. Johnson, M. Baker, and R. Willey, *Phys. Rev.*, **136**, B1111 (1964).
73. G. S. Guralnik and C. R. Hagen, *Nuovo Cimento*, **45**, 959 (1966).
74. G. S. Guralnik and C. R. Hagen, *Phys. Rev.*, **149**, 1017 (1966).
75. C. R. Hagen, Ph.D. dissertation, Massachusetts Institute of Technology, 1962, unpublished.
76. T. D. Lee, *Phys. Rev.*, **95**, 1329 (1954).

# Author Index

Numbers in parentheses are reference numbers and show that an author's work is referred to although his name is not mentioned in the text.   Numbers in *italics* indicate the pages on which the full references appear.

## A

Abarbanel, H. D. I., 448(38), 453(38), *471*, 550, *564*

Abashian, A., 477(14), 483(14), 484(14), *560*

Abolins, M., 30, 31, 89(78), *168*, *171*

Abov, Y. G., 542(102), *564*

Abrams, R. J., 146, 149–151, *174*, 303 (100), 304, 347, 348(99), 353(155), 354, 356(155b), 357(155b), 358(155), *378*, *380*, 477(14), 483(14), 484(14), *560*

Adair, R. K., 334, *379*

Adamson, A.-M., 100(98), *172*

Ademollo, M., 12(5), *167*, 418, 420, *470*

Adler, S. L., 387, 397, 402, 418, 424, *470*, 478, 541, 546, *560*

Alessandrini, V. A., 401(14), 411, *470*

Alff, C., 31, *168*

Alles, W., 453(39), *471*, 549(115), *564*

Allison, J., 491(54), *562*

Alston, M., 8, *167*, 180, 182, 311, 313 (114), 332(124), 353(4), *374*, *379*

Altarelli, G., 534(91), 536(91), *563*

Alvarez, L. W., 8(2), 12(6), 13(6), 29 (137), *167–169*, *174*, 180(4), 182(4), 311(114,115), 313(114), 332(124), 353 (4), *374*, *379*

Alvarez, R., 297, *377*

Amaldi, 149

Amati, D., 418(24), 424(24), 425(24), *471*, 506(67), *562*

Ambler, E., 476(7), 479(20), *560*

Ammar, R., 77, 79, *171*, 334(133), *379*

Anderson, E. W., 291, 294, 295, *377*

Anderson, P. W., 606, 660, *707*, *708*

d'Andlau, C., 49(47), 98(93), 100(98), 109(102), *169*, *172*, 252(46), 253(46), *375*

Ankenbrandt, C. M., 291(86), *377*

Araki, H., 648, 650(52), *707*

Armenise, N., 70(66), 107, 119, 122, *170*, *173*

Armenteros, R., 25, 98(93), *167*, *172*, 307, 331(3), 332(3,106), 333, 336(3), 337(136), 338(140), 339(136), 340–343, 367–371 (173), 372, *374*, *378*–*381*

Asbury, J. G., 62, 65, *170*

Ashkin, J., 188(8), *374*

Astbury, A., 291(87), 292(87), 295(87), *377*, 477(14), 483(14), 484(14), *560*

Astbury, P., 114(106), 116(106), *173*

Astier, A., 25(16), 49(47), 98(93), 100 (98), 109(102), 113(104), *167*, *169*, *172*, 252(46), 253(46), *375*

Atkinson, H. H., 283(78a), 284(78a), *376*

Auslander, V. L., 62, *170*

Auvil, P., 265, 267, 268(63), 269(63), 272(63), 274(63), 283(63), *376*

## B

Baacke, J., 272(69), 274(69), 298(69), *376*

Babu, P., 534(91), 536(91), *563*

Bacci, C., 277(72), *376*

Bachman, A. H., 133(120), 155(120), *173*

Badier, J., 250(42), 350, 352(153), 353 (153), *375*, *380*

Badier, S., 547(113), 550(113), *564*

709

# Subject Index